Lecture Notes in Computer Science 4279

Commenced Publication in 1973
Founding and Former Series Editors:
Gerhard Goos, Juris Hartmanis, and Jan van L

Naoki Kobayashi (Ed.)

Programming Languages and Systems

4th Asian Symposium, APLAS 2006
Sydney, Australia, November 8-10, 2006
Proceedings

 Springer

Volume Editor

Naoki Kobayashi
Tohoku University, Graduate School of Information Sciences
Department of Computer and Mathematical Sciences
6-3-9 Aoba, Aramaki, Aoba-ku, Sendai-shi, Miyagi 980-8579, Japan
E-mail: koba@ecei.tohoku.ac.jp

Library of Congress Control Number: 2006935552

CR Subject Classification (1998): D.3, D.2, F.3, D.4, D.1, F.4.1

LNCS Sublibrary: SL 2 – Programming and Software Engineering

ISSN   0302-9743
ISBN-10   3-540-48937-1 Springer Berlin Heidelberg New York
ISBN-13   978-3-540-48937-5 Springer Berlin Heidelberg New York

Springer is a part of Springer Science+Business Media

springer.com

© Springer-Verlag Berlin Heidelberg 2006
Printed in Germany

Typesetting: Camera-ready by author, data conversion by Scientific Publishing Services, Chennai, India
Printed on acid-free paper   SPIN: 11924661   06/3142   5 4 3 2 1 0

Preface

This volume contains the proceedings of the 4th Asian Symposium on Programming Languages and Systems (APLAS 2006), which took place in Sydney, Japan, November 8-10, 2006. The symposium was sponsored by the Asian Association for Foundation of Software.

In response to the call for papers, 70 full submissions were received. Each submission was reviewed by at least three Program Committee members with the help of external reviewers. The Program Committee meeting was conducted electronically over a 2-week period. After careful discussion, the Program Committee selected 22 papers. I would like to sincerely thank all the members of the APLAS 2006 Program Committee for their excellent job, and all the external reviewers for their invaluable contribution. The submission and review process was managed using the CyberChair system.

In addition to the 22 contributed papers, the symposium also included two invited talks by Jens Palsberg (UCLA, Los Angeles, USA) and Peter Stuckey (University of Melbourne, Melbourne, Australia), and one tutorial by Matthew Flatt (University of Utah, USA).

Many people helped to promote APLAS as a high-quality forum in Asia to serve programming language researchers worldwide. Following a series of well-attended workshops that were held in Singapore (2000), Daejeon (2001), and Shanghai (2002), the first three formal symposiums were held in Beijing (2003), Taipei (2004) and Tsukuba (2005).

I am grateful to the General Co-chairs, Manuel Chakravarty and Gabriele Keller, for their invaluable support and guidance that made our symposium in Sydney possible. I would like to thank the AAFS Chair Tetsuo Ida and the Program Chairs of the past APLAS symposiums, Atsushi Ohori, Wei-Ngan Chin, and Kwangkeun Yi, for their advice. I am also thankful to Eijiro Sumii for serving as the Poster Chair. Last but not least, I thank Kohei Suenaga for his help in handling the CyberChair system and other administrative matters.

September 2006   Naoki Kobayashi

Organization

General Co-chairs

Manuel Chakravarty (University of New South Wales, Australia)
Gabriele Keller (University of New South Wales, Australia)

Program Chair

Naoki Kobayashi (Tohoku University)

Program Committee

Kung Chen (National Chengchi University, Taiwan)
Wei-Ngan Chin (National University of Singapore, Singapore)
Patrick Cousot (ENS, France)
Masahito Hasegawa (Kyoto University, Japan)
Jifeng He (United Nations University, Macau)
Haruo Hosoya (University of Tokyo, Japan)
Bo Huang (Intel China Software Center, China)
Oege de Moor (Oxford University, UK)
George Necula (University of California at Berkeley, USA)
Martin Odersky (EPFL, Switzerland)
Tamiya Onodera (IBM Research, Tokyo Research Laboratory, Japan)
Yunheung Paek (Seoul National University, Korea)
Sriram Rajamani (Microsoft Research, India)
Andrei Sabelfeld (Chalmers University of Technology, Sweden)
Zhong Shao (Yale University, USA)
Harald Sondergaard (University of Melbourne, Australia)
Nobuko Yoshida (Imperial College London, UK)

Poster Chair

Eijiro Sumii (Tohoku University)

External Referees

Amal Ahmed	Stefan Andrei	Benjamin Aziz
Minwook Ahn	Puri Arenas	Nick Benton
Hugh Anderson	Aslan Askarov	Martin Berger

Julien Bertrane
Bruno Blanchet
Frederic Blanqui
Matthias Blume
Hans Boehm
Iovka Boneva
Mihai Budiu
Cristiano Calcagno
Sagar Chaki
Avik Chaudhuri
Siau Cheng Khoo
Shigeru Chiba
Adam Chlipala
Doosan Cho
Jeremy Condit
Florin Craciun
Jason Dai
Cristina David
Xinyu Feng
Jérôme Feret
Cédric Fournet
Stephen Freund
Alexey Gotsman
Dan Grossman
Joshua Guttman
Huu Hai Nguyen
Matthew Harren
Aaron Harwood
Martin Hofmann

Kohei Honda
Hans Huttel
Atsushi Igarashi
Kazuhiro Inaba
Seokgyo Jung
Shin-ya Katsumata
Wonseok Kim
Yongjoo Kim
Yue-Sun Kuo
Akash Lal
Peeter Laud
Jooyeon Lee
Benjamin Leperchey
Francesco Logozzo
Youngmo Lyang
Sergio Maffeis
Laurent Mauborgne
Antoine Miné
Yasuhiko Minamide
David Monniaux
Shin-Cheng Mu
Lee Naish
Aleks Nanevski
Aditya Nori
Atsushi Ohori
Sanghyun Park
Andrew Phllips
Henrik Pilegaard
Bernie Pope

Corneliu Popeea
Shengchao Qin
Xavier Rival
Alejandro Russo
Sriram Sankaranarayanan
Jatin Shah
Alex Simpson
Lex Spoon
Tadahiro Suda
Eijiro Sumii
Yuanhao Sun
Michiaki Tatsubori
Kenjiro Taura
Peter Thiemann
Tayssir Touili
Yoshihito Toyama
Akihiko Tozawa
Daniele Varacca
Manik Varma
Jérôme Vouillon
Keith Wansbrough
Tony Wirth
Wuu Yang
Jonghee W. Yoon
Poonna Yospanya
Jonghee M. Youn
Zhiqiang Yu

Sponsoring Institutions

Asian Association for Foundation of Software (AAFS)
The University of New South Wales

Table of Contents

Invited Talk 1

Type Processing by Constraint Reasoning 1
Peter J. Stuckey, Martin Sulzmann, Jeremy Wazny

Session 1

Principal Type Inference for GHC-Style Multi-parameter Type
Classes 26
Martin Sulzmann, Tom Schrijvers, Peter J. Stuckey

Private Row Types: Abstracting the Unnamed 44
Jacques Garrigue

Type and Effect System for Multi-staged Exceptions 61
Hyunjun Eo, Ik-Soon Kim, Kwangkeun Yi

Session 2

Relational Reasoning for Recursive Types and References 79
Nina Bohr, Lars Birkedal

Proof Abstraction for Imperative Languages 97
William L. Harrison

Reading, Writing and Relations: Towards Extensional Semantics
for Effect Analyses 114
Nick Benton, Andrew Kennedy, Martin Hofmann,
Lennart Beringer

Session 3

A Fine-Grained Join Point Model for More Reusable Aspects 131
Hidehiko Masuhara, Yusuke Endoh, Akinori Yonezawa

Automatic Testing of Higher Order Functions 148
Pieter Koopman, Rinus Plasmeijer

Invited Talk 2

Event Driven Software Quality 165
   Jens Palsberg

Session 4

Widening Polyhedra with Landmarks............................... 166
   Axel Simon, Andy King

Comparing Completeness Properties of Static Analyses and Their
Logics 183
   David A. Schmidt

Polymorphism, Subtyping, Whole Program Analysis and Accurate
Data Types in Usage Analysis 200
   Tobias Gedell, Jörgen Gustavsson, Josef Svenningsson

Session 5

A Modal Language for the Safety of Mobile Values 217
   Sungwoo Park

An Analysis for Proving Temporal Properties of Biological Systems 234
   Roberta Gori, Francesca Levi

Computational Secrecy by Typing for the Pi Calculus 253
   Martín Abadi, Ricardo Corin, Cédric Fournet

Invited Tutorial

Scheme with Classes, Mixins, and Traits 270
   Matthew Flatt, Robert Bruce Findler, Matthias Felleisen

Session 6

Using Metadata Transformations to Integrate Class Extensions
in an Existing Class Hierarchy 290
   Markus Lumpe

Combining Offline and Online Optimizations: Register Allocation
and Method Inlining 307
   Hiroshi Yamauchi, Jan Vitek

A Localized Tracing Scheme Applied to Garbage Collection 323
    Yannis Chicha, Stephen M. Watt

Session 7

A Pushdown Machine for Recursive XML Processing 340
    Keisuke Nakano, Shin-Cheng Mu

XML Validation for Context-Free Grammars 357
    Yasuhiko Minamide, Akihiko Tozawa

A Practical String Analyzer by the Widening Approach 374
    Tae-Hyoung Choi, Oukseh Lee, Hyunha Kim, Kyung-Goo Doh

Session 8

A Bytecode Logic for JML and Types 389
    Lennart Beringer, Martin Hofmann

On Jones-Optimal Specializers: A Case Study Using Unmix 406
    Johan Gade, Robert Glück

Author Index 423

Type Processing by Constraint Reasoning

Peter J. Stuckey[1,2], Martin Sulzmann[3], and Jeremy Wazny[2]

[1] NICTA Victoria Laboratory
[2] Department of Computer Science and Software Engineering
University of Melbourne, 3010 Australia
{pjs, jeremyrw}@cs.mu.oz.au
[3] School of Computing, National University of Singapore
S16 Level 5, 3 Science Drive 2, Singapore 117543
sulzmann@comp.nus.edu.sg

Abstract. Herbrand constraint solving or unification has long been understood as an efficient mechanism for type checking and inference for programs using Hindley/Milner types. If we step back from the particular solving mechanisms used for Hindley/Milner types, and understand type operations in terms of constraints we not only give a basis for handling Hindley/Milner extensions, but also gain insight into type reasoning even on pure Hindley/Milner types, particularly for type errors. In this paper we consider typing problems as constraint problems and show which constraint algorithms are required to support various typing questions. We use a light weight constraint reasoning formalism, Constraint Handling Rules, to generate suitable algorithms for many popular extensions to Hindley/Milner types. The algorithms we discuss are all implemented as part of the freely available Chameleon system.

1 Introduction

Hindley/Milner type checking and inference has long been understood as a process of solving Herbrand constraints, but typically the typing problem is not first mapped to a constraint problem and solved, instead a fixed algorithm, such as algorithm $\mathcal{W}$ using unification, is used to infer and check types. We argue that understanding a typing problem by first mapping it to a constraint problem gives us greater insight into the typing in the first place, in particular:

- Type inference corresponds to collecting the type constraints arising from an expression. An expression has no type if the resulting constraints are *unsatisfiable*.
- Type checking corresponds to checking that the declared type, considered as constraints, *implies* (that is has more information than) the inferred type (constraints collected from the definition).
- Type errors of various classes: ambiguity, subsumption errors; can all be explained better by reasoning on the type constraints.

Strongly typed languages provide the user with the convenience to significantly reduce the number of errors in a program. Well-typed programs can be guaranteed not to "go wrong" [22], with respect to a large number of potential problems.

N. Kobayashi (Ed.): APLAS 2006, LNCS 4279, pp. 1–25, 2006.

Typically type processing of a program either checks that types declared for each program construct are correct, or, better, infers the types for each program construct and checks that these inferred types are compatible with any declared types. If the checks succeed, the program is type correct and cannot "go wrong".

However, programs are often not well-typed, and therefore must be modified before they can be accepted. Another important role of the type processor is to help the author determine why a program has been rejected, what changes need to be made to the program for it to be type correct.

Traditional type inference algorithms depend on a particular traversal of the syntax tree. Therefore, inference frequently reports errors at locations which are far away from the actual source of the problem. The programmer is forced to tackle the problem of correcting his program unaided. This can be a daunting task for even experienced programmers; beginners are often left bewildered.

Our thesis is that by mapping the entire typing problem to a set of constraints, we can use constraint reasoning to (a) concisely and efficiently implement the type processor and (b) accurately determine where errors may occur, and aid the programmer in correcting them. The Chameleon [32] system implements this for rich Hindley/Milner based type languages.

We demonstrate our approach via three examples. Note that throughout the paper we will adopt Haskell [11] style syntax in examples.

Example 1. Consider the following ill-typed program:

```
f 'a' b    True = error "'a'"
f c   True z    = error "'b'"
f x   y    z    = if z then x else y
f x   y    z    = error "last"
```

Here **error** is the standard Haskell function with type $\forall a.[Char] \rightarrow a$. GHC reports:

```
mdef.hs:4:
    Couldn't match 'Char' against 'Bool'
        Expected type: Char
        Inferred type: Bool
    In the definition of 'f': f x y z = if z then x else y
```

What's confusing here is that GHC combines type information from a number of clauses in a non-obvious way. In particular, in a more complex program, it may not be clear at all where the *Char* and *Bool* types it complains about come from. Indeed, it isn't even obvious where the conflict in the above program is. Is it complaining about the two branches of the if-then-else (if so, which is *Char* and which *Bool*?), or about z which might be a *Char*, but as the conditional must be a *Bool*?

The Chameleon system reports:[1]

---

[1] The currently available Chameleon system (July 2005) no longer supports these more detailed error messages, after extensions to other parts of the system. The feature will be re-enabled in the future. The results are given from an earlier version.

```
multi.hs:1: ERROR: Type error - one error found
Problem : Definition clauses not unifiable
Types   : Char -> a -> b -> c
          d -> Bool -> e -> f
          g -> g -> h -> i
Conflict: f 'a' b True = error "'a'"
          f c True z = error "'b'"
          f x y z = if z then x else y
```

Note we do not mention the last definition equation which is irrelevant to the error.

If we assume the actual error is that the **True** in the second definition should be a **'b'** through some copy-and-paste error, then it is clear that the GHC error message provides little help in discovering it. The Chameleon error certainly implicates the **True** in the problem and gives type information that should direct the programmer to the problem quickly.

As part of the diagnosis the system "colours" both the conflicting types and certain program locations. A program location which contributes to any of the reported conflicting types is highlighted in the same style as that type. Locations which contribute to multiple reported types are highlighted in a combination of the styles of the types they contribute to. (There are no such locations in the case above.)

The above example illustrates the fundamental problems with any traditional Hindley/Milner type inference like algorithms $\mathcal{W}$ [22]. The algorithms suffer from a bias derived from the way they traverse the abstract syntax tree (AST). The second problem is that being tied to unification, which is only one particular implementation of a constraint solving algorithm for tree constraints, they do not treat the problem solely as a constraint satisfaction problem.

The problems of explaining type errors are exacerbated when the type system becomes more complex. Type classes [34] are an important extension to Hindley/Milner types, allowing principled (non-parametric) overloading. But the extension introduces new classes of errors and complicates typing questions. Type classes are predicates over types, and now we have to admit that type processing is a form of reasoning over first order formulae about types.

Example 2. Consider the following program which is typical of the sort of mistake that beginners make. The base case **sum [] = []** should read **sum [] = 0**. The complexity of the reported error is compounded by Haskell's overloading of numbers.

```
sum [] = []
sum (x:xs) = x + sum xs

sumLists = sum . map sum
```

GHC does not report the error in **sum** until a monomorphic instance is required, at which point it discovers that no instance of **Num [a]** exists. This means that unfortunately such errors may not be found through type checking alone – it may remain undiscovered until someone attempts to run the program. The function sumLists forces that here, and GHC reports:

```
sum.hs:4:
No instance for (Num [a]) arising from use of 'sum' at sum.hs:3
Possible cause: the monomorphism restriction applied to the following:
  sumLists :: [[[a]]] -> [a] (bound at sum.hs:3)
Probable fix: give these definition(s) an explicit type signature
In the first argument of '(.)', namely 'sum'
In the definition of 'sumLists': sumLists = sum . (map sum)
```

The error message is completely misleading, except for the fact that the problem is there is no instance of Num [a]. The probable fix will not help.

For this program Chameleon reports the following:

```
sum.hs:4: ERROR: Missing instance
Instance:Num [a]: sum [] = []
                  sum (x:xs) = x + sum xs
```

This indicates that the demand for this instance arises from the interaction between [] on the first line of sum and (+) on the second. The actual source of the error is highlighted.

The advantages of using constraint reasoning extend as the type system becomes even more complex. Generalized Algebraic Data Types (GADTs) [3,36] are one of the latest extensions of the concept of algebraic data types. They have attracted a lot of attention recently [24,25,26]. The novelty of GADTs is that the (result) types of constructor may differ. Thus, we may make use of additional type equality assumptions while typing the body of a pattern clause.

Example 3. Consider the following example of a GADT, using GHC style notation, where List a n represents a list of as of length n. Type constructors Z and S are used to represent numbers on the level of types.

```
data Z -- zero
data S n -- successor
data List a n where
  Nil :: List a Z
  Cons :: a -> List a m -> List a (S m)
```

We can now express much more complex behaviour of our functions, for example

```
map :: (a -> b) -> List a n -> List b n
map f Nil = Nil
map f (Cons a l) = Cons (f a) (map f l)
```

which guarantees that the map function returns a list of the same length as its input.

GADTs introduce more complicated typing problems because different bodies of the same function can have different types, since they act under different assumptions. This makes the job of reporting type errors much more difficult.

Example 4. Consider defining another GADT to encode addition among our (type) number representation.

```
data Sum l m n where
  Base :: Sum Z n n
  Step :: Sum l m n -> Sum (S l) m (S n)
```

We make use of the Sum type class to refine the type of the append function. Thus, we can state the desired property that the length of the output list equals the sum of the length of the two input lists.

```
append2 :: Sum l m n -> List a l -> List a m -> List a n
append2 Base Nil ys = Nil -- wrong!! should be ys
append2 (Step p) (Cons x xs) ys = Cons x (append p xs ys)
```

For this program GHC reports

```
append.hs:17:22:
    Couldn't match the rigid variable 'n' against 'Z'
      'n' is bound by the type signature for 'append2'
      Expected type: List a n
      Inferred type: List a Z
    In the definition of 'append2': append2 Base Nil ys = Nil
```

For this program Chameleon currently reports:

```
ERROR: Polymorphic type variable 'n' (from line 13, col. 56) instantiated by
append2 :: Sum l m n -> List a l -> List a m -> List a n
append2 Base Nil ys = Nil -- wrong!! should be ys
```

Here we can determine the actual locations that cause the subsumption error to occur. We could also give information on the assumptions made, though presently Chameleon does not. We aim in the future to produce something like:

```
append.hs:10: ERROR:  Inferred type does not subsume declared type
Problem: The variable 'm' makes the declared type too polymorphic
    Under the assumptions l = Z and m = n arising from
          append2 Base Nil ys = Nil
    Declared: Sum Z m m -> List a Z -> List a m -> List a m
    Inferred: Sum Z m m -> List a Z -> List a m -> List a Z
append2 Base Nil ys = Nil -- wrong!! should be ys
```

Our advantage is that we use a constraint-based system where we maintain information which constraints arise from which program parts. GHC effectively performs unification under a mixed prefix, hence, GHC only knows which 'branch' failed but not exactly where.

As the examples illustrate, by translating type information to constraints with locations attached we can use constraint reasoning on the remaining constraint problem. The constraint reasoning maintains which locations caused any inferences it makes, and we can then use these locations to help report error messages much more precisely. In this paper we show how to translate complex typing problems to constraints and reason about the resulting typing problems.

The rest of the paper is organized as follows. In Section 2 we introduce our language for constraints, and the CHR formalism for constraint reasoning. We show how constraint algorithms for satisfiability and inference are expressible using CHRs. In Section 3 we show how we map a functional program to a CHR program defining the type constraints. We then in Section 4 examine typing in Hindley/Milner using our system, before considering reporting errors in Hindley/Milner in Section 5. We add type classes in Section 6, and show how that changes type inference and checking, and introduces new kinds of type errors. We then briefly consider further extensions such as functional dependencies, programmed type extensions and GADTs in Section 7. We conclude with a brief discussion of related work. Much of the technical underpinnings to material in this paper has appeared previously, and so we leave the presentation as quite informal. For more details the reader is referred to [6,28,29,30,31,35].

2   Constraints and CHRs

In this section we introduce constraints with location annotations, and our framework for constraint reasoning, Constraint Handling Rules.

We use notation $\bar{o}$ to refer to a sequence of objects o, usually types or variables. Out type language is standard, we assume type variables a, function types $t \rightarrow t$ and user definable data types $T\ \bar{t}$. We use common Haskell notation for writing function, pair, list types, etc.

We make use of two kinds of constraints – equations and user-defined constraints. An equation is of the form $t_1 = t_2$, where t_1 and t_2 are types that share the same structure as types in the language. User-defined constraints are written $U\ \bar{t}$ or $f(t)$. We use these two forms to distinguish between constraints representing type class overloading and those arising from function definitions.

Conjunctions of constraints are sometimes written using a comma separator instead of the Boolean connective $\wedge$. We often treat conjunctions as sets of constraints. We assume a special (always satisfiable) constraint $True$ representing the empty conjunction of constraints, and a special never-satisfiable constraint $False$. If C is a conjunction we let C_e be the equations in C and C_u be the user-defined constraints in C. We assume the usual definitions of substitution, most general unifier (mgu), etc. see e.g. [20]. We define $mgu(C)$ to return a most general unifier of the equations C.

We will make use of *justified* constraints which have a list of labels representing program locations attached. The *justification* of a constraint refers to the program locations from which the constraint arose. We shall denote justified constraints using a subscript list of locations, and typically write singleton justified constraints $C_{[i]}$ as simply C_i. We write $J_1 +\!\!+ J_2$ to represent the result of appending justification J_2 to the end of J_1. For our purposes, we can safely remove any repeated location which appears to the right of another occurrence of that location. e.g. $[1, 2, 1, 3, 2]$ becomes $[1, 2, 3]$.

In addition to the Boolean operator $\wedge$ (conjunction), we make use of $\supset$ (implication) and $\leftrightarrow$ (equivalence) and quantifiers $\exists$ (existential) and $\forall$ (universal) to express conditions in formal statements, typing rules etc. We assume that $fv(o)$ computes the free variables not bound by any quantifier in an object o. We write $\bar{\exists}_o.F$ as a short-hand for $\exists fv(F) - fv o.F$ where F is a first-order formula and o is an object. Unless otherwise stated, we assume that formulae are implicitly universally quantified. We refer to [27] for more details on first-order logic.

Constraint Handling Rules with Justifications. We will translate typing problems to a constraint problem where the meaning of the user-defined constraints is defined by Constraint Handling Rules (CHRs) [8]. CHRs manipulate a global set of primitive constraints, using rewrite rules of two forms

$$\text{simplification } (r1) \; c_1, \ldots, c_n \iff d_1, \ldots, d_m$$
$$\text{propagation } (r2) \; c_1, \ldots, c_n \implies d_1, \ldots, d_m$$

where $c_1, \ldots, c_n$ are user-defined constraints, $d_1, \ldots, d_m$ are constraints, and $r1$ and $r2$ are labels by which we can refer to these rules. We will often omit rule labels when they are not necessary. A CHR *program* P is a set of CHRs.

In our use of the rules, constraints occurring on the right hand side of rules have justifications attached. We extend the usual derivation steps of Constraint Handling Rules to maintain and extend these justifications.

A *simplification derivation step* applying a (renamed apart) rule instance $r \equiv c_1, \ldots, c_n \iff d_1, \ldots, d_m$ to a set of constraints C is defined as follows. Let $E \subseteq C_e$ where $\theta = mgu(E)$. Let $D = \{c'_1, \ldots, c'_n\} \subseteq C_u$, and suppose there exists substitution σ on variables in r such that $\{\theta(c'_1), \ldots, \theta(c'_n)\} = \{\sigma(c_1), \ldots, \sigma(c_n)\}$, i.e. a subset of C_u *matches* the left hand side of r under the substitution given by E. The *justification* J of the matching is the union of the justifications of $E \cup D$. Note that there may be multiple subsets of C_e which satisfy the above condition and allow matching to occur. For our purposes, however, we require the subset E to be *minimal*. i.e. no strict subset of E can allow for a match. An algorithm for finding such an E is detailed later in this section.

Then we create a new set of constraints $C' = C - \{c'_1, \ldots, c'_n\} \cup \{\theta(c'_1) = c_1, \ldots, \theta(c'_n) = c_n, (d_1)_{J+}, \ldots, (d_n)_{J+}\}$. Note that the equation $\theta(c'_i) = c_i$ is shorthand for $\theta(s_1) = t_1, \ldots, \theta(s_m) = t_m$ where $c'_i \equiv p(s_1, \ldots, s_m)_{J'}$ and $c_i \equiv p(t_1, \ldots, t_m)$.

The annotation $J+$ indicates that we add the justification set J to the *beginning* of the original justification of each d_i. The other constraints (the equality constraints arising from the match) are given empty justifications. Indeed, this is sufficient. The connection to the original location in the program text is retained by propagating justifications to constraints on the right hand side only.

A *propagation derivation step* applying a (renamed apart) rule instance $r \equiv c_1, \ldots, c_n \implies d_1, \ldots, d_m$ is defined similarly except the resulting set of constraints is $C' = C \cup \{\theta(c'_1) = c_1, \ldots, \theta(c'_n) = c_n, (d_1)_{J+}, \ldots, (d_n)_{J+}\}$.

A derivation step from global set of constraints C to C' using an instance of rule r is denoted $C \longrightarrow_r C'$. A *derivation*, denoted $C \longrightarrow_P^* C'$ is a sequence of derivation steps using rules in P where no derivation step is applicable to C'. The operational semantics of CHRs exhaustively apply rules to the global set of constraints, being careful not to apply propagation rules twice on the same constraints (to avoid infinite propagation). For more details on avoiding re-propagation see e.g. Abdennadher[1].

Example 5. Consider the following CHRs.

$$g(t_4) \iff (t_1 = Char)_1, f(t_2)_2, (t_2 = t_1 \to t_3)_3, (t_4 = t_3)_4$$
$$f(t_7) \iff (t_5 = Bool)_5, (t_6 = Bool)_6, (t_7 = t_5 \to t_6)_7$$

A CHR derivation from the goal g_8 where 8 stands for a hypothetical program location, is shown below. To help the reader, we underline constraints involved in rule applications.

$$\underline{g(t)_8}$$
$$\longrightarrow t = t_4, (t_1 = Char)_{[8,1]}, \underline{f(t_2)_{[8,2]}}, (t_2 = t_1 \to t_3)_{[8,3]}, (t_4 = t_3)_{[8,4]}$$
$$\longrightarrow t = t_4, (t_1 = Char)_{[8,1]}, t_2 = t_7, (t_5 = Bool)_{[8,2,5]}, (t_6 = Bool)_{[8,2,6]},$$
$$(t_7 = t_5 \to t_6)_{[8,2,7]}, (t_2 = t_1 \to t_3)_{[8,3]}, (t_4 = t_3)_{[8,4]}$$

Note that we have not bothered to rename any of the new constraints, since all the variables are already distinct, and no rule is applied more than once. In the first step, the constraint $g(t)_8$ matches the left hand side of the first CHR. We replace $g(t)_8$ by the right hand side. In addition, we add the matching equation $t = t_4$. Note how the justification from $g(t)_8$ is added to each justification set. Thus, by propagating justifications we retain the connection constraints and the program locations from which these constraints were originating from. In the final step, the constraint $f(t_2)_{[8,2]}$ matches the left hand side of the second CHR. Hence, we add $[8, 2]$ to the constraints on the right hand side of g's CHR.

Because of the highly nondeterministic operational semantics, an important property of a CHR program is *confluence*, which demands that each possible order of rule applications leads to the same results (modulo renaming). That is, if $C \longrightarrow C'$ and $C \longrightarrow C''$, then $C' \longrightarrow_P^* D$ and $C'' \longrightarrow_P^* D'$ where $\bar{\exists}_C D \leftrightarrow \bar{\exists}_C D'$. We will demand that the CHR programs we use are confluent. Another important property is termination. A set P of CHRs is *terminating* iff for each C we find D such that $C \longrightarrow_P^* D$. Again we will demand that the CHR programs we use are terminating.

A common restriction on a CHRs $C \iff D$ or $C \implies D$ is *range restriction*, that is, $fv(\phi(D)) \subseteq fv(\phi(C))$ where $\phi = mgu(D_e)$. Usually it holds because $fv(D) \subseteq fv(C)$. Range restrictedness essentially prevents new variables from being introduced by rules. We will also restrict attention to CHR programs where simplification rules are *single-headed*, that is, of the form $c \iff d_1, \ldots, d_m$.

Given a CHR program P which is confluent, terminating, range-restricted and only includes single-headed simplification rules, we can define a number of constraint operations.

Satisfiability. We use an open world assumption for satisfiability of CHR constraints, that is, we assume we can always add a new rule making a new fixed type constraint hold. In that case unsatisfiability can only result from the equations. We can check that C is satisfiable by determining $C \longrightarrow_P^* D$ and checking that D_e is satisfiable.

```
min_unsat(D)                        min_impl(D,∃ā.F)
  M := ∅                             M := ∅
  while satisfiable(M) {             while ¬implies(M,∃ā.F) {
    C := M                             C := M
    while satisfiable(C)               while ¬implies(C,∃ā.F)
      { let e ∈ D - C; C := C ∪ {e} }    { let e ∈ D - C; C := C ∪ {e} }
    D := C; M := M ∪{e}}               D := C; M := M ∪ {e} }
  return M                           return M
              (a)                                 (b)
```

Fig. 1. Constraint manipulation algorithms

Minimal Unsatisfiable Subsets. Given an unsatisfiable constraint D, we will be interested in finding a minimal subset E of D_e such that E is unsatisfiable. An unsatisfiable set is *minimal* if the removal of any constraint from that set leaves it satisfiable. The Chameleon system simply finds an arbitrary minimal unsatisfiable subset. An algorithm is shown in Figure 1(a).

Example 6. Consider the final constraint of Example 5. It is unsatisfiable, applying min_unsat to this constraint yields.

$$(t_1 = Char)_{[8,1]}, t_2 = t_7, (t_5 = Bool)_{[8,2,5]}, (t_7 = t_5 \rightarrow t_6)_{[8,2,7]}, (t_2 = t_1 \rightarrow t_3)_{[8,3]}$$

Ultimately, we are interested in the justifications attached to minimal unsatisfiable constraints. This will allow us to identify problematic locations in the program text.

We can straightforwardly determine which constraints $e \in M$ must occur in all minimal unsatisfiable subsets, since this is exactly those where $D - \{e\}$ is satisfiable. The complexity (for both checks) is $O(|D|^2)$ using an incremental unification algorithm. A detailed analysis of the problem of finding all minimal unsatisfiable constraints can be found in [9].

Implication Testing. Given the restrictions on CHR programs defined above, we can show that they provide a canonical normal form (see [28] for details), that is, every equivalent constraint is mapped to an equivalent (modulo renaming) result. We can use an equivalence check to determine implication of $\exists_V C \supset \exists_V C'$, where we assume C and C' are renamed apart except for V, as follows. We execute $C \longrightarrow_P^* D$ and $C, C' \longrightarrow_P^* D'$, then check that $\phi(D_u)$ is a renaming of $\phi'(D'_u)$, where $\phi = mgu(D_e)$ and $\phi' = mgu(D'_e)$.

Minimal Implicants. We are also interested in finding minimal systems of constraints that imply another constraint. Assume that $C \longrightarrow_P^* D$ where $\models D \supset \exists ā.F$. We want to identify a minimal subset E of D such that $\models E \supset \exists ā.F$. The algorithm for finding minimal implicants is highly related to that for minimal unsatisfiable subsets.

The code for min_impl is identical to min_unsat except the test $satisfiable(S)$ is replaced by $\neg implies(S, \exists ā.F)$. It is shown in Figure 1(b).

Expressions	e	$::= f_l \mid x_l \mid (\lambda x_l.e)_l \mid (e\ e)_l \mid (\text{case } e \text{ of } ([(p_i \to e_i)_l]_{i \in I})_l)_l$
Patterns	p	$::= x_l \mid (K\ p...p)_l$
Types	t	$::= a \mid t \to t \mid T\ \bar{t}$
Primitive Constraints	at	$::= t = t \mid TC\ \bar{t}$
Constraints	C	$::= at \mid C \wedge C$
Type Schemes	σ	$::= t \mid \forall \bar{a}.C \Rightarrow t$
Fun Decls	fd	$::= f :: (C \Rightarrow t)_l \mid f_l = e$
Data Decls	dd	$::= \text{data } T\ \bar{a} = K\ \bar{t}$
Type Class Decls	tc	$::= \text{class } (C \Rightarrow TC\ \bar{a})_l \text{ where } m :: (C \Rightarrow t)_l \mid \text{instance } C \Rightarrow (TC\ \bar{t})_l$
Programs	FP	$::= \epsilon \mid fd\ FP \mid dd\ FP \mid tc\ FP$

Fig. 2. Syntax of Programs

The test $implies(M, \exists \bar{a}.F)$ can be performed as follows. If F is a system of equations only, we build $\phi = mgu(M_e)$ and $\phi' = mgu(M_e \wedge F)$ and check that $\phi(a) = \phi'(a)$ for all variables except those in $\bar{a}$. If F includes user defined constraints, then for each user-defined constraint $c_i \in F_u$ we nondeterministically choose a user-defined constraint $c'_i \in M$. We then check that $implies(M, \exists \bar{a}.(F_e \wedge c_i = c'_i)$ holds as above. We need to check all possible choices for c'_i (although we can omit those which obviously lead to failure, e.g. $c_i = Eq\ a$ and $c'_i = Ord\ b$).

3   Type Processing

Our approach to type processing follows [5] by translating the typing problem into a constraint problem and inferring and checking types by constraint operations. We map the type information to a set of Constraint Handling Rules (CHRs) [8], where the constraints are justified by program locations.

3.1   Expressions, Types and Constraints

The syntax of programs can be found in Figure 2. Using case expressions we can easily encode multiple-clause definitions: and if-then-else expressions which we will make use of in our examples. For brevity we omit nested function definitions and recursive functions. They are straightforward to handle, but messy; for a complete treatment see [35].

Note that our expressions are fully *labeled*, i.e. we label program locations with unique numbers. We indicate these labels by a subscript l following the expression, as can be seen in the language description above. Labels will become important when generating constraints from a source program.

We assume that K refers to constructors of user-defined data types. As usual patterns are assumed to be linear, i.e., each variable occurs at most once. In examples we will use pattern matching notation for convenience. Note that each pattern/action has a location, as well as a location for the list of all pattern/actions and a location for the case.

We assume data type declarations $\text{data } T\ \bar{a} = K\ t_1 \cdots t_n$ are preprocessed and the types of constructors $K : \forall \bar{a}.t_1 \to \cdots \to t_n \to T\ \bar{a}$ are recorded in the environment E.

Type schemes have an additional constraint component which allows us to restrict the set of type instances. We often refer to a type scheme as a type for short. Note that we consider $\forall \bar{a}.t$ as a short-hand for $\forall \bar{a}.True \Rightarrow t$.

We also ignore the bodies of instance declarations for brevity, they don't add any significant extra complication.

3.2   Constraint Generation from Expressions

The basic idea of our translation is that we map a functional program FP to a CHR program P. For each function f defined by the program FP we introduce a unary predicate f in P such that the solutions of $f(t)$ are the types of f.

Constraint generation is formulated as a logical deduction system with clauses of the form $E, \Gamma, e \vdash_{Cons} (F \mid t)$ where the environment E of all pre-defined functions, environment Γ of lambda-bound variables, and expression e are input parameters and constraint C and type t are output parameters.

Each individual sub-expression gives rise to a constraint which is justified by the location attached to this sub-expression. See Figure 3 for details. In rule (Var-x) we simply look up the type of a λ-bound variable in Γ. The rule (Var-x) creates a renamed apart copy of the type of a predefined let-bound function. In rule (Var-f) we generate an "instantiation" constraint, to represent the type of a let-defined function, we use the notation $[\bar{b}/\bar{a}]$ to define a substitution replacing each $a \in \bar{a}$ by the corresponding $b \in \bar{b}$. In rule (Case) we first equate the types of all pattern/actions, and then treat the remainder like an application. In rule (Pat) we make use of auxiliary judgments of the form $p \vdash_{Cons} \forall \bar{b}.(C \mid t \mid \Gamma_p)$ which we use to generate types and constraints from patterns, as well as to extend the type environment with newly bound variables. The other rules are straightforward.

4   Hindley/Milner Types

We begin by restricting ourselves to programs without type classes or instances. This leaves us in the case of pure Hindley/Milner types. Generation of CHRs is straightforward by iteration over the program. The function definition $f = e$ generates the rule $f(t) \iff C$ where $E, \emptyset, e \vdash_{Cons} (C, t)$. This defines the predicate f encoding the type of function f. The function declaration $f : (C \Rightarrow t)_l$ generates the rule $f_a(t') \iff C_l \land (t = t')_l$. This defines the predicate f_a encoding the annotated type of f.

Example 7. For example the (location annotated) program

```
(g = (f2 'a'1)3)4
(f True5 = True6)7
```

is translated to (after some simplification[2]):

$$g(t_4) \iff (t_1 = Char)_1, f(t_2)_2, (t_2 = t_1 \to t_3)_3, (t_4 = t_3)_4$$
$$f(t_7) \iff (t_5 = Bool)_5, (t_6 = Bool)_6, (t_7 = t_5 \to t_6)_7$$

---

[2] The desugared definition of f is $f = \lambda x.(\text{case } x \text{ of } True \to True)$ creating a much bigger but equivalent set of constraints.

(Var-x)
$$\frac{(x : t) \in \Gamma \quad t_l \text{ fresh}}{E, \Gamma, x_l \vdash_{Cons} ((t_l = t)_l \mid t')}$$

(Var-p)
$$\frac{f : \forall \bar{a}.C \Rightarrow t \in E \quad \bar{b}, t_l \text{ fresh}}{E, \Gamma, f_l \vdash_{Cons} ([\overline{b/a}]C)_l \wedge (t_l = [\overline{b/a}]t)_l \mid t')}$$

(Var-f)
$$\frac{f : \sigma \notin E \quad t_l \text{ fresh}}{E, \Gamma, f_l \vdash_{Cons} (f(t_l)_l \mid t_l)}$$

(Abs)
$$\frac{E, \Gamma.x : t_{l_1}, e \vdash_{Cons} (C \mid t) \quad t_{l_1}, t_{l_2}, t' \text{ fresh}}{E, \Gamma, (\lambda x_{l_1}.e)_{l_2} \vdash_{Cons} (C \wedge (t_{l_2} = t' \rightarrow t)_{l_2} \wedge (t_{l_1} = t')_{l_1} \mid t_{l_2})}$$

(App)
$$\frac{E, \Gamma, e_1 \vdash_{Cons} (C_1 \mid t_1) \quad \Gamma, e_2 \vdash_{Cons} (C_2 \mid t_2) \quad t_l \text{ fresh}}{E, \Gamma, (e_1 \ e_2)_l \vdash_{Cons} (C_1 \wedge C_2 \wedge (t_1 = t_2 \rightarrow t_l)_l \mid t_l)}$$

(Case)
$$\frac{\begin{array}{c} E, \Gamma, e \vdash_{Cons} (C_e \mid t_e) \\ E, \Gamma, (p_i \rightarrow e_i) \vdash_{Cons} (C_i \mid t_i) \quad \text{for } i \in I \\ C \equiv \bigwedge_{i \in I} ((t_{l_1} = t_i)_{l_1} \wedge C_i) \wedge (t_{l_1} = t_e \rightarrow t_{l_2})_{l_2} \quad t_{l_1}, t_{l_2} \text{ fresh} \end{array}}{E, \Gamma, (\text{case } e \text{ of } ([p_i \rightarrow e_i]_{i \in I})_{l_1})_{l_2} \vdash_{Cons} (C \mid t_{l_2})}$$

(Pat)
$$\frac{\begin{array}{c} p \vdash_{Cons} (C_p \mid t_p \mid \Gamma') \quad E, \Gamma \cup \Gamma', e \vdash_{Cons} (C_e \mid t_e) \\ C \equiv C_p \wedge C_e \wedge (t_l = t_p \rightarrow t_e)_l \quad t_l \text{ fresh} \end{array}}{E, \Gamma, (p \rightarrow e)_l \vdash_{Cons} (C \mid t_l)}$$

(Pat-Var)
$$\frac{t \text{ fresh}}{x_l \vdash_{Cons} (True \mid t_l \mid \{x : t_l\})}$$

(Pat-K)
$$\frac{\begin{array}{c} p_i \vdash_{Cons} (t_{p_i} \mid C_{p_i} \mid \Gamma_{p_i}) \quad \text{for } i = 1, ..., n \\ K : \forall \bar{a}.t_K \quad \Gamma_p = \Gamma \cup \bigcup_{i=1,...,n} \Gamma_{p_i} \quad t_l \text{ fresh} \\ C' \equiv (t_K = t_{p_1} \rightarrow ... \rightarrow t_{p_n} \rightarrow t_l)_l \wedge \bigwedge_{i \in \{1,...,n\}} C_{p_i} \end{array}}{(K \ p_1 \ ... \ p_n)_l \vdash_{Cons} (C' \mid t_l \mid \Gamma_p)}$$

Fig. 3. Justified Constraint Generation

Example 8. The (location annotated) program

```
h :: (Int -> (Int,Int)))₁
(h x₂ = (x₃, x₄)₅)₆
```

is translated to

$$h_a(t_1) \Longleftrightarrow (t_1 = Int \rightarrow (Int, Int))_1$$
$$h(t_6) \Longleftrightarrow (t_2 = t_x)_2, (t_3 = t_x)_3, (t_4 = t_x)_4, (t_5 = (t_3, t_4))_5, (t_6 = t_2 \rightarrow t_5)_6$$

In this framework it is now easy to see the correspondences between typing questions and constraint algorithms.

Type Inference. Type inference for an expression e corresponds to building a canonical normal form of the constraint generated from e. Type inference of a function f simply involves executing the goal $f(t) \longrightarrow_P^* C$. The type of f is $\bar{\exists}_t C$.

Example 9. For the program of Example 7, if we wish to infer the type of g, we determine C such that $g(t) \longrightarrow_P^* C$. The generated constraint is shown in Example 5. Since the resulting constraints are not satisfiable g has no type.

Example 10. Consider the program in Example 8. The goal $h(t) \longrightarrow_P^* C_1$ generates the constraint

$$C_1 \equiv t = t_6 \wedge (t_2 = t_x)_2 \wedge (t_3 = t_x)_3 \wedge (t_4 = t_x)_4 \wedge (t_5 = (t_3, t_4))_5 \wedge (t_6 = t_2 \to t_5)_6$$

which is satisfiable. A simplified equivalent constraint to $\bar{\exists}_t C_1$ is $\exists t_x. t = t_x \to (t_x, t_x)$ which we report as the type of h as $h : \forall t_x. t_x \to (t_x, t_x)$.

Type Checking. Type checking of a function definition $f = e$ with respect to its declared type $f : C \Rightarrow t$ requires us to test implication. Since we have two constraints defining the inferred and declared type we simply need to check implication. Let $f(t) \longrightarrow_P^* C$ and $f_a(t) \longrightarrow_P^* C'$. Then the declared type is correct if $\bar{\exists}_t C' \supset \bar{\exists}_t C$. We can use the implication checking algorithm discussed in Section 2.

Example 11. Consider the program in Example 8. The goal $h_a(t) \longrightarrow_P^* C_2$ generates

$$C_2 \equiv (l = Int \to (Int, Int)_1$$
$$C_1 \wedge C_2 \equiv (t = Int \to (Int, Int))_1 \wedge C_1$$

The corresponding substitutions are identical on t. Hence the declared type is correct.

5 Type Error Reporting

The most important insight we gain from understanding typing problems as constraint problems in the case of pure Hindley/Milner types is what to do when it goes wrong! Since we have mapped typing questions to constraint questions, we immediately have more insight into why failure occurred. In this section we consider what it means about the corresponding constraint problem when type inference or type checking fails. We then use this to define better error messages.

5.1 Failure of Type Inference

A program is ill-typed if the constraints on its type are unsatisfiable. Before the program can be run, it must be modified, but obviously any such modification must actually fix the problem at hand. Our task then, is to report the type error in such a way that the programmer is directed towards the locations in the source code which are potentially the source of the error, and if modified appropriately, would fix the program.

Suppose type inference fails for a function f, then we have an unsatisfiable set of constraints C arising from $f(t) \longrightarrow_P^* C$. The key insight we obtain from the constraint view is this:

A type error results from a minimal unsatisfiable set of constraints.

We dont need to consider all constraints in C to have a type error. Hence we should report errors as minimal unsatisfiable sets of constraints. Note there are many possible minimal unsatisfiable sets, and different sets will generate different error reports (see [35] for examples).

We can find M a single minimal unsatisfiable subset of C, employing the algorithm of Section 2 (we will just take the first generated). Such a set represents a "smallest" type error, and the corresponding locations give a smallest collection of program locations which caused the error. The simplest scheme for reporting an error is simply to highlight all the locations of the source text which make up a type error.

Example 12. When we try to infer a type for g in Example 7 we obtain the constraints shown in Example 5. Since these are unsatisfiable we find a minimal unsatisfiable subset as shown in Example 6. The set of locations involved are $\{1, 2, 3, 5, 7, 8\}$ The type error can be reported as

```
g = f 'a'
f True = True
```

This indicates a conflict between the application of f to 'a' in g, and f's pattern. Importantly, because we have used a minimal unsatisfiable subset of the inconsistent constraints, we have only highlighted the locations which are actually involved in the error; the True in the body of f is not part of the conflict, and therefore not highlighted.

Note that we do not highlight applications since they have no explicit tokens in the source program. We leave it to the user to understand when we highlight a function position we may also refer to its application.

To remain efficient, we only consider a single minimal unsatisfiable subset of constraints at a time. Given the number of constraints generated during inference, calculating all minimal unsatisfiable subsets is simply not feasible. As mentioned in Section 2, however, it is inexpensive to find any constraints which appear in all minimal unsatisfiable subsets.

For type error reporting purposes, finding a non-empty intersection of all minimal unsatisfiable subsets is significant, since those constraints correspond to source locations which are part of every type conflict present. These common locations are much more likely to be the actual source of the mistake.

Example 13. The following simple program, where functions toUpper and toLower are standard Haskell functions both with type $Char \rightarrow Char$, is ill-typed.

```
(f x₂ = (if₃ x₄ then₅ (toUpper₆ x₇)₈ else₉ (toLower₁₀ x₁₁)₁₂)₁
```

It's plain to see that there is a conflict between the use of x at type *Bool* in the conditional, and at type *Char* in both branches of the if-then-else. Hence, there are two minimal unsatisfiable subsets of the above constraints. Common to both of these are the (location annotated) constraints listed below.

$$(t_3 = Bool)_3, (t_4 = t_1)_4,$$

This strongly suggests that the real source of the mistake in this program lies at location 3 or 4. We might report this by highlighting the source text as follows.

```
f x = (if x then (toUpper x) else (toLower x))
```

Indeed, changing the expression at location 4 to something like x > 'm' would resolve both type conflicts, whereas changing either of the two branches would only fix one.

Just highlighting the locations causing a type error is not very informative. Usually type errors are reported as an incompatibility of two types, an expected type and an inferred type. Given our much more detailed constraint viewpoint we can do better. Our algorithm for generating text error messages with type information, from a minimal unsatisfiable set of justified constraints, is as follows:

1. Select a location from the minimal unsatisfiable set to report the type conflict about
2. Find the types that conflict at that location
   - Assign each a colour and determine which locations contribute to it
3. Diagnose the error in terms of the conflicting types at the chosen location. Highlight each location involved in the colours of the types it contributes to.

Although we can pick any location, we have found that usually the highest location in the abstract syntax tree occuring in the minimal unsatisfiable subset leads to the clearest error messages. If l is the highest location appearing in M, we remove all equations added by location l to obtain M'. Now M' is satisfiable (since we have removed at least one equation from a minimal unsatisfiable set) and we can use it to determine the types reported. We will choose locations l' to report the types of depending on the kind of location l. Importantly if $\phi = mgu(M')$ and $\phi(t_{l'}) = t'$ we report the type of location l' as t' and highlight the locations from M' of a minimal implicant of $t_{l'} = t'$.

We can define a specific type error for each different kind of location. For brevity we just give an example, see [31,35] for more details.

Example 14. For a location corresponding to incompatible types for pattern/ actions in a case $([p_i \to e_i]_{i \in I})_l$ we remove all the constraints of the form $(t_l = t_i)_l$ occuring in M. We now report the types t_i of each pattern/action entry $p_i \to e_i$ as defined by M'.

Example 1 is an example of incompatible types of a pattern/actions (in the desugared version). For this example, we remove the equations forcing each clause for f to have the same type. We then determine the type of each clause independently, and find minimal implicants of these types. By highlighting each type and its implicant locations in the same color we can see why the types arose.

Note that the types only consider constraints in the minimal unsatisfiable subset, so that the type of the first alternative is reported as `Char -> a -> b -> c` rather than `Char -> a -> Bool -> c` which we might expect.

5.2 Failure of Type Checking

When type checking fails for $f : C \to t$; $f = e$ we have that $f(t) \longrightarrow_P^* C$ and $f_a(t) \longrightarrow_P^* C'$ and its not the case that $\exists_t C' \supset \exists_t C$. If $\exists_t C$ is *False* we have a failure of type inference and can report a problem as in the previous subsection. Otherwise we can choose any constraint in $\exists_t C$ not implied by $\exists_t C'$.

There are choices in how to do this. Currently Chameleon chooses in the following way. We consider the substitutions $\phi = mgu(C')$ and $\phi' = mgu(C \wedge C')$. Choose a variable $a \in \phi(t)$ where $\phi'(a) \neq a$. We then determine the minimal subset D of C such that $D \wedge C' \supset a = \phi'(a)$. We make use of the min_impl algorithm described in Section 2 to find D. This describes a minimal reason why the variable a was bound in the inferred type.

Example 15. Consider the following modification of the program in Example 8

```
h :: (a -> (a,b))₁
(h x₂ = (x₃, x₄)₅)₆
```

is translated to

$$h_a(t_1) \Longleftrightarrow (t_1 = (a \to (a, b)))_1$$
$$h(t_6) \Longleftrightarrow (t_2 = t_x)_2, (t_3 = t_x)_3, (t_4 = t_x)_4, (t_5 = (t_3, t_4))_5, (t_6 = t_2 \to t_5)_6$$

We find that $\phi = \{t \mapsto a \to (a, b)\}$ while $\phi' = \{t \mapsto a \to (a, a), t_x \mapsto a, b \mapsto a\}$. We find $\phi'(b) \neq b$. We determine a minimal implicant of $C \wedge C'$ for $b = a$, which is $\{(t_1 = (a \to (a, b)))_1, (t_6 = t_2 \to t_5)_6, (t_5 = (t_3, t_4))_5, (t_2 = t_x)_2, (t_4 = t_x)_4, \}$. The resulting set of locations are highlighted.

```
h.hs:2: ERROR: Inferred type does not subsume declared type
Declared: forall a,b. a -> (a,b)
Inferred: forall a. a -> (a,a)
Problem : The variable 'b' makes the declared type too polymorphic
          h x = (x, x)
```

The GHC error message explains the same problem in inferred and declared type but can't point us at any location that caused the problem.

6   Type Class Overloading

Type classes and instances are a popular extension of Hindley/Milner types that give controlled overloading. We now extend our notion of constraints to incorporate classes and instances. Again we use CHRs to encode their meaning. We then revisit the typing questions once more. The class declaration and instance declaration generate the following CHRs:

$$\text{class } (C \Rightarrow TC\ \bar{a})_{l_1} \text{ where } m :: (D \Rightarrow t)_{l_2} \qquad TC\ \bar{a} \Longrightarrow C_{l_1}$$
$$m_a(t) \Longleftrightarrow t = t_{l_2}, D_{l_2}, (TC\ \bar{a})_{l_2}$$
$$\text{instance } E \Rightarrow (TC\ \bar{t})_{l_3} \qquad\qquad TC\ \bar{t} \Longleftrightarrow E_{l_3}$$

The first rule ensures the super-class constraint hold, that is if $TC\ \bar{a}$ then the super class constraints C also hold. The location annotation ensure we see they arise from the class declaration. The second rule defines the type of the method m. The third rule encodes the proof that an instance is available through the instance rules. We omit instance method declarations for simplicity, they simply create more type checking.

Example 16. The table below shows class and instance declarations below and their translation (where we ignore instance method declarations for brevity).

```
class (Eq a)₁ where                Eq a ⟹ True₁
  (==) :: (a -> a -> Bool)₂   (==)(t₂) ⟺ (t₂=a→ a → Bool)₂, (Eq a)₂
class (Eq a => Ord a)₃ where    Ord a ⟹ (Eq a)₃
  (>) :: (a -> a -> Bool)₄      (>)(t₄) ⟺ (t₄=a →a→Bool)₄, (Ord a)₄
instance (Ord a => Ord [a])₅   Ord [a] ⟺ (Ord a)₅
instance (Ord Bool)₆          Ord Bool ⟺ True₆
```

Note that the super-class relation encoded by the CHR states that each occurrence of $Ord\ a$ implies $(Eq\ a)_3$. Note that right hand sides of CHRs generated are justified, so we can keep track which rules were involved when inspecting justifications attached to constraints.

Our assumptions on CHRs require that the CHRs generated from class and instance declarations are confluent, terminating, range-restricted and single-headed simplification. The last two properties are easy to check, and, fortunately, the first two properties are guaranteed by the conditions imposed on Haskell type classes. An in-depth discussion can be found in [6].

Type inference in the presence of type classes and instances works as follows. To infer the type of f we determine $f(t) \longrightarrow_P^* C$ and give the inferred type of f as $f :: \phi(C_u) \Rightarrow \phi(t)$ where $\phi = mgu(C_e)$.

6.1   Failure of Type Inference

As in the pure Hindley/Milner case a failure of type inference can give an unsatisfiable set of constraints C. Unsatisfiability of a set of constraints can only arise through an unsatisfiable set of term equations, since the assumption is that the classes and instances follow an open world assumption, another instance could be added at any time in order to satisfy any remaining class constraints. Hence we can use the same mechanisms as for pure Hindley/Milner.

But there are two new kinds of type error that can now occur.

Missing Instance Error. In Haskell 98, type classes are single-parameter and each argument of a type class appearing within a functions type $\phi(C_u)$, must be a single variable (a). A non-conforming constraint is one whose arguments have not been reduced to this form, indicating that there is a *missing instance* error.

For a missing instance error to occur a class constraint T a must occur in C such that $\phi(a)$ is not a variable. We can determine the reason this constraint occurs in C using minimal implications. Let L be the set of locations occurring on the constraint $(T \ a)_L$. Now $\phi(a)$ is not a variable (or variable applied to arguments) so it is a term with top level type constructor K of arity n say. We determine the minimal implicants in C of $\exists \bar{y}.a = K \ \bar{y}$. Collecting the locations L' of this minimal implicant with the locations L introducing T a we have the reasons why the missing instance is involved.

Example 17. Re-examining Example 2 from the introduction: the inferred type is $sum :: Num \ [a] \Rightarrow [[a]] \rightarrow [a]$. The missing instance $Num \ [a]$ arise from an initial class constraint $Num \ b$ introduced by + and $b = [a]$ which is implied by the result of sum in the first definition arising from the [] on the right of the equality. Hence we obtain error message shown in Example 2.

Ambiguity Error. An important restriction usually made on types is that they are *unambiguous*. A type $\bar{\exists}_t C$ is unambiguous if fixing t fixes all the existentially quantified variables in $\bar{\exists}_t C$. Programs with ambiguous types can lead to operationally nondeterministic behaviour.

We can use CHRs to check unambiguity as follows. A type $\bar{\exists}_t C$ is unambiguous if ρ is a renaming of $fv(C)$ we determine $C \wedge \rho(C) \wedge t = \rho(t) \longrightarrow^*_P D$. If $D \supset a = \rho(a)$ for all $a \in fv(C)$ then f is unambiguous.

In reporting ambiguity we highlight the locations where the ambiguous variable is part of the type, since each such location could be improved to remove the ambiguity. For ease of reporting we only consider only a variable $a \in \bar{a} = fv(\phi(C_u))$ where $\phi = mgu(C_e)$. If the type $\bar{\exists}_t C$ is ambiguous, then the test must fail for one of these variables. Examining a location variable t_l we can see if a occurs in its type, if $a \in fv(\phi(t_l))$. We highlight all locations where this test succeeds.

Example 18. Consider the following program, where $read :: Read \ a \Rightarrow [Char] \rightarrow a$ and $show :: Show \ a \Rightarrow a \rightarrow [Char]$,

```
f x y z = show (if x then read y else read z)
```

The inferred type is ambiguous since the type a of read y and read z does not appear in the type of f. GHC reports the error as follows

```
amb.hs:3:26:
    Ambiguous type variable 'a' in the constraints:
      'Read a' arising from use of 'read' at amb.hs:3:26-29
      'Show a' arising from use of 'show' at amb.hs:3:10-13
    Probable fix: add a type signature that fixes these type variable(s)
```

Chameleon highlights the positions where the type variable a appears as part of the type:

```
ambig.ch:9: ERROR: Inferred type scheme is ambiguous:
Type scheme: forall a. (Read a,Show a)=> Bool ->[Char] -> [Char] -> [Char]
Suggestion: Ambiguity can be resolved at these locations
            f x y z = show (if x then read y else read z)
```

illustrating that the ambiguity can be removed by type annotations on either call to read, or on the if-then-else. Note how effectively GHC picks just one instance of read to concentrate on.

6.2 Failure of Type Checking

Now type checking can fail in a new way, since the types are no longer simply sets of equations. We now have to consider that a type class constraint is not implied. This ends up actually easier than the case for equations.

Recall that $f(t) \longrightarrow^*_P C$ and $f_a(t) \longrightarrow^*_P C'$. Let $\phi = mgu(C'_e)$ and $\phi' = mgu(C_e \wedge C'_e)$. Suppose we have a constraint $\phi'(T\ \bar{a}) \in \phi'(C_u)$ such that $\phi'(T\ \bar{a}) \notin \phi(C_u)$. Suppose $(T\ \bar{a})_L$ is the location annotated version of this constraint in C_u, we highlight the locations L which causes the unmatched class constraint to arise.

Example 19. Consider the following program

```
notNull :: Eq a => [a] -> Bool
notNull xs = xs > []
```

The inferred type is $Ord\ a \wedge Eq\ a \Rightarrow a \to Bool$, while the declared type is $Eq\ a \Rightarrow a \to Bool$. We determine the locations that cause the $Ord\ a$ class constraint to arise, and highlight them.

We report the following.

```
notNull.hs:2: ERROR: Inferred type does not subsume declared type
Declared: forall a. Eq a => [a] -> Bool
Inferred: forall a. Ord a => [a] -> Bool
Problem : Constraint Ord a, from following location, is unmatched.
          notNull :: Eq a => [a] -> Bool
          notNull xs = xs > []
```

It should be noted that GHC also seems to do well at reporting this sort of error; it appears to record the source location of each user constraint, so it can then report where any unmatched constraints come from.

GHC raises the following error:

```
notNull.hs:2:
   Could not deduce (Ord a) from the context (Eq a)
   arising from use of '>' at notNull.hs:2
   Probable fix:
       Add (Ord a) to the type signature(s) for 'notNull'
   In the definition of 'notNull': notNull xs = xs > []
```

Other Haskell systems such as Hugs [16] and nhc98 [23], however, report the error without identifying the program locations responsible.

7 Extended Type Systems

We now consider further extensions to Hindley/Milner types and how they can be incorporated. Chameleon [32] supports all the features we discuss below.

7.1 Functional Dependencies

Functional dependencies [17] are an important extension for multi-parameter type classes. They allow the programmer to specify depencies between arguments of multi-parameter type classes, and hence improve type inference. Classes with functional dependencies are translated using additional CHRs for each functional dependency, and for each instance and functional dependency.

Example 20. The following type class models a collection relationship ce is a collection of es.

```
class (Collects ce e)₁ | (ce -> e)₂ where
    empty :: ce
    insert :: e -> ce -> ce
instance (Collects Integer Bool)₃ where ...
instance Eq a => (Collects [a] a)₄ where ...
```

The functional dependency $ce \rightarrow e$ states that there is at most one element type e for each collection type ce. Without this empty is ambiguous.

The additional CHRs are

$$Collects\ ce\ e1, Collects\ ce\ e2 \Longrightarrow (e1 = e2)_{2}$$
$$Collects\ Integer\ b \Longrightarrow (b = Bool)_{[2,3]}$$
$$Collects\ [a]\ b \Longrightarrow (b = a)_{[2,4]}$$

The first enforces the functional dependency on two *Collects* constraints with the same collection type. The last two are improvement rules for each instance. Once we know the collection type is *Integer*, we know the element type is *Bool*, and once we know the collection type is $[a]$ we know the element type is a.

We can show (see [6]) that Haskell programs with functional dependencies satisfying the restrictions in [17] lead to confluent, terminating, range-restricted and single-headed simplication programs, so our type framework is usable without modification. The only new difficulty arises in error reporting. Functional dependencies can create unsatisfiable constraints where the location l occuring in a justification but t_l does not appear in the constraints. We overcome this by reporting the error on the usage of the functional dependency.

Example 21. The function

```
f ce = insert 'a' (insert True c)
```

is incorrect since we cannot have a *Bool* and *Char* in the same collection. GHC declares:

```
collects.hs:5:
    Couldn't match 'Bool' against 'Char'
        Expected type: Bool
        Inferred type: Char
    When using functional dependencies to combine
        Collects ce Bool, arising from use of 'insert' at collects.hs:7
        Collects ce Char, arising from use of 'insert' at collects.hs:7
    When generalizing the type(s) for 'f'
```

We report:

```
collects.hs:5: ERROR: Functional dependency causes type error
Types    : Char
           Bool
Problem : class Collects ce e | ce -> e ...
           Enforces: Collects ce e1, Collects ce e2 ==> e1 = e2
           On constraints:
               Collects ce Char (from line 5, col. 7)
               Collects ce Bool (from line 5, col. 19)
Conflict: f c = insert 'a' (insert True c)
```

Note here we have multiple "colour" highlighting. The calls to `insert` both generate *Collects* constraint and define the types of variables $e1$ and $e2$ so they are highlighted in both ways.

The advantage of our error report is that we are not limited to identifying just the locations of the *Collects* constraints above, we can straightforwardly point out all of the other complicit locations, and identify which of the conflicting types they contribute to.

7.2   Adhoc Type Improvements

In Chameleon the user is allowed to write their own CHRs, which become part of the program P. This can be used to improve type inference and checking.

Example 22. Consider the following class and instance building a `zip`-like function `zipall` for zipping an arbitrary number of arguments:

```
class Zip a b c | c -> b, c -> a where
    zipall :: [a] -> [b] -> c
instance Zip a b [(a,b)] where zipall = zip
instance Zip (a,b) c e => Zip a b ([c]->e) where
    zipall as bs cs = zipall (zip as bs) cs
```

As it stands type inference for

```
e = head (zipall ['a','b'] [True,False] ['c'])
```

will return $e :: \forall a. Zip\ (Char, Bool)\ Char\ [a] \Rightarrow a$. We can add an improving propagation rules to enforce that whenever the third argument of a *Zip* constraint is a list type, rather than a function type, it is a list of pairs of the first two. In Chameleon format this is

```
rule Zip a b [c] ==> c = (a,b)
```

With this rule we infer $e :: ((Char, Bool), Char)$ as expected.

Arbitrary rule additions may break confluence, termination, range-restrictedness and single-headed simplification (the last two of which we can check). Currently we assume the user enforces confluence and termination. We can handle type error reporting with adhoc rules using the same approach as for functional dependencies, choosing the last rule fired. This does highlight the future need for better error reporting by explaining a sequence of CHR rule firings.

7.3   Extended Algebraic Data Types

Guarded algebraic data types illustrated in Example 4 significantly complicate type processing. Chameleon supports GADTs through a more generalized form, Extended Algebraic Data Types (EADTs) [33] which also generalizes existential types. EADTs extend the translation to constraints to include quantified implication constraints of the form

$$\text{ImpConstraints } F ::= C \mid \forall \bar{b}.(C \supset \exists \bar{a}.F) \mid F \wedge F$$

This makes type inference in general impossible, since there may be an infinite number of maximal types, so we concentrate on type checking. Essentially the type checking procedure must check that the implication constraint $\forall \bar{b}.(C \supset \exists \bar{a}.F)$ is implied by the declared type C'. In checking this implication we effectively check if $C \wedge C' \supset \exists \bar{a}.F$. If the implication fails we have a subsumption error like that illustrated in Example 4. See [35] for an extended discussion of type errors for EADTs.

8   Related Work

The starting point for this work was [5] which translated Hindley/Milner types to a set of Horn clauses rather than CHRs. The advantage of CHRs is that we can easily accommodate more advanced type extensions like type classes. Another difference to [5] is that we attach justifications to constraints to keep track of program locations.

Despite recent efforts [4,21,15,10], we believe there remains a lot of scope for improving the quality of type error diagnoses. For example, almost all other work we are aware of has focused on the plain Hindley/Milner type system and excludes features like type-class overloading [34] which are critical in languages like Haskell and Clean (the one exception is the recent paper by Heeren and Hage [13]).

The standard algorithm, $\mathcal{W}$, tends to find errors too late in its traversal of a program [18,37]. $\mathcal{W}$ has been generalised [18] so that the point at which substitutions are applied can be varied. Despite this, there are cases where it is not clear which variation provides the most appropriate error report. Moreover, all of these algorithms suffer from a left-to-right bias when discovering errors during abstract syntax tree (AST) traversal.

One way to overcome this problem, as we have seen, is to avoid the standard inference algorithms altogether and focus directly on the constraints involved. Although our work bears a strong resemblance to [12,14,15], our aims are different. We attempt to explain errors involving advanced type system features, such as overloading, whereas the Helium system [15], which is based on a beginner-friendly variant of Haskell, omits such features by design. Their focus has been on inventing heuristics which allow them to present type errors from a more useful perspective, as well as automatically suggesting "probable fixes." More recently [13] they propose extending their source language with so-called 'type class directives', which provide restrictions on certain forms of type classes (such as making Num $[a]$ illegal). These can be straightforwardly encoded using Chameleon rules.

Closest to our work is probably that of Haack and Wells [10] who also, independently, propose using minimal unsatisfiable subsets of typing constraints to identify problematic program locations. The main difference between their work and ours is that they focus entirely on the standard Hindley/Milner system, limiting their constraint domain to equations, and only report errors by highlighting the locations involved. Another limitation of their proposal is that it lacks any way to generate type explanations, which we do by finding minimal implicants. Such a facility is necessary for explaining subsumption errors.

Another related research direction is error explanation systems [7,2], which allow the user to examine the process by which specific types are inferred for program variables. By essentially recording the effects of the inference procedure on types a step at a time, a complete history can be built up. Unfortunately, a common shortcoming of such systems is the excessive size of of explanations. Although complete, such explanations are full of repetitive and redundant information which can be a burden to sort through. Furthermore, since these systems are layered on top of an existing inference algorithm, they suffer from the same left-to-right bias when discovering errors.

9   Conclusion

We have presented a flexible type processing system for Hindley/Milner types and extensions which naturally supports advanced type error reporting and reasoning techniques. The central idea of our approach is to translate the typing problem to a constraint problem, i.e. a set of constraints where function relations are expressed in terms of CHRs. Individual constraints are justified by the location of their origin. During CHR solving we retain these locations. CHRs are a sufficiently rich constraint language to encode the typing problem for a wide range of extensions of the Hindley/Milner system such as type-class overloading and functional dependencies. The techniques explained in this paper have all been implemented as part of the Chameleon system [32] which is freely available.

The basic machinery we use here can also be used in an interactive type debugging framework (see [29,30]). Clearly as type systems become more and more complicated these interactive forms of type debugging, which for example can explain why a function has an inferred type of a certain shape, become much important. We can also straightforwardly extend our approach to create specialised error messages for library functions or CHR rules in the manner of Helium (see [35] for details).

By lifting type algorithms from adhoc specialized algorithms to generic constraint reasoning algorithms our approach offers the advantages of uniformity (allowing easier handling of extensions) as well as a clear semantics (which for example allowed us to give the first proof of the soundness and completeness of Jones functional dependency restrictions [6]). As types become more complicated, we need to make use of the existing deep understanding of constraints and first order predicate logic, in order to handle them correctly. Typing problems will also inevitably push us to develop new constraint algorithms, for example constraint abduction [19] seems required for inference of GADTs.

References

1. S. Abdennadher. Operational semantics and confluence of constraint propagation rules. In *Proc. of CP'97*, volume 1330 of *LNCS*, pages 252–266. Springer-Verlag, 1997.
2. M. Beaven and R. Stansifer. Explaining type errors in polymorphic languages. In *ACM Letters on Programming Languages*, volume 2, pages 17–30, December 1993.
3. J. Cheney and R. Hinze. First-class phantom types. Technical Report CUCIS TR2003-1901, Cornell University, 2003.
4. O. Chitil. Compositional explanation of types and algorithmic debugging of type errors. In *Proc. of ICFP'01*, pages 193–204. ACM Press, 2001.
5. B. Demoen, M. García de la Banda, and P.J. Stuckey. Type constraint solving for parametric and ad-hoc polymorphism. In *Proc. of the 22nd Australian Computer Science Conference*, pages 217–228. Springer-Verlag, 1999.
6. G. J. Duck, S. Peyton-Jones, P. J. Stuckey, and M. Sulzmann. Sound and decidable type inference for functional dependencies. In *Proc. of ESOP'04*, volume 2986 of *LNCS*, pages 49–63. Springer-Verlag, 2004.
7. D. Duggan and F. Bent. Explaining type inference. *Science of Computer Programming*, 27(1):37–83, 1996.
8. T. Frühwirth. Constraint handling rules. In *Constraint Programming: Basics and Trends*, volume 910 of *LNCS*. Springer-Verlag, 1995.
9. M. García de la Banda, P.J. Stuckey, and J. Wazny. Finding all minimal unsatisfiable constraints. In *Proc. of PPDP'03*, pages 32–43. ACM Press, 2003.
10. C. Haack and J. B. Wells. Type error slicing in implicitly typed, higher-order languages. In *Proc. of ESOP'03*, volume 2618 of *LNCS*, pages 284–301. Springer-Verlag, 2003.
11. Haskell 98 language report. http://research.microsoft.com/Users/simonpj/haskell98-revised/haskell98-report-html/.
12. B. Heeren and J. Hage. Parametric type inferencing for Helium. Technical Report UU-CS-2002-035, Utrecht University, 2002.
13. B. Heeren and J. Hage. Type class directives. In *Proc. of PADL 2005*, 2005.
14. B. Heeren, J. Hage, and D. Swierstra. Generalizing Hindley-Milner type inference algorithms. Technical Report UU-CS-2002-031, Utrecht University, 2002.
15. Helium home page. http://www.cs.uu.nl/~afie/helium/.
16. Hugs home page. http://www.haskell.org/hugs/.
17. M. P. Jones. Type classes with functional dependencies. In *Proc. ESOP'00*, volume 1782 of *LNCS*, pages 230–244. Springer-Verlag, March 2000.
18. O. Lee and K. Yi. A generalized let-polymorphic type inference algorithm. Technical Memorandum ROPAS-2000-5, National Creative Research Center, Korea Advanced Institute of Science and Technology, March 2000.
19. M.J. Maher. Herbrand constraint abduction. In *20th IEEE Symposium on Logic in Computer Science (LICS 2005)*, pages 397–406. IEEE Computer Society, 2005.
20. K. Marriott and P.J. Stuckey. *Programming with Constraints: an Introduction*. MIT Press, 1998.

21. B.J. McAdam. Generalising techniques for type debugging. In *Trends in Functional Programming*, pages 49–57, March 2000.
22. R. Milner. A theory of type polymorphism in programming. *Journal of Computer and System Sciences*, 17:348–375, Dec 1978.
23. nhc98 home page. haskell.org/nhc98/.
24. H. Nilsson. Dynamic optimization for functional reactive programming using generalized algebraic data types. In *Proc. of ICFP'05*, pages 54–65. ACM Press, 2005.
25. F. Pottier and N. Gauthier. Polymorphic typed defunctionalization. In *Proc. of POPL'04*, pages 89–98. ACM Press, January 2004.
26. T. Sheard and E. Pasalic. Meta-programming with built-in type equality. In *Fourth International Workshop on Logical Frameworks and Meta-Languages*, 2004.
27. J.R. Shoenfield. *Mathematical Logic*. Addison-Wesley, 1967.
28. P.J. Stuckey and M. Sulzmann. A theory of overloading. *ACM Transactions on Programming Languages and Systems*, 27(6):1216–1269, 2005.
29. P.J. Stuckey, M. Sulzmann, and J. Wazny. The Chameleon type debugger (tool demonstration). In M. Ronsse, editor, *Proceedings of the Fifth International Workshop on Automated Debugging*, pages 247–260, 2003. http://arxiv.org/html/cs.SE/0309027.
30. P.J. Stuckey, M. Sulzmann, and J. Wazny. Interactive type debugging in Haskell. In J. Juring, editor, *Proceedings of the ACM SIGPLAN 2003 Haskell Workshop*, pages 72–83. ACM Press, 2003.
31. P.J. Stuckey, M. Sulzmann, and J. Wazny. Improving type error diagnosis. In *Proceedings of the ACM SIGPLAN 2004 Haskell Workshop*, pages 80–91. ACM Press, 2004.
32. M. Sulzmann and J. Wazny. Chameleon. http://www.comp.nus.edu.sg/~sulzmann/chameleon.
33. M. Sulzmann, J. Wazny, and P.J. Stuckey. A framework for extended algebraic data types. In P. Wadler and M. Hagiya, editors, *Proceedings of 8th International Symposium on Functional and Logic Programming*, number 3945 in LNCS, pages 47–64. Springer-Verlag, April 2006.
34. P. Wadler and S. Blott. How to make *ad-hoc* polymorphism less *ad-hoc*. In *Proc. of POPL'89*, pages 60–76. ACM Press, 1989.
35. J. Wazny. *Type inference and type error diagnosis for Hindley/Milner with extensions*. PhD thesis, University of Melbourne, 2006. http://www.comp.nus.edu.sg/~sulzmann/chameleon/thesis.ps.gz.
36. H. Xi, C. Chen, and G. Chen. Guarded recursive datatype constructors. In *Proc. of POPL'03*, pages 224–235. ACM Press, 2003.
37. J. Yang, J. Wells, P. Trinder, and G. Michaelson. Improved type error reporting. In *Proceedings of 12th International Workshop on Implementation of Functional Languages*, pages 71–86, 2000.

Principal Type Inference for GHC-Style Multi-parameter Type Classes

Martin Sulzmann[1], Tom Schrijvers[2,*], and Peter J. Stuckey[3]

[1] School of Computing, National University of Singapore
S16 Level 5, 3 Science Drive 2, Singapore 117543
sulzmann@comp.nus.edu.sg
[2] Department of Computer Science
Katholieke Universiteit Leuven
Celestijnenlaan 200A, B-3001 Heverlee, Belgium
tom.schrijvers@cs.kuleuven.be
[3] NICTA Victoria Laboratory
Department of Computer Science and Software Engineering
The University of Melbourne, Vic. 3010, Australia
pjs@cs.mu.oz.au

Abstract. We observe that the combination of multi-parameter type classes with existential types and type annotations leads to a loss of principal types and undecidability of type inference. This may be a surprising fact for users of these popular features. We conduct a concise investigation of the problem and are able to give a type inference procedure which, if successful, computes principal types under the conditions imposed by the Glasgow Haskell Compiler (GHC). Our results provide new insights on how to perform type inference for advanced type extensions.

1 Introduction

Type systems are important building tools in the design of programming languages. They are typically specified in terms of a set of typing rules which are formulated in natural deduction style. The standard approach towards establishing type soundness is to show that any well-typed program cannot go wrong at run-time. Hence, one of the first tasks of a compiler is to verify whether a program is well-typed or not.

The trouble is that typing rules are often not syntax-directed. Also, we often have a choice of which types to assign to variables unless we demand that the programmer supplies the compiler with this information. However, using the programming language may then become impractical. What we need is a type inference algorithm which automatically checks whether a program is well-typed and as a side-effect assigns types to program text.

---

* Research Assistant of the fund for Scientific Research - Flanders (Belgium)(F.W.O. - Vlaanderen).

N. Kobayashi (Ed.): APLAS 2006, LNCS 4279, pp. 26–43, 2006.

For programming languages based on the Hindley/Milner system [19] we can typically verify that type inference is *complete* and the inferred type is *principal* [1]. Completeness guarantees that if the program is well-typed type inference will infer a type for the program whereas principality guarantees that any type possibly given to the program can be derived from the inferred type.

Here, we ask the question whether this happy situation continues in the case of multi-parameter type classes (MPTCs) [13], a popular extension of the Hindley/Milner system and available as part of Haskell [21] implementations such as GHC [5] and HUGS [9]. GHC and HUGS also support (boxed) existential types [17] and type annotations [20].[1] It is the combination of all these features that make MPTCs so popular among programmers.

In this paper, we make the following contributions:

- We answer the above question negatively. We show that the combination of MPTCs with type annotations and existential types does not enjoy principal types and type inference is undecidable in general (Section 2).
- However, under the GHC [5] multi-parameter type class conditions, we can give a procedure where every inferred type is principal among all types (Section 4).

We omit proofs for brevity, sketches can be found in [26].

To the best of our knowledge, we are the first to point out precisely the problem behind type inference for MPTCs. Previous work [3] only reports the loss of principal types but does not provide many clues about how to tackle the inference problem.

We have written this introduction as if Haskell (GHC and HUGS) is the only language (systems) that supports MPTCs. Type classes are also supported in a number of other languages such as Mercury [7,10], HAL [2] and Clean [22]. However, as far as we know there is no formal description of multi-parameter type classes and the combination with existential types and type annotations. From now on, we will use MPTCs to refer to the system that combines all these features. For example, Läufer [16] only considered the combination of single-parameter type classes and existential types. The only formal description available is our own previous work [27] where we introduce the more general system of extended algebraic data types (EADTs). Notice that in [27] we discuss type checking but not type inference.

In the next section, we give a cursory introduction to MPTCs as supported in GHC based on a simple example. We refer to [13] for further examples and background material on MPTCs.

2   Multi-parameter Type Classes

Example. We use MPTCs for the implementation of a stack ADT.

---

[1] For the purposes of this paper, we will use the term "type inference" to refer to type inference and checking in the presence of type annotations.

```
class StackImpl s a where
    pushImpl          :: a->s->s
    popAndtopImpl   :: s->Maybe (s,a)
instance StackImpl [a] a where
    pushImpl           = (:)
    popAndtopImpl []      = Nothing
    popAndtopImpl (x:xs) = Just (xs, x)
```

In contrast to a *single*-parameter type class, a *multi*-parameter type class such as StackImpl describes a relation among its type parameters s (the stack) and a (the type of elements stored in a stack). The methods pushImpl and popAndtopImpl provide a minimal interface to a stack. We also provide a concrete implementation using lists.

With the help of an existential type, the stack implementation can be encapsulated:

```
data Stack a = forall s. StackImpl s a => Stck s
```

Each stack is parameterized in terms of the element type a whereas the actual stack s is left abstract as indicated by the forall keyword. We generally refer to variables such as s as *abstract* variables. When scrutinizing a stack we are not allowed to make any specific assumptions about s. The type class constraint (a.k.a. context) StackImpl s a supplies each stack with its essential operations. We use here a combination of multi-parameter type classes and existential types.

It is then straightforward to implement the common set of stack operations.

```
push :: a -> Stack a -> Stack a
push x (Stck s) = Stck (pushImpl x s)
pop :: Stack a -> Stack a
pop (Stck s) = case (popAndtopImpl s) of
                  Just (s',x::a) -> Stck s'     -- (1)

top :: Stack a -> a
top (Stck s) = case (popAndtopImpl s) of
                  Just (_,x) -> x
empty :: Stack a -> Bool
empty (Stck s) = case (popAndtopImpl s) of
                    Just (s'::s,x::a) -> False -- (2)
                    Nothing          -> True
```

In case of function push, the pattern Stck s brings into scope the type class StackImpl s a. Thus, we can access specific methods such as pushImpl x s to push new elements onto the stack. Functions pop and empty require lexically scoped type annotations at locations (1) and (2). For example, in case of function pop the call popAndtopImpl s yields a value of type Stack b for some b and demands the presence of a type class StackImpl s b. Though, the pattern match Stck s only makes available the type class StackImpl s a. Via the lexically scoped annotation x::a, notice that a refers to pop's annotation, we convince the type inferencer that a=b. Then, the program is accepted.[2]

The informed reader will notice that instead of lexically scoped type annotations we could use functional dependencies [12] to enforce that a=b. In our opinion, for many practical examples the reverse argument applies as well. Furthermore, lexically scoped type annotations are a more light-weight extension than functional dependencies. Hence, we will ignore functional dependencies for the purpose of this paper.

What we discover next is that MPTC type inference is not tractable in general. **Loss of Principal Types and Undecidability of Type Inference.** Consider the following (contrived) program.

```
class Foo a b where foo :: a->b->Int
instance Foo Int b            -- (F1)
instance Foo a b => Foo [a] b  -- (F2)
data Bar a = forall b. K a b
f (K x y) = foo x y
```

The surprising observation is that function f can be given the following infinite set of types

$$f :: Bar\ [Int]^n \rightarrow Int$$

for any $n \geq 0$, where $[Int]^n$ is a list of lists ... of lists (n times) of integers. We postpone a discussion on why the above types arise to the next section.

The devastating conclusion we draw is that principal types are lost in general. We even cannot hope for complete and decidable type inference because the set of maximal types given to a program may be infinite. We say a type is *maximal* if there is no other more general type. The above types are all clearly maximal.

Function f makes use of multi-parameter type classes and "pure" existential types. That is, the type class context of the existential data type definition is empty. This shows that type inference is already a problem for "simple" examples. We do not have to resort to "fancy" examples where we constrain the parameters of constructors by a multi-parameter type class.

The "simple" combination of multi-parameter type classes and type annotations poses the same problems. The following function where we assume the above instances

```
g y = let h :: c->Int
          h x = foo y x
      in h y
```

has a similar infinite set of types $g :: [Int]^n \rightarrow Int$ for any $n \geq 0$.

It should be intuitively clear that to establish completeness and decidability of type inference in the MPTC type system we would need to demand an excessive amount of type annotations, something which would seriously impair the practical usefulness of MPTCs.

---

[2] GHC requires the somewhat redundant pattern annotation pop (Stck s::Stack a) which we omit here for simplicity.

Therefore, we seek for a compromise and give up on having both complete-ness and decidability. As is usual in the Hindley/Milner type system, we sacrifice completeness for the sake of decidability. For example, some well-typed programs with polymorphic recursion are rejected because it makes type inference unde-cidable [8]. Instead, we demand that if type inference succeeds, the inferred type must be principal.

An incomplete type inference has already been implemented in GHC; for example it does not produce a type for either f or g. The incompleteness of the GHC implementation is captured in a number of conditions on programs. Programs that do not satisfy these conditions are rejected. Unfortunately, there exists neither a formalization of GHC's inference, nor a proof that its conditions guarantee principal types. We will show that the GHC conditions are indeed sufficient, and we present a formal type inference that computes principal types under these conditions.

3   MPTC Inference Overview

We investigate in more detail why MPTC inference is so hard. Then, we motivate our MPTC inference procedure. We postpone a description of the GHC MPTC conditions to the next section.

3.1   Preliminaries

We introduce some basic assumptions and notation which we will use throughout the paper.

We often write $\bar{o}$ as a short-hand for a sequence of objects $o_1, ..., o_n$ (e.g. types etc). We write $fv(o)$ to denote the free variables in some object o. We write "$-$" to denote set subtraction.

We assume that t refers to types consisting of type variables a, function types $t_1 \rightarrow t_2$ and user-definable types $T\ \bar{t}$. We assume primitive constraints of the form $t_1 = t_2$ (type equations) and $TC\ \bar{t}$ (type class constraints).

We generally assume that the reader is familiar with the concepts of substi-tutions, unifiers, most general unifiers (m.g.u.) etc [15] and first-order logic [23]. We write $[\bar{t}/a]$ to denote the simultaneous substitution of variables a_i by types t_i for $i = 1, .., n$. We use common notation for Boolean conjunction ($\wedge$), implication ($\supset$) and universal ($\forall$) and existential quantifiers ($\exists$). Often, we abbreviate $\wedge$ by ",", and use set notation for conjunctions of formulae. We sometimes use $\bar{\exists}_V.Fml$ as a short-hand for $\exists fv(Fml) - V.Fml$ where Fml is some first-order formula and V a set of variables, that is existential quantification of all variables in Fml apart from V. We write $\models$ to denote the model-theoretic entailment relation. When writing logical statements we often leave (outermost) quantifiers implicit. E.g., let Fml_1 and Fml_2 be two formulae where Fml_1 is closed (contains no free vari-ables). Then, $Fml_1 \models Fml_2$ is a short-hand for $Fml_1 \models \forall fv(Fml_2).Fml_2$ stating that in any (first-order) model for Fml_1 formula $\forall fv(Fml_2).Fml_2$ is satisfied.

3.2   Type Inference Via Implication Constraints

The examples we have seen so far suggest that we need to perform type inference under "local assumptions." That is, the assumption constraints resulting from type annotations and pattern matches over existential types must satisfy the constraints resulting from the program body. In the case of multiple pattern clauses, the individual assumptions for each pattern clause do not interact with the other clauses. Hence, their effect is localized. This is a significant departure from standard Hindley/Milner inference where we are only concerned with solving sets of primitive constraints such as type equations and type classes.

Our MPTC type inference method makes use of the richer form of implication constraints.

$$
\begin{array}{lll}
\text{Type Classes} & tc ::= TC\ \bar{t} \\
\text{Context} & D ::= tc \mid D \wedge D \\
\text{Constraints} & C ::= t = t \mid TC\ \bar{t} \mid C \wedge C \\
\text{Implication Constraints}\ F & ::= C \mid \forall \bar{b}.(D \supset \exists \bar{a}.F) \mid F \wedge F
\end{array}
$$

Constraints on the left-hand side of the implication symbol $\supset$ represent local assumptions arising from constraints in type annotations and data type definitions. For MPTC programs we can guarantee that only type classes appear on the left-hand side. Constraints on the right-hand side arise from the actual function body by generating constraints out of expressions following a standard procedure such as algorithm W [19]. Universally quantified type variables refer to variables in type annotations and abstract variables. Recall that abstract variables are introduced by the `forall` keyword in data type definitions. Existentially quantified type variables belong to right-hand side constraints.

The example from before

```
pop :: Stack a -> Stack a
pop (Stck s) = case (popAndtopImpl s) of
                 Just (s',x::a) -> Stck s'     -- (1)
```

gives rise to the implication constraint

$$\forall a.\forall s.(StackImpl\ s\ a \supset \exists t_x.(StackImpl\ s\ t_x \wedge t_x = a))$$

For example, constraint $StackImpl\ s\ t_x$ arises from the program text `popAndtopImpl s` and constraint $t_x = a$ arises from `x::a`. On the other hand, the constraint $StackImpl\ s\ a$ on the left-hand side of $\supset$ arises from the pattern match `Stck s`. The above implication constraint is clearly a universally true statement. Hence, we can argue that the type of `pop` is correct.

If we replace the lexically scoped annotation `x::a` by `x` we find the following variation of the above implication constraint.

$$\forall a.\forall s.(StackImpl\ s\ a \supset \exists t_x.StackImpl\ s\ t_x)$$

This is also a universally true statement. But verifying this statement is more difficult. Checking is not enough here, we need to find a solution for t_x. The problem is that the solving procedure which we outline below will not necessarily find the answer $t_x = a$. The GHC type inferencer will fail as well.

The crucial observation is that without the annotation x::a, the program is in fact "ambiguous", hence, illegal. The type t_x of program variable x does not appear in the type of function pop. Therefore, several solutions for t_x may exist but this choice is not reflected in the type. Haskell type classes follow the open-world assumption. That is, at some later stage we can add further instances such as instance StackImpl s Int and thus we find besides $t_x = a$ a second solution $t_x = Int$.

The danger then is that the meaning of programs may become ambiguous. This is a well-recognized problem [11,24]. For this reason, Haskell demands that programs must be unambiguous. We therefore follow Haskell and rule out ambiguous programs. In terms of implication constraints, the unambiguity condition says that all existentially quantified type variables which do not appear in the final type must be unique. It is certainly not a coincidence that unambiguity also prevents us from guessing solutions.

For our specific case, we could argue that the declaration instance StackImpl s Int itself is illegal because it overlaps with the one from before. Hence, there should be only one valid solution $t_x = a$. The point is that the unambiguity check is a conservative check and does not take into account any of the specific conditions which we impose on instances. Hence, the program without the annotation x::a fails not because it does not type check, the program is simply plain illegal.

Let's consider the implication constraint for the "devious" program

$$\text{f (K x y) = foo x y}$$

We find that $t_f = Bar\ t_x \rightarrow t_r \wedge \forall t_y.(Foo\ t_x\ t_y \supset t_r = Int)$ where t_f, t_x and t_y are respectively the types of f, x and y respectively, and t_r is the result type. The implication constraint restricts the set of solutions that can be given to these variables. The function body demands that $t_r = Int$ and the call foo x y demands $Foo\ t_x\ t_y$. The universal quantifier $\forall t_y$ captures the fact that variable y is abstract.

In the previous example, we only had to check that the implication constraint is correct. Here, we actually need to find a solution. The problem becomes now apparent. The constraint $t_f = Bar\ [Int]^n \rightarrow Int$ is a solution of the above implication constraint for any $n \geq 0$. More formally,

$$\forall t_f.(t_f = Bar\ [Int]^n \rightarrow Int) \supset$$
$$(\exists t_r.\exists t_x.t_f = Bar\ t_x \rightarrow t_r \wedge \forall t_y.(Foo\ t_x\ t_y \supset t_r = Int))$$

is a true statement under the assumption that $Foo\ [Int]^n\ t_y$ holds for any t_y, which is implied by the above instances (F1) and (F2). Each one of maximal types f :: $Bar\ [Int]^n \rightarrow Int$ corresponds to one of the solutions $t_f = Bar\ [Int]^n \rightarrow Int$.

A naive "solution" would be to consider the implication constraint itself as the solution. Although, we (trivially) obtain complete inference, this approach is not practical. First, types become unreadable. In the type system, we now admit implication constraints (and not only sets of primitive constraints). Second, type inference becomes intractable. The implication constraints arising from the program text may now have implication constraints on the left-hand side of $\supset$. But then solving these "extended" implication constraints is very close to solving of first-order formulae. Previous work [14] shows that solving of first-order formula with subtype constraints is decidable but has a non-elementary complexity. Note that via Haskell type classes we can encode complex relations such as subtyping. Hence, we abandon this path and consider how to solve implication constraints in terms of sets of primitive constraints.

3.3   Highlights of MPTC Implication Solver

In its simplest form, we need a solving procedure for implication constraints of the form $D \supset C$ where D consists of sets of type class constraints whereas C additionally contains Hindley/Milner constraints (i.e. type equations). Before we attempt solving, let's consider how to check that $D \supset C$ holds. Checking is a natural first step to achieve solving.

We apply the law that $D \supset C$ iff $D \leftrightarrow D \wedge C$. Thus, checking can be turned into an equivalence test among constraints. The standard method to test for equivalence is to build the canonical normal forms of D and $D \wedge C$ and check whether both forms are identical. In case of type equations, we can build canonical normal forms by building most general unifiers. Here, we additionally find type classes.

The meaning of type classes is specified by instance declarations which effectively define a rewrite relation among constraints. For example, the **instance** **StackImpl [a]** a declaration from Section 2 implies that the *StackImpl [a]* a constraint can be rewritten to *True*. In Haskell speak, this process is known as context reduction, although, we will use the term constraint rewriting/solving here. In Section 4.1, we formalize how to derive these rewriting steps from instance declarations. For the moment, let's assume a rewrite relation $\rightarrowtail^*$ among constraints where we exhaustively apply instance rules on type classes and rewrite type equations into most general unifiers.

Based on this assumption, we check $D \leftrightarrow D \wedge C$ by executing $C \rightarrowtail^* C'$ for some final constraint C' and testing whether D and C' are identical. Notice that we do not rewrite D which is due to the GHC assumption that constraints D are already in canonical normal form. If D and C' are identical, the check succeeds. Otherwise, we need to infer some missing hypotheses, i.e. constraint. The obvious approach is to take the set difference between C' and D. Recall that we can treat a conjunction of primitive constraints as a set. Then, $C' - D$ is a solution of $D \supset C$. We have that $(C' - D) \supset (D \supset C)$ iff $((C' - D) \wedge D) \supset C$ iff $C' \supset C$ which clearly holds. To summarize, the main idea behind our solving procedure is to rewrite constraints to some canonical normal form. We take the set difference between canonical normal forms to infer the missing assumptions.

To illustrate this solving procedure, we consider a simple example.

```
class F a
class B a b where b :: a -> b
instance F a => B a [a]
data T a = F a => Mk a        -- (T)
f (Mk x) = b x
```

In the data type definition (T), $F\ a$ constrains the type of the constructor Mk. Function g gives rise to the following implication constraint

$$t_f = T\ t_x \rightarrow b \wedge (F\ t_x \supset B\ t_x\ b)$$

This case is slightly more general than above. Constraints $t_f = T\ t_x \rightarrow b$ will be definitely part of the solution. Solving of $(F\ t_x \supset B\ t_x\ b)$ yields the solution $B\ t_x\ b$. There are no instance rules applicable to $B\ t_x\ b$. Hence, the difference between $B\ t_x\ b$ and $F\ t_x$ is $B\ t_x\ b$. Hence, $t_f = T\ t_x \rightarrow b \wedge B\ t_x\ b$ is a solution. Hence, f can be given the type $\forall t_x, b.B\ t_x\ b \Rightarrow t_x \rightarrow b$.

In general, our solving procedures needs to deal with multiple branches (i.e. conjunctions of implications). Universally quantified variables refer to type annotations and abstract variables whereas existentially quantified variables refer to Hindley/Milner constraints. Universal variables are more "problematic" because they cannot be instantiated and are not allowed to escape. In the following, we give an informal discussion of how our solving procedure deals with such cases. The exact details are presented in the upcoming section.

For example, $B\ a\ b \wedge t_r = Int$ is not a valid solution of

$$\forall b.\ True \supset (B\ a\ b \wedge t_r = Int)$$

because the variable b escapes. We will check for escaping of universal variables by applying a well-known technique known as Skolemization [18]. Skolemization of $\forall b.\ True \supset (B\ a\ b \wedge t_r = Int)$ yields $True \supset (B\ a\ Sk \wedge t_r = Int)$. The constraint $B\ a\ Sk \wedge t_r = Int$ is clearly not a valid solution because of the Skolem constructor Sk.

We explore solving of multiple branches. The idea is consider one branch at a time.

```
class Foo a b where foo::a->b->Int
instance Foo Int b -- (F)
class Bar a b where bar :: b->a->a
data Erk a = forall b. Bar a b => K1 (a,b)
           | forall b. K2 (a,b)
g (K1 (a,b)) = bar b a
g (K2 (a,b)) = foo a b
```

Function g's program text gives rise to

$$
\begin{aligned}
t = Erk\ a \rightarrow t_3 \wedge t_3 = t_1 \wedge t_3 = t_2 \wedge &&& (C_0)\\
(Bar\ a\ Sk_1 \supset Bar\ a\ Sk_1 \wedge t_1 = a) \wedge &&& (F_1)\\
(True \supset Foo\ a\ Sk_2 \wedge t_2 = Int) &&& (F_2)
\end{aligned}
$$

where each branch corresponds to a pattern clause. Universal quantifiers have already been replaced by fresh Skolem constructors.

We start solving the first branch F_1. Based on our method for solving for single implications, we find that $C_0 \wedge t_1 = a$ is a solution for $C_0 \wedge F_1$. We make this solving step explicit by writing

$$C_0 \wedge F_1 \wedge F_2 \gg C_0 \wedge t_1 = a \wedge F_2$$

We will formally define this rewriting relation $\gg$ among implication constraints in the upcoming section. Each time we solve a single implication constraint we replace the implication constraint with its solution. Thus, we incrementally build up the solution for the entire set of implication constraints. Solving of the remaining second branch yields the solution $C_0 \wedge t_1 = a \wedge t_2 = Int$. Hence, we find that $C_0 \wedge F_1 \wedge F_2 \gg^* C_0 \wedge t_1 = a \wedge t_2 = Int$. Notice that $C_0 \wedge t_1 = a \wedge t_2 = Int$ implies $a = Int$ and therefore we can rewrite $Foo\ a\ Sk_2$ to $True$ and thus solve (F_2). We obtain that g has type `Erk Int->Int`.

If we start solving F_2 first, we cannot immediately "fully" solve this implication constraint. The constraint $Foo\ a\ Sk_2 \wedge t_2 = Int$ is not a valid solution because of the Skolem constructor. We can only infer, i.e. add, the *partial* solution $t_2 = Int$. That is, we make the following progress

$$C_0 \wedge F_1 \wedge F_2 \gg C_0 \wedge t_2 = Int \wedge F_1 \wedge F_2$$

If we continue solving F_2 we are stuck. No further constraints can be added at this stage. Our solving method only observes the canonical normal forms of the constraints involved. Based on this information, we cannot infer the missing information $t_1 = a$. Hence, we consider solving of F_1. We find that $C_0 \wedge t_2 = Int \wedge F_1 \wedge F_2 \gg C_0 \wedge t_2 = Int \wedge t_1 = a \wedge F_2$. Finally, we can verify that $C_0 \wedge t_2 = Int \wedge t_1 = a \wedge F_2 \gg C_0 \wedge t_2 = Int \wedge t_1 = a$.

The point is that it may not be possible to solve a single implication without solving other implications first. In case we cannot make progress, i.e. no further constraints can be added, we consider a different branch. In general, a different solving order may yield a different result. Under the conditions imposed by GHC, we can verify that we always obtain the same result. The above example satisfies the GHC conditions and indeed we infer both times the same result.

4   Inferring Principal Types Under the GHC Conditions

In our approach, type inference boils down to solving of implication constraints. In a first step, we review some material on type class constraint solving, i.e. solving of sets of primitive constraints. Then, we formalize the MPTC implication solver. Along the way, we introduce the conditions imposed by GHC sufficient to verify our main result: The MPTC implication solver computes principal solutions, therefore type inference computes principal types, under the GHC MPTC Conditions.

For space reasons, we omit the details of how to generate implication constraints out of the program text. This is by now a standard exercise. For full details see the technical report version of this paper [26].

4.1   Type Class Constraint Solver

In case we only consider multi-parameter type classes (i.e. no existential types and type annotations are involved), type inference boils down to solving of sets of primitive constraints. Instance declarations define a rewrite relation among type class constraints. Hence, the type class constraint solver is parameterized in terms of these rewrite relations.

Following our earlier work [24], we formally define these rewrite relations in terms of Constraint Handling Rules (CHRs) [4]. For each declaration

$$\texttt{instance } D \;\Rightarrow\; TC\ \bar{t}$$

we introduce the single-headed CHR $\texttt{rule } TC\ \bar{t} \iff D$. In case, the context D is empty, we generate $\texttt{rule } TC\ \bar{t} \iff True$. The set of all such generated constraint rules is collected in the *MPTC program logic* P.

Logically, the symbol $\iff$ corresponds to Boolean equivalence. Operationally, we can apply a renamed $\texttt{rule } TC\ \bar{t} \iff D$ to a set of constraints C if we find a matching copy $TC\ \bar{s} \in C$ such that $\phi(\bar{t}) = \bar{s}$ for some substitution ϕ. Then, we replace $TC\ \bar{s}$ by the right-hand side under the matching substitution $\phi(D)$ More formally, we write $C \rightarrowtail (C - \{TC\ \bar{s}\}) \cup \phi(D)$ to denote this derivation step. We write $C \rightarrowtail^*_P C'$ to denote the exhaustive application of all rules in P, starting with the *initial* constraint C and resulting in the *final* constraint C'. If the program logic P is fixed by the context, we sometimes also write $C \rightarrowtail^* C'$.

Here is an example to show some CHRs in action. Under the CHRs

```
rule StackImpl (Tree a) a <==> Eq a
rule Eq [a] <==> Eq a
```

we find that $StackImpl\ (Tree[a])[a] \rightarrowtail Eq\ [a] \rightarrowtail Eq\ a$.

We repeat the CHR soundness result [4] which states that CHR rule applications perform equivalence transformations. Recall that $P \models F$ means that any model M satisfying P (treating $\iff$ as Boolean equivalence) also satisfies F.

Lemma 1 (CHR Soundness [4]). *Let* $C \rightarrowtail^*_P C'$. *Then* $P \models C \leftrightarrow \bar{\exists}_{fv(C)}.C'$.

We say P is *terminating* if for each initial constraint we find a final constraint. We say P is *confluent* if different derivations starting from the same point can always be brought together again.

We will demand that CHRs resulting from instances satisfy these properties. Termination obviously guarantee decidability. Confluence guarantees canonical normal forms. Otherwise, we may need to back-track and exhaustively explore all possibilities during solving which may increase the complexity of the solver significantly.

To guarantee confluence and termination, GHC imposes the following conditions on programs.

Definition 1 (Well-Behaved Instances)

Termination Order: *The context of an instance declaration can mention only type variables, not type constructors, and in each individual class constraint all the type variables are distinct.*

In an instance declaration instance $D \Rightarrow TC\ t_1 \ldots t_n$, at least one of the types t_i must not be a type variable and $fv(D) \subseteq fv(t_1, \ldots, t_n)$.

Non-Overlapping: *The instance declarations must not overlap: For any two declarations* instance $D \Rightarrow TC\ t_1 \ldots t_n$ *and* instance $D' \Rightarrow TC\ t'_1 \ldots t'_n$ *there is no substitution ϕ such that $\phi(t_1) = \phi(t'_1), \ldots, \phi(t_n) = \phi(t'_n)$.*

From now on we assume that the MPTC program logic satisfies the Well-Behaved Instances Conditions. They are sufficient, but not necessary[3] conditions for the essential property that the type class constraint solver is terminating and confluent.

4.2   MPTC Implication Solver

Solutions and Normalization. We first apply three normalization steps to the implication constraints for convenience.

In the first normalization step, we flatten nested implications and pull up quantifiers, based on the following first-order equivalences: (i) $(F_1 \supset Qa.F_2) \leftrightarrow Qa.(F_1 \supset F_2)$ where $a \notin fv(F_1)$ and $Q \in \{\exists, \forall\}$; (ii) $(Qa.F_1) \wedge (Qb.F_2) \leftrightarrow Qa, b.(F_1 \wedge F_2)$ where $a \notin fv(F_2)$, $b \notin fv(F_1)$ and $Q \in \{\exists, \forall\}$; and (iii) $C_1 \supset (C_2 \supset C_3) \leftrightarrow (C_1 \wedge C_2) \supset C_3$. We exhaustively apply the above identities from left to right until we reach the *pre-normal* form

$$C_0 \wedge \mathcal{Q}.((D_1 \supset C_1) \wedge \ldots \wedge (D_n \supset C_n))$$

where $\mathcal{Q}$ is a mixed prefix of the form $\exists \overline{b_0}.\forall \overline{a_1}.\exists \overline{b_1} \ldots \forall \overline{a_n}.\exists \overline{b_n}$. Variables in C_0 are free. Our goal is to find solutions (in terms of types) to these variables.

Definition 2 (Solutions for Fixed Assumption Constraints). *Let P be a MPTC program logic, $F \equiv C_0 \wedge \mathcal{Q}.((D_1 \supset C_1) \wedge \ldots \wedge (D_n \supset C_n))$ an implication constraint and C a constraint. We say that C is a* solution *of F w.r.t. P iff*

1. $C, C_0 \rightarrowtail \ldots \rightarrowtail C,$
2. $\models \mathcal{Q}.(C \wedge D_i \leftrightarrow C'_i)$ *where $C, C_i \rightarrowtail^*_P C'_i$ for $i = 1, \ldots, n$, and*
3. $C \wedge \mathcal{Q}.(D_i \wedge C_i)$ *is satisfiable in P for each $i = 1, \ldots, n$.*

In such a situation, we say that C satisfies the Fixed Assumption Constraint Condition.

We say that C is a principal solution *iff (i) C is a solution, and (ii) for any other solution C' we have that $P \models C' \supset \overline{\exists}_{fv(F)}.C$.*

The first two conditions define solutions in terms of the operational reading of instances as CHRs. They imply the logical statement $P \models C \supset F$. This can be verified by straightforward application of the CHR Soundness Lemma. The reason for defining solutions operationally rather than logically is due to the type-preserving dictionary-passing translation scheme [6] employed in GHC. Briefly, assumption constraints D are taken literally and turned into dictionaries.

---

[3] There are other more liberal instance conditions [25] which guarantee the same.

Primitive: We define $F \gg_P^* C'$ where $C \rightarrowtail_P^* C'$ if $F \equiv C$.

General: Otherwise $F \equiv C_0 \wedge (D \supset C) \wedge F'$. We assume that the most general unifier of type equations in C_0 has been applied to D and C. We execute $C_0, D, C \rightarrowtail_P^* C'$ for some C'. We distinguish among the following cases:

Fail: If *False* $\in C'$ we immediately fail.

Solved: If $C' - (C_0 \wedge D)$ yields the empty set (i.e. C' and $C_0 \wedge D$ are logically equivalent), we consider $D \supset C$ as solved. We define $F \gg_P^* C''$ if $C_0 \wedge F' \gg_P^* C''$.

Add: Otherwise, we set S to be the subset of all constraints in $C' - (C_0 \wedge D)$ which do not refer to a Skolem constructor.

    (a) In case S is non-empty, we define $F \gg_P^* C''$ if $C_0 \wedge S \wedge (D \supset C) \wedge F' \gg_P^* C''$.

    (b) In case S is empty, we pick some $(D_1 \supset C_1) \in F'$ and define $F \gg_P^* C''$ if $C_0 \wedge (D_1 \supset C_1) \wedge (F' - (D_1 \supset C_1)) \wedge (D \supset C) \gg_P^* C''$.

    (c) Otherwise, we fail.

Fig. 1. MPTC Implication Solver

Rewriting them would break separate compilation. Hence, in our definition of solutions we guarantee that assumption constraints are fixed. Interestingly, the Fixed Assumption Constraint Condition is essential to guarantee principal types as we will see later.

The last condition demands that for each particular branch the constraints arising do not contradict each other (i.e. they must be satisfiable). In particular, we reject thus the always false constraint *Int = Bool* as a solution. Such solutions are clearly non-sensical because they solve any implication constraint. In terms of the GHC translation scheme, unsatisfiable branches represent dead-code, hence, we can ignore them.

In the second normalization step we eliminate all universally quantified variables by Skolemization [18]. That is, we transform $\exists \bar{b}. \forall \bar{a}. F$ into $\exists \bar{b}. [\overline{Sk_a(\bar{b})}/\bar{a}]F$ where Sk_{a_i}'s are some fresh Skolem constructors. We apply this step repeatedly on implication constraints in pre-normal form until we reach the *Skolemized, pre-normal* form

$$C_0 \wedge \exists \bar{b}. ((D'_1 \supset C'_1) \wedge \ldots \wedge (D'_n \supset C'_n))$$

For solutions C of Skolemized implication constraints, we additionally demand that no Skolem constructor appears in C.

The Skolemization preserves the set of solutions. It is sufficient to verify this statement for a single branch.

Lemma 2 (Solution Equivalence). *Let P be a MPTC program logic, S a constraint, $Q.(D \supset C)$ a implication constraint and $\exists \bar{b}.(D' \supset C')$ its Skolemized form. Then, S is a solution of $Q.(D \supset C)$ iff S is a solution of $\exists \bar{b}.(D' \supset C')$.*

In the last normalization step we drop the outermost existential quantifier $\exists \bar{b}$. However, the choice of variables $\bar{b}$ may not be unique. If this is the case we face the ambiguity problem mentioned in Section 3. Therefore, we only consider unambiguous implication constraints where we can safely drop the existential quantifier.

We say that $C_0 \wedge \exists \bar{b}.((D_1 \supset C_1) \wedge ... \wedge (D_n \supset C_n))$ is *unambiguous* iff $fv(\phi(D_i), \phi(C_i)) \subseteq fv(\phi(C_0))$ for each $i = 1, ..., n$ where ϕ is the m.g.u. of type equations in C_0.[4] The above says that fixing the variables in C_0 will fix the variables in each branch. Checking for ambiguity is obviously decidable.

Next, we introduce a solving procedure for implication constraints in *normal* form, i.e. unambiguous, Skolemized, pre-normal implications constraints of the form

$$C_0 \wedge (D_1 \supset C_1) \wedge ... \wedge (D_n \supset C_n)$$

Solving Method. We formalize the solving method motivated in Section 3.3. In Figure 1, we define a solver $F \gg_P^* C$ for implication constraints F in normal form w.r.t. the program logic P which, if successful, yields a solution C. The case **Add** subcase **(b)** deals with the situation where we cannot make any further progress, hence, we switch to a different branch. We assume that if none of the branches makes progress we reach subcase **(c)**.

We can establish soundness by a straightforward application of the CHR Soundness and Solution Equivalence Lemma.

Lemma 3 (Soundness of Solving). *Let P be a program logic If $F \gg_P^* C$ for some C then C is a solution of F.*

4.3 Main Result

In addition to the Well-Behaved Instances and the Fixed Assumption Constraint Conditions, GHC imposes a third condition on programs.

Definition 3 (GHC MPTC Conditions). *We say a program satisfies the* GHC MPTC Conditions *iff*

- *Instances are well-behaved (see Definition 1).*
- *Each implication constraint in normal-form arising out of a program is unambiguous and has a solution which satisfies the Fixed Assumption Constraint Conditions (see Definition 2).*
- *Each data type definition satisfies the* Bound Type Class Context Condition. *That is, for any*

```
data T a1 ... am = forall b1,...,bn. D => K t1 ... tl
```

and each $TC \ \overline{t'} \in D$ we have that $fv(\overline{t'}) \cap fv(\overline{b}) \neq \emptyset$.

In fact, GHC 6.4.1 accepts `data T a = forall b. F a => Mk a b` which breaks the Bound Type Class Context Condition. However, in GHC such declarations are interpreted as `data F a => T a = forall b. Mk a b`. That is, `F a` needs to be satisfied when building any value of type `T a`, but `F a` will not appear in a local assumption constraint.

---

[4] We assume that $fv(a = Int) = \emptyset$ because a type is bound by the monomorphic type Int.

Our main result says:

Theorem 1 (Principal Types for GHC MPTC Programs). *If successful, our solving method computes principal solutions for programs satisfying the GHC MPTC Conditions.*

Before we explain the proof steps necessary to verify the above result, we highlight the importance of the GHC MPTC Conditions.

The Well-Behaved Instances Conditions are not essential. We could replace them with alternative conditions as long as we the type class constraint solver remains confluent and terminating.

GHC imposes the Fixed Assumption Constraint Condition because of dictionary-passing translation scheme. The next example shows that without this condition we may infer non-principal types.

```
class Bar a b c d where bar ::d->c->a->b
class Bar2 a b
class Foo a b d
class Foo2 a
instance Bar2 a b => Bar a b c T2 -- (B)
instance Foo2 a => Foo a b T2       -- (F)
instance Foo2 a => Bar2 a [a]       -- (B2)
data T2 = K
data Erk a d = forall c. Foo a c d => Mk a c d
f (Mk a c K) = bar K c a
```

The program logic P consists of the following rules.

```
rule Bar a b c T2 <==> Bar2 a b  -- (B)
rule Foo a b T2   <==> Foo2 a    -- (F)
rule Bar2 a [a]   <==> Foo2 a    -- (B2)
```

The program text of f yields the (simplified) implication constraint (*Foo a Sk T2 ⊃ Bar a b Sk T2*).

Application of our solving method yields the solution *Bar2 a b* which implies the type $\forall a, b. Bar2\ a\ b \Rightarrow Erk\ a\ T2 \rightarrow b$ for f. However, this solution is not principal. We claim there is another incomparable solution $b = [a]$ which corresponds to the type $\forall a. Erk\ a\ T2 \rightarrow [a]$. Both solutions (types) are incomparable and there is no more general solution (type).

We verify that $b = [a]$ is indeed a solution by checking that $b = [a] \wedge$ (*Foo a Sk T2 ⊃ Bar a b Sk T2*) holds w.r.t. P. From the earlier Section 3, we know that the checking problem $b = [a] \wedge$ (*Foo a Sk T2 ⊃ Bar a b Sk T2*) can equivalently be phrased as an equivalence testing problem $(b = [a] \wedge Foo\ a\ Sk\ T2)$ $\leftrightarrow (b = [a] \wedge Foo\ a\ Sk\ T2 \wedge Bar\ a\ b\ Sk\ T2)$. Then, we rewrite the left-hand and right-hand side and check whether resulting constraints are logically equivalent.

$$(1) \qquad b = [a], Foo\ a\ Sk\ T2$$
$$\rightarrowtail_F b = [a], Foo2\ a \qquad (*)$$

$$(2) \qquad b = [a], Foo\ a\ Sk\ T2, Bar\ a\ b\ Sk\ T2$$
$$\leftrightarrow \quad b = [a], Foo\ a\ Sk\ T2, Bar\ a\ [a]\ Sk\ T2$$
$$\rightarrowtail_B b = [a], Foo\ a\ Sk\ T2, Bar2\ a\ [a]$$
$$\rightarrowtail_{B2} b = [a], Foo\ a\ Sk\ T2, Foo2\ a$$
$$\rightarrowtail_F b = [a], Foo2\ a$$

The final constraints $b = [a]$, *Foo2* a are equivalent. Hence, $b = [a]$ is a solution. However, $b = [a]$ is not a valid solution under the GHC MPTC Conditions. To obtain the solution $b = [a]$, it is crucial to rewrite the assumption constraint, see the derivation step (∗). This violates the Fixed Assumption Constraint Condition.

The Bound Type Class Context Condition is essential as well. Here are excerpts of an example which we have seen earlier in Section 3.3.

```
data T a = F a => Mk a        -- (T)
f (Mk x) = b x
```

The definition (T) violates the Bound Type Class Context Condition. Variable a is not bound by the `forall` quantifier. Our solving procedure infers the type $\forall t_x, b.B\ t_x\ b \Rightarrow T\ t_x \to b$. But this type is not principal. Function f can also be given the incomparable type $\forall a.T\ a \to [a]$ and there is no more general type.

We conclude this section by stating the essential result to verify the above theorem. The crucial observation is that under the GHC MPTC Conditions, the "incremental" solutions S which we compute in solving step **Add** are part of the principal solution (if one exists). Here is the formal result.

Lemma 4 (Principal Progress). *Let P be a program logic derived from instance declarations which satisfy the GHC MPTC Conditions. Let $(D \supset C)$ be a implication constraint in normal form such that (a) $D \rightarrowtail^* D$ and (b) each primitive constraint in D contains at least one Skolem constructor. Let S be a Skolem-free subset of $C' - D$ where $C \rightarrowtail^*_P C'$ from some C' and False $\notin C' - D$. If $(D \supset C)$ has a principal solution, then S is a subset of this principal solution.*

Assumption (a) effectively represents the Fixed Assumption Condition and assumption (b) represents the Bound Type Class Context Condition. The Bound Type Class Context Condition guarantees that for all implication constraints $(D \supset C)$ in normal form we have that each type class constraint in D contains at least one Skolem constructor. Implication constraints resulting from type annotations always satisfy this property.

In combination with Lemma 3, the above results guarantee that our solving method makes progress towards a principal solution. Thus, we can verify the above theorem.

Under the GHC Conditions, we can also verify that the final result is independent of the order of solving. Recall that in solver case **Add**, subcase **(b)** the choice which implication $(D_1 \supset C_1)$ to consider next is not fixed. Effectively, the result below is saying that the implication solver is confluent.

Lemma 5 (Deterministic Progress). *Under the GHC MPTC Conditions, different runs of the MPTC implication solver will yield the same result where we either report a solution or reach one of the failure states. Every implication constraint is considered at most twice.*

5   Conclusion

We have pointed out subtle problems when performing type inference for multi-parameter type classes with existential types and type annotations. In general, we lose principality and decidability of type inference. Under the GHC MPTC Conditions, we give a procedure that infers principal types. To the best of our knowledge, there is no formal description available of the GHC type inference engine or any of the other systems which we have mentioned. Nevertheless, we believe that our procedure is fairly close to the actual GHC implementation. Formalizing the GHC type inference engine based on the principles and methods introduced in this paper is something which we plan to pursue in the future.

Our main result guarantees that every inferred type is principal. The question is whether failure of our inference method implies that no principal type exists?

```
class Foo a b where foo :: a->b
data Bar a = forall b. Foo b a => Mk b
f (Mk x) = foo x
```

Function f's program text generates $t = Bar\ a \rightarrow c \land (Foo\ Sk\ a \supset Foo\ Sk\ c)$. Our solving method fails (and so does GHC). It almost seems that $t = Bar\ a \rightarrow a$ is a principal solution. Hence, f has the principal type $\forall a. Bar\ a \rightarrow a$. But this is only true if we assume a "closed" world where the set of instances (here none) are fixed. Haskell type classes follow the open world assumption. At some later stage, we may introduce **instance Foo b Int**. Then, f can be given the incomparable type $Bar\ a \rightarrow Int$. The point is that the principal types inferred by our MPTC implication solving method are "stable". That is, they remain principal if we add further instances (which must satisfy the GHC MPTC Conditions of course). Failure of our inference method seems to imply that no stable principal type exists. This is something which we plan to investigate further.

Acknowledgments

We thank the reviewers for their comments.

References

1. L. Damas and R. Milner. Principal type-schemes for functional programs. In *Proc. of POPL'82*, pages 207–212. ACM Press, January 1982.
2. B. Demoen, M. García de la Banda, W. Harvey, K. Marriott, and P.J. Stuckey. An overview of HAL. In J. Jaffar, editor, *Proceedings of the Fourth International Conference on Principles and Practices of Constraint Programming*, LNCS, pages 174–188. Springer-Verlag, October 1999.
3. K. F. Faxén. Haskell and principal types. In *Proc. of Haskell Workshop'03*, pages 88–97. ACM Press, 2003.
4. T. Frühwirth. Constraint Handling Rules. In *Constraint Programming: Basics and Trends*, LNCS. Springer-Verlag, 1995.
5. Glasgow haskell compiler home page. http://www.haskell.org/ghc/.
6. C. V. Hall, K. Hammond, S. L. Peyton Jones, and P. L. Wadler. Type classes in Haskell. *ACM Transactions on Programming Languages and Systems*, 18(2):109–138, 1996.

7. F. Henderson et al. The Mercury language reference manual, 2001. http://www.cs.mu.oz.au/research/mercury/.
8. Fritz Henglein. Type inference with polymorphic recursion. *Transactions on Programming Languages and Systems*, 15(1):253–289, April 1993.
9. Hugs home page. haskell.cs.yale.edu/hugs/.
10. D. Jeffery, F. Henderson, and Z. Somogyi. Type classes in Mercury. In J. Edwards, editor, *Proc. Twenty-Third Australasian Computer Science Conf.*, volume 22 of *Australian Computer Science Communications*, pages 128–135. IEEE Computer Society Press, January 2000.
11. M. P. Jones. Coherence for qualified types. Research Report YALEU/DCS/RR-989, Yale University, Department of Computer Science, September 1993.
12. M. P. Jones. Type classes with functional dependencies. In *Proc. of ESOP'00*, volume 1782 of *LNCS*. Springer-Verlag, 2000.
13. S. Peyton Jones, M. P. Jones, and E. Meijer. Type classes: an exploration of the design space. In *Haskell Workshop*, June 1997.
14. V. Kuncak and M. Rinard. Structural subtyping of non-recursive types is decidable. In *Proc. of LICS'03*, pages 96–107. IEEE Computer Society, 2003.
15. J. Lassez, M. Maher, and K. Marriott. Unification revisited. In *Foundations of Deductive Databases and Logic Programming*. Morgan Kauffman, 1987.
16. K. Läufer. Type classes with existential types. *Journal of Functional Programming*, 6(3):485–517, 1996.
17. K. Läufer and M. Odersky. Polymorphic type inference and abstract data types. *ACM Trans. Program. Lang. Syst.*, 16(5):1411–1430, 1994.
18. Dale Miller. Unification under a mixed prefix. *J. Symb. Comput.*, 14(4):321–358, 1992.
19. R. Milner. A theory of type polymorphism in programming. *Journal of Computer and System Sciences*, 17:348–375, Dec 1978.
20. M. Odersky and K. Läufer. Putting type annotations to work. In *Proc. of POPL'96*, pages 54–67. ACM Press, 1996.
21. S. Peyton Jones, editor. *Haskell 98 Language and Libraries: The Revised Report*. Cambridge University Press, 2003.
22. M.J. Plasmeijer and M.C.J.D. van Eekelen. Language report Concurrent Clean. Technical Report CSI-R9816, Computing Science Institute, University of Nijmegen, Nijmegen, The Netherlands, June 1998. ftp://ftp.cs.kun.nl/pub/Clean/Clean13/doc/refman13.ps.gz.
23. J.R. Shoenfield. *Mathematical Logic*. Addison-Wesley, 1967.
24. P. J. Stuckey and M. Sulzmann. A theory of overloading. *ACM Transactions on Programming Languages and Systems (TOPLAS)*, 27(6):1–54, 2005.
25. M. Sulzmann, G. J. Duck, S. Peyton Jones, and P. J. Stuckey. Understanding functional dependencies via Constraint Handling Rules. *Journal of Functional Programming*, 2006. To appear.
26. M. Sulzmann, T. Schrijvers, and P.J.Stuckey. Principal type inference for GHC-style multi-parameter type classes. Technical report, The National University of Singapore, 2006.
27. M. Sulzmann, J. Wazny, and P.J.Stuckey. A framework for extended algebraic data types. In *Proc. of FLOPS'06*, volume 3945 of *LNCS*, pages 47–64. Springer-Verlag, 2006.

Private Row Types: Abstracting the Unnamed

Jacques Garrigue

Graduate School of Mathematical Sciences,
Nagoya University, Chikusa-ku, Nagoya 464-8602
garrigue@math.nagoya-u.ac.jp

Abstract. In addition to traditional record and variant types, Objective Caml has structurally polymorphic types, for objects and polymorphic variants. These types allow new forms of polymorphic programming, but they have a limitation when used in combination with modules: there is no way to abstract their polymorphism in a signature. Private row types remedy this situation: they are manifest types whose "row-variable" is left abstract, so that an implementation may instantiate it freely. They have useful applications even in the absence of functors. Combined with recursive modules, they provide an original solution to the expression problem.

1 Introduction

Polymorphic objects and variants, as offered by Objective Caml, allow new forms of polymorphic programming. For instance, a function may take an object as parameter, and call some of its methods, without knowing its exact type, or even the list of its methods [1]. Similarly, a list of polymorphic variant values can be used in different contexts expecting different sets of constructors, as long as the types of constructor arguments agree, and all constructors present in the list are allowed [2].

These new types are particularly interesting in programming situations where one gradually extends a type with new methods or constructors. This is typically supported by classes for objects, but this is also possible with polymorphic variants, thanks to the dispatch mechanism which was added to pattern matching. This is even possible for recursive types, but then one has to be careful about making fix-points explicit, so as to allow extension. A typical example of this style is the expression problem, where one progressively and simultaneously enriches a small expression language with new constructs and new operations [3]. This problem is notoriously difficult to solve, and Objective Caml was, to the best of our knowledge, the first language to do it in a type safe way, using either polymorphic variants [4] or classes [5].

If we think of these situations as examples of incremental modular programming, we realize that an essential ML feature does not appear in this picture: functors. This is surprising, as they are supposed to be the main mechanism providing high-level modularity in ML. There is a simple reason for this situation: it is currently[1] impossible to express structural polymorphism in functors. One may of course specify polymorphic values in interfaces, but this does not provide for the main feature of functors, namely the ability to have types in the result of a functor depend on its parameters. To understand this, let's see how functor abstraction works.

---

[1] As of Objective Caml 3.08.

N. Kobayashi (Ed.): APLAS 2006, LNCS 4279, pp. 44–60, 2006.
© Springer-Verlag Berlin Heidelberg 2006

```
let add (p1 : float array) (p2 : float array) =
  let l1 = Array.length p1 and l2 = Array.length p2 in
  Array.init (max l1 l2)
    (fun i -> if i < l1 then if i < l2 then p1.(i) +. p2.(i)
              else p1.(i) else p2.(i))
```

This program computes the sum of two polynomials. We might want to abstract the representation of arrays, to emphasize that this program uses them functionally (arrays in OCaml are mutable.)

```
module type Vect = sig
  type t
  val init : int -> (int -> float) -> t
  val length : t -> int
  val get : t -> int -> float
end
module Poly (V : Vect) = struct
  let add p1 p2 =
    let l1 = V.length p1 and l2 = V.length p2 in
    V.init (max l1 l2)
      (fun i -> if i < l1 then if i < l2 then V.get p1 i +. V.get p2 i
                else V.get p1 i else V.get p2 i)
end
```

We have given the name t to float array, and made it abstract as a parameter. The type inferred for add is V.t -> V.t -> V.t, which depends on what implementation of Vect we will pass as parameter to Poly.

What happens now if we want to make explicit that vectors are to be represented as objects, calling methods inside the functor? Here is a first attempt.

```
module type OVect = sig
  type t = <length: int; get: int -> float>
  val init : int -> (int -> float) -> t
end
module OPoly (V : OVect) = struct
  let add (p1 : V.t) (p2 : V.t) : V.t =
    let l1 = p1#length and l2 = p2#length in
    V.init (max l1 l2)
      (fun i -> if i < l1 then if i < l2 then p1#get i +. p2#get i
                else p1#get i else p2#get i)
end
```

Type t is an *object type*. It gives the list of methods in the object, and their types. Methods are called with the *obj#method* notation. Objects and their types in OCaml are fully structural, and they can be seen as polymorphic records[6], extended with explicit structural subtyping. The code above typechecks correctly, but it doesn't give us enough polymorphism. Since t has a concrete definition in OVect, any module implementing OVect will have to include exactly the same definition. Structural subtyping allows coercing an object with more methods to type t, returning it in init or passing it to add, but other methods become inaccessible. That is, the result of add would still have only methods length and get. What we would like is to be able to define implementations where t has more methods than in OVect, so that we could still access them in the result of add. Intuitively, this amounts to defining t in OVect as

```
type t = <length: int; get: int -> float; ..>
```

where the ellipsis "`..`" allows extra methods. But free type variables are not allowed in types definition (think of type t = 'a,) and the "`..`" in the above type represents an internal type variable, usually called the *row variable*, which is free here. The first solution that comes to mind is to do as we would with normal type variables, and define an abstract type corresponding to this "`..`".

```
type t_row
type t = <length: int; get: int -> float; t_row>
```

This requires the ability to name the row variable, which is anonymous in OCaml. We formalize this idea at the beginning of section 3. We also find that it is only a first step, as incremental refinement of type definitions would be clumsy, and this formalization cannot fully handle polymorphic variant types.

A better approach to this problem is to find a middle-ground between abstract types, which are completely opaque, and concrete types, which cannot be further refined.

One option to introduce such semi-abstract types would be to exploit subtyping: one might allow defining upper or lower bounds for abstract types. This is the idea behind F-bounded polymorphism [7], which has been integrated into a number of languages such as Generic Java [8], Moby [9], or Scala [10]. In particular, Moby and Scala do have a module system able to express functors, and Scala gives an elegant solution to the expression problem [11].

In a language offering complete type inference, like Objective Caml does, subtyping has to be explicit, if we are to keep types simple. This makes the F-bounded polymorphism approach impractical, because any use of a value whose type is semi-abstract would require an explicit coercion. It is more natural to stick with the fully structural approach inherent to OCaml, simply abstracting extensibility (rather than the whole type) as if it were a type variable. This means that we actually follow the idea of adding an abstract t_row, but that we will keep it unnamed. Here is our syntax for it.

```
type t = private <length: int; get: int -> float; ..>
```

A private row type[2] is defined by a structural type, either object or variant, where the only free type variable is the row variable. Superficially, this looks exactly like the definition we just rejected as not well-formed. But here the "private" keyword implicitly binds the row variable as an anonymous abstract type, at the same level as the type definition. Using this definition in OVect, the functor OPoly now accepts any object type having at least the methods length and get with proper types.

There have been examples in the past combining classes with functors. Such a combination has been used by the FOC project for instance [12]. But in the absence of private row types, classes were only used to provide late-binding at the value level, and classes or object types did not appear in parameters of functors. We will also see that

---

[2] The "private" part of the naming will get clearer in section 2.2. The qualifiers "row" and "structural" are more or less interchangeable in this paper. The author somehow prefers structural, but some people seem to find the concept of row easier to grasp.

private row types, in combination with recursive modules, are even more interesting for polymorphic variants, as they provide a powerful way to structure programs using them.

The body of this paper is composed of two sections. The next one presents various examples using private row types, for functors, privacy, and extensible recursion. Section 3 formalizes the definitions, combining structural polymorphism with applicative functors.

2 Using Private Row Types

In this section we give examples of various uses of private row types, in combination with other features. All examples were type-checked using Objective Caml 3.09. The only new syntax compared to previous versions of the language is the "private" keyword, which indicates a private row type. While some function definitions contain type annotations, they are only there for demonstrative purposes, and the definitions would still be typable without them, leading to a more general type —*i.e.* type inference is still principal.

2.1 Simple Functors

Private row types are essential in combining functors with structural polymorphism. A natural application is our introduction example. For definitions prefixed with #, we show in italic the types inferred, as in an interactive session.

```
module type OVect = sig
  type t = private <length: int; get: int -> float; ..>
  val init : int -> (int -> float) -> t
end
# module OPoly (V : OVect) = struct ... end ;;
```
module OPoly : functor (V: OVect) -> sig val add : V.t -> V.t -> V.t end

We can develop it more, by adding a map method and using it in a function mul for external product.

```
module type OVect2 = sig
  type t = private
      <length: int; get: int -> float; map: (float -> float) -> t; ..>
  val init : int -> (int -> float) -> t
end
# module OPoly2 (V : OVect2) = struct
    include OPoly(V)
    let mul x (p : V.t) = p#map (fun y -> x *. y)
  end ;;
```
module OPoly2 : functor (V : OVect2) ->
sig
*   val add : V.t -> V.t -> V.t*
*   val mul : float -> V.t -> V.t*
end

Since we wish to extend OPoly, we include an instance of it. Note how we pass an argument of type OVect2 to OPoly which expects an OVect. This is accepted as OVect2.t is an instance of OVect.t.

Another typical case where we need to use functors with objects, is when the functionality we need is already provided as a functor.

```
module OMap(X : sig type t = private <compare : t -> int; ..> end)
  = Map.Make(struct type t = X.t let compare (x:t) y = x#compare y end)
class vector (n : int) (f : int -> float) = object (s : 's)
  val v = Array.init n f
  method length = n
  method get i = v.(i)
  method map f = < v = Array.map f v >
  method compare (vec : 's) = compare v (Array.init vec#length vec#get)
end
module VMap = OMap(struct type t = vector end)
module VPoly = OPoly2(struct type t = vector let init = new vector end)
```

Here the functor Map.Make from the standard library expects a type t and a function compare : t -> t -> int. Since t is not allowed any polymorphism, we have to wrap it in a new functor expecting only one type, which provides this time a method compare. We define a class vector —which implicitly also defines a type vector for its objects—, with all the methods required by OMap and OPoly2, so we can pass its type as parameter to both. Here the type annotations on f and vec are required, as class definitions may not contain free type variables.

Examples involving polymorphic variants also arise naturally. Consider for instance a simple property base, such that we may add new types of properties.

```
type basic = ['Bool of bool | 'String of string]
module Props(X : sig type t = private [> basic] end) =
  struct
    let base : (string,X.t) Hashtbl.t = Hashtbl.create 17
    let put_bool k b = Hashtbl.add k ('Bool b)
    let put_str k s = Hashtbl.add k ('String s)
    let to_string (v : X.t) = match v with
        'Bool b   -> if b then "true" else "false"
      | 'String s -> s
      | _ -> "other" (* required by typing *)
  end
```

The notation [> basic] is an abbreviation for [> 'Bool of bool | 'String of string]. It means that the actual variant type X.t will have to contain at least the constructors of basic, and eventually more. The ">" implies the presence of a row variable. This notation is not new to this proposal, but the "private" keyword is needed to bind the implicit row variable in a type definition. An interesting consequence of extensibility is that any pattern-matching on X.t needs to contain a default case, as it may actually contain more cases than basic. This is similar to Zenger&Odersky's approach to extensible datatypes, which also requires defaults [13].

In order to extend this basic property type, we only need to define a new type and apply the functor.

```
# type extended = [basic | 'Int of int] ;;
type extended = [ 'Bool of bool | 'Int of int | 'String of string ]
# module MyProps = Props(struct type t = extended end) ;;
module MyProps :
  sig
    val base : (string, extended) Hashtbl.t
    val put_bool : string -> bool -> unit
    val put_str : string -> string -> unit
    val to_string : extended -> string
  end
```

Note that here, extended is a "final" type, not extensible, thus we may write complete pattern-matchings for it. We may want to use this property to refine the to_string function. The notation #basic is an abbreviation for the or-pattern collecting all cases from basic, *i.e.* ('Bool _ | 'String _).

```
# let to_string (v : extended) = match v with
    'Int n -> string_of_int n
  | #basic -> MyProps.to_string v ;;
val to_string : extended -> string
```

The functorial approach is also useful when combining polymorphic variants and mutable values. It allows to extend the type of a polymorphic variant in a different compilation unit, which was not possible before. Here is an example which causes a compile time error.

```
(* base.ml *)
type basic = ['Bool of bool | 'String of string]
let base : (string, [>basic]) Hashtbl.t = Hashtbl.create 17
$ ocamlc -c base.ml
File "base.ml", line 2, characters 41-58:
The type of this expression, (string, _[> basic ]) Hashtbl.t,
contains type variables that cannot be generalized
```

Since base is not a value, its type cannot be made polymorphic. A final type for it should be determined in the same compilation unit. Since no such type is given here, this results in an error. Using the above functor avoids the problem, by delaying the creation of the hash table to the application of the functor. Note that using a functor means that any code accessing the property base must be functorized too. This is a classical downside of doing linking through functor application. As a counter part, this enhances modularity, allowing to use several property bases in the same program for instance.

2.2 Relation to Private Types

Since version 3.07, released in 2003, Objective Caml has *private types*, introduced by Pierre Weis [14]. Like private row types, private types are intended to appear in signatures, abstracting some behavior of the implementation. To do that, they simply restrict (non-polymorphic) variants and records, prohibiting the creation of values outside of the module where they were defined, while still allowing pattern-matching or field access. Contrary to private row types, they do not allow refinement of type definitions. Their main intent is to allow to enforce invariant properties on concrete types, like it is possible with abstract datatypes, while avoiding any overhead.

```
module Relative : sig
   type t = private Zero | Pos of int | Neg of int
   val inj : int -> t
end = struct
   type t = Zero | Pos of int | Neg of int
   let inj n = if n=0 then Zero else if n>0 then Pos n else Neg (-n)
end
# open Relative ;;
# let string_of_rel = function
     Zero -> "0"
   | Pos n -> string_of_int n
   | Neg n -> "-" ^ string_of_int n;;
val string_of_rel : rel -> string
# Zero;;
Cannot create values of the private type Relative.t
```

Interestingly, we can simulate private types with private row types. The kind of variant refinement used here is opposite to the previous section: we model restrictions on construction by assuming that some constructors may actually not be there. This gives us more flexibility than with the original private types, as some constructors may be declared as present, to make them public.

```
module Relative : sig
   type t = private [< 'Zero | 'Pos of int | 'Neg of int > 'Zero]
   val inj : int -> t
end = struct
   type t = ['Zero | 'Pos of int | 'Neg of int]
   let inj n = if n=0 then 'Zero else if n>0 then 'Pos n else 'Neg (-n)
end
# let zero : Relative.t = 'Zero;;
val zero : Relative.t = 'Zero
# let one : Relative.t = 'Pos (-1);;
This expression has type [> 'Pos of int ] but is here used with type
   Relative.t
```

The private definition of t has one public constructor, 'Zero, as implied by the "> 'Zero" bit of the definition, which says that it must be present in the implementation, but 'Pos and 'Neg are allowed to be absent, so they are private. As a result, 'Zero can be given type Relative.t, but 'Pos(-1) cannot, which protects abstraction.

Private record types can be modeled by object types, this time in the usual way. As an extra feature we naturally gain the possibility of hiding some fields. This allows to define module-private (or friend) methods, like in Java, while OCaml only has object-private methods.

```
module Vector : sig
  type 'a c = private
      < length: int; get: int -> 'a; compare: 'a c -> int; .. >
  val init : int -> (int -> 'a) -> 'a c
  val map : ('a -> 'b) -> 'a c -> 'b c
end = struct
  class ['a] c v = object (s : 's)
    method v = v
    method length = Array.length v
    method get i : 'a = v.(i)
    method compare (vec : 's) = compare v vec#v
  end
  let init n f = new c (Array.init n f)
  let map f v = new c (Array.map f v#v)
end
```

Here we have used a private object type to hide the method v, while enforcing its presence in the actual object. This allows accessing the contents of the object in a more efficient way. If v were visible outside of Vector, encapsulation would be broken, as one could use it to mutate these contents.

One might think that it would be enough to use an abstract type for the array returned by v, without hiding v itself. However, object typing in OCaml is purely structural: one can freely create an object by hand, and give it the same type as an existing class, even though its methods might cunningly call methods from different objects, breaking the coherence of the definitions. Only private object types can protect against this, while still allowing the programmer to call methods in a natural way. As with private types, this allows to enforce invariants, for instance saying that for a value v of type Vector.c, calling v#get i always succeeds when $0 \leq i < $ v#length.

Note that private object types do not interact directly with classes, and as such they are not as expressive as abstract views for instance [15]. In particular one cannot inherit from a private type.

2.3 Recursion and the Expression Problem

Examples in previous sections have kept to a simple structure. In particular, the variant types involved were not recursive. As we indicated in introduction, polymorphic variants are known to provide a very simple solution to the expression problem, allowing one to extend a recursive type with new constructors, with full type safety, and without any recompilation. However, the original solution has a small drawback: one has to close the recursion individually for each operation defined on the datatype. Moreover it relies quite heavily on type inference to produce polymorphic types.

With the introduction of recursive modules, a natural way to make things more explicit is to close the recursion at the module level. However, this also requires private row types, to allow extension without introducing mind-boggling coercions (see mixmod.ml at [4] for an example with coercions.)

We present here a variation on the expression problem, where we insist only on the addition of new constructors, since adding new operations is trivial in this setting. If you find it difficult to follow our approach, reading [4] first should help a lot. We first define a module type describing the operations involved.

```
module type Ops = sig
  type expr
  val eval : expr -> expr
  val show : expr -> string
end
```

We then define a first language, with only integer constants and addition. To keep it extensible, we leave the recursion open in the variant type, and have operations recurse through the parameter of a functor.

```
module Plus = struct
  type 'a expr0 = ['Num of int | 'Plus of 'a * 'a]
  module F(X : Ops with type expr = private [> 'a expr0] as 'a) =
    struct
      type expr = X.expr expr0
      let eval : expr -> X.expr = function
          'Num _ as e  -> e
        | 'Plus(e1,e2) -> match X.eval e1, X.eval e2 with
                            'Num m, 'Num n -> 'Num(m+n)
                          | e12            -> 'Plus e12
      let show : expr -> string = function
          'Num n -> string_of_int n
        | 'Plus(e1,e2) -> "("^X.show e1^"+"^X.show e2^")"
    end
  module rec L : (Ops with type expr = L.expr expr0) = F(L)
end
```

Observe how closing the recursion is now easy: we just have to take a fix-point of the functor.

The next step is to define a second language, adding multiplication. Inside the functor, we instantiate the original addition language, and use it to delegate known cases in operations, using variant dispatch.

```
module Mult = struct
  type 'a expr0 = ['a Plus.expr0 | 'Mult of 'a * 'a]
  module F(X : Ops with type expr = private [> 'a expr0] as 'a) =
    struct
      type expr = X.expr expr0
      module L = Plus.F(X)
      let eval : expr -> X.expr = function
          #L.expr as e -> L.eval e
        | 'Mult(e1,e2) -> match X.eval e1, X.eval e2 with
                            'Num m, 'Num n -> 'Num(m*n)
                          | e12            -> 'Mult e12
      let show : expr -> string = function
          #L.expr as e -> L.show e
        | 'Mult(e1,e2) -> "("^X.show e1^"*"^X.show e2^")"
    end
  module rec L : (Ops with type expr = L.expr expr0) = F(L)
end
```

That's it. Here is a simple example using the final language.

```
# Mult.L.show('Plus('Num 2,'Mult('Num 3,'Num 5)));;
- : string = "(2+(3*5))"
```

This whole approach may seem verbose at first, but a large part of it appears to be boilerplate. Half of the lines of Plus have to be repeated in Mult, and would actually be in any similar code. From a more theoretical point of view, this example makes clearer the relation between solutions to the expression problem that use type abstraction, such as [11], and our original solution which used only polymorphism.

Combining object types with recursive modules also has applications, but they are less immediate, as classes already provide a form of open recursion.

3 Formalization

Before giving a complete formalization, we first describe a much simpler one, which is limited to private object types. The idea is to formalize objects as rows, in the style of Rémy [16]. Here are our core types.

$$
\begin{array}{lll}
\nu ::= \alpha \mid t(\vec{\tau\rho}) & \text{abstractions} \\
\tau ::= \nu \mid \tau \to \tau \mid \langle \rho \rangle & \text{types} \\
\rho ::= \nu \mid \emptyset \mid l : \tau; \rho & \text{rows} \\
k ::= \star \mid \diamond & \text{kinds} \\
\sigma ::= \tau \mid \forall \alpha{:}k.\sigma & \text{polytypes}
\end{array}
$$

Types are composed of abstractions, function types, and object types. An object type is described by a row, which is a list of pairs label-type, terminated either by the empty list or an abstraction. Abstractions are either type variables or abstract types (which may have parameters, types or rows.) In order to indicate the contexts where an abstraction may be used, we introduce two kinds: $\star$ for types and $\diamond$ for rows. We allow fields to commute in rows, that is

$$
l_1 : \tau_1; l_2 : \tau_2; \rho = l_2 : \tau_2; l_1 : \tau_1; \rho \quad \text{if } l_1 \neq l_2
$$

The same label may occur twice in a row (as for labeled arguments [17].) This simplifies kinds —they don't need to track which labels are used—, but this has no practical impact, as there is no way to create such an object.

If we start with this core type system, moving to the module level is trivial: we just need to add kinds to abstract types. This creates no difficulty, as Leroy's modular module system already handles simple kinds [18]. In such a system, the signature OVect would be:

```
module type OVect = sig
  type t_row : ◇
  type t : ⋆ = <length: int; get: int → float; t_row>
  val init : int → (int → float) → t
end
```

Then defining a particular instance just requires providing a concrete definition for t_row.

Unfortunately, type refinement in this system proves to be very clumsy. The trouble is that the natural encoding of OVect2 would not be an instance of OVect. We need extra type definitions to make it possible.

```
module type OVect2 = sig
  type t_row' : ◇
  type t_row : ◇ = map : (float → float) → t; t_row'
  type t : ⋆ = <length: int; get: int → float; t_row>
  val init : int → (int → float) → t
end
```

The fact one has to change the name of the abstract row is particularly confusing.

This clumsiness leads to our implicit syntax for private row types: rather than make abstract rows explicit, and have them pollute signatures, we prefer to leave them implicit, just indicating their presence. Implementations do not need to give a concrete definition for abstract rows, as the type system can recover them by comparing a private type definition and its implementation. Technically this amounts to an extension of the subtyping relation for modules. And as we keep rows implicit, we can omit kinds from the surface language.

We might have gone even further, and allowed any free variable to be automatically converted into an anonymous abstract type. We refrained from this for two reasons. This contradicts the principle of minimality in language changes, and this doesn't fit well the intuition of "private" type. Yet this might be an interesting choice when designing a more implicit type system for modules.

While this sketch of a formalization gives a good intuition of what private row types are, sufficient for practical uses, we will use a different formalization for our core language. The main reason is that this system does not extend nicely to private variant types. As can be seen in Rémy's paper, allowing variant tags to disappear from a type require additional *presence* variables. If we were to apply this scheme, we would need an abstract presence type for each constructor we want to keep private, adding a lot of complexity[3].

We provide in the rest of this section a condensed description of the formal system underlying private row types. It is based on our formalism for structural polymorphism [19] for the core language part, combined with Leroy's description of an applicative functor calculus [20]. A combination of these two systems already provides a complete description of Objective Caml's type system (without polymorphic methods, labeled parameters, and extensions.)

We will not give full details of these two systems, as both of them are rather complex, yet very few changes are needed. One is the ability to specify inside structural types that they have an identity (a name), and are only compatible with types having the same identity. The other is to allow refining private row types through module subtyping, and check that all such refinements are legal.

While we will still internally use an abstract type to represent a "virtual" row variable, the formalism we describe here does not have explicit row variables. It is rather

---

[3] The internal representation of polymorphic variant types in the Objective Caml compiler does use such presence variables, but they are not shown to the programmer, and they are not abstracted individually.

$$\tau ::= \alpha \qquad\qquad\qquad \text{type variable}$$
$$| \; t(\vec{\tau}) \qquad\qquad\qquad \text{abstract type}$$
$$| \; \tau \to \tau \qquad\qquad\qquad \text{function type}$$
$$K ::= \emptyset \; | \; K, \alpha :: (C,R) \qquad \text{kinding environment}$$
$$\theta ::= \tau \; | \; K \triangleright \tau \qquad\qquad \text{kinded type}$$
$$\sigma ::= \theta \; | \; \forall \bar{\alpha}.\theta \qquad\qquad \text{polytype}$$

Fig. 1. Types and kindings

$$<l_1 : \tau_1; \dots; l_n : \tau_n; ..> \;\overset{\text{def}}{=}\; \alpha :: (\mathsf{o}, \{l_1, \dots, l_n\}, \mathcal{L}, 0, \{l_1 \mapsto \tau_1, \dots, l_n \mapsto \tau_n\}) \triangleright \alpha$$

$$<l_1 : \tau_1; \dots; l_n : \tau_n> \;\overset{\text{def}}{=}\; \alpha :: (\mathsf{o}, \{l_1, \dots, l_n\}, \{l_1, \dots, l_n\}, 0, \{l_1 \mapsto \tau_1, \dots, l_n \mapsto \tau_n\}) \triangleright \alpha$$

$$[> l_1 \text{ of } \tau_1 \; | \dots | \; l_n \text{ of } \tau_n] \;\overset{\text{def}}{=}\; \alpha :: (\mathsf{v}, \{l_1, \dots, l_n\}, \mathcal{L}, 0, \{l_1 \mapsto \tau_1, \dots, l_n \mapsto \tau_n)\}) \triangleright \alpha$$

$$[< l_1 \text{ of } \tau_1 \; | \dots | \; l_n \text{ of } \tau_n > l_1 \dots l_k] \;\overset{\text{def}}{=}\;$$
$$\alpha :: (\mathsf{v}, \{l_1, \dots, l_k\}, \{l_1, \dots, l_n\}, 0, \{l_1 \mapsto \tau_1, \dots, l_n \mapsto \tau_n\}) \triangleright \alpha$$

Fig. 2. Kindings corresponding to surface syntax

based on an expressive kinding relation [6], which describes constraints on types rather than simply categories.

3.1 Core Type System

We will directly use the formalism from [19], as it is already general enough. We only have to add parameterized abstract types. This section may seem obscure without a good understanding of the formalism used, yet understanding figure 2 and the entailment relation should be sufficient to go on to the module level. An important point is that the definitions here ensure automatically subject reduction (leading to type soundness) and principal type inference, without need of extra proofs.

The syntax for types and kindings is given in figure 1. Simple types τ are defined as usual. They include type variables, function types, and named abstract types with type parameters. Polytypes σ are extended with a kinding environment K that restricts possible instances for constrained variables. K is a set of bindings $\alpha :: (C,R)$, C a constraint and R a set of relations from labels to types, describing together the possible values admitted for the type α. There is no specific syntax in types for object and variants, as they are denoted by type variables constrained in a kinding environment. The kindings corresponding to the syntax used in previous sections, using the constraint domain defined lower, are given in figure 2, respectively for open or closed, object and variant types. The only relation we use in kindings, $\mapsto$, is not a function: a label may be related to several types. Recursive types can be defined using a mutually recursive kinding environment, *i.e.* where kinds are related to each other. It should be clear by now that the notion of kind in this type system bears no resemblance to the simple kinds we considered first. Note that we only introduce abstract types here; type abbreviations can be seen as always expanded.

In order to have a proper type system, we only need to define a constraint domain. Our constraint domain includes both object and variant types, and support for identifying a type by its name. We assume a set $\mathcal{L}$ of labels, denoting methods or variant constructors. $\mathcal{L}$ includes a special label *row* used to encode our virtual row. The C in a kind is an element of the following set.

$$(k, L, U, p) \in \{o, v\} \times P_{fin}(\mathcal{L}) \times (P_{fin}(\mathcal{L}) \cup \{\mathcal{L}\}) \times \{0, 1\}$$

k distinguishes objects and variants. L represents a lower bound on available methods or constructors (*required* or *present* ones), and should be a finite subset of $\mathcal{L}$. U represents an upper bound, and should be either a finite subset of $\mathcal{L}$, or $\mathcal{L}$ itself. p is 0 for normal types, 1 for private types, and will be used at the module level. For both of objects and variants, we obtain a "final" (non-refinable) type by choosing $L = U$.

We define an entailment relation on constraints, noted "$C \models C'$", which is reflexive and transitive. We first distinguish inconsistent constraints.

$$(o, L, U, p) \models \perp \text{ if } U \neq L \text{ and } U \neq \mathcal{L}$$
$$(v, L, U, p) \models \perp \text{ if } L \not\subseteq U$$

An object type can only be extensible or final: its upper bound is either L or all labels. On the other hand, a variant type with a finite upper bound may still be refined by removing tags, so that the only restriction is that the lower bound should be included in the upper bound.

Entailment can refine a constraint as long as it is not private. Note that refinement goes backward: a variable with the kind on the right of the entailment relation can be instantiated to one with the kind on the left.

$$(k, L', U', p) \models (k, L, U, 0) \text{ if } L \subset L' \text{ and } U \supset U'$$

Next we use our constraints to selectively propagate type equalities. For a constraint $C = (k, L, U, p)$ and a label l:

$$C \vdash uniq(l) \overset{\text{def}}{=} k = o \vee l \in L \vee (p = 1 \wedge l \in U) \vee l = row$$
$$l \mapsto \alpha_1 \wedge l \mapsto \alpha_2 \wedge uniq(l) \Rightarrow \alpha_1 = \alpha_2.$$

The first line defines a predicate *uniq*, denoting when only one type can be associated to a label. The second line is a propagation rule. It means that, for a kind (C, R), when a label satisfies the property *uniq*, then types associated to this label in R should be unified. In the original system without private rows, the definition of *uniq* was $k = o \vee l \in L$, meaning that unification is triggered either if we consider an object type, or a required label in a variant type. Now it is also triggered for possible labels in private variant types. That is, all possible labels in private types must have unique types. Combined with that fact their constraint cannot be further refined, this ensures that no typing information will be added to them. The special label *row* is always unique, and will be associated to an abstract type denoting the identity of a private row type.

It is easy to see that these definitions satisfy the conditions for a valid constraint domain, as stated in [19].

Note that this extension of the core type system is also required in order to handle first-class polymorphism, available through polymorphic methods and record fields. In that case, *row* is only associated with a universal type variable.

3.2   Module Type System

The second part is at the module level: we must introduce private type definitions, and allow refinement through module subtyping. In order to formalize this, we will switch to Leroy's module calculus [20], which has 4 kinds of judgements: well-formedness ($E \vdash \sigma$ type), module typing ($E \vdash s : S$), type equivalence ($E \vdash \theta \approx \theta'$), and module subtyping ($E \vdash S <: S'$.) We will proceed by adding and modifying rules in this calculus, without reproducing all rules for the sake of space.

Leroy leaves the base language unspecified. We have to be more specific, in particular allowing parameterized type definitions. We will see manifest type definitions as kinded types: type $t_i(\vec{\alpha}) = K \triangleright \tau$. Note that while variables of refinable kinds must all appear in $\vec{\alpha}$, as there is no way to quantify a variable explicitly outside of the type definition, variables whose kind is no longer refinable, $i.e.$ either $L = U$ or $p = 1$, are seen as implicitly quantified, and may appear in K but not in $\vec{\alpha}$. "$E \vdash \sigma$ type" checks that σ is a valid polytype under environment E, and that no refinable type variable is free.

The basic typing rule for type definitions is unchanged, up to our addition of type parameters.

$$\frac{E \vdash \forall \vec{\alpha}.\theta \text{ type} \quad t_i \notin BV(E) \quad E; \text{type } t_i(\vec{\alpha}) = \theta \vdash s : S}{E \vdash (\text{type } t_i(\vec{\alpha}) = \theta; s) : (\text{type } t_i(\vec{\alpha}) = \theta; S)}$$

As it does not handle directly private row types, we first need to translate private definitions into normal ones, both inside modules and signatures. As we have explained before, we do it by defining an abstract type t_{row} along with the manifest type t, using it as row.

$$\text{type } t_i(\vec{\alpha}) = \text{private } \theta_0 \overset{\triangle}{=} \text{type } t_{rowi}(\vec{\alpha}); \text{type } t_i(\vec{\alpha}) = \theta$$

$$\text{where} \quad \begin{aligned} \theta_0 &= K, \beta :: (k, L, U, 0, R) \triangleright \beta \quad L \neq U \\ \theta &= K, \beta :: (k, L, U, 1, R \cup \{row \mapsto t_{rowi}(\vec{\alpha})\}) \triangleright \beta \end{aligned}$$

θ_0 is a row type, with a single non-quantified refinable type variable β. In θ, we make its kind private, and mark it with the abstract type t_{rowi}, which is defined along t_i.

Once we have introduced private row types, we should allow refinement through subtyping. However, the standard approach of having t_{rowi} manifest on one side, and abstract on the other, will not work here, as we want to allow the enclosing kinds to be different. Here is the original rule for subtyping.

$$\frac{E \vdash \theta \approx \theta'}{E \vdash (\text{type } t_i(\vec{\alpha}) = \theta) <: (\text{type } t_i(\vec{\alpha}) = \theta')}$$

As you can see, the trouble here is that this rule is limited to equivalent type representations. In order to accommodate refinement, we add a new rule, using entailment.

$$\frac{(k, L, U, 0) \models (k, L', U', 0) \quad E \vdash K \approx K' \quad row \mapsto t_{rowi}(\vec{\alpha}) \in R'}{E \vdash (\text{type } t_i(\vec{\alpha}) = K, \beta :: (k, L, U, p, R) \triangleright \beta)}{ <: (\text{type } t_i(\vec{\alpha}) = K', \beta :: (k, L', U', 1, R') \triangleright \beta)}$$

This rule says that, a row type definition (either private or not) subsumes a private row type definition when: (1) the original definition entails the private one (both assumed public), (2) kinding environments K and K' are identical, up to the equivalence of the types they contain, (3) all labels common to both definitions are associated to equivalent types, which also implies that if $row \mapsto \tau \in R$, then $E \vdash \tau \approx t_{rowi}(\vec{\alpha})$. The requirement $row \mapsto t_{rowi}(\vec{\alpha}) \in R'$ additionally ensures that the abstract row is declared inside the same signature.

Another slight modification we need is to allow the introduction of hidden types in subtyping. This accounts for two situations. The first one is when the original type definition is public, and we make it private through subtyping. We need to introduce a new abstract t_{rowi} in the subtype, matching the implicit one in the supertype.

$$\frac{t_{rowi} \notin BV(D_i) \quad (1 \le i \le n)}{E \vdash \text{sig } D_1; ...; D_n \text{ end} <: \text{sig } D_1; ...; D_k; \text{type } t_{rowi}(\vec{\alpha}); D_{k+1}; ...; D_n \text{ end}}$$

The second one occurs when we define a type alias for a private type, and then export it as being itself a private type. Here is an example.

```
module M : sig type t = private [> 'A] end = struct
   module M1 = struct type t = private [> 'A | 'B] end
   type t = M1.t
end
```

We need to add type $t_{rowi} = M_1.t_{rowi}$ in the signature of our implementation, in order to use the subtyping rule for private row types:

$$\frac{t_{rowi} \notin BV(D_i) \quad D_k = (\text{type } t_i(\vec{\alpha}) = K, \beta :: (k, L, U, 1, R) \rhd \beta) \quad row \mapsto \tau \in R}{E \vdash \text{sig } D_1; ...; D_k; S \text{ end} <: \text{sig } D_1; ...; D_{k-1}; \text{type } t_{rowi}(\vec{\alpha}) = \tau; D_k; S \text{ end}}$$

These rules together provide a complete formalization of private row types.

3.3   Extra Features

Independently of these questions of formalism, another issue appears with the introduction of the `with` construct for signatures. This construct is not present in [20], but it is needed in practice for any implementation, to avoid expanding all signatures by hand. We are using it in our own example of section 2.3. The technical difficulty with `with` comes from the fact it only substitutes one definition at a time, and the environment of the signature to be modified is not available in the new definition. It had to be extended to allow private row types, particularly recursive ones. This is not yet enough for mutually recursive types, and it seems that there are approaches more promising than `with` to manipulate signatures [21].

A last design decision is related to the handling of variance. In order to allow more subtyping, in OCaml both abstract types and algebraic datatypes have variances associated to their type parameters. For instance the type $list(\alpha)$ is covariant, which can be written type $list(+\alpha)$ in its type definition. For abstract types variance annotations are explicit, but for algebraic datatypes they are inferred from the definition of the type. As private row types have a structural definition, one might think of inferring their variance. However, the presence of an associated abstract type clearly indicates that variance should be explicit. This also means that this variance must be respected:

i.e. an implementation should have a stronger variance than the private row type it replaces, and variance can only be weakened through subtyping. This reasoning can be used to explain why private types, while they do not allow refinement, use also explicit variances.

4 Conclusion

We have introduced a new form of type definition, which is both manifest and abstract at the same time. We branded it as private, as it behaves in a way very similar to both private types in OCaml, and private methods as they are understood in Java. Nonetheless, the power of this new feature is not limited to privacy, but goes a long way towards abstraction allowing incremental extension. As this feature relies heavily on the expressive power of modules, it is most interesting when combined with recent extensions of module systems, such as recursive modules [22,23,24] or, in an hopefully close future, combinable signatures [21].

Another desirable addition is support for unions of private variant types. One can already define unions of concrete polymorphic variant types, and use them through dispatch. The private case is more complex, as one must ensure that the combined types are compatible. We are currently working on this question.

Acknowledgements

Comments from Didier Rémy, Keiko Nakata, Romain Bardou, and anonymous referees were a great help in improving this paper. I thank them all.

References

1. Rémy, D., Vouillon, J.: Objective ML: An effective object-oriented extension to ML. Theory and Practice of Object Systems **4** (1998) 27–50
2. Garrigue, J.: Programming with polymorphic variants. In: ML Workshop, Baltimore (1998)
3. Wadler, P.: The expression problem. Java Genericity mailing list (1998) http://www.daimi.au.dk/~madst/tool/papers/expression.txt.
4. Garrigue, J.: Code reuse through polymorphic variants. In: Workshop on Foundations of Software Engineering, Sasaguri, Japan (2000) http://www.math.nagoya-u.ac.jp/~garrigue/papers/fose2000.html.
5. Rémy, D., Garrigue, J.: On the expression problem. http://pauillac.inria.fr/~remy /work/expr/(2004)
6. Ohori, A.: A polymorphic record calculus and its compilation. ACM Transactions on Programming Languages and Systems **17** (1995) 844–895
7. Canning, P., Cook, W., Hill, W., Olthoff, W., Mitchell, J.C.: F-bounded polymorphism for object-oriented programming. In: Proc. ACM Symposium on Functional Programming and Computer Architectures. (1989) 273–280
8. Bracha, G., Odersky, M., Stoutamire, D., Wadler, P.: Making the future safe for the past: Adding genericity to the Java programming language. In: Proc. ACM Symposium on Object Oriented Programming, Systems, Languages and Applications. (1998)

9. Fisher, K., Reppy, J.: The design of a class mechanism for Moby. In: Proc. ACM Conference on Programming Language Design and Implementation. (1999)
10. Odersky, M., Crémet, V., Röckl, C., Zenger, M.: A nominal theory of objects with dependent types. In: Proc. European Conference on Object-Oriented Programming. (2003)
11. Zenger, M., Odersky, M.: Independently extensible solutions to the expression problem. In: Workshop on Foundations of Object-Oriented Languages. (2005)
12. Boulmé, S., Hardin, T., Rioboo, R.: Polymorphic data types, objects, modules and functors: is it too much? RR 014, LIP6, Université Paris 6 (2000)
13. Zenger, M., Odersky, M.: Extensible algebraic datatypes with defaults. In: Proc. ACM International Conference on Functional Programming. (2001) 241–252
14. Leroy, X., Doligez, D., Garrigue, J., Rémy, D., Vouillon, J.: The Objective Caml system release 3.09, Documentation and user's manual. Projet Cristal, INRIA. (2005)
15. Vouillon, J.: Combining subsumption and binary methods: an object calculus with views. In: Proc. ACM Symposium on Principles of Programming Languages. (2001) 290–303
16. Rémy, D.: Type inference for records in a natural extension of ML. In Gunter, C.A., Mitchell, J.C., eds.: Theoretical Aspects Of Object-Oriented Programming. Types, Semantics and Language Design. MIT Press (1993)
17. Garrigue, J., Aït-Kaci, H.: The typed polymorphic label-selective λ-calculus. In: Proc. ACM Symposium on Principles of Programming Languages. (1994) 35–47
18. Leroy, X.: A modular module system. Journal of Functional Programming 10 (2000) 269–303
19. Garrigue, J.: Simple type inference for structural polymorphism. In: Workshop on Foundations of Object-Oriented Languages, Portland, Oregon (2002)
20. Leroy, X.: Applicative functors and fully transparent higher-order modules. In: Proc. ACM Symposium on Principles of Programming Languages. (1995) 142–153
21. Ramsey, N., Fisher, K., Govereau, P.: An expressive language of signatures. In: Proc. ACM International Conference on Functional Programming. (2005)
22. Crary, K., Harper, R., Puri, S.: What is a recursive module? In: Proc. ACM Conference on Programming Language Design and Implementation. (1999) 50–63
23. Russo, C.V.: Recursive structures for Standard ML. In: Proc. ACM International Conference on Functional Programming. (2001) 50–61
24. Nakata, K., Garrigue, J.: Recursive modules for programming. In: Proc. ACM International Conference on Functional Programming, Portland, Oregon (2006)

Type and Effect System for Multi-staged Exceptions*

Hyunjun Eo[1], Ik-Soon Kim[2], and Kwangkeun Yi[1]

[1] Seoul National University, Korea
[2] École Polytechnique, France

Abstract. We present a type and effect system for a multi-staged language with exceptions. The proposed type and effect system checks if we safely synthesize complex controls with exceptions in multi-staged programming. The proposed exception constructs in multi-staged programming has no artificial restriction. Exception-raise and -handle expressions can appear in expressions of any stage, though they are executed only at stage 0. Exceptions can be raised during code composition and may escape before they are handled. Our effect type system support such features. We prove our type and effect system sound: empty effect means the input program has no uncaught exceptions during its execution.

1 Introduction

Staged computation, which explicitly divides a computation into separate stages, is a unifying framework for existing program generation systems: partial evaluation [5,1], run-time code generation [7,10], function inlining and macro expansion [11,3] are all instances of staged computation. The stage levels are determined by the nesting depth of program generations: stage 0 generates a program of stage 1 that generates a program of stage 2, and so on. The key aspect of multi-staged language is to have code templates (program fragments) as first-class objects. Code templates are freely passed, composed with code of other stages, and executed. At stage 0, computation include all normal computation plus generating code and executing generated code. At stage > 0, computation is just code-composition: it just visits expression's sub-expressions and substitutes code into code when appropriate.

Example 1. As a specializer example in multi-stage programming, consider a recursive map function:

```
fun map f nil = nil
  | map f (x::r) = (f x) :: (map f r)
```

---

* Eo and Yi were partially supported by Brain Korea 21 Project of Korea Ministry of Education and Human Resources, by IT Leading R& D Support Project of Korea Ministry of Information and Communication, by Korea National Security Research Institute, and by Microsoft Research Asia. Kim was supported by post-doctoral grants from École Polytechnique and École Normale Supérieure in France.

N. Kobayashi (Ed.): APLAS 2006, LNCS 4279, pp. 61–78, 2006.

The map function applies function f to each element in the input list, and builds a list with the results returned by f. If we know which list is available, we can specialize map function with the input list. For example, if input list is 1::2::nil, we specialize the map function to fn f => (f 1)::(f 2):::nil. The specialized function is more efficient than the original map function because it does not need to traverse the list structure. This specialization can be achieved by the following two functions in Lisp's quasi-quote syntax [11]:

```
fun map_ls nil = 'nil
  | map_ls (x::r) = '((f ,x) :: ,(map_ls r))
fun smap ls = eval '(fn f => ,(map_ls ls))
```

At stage 0, the function smap, along with map_ls, traverses input list ls and generates a specialized function of stage 1: the stage increases by the number of surrounding backquotes ('), and decreases by the number of commas (,). Because the application (f ,x) in map_ls is at stage 1 (surrounded by one backquote), it will not be evaluated. However, the recursive call (map_ls r) will be evaluated because it is at stage 0 (surrounded by one backquote and one comma). ∎

Exception handling allows the programmer to define, raise and handle exceptional conditions. Exceptional conditions are brought (by a raise expression) to the attention of another expression where the raised exceptions may be handled. Raised exceptions abort the usual program continuation, transfer ("long jump") the control to its handling point, and continue there with the handler expression. Hence by using exceptions programmers can divert any control structure to a point where the corresponding exception is handled. The exception facilities, however, can provide a hole for program safety. Programs can abruptly halt when an exception is raised and never handled.

In this paper we extend the Lisp-like multi-staged language λ_{open}^{sim} [6] with such exceptions and then present a sound type and effect system that statically estimate may-uncaught exceptions in the input programs.

The proposed exception facility in the multi-staged language has no artificial restriction. Lexically, exception-raise and -handle expressions can appear in expressions of any stage. Only restriction, which is natural, is on their dynamics: exceptions must be raised and handled only at stage 0 (at normal computation). Hence, the most interesting feature of our language is exceptions raised during code composition. During computation at stage > 0 (during code composition) an expression can be brought to stage 0 and evaluated there to return a code to substitute for the expression at the code composition. During this stage-0 evaluation an exception can be raised. This raised exception can be caught by a handler only at stage 0. Which handler is that? Any handler at stage 0 in the continuation of the raised exception. A handler that is installed during the stage-0 evaluation can catch it. Or, a handler that is installed at stage 0 before the code composition can catch it and continue.

Example 2. We explain this staged exception semantics by an example. The following function f gets a list ls and generates a code that multiplies free variable a with every element in ls.

```
fun g nil = '1
  | g x::r = '(,x * ,(g r))
fun f ls = '(a * ,(g ls))
```

When the input list ls is '2::'0::'3::nil, the result code will be '(a * 2 * 0 * 3 * 1). We can prepare a more efficient code by using exceptions. We change g to raise Zero whenever an element of ls is '0.

```
fun g1 nil = '1
  | g1 x::r = if x = '0 then raise Zero
                 else '(,x * ,(g1 r))
```

Then, to catch the raised exception Zero, we can install a handler during the stage-0 evaluation inside the code composition:

```
fun f1 ls = '(a * ,((g1 ls) handle Zero => '0))
```

Or, we can install a handler at stage 0 before the code composition:

```
fun f2 ls = '(a * ,(g1 ls)) handle Zero => '0
```

Note that f1 and f2 behave differently. When the input ls has '0, f1 generates '(a * 0) while f2 generates '0.   ∎

We extend the effect type system [12,13,14] for exception analysis of ML [4,9] to have staged effect types. The extension consists of annotating the box type constructor □ for the code type with the set of possible exceptions that may be raised during the code execution. Every exception effect has an associated non-negative integer that denotes the number of stages that the raised exception must escape to be handled at stage 0. For example, $Zero^n$ in an effect means that uncaught exception Zero can be handled at stage 0 after escaping n stages.

The type of a code with raise c (c for an exception name) would be:

$$\text{'(raise } c) : \Box(\varnothing \triangleright A, \{c^0\}), \emptyset.$$

The box type $\Box(\varnothing \triangleright A, \{c^0\})$ means that the above expression is a closed code of type A, and may raise an exception c when evaluated. The empty effect $\emptyset$ means that this code does not raise any exception. The type of executing the above code template by eval would be:

$$\text{eval '(raise } c) : A, \{c^0\}.$$

The effect $\{c^0\}$ means that the above expression may raise exception c. The superscript 0 means that the raised exception c can be handled by a proper handler at the current stage.

Example 3. We will explain such exceptions and their corresponding types by an example program in Fig. 1. The function codegen compiles a program in language L into an ML program of int type. During compilation, it may raise an exception CompileError. The type of codegen would be:

$$\text{codegen} : L \xrightarrow{\{CompileError^0\}} \Box(\varnothing \triangleright \text{int}), \emptyset.$$

```
exception CompileError

type L = CONST of int | PLUS of L * L | ···

fun codegen e =
  case e of
    CONST x => `,x
  | PLUS(e1,e2) => `(,(codegen e1) + ,(codegen e2))
    ...
  | _ => raise CompileError

fun compile program =
    (codegen (parse program))
    handle CompileError => print "Compile Error"; `0
```

Fig. 1. An example: compiling L into ML

It means that exception CompileError may be raised when we apply codegen. Hence, the type of application (codegen e1) is:

$$(\text{codegen e1}) : \Box(\varnothing \rhd \text{int}, \emptyset), \{\text{CompileError}^0\}.$$

In order to plug the above code inside another code (i.e., inside a backquote expression), we have to comma it: `(,(codegen e1)). The type of ,(codegen e1) is:

$$,(\text{codegen e1}) : \text{int}, \{\text{CompileError}^1\}.$$

Because this expression is inside a code template (stage 1), the raised exception CompileError cannot be handled at the current stage: it can be handled only after escaping 1 stage. The superscript 1 in CompileError^1 describes this situation. The type of the enclosing code template of the above expression is:

$$`(,(\text{codegen e1})) : \Box(\varnothing \rhd \text{int}, \emptyset), \{\text{CompileError}^0\}.$$

It means that the above expression may raise exception CompileError. The superscript 0 in CompileError^0 means that CompileError can be handled at the current stage. Hence a handler at stage 0 can catch it

$$\begin{array}{l}`(,(\text{codegen e1}))\\ \text{handle CompileError => } `0\end{array} : \Box(\varnothing \rhd \text{int}, \emptyset), \emptyset$$

while a handler inside code template (at stage > 0) cannot handle it

$$\begin{array}{l}`(,(\text{codegen e1})\\ \text{handle CompileError => } 0)\end{array} : \Box(\varnothing \rhd \text{int}, \emptyset), \{\text{CompileError}^0\}$$

∎

Recently, Nanevski has proposed an exception type for staged language in a different formulation [8]: his language requires programmer to explicitly name each code composition, while our type system (in an implicit style) allows unnamed code composition[1]. Though explicitly naming code composition may make type system simple (such that it is not necessary to annotate effects with stage levels), we chose to use the implicit style. Our reason is pragmatic: to have an exception type system to support Lisp's quasi-quote system. Lisp's quasi-quote system is an implicit multi-staged language that has evolved to comply with the demands from multi-staged programming practices. Moreover, our type system enjoys the advantage of [6] that supports open code as first-class objects.

In the rest of our paper, we introduce the syntax and semantics of our language (Section 2), define the exception types and effects (Section 3.1), describe typing rules (Section 3.2), and prove the soundness of our effect type system (Section 3.3).

2 Language

2.1 Syntax

Our language λ_{exn}^{stage} has the staging constructs á la λ_{open}^{sim} [6] with the exception-raise and -handle constructs. We exclude references and gensyms from λ_{open}^{sim} in order to focus on exceptions.

$$e \in Exp ::= i \mid c \mid x \mid \lambda x.e \mid e_1 e_2$$
$$\mid \text{box } e \mid \text{eval } e \mid \text{unbox}_k \, e$$
$$\mid \text{raise } e \mid \text{handle } e_1 \, c \, e_2$$

Expression i is an integer constant, c is an exception name. Expression box e, $\text{unbox}_k \, e$ ($k > 0$), and eval e are for manipulating code templates that respectively correspond to the backquote('), the comma(,) .... k stages, and the eval in Lisp's quasi-quote notation. At stage 0, raise e raises an exception returned from evaluating e. Handle expression handle $e_1 \, c \, e_2$ evaluates e_1 first. If it does not raise an exception, its result is the handle expression's result. If it raises exception c, then the handler catches it and evaluates e_2. If it raises an exception other than c, then the raised exception is the result.

2.2 Operational Semantics

Fig. 2 shows a big-step operational semantics of our language λ_{exn}^{stage}. Evaluation

$$e \xrightarrow{\ n\ } r$$

denotes that expression e is evaluated to result r at stage n.

Values V^n are the values of stage n. In multi-staged languages, values exists at every stage. Values at stage 0 are normal ones plus code. Values at stages> 0 are code only. A staged value v^n ($n > 0$) is an expression that is to be evaluated later when it is demoted to stage 0 by the eval construct. Results R^n at stage

---

[1] Davies and Pfenning have shown that both explicit and implicit formulations are inter-translatable [2].

Normal computations (at stage 0) and   Propagation of
code compositions (at stage $n > 0$)   raised exceptions

(EINT) $i \xrightarrow{n} i \ (n \geq 0)$

(EEXN) $c \xrightarrow{n} c \ (n \geq 0)$

(EVAR) $x \xrightarrow{n} x \ (n > 0)$

(EABS) $\lambda x.e \xrightarrow{0} \lambda x.e$

$$\frac{e \xrightarrow{n} v}{\lambda x.e \xrightarrow{n} \lambda x.v}(n>0) \qquad\qquad \frac{e \xrightarrow{n} \overline{c}}{\lambda x.e \xrightarrow{n} \overline{c}}(n>0)$$

(EAPP) $$\frac{e_1 \xrightarrow{0} \lambda x.e \quad e_2 \xrightarrow{0} v_2 \quad [x \xmapsto{0} v_2]e \xrightarrow{0} v}{e_1\, e_2 \xrightarrow{0} v} \qquad \frac{e_1 \xrightarrow{n} \overline{c}}{e_1\, e_2 \xrightarrow{n} \overline{c}}(n \geq 0)$$

$$\frac{e_1 \xrightarrow{n} v_1 \quad e_2 \xrightarrow{n} v_2}{e_1\, e_2 \xrightarrow{n} v_1\, v_2}(n>0) \qquad \frac{e_2 \xrightarrow{n} \overline{c}}{e_1\, e_2 \xrightarrow{n} \overline{c}}(n \geq 0)$$

(EBOX) $$\frac{e \xrightarrow{n+1} v}{\mathbf{box}\ e \xrightarrow{n} \mathbf{box}\ v}(n \geq 0) \qquad \frac{e \xrightarrow{n+1} \overline{c}}{\mathbf{box}\ e \xrightarrow{n} \overline{c}}(n \geq 0)$$

(EUNBOX) $$\frac{e \xrightarrow{0} \mathbf{box}\ v}{\mathbf{unbox}_n\ e \xrightarrow{n} v}(n>0)$$

$$\frac{e \xrightarrow{n-k} v}{\mathbf{unbox}_k\ e \xrightarrow{n} \mathbf{unbox}_k\ v}(n>k>0) \qquad \frac{e \xrightarrow{n-k} \overline{c}}{\mathbf{unbox}_k\ e \xrightarrow{n} \overline{c}}(n \geq k>0)$$

(EEVAL) $$\frac{e \xrightarrow{0} \mathbf{box}\ v^1 \quad v^1 \xrightarrow{0} v^0}{\mathbf{eval}\ e \xrightarrow{0} v^0}$$

$$\frac{e \xrightarrow{n} v}{\mathbf{eval}\ e \xrightarrow{n} \mathbf{eval}\ v}(n>0) \qquad \frac{e \xrightarrow{n} \overline{c}}{\mathbf{eval}\ e \xrightarrow{n} \overline{c}}(n \geq 0)$$

(ERAISE) $$\frac{e \xrightarrow{0} c}{\mathbf{raise}\ e \xrightarrow{0} \overline{c}}$$

$$\frac{e \xrightarrow{n} v}{\mathbf{raise}\ e \xrightarrow{n} \mathbf{raise}\ v}(n>0) \qquad \frac{e \xrightarrow{n} \overline{c}}{\mathbf{raise}\ e \xrightarrow{n} \overline{c}}(n \geq 0)$$

(EHANDLE) $$\frac{e_1 \xrightarrow{0} v}{\mathbf{handle}\ e_1\ c\ e_2 \xrightarrow{0} v} \qquad \frac{e_1 \xrightarrow{n} \overline{c}}{\mathbf{handle}\ e_1\ c\ e_2 \xrightarrow{n} \overline{c}}(n>0)$$

$$\frac{e_1 \xrightarrow{0} \overline{c} \quad e_2 \xrightarrow{0} v}{\mathbf{handle}\ e_1\ c\ e_2 \xrightarrow{0} v} \qquad \frac{e_1 \xrightarrow{n} \overline{c}}{\mathbf{handle}\ e_1\ c'\ e_2 \xrightarrow{n} \overline{c}}(n>0)$$

$$\frac{e_1 \xrightarrow{0} \overline{c}}{\mathbf{handle}\ e_1\ c'\ e_2 \xrightarrow{0} \overline{c}} \qquad \frac{e_2 \xrightarrow{n} \overline{c}}{\mathbf{handle}\ e_1\ c\ e_2 \xrightarrow{n} \overline{c}}(n>0)$$

$$\frac{e_1 \xrightarrow{n} v_1 \quad e_2 \xrightarrow{n} v_2}{\mathbf{handle}\ e_1\ c\ e_2 \xrightarrow{n} \mathbf{handle}\ v_1\ c\ v_2}(n>0) \qquad \frac{e_2 \xrightarrow{n} \overline{c}}{\mathbf{handle}\ e_1\ c'\ e_2 \xrightarrow{n} \overline{c}}(n>0)$$

Fig. 2. Operational semantics of λ_{exn}^{stage}

$$[x \overset{n}{\mapsto} v]i = i$$
$$[x \overset{n}{\mapsto} v]c = c$$
$$[x \overset{n}{\mapsto} v]y = v, \quad \text{if } x = y \text{ and } n = 0$$
$$= y, \quad \text{otherwise}$$
$$[x \overset{n}{\mapsto} v](\lambda y.e) = \lambda y.e, \quad \text{if } x = y \text{ and } n = 0$$
$$= \lambda y.([x \overset{n}{\mapsto} v]e), \quad \text{otherwise}$$
$$[x \overset{n}{\mapsto} v](e_1 \ e_2) = ([x \overset{n}{\mapsto} v]e_1) \ ([x \overset{n}{\mapsto} v]e_2)$$
$$[x \overset{n}{\mapsto} v](\mathbf{box} \ e) = \mathbf{box} \ ([x \overset{n+1}{\mapsto} v]e)$$
$$[x \overset{n}{\mapsto} v](\mathbf{unbox}_k \ e) = \mathbf{unbox}_k \ ([x \overset{n-k}{\mapsto} v]e)$$
$$[x \overset{n}{\mapsto} v](\mathbf{eval} \ e) = \mathbf{eval} \ ([x \overset{n}{\mapsto} v]e)$$
$$[x \overset{n}{\mapsto} v](\mathbf{raise} \ e) = \mathbf{raise} \ ([x \overset{n}{\mapsto} v]e)$$
$$[x \overset{n}{\mapsto} v](\mathbf{handle} \ e_1 \ c \ e_2) = \mathbf{handle} \ ([x \overset{n}{\mapsto} v]e_1) \ c \ ([x \overset{n}{\mapsto} v]e_2)$$

Fig. 3. Substituting v for free variable x of stage 0 at stage n

n are either values at stage n or raised exceptions. We write $\bar{c}$ for a raised c exception.

$$v^n \in V^n ::= i \mid c \mid \lambda x.e \mid \mathbf{box} \ v^1 \qquad \text{if } n = 0$$
$$::= i \mid c \mid x \mid \lambda x.v^n \mid v^n v^n$$
$$\mid \mathbf{box} \ v^{n+1} \mid \mathbf{eval} \ v^n \mid \mathbf{unbox}_k \ v^{n-k}$$
$$\mid \mathbf{raise} \ v^n \mid \mathbf{handle} \ v_1^n \ c \ v_2^n \qquad \text{if } n > k \geq 0$$

$$r^n \in R^n ::= v^n \mid \bar{c}$$

Staging semantics of λ_{exn}^{stage} is the same as in λ_{open}^{sim} [6], conservatively extended with exceptions.

At stage 0, computation include, in addition to normal computation, generating code and executing generated code. (EINT), (EEXN), (EABS), and (EAPP) are as usual. (EAPP) defines the beta reduction. The definition of the staged substitution operator $[x \overset{n}{\mapsto} v]$ is in Fig. 3. (EBOX) defines code generation. (EEVAL) at stage 0 executes generated code: a code template $\mathbf{box} \ v^1$ becomes an expression v^1 then is evaluated. By the type system, v^1 is restricted to closed code. (See section 3). Because only closed code can be evaluated at stage 0, we don't have an evaluation rule for variable at stage 0.

At stage > 0, only meaningful computation is code substitution. It consists of just visiting every sub-expressions and substitute code into code when appropriate. Code substitution is by the $\mathbf{unbox}_k$ expression. At stage n, expression $\mathbf{unbox}_n \ e$ executes the sub-expression e at stage 0 then substitute its result code for the $\mathbf{unbox}_n$ expression: (EUNBOX).

(ERAISE) raises an exception only at stage 0. The right side of Fig. 2 shows that the propagation of raised exception $\bar{c}$. A raised exception $\bar{c}$ is propagated to the nearest handler that handles exception c at stage 0: (EHANDLE). Raised exceptions can escape any control structure including stages.

Example 4. In the following expression, an exception c is initially raised at stage 0, is "promoted" to stage 2 (by unbox_2), and then escapes to stage 0 (by two boxes).

$$\cfrac{\cfrac{\cfrac{\cfrac{c \xrightarrow{0} c}{\text{raise}\,c \xrightarrow{0} \bar{c}}}{\text{unbox}_2\,\text{raise}\,c \xrightarrow{2} \bar{c}}}{\text{box}\,(\text{unbox}_2\,\text{raise}\,c) \xrightarrow{1} \bar{c}}}{\text{box}\,(\text{box}\,(\text{unbox}_2\,\text{raise}\,c)) \xrightarrow{0} \bar{c}}$$

$\bar{c}$ is raised at stage 0

$\bar{c}$ is promoted to stage 2

$\bar{c}$ is demoted to stage 1

$\bar{c}$ is demoted to stage 0

∎

Like exceptions raised during normal computation, stage-escaping exceptions (raised during code composition) are handled only at stage 0. Hence, handle expressions at stage> 0 cannot handle a raised exceptions.

Example 5. The following expression evaluates to $(\text{box}\,0)$ because raised exception $\bar{c}$ is propagated to stage 0, and handled there to evaluate into code 0.

$$\cfrac{\cfrac{\cfrac{\cfrac{c \xrightarrow{0} c}{\text{raise}\,c \xrightarrow{0} \bar{c}}}{\text{unbox}_1\,\text{raise}\,c \xrightarrow{1} \bar{c}}}{\text{box}\,(\text{unbox}_1\,\text{raise}\,c) \xrightarrow{0} \bar{c}} \quad \cfrac{0 \xrightarrow{1} 0}{\text{box}\,0 \xrightarrow{0} \text{box}\,0}}{\text{handle}\,(\text{box}\,(\text{unbox}_1\,\text{raise}\,c))\,c\,(\text{box}\,0) \xrightarrow{0} \text{box}\,0} \quad \text{handle at stage 0 catches } \bar{c}$$

∎

Example 6. The following expression raises uncaught exception $\bar{c}$ because handle expression inside the code template cannot handle $\bar{c}$ and just propagates it to stage 0 escaping the code template of stage 1.

$$\cfrac{\cfrac{\cfrac{\cfrac{c \xrightarrow{0} c}{\text{raise}\,c \xrightarrow{0} \bar{c}}}{\text{unbox}_1\,(\text{raise}\,c) \xrightarrow{1} \bar{c}}}{\text{handle}\,(\text{unbox}_1\,(\text{raise}\,c))\,c\,0 \xrightarrow{1} \bar{c}}}{\text{box}\,(\text{handle}\,(\text{unbox}_1\,(\text{raise}\,c))\,c\,0) \xrightarrow{0} \bar{c}}$$

handle at stage 1 cannot catch c

∎

As in λ_{open}^{sim} [6], at stages> 0 (at code composition stages) no alpha-equivalence is supported, i.e., variable-capturing substitution is allowed. If we change a bound name in expressions of stages> 0, the resulting program's semantics changes. On the other hand at stage 0 (at the normal computation stage) alpha-equivalence is preserved as usual. (We enforce only closed code to be evaluated at stage 0. See (TEVAL) in Section 3).

3   Effect Type System

3.1   Exception Types and Effects

We use A, B for types, φ for effects, and ψ for a set of exceptions.

$$A, B \in \textit{Type} ::= \texttt{int} \mid \texttt{exn}(\psi) \mid A \xrightarrow{\varphi} B \mid \square(\Gamma \triangleright A, \varphi)$$

Exception type $\texttt{exn}(\psi)$ has a set of exceptions that an expression of that type can have. As in usual effect systems, function type $A \xrightarrow{\varphi} B$ has a latent effect φ that describes exceptions that may be raised during the evaluation of the function's body. Code type $\square(\Gamma \triangleright A, \varphi)$ is a conditional modal type in which condition Γ specifies the types of free variables in the code template of type A. Our code type is also annotated by a latent effect φ that describes exceptions that may be raised when the code template of that type is evaluated by $\texttt{eval}$.

$$
\begin{aligned}
\varphi &\in \textit{Effects} &&= 2^{\textit{Exn} \times \mathbb{N}} \\
\psi &\in \textit{Exceptions} &&= 2^{\textit{Exn}} \\
c &\in \textit{Exn} &&= \text{set of exception names}
\end{aligned}
$$

Effects in our types are sets of exceptions, where each exception has the number of stages to escape. The stage-escaping numbers denote how many stages should those exceptions escape to be handled at stage 0. For $\psi \in \textit{Exceptions}$, ψ^n means $\{c^n \mid c \in \psi\} \in \textit{Effects}$.

Normal Exceptions vs. Stage-Escaping Exceptions
Normal exceptions, which may be raised during normal computation, and stage-escaping exceptions, which may be raised during code composition, have a different behavior. If they are in a code template, stage-escaping exceptions can escape stages, while normal exceptions cannot. For example, $\texttt{raise}\,c$ raises a normal exception, while $\texttt{unbox}_1\,(\texttt{raise}\,c)$ raises a stage-escaping exception. Hence $\texttt{box}\,(\texttt{raise}\,c)$ does not raise exception c, while $\texttt{box}\,(\texttt{unbox}_1\,(\texttt{raise}\,c))$ raises exception c.

Definition 1. *For an effect φ, and a unary predicate $P : \mathbb{N} \rightarrow \{true, false\}$, we define P-restricted effect φ, denoted φ^P, as follows:*

$$\varphi^P \stackrel{def}{=} \{c^n \mid c^n \in \varphi \wedge P(n)\}$$

We can decompose an effect φ into a normal effect $\varphi^{=0}$ and a stage-escaping effect $\varphi^{>0}$, where "$= 0$" is a unary predicate "is equal to 0" and "> 0" is a unary predicate "is greater than 0". Hence the normal effect $\varphi^{=0}$ means exceptions which escape 0 stages (cannot escape stages), and the stage-escaping effect $\varphi^{>0}$ means exceptions which escape at least one stage.

Promotion and Demotion of Effects
As shown in Example 4, stage-escaping exceptions can cross stages upwards (by $\texttt{unbox}_k$) or downwards (by $\texttt{box}$). When stage-escaping exceptions are promoted or demoted to other stages, the effects that estimate those exceptions should also be promoted or demoted, respectively.

Definition 2. *A promotion $\uparrow_k$ is a function from Effects to Effects such that*

$$\uparrow_k \varphi \overset{def}{=} \{c^{n+k} \mid c^n \in \varphi\}, \ where \ n \geq 0 \ and \ k > 0.$$

A demotion $\downarrow$ is a function from Effects to Effects such that

$$\downarrow \varphi \overset{def}{=} \{c^{n-1} \mid c^n \in \varphi\}, \ where \ n > 0.$$

3.2 Typing Rules

The typing judgment

$$\Gamma_0 \cdots \Gamma_n \vdash e : A, \varphi$$

means that an expression e, under type environment $\Gamma_0 \cdots \Gamma_n$ has type A and effect φ at stage n. $\Gamma_0 \cdots \Gamma_n$ is a sequence of type environments $\Gamma_0, \cdots, \Gamma_n$. Γ_n is the current type environment. Subscripts $0, \cdots, n$ are stage numbers. Fig. 4 shows our typing rules for λ_{exn}^{stage}.

For exception name c, we include it inside its exception type **exn**. For instance, the type of c must be of the form $\mathbf{exn}(\psi)$ such that $c \in \psi$:

$$\frac{c \in \psi}{\Gamma_0 \cdots \Gamma_n \vdash c : \mathbf{exn}(\psi), \emptyset} \qquad \text{(TEXN)}$$

The type of raise expression **raise** e can be any arbitrary type A. Because exceptions ψ are raised at the current stage, **(TRAISE)** collects ψ^0 and the effect φ of its sub-expression e.

$$\frac{\Gamma_0 \cdots \Gamma_n \vdash e : \mathbf{exn}(\psi), \varphi}{\Gamma_0 \cdots \Gamma_n \vdash \mathbf{raise} \ e : A, \psi^0 \cup \varphi} \qquad \text{(TRAISE)}$$

Handle expression **handle** $e_1 \ c \ e_2$ catches exception c of e_1 only when the handle expression is evaluated at stage 0, its effect catches only c^0.

$$\frac{\Gamma_0 \cdots \Gamma_n \vdash e_1 : A, \varphi \quad \Gamma_0 \cdots \Gamma_n \vdash e_2 : A, \varphi' \quad \varphi'' = (\varphi \setminus \{c^0\}) \cup \varphi'}{\Gamma_0 \cdots \Gamma_n \vdash \mathbf{handle} \ e_1 \ c \ e_2 : A, \varphi''} \ \text{(THANDLE)}$$

For box expression **box** e, **(TBOX)** injects normal exceptions $\varphi^{=0}$ of the sub-expression e into the latent effect of the box type, because they can not escape stages: the box expression would not raise them until unboxed or evaluated. Stage-escaping exceptions $\varphi^{>0}$ of e can escape to the outside of the box expression, hence the effect of the box expression must include them. Because the evaluation $(\mathbf{box} \ e) \overset{n}{\longrightarrow} \overline{c}$ and its premise $e \overset{n+1}{\longrightarrow} \overline{c}$ imply that the raised exception $\overline{c}$ escapes one stage (from $n+1$ to n), stage-escaping exceptions $\varphi^{>0}$ of e should be demoted to $\downarrow \varphi^{>0}$.

(TINT)	$\Gamma_0 \cdots \Gamma_n \vdash i : \mathbf{int}, \emptyset$

$$(\text{TEXN}) \quad \frac{c \in \psi}{\Gamma_0 \cdots \Gamma_n \vdash c : \mathbf{exn}(\psi), \emptyset}$$

$$(\text{TVAR}) \quad \frac{\Gamma_n(x) = A}{\Gamma_0 \cdots \Gamma_n \vdash x : A, \emptyset}$$

$$(\text{TABS}) \quad \frac{\Gamma_0 \cdots \Gamma_n + x : A \vdash e : B, \varphi}{\Gamma_0 \cdots \Gamma_n \vdash \lambda x.e : A \xrightarrow{\varphi=0} B, \varphi^{>0}}$$

$$(\text{TAPP}) \quad \frac{\Gamma_0 \cdots \Gamma_n \vdash e_1 : A \xrightarrow{\varphi''} B, \varphi \quad \Gamma_0 \cdots \Gamma_n \vdash e_2 : A, \varphi'}{\Gamma_0 \cdots \Gamma_n \vdash e_1\, e_2 : B, \varphi \cup \varphi' \cup \varphi''}$$

$$(\text{TBOX}) \quad \frac{\Gamma_0 \cdots \Gamma_n \Gamma \vdash e : A, \varphi}{\Gamma_0 \cdots \Gamma_n \vdash \mathbf{box}\, e : \Box(\Gamma \rhd A, \varphi^{=0}), \downarrow \varphi^{>0}}$$

$$(\text{TUNBOX}) \quad \frac{\Gamma_0 \cdots \Gamma_{n-k} \vdash e : \Box(\Gamma_n \rhd A, \varphi), \varphi' \quad n \geq k > 0}{\Gamma_0 \cdots \Gamma_n \vdash \mathbf{unbox}_k\, e : A, \varphi \cup (\uparrow_k \varphi')}$$

$$(\text{TEVAL}) \quad \frac{\Gamma_0 \cdots \Gamma_n \vdash e : \Box(\emptyset \rhd A, \varphi), \varphi'}{\Gamma_0 \cdots \Gamma_n \vdash \mathbf{eval}\, e : A, \varphi \cup \varphi'}$$

$$(\text{TRAISE}) \quad \frac{\Gamma_0 \cdots \Gamma_n \vdash e : \mathbf{exn}(\psi), \varphi}{\Gamma_0 \cdots \Gamma_n \vdash \mathbf{raise}\, e : A, \psi^0 \cup \varphi}$$

$$(\text{THANDLE}) \quad \frac{\Gamma_0 \cdots \Gamma_n \vdash e_1 : A, \varphi \quad \Gamma_0 \cdots \Gamma_n \vdash e_2 : A, \varphi' \quad \varphi'' = (\varphi \setminus \{c^0\}) \cup \varphi'}{\Gamma_0 \cdots \Gamma_n \vdash \mathbf{handle}\, e_1\, c\, e_2 : A, \varphi''}$$

$$(\text{TSUB}) \quad \frac{\Gamma_0 \cdots \Gamma_n \vdash e : A, \varphi \quad \varphi \subseteq \varphi'}{\Gamma_0 \cdots \Gamma_n \vdash e : A, \varphi'}$$

Fig. 4. Typing rules of λ_{exn}^{stage}

$$\frac{\Gamma_0 \cdots \Gamma_n \Gamma \vdash e : A, \varphi}{\Gamma_0 \cdots \Gamma_n \vdash \mathbf{box}\, e : \Box(\Gamma \rhd A, \varphi^{=0}), \downarrow \varphi^{>0}} \quad (\text{TBOX})$$

For unbox expression $\mathbf{unbox}_k\, e\ (k > 0)$, the only normal exceptions the unbox expression may have are exceptions in the latent effect φ of e. Note that the evaluation $(\mathbf{unbox}_k\, e) \xrightarrow{n} \bar{c}$ and its premise $e \xrightarrow{n-k} \bar{c}$ imply that the stage of the raised exception $\bar{c}$ would be increased by k: from $n-k$ to n. Hence, to be handled, the uncaught exceptions of the unbox expression should escape k more stages than those of its sub-expression. Hence we promote the effect φ' of e to $\uparrow_k \varphi'$.

$$\frac{\Gamma_0 \cdots \Gamma_{n-k} \vdash e : \Box(\Gamma_n \rhd A, \varphi), \varphi' \quad n \geq k > 0}{\Gamma_0 \cdots \Gamma_n \vdash \mathbf{unbox}_k\, e : A, \varphi \cup (\uparrow_k \varphi')} \quad (\text{TUNBOX})$$

For eval expression $\mathbf{eval}\, e$, (TEVAL) allows only closed code to be evaluated by **eval** construct. When we evaluate a code with free variables, those free variables may cause unintended variable capture, because of the alpha-conversion at stage

0. Recall that we assume that variables in a code template can not be alpha-converted (for the sake of unhygienic macros), but variables at stage 0 can be alpha-converted. Hence we force to evaluate only colosed code: the code template type $\Box(\varnothing \rhd A, \varphi)$ of e should have empty environment. Like unbox expression, the effect of eval expression should have both of the latent effect φ and the effect φ' of e. We don't need to promote the effect φ' because the stage of e and that of eval e are the same.

$$\frac{\Gamma_0 \cdots \Gamma_n \vdash e : \Box(\varnothing \rhd A, \varphi), \varphi'}{\Gamma_0 \cdots \Gamma_n \vdash \texttt{eval}\, e : A, \varphi \cup \varphi'} \tag{TEVAL}$$

Abstraction $\lambda x.e$ is a value at stage 0, while it can be an evaluable expression at stage $n > 0$. Hence the normal exception $\varphi^{=0}$ of e should be injected to the latent effect of the function, and might be raised where the function is applied. Stage-escaping exception $\varphi^{>0}$ of e should be propagated to $\lambda x.e$. Note that $c^0 \in \varphi^{=0}$ means that e may raise exception c at stage 0 ($e \xrightarrow{0} \bar{c}$), and $c^n \in \varphi^{>0}$ means that e may be evaluated to the raised exception $\bar{c}$ at stage $n > 0$ ($e \xrightarrow{n} \bar{c}$).

$$\frac{\Gamma_0 \cdots \Gamma_n + x : A \vdash e : B, \varphi}{\Gamma_0 \cdots \Gamma_n \vdash \lambda x.e : A \xrightarrow{\varphi^{=0}} B, \varphi^{>0}} \tag{TABS}$$

For application $e_1\, e_2$, (TAPP) is conventional. All effects from evaluating e_1, e_2, and the function's body are collected. The function body's effect is the latent effect in the type of e_1.

$$\frac{\Gamma_0 \cdots \Gamma_n \vdash e_1 : A \xrightarrow{\varphi''} B, \varphi \quad \Gamma_0 \cdots \Gamma_n \vdash e_2 : A, \varphi'}{\Gamma_0 \cdots \Gamma_n \vdash e_1\, e_2 : B, \varphi \cup \varphi' \cup \varphi''} \tag{TAPP}$$

The subsumption rule (TSUB) allows any expression to be treated as having more effect than it actually does. By applying subsumption rule to the latent effect, abstractions or the code templates can be treated as having more effect than reality. Without the subsumption rule, a value of type $\Box(\Gamma \rhd A, \emptyset)$ and a value of type $\Box(\Gamma \rhd A, \{c^0\})$ could not both be passed as arguments to the same function, because the function and argument types would have to match exactly.

$$\frac{\Gamma_0 \cdots \Gamma_n \vdash e : A, \varphi \quad \varphi \subseteq \varphi'}{\Gamma_0 \cdots \Gamma_n \vdash e : A, \varphi'} \tag{TSUB}$$

Example 7. A code template box (raise c), which raises an exception c when evaluated, has the following typing:

$$\frac{\dfrac{\varnothing\varnothing \vdash c : \texttt{exn}(\{c\}), \emptyset}{\varnothing\varnothing \vdash \texttt{raise}\, c : A, \{c^0\}}}{\varnothing \vdash \texttt{box}\,(\texttt{raise}\, c) : \Box(\varnothing \rhd A, \{c^0\}), \emptyset.}$$

The empty effect $\emptyset$ implies that the code template will not raise any exception, and the type $\Box(\emptyset \triangleright A, \{c^0\})$ implies that the exception c may be raised when we execute the code template.   ∎

Example 8. Exceptions may be raised during code composition. Recall the expression in Example 4.

$$\frac{\dfrac{c \xrightarrow{0} c}{\mathbf{raise}\, c \xrightarrow{0} \bar{c}}}{\dfrac{\mathbf{unbox}_2\, \mathbf{raise}\, c \xrightarrow{2} \bar{c}}{\dfrac{\mathbf{box}\,(\mathbf{unbox}_2\, \mathbf{raise}\, c) \xrightarrow{1} \bar{c}}{\mathbf{box}\,(\mathbf{box}\,(\mathbf{unbox}_2\, \mathbf{raise}\, c)) \xrightarrow{0} \bar{c}}}}$$

$\bar{c}$ is raised at stage 0

$\bar{c}$ is promoted to stage 2

$\bar{c}$ is demoted to stage 1

$\bar{c}$ is demoted to stage 0

The above expression has the following typing:

$$\frac{\dfrac{\dfrac{\dfrac{\emptyset \vdash c : \mathbf{exn}(\{c\}), \emptyset}{\emptyset \vdash \mathbf{raise}\, c : \Box(\emptyset \triangleright A, \emptyset), \{c^0\}}}{\emptyset\emptyset\emptyset \vdash \mathbf{unbox}_2\, \mathbf{raise}\, c : A, \{c^2\}}}{\emptyset\emptyset \vdash \mathbf{box}\,(\mathbf{unbox}_2\, \mathbf{raise}\, c) : \Box(\emptyset \triangleright A, \emptyset), \{c^1\}}}{\emptyset \vdash \mathbf{box}\,(\mathbf{box}\,(\mathbf{unbox}_2\, \mathbf{raise}\, c)) : \Box(\emptyset \triangleright \Box(\emptyset \triangleright A, \emptyset), \emptyset), \{c^0\}.}$$

This typing means that the expression is a code template of a code template, and may raise uncaught exception c. The stage-escaping numbers n of c^n in the proof tree exactly capture the dynamic stages of $\bar{c}$ ($0 \to 2 \to 1 \to 0$).   ∎

Example 9. An exception raised during code composition can be handled by a proper handler installed at stage 0. Recall the expression in Example 5. A raised exception c at stage 0 can be caught by a handler at stage 0:

$$\mathbf{handle}\,(\mathbf{box}\,(\mathbf{unbox}_1\, \mathbf{raise}\, c))\, c\, (\mathbf{box}\, 0) \xrightarrow{0} \mathbf{box}\, 0$$

Our effect type system decides that the above expression has no uncaught exception:

$$\frac{\dfrac{\dfrac{\dfrac{\emptyset \vdash c : \mathbf{exn}(\{c\}), \emptyset}{\emptyset \vdash \mathbf{raise}\, c : \Box(\emptyset \triangleright \mathbf{int}, \emptyset), \{c^0\}}}{\emptyset\emptyset \vdash \mathbf{unbox}_1\, \mathbf{raise}\, c : \mathbf{int}, \{c^1\}}}{\emptyset \vdash \mathbf{box}\,(\mathbf{unbox}_1\, \mathbf{raise}\, c) : \Box(\emptyset \triangleright \mathbf{int}, \emptyset), \{c^0\}} \quad \dfrac{\dfrac{\emptyset\emptyset \vdash 0 : \mathbf{int}, \emptyset}{}}{\emptyset \vdash \mathbf{box}\, 0 : \Box(\emptyset \triangleright \mathbf{int}, \emptyset), \emptyset}}{\emptyset \vdash \mathbf{handle}\,(\mathbf{box}\,(\mathbf{unbox}_1\, \mathbf{raise}\, c))\, c\, (\mathbf{box}\, 0) : \Box(\emptyset \triangleright \mathbf{int}, \emptyset), \emptyset}$$

∎

Example 10. A raised exception c at stage 0 can not be caught by a handler in a code template (at stage 1). Recall the expression in Example 6. It raises exception c in the code template, and does not handle the exception because the handler is inside the code template:

$$\texttt{box}\,(\texttt{handle}\,(\texttt{unbox}_1\,\texttt{raise}\,c)\,c\,0) \xrightarrow{\ 0\ } \overline{c}$$

Our effect type system safely estimates that the above expression may raise an uncaught exception c:

$$\frac{\dfrac{\dfrac{\varnothing \vdash c : \mathbf{exn}(\{c\}), \emptyset}{\varnothing \vdash \mathbf{raise}\,c : \Box(\varnothing \triangleright \mathbf{int}, \emptyset), \{c^0\}}}{\dfrac{\varnothing\varnothing \vdash \mathbf{unbox}_1\,\mathbf{raise}\,c : \mathbf{int}, \{c^1\} \quad \varnothing\varnothing \vdash 0 : \mathbf{int}, \emptyset}{\varnothing\varnothing \vdash \mathbf{handle}\,(\mathbf{unbox}_1\,\mathbf{raise}\,c)\,c\,0 : \mathbf{int}, \{c^1\}}}}{\varnothing \vdash \mathbf{box}\,(\mathbf{handle}\,(\mathbf{unbox}_1\,\mathbf{raise}\,c)\,c\,0) : \Box(\varnothing \triangleright \mathbf{int}, \emptyset), \{c^0\}}$$

∎

Example 11. Let's consider the following code template.

$$\texttt{box}\,(\texttt{handle}\,(\texttt{raise}\,c)\,c\,0)$$

The handler inside the code template catches exception c when the code template is executed. The above code template has the following typing:

$$\frac{\dfrac{\dfrac{\varnothing\varnothing \vdash c : \mathbf{exn}(\{c\}), \emptyset}{\varnothing\varnothing \vdash \mathbf{raise}\,c : \mathbf{int}, \{c^0\} \quad \varnothing\varnothing \vdash 0 : \mathbf{int}, \emptyset}}{\varnothing\varnothing \vdash \mathbf{handle}\,(\mathbf{raise}\,c)\,c\,0 : \mathbf{int}, \emptyset}}{\varnothing \vdash \mathbf{box}\,(\mathbf{handle}\,(\mathbf{raise}\,c)\,c\,0) : \Box(\varnothing \triangleright \mathbf{int}, \emptyset), \emptyset}$$

Our system gives a correct effect typing for every stage. ∎

3.3 Soundness

In our evaluation rule (in Fig. 2), there are two rules which convert values at stage n to values at another stage m. The eval at stage 0 converts $\texttt{box}\,v^1$ into v^1 and evaluate v^1 at stage 0; it demotes values at stage $n > 0$ to expressions at stage $(n-1)$. The $\texttt{unbox}_k$ at stage $k > 0$ converts $\texttt{box}\,v^1$ into v^k; it promotes values at stage $(n+1)$ to values at stage $(n+k)$. The following lemma shows that such demotion and promotion preserve types and effects. We can freely promote or demote values, because our types and effects only depend on the structure of their sub-expressions and do not depend on the stages where they are. The only restriction of demotion is that Γ_1 should be $\varnothing$, because a value at stage 1 must not have a free variable of stage 1 to be demoted (or to be evaluated by eval).

Lemma 1 (Demotion and Promotion). *Suppose* $\varnothing\Gamma_1 \cdots \Gamma_n \vdash v : A, \varphi$.

1. *If* $\Gamma_1 = \varnothing$ *then* $\Gamma_1 \cdots \Gamma_n \vdash v : A, \varphi$.
2. $\varnothing\Gamma_1' \cdots \Gamma_m'\Gamma_1 \cdots \Gamma_n \vdash v : A, \varphi$ *for all* $\Gamma_1' \cdots \Gamma_m'$.

Proof. We prove the lemma by induction on the structure of v.   ∎

Values at stage $n > 0$ may raise exceptions when demoted to stage 0 (or evaluated by `eval`). Hence we can not claim that values at any stage have empty effect. However, any value v^0 at stage 0 has an empty effect (does not raise any exception):

Lemma 2 (Empty Effect of v^0). *If $\Gamma_0 \vdash v : A, \varphi$ then $\Gamma_0 \vdash v : A, \emptyset$.*

Proof. We first prove that $\Gamma_0 \cdots \Gamma_n \vdash v : A, \varphi^{<n}$, if $\Gamma_0 \cdots \Gamma_n \vdash v : A, \varphi$. It can be shown by induction on the structure of v. Then the lemma immediately follows from $\forall \varphi : (\varphi^{<0}) = \emptyset$.   ∎

The soundness theorem shows that every exception that may be raised and uncaught during the evaluation of an expression should be collected inside the expression's effect. For the proof of the soundness theorem, we need Lemma 1 and Lemma 2.

Theorem 1 (Soundness). *Suppose $\varnothing \Gamma_1 \cdots \Gamma_n \vdash e : A, \varphi$.*

1. *If $e \xrightarrow{n} v$ then $\varnothing \Gamma_1 \cdots \Gamma_n \vdash v : A, \varphi$.*
2. *If $e \xrightarrow{n} \bar{c}$ then $\varphi \supseteq \{c^n\}$.*

Proof. We prove the theorem by induction on the proof tree size of evaluation rule. We show the representative cases (EUNBOX), (EBOX), and (EHANDLE) in Appendix A.   ∎

4   Conclusion

We have presented type and effect system for multi-staged language with exceptions. The proposed type and effect system checks if we safely synthesize complex controls with exceptions (long jumps) in multi-staged programming. The proposed exception constructs in multi-staged programming has no artificial restriction. Exception-raise and -handle expressions can appear in expressions of any stage. Exceptions can be raised during code composition and may escape stages and can be handled only at stage 0. Our effect type system support such features and is proven safe that empty effect means the input program has no uncaught exceptions during its evaluation. The obvious next step is to extend our system to support the let-polymorphism and imperative operations.

References

1. Olivier Danvy. Type-directed partial evaluation. In *Proceedings of the Symposium on Principles of Programming Languages*, pages 242–257. ACM, Jan 1996.
2. Rowan Davies and Frank Pfenning. A modal analysis of staged computation. *Journal of the ACM*, 48(3):555–604, 2001.
3. Paul Graham. *On Lisp: an advanced techniques for Common Lisp*. Prentice Hall, 1994.
4. Juan Carlos Guzmán and Ascánder Suárez. A type system for exceptions. In *Proceedings of the ACM SIGPLAN Workshop on ML and its Applications*, June 1994.
5. Neil D. Jones, Carsten K. Gomard, and Peter Sestoft. *Partial evaluation and automatic program generation*. Prentice-Hall, 1993.

6. Ik-Soon Kim, Kwangkeun Yi, and Cristiano Calcagno. A polymorphic modal type system for Lisp-like multi-staged languages. In *Proceedings of The ACM SIGPLAN-SIGACT Symposium on Principles of Programming Languages*, pages 257–268. ACM, January 2006.
7. M. Leone and Peter Lee. Optimizing ML with run-time code generation. In *Proceedings of the ACM SIGPLAN'96 Conference on Programming Language Design and Implementation*, pages 137–148. ACM Press, June 1996.
8. Aleksandar Nanevski. A modal calculus for exception handling. In *Proceedings of the Intuitionistic Modal Logic and Applications Workshop*, June 2005.
9. François Pessaux and Xavier Leroy. Type-based analysis of uncaught exceptions. In *Proceedings of The ACM SIGPLAN-SIGACT Symposium on Principles of Programming Languages*, pages 276–290, January 1999.
10. Massimilian Poletto, Wilson C. Hsieh, Dawson R. Engler, and M. Frans Kaashoek. C and tcc:a language and compiler for dynamic code generation. *ACM Transactions on Programming Languages and Systems*, 21:324–369, March 1999.
11. Guy L. Steele. *Common Lisp the Language, 2nd edition*. Digital Press, 1990.
12. Jean-Pierre Talpin and Pierre Jouvelot. Polymorphic type, region and effect inference. *Journal of Functional Programming*, 2(3):245–271, July 1992.
13. Jean-Pierre Talpin. *Theoretical and Practical Aspects of Type and Effect Inference*. PhD thesis, University of Paris VI, May 1993.
14. Mads Tofte and Jean-Pierre Talpin. Implementation of the typed call-by-value λ-calculus using a stack of regions. In *Proceedings of The ACM SIGPLAN-SIGACT Symposium on Principles of Programming Languages*, pages 188–201, January 1994.

A   Proof of Soundness Theorem

Theorem 1 (Soundness). *Suppose* $\varnothing \Gamma_1 \cdots \Gamma_n \vdash e : A, \varphi.$

1. *If* $e \xrightarrow{n} v$ *then* $\varnothing \Gamma_1 \cdots \Gamma_n \vdash v : A, \varphi.$
2. *If* $e \xrightarrow{n} \bar{c}$ *then* $\varphi \supseteq \{c^n\}.$

Proof. By induction on the proof tree size of evaluation rule $\xrightarrow{n}$. We prove the representative cases (EEVAL), (EUNBOX), (EBOX), and (EHANDLE). We can similarly prove other cases

- (EEVAL)
  - Case for eval $e \xrightarrow{0} v^0$.
(1)	$\varnothing \vdash$ eval $e : A, \varphi \cup \varphi'$	Assumption
(2)	$e \xrightarrow{0}$ box v^1	By (EEVAL)
(3)	$v^1 \xrightarrow{0} v^0$	By (EEVAL)
(4)	$\varnothing \vdash e : \square(\varnothing \triangleright A, \varphi), \emptyset$	By (TEVAL),Lemma 2
(5)	$\varnothing \vdash$ box $v^1 : \square(\varnothing \triangleright A, \varphi), \emptyset$	By I.H. (induction hypothesis)
(6)	$\varnothing\varnothing \vdash v^1 : A, \varphi$	By (TBOX)
(7)	$\varnothing \vdash v^1 : A, \varphi$	By Lemma 1
(8)	$\varnothing \vdash v^0 : A, \varphi$	By I.H.
(9)	$\varnothing \vdash v^0 : A, \varphi \cup \varphi'$	By (TSUB)
  - Case for eval $e \xrightarrow{n}$ eval v where $n > 0$.
(1)	$\varnothing \Gamma_1 \cdots \Gamma_n \vdash$ eval $e : A, \varphi \cup \varphi'$	Assumption
(2)	$e \xrightarrow{n} v$	By (EEVAL)
(3)	$\varnothing \Gamma_1 \cdots \Gamma_n \vdash e : \square(\varnothing \triangleright A, \varphi), \varphi'$	By (TEVAL)
(4)	$\varnothing \Gamma_1 \cdots \Gamma_n \vdash v : \square(\varnothing \triangleright A, \varphi), \varphi'$	By I.H.
(5)	$\varnothing \Gamma_1 \cdots \Gamma_n \vdash$ eval $v : A, \varphi \cup \varphi'$	By (TEVAL)

- Case for $\texttt{eval}\ e \xrightarrow{n} \bar{c}$.
  - (1) $\varnothing \Gamma_1 \cdots \Gamma_n \vdash \texttt{eval}\ e : A, \varphi \cup \varphi'$ Assumption
  - (2) $e \xrightarrow{n} \bar{c}$ By (EEVAL)
  - (3) $\varnothing \Gamma_1 \cdots \Gamma_n \vdash e : \Box(\varnothing \rhd A, \varphi), \varphi'$ By (TEVAL)
  - (4) $\varphi' \supseteq \{c^n\}$ By I.H.
  - (5) $\varphi \cup \varphi' \supseteq \{c^n\}$ By (4)

- (EUNBOX)

  - Case for $\texttt{unbox}_n\ e \xrightarrow{n} v$ where $n > 0$.
    - (1) $\varnothing \Gamma_1 \cdots \Gamma_n \vdash \texttt{unbox}_n\ e : A, \varphi \cup (\uparrow_n \varphi')$ Assumption
    - (2) $e \xrightarrow{0} \texttt{box}\ v$ By (EUNBOX)
    - (3) $\varnothing \vdash e : \Box(\Gamma_n \rhd A, \varphi), \varphi'$ By (TUNBOX)
    - (4) $\varnothing \vdash \texttt{box}\ v : \Box(\Gamma_n \rhd A, \varphi), \emptyset$ By I.H.,Lemma 2
    - (5) $\varnothing \Gamma_n \vdash v : A, \varphi$ By (TBOX)
    - (6) $\varnothing \Gamma_1 \cdots \Gamma_n \vdash v : A, \varphi$ By Lemma 1
    - (7) $\varnothing \Gamma_1 \cdots \Gamma_n \vdash v : A, \varphi \cup (\uparrow_n \varphi')$ By (TSUB)

  - Case for $\texttt{unbox}_k\ e \xrightarrow{n} \texttt{unbox}_k\ v$ where $n > k \geq 0$.
    - (1) $\varnothing \Gamma_1 \cdots \Gamma_n \vdash \texttt{unbox}_k\ e : A, \varphi \cup (\uparrow_k \varphi')$ Assumption
    - (2) $e \xrightarrow{n-k} v$ By (EUNBOX)
    - (3) $\varnothing \Gamma_1 \cdots \Gamma_{n-k} \vdash e : \Box(\Gamma_n \rhd A, \varphi), \varphi'$ By (TUNBOX)
    - (4) $\varnothing \Gamma_1 \cdots \Gamma_{n-k} \vdash v : \Box(\Gamma_n \rhd A, \varphi), \varphi'$ By I.H.
    - (5) $\varnothing \Gamma_1 \cdots \Gamma_n \vdash \texttt{unbox}_k\ v : A, \varphi \cup (\uparrow_k \varphi')$ By (TUNBOX)

  - Case for $\texttt{unbox}_k\ e \xrightarrow{n} \bar{c}$.
    - (1) $\varnothing \Gamma_1 \cdots \Gamma_n \vdash \texttt{unbox}_k\ e : A, \varphi \cup (\uparrow_k \varphi')$ Assumption
    - (2) $e \xrightarrow{n-k} \bar{c}$ By (EUNBOX)
    - (3) $\varnothing \Gamma_1 \cdots \Gamma_{n-k} \vdash e : \Box(\Gamma_n \rhd A, \varphi), \varphi'$ By (TUNBOX)
    - (4) $\varphi' \supseteq \{c^{n-k}\}$ By I.H.
    - (5) $\uparrow_k \varphi' \supseteq \{c^n\}$ By definition of $\uparrow_k$
    - (6) $\varphi \cup (\uparrow_k \varphi') \supseteq \{c^n\}$ By (5)

- (EBOX)

  - Case for $\texttt{box}\ e \xrightarrow{n} \texttt{box}\ v$.
    - (1) $\varnothing \Gamma_1 \cdots \Gamma_n \vdash \texttt{box}\ e : \Box(\Gamma \rhd A, \varphi^{-0}), \downarrow \varphi^{>0}$ Assumption
    - (2) $e \xrightarrow{n+1} v$ By (EBOX)
    - (3) $\varnothing \Gamma_1 \cdots \Gamma_n \Gamma \vdash e : A, \varphi$ By (TBOX)
    - (4) $\varnothing \Gamma_1 \cdots \Gamma_n \Gamma \vdash v : A, \varphi$ By I.H.
    - (5) $\varnothing \Gamma_1 \cdots \Gamma_n \vdash \texttt{box}\ v : \Box(\Gamma \rhd A, \varphi^{=0}), \downarrow \varphi^{>0}$ By (TBOX)

  - Case for $\texttt{box}\ e \xrightarrow{n} \bar{c}$.
    - (1) $\varnothing \Gamma_1 \cdots \Gamma_n \vdash \texttt{box}\ e : \Box(\Gamma \rhd A, \varphi^{=0}), \downarrow \varphi^{>0}$ Assumption
    - (2) $e \xrightarrow{n+1} \bar{c}$ By (EBOX)
    - (3) $\varnothing \Gamma_1 \cdots \Gamma_n \Gamma \vdash e : A, \varphi$ By (TBOX)
    - (4) $\varphi \supseteq \{c^{n+1}\}$ By I.H.
    - (5) $\varphi^{>0} \supseteq \{c^{n+1}\}$ By definition of $\varphi^{>0}$
    - (6) $\downarrow \varphi^{>0} \supseteq \{c^n\}$ By definition of $\downarrow$

- (EHANDLE)

  - Case for $\texttt{handle}\ e_1\ c\ e_2 \xrightarrow{0} v$.
    - (1) $\varnothing \vdash \texttt{handle}\ e_1\ c\ e_2 : A, \varphi$ Assumption
    - (2) $\varnothing \vdash e_1 : A, \varphi_1$ By (THANDLE)
    - (3) $\varnothing \vdash e_2 : A, \varphi_2$ By (THANDLE)
    - (4) $\varphi = (\varphi_1 \setminus \{c^0\}) \cup \varphi_2$ By (THANDLE)

* $e_1 \xrightarrow{0} v$.

    (5) $\varnothing \vdash v : A, \varphi_1$ By I.H.

    (6) $\varnothing \vdash v : A, \emptyset$ By Lemma 2

    (7) $\varnothing \vdash v : A, \varphi$ By (TSUB)

* $e_1 \xrightarrow{0} \bar{c}$ and $e_2 \xrightarrow{0} v$.

    (5) $\varnothing \vdash v : A, \varphi_2$ By I.H.

    (6) $\varnothing \vdash v : A, \varphi$ By (TSUB)

- Case for **handle** $e_1\, c'\, e_2 \xrightarrow{0} \bar{c}$.

    (1) $\varnothing \vdash$ **handle** $e_1\, c'\, e_2 : A, \varphi$ Assumption

    (2) $e_1 \xrightarrow{0} \bar{c}$ By (EHANDLE)

    (3) $\varnothing \vdash e_1 : A, \varphi_1$ By (THANDLE)

    (4) $\varnothing \vdash e_2 : A, \varphi_2$ By (THANDLE)

    (5) $\varphi = (\varphi_1 \setminus \{c'^0\}) \cup \varphi_2$ By (THANDLE)

    (6) $\varphi_1 \supseteq \{c^0\}$ By I.H.

    (7) $\varphi \supseteq (\varphi_1 \setminus \{c'^0\}) \cup \varphi_2 \supseteq \{c^0\}$ By (6)

- Case for **handle** $e_1\, c\, e_2 \xrightarrow{n} v_2$ where $n > 0$.

    (1) $\Gamma_0 \cdots \Gamma_n \vdash$ **handle** $e_1\, c\, e_2 : A, \varphi$ Assumption

    (2) $e_1 \xrightarrow{n} v_1$ By (EHANDLE)

    (3) $e_2 \xrightarrow{n} v_2$ By (EHANDLE)

    (4) $\Gamma_0 \cdots \Gamma_n \vdash e_1 : A, \varphi_1$ By (THANDLE)

    (5) $\Gamma_0 \cdots \Gamma_n \vdash e_2 : A, \varphi_2$ By (THANDLE)

    (6) $\varphi = (\varphi_1 \setminus \{c^0\}) \cup \varphi_2$ By (THANDLE)

    (7) $\Gamma_0 \cdots \Gamma_n \vdash v_1 : A, \varphi_1$ By I.H.

    (8) $\Gamma_0 \cdots \Gamma_n \vdash v_2 : A, \varphi_2$ By I.H.

    (9) $\Gamma_0 \cdots \Gamma_n \vdash v_2 : A, \varphi$ By (TSUB)

- Case for **handle** $e_1\, c\, e_2 \xrightarrow{n} \bar{c}$ where $n > 0$.

    (1) $\Gamma_0 \cdots \Gamma_n \vdash$ **handle** $e_1\, c\, e_2 : A, \varphi$ Assumption

    (2) $\Gamma_0 \cdots \Gamma_n \vdash e_1 : A, \varphi_1$ By (THANDLE)

    (3) $\Gamma_0 \cdots \Gamma_n \vdash e_2 : A, \varphi_2$ By (THANDLE)

    (4) $\varphi = (\varphi_1 \setminus \{c^0\}) \cup \varphi_2$ By (THANDLE)

* $e_1 \xrightarrow{n} \bar{c}$.

    (5) $\varphi_1 \supseteq \{c^n\}$ By I.H.

    (6) $\varphi = (\varphi_1 \setminus \{c^0\}) \cup \varphi_2 \supseteq \{c^n\}$ By (5)

* $e_2 \xrightarrow{n} \bar{c}$.

    (5) $\varphi_2 \supseteq \{c^n\}$ By I.H.

    (6) $\varphi = (\varphi_1 \setminus \{c^0\}) \cup \varphi_2 \supseteq \{c^n\}$ By (5)

- Case for **handle** $e_1\, c'\, e_2 \xrightarrow{n} \bar{c}$ where $n > 0$.

    (1) $\Gamma_0 \cdots \Gamma_n \vdash$ **handle** $e_1\, c\, e_2 : A, \varphi$ Assumption

    (2) $\Gamma_0 \cdots \Gamma_n \vdash e_1 : A, \varphi_1$ By (THANDLE)

    (3) $\Gamma_0 \cdots \Gamma_n \vdash e_2 : A, \varphi_2$ By (THANDLE)

    (4) $\varphi = (\varphi_1 \setminus \{c'^0\}) \cup \varphi_2$ By (THANDLE)

* $e_1 \xrightarrow{n} \bar{c}$.

    (5) $\varphi_1 \supseteq \{c^n\}$ By I.H.

    (6) $\varphi = (\varphi_1 \setminus \{c'^0\}) \cup \varphi_2 \supseteq \{c^n\}$ By (5)

* $e_2 \xrightarrow{n} \bar{c}$.

    (5) $\varphi_2 \supseteq \{c^n\}$ By I.H.

    (6) $\varphi = (\varphi_1 \setminus \{c'^0\}) \cup \varphi_2 \supseteq \{c^n\}$ By (5)

Relational Reasoning for Recursive Types and References

Nina Bohr and Lars Birkedal

IT University of Copenhagen (ITU)
{ninab, birkedal}@itu.dk

Abstract. We present a local relational reasoning method for reasoning about contextual equivalence of expressions in a λ-calculus with recursive types and general references. Our development builds on the work of Benton and Leperchey, who devised a nominal semantics and a local relational reasoning method for a language with simple types and simple references. Their method uses a parameterized logical relation. Here we extend their approach to recursive types and general references. For the extension, we build upon Pitts' and Shinwell's work on relational reasoning about recursive types (but no references) in nominal semantics. The extension is non-trivial because of general references (higher-order store) and makes use of some new ideas for proving the existence of the parameterized logical relation and for the choice of parameters.

1   Introduction

Proving equivalence of programs is important for verifying the correctness of compiler optimizations and other program transformations. Program equivalence is typically defined in terms of *contextual equivalence*, which expresses that two program expressions are equivalent if they have the same observable behaviour when placed in any program context C. It is generally quite hard to show directly that two program expressions are contextually equivalent because of the universal quantification over all contexts. Thus there has been an extensive research effort to find reasoning methods that are easier to use for establishing contextual equivalence, in particular to reduce the set of contexts one has to consider, see, e.g., [7,3,1,6] and the references therein. For programming languages with references, it is not enough to restrict attention to fewer contexts, since one also needs to be able to reason about equivalence under *related* stores. To address this challenge, methods based on logical relations and bisimulations have been proposed, see, e.g., [8,2,13]. The approaches based on logical relations have so far been restricted to deal only with simple integer references (or references to such). To extend the method to general references in typed languages, one also needs to extend the method to work in the presence of recursive types. The latter is a challenge on its own, since one cannot easily establish the existence of logical relations by induction in the presence of recursive types. Thus a number of research papers have focused on relational reasoning methods for recursive types without references, e.g., [3,1]. Recently, the bisimulation approach has been simplified

N. Kobayashi (Ed.): APLAS 2006, LNCS 4279, pp. 79–96, 2006.

and extended to work for untyped languages with general references [5,4]. For effectiveness of the reasoning method, we seek *local* reasoning methods, which only require that we consider the accessible part of a store and which works in the presence of a separated (non-interfering) invariant that is preserved by the context. In [2], Benton and Leperchey developed a relational reasoning method for a language with simple references that does allow for local reasoning. Their approach is inspired by related work on separation logic [10,9]. In particular, an important feature of the state relations of Benton and Leperchey is that they depend on only part of the store: that allows us to reason that related states are still related if we update them in parts on which the relation does not depend. In this paper we extend the work of Benton and Leperchey to relational reasoning about contextual equivalence of expressions in a typed programming language with general recursive types *and* general references (thus with higher-order store). We arrive at a useful reasoning method. In particular, we have used it to verify all the examples of [5]. We believe that the method is simple to use, but more work remains to compare the strengths and weaknesses of the method we present here with that of *loc. cit.*

Before giving an overview of the technical development, we now present two examples of pairs of programs that can easily be shown contextually equivalent with the method we develop. The examples are essentially equivalent to (or perhaps slightly more involved than) examples in [5]. Section 5 contains the proofs of contextual equivalence.

The programs M and N shown below both take a function as argument and returns two functions, set and get. In M, there is one hidden reference y, which set can use to store a function. The get function returns the contents of y. The program N uses three local references y_0, y_1 and p. The p reference holds a integer value. The set function updates p and depending on the value of p it stores its argument in either y_0 or y_1. The get function returns the contents of y_0 or y_1, depending on the value of p. Note that the programs store functions in the store. Intuitively, the programs M and N are contextually equivalent because they use *local storage*. The proof method we develop allows us to prove that they are contextually equivalent via local reasoning.

$$M = \text{rec } f \ (g: \tau \to T\tau'): T(((\tau \to T\tau') \to T\text{unit}) \times (\text{unit} \to T(\tau \to T\tau'))) =$$
$$\text{let } y \Leftarrow \text{ref } g \text{ in}$$
$$\text{let set} \Leftarrow \text{val (rec } f_{1M}(g_1 : \tau \to T\tau') : T\text{unit} = y := g_1) \text{ in}$$
$$\text{let get} \Leftarrow \text{val (rec } f_{2M}(x : \text{unit}) : T(\tau \to T\tau') = !y) \text{ in}$$
$$(\text{set,get})$$

$$N = \text{rec } f \ (g: \tau \to T\tau'): T(((\tau \to T\tau') \to T\text{unit}) \times (\text{unit} \to T(\tau \to T\tau'))) =$$
$$\text{let } y_0 \Leftarrow \text{ref } g \text{ in}$$
$$\text{let } y_1 \Leftarrow \text{ref } g \text{ in}$$
$$\text{let } p \Leftarrow \text{ref } 0 \text{ in}$$
$$\text{let set} \Leftarrow \text{val (rec } f_{1N}(g_1 : \tau \to T\tau') : T\text{unit} =$$
$$\text{if iszero}(!p) \text{ then}$$
$$(p := 1; \ y_1 := g_1)$$
$$\text{else}$$

$$(p := 0; \ y_0 := g_1)) \text{ in}$$
$$\text{let } get \Leftarrow \text{val } (\text{rec } f_{2N}(x : \text{unit}) : (\tau \to T\tau') =$$
$$\text{if iszero}(!p) \text{ then } !y_0 \text{ else } !y_1) \text{ in}$$
$$(set, get)$$

Next consider the programs M' and N' below. They both have a free variable g of function type. In M', g is applied to a function that just returns unit and then M' returns the constant unit function. In N', g is applied to a function that updates a reference local to N', maintaining the invariant that the value of the local reference is always greater than zero. After the call to g, N' returns the constant unit function if the value of the local reference is greater than zero; otherwise it diverges (Ω stands for a diverging term). Intuitively, it is clear that M' and N' are contextually equivalent, since the local reference in N' initially is greater than zero and g can only update the local reference via the function it is given as argument and, indeed, we can use our method to prove formally that M' and N' are contextually equivalent via local reasoning.

$$M' = \text{let } f \Leftarrow \text{val } (\text{rec } f'(a : \text{unit}) : T\text{unit} = \text{val } ()) \text{ in}$$
$$\text{let } w \Leftarrow gf \text{ in}$$
$$\text{val } f$$

$$N' = \text{let } x \Leftarrow \text{ref } 1 \text{ in}$$
$$\text{let } f \Leftarrow \text{val } (\text{rec } f'(a : \text{unit}) : T\text{unit}) = x := !x + 1) \text{ in}$$
$$\text{let } w \Leftarrow gf \text{ in}$$
$$\text{let } z \Leftarrow \text{if iszero}(!x) \text{ then } \Omega \text{ else } (\text{rec } f'(a : \text{unit}) : T\text{unit} = \text{val } ()) \text{ in}$$
$$\text{val } z$$

We now give an overview of the technical development, which makes use of a couple of new ideas for proving the existence of the parameterized logical relation and for the choice of parameters.

In Section 2 we first present the language and in Section 3 we give a denotational semantics in the category of FM-cpo's. Adapting methods developed by Pitts [7] and Shinwell [11,12] we prove the existence of a recursive domain in $(\text{FM-Cpo}_\perp)^4$, $\mathbb{D} = (\mathbb{V}, \mathbb{K}, \mathbb{M}, \mathbb{S})$, such that $i : F(\mathbb{D}, \mathbb{D}) \cong \mathbb{D}$ where F is our domain constructor. The 4-tuple of domains $\mathbb{D}$ has the minimal invariant property, that is, $id_\mathbb{D}$ is the least fixed point of $\delta : (\mathbb{D} \to \mathbb{D}) \to (\mathbb{D} \to \mathbb{D})$ where $\delta(e) = i \circ F(e, e) \circ i^{-1}$. Denotations of values are given in $\mathbb{V}$, continuations in $\mathbb{K}$, computations in $\mathbb{M}$ and stores in $\mathbb{S}$. We show adequacy via a logical relation, the existence of which is established much as in [11].

The denotational semantics can be used to establish simple forms of contextual equivalence qua adequacy. For stronger proofs of contextual equivalences we define a parameterized relation between pairs of denotations of values, pairs of denotations of continuations, pairs of denotations of computations, pairs of denotations of stores. We can express contextual equivalence for two computations by requiring that they have the same terminaton behaviour when placed in the same arbitrary closing contexts.

Since our denotations belong to a recursive domain, the existence of the parameterized logical relation again involves a separate proof. The proof requires that the relations are preserved under approximations. On the other hand we want the parameters to express invariants for hidden local areas of related stores, and such properties of stores will not be preserved under approximations. Therefore our relations are really given by 4-tuples, which we think of as two pairs: the 4-tuples have the form (d_1', d_1, d_2', d_2), where $d_1' \sqsubseteq d_1$ and $d_2' \sqsubseteq d_2$. We can now let the approximation be carried out over the primed domain elements d_1', d_2', and preserve the invariant on the non-primed elements d_1, d_2. Correspondingly, relatedness of computations is stated as a two-sided termination approximation. Termination of application of an approximated computation m_1' to an approximated continuation k_1' and an approximated store S_1' implies termination in the other side of the non-approximated elements, $m_1' k_1' S_1' = \top \implies m_2 k_2 S_2 = \top$, and similarly for the other direction. With this separation of approximation from the local properties that the parameters express, we can prove that the relation exists. We can then extract a binary relation, defined via reference to the 4-ary relation, such that the binary relation implies contextual equivalence.

A parameter expresses properties of two related stores; and computations are related under a parameter if they have equivalent termination behaviour when executed in stores, which preserve at least the invariants expressed by the parameter. Our parameters are designed to express relatedness of pairs in the presence of higher-order store and therefore they are somewhat more complex than the parameters used by Benton and Leperchey [2]. As we have seen in the examples above, we can prove contextual equivalence of two functions, which allocate local store in different ways, and then return functions set and get that access the hidden local storage. These local locations can be updated later by application of the exported set-functions to related arguments. In between the return of the functions and the application of the returned set-functions, there might have been built up additional local store invariants. Thus functions stored by a later call to the returned set-function may require further properties of stores in order to have equivalent behaviour, than was the case when our set and get functions were returned. To handle this possibility our parameters include pairs of locations; two stores are then related wrt. such pairs of locations if the pair of locations contain values that are related relative to the invariants that hold for the two stores.

In more detail, a parameter has the form $\Delta\{r_1, \ldots, r_n\}$. Here Δ is a store type that types a finite set of locations; these are intuitively our "visible locations." The $r_1, \ldots, r_n$ are local parameters. A local parameter r_i has its own finite area of store in each side, disjoint from the visible area and from all the other local parameters' store areas. A local parameter r_i has the form $(P_1, LL_1) \vee \cdots \vee (P_m, LL_m)$. The Ps express properties of two stores and the LLs are lists of location pairs. It is possible to decide if two states fulfill the properties expressed by the Ps by only considering the contents of r_is private areas of store. At least one P must hold and the corresponding LL must hold values related relative to the invariants that hold for the two stores (we can also think of this as related at the given time in computation). Using FM domain theory makes it possible for us to express the parameters directly by location names.

We present the definition of our relation, state its existence and the theorem that relatedness implies contextual equivalence in Section 4. In the following Section 5 we show how we prove contextual equivalence of our example programs. We hope that the proofs will convince the reader that our logical relations proof method is fairly straightforward to apply; in particular the choice of parameters is very natural. We conclude in Section 6.

For reasons of space most proofs have been omitted from this extended abstract.

2 Language

The language we consider is a call-by-value, monadically-typed λ-calculus with recursion, general recursive types, and general dynamically allocated references. Types are either *value types* τ or *computation types* $T\tau$. Values of any closed value type can be stored in the store.

$$\tau ::= \alpha \mid \text{unit} \mid \text{int} \mid \tau \times \tau \mid \tau + \tau \mid \tau\text{ref} \mid \tau \to T\tau \mid \mu\alpha.\tau$$
$$\gamma ::= \tau \mid T\tau$$

Typing contexts, Γ, are finite maps from variables to closed value types. We assume infinite sets of variables, ranged over by x, type variables, ranged over by α, and locations, ranged over by l. We let $\mathbb{L}$ denote the set of locations. Store types Δ are finite maps from locations to value types. Terms G are either *values* V or *computations* M:

$$
\begin{aligned}
V ::=&\ x \mid \underline{n} \mid \underline{l} \mid () \mid (V,V') \mid \text{in}_i V \mid \text{rec } f(x:\tau) = M \mid \text{fold } V \\
M ::=&\ VV' \mid \text{let } x \Leftarrow M \text{ in } M' \mid \text{val } V \mid \pi_i V \mid \text{ref } V \mid !V \mid \\
&\ V := V' \mid \text{case } V \text{ of in}_{1x1} \Rightarrow M_1; \text{in}_{2x2} \Rightarrow M_2 \mid \\
&\ V = V' \mid V + V' \mid \text{iszero } V \mid \text{unfold } V \\
G ::=&\ M \mid V.
\end{aligned}
$$

Continuations K take the following form:

$$K ::= \text{val } x \mid \text{let } y \Leftarrow M \text{ in } K$$

The typing judgments take the form

$$\Delta; \Gamma \vdash V : \tau \qquad \Delta; \Gamma \vdash M : T\tau \qquad \Delta; \vdash K : (x : \tau)^\top$$

The typing rules for values and terms are as in [2] extended with rules for recursive types, except that the type for references is not restricted. Here we just include the following three selected rules:

$$\frac{\Delta; \Gamma \vdash V : \tau}{\Delta; \Gamma \vdash \mathit{ref} V : T(\tau\text{ref})}$$

$$\frac{\Delta; \Gamma \vdash V : \tau[\mu\alpha.\tau/\alpha]}{\Delta; \Gamma \vdash \mathit{fold} V : \mu\alpha.\tau} \qquad \frac{\Delta; \Gamma \vdash V : \mu\alpha.\tau}{\Delta; \Gamma \vdash \mathit{unfold} V : T(\tau[\mu\alpha.\tau/\alpha])}$$

Stores Σ are finite maps from locations to closed values. A store Σ has store type Δ, written $\Sigma : \Delta$, if, for all l in the domain of Δ, $\Delta; \vdash \Sigma(l) : \Delta(l)$.

The operational semantics is defined via a termination judgment Σ, let $x \Leftarrow M$ in $K \downarrow$, where M is closed and K is a *continuation term in* x. Typed continuation terms are defined by:

$$\frac{}{\Delta; \vdash val \; x : (x : \tau)^\top} \qquad \frac{\Delta; x : \tau \vdash M : T\tau' \quad \Delta; \vdash K : (y : \tau')^\top}{\Delta; \vdash let \; y \Leftarrow M \; in \; K : (x : \tau)^\top}$$

The defining rules for the termination judgment Σ, let $x \Leftarrow M$ in $K \downarrow$ are standard given that the language is call-by-value, with left-to-right evaluation order. We just include one rule as an example:

$$\frac{\Sigma, let \; x \Leftarrow val \; V \; in \; K \downarrow}{\Sigma, let \; x \Leftarrow unfold(fold \; V) \; in \; K \downarrow}$$

A *context* is a computation term with a hole, and we write $C[.] : (\Delta; \Gamma \vdash \gamma) \Rightarrow (\Delta; - \vdash T\tau)$ to mean that whenever $\Delta; \Gamma \vdash G : \gamma$ then $\Delta; - \vdash C[G] : T\tau$.

The definition of contextual equivalence is standard and as in [2].

Definition 1. *If* $\Delta; \Gamma \vdash G_i : \gamma$, *for* $i = 1, 2$ *then* G_1 *and* G_2 *are* contextually equivalent, *written*

$$\Delta; \Gamma \vdash G_1 =_{ctx} G_2,$$

if, for all types τ, *for all contexts* $C[.] : (\Delta; \Gamma \vdash \gamma) \Rightarrow (\Delta; - \vdash T\tau)$ *and for all stores* $\Sigma : \Delta$,

$$\Sigma, let \; x \Leftarrow C[G_1] \; in \; val \; x \downarrow \Longleftrightarrow \Sigma, let \; x \Leftarrow C[G_2] \; in \; val \; x \downarrow .$$

3   Denotational Semantics

We define a denotational semantics of the language from the previous section and show that the semantics is *adequate*. The denotational semantics is defined using FM-domains [11]. The semantics and the adequacy proof, in particular the existence proof of the logical relation used to prove adequacy, builds on Shinwell's work on semantics of recursive types in FM-domains [11]. Our approach is slightly different from that of Shinwell since we make use of universal domains to model the fact that any type of value can be stored in the store, but technically it is a minor difference.

We begin by calling to mind some basic facts about FM-domains; see [11] for more details. Fix a countable set of atoms, which in our case will be the locations, $\mathbb{L}$. A *permutation* is a bijective function $\pi \in (\mathbb{L} \to \mathbb{L})$ such that the set $\{l \mid \pi(l) \neq l\}$ is finite. An FM-set X is a set equipped with a permutation action: an operation $\pi \bullet - : perms(\mathbb{L}) \times X \to X$ that preserves composition and identity, and such that each element $x \in X$ is finitely supported: there is a finite set $L \subset \mathbb{L}$ such that whenever π fixes each element of L, the action of π fixes x: $\pi \bullet x = x$. There is a smallest such set, which we write $supp(x)$. A morphism of FM-sets is a function $f : D \to D'$ between the underlying sets that is equivariant: $\forall x.\pi \bullet (fx) = f(\pi \bullet x)$. An FM-cpo is an FM-set with an equivariant partial order relation $\sqsubseteq$ and least upper bounds of all finitely-supported ω-chains. A morphism of FM-cpos is a morphism of their underlying FM-sets that is monotone and preserves lubs of finitely-supported chains. We only require the existence and preservation of lubs of finitely-supported chains, so an FM-cpo may not be a cpo in the usual sense. The sets $\mathbb{Z}$, $\mathbb{N}$, etc., are discrete FM-cpos with the trivial action. The set of locations, $\mathbb{L}$, is a discrete FM-cpo with the action $\pi \bullet l = \pi(l)$. The category of FM-cpos is bicartesian closed: we write 1 and $\times$ for the finite products, $D \Rightarrow D'$ for the internal hom and $0, +$ for the coproducts. The action on products is pointwise, and on functions is given by conjugation: $\pi \bullet f = \lambda x.\pi \bullet (f(\pi^{-}1 \bullet x))$. The category is not well-pointed: morphisms $1 \to D$ correspond to elements of $1 \Rightarrow D$ with empty support. The lift monad, $(-)_L$, is defined as usual with the obvious action. The Kleisli category FM-Cpo$_\perp$ is the category of pointed FM-cpos (FM-cppos) and strict continuous maps, which is symmetric monoidal closed, with smash product $\otimes$ and strict function space $\multimap$. If D is a pointed FM-cpo then $\mathit{fix} : (D \Rightarrow D) \multimap D$ is defined by the lub of an ascending chain in the usual way. We write $\mathbb{O}$ for the discrete FM-cpo with elements $\perp$ and $\top$, ordered by $\perp \sqsubseteq \top$.

As detailed in [11], one may solve recursive domain equations in FM-Cpo$_\perp$. For the denotational semantics, we use minimal invariant recursive domains:

$$\begin{aligned}
\mathbb{V} &\cong 1_\perp \oplus \mathbb{Z}_\perp \oplus \mathbb{L}_\perp \oplus (\mathbb{V} \oplus \mathbb{V}) \oplus (\mathbb{V} \otimes \mathbb{V}) \oplus (\mathbb{V} \multimap \mathbb{M})_\perp \oplus \mathbb{V} \\
\mathbb{K} &\cong (\mathbb{S} \multimap (\mathbb{V} \multimap \mathbb{O})) \\
\mathbb{M} &\cong (\mathbb{K} \multimap (\mathbb{S} \multimap \mathbb{O})) \\
\mathbb{S} &\cong \mathbb{L}_\perp \multimap \mathbb{V}.
\end{aligned}$$

Formally, these are obtained as the minimal invariant solution to a locally FM-continuous functor $F : (\text{FM-Cpo}_\perp^4)^{\text{op}} \times \text{FM-Cpo}_\perp^4 \to \text{FM-Cpo}_\perp^4$. We write $\mathbb{D}$ for $(\mathbb{V}, \mathbb{K}, \mathbb{M}, \mathbb{S})$ and i for the isomorphism $i : F(\mathbb{D}, \mathbb{D}) \cong \mathbb{D}$. We will often omit the isomorphism i and the injections into the sum writing, e.g., simply (v_1, v_2) for an element of $\mathbb{V}$.

Types, τ are interpreted by $[\![\tau]\!] = \mathbb{V}$, computation types $T\tau$ are interpreted by $[\![T\tau]\!] = \mathbb{M}$, continuation types $(x : \tau)^\top$ are interpreted by $[\![(x : \tau)^\top]\!] = \mathbb{K}$, and store types Δ are interpreted by $[\![\Delta]\!] = \mathbb{S}$. Type environments $\Gamma = x_1 : \tau_1, \ldots, x_n : \tau_n$ are interpreted by $\mathbb{V}^n$.

Typing judgments are interpreted as follows:

- $[\![\Delta; \Gamma \vdash V : \tau]\!] \in ([\![\Gamma]\!] \multimap [\![\tau]\!])$
- $[\![\Delta; \Gamma \vdash M : T\tau]\!] \in ([\![\Gamma]\!] \multimap [\![T\tau]\!])$
- $[\![\Delta; \vdash K : (x : \tau)^\top]\!] \in \mathbb{K}$

The actual definition of the interpretations is quite standard, except for allocation which makes use of the properties of FM-cpo's:

$$\begin{aligned}
&[\![\Delta; \Gamma \vdash \text{ref}V : T(\tau\text{ref})]\!] \rho = \lambda k.\lambda S. \\
&\quad k(S([l \mapsto [\![\Delta; \Gamma \vdash V : \tau]\!] \rho]))l \\
&\quad \text{for some/any } l \notin \mathit{supp}(\lambda l'.k(S[l' \mapsto [\![\Delta; \Gamma \vdash V : \tau]\!] \rho])l')
\end{aligned}$$

The definition is much as in [2]. The use of FM-cpo's ensure that it is a good definition. As in [2], we use the monad T to combine state with continuations to get a good control over what the new location has to be fresh for.

We only include two additional cases of the semantic definition, namely the one for unfold and the one for continuations:

$$[\![\Gamma \vdash \text{unfold } V : T(\tau[\mu\alpha.\tau/\alpha])]\!]\, \rho = \lambda k.\lambda S.$$
$$\text{case } [\![\Delta; \Gamma \vdash V : \mu\alpha.\tau]\!]\, \rho \text{ of } i_1 \circ in_\mu(d) \text{ then } kSd; \text{ else}\bot,$$

where in_μ is the appropriate injection of $\mathbb{V}$ into $1_\bot \oplus \mathbb{Z}_\bot \oplus \mathbb{L}_\bot \oplus (\mathbb{V} \oplus \mathbb{V}) \oplus (\mathbb{V} \otimes \mathbb{V}) \oplus (\mathbb{V} \multimap \mathbb{M})_\bot \oplus \mathbb{V}$ and i_1 is the isomorphism from this sum into $\mathbb{V}$.

$$[\![\Delta; \vdash K : (x : \tau)^\top]\!] = \lambda S.\lambda d.$$
$$[\![\Delta; x : \tau \vdash K : T\tau']\!]\{x \mapsto d\}(\lambda S'.(\lambda d'.\top)_\bot)_\bot S$$

Theorem 1 (Soundness and Adequacy). *If* $\Delta; \vdash M : T\tau$, $\Delta; \vdash K : (x : \tau)^\top$, $\Sigma : \Delta$ *and* $S \in [\![\Sigma : \Delta]\!]$ *then*

$$\Sigma, \text{let } x \Leftarrow M \text{ in } K \downarrow \quad \text{iff} \quad [\![\Delta; \vdash M : T\tau]\!] * [\![\Delta; \vdash K : (x : \tau)^\top]\!]\, S = \top.$$

Soundness is proved by induction and to show adequacy one defines a formal approximation relation between the denotational and the operational semantics. The existence proof of the relation is non-trivial because of the recursive types, but follows from a fairly straightforward adaptation of Shinwell's existence proof in [11] (Shinwell shows adequacy for a language with recursive types, but without references).

Corollary 1. $[\![\Delta; \Gamma \vdash G_1 : \gamma]\!] = [\![\Delta; \Gamma \vdash G_2 : \gamma]\!]$ *implies* $\Delta; \Gamma \vdash G_1 =_{ctx} G_2$.

4   A Parameterized Logical Relation

In this section we define a parameterized logical relation on $\mathbb{D}$ and $F(\mathbb{D}, \mathbb{D})$, which we can use to prove contextual equivalence. (In the following we will sometimes omit the isomorphism i, i^{-1} between $F(\mathbb{D}, \mathbb{D})$ and $\mathbb{D}$).

4.1   Accessibility Maps, Simple State Relations and Parameters

Intuitively, the parameters express properties of two related states by expressing requirements of disjoint areas of states. There is a "visible" area and a finite number of "hidden invariants." In the logical relation, computations are related under a parameter if they have corresponding termination behaviour under the assumption that they are executed in states satisfying the properties expressed by the parameter.

Definition 2. *A function* $A : \mathbb{S} \to \mathcal{P}_{\text{fin}}(\mathbb{L})$ *from* $\mathbb{S}$ *to the set of finite subsets of* $\mathbb{L}$ *is an* accessibility map *if*

$$\forall S_1, S_2. \ (\forall l \in A(S_1). \ S_1 l = S_2 l) \Rightarrow A(S_1) = A(S_2)$$

We let $A_\emptyset$ denote the accessibility map defined by $\forall S.A_\emptyset(S) = \emptyset$, and we let $A_{\{l_1,\dots,l_k\}}$ denote the accessibility map defined by $\forall S.A_{\{l_1,\dots,l_k\}}(S) = \{l_1,\dots,l_k\}$.

Definition 3. *A simple state relation P is a triple $(\hat{p}, A_{p1}, A_{p2})$ satisfying that A_{p1} and A_{p2} are accessibility maps and $\hat{p}$ is a relation on $\mathbb{S}$ satisfying, for all states $S_1, S_2, S_1', S_2' \in \mathbb{S}$,*

$$(\forall l_1 \in A_{p1}(S_1).S_1 l_1 = S_1' l_1 \ \wedge \ \forall l_2 \in A_{p2}(S_2).S_2 l_2 = S_2' l_2)$$
$$\Rightarrow ((S_1, S_2) \in \hat{p} \Leftrightarrow (S_1', S_2') \in \hat{p}).$$

Note that a simple state relation is essentially a relation on states for which it can be decided whether a pair of states belong to the relation only on the basis of some parts of the states, defined by a pair of accessibility maps.

We denote the "always true" simple state relation $(\mathbb{S} \times \mathbb{S}, A_\emptyset, A_\emptyset)$ by T.

We now define the notion of a local parameter, which we will later use to express hidden invariants of two related states. Intuitively, a local parameter has its own private areas of the states. These areas are used for testing conditions and for storing related values. The testing condition is a disjunction of simple state relations, where to each disjunct there is an associated list of pairs of locations from the two related states. At least one condition must be satisfied and the corresponding list of locations hold related values.

Definition 4. *A local parameter r is a finite non-empty set of pairs $\{(P_1, LL_1), .., (P_m, LL_m)\}$, where each P_i is a simple state relation $P_i = (\hat{p}_i, A_{pi1}, A_{pi2})$ and each LL_i is a finite set of location pairs and closed value types $LL_i = \{ (l_{i11}, l_{i12}, \tau_{i1}), \dots, (l_{in_i1}, l_{in_i2}, \tau_{n_i}) \}$. $(n_i \geq 0)$.*

We often write a local parameter as $r = ((P_1, LL_1) \vee \dots \vee (P_m, LL_m))$. For a location list LL, we write L_1 resp. L_2 for the set of locations that occur as first resp. second components in the location list LL. For a local parameter r, there are associated accessibility maps A_{r1} and A_{r2} given by $\forall S.\ A_{r1}(S) = \bigcup_i A_{pi1}(S) \cup L_1$ and $\forall S.\ A_{r2}(S) = \bigcup_i A_{pi2}(S) \cup L_2$.

We denote the "always true" local parameter $\{(T, \emptyset)\}$ also simply by T. It has the associated accessibility maps $A_\emptyset, A_\emptyset$.

As explained in the introduction we have included the LL-list to be used for storing related values which may later be updated by exported updating functions. The updated values may require more invariants to hold for the stores in order to have equivalent behaviour. This interpretation of the local parameter is expressed in the definition of our invariant relation $F(\nabla, \nabla)$ below.

Definition 5. *A parameter Δr is a pair (Δ, r), with Δ a store type, and $r = \{r_1, .., r_n\}$ a finite set of local parameters such that $T \in r$.*

For a parameter Δr we associate accessibility maps A_{r1} and A_{r2}, given by $\forall S.\ A_{r1}(S) = \bigcup A_{r_i 1}(S)$ and $\forall S.\ A_{r2}(S) = \bigcup A_{r_i 2}(S)$.

For each store type Δ we have a special the "always true" parameter $\Delta id_\emptyset = \Delta\{T\}$.

Definition 6. *For parameters $\Delta'r'$ and Δr define*

$\Delta'r' \rhd \Delta r \overset{def}{\Longleftrightarrow} \Delta' \supseteq \Delta$ *and* $r' \supseteq r$.

The ordering relation $\rhd$ is reflexive, transitive and antisymmetric. For all parameters Δr it holds that there are only finitely many parameters $\Delta_0 r_0$ such that $\Delta r \rhd \Delta_0 r_0$. For convenience we sometimes write $\Delta r \lhd \Delta'r'$ for $\Delta'r' \rhd \Delta r$.

4.2 Parameterized Relations and Contextual Equivalence

In this section we will define a parameterized logical relation on $\mathbb{D}$ and $F(\mathbb{D},\mathbb{D})$. Let $D = (D_V, D_K, D_M, D_S) \in \{\mathbb{D}, F(\mathbb{D},\mathbb{D})\}$. We define the set of relations $\mathcal{R}(D)$ on D as follows.

$\mathcal{R}(D) = \hat{R}_V \times \hat{R}_K \times \hat{R}_M \times \hat{R}_S$ where

$\hat{R}_V =$ all subsets of
$D_V^4 \times \{\tau \mid \tau$ is a closed value type$\} \times \{$parameter$\}$ that include
$\{(\bot, v_1, \bot, v_2, \tau, \Delta r) \mid v_1, v_2 \in D_V,\ \tau$ closed value type, Δr parameter$\}$
$\hat{R}_K =$ all subsets of
$D_K^4 \times \{(x:\tau)^\top \mid (x:\tau)^\top$ is a continuation type$\} \times \{$parameter$\}$ that include
$\{(\bot, k_1, \bot, k_2, (x:\tau)^\top, \Delta r) \mid$
$\qquad k_1, k_2 \in D_K, (x:\tau)^\top$ continuation type, Δr parameter$\}$
$\hat{R}_M =$ all subsets of
$D_M^4 \times \{T\tau \mid T\tau$ is a closed computation type$\} \times \{$parameter$\}$ that include
$\{(\bot, m_1, \bot, m_2, T\tau, \Delta r) \mid$
$\qquad m_1, m_2 \in D_M, T\tau$ closed computation type, Δr parameter$\}$
$\hat{R}_S =$ all subsets of $D_S^4 \times \{$parameter$\}$ that include
$\{(\bot, S_1, \bot, S_2, \Delta r) \mid S_1, S_2 \in D_S, \Delta r$ parameter$\}$

A relation $(R_1, R_2, R_3, R_4) \in \mathcal{R}(D)$ is *admissible* if, for each i, R_i is closed under least upper bounds of finitely supported chains of the form $(d_1^i, d_1, d_2^i, d_2, (type), \Delta r)_{i \in \omega}$ where $d_1, d_2, type, \Delta r$ are constant. We let $\mathcal{R}_{adm}(D)$ denote the admissible relations over D.

Theorem 2. *There exists a relational lifting of the functor F to $(\mathcal{R}(\mathbb{D})^{op} \times \mathcal{R}(\mathbb{D})) \to \mathcal{R}(F(\mathbb{D},\mathbb{D}))$ and an* admissible *relation $\nabla = (\nabla_V, \nabla_K, \nabla_M, \nabla_S) \in \mathcal{R}_{adm}(\mathbb{D})$ satisfying the equations in Figure 1 and $(i,i) : F(\nabla, \nabla) \subset \nabla \wedge (i^{-1}, i^{-1}) : \nabla \subset F(\nabla, \nabla)$.*

Proof (Theorem 2, existence of an invariant relation ∇). The proof makes use of the ideas mentioned in the Introduction in combination with a proof method inspired from Pitts [7]. We have defined a relational structure on the domains $\mathbb{D}$ and $F(\mathbb{D},\mathbb{D}) \in$ FM-Cpo$_\bot^4$ as products of relations on each of their four domain-projections. Each of these relations is a 4-ary relation with elements $(d_1', d_1, d_2', d_2, (type), \Delta r)$ where $d_1' = d_2' = \bot$ relates to everything.

We define the action of $F(-,+)$ on relations $R^-, R^+ \in \mathbb{D}$ such that it holds that $d_1' \sqsubseteq d_1$ and $d_2' \sqsubseteq d_2$ in elements $(d_1', d_1, d_2', d_2, (type), \Delta r)$ of $F(R^-, R^+)_n$, $n \in \{V, K, M, S\}$. In the definition of $F(R^-, R^+)_S \in \mathcal{R}(i^{-1}\mathbb{S})$ the accessibility

$$F(\nabla, \nabla)_V = \{(\bot,\ v_1,\ \bot,\ v_2,\ \tau,\ \Delta r)\ \} \cup$$
$$\{(v_1',\ v_1,\ v_2',\ v_2, \tau, \Delta r)\ |$$
$$v_1' \sqsubseteq v_1 \neq \bot\ \wedge\ v_2' \sqsubseteq v_2 \neq \bot\ \wedge$$
$$(v_1',\ v_1,\ v_2',\ v_2, \tau, \Delta r) \in \Diamond\ \}$$
where
$$\Diamond\quad = \{(in_1*,\ in_1*,\ in_1*,\ in_1*,\ \text{unit},\ \Delta r)\ \} \cup$$
$$\{(in_{\mathbb{Z}}n,\ in_{\mathbb{Z}}n,\ in_{\mathbb{Z}}n,\ in_{\mathbb{Z}}n,\ \text{int},\ \Delta r)\ |\ n \in \mathbb{Z}\ \} \cup$$
$$\{(in_{\mathbb{L}}l,\ in_{\mathbb{L}}l,\ in_{\mathbb{L}}l,\ in_{\mathbb{L}}l,\ (\Delta l)\text{ref},\ \Delta r)\ |\ l \in dom(\Delta)\ \} \cup$$
$$\{(in_{\oplus}in_i d_1',\ in_{\oplus}in_i d_1,\ in_{\oplus}in_i d_2',\ in_{\oplus}in_i d_2,\ \tau_1 + \tau_2,\ \Delta r)\ |$$
$$\exists \Delta_0 r_0 \lhd \Delta r.\ (d_1',\ d_1,\ d_2',\ d_2,\ \tau_i,\ \Delta_0 r_0) \in \nabla_V,\ i \in \{1,2\}\ \} \cup$$
$$\{(in_{\otimes}(d_{1a}',d_{1b}'),\ in_{\otimes}(d_{1a},d_{1b}),\ in_{\otimes}(d_{2a}',d_{2b}'),\ in_{\otimes}(d_{2a},d_{2b}),$$
$$\tau_a \times \tau_b,\ \Delta r)\ |$$
$$\exists \Delta_0 r_0 \lhd \Delta r.\ (d_{1a}',\ d_{1a},\ d_{2a}',\ d_{2a}',\ \tau_a,\ \Delta_0 r_0) \in \nabla_V\ \text{and}$$
$$(d_{1b}',\ d_{1b},\ d_{2b}',\ d_{2b},\ \tau_b,\ \Delta_0 r_0) \in \nabla_V\ \} \cup$$
$$\{(in_{\bullet}d_1',\ in_{\bullet}d_1,\ in_{\bullet}d_2'\ in_{\bullet}d_2,\ \tau \to T\tau',\ \Delta r)\ |$$
$$\forall \Delta'r' \rhd \Delta r,\ (v_1'\ ,v_1,\ v_2',\ v_2,\ \tau,\ \Delta'r') \in \nabla_V.$$
$$(d_1'v_1',\ d_1v_1,\ d_2'v_2',\ d_2v_2,\ T\tau',\ \Delta'r') \in \nabla_M\ \} \cup$$
$$\{(in_{\mu}d_1',\ in_{\mu}d_1,\ in_{\mu}d_2',\ in_{\mu}d_2,\ \mu\alpha.\tau, \Delta r)\ |$$
$$\exists \Delta_0 r_0 \lhd \Delta r.\ (d_1',\ d_1,\ d_2',\ d_2,\ \tau[\mu\alpha.\tau/\alpha],\ \Delta_0 r_0) \in \nabla_V\ \}$$

$$F(\nabla, \nabla)_K = \{(k_1',\ k_1,\ k_2',\ k_2,\ (x:\tau)^\top,\ \Delta r)\ |$$
$$k_1' \sqsubseteq k_1\ \wedge\ k_2' \sqsubseteq k_2\ \wedge\ \forall \Delta'r' \rhd \Delta r.$$
$$\forall (S_1',\ S_1,\ S_2',\ S_2,\ \Delta'r') \in \nabla_S.$$
$$\forall (v_1',\ v_1,\ v_2',\ v_2,\ \tau,\ \Delta'r') \in \nabla_V.$$
$$(k_1'S_1'v_1' = \top \Rightarrow k_2 S_2 v_2 = \top)\ \wedge$$
$$(k_2'S_2'v_2' = \top \Rightarrow k_1 S_1 v_1 = \top)\ \}$$

$$F(\nabla, \nabla)_M = \{(m_1',\ m_1,\ m_2',\ m_2,\ T\tau,\ \Delta r)\ |$$
$$m_1' \sqsubseteq m_1\ \wedge\ m_2' \sqsubseteq m_2\ \wedge\ \forall \Delta'r' \rhd \Delta r.$$
$$\forall (k_1',\ k_1,\ k_2',\ k_2,\ (x:\tau)^\top,\ \Delta'r') \in \nabla_K.$$
$$\forall (S_1',\ S_1,\ S_2',\ S_2,\ \Delta'r') \in \nabla_S.$$
$$(m_1'k_1'S_1' = \top \Rightarrow m_2 k_2 S_2 = \top)\ \wedge$$
$$(m_2'k_2'S_2' = \top \Rightarrow m_1 k_1 S_1 = \top)\ \}$$

$$F(\nabla, \nabla)_S = \{(\bot,\ S_1,\ \bot,\ S_2,\ \Delta r)\ \} \cup$$
$$\{(S_1',\ S_1,\ S_2',\ S_2,\ \Delta r)\ |\ r = \{r_1, \ldots, r_n\}\ \wedge$$
$$S_1' \sqsubseteq S_1 \neq \bot\ \wedge\ S_2' \sqsubseteq S_2 \neq \bot\ \wedge\ \forall i \neq j,\ i,j \in 1, \ldots, n.$$
$$A_{ri1}(S_1) \cap A_{rj1}(S_1) = \emptyset\ \wedge\ A_{ri2}(S_2) \cap A_{rj2}(S_2) = \emptyset\ \wedge$$
$$dom(\Delta) \cap A_{r1}(S_1) = \emptyset\ \wedge\ dom(\Delta) \cap A_{r2}(S_2) = \emptyset\ \wedge$$
$$\forall l \in dom(\Delta).(S_1'l,\ S_1l,\ S_2'l,\ S_2l,\ \Delta l,\ \Delta r) \in \nabla_V\ \wedge$$
$$\forall r_a \in r.\exists (P_b, LL_b) \in r_a.\ (S_1, S_2) \in \hat{p}_b\ \wedge$$
$$\forall (l_1, l_2, \tau) \in LL_b.(S_1'l_1, S_1l_1, S_2'l_2, S_2l_2, \tau, \Delta r) \in \nabla_V$$

Fig. 1. Invariant Relation ∇

maps and the simple state relations mentioned in a parameter Δr are only used on the non-primed elements s_1, s_2 from $(s_1', s_1, s_2', s_2, \Delta r)$. As explained, approximation will be carried out on the primed domain elements. Therefore, we define application of a pair of functions (f, j) to a relation only for $f \sqsubseteq j$ with j an isomorphism $j \in \{i, i^{-1}, id_{\mathbb{D}}, id_{F(\mathbb{D}, \mathbb{D})}\}$. In an application $(f, j)R$ we apply f to the elements in the primed positions, and j to the elements of the non-primed positions. Then we define $(f, j) : R \subset S$ to mean that set theoretically $(f, j)R \subseteq S$. It holds that $F(R^-, R^+)$ preserves admissibility of R^+. It also holds that $R^-, R^+, S^-, S^+ \in \mathcal{R}(\mathbb{D})$ with $(f^-, id_{\mathbb{D}}) : S^- \subset R^-$ and $(f^+, id_{\mathbb{D}}) : R^+ \subset S^+$ implies $(F(f^-, f^+), id_{F(\mathbb{D}, \mathbb{D})}) : F(R^-, R^+) \subset F(S^-, S^+)$. These properties are essential for the proof of existence of the invariant relation ∇.

Proposition 1 (Weakening). *For all* $\Delta' r' \rhd \Delta r$,

- $(v_1', v_1, v_2', v_2, \tau, \Delta r) \in \nabla_V \Rightarrow (v_1', v_1, v_2', v_2, \tau, \Delta' r') \in \nabla_V$,
- $(k_1', k_1, k_2', k_2, (x : \tau)^\top, \Delta r) \in \nabla_K \Rightarrow (k_1', k_1, k_2', k_2, (x : \tau)^\top, \Delta' r') \in \nabla_K$,
- $(m_1', m_1, m_2', m_2, T\tau, \Delta r) \in \nabla_M \Rightarrow (m_1', m_1, m_2', m_2, T\tau, \Delta' r') \in \nabla_M$.

Below we define a binary relation between denotations of typing judgement conclusions. This relation will be used as basis for proofs of contextual equivalence. The relation is defined by reference to the 4-ary relations from ∇. For two closed terms, two continuations, or two states the binary relation requires that their denotations d_1, d_2 are related as two pairs $(d_1, d_1, d_2, d_2, (type), parameter) \in \nabla_j$. The denotations of open value-terms with n free variables belong to $\mathbb{V}^n \multimap \mathbb{V}$, denotations of open computation terms to $\mathbb{V}^n \multimap \mathbb{M}$. They must give related elements in ∇ whenever they are applied to n-tuples of ∇-related elements form $\mathbb{V}$.

Definition 7 (Relating denotations of open expressions)

- *For all* $\Gamma = x_1 : \tau_1, \ldots, x_n : \tau_n$ *and* $\Delta; \Gamma \vdash V_1 : \tau$ *and* $\Delta; \Gamma \vdash V_2 : \tau$
  let $v_1 = [\![\Delta; \Gamma \vdash V_1 : \tau]\!]$ *and* $v_2 = [\![\Delta; \Gamma \vdash V_2 : \tau]\!]$, *and define*

$$(v_1, v_2, \tau, \Delta r) \in \nabla_V^\Gamma \overset{\text{def}}{\Longleftrightarrow}$$
$$\forall \Delta' r' \rhd \Delta r. \forall i \in \{1, \ldots, n\}. \forall (v_{1i}', v_{1i}, v_{2i}', v_{2i}, \tau_i, \Delta' r') \in \nabla_V.$$
$$(v_1(\overline{v_{1i}'}), v_1(\overline{v_{1i}}), v_2(\overline{v_{2i}'}), v_2(\overline{v_{2i}}), \tau, \Delta' r') \in \nabla_V.$$

- *For all* $\Gamma = x_1 : \tau_1, \ldots, x_n : \tau_n$, $\Delta; \Gamma \vdash M_1 : T\tau$ *and* $\Delta; \Gamma \vdash M_2 : T\tau$,
  let $m_1 = [\![\Delta; \Gamma \vdash M_1 : T\tau]\!]$ *and* $m_2 = [\![\Delta; \Gamma \vdash M_2 : T\tau]\!]$, *and define*

$$(m_1, m_2, T\tau, \Delta r) \in \nabla_M^\Gamma \overset{\text{def}}{\Longleftrightarrow}$$
$$\forall \Delta' r' \rhd \Delta r. \forall i \in \{1, \ldots, n\}. \forall (v_{1i}', v_{1i}, v_{2i}', v_{2i}, \tau_i, \Delta' r') \in \nabla_V.$$
$$(m_1(\overline{v_{1i}'}), m_1(\overline{v_{1i}}), m_2(\overline{v_{2i}'}), m_2(\overline{v_{2i}}), T\tau, \Delta' r') \in \nabla_M.$$

- *For all* $\Delta; \vdash K_1 : (x : \tau)^\top$ *and* $\Delta; \vdash K_2 : (x : \tau)^\top$,
  let $k_1 = [\![\Delta; \vdash K_1 : (x : \tau)^\top]\!]$ *and* $k_2 = [\![\Delta; \vdash K_2 : (x : \tau)^\top]\!]$, *and define*

$$(k_1, k_2, (x : \tau)^\top, \Delta r) \in \nabla_K^\emptyset \overset{\text{def}}{\Longleftrightarrow} (k_1, k_1, k_2, k_2, (x : \tau)^\top, \Delta r) \in \nabla_K.$$

– *For all* $\Sigma_1 : \Delta$, $\Sigma_2 : \Delta$, *let* $S_1 \in [\![\Sigma_1 : \Delta]\!]$ *and* $S_2 \in [\![\Sigma_2 : \Delta]\!]$, *and define*

$$(S_1, S_2, \Delta r) \in \nabla_S^\emptyset \overset{def}{\Longleftrightarrow} (S_1, S_1, S_2, S_2, \Delta r) \in \nabla_S.$$

Lemma 1

1. *Suppose* $(m_1, m_2, T\tau, \Delta r) \in \nabla_M^\Gamma$. *We then have that*

$$\forall \Delta' r' \rhd \Delta r. \forall (v_{1j}, v_{2j}, \tau_j, \Delta' r') \in \nabla_V^\emptyset. \forall j \in \{1, \dots, n\}.$$
$$\forall (k_1, k_2, (x : \tau)^\top, \Delta' r') \in \nabla_K^\emptyset. \forall (S_1, S_2, \Delta' r') \in \nabla_S^\emptyset.$$
$$(i^{-1}(m_1(\overline{v_{1j}})))k_1 S_1 = \top \Longleftrightarrow (i^{-1}(m_2(\overline{v_{2j}})))k_2 S_2 = \top.$$

Theorem 3 (Fundamental Theorem). *For all parameters* Δr *it holds that*

– *if* $\Delta; \Gamma \vdash V : \tau$ *then* $([\![\Delta; \Gamma \vdash V : \tau]\!], [\![\Delta; \Gamma \vdash V : \tau]\!], \tau, \Delta r) \in \nabla_V^\Gamma$,
– *if* $\Delta; \Gamma \vdash M : T\tau$ *then* $([\![\Delta; \Gamma \vdash M : T\tau]\!], [\![\Delta; \Gamma \vdash M : T\tau]\!], T\tau, \Delta r) \in \nabla_M^\Gamma$.

The Fundamental Theorem is proved in the standard way by showing that all the typing rules preserve relatedness in ∇^Γ; weakening (Proposition 1) is used in several proof cases.

Lemma 2

– $\forall r.\ ([\![\Delta; \vdash val\ x : (x : \tau)^\top]\!], [\![\Delta; \vdash val\ x : (x : \tau)^\top]\!], (x : \tau)^\top, \Delta r) \in \nabla_K^\emptyset$,
– *if* $S \in [\![\Delta]\!]$ *then* $(S, S, \Delta id_\emptyset) \in \nabla_S^\emptyset$.

The following theorem expresses that we can show two computations or two values to be contextually equivalent by showing that they are related in ∇^Γ under a parameter $\Delta id_\emptyset$, which does not require that any hidden invariants hold for states. The computations may themselves be able to build up local state invariants and a proof of relatedness will often require one to express these invariants; see the examples in the next section.

Theorem 4 (Contextual Equivalence). *Let* $C[\_] : (\Delta; \Gamma \vdash \gamma) \Rightarrow (\Delta; \vdash T\tau)$ *be a context. If* $\Delta; \Gamma \vdash G_1 : \gamma$ *and* $\Delta; \Gamma \vdash G_2 : \gamma$ *and*

$$([\![\Delta; \Gamma \vdash G_1 : \gamma]\!], [\![\Delta; \Gamma \vdash G_2 : \gamma]\!], \gamma, \Delta id_\emptyset) \in \nabla_j^\Gamma,\ j \in \{V, M\}$$

then

$$\forall \Sigma : \Delta.\ (\Sigma, let\ x \Leftarrow C[G_1]\ in\ val\ x \downarrow \Longleftrightarrow \Sigma, let\ x \Leftarrow C[G_2]\ in\ val\ x \downarrow).$$

5 Examples

Before presenting our examples, we will first sketch how a typical proof of contextual equivalence proceeds. Thus, suppose we wish to show that two computations m_1 and m_2 are contextually equivalent. We then need to show that they are related in a parameter $\Delta id_\emptyset$ or, equivalently, in Δr, for any r. This requires us to show, for any extended parameter $\Delta^1 r^1$, any pair[1] of continuations k_1 and k_2

---

[1] Formally, we consider 4-tuples.

related in $\Delta^1 r^1$, and any pair of states S_1 and S_2 related in $\Delta^1 r^1$, $m_1 k_1 S_1$ and $m_2 k_2 S_2$ have the same termination behaviour. The latter amounts to showing that $k_1(S_1[\ldots])v_1$ and $k_2(S_2[\ldots])v_2$ have the same termination behaviour, where $S_1[\ldots]$ and $S_2[\ldots]$ are potentially updated versions of S_1 and S_2; and v_1 and v_2 are values. Since k_1 and k_2 are assumed related in $\Delta^1 r^1$, it suffices to define a parameter $\Delta^2 r^2$ extending $\Delta^1 r^1$ and show that $S_1[\ldots]$ and $S_2[\ldots]$ are related in $\Delta^2 r^2$ and that v_1 and v_2 are related in $\Delta^2 r^2$. Typically, the definition of the parameter $\Delta^2 r^2$ essentially consists of defining one or more local parameters, which capture the intuition for why the computations are related.

In the first example below we prove that M and N from the Introduction are contextually equivalent. In this case, the only local parameter we have to define is $\tilde{r}^3 = ((P_1, LL_1) \vee (P_2, LL_2))$, where

$$P_1 = (\{(S_1, S_2) \mid S_2 l_p = 0\}, A_\emptyset, A_{\{l_p\}}), \qquad LL_1 = \{(l_y, l_{y0})\},$$
$$P_2 = (\{(S_1, S_2) \mid S_2 l_p = n \neq 0\}, A_\emptyset, A_{\{l_p\}}), \qquad LL_2 = \{(l_y, l_{y1})\}.$$

This local parameter expresses that, depending on the value of $S_2(l_p)$, either the locations (l_y, l_{y0}) or the locations (l_y, l_{y1}) contain related values.

In the first subsection below we present the proof of contextual equivalence of M and N in detail. Formally, there are several cases to consider, but do note that the proof follows the outline given above and is almost automatic except for the definition of the local parameter shown above.

5.1   Example 1

Consider the programs M and N from the Introduction.

We want to show that M and N are related in any parameter Δr, that is $\forall \Delta r.\ ([\![\emptyset; \vdash M : \sigma]\!], [\![\emptyset; \vdash N : \sigma]\!]), \sigma, \Delta r) \in \nabla_V^\emptyset$. Here $\sigma = (\tau \to T\tau') \to T(\sigma_1 \times \sigma_2)$, and $\sigma_1 = (\tau \to T\tau') \to T\text{unit}$ and $\sigma_2 = \text{unit} \to (\tau \to T\tau')$). As M and N are values of function type, their denotations have the forms $in_\bullet d_M$ and $in_\bullet d_N$. We need to show $\forall \Delta^1 r^1 \rhd \Delta r.\forall (v_1', v_1, v_2', v_2, \tau \to T\tau', \Delta^1 r^1) \in \nabla_V$. $(d_M v_1', d_M v_1, d_N v_2', d_N v_2, T(\sigma_1 \times \sigma_2), \Delta^1 r^1) \in \nabla_M$.

It suffices to show that $\forall \Delta^2 r^2 \rhd \Delta^1 r^1.\forall (k_1', k_1, k_2', k_2, (x : \sigma_1 \times \sigma_2)^\top, \Delta^2 r^2) \in \nabla_K.\forall (S_1', S_1, S_2', S_2, \Delta^2 r^2) \in \nabla_S$ it holds that $(d_M v_1')k_1' S_1' = \top \implies (d_N v_2)k_2 S_2 = \top$ and $(d_N v_2')k_2' S_2' = \top \implies (d_M v_1)k_1 S_1 = \top$.

Now, $(d_M v_1)k_1 S_1 = k_1(S_1[l_y \mapsto v_1])([\![\emptyset; y \vdash recf_{1M}]\!](y \mapsto l_y), [\![\emptyset; y \vdash recf_{2M}]\!](y \mapsto l_y))$, where l_y is a location that is fresh wrt. the store S_1 in combination with the parameter $\Delta^2 r^2$, i.e.,

$$l_y \notin dom(\Delta^2) \cup A_{r^2 1}(S_1). \tag{1}$$

The value of $(d_M v_1')k_1' S_1'$ is similar.
Moreover,

$$(d_N v_2)k_2 S_2 = k_2\,(S_2[l_p \mapsto in_\mathbb{Z} 0, l_{y0} \mapsto v_2, l_{y1} \mapsto v_2])$$
$$([\![\emptyset; p, y_0, y_1 \vdash recf_{1N}]\!](p \mapsto l_p, y_0 \mapsto l_{y0}, y_1 \mapsto l_{y1}),$$
$$[\![\emptyset; p, y_0, y_1 \vdash recf_{2N}]\!](p \mapsto l_p, y_0 \mapsto l_{y0}, y_1 \mapsto l_{y1})),$$

where l_p, l_{y0}, l_{y1} are locations that are fresh wrt. the store S_2 in combination with the parameter $\Delta^2 r^2$, i.e

$$l_p, l_{y0}, l_{y1} \notin dom(\Delta^2) \cup A_{r^2 2}(S_2). \tag{2}$$

The value of $(d_N v_2')k_2' S_2'$ is similar.

Since the continuations are related in the parameter $\Delta^2 r^2$ it suffices to show that, if $S_1' \neq \perp \vee S_2' \neq \perp$ then we can give an extended parameter $\Delta^3 r^3 \rhd \Delta^2 r^2$ such that the updated states and the values (pairs of (set,get)) are related in the extended parameter $\Delta^3 r^3$.

We let $\Delta^3 r^3 = \Delta^2(r^2 \cup \{\tilde{r}^3\})$, where $\tilde{r}^3 = ((P_1, LL_1) \vee (P_2, LL_2))$, and

$$P_1 = (\{(S_1, S_2) \mid S_2 l_p = 0\}, A_\emptyset, A_{\{l_p\}}), \qquad LL_1 = \{(l_y, l_{y0}, \tau \to T\tau')\},$$
$$P_2 = (\{(S_1, S_2) \mid S_2 l_p = n \neq 0\}, A_\emptyset, A_{\{l_p\}}), \qquad LL_2 = \{(l_y, l_{y1}, \tau \to T\tau')\}.$$

Recall $\forall S. \ A_\emptyset(S) = \emptyset \ \wedge \ \forall S. \ A_{\{l_p\}}(S) = \{l_p\}$.

Then it holds that the accessibility maps associated with the local parameter $\tilde{r}^3$, are given by $\forall S. A_{\tilde{r}^3 1}(S) = \{l_y\}$ and $\forall S. A_{\tilde{r}^3 2}(S) = \{l_p, l_{y0}, l_{y1}\}$.

We now verify that

$$(\ S_1'[l_y \mapsto v_1'], S_1[l_y \mapsto v_1], S_2'[l_p \mapsto in_\mathbb{Z} 0, l_{y0} \mapsto v_2', l_{y1} \mapsto v_2'], \tag{3}$$
$$S_2[l_p \mapsto in_\mathbb{Z} 0, l_{y0} \mapsto v_2, l_{y1} \mapsto v_2], \Delta^3 r^3) \in \nabla_S.$$

By (1) and (2), all locations viewed by the local parameter $\tilde{r}^3$ are disjoint from $dom(\Delta^2)$ and from all local areas viewed by r^2. The stores have only been changed in locations viewed by $\tilde{r}^3$. Since values related in a parameter are also related in any extending parameter (weakening) every requirement from $\Delta^2 r^2$ still holds. Finally, since $S_2[l_p \mapsto in_\mathbb{Z} 0, l_{y0} \mapsto v_2, l_{y1} \mapsto v_2](l_p) = 0$ and the values stored in locations l_y and l_{y0} in the updated stores, namely v_1', v_1, v_2', v_2, are related in $\Delta^1 r^1$ and then by weakening also in $\Delta^3 r^3$, the first disjunct of $\tilde{r}^3$ is satisfied, and hence (3) holds.

It remains to show
A: $([\emptyset; y \vdash recf_{1M}](y \mapsto l_y), [\emptyset; y \vdash recf_{1M}](y \mapsto l_y), [\emptyset; p, y_0, y_1 \vdash f_{1N}](p \mapsto l_p, y_0 \mapsto l_{y0}, y_1 \mapsto l_{y1}), [\emptyset; p, y_0, y_1 \vdash recf_{1N}](p \mapsto l_p, y_0 \mapsto l_{y0}, y_1 \mapsto l_{y1}), (\tau \to T\tau') \to T\text{unit}, \Delta^3 r^3) \in \nabla_V$ and

B: $([\emptyset; y \vdash recf_{2M}](y \mapsto l_y), [\emptyset; y \vdash recf_{2M}](y \mapsto l_y), [\emptyset; p, y_0, y_1 \vdash recf_{2N}](p \mapsto l_p, y_0 \mapsto l_{y0}, y_1 \mapsto l_{y1}) [\emptyset; p, y_0, y_1 \vdash recf_{2N}](p \mapsto l_p, y_0 \mapsto l_{y0}, y_1 \mapsto l_{y1}), (\tau \to T\tau') \to T\text{unit}, \Delta^3 r^3) \in \nabla_V.$

Now let $\Delta^4 r^4 \rhd \Delta^3 r^3$, $(w_1', w_1, w_2', w_2, \tau \to T\tau', \Delta^4 r^4) \in \nabla_V$, and let $\Delta^5 r^5 \rhd \Delta^4 r^4, (K_1', K_1, K_2', K_2, (x : \tau \to T\tau')^\top \Delta^5 r^5) \in \nabla_K, (S_1', S_1, S_2', S_2, \Delta^5 r^5) \in \nabla_S, (c_1', c_1, c_2', c_2, (x : \text{unit})^\top, \Delta^5 r^5) \in \nabla_K.$

We have denotations $[\emptyset; y \vdash recf_{1M}](y \mapsto l_y) = in_\bullet d_{M1}, [\emptyset; p, y_0, y_1 \vdash recf_{1N}](p \mapsto l_p, y_0 \mapsto l_{y0}, y_1 \mapsto l_{y1}) = in_\bullet d_{N1}, [\emptyset; y \vdash recf_{2M}](y \mapsto l_y) = in_\bullet d_{M2}, [\emptyset; p, y_0, y_1 \vdash recf_{2N}](p \mapsto l_p, y_0 \mapsto l_{y0}, y_1 \mapsto l_{y1}) = in_\bullet d_{N2}.$

<u>A:</u> Now we want to show relatedness of the setters. As before if $w'_1 = w'_2 = \bot$ or $S'_1 = S'_2 = \bot$ we are done. Otherwise we reason as follows.

Observe that $(d_{M1}w_1)c_1S_1 = c_1(S_1[l_y \mapsto w_1])in_1*$ and similarly $(d_{M1}w_1)c'_1S'_1 = c'_1(S'_1[l_y \mapsto w'_1])in_1*$. Also, $(d_{N1}w_2)c_2S_2 = c_2(S_2[l_p \mapsto in_{\mathbb{Z}}0, l_{y0} \mapsto w_2])in_1*$, if $S_2l_P \neq 0$, and $(d_{N1}w_2)c_2S_2 = c_2(S_2[l_p \mapsto in_{\mathbb{Z}}1, l_{y1} \mapsto w_2])in_1*$, if $S_2l_P = 0$. Similarly for the approximation $(d_{N1}w'_2)c'_2S'_2$.

Since the states are related in Δ^5r^5 which is an extension of Δ^3r^3 we know that the content of S_2l_p is $in_{\mathbb{Z}}n$ for some n. We know that the continuations c'_1, c_1, c'_2, c_2 are related in Δ^5r^5. $(in_1*, in_1*, in_1*, in_1*, \text{unit}, \Delta^5r^5)$ since they are related in any parameter. So if we can show that the updated states are related in Δ^5r^5 we are done.

The states S'_1, S_1, S'_2, S_2 are related in Δ^5r^5. All changes are only within the store areas belonging to $\tilde{r}^3$ and the changes preserve the invariant for $\tilde{r}^3$, hence the updated states are still related in Δ^5r^5. We conclude that the setters are related in ∇^3r^3.

<u>B:</u> Now we want to show relatedness of the getters. As before, if the denotations are applied to related unit type values where the approximations are $\bot$ or if $S'_1 = S'_2 = \bot$ we are done. Otherwise we reason as follows. Note that $(d_{M2}in_1*)K_1S_1 = K_1S_1(S_1l_y)$ and similarly $(d_{M2}in_1*)K'_1S'_1 = K'_1S'_1(S'_1l_y)$. Since the states are not $\bot$ and are related in Δ^5r^5 which is an extension of Δ^3r^3 we know that the content of S_2l_p is $in_{\mathbb{Z}}n$ for some n. We have that $(d_{N2}in_1*)K_2S_2 = K_2S_2(S_2l_{y0})$, if $n = 0$, and $(d_{N2}in_1*)K_2S_2 = K_2S_2(S_2l_{y1})$, if $n \neq 0$. Similarly for the approximation $(d_{N2}in_1*)K'_2S'_2$.

We know that the continuations K'_1, K_1, K'_2, K_2 and the states S'_1S_1, S'_2, S_2 are related in Δ^5r^5. So if we can show that the retrieved values are related in Δ^5r^5 we are done.

Since the states S'_1S_1, S'_2, S_2 are related in Δ^5r^5 they satisfy the invariant of $\tilde{r}^3$. So the content of S_2l_p is $in_{\mathbb{Z}}n$ for some n. If $n = 0$ then $S'_1l_y, S_1l_y, S'_2l_{y0}, S_2l_{y0}$ are related in Δ^5r^r, and if $n \neq 0$ then $S'_1l_y, S_1l_y, S'_2l_{y1}, S_2l_{y1}$ are related in Δ^5r^r, again by the requirement from $\tilde{r}^3$. This is what we need for the retrieved values to be related. We conclude that the getters are related in ∇^3r^3.

Then we can conclude that $(\llbracket M \rrbracket, \llbracket N \rrbracket, \sigma, \Delta r) \in \nabla^{\emptyset}_V$, and as Δr was arbitrary that they are related in any parameter. Hence the programs M and N are contextually equivalent.

5.2   Example 2

Consider the computation terms M' and N' from the Introduction. They both have a free variable g of function type. We want to show that M' and N' are related in any parameter Δr.

We need to show $\forall \Delta^1r^1 \rhd \Delta r.\forall(g'_1, g_1, g'_2, g_2, \sigma, \Delta^1r^1) \in \nabla_V.\forall \Delta^2r^2 \rhd \Delta^1r^1.\forall(k'_1, k_1, k'_2, k_2, (x:\sigma_1)^\top, \Delta^2r^2 \in \nabla_K).\forall(S'_1, S_1, S'_2, S_2, \Delta^2r^2) \in \nabla_S.$ $\llbracket \emptyset; g:\sigma \vdash M' : T\sigma_1 \rrbracket(g \mapsto g'_1)k'_1S'_1 = \top \implies \llbracket \emptyset; g:\sigma \vdash N' : T\sigma_1 \rrbracket(g \mapsto g_2)k_2S_2 = \top$ and $\llbracket \emptyset; g:\sigma \vdash N' : T\sigma_1 \rrbracket(g \mapsto g'_2)k'_2S'_2 = \top \implies \llbracket \emptyset; g:\sigma \vdash M' : T\sigma_1 \rrbracket(g \mapsto g_1)k_1S_1 = \top.$ Here $\sigma = \sigma_1 \to T\text{unit}$, and $\sigma_1 = \text{unit} \to T\text{unit}$.

For the proof of this we define a local parameter $\tilde{r}^3 = (P^3, \emptyset)$ for $P^3 = (\{(S_a, S_b)| \ S_b l_x = in_{\mathbb{Z}} n > 0)\}, A_\emptyset, A_{\{l_x\}})$, where l_x is fresh for $dom(\Delta^2) \cup A_{r^2 2}(S_2)$. Then we have a parameter $\Delta^3 r^3$ where $\Delta^3 = \Delta^2$ and $r^3 = r^2 \cup \{\tilde{r}^3\}$ which we use in the proof.

6   Conclusion

We have presented a local relational proof method for establishing contextual equivalence of expressions in a language with recursive types and general references, building on earlier work of Benton and Leperchey [2]. The proof of existence of the logical relation is fairly intricate because of the interplay between recursive types and local parameters for reasoning about higher-order store. However, the method is easy to use on examples: the only non-trivial steps are to guess the right local parameters — but since the local parameters express the intuitive reason for contextual equivalence, the non-trivial steps are really fairly straightforward. It is possible to extend our method to a language also with impredicative polymorphism; we will report on that on another occasion.

References

1. A. Ahmed. Step-indexed syntactic logical relations for recursive and quantified types. In P. Sestoft, editor, *Programming Languages and Systems. 15th European Symposium on Programming, ESOP 2006*, volume 3924 of *Lecture Notes in Computer Science*, pages 69–83. Springer, 2006.
2. N. Benton and B. Leperchey. Relational reasoning in a nominal semantics for storage. In *Proceedings of the Seventh International Conference on Typed Lambda Calculi and Applications (TLCA'05)*, volume 3461 of *Lecture Notes in Computer Science*. Springer, 2005.
3. L. Birkedal and R. Harper. Constructing interpretations of recursive types in an operational setting. *Information and Computation*, 155:3–63, 1999.
4. V. Koutavas and M. Wand. Bisimulations for untyped imperative objects. In P. Sestoft, editor, *Programming Languages and Systems, 15th European Symposium on Programming, ESOP 2005, Vienna, Austria.*, volume 3924 of *Lecture Notes in Computer Science*. Springer, 2006. to appear.
5. V. Koutavas and M. Wand. Small bisimulations for reasoning about higher-order imperative programs. In *POPL '06: Proceedings of the 33rd ACM SIGPLAN-SIGACT symposium on Principles of Programming Languages*, pages 141–152, New York, NY, USA, 2006. ACM Press.
6. I. A. Mason, S. Smith, and C. L. Talcott. From operational semantics to domain theory. *Information and Computation*, 128(1):26–47, 1996.
7. A. Pitts. Relational properties of domains. *Information and Computation*, 127:66–90, 1996.
8. A. Pitts and I. Stark. Observable properties of higher order functions that dynamically create local names, or: What's new? In *Mathematical Foundations of Computer Science, Proc. 18th Int. Symp., Gdańsk, 1993*, volume 711 of *Lecture Notes in Computer Science*, pages 122–141. Springer-Verlag, Berlin, 1993.

9. U. Reddy and H. Yang. Correctness of data representations involving heap data structures. *Science of Computer Programming*, 50(1-3):129–160, Mar. 2004.

10. J. C. Reynolds. Separation logic: A logic for shared mutable data structures. In *Proc. of the 17th Annual IEEE Symposium on Logic in Computer Science (LICS'02)*, pages 55–74, Copenhagen, Denmark, July 2002. IEEE Press.

11. M. Shinwell. *The Fresh Approach: Functional Programming with Names and Binders*. PhD thesis, Computer Laboratory, Cambridge University, Dec. 2004.

12. M. R. Shinwell and A. M. Pitts. On a monadic semantics for freshness. *Theoretical Computer Science*, 342:28–55, 2005.

13. E. Sumii and B. C. Pierce. A bisimulation for type abstraction and recursion. In *ACM SIGPLAN–SIGACT Symposium on Principles of Programming Languages (POPL), Long Beach, California*, 2005.

Proof Abstraction for Imperative Languages[*]

William L. Harrison

Dept. of Computer Science, University of Missouri,
Columbia, Missouri, USA

Abstract. Modularity in programming language semantics derives from abstracting over the structure of underlying denotations, yielding semantic descriptions that are more abstract and reusable. One such semantic framework is Liang's modular monadic semantics in which the underlying semantic structure is encapsulated with a monad. Such abstraction can be at odds with program verification, however, because program specifications require access to the (deliberately) hidden semantic representation. The techniques for reasoning about modular monadic definitions of imperative programs introduced here overcome this barrier. And, just like program definitions in modular monadic semantics, our program specifications and proofs are representation-independent and hold for whole classes of monads, thereby yielding proofs of great generality.

Keywords: Monads, Monad Transformers, Language Semantics, Program Specification and Verification.

1 Introduction

Modular monadic semantics (MMS) provides a powerful abstraction principle for denotational definitions via the use of monads and monad transformers [13,2,21] and MMS supports a modular, "mix and match" approach to semantic definition. MMS has been successfully applied to a wide variety of programming languages as well as to language compilers [8,6].

What is not well-recognized is the impact that the semantic factorization by monad transformers in MMS has on program specification and verification. Modularity comes with a price! The monad parameter to an MMS definition is a "black box" (i.e., its precise type structure is unknown) and must remain so if program abstraction is to be preserved. Yet, this makes reasoning with MMS language definitions using standard techniques frequently impossible. How does one reason about MMS specifications without sacrificing modularity and reusability? Furthermore, is there a notion of *proof* abstraction for MMS akin to its notion of *program* abstraction? This paper provides answers in the affirmative to these questions for imperative languages.

* This research supported in part by subcontract GPACS0016, System Information Assurance II, through OGI/Oregon Health & Sciences University.

N. Kobayashi (Ed.): APLAS 2006, LNCS 4279, pp. 97–113, 2006.

This paper presents a novel form of specification for reasoning about MMS definitions called *observational program specification* (OPS), as well as related proof techniques useful for proving such specifications. To reason about MMS definitions (which are parameterized by monads), it is necessary to parameterize the specifications themselves by monads as well. This is precisely what OPS does by lifting predicates to the computational level, and we refer to such lifted predicates as *observations*. Both MMS definitions and OPS specifications are parameterized by a monad that hides underlying denotational structure, thereby allowing greater generality in both programs and proofs alike. And just as MMS provides a notion of program abstraction, OPS provides a notion of *proof* abstraction. Observational program specifications and proofs are representation-independent, holding for whole classes of monads, thereby yielding proofs of great generality.

The methodology pursued here is as follows. Axioms characterizing algebraically the behavior of state monads are defined, and it is demonstrated that these axioms are preserved under monad transformer application. Then, a denotational semantics for the simple imperative language with loops is given in terms of state monads. Using OPS and "observation" computations, Hoare's classic programming logic [9] for this language is embedded into its own state-monadic semantics. Furthermore, it is demonstrated that the inference rules of this logic are derivable from the embedding, relying only on the state monad axioms and facts about observations. This provides a notion of proof abstraction for the simple imperative language because proofs in Hoare logic can now be lifted to any monad with state regardless of other effects it encapsulates!

This paper has the following structure. Section 2 motivates OPS, and Section 3 outlines background material necessary to understand this paper, including overviews of monads and monad transformers. In Section 4, the axiomatization of state monads and their preservation properties with respect to monad transformer application are stated and proved. In Section 5, the notion of observations is made precise. Section 6 presents the embedding of Hoare logic, and also the proof of soundness of this embedding. Section 7 compares the present work with related research. Conclusions and future work are outlined in Section 8.

2   Introducing Observational Specifications

As an example, consider the correctness of an imperative construct p! defined in a monad with a state Sto. Generally [26,15], a partial correctness specification of an imperative feature like this would take the form of a relation $\Re$ between input and output states σ_0 and σ_1, so that $\sigma_0 \, \Re \, \sigma_1$ means that the state σ_1 may result from the execution of p! in σ_0. If p! were defined in the single state monad $St\, a = Sto \to a \times Sto$, then the correctness of p! would be written:

$$\forall \sigma_0 : Sto. \ \sigma_0 \, \Re \, (\pi_2(\text{p!} \, \sigma_0)) \tag{1}$$

where π_2 is the second projection function $\lambda(-, x).x$. However, if p! were reinterpreted in the "Environment+State" monad $EnvSt\, a = Env \to Sto \to a \times Sto$, then the above correctness specification would be rewritten as:

$$\forall \rho_0 : Env. \ \forall \sigma_0 : Sto. \ \sigma_0 \, \Re \, (\pi_2(\mathsf{p}! \ \rho_0 \ \sigma_0)) \tag{2}$$

One can see from these two examples that every monad in which p! is interpreted requires a new correctness specification! Because specifications (1) and
(2) rely on the fixed structure of St and EnvSt, respectively, there is no way
of reusing them when p! is reinterpreted in another monad; or in other words,
they are *representation-dependent* specifications. Consequently, each new specification will require a new proof as well. Because state monads may be arbitrarily
complex—consider those in Figure 1—this makes proof abstraction attractive.

How does one develop a notion of *proof* abstraction akin to MMS *program*
abstraction? The key insight here is that, because the language definitions we
use are parameterized by a monad, it is necessary to develop a specification
style that is also parameterized by a monad. The first step is to add a new,
distinguished value type *prop*, denoted by the discrete CPO {tt, ff}. The type
prop must be distinguished from the *Bool* type in languages which have recursive
Bool-valued functions because the denotation of *Bool* in such cases is a pointed
CPO. In the present work, it is sufficient to identify *prop* with *Bool* because the
language considered here does not allow recursion over booleans.

Assume that g is a monadic operator which reads the current *Sto* state. For
example in St, it would simply be $\lambda\sigma.(\sigma, \sigma)$, and it would have a similar definition in EnvSt. Then, the correctness condition $(\sigma_0 \, \Re \, \sigma_1) \in prop$ may then be a
computed value for appropriate stores σ_0 and σ_1:

$$
\begin{array}{ccc}
\mathsf{g} \star \lambda\sigma_0. & & \\
\mathsf{p}! \star \lambda\_. & & \mathsf{p}! \star \lambda\_. \\
\mathsf{g} \star \lambda\sigma_1. & = & \eta(\mathsf{tt}) \\
\eta(\sigma_0 \, \Re \, \sigma_1) & &
\end{array}
\tag{3}
$$

What does this equation mean? Examining the left-hand side of Equation 3, the
execution of p! is couched between two calls to g, of which the first call returns
the input store σ_0 and the second call returns the output store σ_1 resulting
from executing p!. Note that σ_1 will reflect any updates to the store made by
p!. Finally, the truth-value of the *prop* expression $(\sigma_0 \, \Re \, \sigma_1)$ is returned. The
right-hand side of Equation 3 executes p! and then always returns tt. Observe
also that it was necessary to execute p! on the right-hand side so that identical
effects (e.g., store updates and non-termination) would occur on both sides of
the equation. Equation 3 requires that $(\sigma_0 \, \Re \, \sigma_1)$ be tt for all input and output
stores σ_0 and σ_1, respectively, which is precisely what we want.

Equation 3 is a representation-*independent* specification of p!. In the single
store monad St, it means precisely the same thing as (1), while in the monad
EnvSt, (3) means exactly the same thing as (2). In fact, Equation 3 makes sense
in any monad where p! makes sense—consider the state monads in Figure 1.
Such monads are called *state* monads—a notion made precise in Section 4. It
is called an *observational* specification because the left-hand side of (3) gathers
certain data from different stages in the computation (i.e., stores σ_0 and σ_1) and
"observes" whether or not $(\sigma_0 \, \Re \, \sigma_1)$ holds.

$M_0\alpha = Sto \to \alpha \times Sto$

$M_1\alpha = e_1 \to (s_1 \to (s_2 \to (Sto \to ((((\alpha \times s_1) \times s_2) \times Sto) + err_1)))))$

$M_2\alpha = e_1 \to ((\alpha \to (Sto \to ((ans_1 \times Sto) + err_1))) \to (Sto \to ((ans_1 \times Sto) + err_1)))$

$M_3\alpha = e_1 \to (e_2 \to$
$\qquad ((\alpha \to ((ans_1 \to (Sto \to (((ans_2 \times Sto) + err_1) + err_2)))$
$\qquad\qquad \to (Sto \to (((ans_2 \times Sto) + err_1) + err_2))))$
$\qquad\qquad\qquad \to ((ans_1 \to (Sto \to (((ans_2 \times Sto) + err_1) + err_2)))$
$\qquad\qquad\qquad\qquad \to (Sto \to (((ans_2 \times Sto) + err_1) + err_2)))))$

$$\vdots$$

Fig. 1. State Monads on store Sto may be arbitrarily complex, complicating "brute force" induction on their types. Each of these monads may be created through applications of the state, environment, CPS, and error monad transformers (see Figure 2).

3 Background

This section outlines the background material necessary to understand the present work. Due to space constraints, we must assume of necessity that the reader is familiar with monads. Below we present a brief overview of monad transformers and modular monadic semantics and discuss how program modularity and abstraction arise within MMS language specifications.

Monads, Monad Transformers and Liftings. This section provides a brief overview and readers requiring more background should consult the related work (especially, Liang et al. [14]).

A structure $(M, \eta, \star)$ is a *monad* if, and only if, M is a type constructor (functor) with associated operations *bind* $(\star : M\alpha \to (\alpha \to M\beta) \to M\beta)$ and *unit* $(\eta : \alpha \to M\alpha)$ obeying the well-known "monad laws" [14]:

$$(\eta\, a) \star k = k\, a \qquad \text{(left unit)}$$
$$x \star \eta = x \qquad \text{(right unit)}$$
$$x \star (\lambda a.(k\, a \star h)) = (x \star k) \star h \qquad \text{(assoc)}$$

Given two monads, M and M', it is natural to ask if their composition, $M \circ M'$, is also a monad, but it is well-known that monads generally do not compose in this simple manner [2]. However, *monad transformers* do provide a form of monad composition [2,14,21]. When applied to a monad M, a monad transformer T creates a new monad M'. For example, the state monad transformer, (StateT s), is shown in Figure 2. (Here, the s is a type argument, which can be replaced by any type which is to be "threaded" through the computation.) Note that (StateT s Id) is identical to the state monad (St $a = s \to a \times s$). The state monad transformer also provides *update* u and *get* g operations to update and read, respectively, the new state in the "larger" monad. Figure 2 also presents (the endofunction parts of) three other commonly-used monad transformers: *environments* EnvT, *continuation-passing* ContT, and *exceptions* ErrorT. The monad

---

State Monad Transformer (StateT s)	Environment Transformer (EnvTe)

$S\alpha = $ StateT s M $\alpha = s \to $ M$(\alpha \times s)$

$\eta_S : \alpha \to S\alpha$
$\eta_S\, x = \lambda\sigma.\,\eta_M(x, \sigma)$

$(\star_S) : (S\alpha) \to (\alpha \to S\beta) \to (S\beta)$
$x \star_S f = \lambda\sigma_0.\,(x\,\sigma_0) \star_M (\lambda(a,\sigma_1).f\,a\,\sigma_1)$

$\mathrm{lift}_S : M\alpha \to S\alpha$
$\mathrm{lift}_S\, x = \lambda\sigma.\,x \star_M \lambda y.\,\eta_M(y, \sigma)$

$u : (s \to s) \to S()$
$u(\Delta : s \to s) = \lambda\sigma.\,\eta_M((), \Delta\,\sigma)$

$g : Ss$
$g = \lambda\sigma.\,\eta_M(\sigma, \sigma)$

$E\alpha\ =\ $EnvT e M $\alpha\ =\ e \to M\,\alpha$
$\mathrm{lift}_E\, x\ =\ \lambda\,(\rho : e).\,x$
rdEnv $:\ E\,e$
rdEnv $=\ \lambda\,(\rho : e).\,\eta_M\,\rho$
inEnv $:\ e \to E\alpha \to E\alpha$
inEnv $\rho\,\varphi\ =\ \lambda\,(\_ : e).\,\varphi\,\rho$

CPS Transformer (ContT ans)

$C\alpha\ =\ $ContT ans M α
$\qquad =\ (\alpha \to M\ ans) \to M\ ans$
$\mathrm{lift}_C\, x\ =\ (x \star_M)$

Error Transformer (ErrorT err)

Err $\alpha\ =\ $ErrorT err M $\alpha\ =\ M\alpha\ +\ err$
$\mathrm{lift}_{Err}\, x\ =\ x \star_M \lambda\,v.\,\eta_M(\mathrm{inj}_l v)$

Fig. 2. Examples of Monad Transformers: state (left); environment, cps and error (right) monad transformers

laws are preserved by monad transformers [13,2]. Please see Liang et al. [14] for further details.

Observe that, if M has operators defined by earlier monad transformer applications, then those operators must be redefined for the "larger" monad (T M). This is known as *lifting* the operators through T. Lifting is the main technical issue in [2,14]; it is related to, but should not be confused with, the lift operators in Figure 2). For each monad transformer T presented in Figure 2, the liftings of the update and get operators from M to (T M) are $(\mathrm{lift}_T \circ u)$ and $(\mathrm{lift}_T\, g)$.

The Lifting Laws capture the behavior of the lift function [14] associated with a monad transformer. Liang's definition of monad transformer requires that a lift function obeying the Lifting Laws be defined and, in his thesis[13], he defines lift operators for a wide range of monad transformers (including those in Figure 2) and verifies the Lifting Laws for them.

Definition 1 (Lifting Laws). *For monad transformer t, and monad m:* lift $\circ$ $\eta_m = \eta_{tm}$ *and* $\mathrm{lift}(x \star_m f) = (\mathrm{lift}\, x) \star_{tm} (\mathrm{lift} \circ f)$.

Modular Monadic Semantics & Program Abstraction. The principal advantage of the MMS approach to language definition is that the underlying denotational *model* can be arbitrarily complex without complicating the denotational *description* unnecessarily—what we have referred to earlier as separability. The beauty of MMS is that the equations defining $[\![t]\!]$ can be reinterpreted in a variety of monads M. To borrow a term from the language of abstract data types, the monadic semantics of programming languages yields *representation-independent* definitions. This is what prompts some authors (notably Espinosa [2]) to refer to MMS as the "ADT approach to language definition."

Functional	Modular Monadic
$\mathcal{F}[\![t]\!] : Int$	$\mathcal{M}[\![t]\!] : \mathsf{Id}\ Int$
$\mathcal{F}[\![i]\!] = i$	$\mathcal{M}[\![i]\!] = \eta(i)$
$\mathcal{F}[\![-e]\!] = -\mathcal{F}[\![e]\!]$	$\mathcal{M}[\![-e]\!] = \mathcal{M}[\![e]\!] \star \lambda v.\eta(-v)$
$\mathcal{F}[\![t]\!] : Sto \to Int \times Sto$	$\mathcal{M}[\![t]\!] : \mathsf{St}\ Int$
$\mathcal{F}[\![i]\!]\sigma = (i,\sigma)$	$\mathcal{M}[\![i]\!] = \eta(i)$
$\mathcal{F}[\![-e]\!]\sigma = \mathrm{let}\ (v,\sigma') = \mathcal{F}[\![e]\!]\sigma$ $\mathrm{in}\ (-v,\sigma')$	$\mathcal{M}[\![-e]\!] = \mathcal{M}[\![e]\!] \star \lambda v.\eta(-v)$

Fig. 3. Program Abstraction via Modular Monadic Semantics. When the functional definition (left column, top row) is re-interpreted in a different type (left column, bottom row), the text of its definition changes radically. In the MMS setting (right column), no such change is required.

Let us consider standard functional-style language definitions and why they are representation-dependent. Consider the left column in Figure 3; it gives functional-style definitions for a simple expression language *Exp* with constants and negation. Note that the two functional semantics, $\mathcal{F}[\![-]\!]$, are defined in two settings corresponding to the identity and state monads. Both definitions of $\mathcal{F}[\![-]\!]$ are very representation-dependent—the very text of the definitions must be completely rewritten when the semantic setting changes. In contrast, MMS semantic equations ($\mathcal{M}[\![-]\!]$ in the right column of Figure 3) are free from the details of the underlying denotation because the monadic unit and bind operations handle any extra computational "stuff" (stores, environments, continuations, etc.). Since negation does not use any of this data, the same equations for $\mathcal{M}[\![-]\!]$ define *Exp* for all monads!

4 State Monads and Their Axiomatization

State monads are monads that capture the notion of computation associated with imperative programs. This section introduces the axiomatization for state monads. First, the appropriate signature is defined (state monad structures), and then the state monad axioms are given as equations on this signature. Theorem 1 shows how state monads may be created, and Theorem 2 demonstrates that any monad transformer (according to Liang's definition [14,13]) preserves imperative behavior. Lemma 1 provides a convenient generalization of the state monad axioms.

State Monad Structure. The quintuple $(\mathsf{M},\eta,\star,\mathsf{u},\mathsf{g},\tau)$ is a *state monad structure* when: $(\mathsf{M},\eta,\star)$ is a monad with operations unit $\eta : \alpha \to \mathsf{M}\alpha$ and bind $\star : \mathsf{M}\alpha \to (\alpha \to \mathsf{M}\beta) \to \mathsf{M}\beta$, and additional operations on τ update $\mathsf{u} : (\tau \to \tau) \to \mathsf{M}()$ and get $\mathsf{g} : \mathsf{M}\tau$. We will refer to a state monad structure $(\mathsf{M},\eta,\star,\mathsf{u},\mathsf{g},\tau)$ simply as M if the associated operations and state type τ are clear from context. Please note that a single monad $(M, \eta, \star)$ may have multiple state effects, each corresponding to multiple state monad structures.

State Monad Axiomatization. Let $M = (M, \eta, \star, u, g, \tau)$ be a state monad structure. M is a *state monad* if the following equations hold for any $f, g : \tau \to \tau$,

$$u\,f \star \lambda\_.u\,g = u\,(g \circ f) \qquad \text{(sequencing)}$$
$$g \star \lambda\sigma_0.g \star \lambda\sigma_1.\eta(\sigma_0, \sigma_1) = g \star \lambda\sigma.\eta(\sigma, \sigma) \qquad \text{(get-get)}$$
$$g \star \lambda\sigma_0.u\,f \star \lambda\_.g \star \lambda\sigma_1.\eta(\sigma_0, \sigma_1) = g \star \lambda\sigma.u\,f \star \lambda\_.\eta(\sigma, f\sigma) \quad \text{(get-update-get)}$$

Axiom (sequencing) shows how updating by f and then updating by g is the same as just updating by their composition $(g \circ f)$. Axiom (get-get) requires that performing two g operations in succession retrieves precisely the same value. Axiom (get-update-get) states that retrieving the state before and after updating with f is the same as retrieving the state before and applying f directly.

Theorem 1 shows that a state monad may be created from any monad through the application of the state monad transformer. Theorem 2 shows that the monad resulting from a monad transformer application to a state monad (i.e., one obeying the state monad axioms) will also obey the state monad axioms. Proofs of both theorems appear in [7].

Theorem 1 (StateT creates a state monad). *For any monad M, let monad $M' = \text{StateT } sto\,M$ and also $u : (sto \to sto) \to M'()$ and $g : M'sto$ be the nonproper morphisms added by $(\text{StateT } sto)$. Then $(M', \eta_{M'}, \star_{M'}, u, g, sto)$ is a state monad.*

Theorem 2 (Monad transformers preserve stateful behavior). *For any state monad $M = (M, \eta, \star, u, g, sto)$ and monad transformer T (see Figure 2), the following state monad structure is a state monad:*

$$(T\,M, \eta', \star', (\text{lift} \circ u), \text{lift}(g))$$

where η', $\star'$, and lift *are the monadic unit, bind, and lifting operations, respectively, defined by T.*

Lemma 1 states a number of properties of the g and u morphisms which will be useful later in the case study of Section 6.

Lemma 1. *Let $(M, \star, \eta, u, g, \tau)$ be a state monad and* getloc(x) $= g \star \lambda\sigma.\eta(\sigma\,x)$ *(*getloc(x) *reads location x). For any $\mathcal{F} : \tau \times \tau \to Ma$ and $\Delta : \tau \to \tau$:*

$$g \star \lambda\sigma.g \star \lambda\sigma'.\mathcal{F}(\sigma, \sigma') = g \star \lambda\sigma.g \star \lambda\sigma'.\mathcal{F}(\sigma, \sigma) \qquad \text{(a)}$$
$$g \star \lambda\sigma.u\Delta \star \lambda\_.g \star \lambda\sigma'.\mathcal{F}(\sigma, \sigma') = g \star \lambda\sigma.u\Delta \star \lambda\_.\mathcal{F}(\sigma, \Delta\sigma) \qquad \text{(b)}$$
$$u[x \mapsto v] \star \lambda\_.\text{getloc}(x) = u[x \mapsto v] \star \lambda\_.\eta(v) \qquad \text{(c)}$$

5   Formalizing Observations

An *observation* is a computation which reads (and only reads!) data such as states and environments, and then observes the truth or falsity of a relation. With OPS, one inserts observations within a computation to capture information about its state or progress. In this way, they are rather reminiscent of the pre- and post-conditions of Hoare semantics, and we formalize this intuition below in Section 6. This section investigates the properties that must hold of a computation for it to be considered an observation.

Obviously, observations must manifest no observable effects (e.g., changing states, throwing exceptions, or calling continuations) or else they will affect the computation being specified. This property—called *innocence*—requires that the outcome of the computation being specified must be the same with or without interspersed observations and is defined below. Secondly, observing a relation twice in succession must yield the same truth value as observing a relation just once; this property is called *idempotence* below. Finally, the order in which two successive observations should be irrelevant. This property is called *non-interference* below.

An M-computation φ is *innocent*, if, and only if, for all M-computations γ,

$$\varphi \star \lambda_{-}. \gamma = \gamma \star \lambda v. \varphi \star \lambda_{-}. \eta\, v = \gamma$$

This says that the effects manifested by φ are irrelevant to γ and may be discarded. Computations φ and γ are *non-interfering* (written $\varphi \,\#\, \gamma$) means:

$$\varphi \star \lambda v.\gamma \star \lambda w.\eta(v, w) = \gamma \star \lambda w.\varphi \star \lambda v.\eta(v, w)$$

If $\varphi \# \gamma$, then their order is of no consequence. The relation $\#$ is clearly symmetric. Lastly, a computation φ is *idempotent* if, and only if,

$$\varphi \star \lambda v.\varphi \star \lambda w.\eta(v, w) = \varphi \star \lambda w.\eta(w, w)$$

That is, successive φ are identical to a single φ. The following lemma shows that idempotence may be used in a more general setting. A similar result for non-interference (not shown) holds by similar reasoning.

Lemma 2. *If $\varphi : \mathsf{M}\alpha$ is idempotent and $f : \alpha \times \alpha \to \mathsf{M}\beta$, then*

$$\varphi \star \lambda v.\varphi \star \lambda w.f(v, w) = \varphi \star \lambda w.f(w, w)$$

Proof. Applying the function "$\star f$" to both sides of the idempotence definition and using the associative and left-unit monad laws yields:

$$\begin{aligned}(\varphi \star \lambda v.\varphi \star \lambda w.\eta(v, w)) \star f &= \varphi \star \lambda v.\varphi \star \lambda w.(\eta(v, w) \star f) \\ &= \varphi \star \lambda v.\varphi \star \lambda w.f(v, w) \\ (\varphi \star \lambda w.\eta(w, w)) \star f &= \varphi \star \lambda w.(\eta(w, w) \star f) \\ &= \varphi \star \lambda w.f(w, w)\end{aligned}$$

$\square$

Notice that stateful computation can easily lose innocence:

$$\mathsf{g} \neq \mathsf{u}[\lambda l.l + 1] \star \lambda_{-}.\mathsf{g}, \text{ and } \mathsf{g} \neq \mathsf{g} \star \lambda\sigma.\mathsf{u}[\lambda l.l + 1] \star \lambda_{-}.\eta(\sigma)$$

Continuation-manipulating computations like `callcc` (*"call with current continuation"*) can also lose innocence, because they can jump to an arbitrary continuation κ_0:

$$\eta(5) \neq \eta(5) \star \lambda v.(\texttt{callcc } \lambda\kappa.\kappa_0 7) \star \lambda\_.\eta(v)$$

If Ω produces an error or is non-terminating, then it is not innocent:

$$\eta(5) \neq \eta(5) \star \lambda v.\Omega \star \lambda\_.\eta(v) = \Omega,$$

Examples of innocent computations. Some computations are always innocent. For example, any computation constructed from an environment monad's "read" operators (e.g., rdEnv), an environment monad's "in" operators (e.g., inEnv, assuming its argument are innocent), or from the "get" operators of a state monad (e.g., g) are always innocent. Unit computations (such as $\eta(x)$, for any x) are also always innocent. Knowing that a computation is innocent is useful in the proofs developed below, not only because an innocent computation commutes with any other computation, but because it can be also be added to any computation without effect. That is, for any arbitrary computations φ_1, φ_2 and innocent computation Υ,

$$\varphi_1 \star \lambda v.\varphi_2 = \Upsilon \star \lambda x.\varphi_1 \star \lambda v.(\Upsilon \star \lambda y.\varphi_2)$$

The values x and y computed by Υ can be used as snapshots to characterize the "before" and "after" behavior of φ_1 just as the states σ_0 and σ_1 computed by g were used in Equation 3.

Are innocent computations "pure"? A similar, but less general, notion to innocence is *purity* (attributed sometimes, apparently erroneously [18], to Moggi although the origins of the term are unclear). An M-computation φ is *pure* if, and only if, $\exists v.\varphi = \eta_M(v)$. An innocent computation may be seen as "pure in any context." Consider the (innocent, but not pure) computation g. It is not the case that $\exists v.g = \eta_M(v)$, because g will return a different state depending on the context in which it occurs.

Three operations are used with observations. The first of these, ITE : M *prop* $\times$ $M(\tau) \times M(\tau) \to M(\tau)$, defines an observational version of if-then-else, while the last two, AND, $\Rightarrow$: M($prop$)$\times$M($prop$)$\to$M($prop$), are computational liftings of propositional connectives. These functions are defined as:

$$\text{ITE}(\theta, u, v) = \theta \star \lambda test.\text{if } test \text{ then } u \text{ else } v$$
$$\theta_1 \text{ AND } \theta_2 = \theta_1 \star \lambda p_1.\theta_2 \star \lambda p_2.\eta(p_1 \wedge p_2)$$
$$\theta_1 \Rightarrow \theta_2 = \theta_1 \star \lambda p_1.\theta_2 \star \lambda p_2.\eta(p_1 \supset p_2)$$

Here, $\wedge$, $\neg$, and $\supset$ are the ordinary propositional connectives on *prop* with the usual truth table definitions. The AND connective could be written using "short-circuit" evaluation so that it would not evaluate its second argument when the first produces ff. However, AND is intended to be applied only to innocent computations and its "termination behavior" on that restricted domain is identical to a short-circuiting definition. Lemma 3 is a property of ITE used in Section 6.

Lemma 3. $\text{ITE}(\theta, x, y) \star f = \text{ITE}(\theta, x \star f, y \star f)$ *for* $\theta : \mathsf{M}\,prop.$

Proof of Lemma 3.

$$
\begin{aligned}
\text{ITE}(\theta, x, y) \star f &= (\theta \star \lambda\beta.\ \text{if } \beta \text{ then } x \text{ else } y) \star f \\
&= \theta \star (\lambda\beta.(\text{if } \beta \text{ then } x \text{ else } y) \star f) \\
&= \theta \star (\lambda\beta.\ \text{if } \beta \text{ then } x \star f \text{ else } y \star f) \\
&= \text{ITE}(\theta, x \star f, y \star f)
\end{aligned}
$$

$\square$

6   A Case Study in OPS: Hoare Logic Embedding

In this section, we show how OPS may be used to derive a programming logic for the simple imperative language with loops from its state-monadic denotational semantics. The programming logic developed here is the familiar axiomatic semantics of Hoare [9]. The soundness of the derived logic relies entirely on properties of monads and the state monad transformer; specifically, these are the state monad creation and preservation theorems (Theorems 1 and 2). These properties are key to the proof abstraction technique presented in this paper because they allow the logic to be interpreted soundly in *any* layered monad constructed with the state monad transformer.

First, we provide an overview of the syntax, semantics, and programming logic for simple imperative language with loops. Then, we develop the embedding of Hoare logic within OPS, and here is the first use of observations to model assertions (e.g., $\{x = 0\}$). The main result, Theorem 3, states that the rules of Hoare logic may be derived from the observational embedding of Hoare triples within any state-monadic semantics $[\![-]\!]$.

Syntax, Semantics, & Logic of the While Language. Figure 4 presents the syntax of the while language $\mathcal{L}$ and its programming logic. In most respects, it is entirely conventional, and it is expected that the reader has seen such definitions many times. Hoare's original logic [9], which is considered here, has a simple assertion logic, amounting to a quantifier-free logic with a single predicate $\leq$. For the sake of simplicity, we identify boolean expressions with assertions, and place them in the same syntactic class $\mathcal{B}$.

Figure 5 presents an MMS definition for $\mathcal{L}$ defined for any state monad. It is entirely conventional, except that the meaning of booleans is defined in terms of the observational embedding of assertions. The assertion embedding $\lceil - \rceil$ is the usual definition of boolean expressions.

Innocence, Non-interference, & Idempotence of $[\![e]\!]$ and $\lceil P \rceil$. It is necessary to demonstrate that the derivation of Hoare logic (presented below) is sound and the proof of this (in Theorem 3) relies on the interaction properties from Section 5 (namely, innocence, non-interference, and idempotence) hold for the assertion embedding and expression semantics of Figure 5; Lemma 4 shows just that.

(Values)	$\mathcal{V} = () + Int + prop$
(Language)	$\mathcal{L} ::= \mathcal{C} \mid \mathcal{E} \mid \mathcal{B}$
(Assertions)	$\mathcal{B} ::= \mathbf{true} \mid \mathbf{false} \mid \mathcal{E} \, \mathbf{leq} \, \mathcal{E} \mid \mathcal{B} \, \mathbf{and} \, \mathcal{B} \mid \mathbf{not} \, \mathcal{B}$
(Expressions)	$e \in \mathcal{E} ::= Var \mid Int \mid -\mathcal{E} \mid \mathcal{E}+\mathcal{E}$
(Commands)	$c \in \mathcal{C} ::= \mathbf{skip} \mid Var\!:=\!\mathcal{E} \mid \mathcal{C} \; ; \; \mathcal{C} \mid \mathbf{if} \; \mathcal{B} \; \mathbf{then} \; \mathcal{C} \; \mathbf{else} \; \mathcal{C} \mid \mathbf{while} \; \mathcal{B} \; \mathbf{do} \; \mathcal{C}$
(Triples)	$\mathcal{T} ::= \{\mathcal{B}\} \, \mathcal{C} \, \{\mathcal{B}\}$

$$\frac{}{\{P\} \; \mathbf{skip} \; \{P\}} \; \text{(Skip)}$$

$$\frac{\{P \, \mathbf{and} \, b\} \; c_1 \; \{Q\} \quad \{P \, \mathbf{and} \, (\mathbf{not} \, b)\} \; c_2 \; \{Q\}}{\{P\} \; \mathbf{if} \; b \; \mathbf{then} \; c_1 \; \mathbf{else} \; c_2 \; \{Q\}} \; \text{(Cond)}$$

$$\frac{}{\{P[x/e]\} \; x\!:=\!e \; \{P\}} \; \text{(Assign)}$$

$$\frac{\{P\} \; c_1 \; \{Q\} \quad \{Q\} \; c_2 \; \{R\}}{\{P\} \; c_1 \; ; \; c_2 \; \{R\}} \; \text{(Seq)}$$

$$\frac{\{P \, \mathbf{and} \, b\} \; c \; \{P\}}{\{P\} \; \mathbf{while} \; b \; \mathbf{do} \; c \; \{P \, \mathbf{and} \, (\mathbf{not} \, b)\}} \; \text{(Iter)}$$

$$\frac{P' \supset P \quad \{P\} \, c \, \{Q\} \quad Q \supset Q'}{\{P'\} \, c \, \{Q'\}} \; \text{(Weaken)}$$

Fig. 4. Abstract Syntax & Inference rules for Simple Imperative Language. Lower case latin letters e and c typically refer to expressions and commands, respectively.

Lemma 4. *Let* $e, e' \in \mathcal{E}$ *and* $P, P' \in \mathcal{B}$. *Then,* $[\![e]\!]$ *and* $\lceil P \rceil$ *are innocent and idempotent, and* $[\![e]\!]\#[\![e']\!]$, $[\![e]\!]\#\lceil P \rceil$, *and* $\lceil P \rceil\#\lceil P' \rceil$.

Lemma 4 follows directly from Axiom (get-get) by straightforward structural induction on the structure of terms.

Embedding Hoare Logic within Monadic Semantics. This section describes how Hoare logic may be interpreted within the state-monadic semantics of Figure 5. First, triples (i.e., "$\{P\} \, c \, \{Q\}$") are interpreted as particular computations, and then their satisfaction is defined as particular equations between computations. We extend the assertion embedding to triples so that:

$$\lceil \{P\} \, c \, \{Q\} \rceil = \lceil P \rceil \star \lambda pre.[\![c]\!] \star \lambda\_.\lceil Q \rceil \star \lambda post.\eta(pre \supset post)$$

Triple satisfaction, written "$\models \{P\} \, c \, \{Q\}$," is defined when:

$$\lceil \{P\} \, c \, \{Q\} \rceil = [\![c]\!] \star \lambda\_.\eta(\mathsf{tt})$$

We also define the satisfaction of an implication "$\models P \supset Q$" as the following equation:

$$(\lceil P \rceil \Rightarrow \lceil Q \rceil) = \eta(\mathsf{tt})$$

We now have the tools to derive the inference rules from Figure 4 from the semantics in Figure 5. Each hypothesis and conclusion gives rise to an interpretation in the semantics via the satisfaction predicate $\models \{P\} \, c \, \{Q\}$ and the observational implication $\Rightarrow$ from Section 5. Soundness for the Hoare logic embedding is what one would expect: an inference rule from Figure 4 with hypotheses $\{hyp_0, \ldots, hyp_n\}$ and conclusion c is *observationally sound* with respect to a state monad semantics, if, whenever each $\models hyp_i$ holds, so does $\models c$.

Assertion Embedding:

$\lceil - \rceil : \mathcal{B} \to M(prop)$ $\lceil e_1 \, \mathbf{leq} \, e_2 \rceil = [\![e_1]\!] \star \lambda v_1.[\![e_2]\!] \star \lambda v_2.\eta(v_1 \leq v_2)$

$\lceil \mathbf{true} \rceil = \eta(\mathbf{tt})$ $\lceil \mathbf{not} \, b \rceil = \lceil b \rceil \star \lambda \beta.\eta(\neg\beta)$

$\lceil \mathbf{false} \rceil = \eta(\mathbf{ff})$ $\lceil b_1 \, \mathbf{and} \, b_2 \rceil = \lceil b_1 \rceil \, \text{AND} \, \lceil b_2 \rceil$

State-monadic Semantics:

$[\![-]\!] : \mathcal{L} \to M\mathcal{V}$ $[\![-e]\!] = [\![e]\!] \star \lambda v.\eta(-v)$

$[\![i]\!] = \eta i$ $[\![e_0 + e_1]\!] = [\![e_0]\!] \star \lambda v_0.[\![e_1]\!] \star \lambda v_1.\eta(v_0 + v_1)$

$[\![x]\!] = \mathbf{getloc}(x)$ $[\![\mathbf{skip}]\!] = \eta\,()$

$[\![b]\!] = \lceil b \rceil$ $[\![c_1 \, ; \, c_2]\!] = [\![c_1]\!] \star \lambda\_.[\![c_2]\!]$

                   $[\![x := e]\!] = [\![e]\!] \star \lambda v.\mathsf{u}[x \mapsto v]$

$[\![\mathbf{if} \, b \, \mathbf{then} \, c_1 \, \mathbf{else} \, c_2]\!] = [\![b]\!] \star \lambda\beta.\mathbf{if} \, \beta \, \mathbf{then} \, [\![c_1]\!] \, \mathbf{else} \, [\![c_2]\!]$

$[\![\mathbf{while} \, b \, \mathbf{do} \, c]\!] = \mathrm{fix}(\mathrm{unwind} \, [\![b]\!] \, [\![c]\!])$

$\mathrm{unwind} : Mprop \to M() \to M() \to M()$

$\mathrm{unwind} \, \gamma_b \, \gamma_c \, \varphi = \gamma_b \star \lambda\beta.\mathbf{if} \, \beta \, \mathbf{then} \, (\gamma_c \star \lambda\_.\varphi) \, \mathbf{else} \, \eta()$

Fig. 5. Assertion Embedding $\lceil - \rceil$ and State-monadic Semantics $[\![-]\!]$ of $\mathcal{L}$. Both the embedding and semantics are defined for *any* state monad $(M, \eta, \star, \mathsf{u}, \mathsf{g}, Var \to Int)$.

Lemma 5 is a substitution lemma for assertions. Below in the statement of Lemma 5, we distinguish numbers from numerals with an underscore "_"; that is, $\underline{v} \in \mathcal{E}$ is the numeral corresponding to the number v. Lemma 5 follows by straightforward structural induction.

Lemma 5 (Substitution Lemma for Assertions). *For expression $e \in \mathcal{E}$, assertion $P \in \mathcal{B}$, and function $f : Int \to prop \to M\alpha$,*

$$[\![e]\!] \star \lambda v.\lceil P[x/e] \rceil \star (f \, v) = [\![e]\!] \star \lambda v.\lceil P[x/\underline{v}] \rceil \star (f \, v) \tag{a}$$

$$\mathsf{u}[x \mapsto v] \star \lambda\_.\lceil P \rceil = \lceil P[x/\underline{v}] \rceil \star \lambda cond.\mathsf{u}[x \mapsto v] \star \lambda\_.\eta(cond) \tag{b}$$

Derivation of Inference Rules. This section states the observational soundness of the Hoare logic embedding presented above in Theorem 3 and presents part of its proof.

Theorem 3 ($\lceil - \rceil$ is observationally sound). *The inference rules of Hoare logic are observationally sound with respect to any state-monadic semantics $[\![-]\!] : \mathcal{L} \to M\mathcal{V}$.*

The proof of Theorem 3 proceeds by structural induction on the inference rules using straightforward equational reasoning. Each case in the proof depends on properties of effects developed above; namely, these are innocence, idempotence and non-interference. The cases for the Skip, Assign and Weaken rules are presented below. The cases for Seq and Cond are similar to those below while the Iter rule follows by fixed-point induction; lack of space prohibits presentation of their proofs here.

Case: Skip Rule.

$$\lceil \{P\} \text{ skip } \{P\} \rceil$$
$$= \lceil P \rceil \star \lambda pre. \llbracket \text{skip} \rrbracket \star \lambda \_. \lceil P \rceil \star \lambda post. \eta(pre \supset post)$$

{ defn. $\llbracket \text{skip} \rrbracket$ }
$$= \lceil P \rceil \star \lambda pre. \eta() \star \lambda \_. \lceil P \rceil \star \lambda post. \eta(pre \supset post)$$

{ innocence of $\eta()$ }
$$= \lceil P \rceil \star \lambda pre. \lceil P \rceil \star \lambda post. \eta(pre \supset post)$$

{ $\lceil P \rceil$ is idempotent, Lemma 4 }
$$= \lceil P \rceil \star \lambda p. \eta(p \supset p)$$

{ logically valid }
$$= \lceil P \rceil \star \lambda p. \eta \, \text{tt}$$

{ innocence of $\lceil P \rceil$ & $\eta()$ }
$$= \eta() \star \lambda \_. \eta \, \text{tt} = \llbracket \text{skip} \rrbracket \star \lambda \_. \eta \text{tt}$$

Case: Assign Rule.

$$\lceil \{P[x/e]\} \; x := e \; \{P\} \rceil$$
$$= \lceil P[x/e] \rceil \star \lambda pre. \llbracket x := e \rrbracket \star \lambda \_. \lceil P \rceil \star \lambda post. \eta(pre \supset post)$$

{ $defn. \; \llbracket x := e \rrbracket$ }
$$= \lceil P[x/e] \rceil \star \lambda pre. \llbracket e \rrbracket \star \lambda v. \mathsf{u}[x \mapsto v] \star \lambda \_. \lceil P \rceil \star \lambda post. \eta(pre \supset post)$$

{ $\llbracket e \rrbracket \# \lceil P \rceil$, Lemma 4 }
$$= \llbracket e \rrbracket \star \lambda v. \lceil P[x/e] \rceil \star \lambda pre. \mathsf{u}[x \mapsto v] \star \lambda \_. \lceil P \rceil \star \lambda post. \eta(pre \supset post)$$

{ $Lemma \; 5(a)$ }
$$= \llbracket e \rrbracket \star \lambda v. \lceil P[x/\underline{v}] \rceil \star \lambda pre. \mathsf{u}[x \mapsto v] \star \lambda \_. \lceil P \rceil \star \lambda post. \eta(pre \supset post)$$

{ $Lemma \; 5(b)$ }
$$= \llbracket e \rrbracket \star \lambda v. \lceil P[x/\underline{v}] \rceil \star \lambda pre. \lceil P[x/\underline{v}] \rceil \star \lambda post. \mathsf{u}[x \mapsto v] \star \lambda \_. \eta(pre \supset post)$$

{ idempotence of $\lceil P[x/\underline{v}] \rceil$, Lemma 4 }
$$= \llbracket e \rrbracket \star \lambda v. \lceil P[x/\underline{v}] \rceil \star \lambda post. \mathsf{u}[x \mapsto v] \star \lambda \_. \eta(post \supset post)$$

{ logical validity }
$$= \llbracket e \rrbracket \star \lambda v. \lceil P[x/\underline{v}] \rceil \star \lambda post. \mathsf{u}[x \mapsto v] \star \lambda \_. \eta(\text{tt})$$

{ innocence of $\lceil P[x/\underline{v}] \rceil$, Lemma 4 }
$$= \llbracket e \rrbracket \star \lambda v. \mathsf{u}[x \mapsto v] \star \lambda \_. \eta(\text{tt})$$
$$= \llbracket x := e \rrbracket \star \lambda \_. \eta(\text{tt})$$

Case: Weakening Rule. Assume $S \Rightarrow P$ and $\models \{P\} \, c \, \{Q\}$.
To show: $\models \{S\} \, c \, \{Q\}$. Rewriting the hypotheses of the inference rule in observational form:

$$\lceil S \rceil \star \lambda s. \lceil P \rceil \star \lambda p. \eta(s \supset p) = \eta(\text{tt})$$
$$\lceil P \rceil \star \lambda p. \llbracket c \rrbracket \star \lambda \_. \lceil Q \rceil \star \lambda q. \eta(p \supset q) = \llbracket c \rrbracket \star \lambda \_. \eta(\text{tt})$$

From the innocence of S and because $(\text{tt} \wedge x) \equiv x$:

$$\lceil S \rceil \star \lambda s. \lceil P \rceil \star \lambda p. \llbracket c \rrbracket \star \lambda \_. \lceil Q \rceil \star \lambda q. \eta(s \supset p \wedge p \supset q) = \llbracket c \rrbracket \star \lambda \_. \eta(\text{tt})$$

Since $(s \supset p \wedge p \supset q) = \text{tt}$ and $(s \supset p \wedge p \supset q) \supset (s \supset q)$:

$$\lceil S \rceil \star \lambda s. \lceil P \rceil \star \lambda p. \llbracket c \rrbracket \star \lambda \_. \lceil Q \rceil \star \lambda q. \eta(s \supset q) = \llbracket c \rrbracket \star \lambda \_. \eta(\text{tt})$$

By the innocence of $\lceil P \rceil$ (and because "p" is a dummy variable like "$\_$"):

$$\lceil S \rceil \star \lambda s.\llbracket c \rrbracket \star \lambda\_.\lceil Q \rceil \star \lambda q.\eta(s \supset q) = \llbracket c \rrbracket \star \lambda\_.\eta(\mathsf{tt})$$

$$\therefore \; \models \{S\}\, c\, \{Q\} \hspace{6cm} \square$$

7   Related Work

Structuring denotational semantics with monads and monad transformers was originally proposed by Moggi [21]. There are two complementary applications of monads in denotational semantics. The first is to use monads to provide a precise typing for effects in a language, while the second uses monads for modularity via monadic encapsulation of the underlying denotational structure. MMS fits squarely in this second category. Hudak, Liang, and Jones [14] and Espinosa [2] use monads and monad transformers to create modular, extensible interpreters. Recent promising work in categorical semantics [25,4] investigates more general approaches to combining monads than with monad transformers, although the cases for certain computational monads (chiefly, the continuation monad) are apparently still open problems as of this writing.

Modularity in programming language semantics is provided by a number of semantic frameworks including *action semantics* [22], *high-level semantics* [12], and *modular monadic semantics* [14,13]. Modularity in these frameworks stems from their organization according to a notion of program abstraction called *separability* [12]: they all provide a mechanism for separating the denotational description of a language (e.g., semantic equations) from its underlying denotational representation. Modularity—or rather the separability principle underlying it—can be at odds with program verification, however, because program specifications (i.e., predicates) are typically written with respect to a *fixed* denotational structure.

Liang [13] addresses the question of reasoning about MMS definitions for monads involving a single environment. He axiomatizes the environment operators rdEnv and inEnv, and shows that these axioms hold in any monad constructed with standard monad transformers (with a weak restriction on the order of transformer application—cf. Section 3). Liang's work provided an early inspiration for this one, but OPS is more powerful in a number of respects. Firstly, observations allow specifications to make finer-grained distinctions based on predicates applied to semantic data internal to the underlying monad. The work developed in [13] only allows equations between terms in the signature $\star$ (bind), η, rdEnv, and inEnv—no statements about the computed environments are possible. Secondly, observations may characterize relationships between any data internal to the underlying monad as well.

OPS was developed to verify a particular form of MMS definition, namely, *modular compilers* [8,6]. Modular compilation is a compiler construction technique allowing the assembly of compilers for high-level programming languages from reusable compiler building blocks (RCBBs). Each RCBB is, in fact, a denotational language definition factored by a monad transformer. Modular compiler verification involves specifying the behavior and interaction of multiple, "layered" effects, instead of just a single state as is presented here. The non-interference property for observations has also been used to characterize "non-interference" information security [5] by controlling "inter-layer" interaction between security levels [7].

OPS is reminiscent of programming logics such as specification and Floyd-Hoare logics [26,23,15] with observations playing a similar role to assertions (e.g., "$\{x = 0\}$"). Evaluation logic [24] is a typed, modal logic extending the computational lambda calculus [17]. It is equipped with "evaluation" modalities signifying such properties as "if E evaluates to x, then $\phi(x)$ holds". Moggi sketches how a number of programming logics, including Hoare logic, may be embedded into evaluation logic [19] and provides a similar, but less general, axiomatization of state. Führmann [3] introduces classifications for monadic effects called "effectoids". Among these are "discardable," "copyable" and "disjoint" effectoids that correspond closely to innocent, idempotent, and non-interfering computations, respectively. Schröder and Mossakowski [27] define a similar notion to discardable/innocent as well called "side-effect free". Instead of using observations to access intermediate data from a computation, their work incorporates a modality rather like the aforementioned evaluation logic modality to interpret Hoare logic monadically. The present work differs from theirs also in that here all monads are layered (i.e., produced by applications of monad transformers). Here, the monads in which the Hoare logic embedding is valid are determined by construction alone; this is valuable considering their potential complexity (see Figure 1).

Launchbury and Sabry [11] produced an axiomatization of monadic state, later used by Ariola and Sabry [1] to prove the correctness of an implementation of monadic state. Their axioms fulfill a similar role to the state monad axioms described in Section 4. They introduce an observation-like construct for describing the shape of the store, sto σ c, where σ is a store and c is a computation to be executed in σ. Observations may be seen as generalizing this sto by relating *any* data (states, environments, etc.) internal to the monad.

Kleene algebras with tests (KAT) are two-sorted algebraic structures which form an equational system for reasoning about programs [10]. A KAT has one sort for "programs" and another sort for "tests." These tests play a similar role to observations in OPS. Non-interference and idempotence properties of observations correspond to multiplicative commutation and idempotence of tests, while innocence corresponds to the commutation of non-test elements. OPS and KAT are both equational systems, although OPS, being embedded in the host language semantics, is less abstract in some sense. An interesting open question is whether OPS may form a general class of computational models of KATs, thereby providing a more compact algebraic way of reasoning with observations.

8   Concluding Remarks

OPS is a powerful and expressive specification technique for reasoning about modular definitions without sacrificing modularity. Semantic frameworks which promote modularity (like the MMS framework considered here) do so at a cost:

reasoning about such definitions is complicated by the separability principle used to gain modularity in the first place. In the case of MMS, the source of this difficulty lies in the disparity between the incompatible settings (i.e., computational and value, respectively) of programs and specifications. The solution presented here resolves this disparity by making specifications compatible with programs through the lifting of predicates to the computational level.

Monad transformers are well known as a structure for program abstraction and this article demonstrates how they give rise to a corresponding notion of proof abstraction as well. With OPS, program proofs hold in any monad in which the program itself makes sense. If an MMS program is written for a particular signature (i.e., those operators added by monad transformers) and behavior-preserving liftings exist for that signature, then the program makes sense—that is, after all, what "liftings exist" means. It is not surprising that if a monadic interface adequately captures the behavior of that same signature, then a program proof relying on that interface should hold as well.

OPS was originally developed for verifying modular compilers [6], and its application within formal methods and high-assurance software development remains an active area of research. To that end, establishing connections between OPS and other verification formalisms—programming logics such as evaluation logic [20] and semantics-based reasoning techniques such as logical relations [16]—is expected to yield useful results.

References

1. Zena M. Ariola and Amr Sabry. Correctness of monadic state: an imperative call-by-need calculus. In *Conference Record of POPL 98: The 25TH ACM SIGPLAN-SIGACT Symposium on Principles of Programming Languages, San Diego, California*, pages 62–73, New York, NY, 1998.
2. David Espinosa. *Semantic Lego*. PhD thesis, Columbia University, 1995.
3. Carsten Führmann. Varieties of effects. In *FoSSaCS '02: Proceedings of the 5th International Conference on Foundations of Software Science and Computation Structures*, pages 144–158, London, UK, 2002. Springer-Verlag.
4. Neil Ghani and Christoph Lüth. Composing monads using coproducts. In *ACM International Conference on Functional Programming*, pages 133–144, 2002.
5. Joseph A. Goguen and José Meseguer. Security policies and security models. In *Proceedings of the 1982 Symposium on Security and Privacy (SSP '82)*, pages 11–20. IEEE Computer Society Press, 1990.
6. William Harrison. *Modular Compilers and Their Correctness Proofs*. PhD thesis, University of Illinois at Urbana-Champaign, 2001.
7. William Harrison and James Hook. Achieving information flow security through precise control of effects. In *18th IEEE Computer Security Foundations Workshop (CSFW05)*, June 2005.
8. William Harrison and Samuel Kamin. Metacomputation-based compiler architecture. In *5th International Conference on the Mathematics of Program Construction, Ponte de Lima, Portugal*, volume 1837 of *Lecture Notes in Computer Science*, pages 213–229. Springer-Verlag, 2000.
9. C. A. R. Hoare. An axiomatic basis for computer programming. *Communications of the ACM*, 12(10):576–580, 1969.

10. Dexter Kozen. On Hoare logic and Kleene algebra with tests. *ACM Transactions on Computational Logic*, 1(1):60–76, 2000.
11. John Launchbury and Amr Sabry. Monadic state: Axiomatization and type safety. In *ACM SIGPLAN International Conference on Functional Programming*, pages 227–238, 1997.
12. Peter Lee. *Realistic Compiler Generation*. Foundations of Computing Series. MIT Press, 1989.
13. Sheng Liang. *Modular Monadic Semantics and Compilation*. PhD thesis, Yale University, 1997.
14. Sheng Liang, Paul Hudak, and Mark Jones. Monad transformers and modular interpreters. In *Proceedings of the 22nd ACM SIGPLAN-SIGACT Symposium on Principles of Programming Languages (POPL)*, pages 333–343. ACM Press, 1995.
15. Jacques Loeckx, Kurt Sieber, and Ryan D. Stansifer. *The Foundations of Program Verification*. Wiley-Teubner Series in Computer Science. Wiley, Chichester, second edition edition, 1987.
16. John C. Mitchell. Type systems for programming languages. In J. van Leeuwen, editor, *Handbook of Theoretical Computer Science*, volume B: Formal Models and Semantics, chapter 8, pages 365–458. North-Holland, New York, NY, 1990.
17. E. Moggi. Notions of computation and monads. *Information and Computation*, 93(1):55–92, 1991.
18. Eugenio Moggi. Personal communication with author.
19. Eugenio Moggi. Representing program logics in evaluation logic. Unpublished manuscript, available online., 1994.
20. Eugenio Moggi. A semantics for evaluation logic. *FUNDINF: Fundamenta Informatica*, 22, 1995.
21. Eugenio Moggi. An abstract view of programming languages. Technical Report ECS-LFCS-90-113, Dept. of Computer Science, Edinburgh Univ., 90.
22. Peter D. Mosses. *Action Semantics*. Number 26 in Cambridge Tracts in Theoretical Computer Science. Cambridge University Press, 1992.
23. David A. Naumann. Calculating sharp adaptation rules. *Information Processing Letters*, 77(2–4):201–208, 2001.
24. Andrew M. Pitts. Evaluation logic. In G. Birtwistle, editor, *IVth Higher Order Workshop, Banff 1990*, Workshops in Computing, pages 162–189. Springer-Verlag, Berlin, 1991.
25. Gordon Plotkin and John Power. Algebraic operations and generic effects. *Applied Categorical Structures*, 11:69–94, 2003.
26. John C. Reynolds. *The Craft of Programming*. Prentice Hall, 1981.
27. Lutz Schröder and Till Mossakowski. Monad-independent Hoare logic in HasCASL. In *Fundamental Approaches to Software Engineering*, volume 2621 of *LNCS*, pages 261–277. Springer, 2003.

Reading, Writing and Relations
Towards Extensional Semantics for Effect Analyses

Nick Benton[1], Andrew Kennedy[1], Martin Hofmann[2], and Lennart Beringer[2]

[1] Microsoft Research, Cambridge
[2] Ludwig-Maximilians-Universität, München

Abstract. We give an elementary semantics to an effect system, tracking read and write effects by using relations over a standard extensional semantics for the original language. The semantics establishes the soundness of both the analysis and its use in effect-based program transformations.

1 Introduction

Many analyses and logics for imperative programs are concerned with establishing whether particular mutable variables (or references or heap cells or regions) may be read or written by a phrase. For example, the equivalence of while-programs

```
C ; if B then C' else C''  =  if B then (C;C') else (C;C'')
```

is valid when B does not read any variable which C might write. Hoare-style programming logics often have rules with side-conditions on possibly-read and possibly-written variable sets, and reasoning about concurrent processes is dramatically simplified if one can establish that none of them may write a variable which another may read.[1]

Effect systems, first introduced by Gifford and Lucassen [8,11], are static analyses that compute upper bounds on the possible side-effects of computations. The literature contains many effect systems that analyse which storage cells may be read and which storage cells may be written (as well as many other properties), but no truly satisfactory account of the semantics of this information, or of the uses to which it may be put. Note that because effect systems *over*estimate the possible side-effects of expressions, the information they capture is of the form that particular variables will definitely *not* be read or will definitely *not* be written. But what does that mean?

Thinking operationally, it may seem entirely obvious what is meant by saying that a variable X will not be read (written) by a command C, viz. no execution trace of C contains a read (resp. write) operation to X. But, as we have argued before [3,6,4], such intensional interpretations of program properties are over-restrictive, cannot be interpreted in a standard semantics, do not behave well with respect to program equivalence or contextual reasoning and are hard to

---

[1] Though here we restrict attention, in an essential manner, to sequential programs.

N. Kobayashi (Ed.): APLAS 2006, LNCS 4279, pp. 114–130, 2006.

maintain during transformations. Thus we seek extensional properties that are more liberal than the intensional ones yet still validate the transformations or reasoning principles we wish to apply.

In the case of not writing a variable, a naive extensional interpretation seems clear: a command C *does not observably write the variable* X if it leaves the value of X unchanged:

$$\forall S, S'.\ C, S \Downarrow S' \implies S'(X) = S(X)$$

Note that this definition places no constraint on diverging executions or the value of X at intermediate states. Operationally, C may read and write X many times, so long as it always restores the original value before terminating. Furthermore, the definition is clearly closed under behavioural equivalence. If we have no non-termination and just two integer variables, X and Y, and the denotation of C is $[\![C]\!] : \mathbb{Z} \times \mathbb{Z} \to \mathbb{Z} \times \mathbb{Z}$ then our simple-minded definition of what it means for C not to write X can be expressed denotationally as

$$\exists f_2 : \mathbb{Z} \times \mathbb{Z} \to \mathbb{Z}.\forall X, Y.\ [\![C]\!](X, Y) = (X, f_2(X, Y))$$

which is the same as saying $[\![C]\!] = \langle \pi_1, f_2 \rangle$.

The property of *neither reading nor writing* X, i.e. of being *observationally pure in* X is also not hard to formalize extensionally:

$$\forall S, S', n.\ C, S \Downarrow S' \iff C, S[X \mapsto n] \Downarrow S'[X \mapsto n]$$

Alternatively $\exists f_2 : \mathbb{Z} \to \mathbb{Z}.\forall X, Y.\ [\![C]\!](X, Y) = (X, f_2(Y))$, which is the same as saying $[\![C]\!] = 1 \times f_2$.

The property of *not observably reading* X is rather more subtle, since X may, or may not, be written. We want to say that the final values of all the other variables are independent of the initial value of X, but the final value of X itself is either a function of the other variables or is the initial value of X:

$$\exists f_1 : \mathbb{Z} \to \mathbb{B}, f_2, f_3 : \mathbb{Z} \to \mathbb{Z}.\forall X, Y.\ [\![C]\!](X, Y) = (f_1(Y) \supset X \mid f_2(Y), f_3(Y))$$

This is clearly a more complex property than the others. Another way to think of it is that the final values of the variables other than X are functions of the initial values of those variables and that for each value of those other variables, the (curried) function mapping the initial value of X to its final value is either constant or the identity. The tricky nature of the 'does not read' property also shows up if one tries to define a family of monads in a synthetic, rather than an analytic fashion (as in Tolmach's work [20]): neither reading nor writing corresponds to the identity monad; not writing corresponds to the reader (environment) monad; but there is no *simple* definition of a 'writer' monad.

Our basic approach to the soundness of static analyses and optimizing transformations is to interpret the program properties (which may be expressed as points in an abstract domain, or as non-standard types) as binary relations over a standard, non-instrumented (operational or denotational) semantics of the language. We have previously [3] described how such an extensional relational interpretation of static analyses allows one both to express constancy and dependency properties for simple imperative programs, and to reason about the transformations they enable. But the non-parametric relations used in that work turn out to be insufficient to admit a compositional, generic translation of perhaps the simplest static analysis there is: the obvious inductive definition of possibly-read and possibly-written variable sets for while-programs.

In earlier, operationally-based, work [6] we expressed the meaning of some simple global (i.e. treating the whole store monolithically) effects using sets of cotermination tests (pairs of contexts) written explicitly in the language, but those definitions were *very* unwieldy and phrased in a way that would not generalize easily to other types. Here we will show how reading, writing and allocating properties for a higher-order language with state can be elegantly captured using parametric logical relations over a simple denotational semantics for the original language. This new interpretation of effects is dramatically slicker and more compelling than previous ones.

1.1 Relations

We just recall some basic facts and notation. A (binary) relation R on a set A is a subset of $A \times A$. If R is a relation on A and Q a relation on B, then we define relations on Cartesian products and function spaces by

$$R \times Q = \{((a,b),(a',b')) \in (A \times B) \times (A \times B) \mid (a,a') \in R, \ (b,b') \in Q\}$$
$$R \to Q = \{(f,f') \in (A \to B) \times (A \to B) \mid \forall (a,a') \in R. \ (f\,a, \ f'\,a') \in Q\}$$

A binary relation on a set is a *partial equivalence relation* (PER) if it is symmetric and transitive. The set of PERs on a set is closed under arbitrary intersections and disjoint unions. If R and Q are PERs, so are $R \to Q$ and $R \times Q$. Write Δ_A for the diagonal relation $\{(a,a) \mid a \in A\}$, and $a : R$ for $(a,a) \in R$.

1.2 The Basic Idea

Our starting point is the following simple, yet striking, observation, which seems not to have been made before:

Lemma 1. *For total commands operating on two integer variables, as above,*

1. *The property of not observably writing X is equivalent to*

$$\forall R \subseteq \Delta. \ [\![C]\!] : R \times \Delta \to R \times \Delta$$

   i.e. preserving all relations less than or equal to the identity on X.
2. *The property of neither observably reading nor observably writing X is equivalent to*

$$\forall R. \ [\![C]\!] : R \times \Delta \to R \times \Delta$$

   i.e. preserving all relations on X.

3. *The property of not reading X is equivalent to*

$$\forall R \supseteq \Delta. \ [\![C]\!] : R \times \Delta \to R \times \Delta$$

i.e. preserving all relations greater than or equal to the identity on X.

Proof. We write f for $[\![C]\!]$ and just consider the last case. Assume $f(X, Y) = (f_1(Y) \implies X \mid f_2(Y), f_3(Y))$ and $R \supseteq \Delta$. Then if $(X, X') \in R$ and $(Y, Y') \in \Delta$ so $Y = Y'$, we have

$$(f(X,Y), f(X',Y')) = ((f_1(Y) \implies X \mid f_2(Y), f_3(Y)),$$
$$(f_1(Y) \implies X' \mid f_2(Y), f_3(Y)))$$

Clearly $(f_3(Y), f_3(Y)) \in \Delta$. In the first component, if $f_1(Y) = true$ then we get $(X, X') \in R$ and if $f_1(Y) = false$ we get $(f_2(Y), f_2(Y)) \in \Delta \subseteq R$ so we're done.

Going the other way, preservation of $\mathbb{T} \times \Delta$ deals with the independence of the second component. In the first component we need to show that for each Y, $\pi_1 f(-, Y) : \mathbb{Z} \to \mathbb{Z}$ is uniformly either constant or the identity. Pick any two distinct elements X, X' and let $R = \Delta \cup \{(X, X')\}$, which contains Δ and is therefore preserved by the first component of f. Thus $(\pi_1 f(X, Y), \pi_1 f(X', Y)) \in R$ means either $\pi_1 f(X, Y) = \pi_1 f(X', Y)$ or $\pi_1 f(X, Y) = X$ and $\pi_1 f(X', Y) = X'$. □

(Note that preservation of relations is closed under unions, so it actually suffices to consider singleton relations in the first two cases and singleton extensions of the identity relation in the last case.)

In the next section we develop the result above to give a semantics for a simple effect system for a higher-order language with global variables, in the process explaining where the faintly mysterious bounded quantification really 'comes from'. The language and effect system is purposefully kept very minimal, so we may explore the key idea without getting bogged down in too much auxiliary detail.

2   Effects for Global Store

2.1   Base Language

We consider a monadically-typed, normalizing, call-by-value lambda calculus with a collection of global integer references. The use of monadic types, making an explicit distinction between values and computations, simplifies the presentation of the effect system and cleans up the equational theory of the language. A more conventionally-typed impure calculus may be translated into the monadic one via the usual 'call-by-value translation' [5], and this extends to the usual style of presenting effect systems in which every judgement has an effect, and function arrows are annotated with 'latent effects' [21].

We assume a finite set $\mathcal{L}$ of global variable names, ranged over by ℓ, and define value types A, computation types TA and contexts Γ as follows:

$$A, B := \mathtt{unit} \mid \mathtt{int} \mid \mathtt{bool} \mid A \times B \mid A \to TB$$
$$\Gamma := x_1 : A_1, \ldots, x_n : A_n$$

$$\Gamma \vdash n : \text{int} \qquad \Gamma \vdash b : \text{bool} \qquad \Gamma \vdash () : \text{unit} \qquad \Gamma, x : A \vdash x : A$$

$$\frac{\Gamma \vdash V_1 : \text{int} \quad \Gamma \vdash V_2 : \text{int}}{\Gamma \vdash V_1 + V_2 : \text{int}} \qquad \frac{\Gamma \vdash V_1 : \text{int} \quad \Gamma \vdash V_2 : \text{int}}{\Gamma \vdash V_1 > V_2 : \text{bool}}$$

$$\frac{\Gamma \vdash V_1 : A \quad \Gamma \vdash V_2 : B}{\Gamma \vdash (V_1, V_2) : A \times B} \qquad \frac{\Gamma \vdash V : A_1 \times A_2}{\Gamma \vdash \pi_i V : A_i}$$

$$\frac{\Gamma, x : A \vdash M : TB}{\Gamma \vdash \lambda x : A.M : A \to TB} \qquad \frac{\Gamma \vdash V_1 : A \to TB \quad \Gamma \vdash V_2 : A}{\Gamma \vdash V_1 V_2 : TB} \qquad \frac{\Gamma \vdash V : A}{\Gamma \vdash \text{val } V : TA}$$

$$\frac{\Gamma \vdash M : TA \quad \Gamma, x : A \vdash N : TB}{\Gamma \vdash \text{let } x \Leftarrow M \text{ in } N : TB} \qquad \frac{\Gamma \vdash V : \text{bool} \quad \Gamma \vdash M : TA \quad \Gamma \vdash N : TA}{\Gamma \vdash \text{if } V \text{ then } M \text{ else } N : TA}$$

$$\frac{}{\Gamma \vdash \text{read}(\ell) : T\text{int}} \qquad \frac{\Gamma \vdash V : \text{int}}{\Gamma \vdash \text{write}(\ell, V) : T\text{unit}}$$

Fig. 1. Simple computation type system

Note that variables are always given value types, as this is all we shall need to interpret a CBV language. There are two forms of typing judgement: value judgements $\Gamma \vdash V : A$ and computation judgements $\Gamma \vdash M : TA$, defined inductively by the rules in Figure 1. Note that the presence of types on lambda-bound variables makes typing derivations unique and that addition and comparison should be considered just representative primitive operations.

Since our simple language has no recursion, we can give it an elementary denotational semantics in the category of sets and functions. Writing S for $\mathcal{L} \to \mathbb{Z}$, the semantics of types is as follows:

$$[\![\text{unit}]\!] = 1 \qquad [\![\text{int}]\!] = \mathbb{Z} \qquad [\![\text{bool}]\!] = \mathbb{B} \qquad [\![A \times B]\!] = [\![A]\!] \times [\![B]\!]$$

$$[\![A \to TB]\!] = [\![A]\!] \to [\![TB]\!] \qquad [\![TA]\!] = S \to S \times [\![A]\!]$$

The interpretation of the computation type constructor is the usual state monad. The meaning of contexts is given by $[\![x_1 : A_1, \ldots, x_n : A_n]\!] = [\![A_1]\!] \times \cdots \times [\![A_n]\!]$, and we can then give the semantics of judgements

$$[\![\Gamma \vdash V : A]\!] : [\![\Gamma]\!] \to [\![A]\!] \qquad \text{and} \qquad [\![\Gamma \vdash M : TA]\!] : [\![\Gamma]\!] \to [\![TA]\!]$$

inductively, though we omit the completely standard details here. The semantics is adequate for the obvious operational semantics and ground contextual equivalence (observing, say, the final boolean value produced by a closed program).

2.2 Effect System

We now present our effect analysis as a type system that refines the simple type system by annotating the computation type constructor with information about

$$\frac{}{X \leq X} \qquad \frac{X \leq Y \quad Y \leq Z}{X \leq Z} \qquad \frac{X \leq X' \quad Y \leq Y'}{X \times Y \leq X' \times Y'}$$

$$\frac{X' \leq X \quad T_\varepsilon Y \leq T_{\varepsilon'} Y'}{(X \to T_\varepsilon Y) \leq (X' \to T_{\varepsilon'} Y')} \qquad \frac{\varepsilon \subseteq \varepsilon' \quad X \leq X'}{T_\varepsilon X \leq T_{\varepsilon'} X'}$$

Fig. 2. Subtyping refined types

whether a computation may read or write particular locations. Formally, define *refined* value types X, computation types $T_\varepsilon X$ and contexts Θ by

$$X, Y := \text{unit} \mid \text{int} \mid \text{bool} \mid X \times Y \mid X \to T_\varepsilon Y$$
$$\varepsilon \subseteq \bigcup_{\ell \in \mathcal{L}} \{r_\ell, w_\ell\}$$
$$\Theta := x_1 : X_1, \ldots, x_n : X_n$$

There is a subtyping relation on refined types, axiomatised in Figure 2. The evident erasure map, $U(\cdot)$, takes refined types to simple types (and contexts) by forgetting the effect annotations:

$$U(\text{int}) = \text{int} \qquad U(\text{bool}) = \text{bool} \qquad U(\text{unit}) = \text{unit}$$
$$U(X \times Y) = U(X) \times U(Y)$$
$$U(X \to T_\varepsilon Y) = U(X) \to U(T_\varepsilon Y)$$
$$U(T_\varepsilon X) = T(U(X))$$

$$U(x_1 : X_1, \ldots, x_n : X_n) = x_1 : U(X_1), \ldots, x_n : U(X_n)$$

Lemma 2. *If $X \leq Y$ then $U(X) = U(Y)$, and similarly for computations.* $\square$

The refined type assignment system is shown in Figure 3. Note that the subject terms are the same (we still only have simple types on λ-bound variables).

Lemma 3. *If $\Theta \vdash V : X$ then $U(\Theta) \vdash V : U(X)$, and similarly for computations.* $\square$

Note that the refined system doesn't rule out any terms from the original language. Define a map $G(\cdot)$ from simple types to refined types that adds the 'top' annotation $\bigcup_{\ell \in \mathcal{L}} \{r_\ell, w_\ell\}$ to all computation types, and then

Lemma 4. *If $\Gamma \vdash V : A$ then $G(\Gamma) \vdash V : G(A)$ and similarly for computations.* $\square$

2.3 Semantics of Effects

The meanings of simple types are just sets, out of which we now carve the meanings of refined types as subsets, *together* with a coarser notion of equality.

$$\Theta \vdash n : \texttt{int} \qquad \Theta \vdash b : \texttt{bool} \qquad \Theta \vdash () : \texttt{unit} \qquad \Theta, x : X \vdash x : X$$

$$\frac{\Theta \vdash V_1 : \texttt{int} \quad \Theta \vdash V_2 : \texttt{int}}{\Theta \vdash V_1 + V_2 : \texttt{int}} \qquad \frac{\Theta \vdash V_1 : \texttt{int} \quad \Theta \vdash V_2 : \texttt{int}}{\Theta \vdash V_1 > V_2 : \texttt{bool}}$$

$$\frac{\Theta \vdash V_1 : X \quad \Theta \vdash V_2 : Y}{\Theta \vdash (V_1, V_2) : X \times Y} \qquad \frac{\Theta \vdash V : X_1 \times X_2}{\Theta \vdash \pi_i V : X_i} \qquad \frac{\Theta, x : X \vdash M : T_\varepsilon Y}{\Theta \vdash \lambda x : U(X).M : X \to T_\varepsilon Y}$$

$$\frac{\Theta \vdash V_1 : X \to T_\varepsilon Y \quad \Theta \vdash V_2 : X}{\Theta \vdash V_1 V_2 : T_\varepsilon Y} \qquad \frac{\Theta \vdash V : X}{\Theta \vdash \texttt{val } V : T_\emptyset X}$$

$$\frac{\Theta \vdash M : T_\varepsilon X \quad \Theta, x : X \vdash N : T_{\varepsilon'} Y}{\Theta \vdash \texttt{let } x \Leftarrow M \texttt{ in } N : T_{\varepsilon \cup \varepsilon'} Y} \qquad \frac{\Theta \vdash V : \texttt{bool} \quad \Theta \vdash M : T_\varepsilon X \quad \Theta \vdash N : T_\varepsilon X}{\Theta \vdash \texttt{if } V \texttt{ then } M \texttt{ else } N : T_\varepsilon X}$$

$$\frac{}{\Theta \vdash \texttt{read}(\ell) : T_{\{r_\ell\}}(\texttt{int})} \qquad \frac{\Theta \vdash V : \texttt{int}}{\Theta \vdash \texttt{write}(\ell, V) : T_{\{w_\ell\}}(\texttt{unit})}$$

$$\frac{\Theta \vdash V : X \quad X \leq X'}{\Theta \vdash V : X'} \qquad \frac{\Theta \vdash M : T_\varepsilon X \quad T_\varepsilon X \leq T_{\varepsilon'} X'}{\Theta \vdash M : T_{\varepsilon'} X'}$$

Fig. 3. Refined type system

More formally, the semantics of each refined type is a partial equivalence relation on the semantics of its erasure, defined as follows:

$$[\![X]\!] \subseteq [\![U(X)]\!] \times [\![U(X)]\!]$$

$$[\![\texttt{int}]\!] = \Delta_\mathbb{Z} \qquad [\![\texttt{bool}]\!] = \Delta_\mathbb{B} \qquad [\![\texttt{unit}]\!] = \Delta_1$$

$$[\![X \times Y]\!] = [\![X]\!] \times [\![Y]\!]$$

$$[\![X \to T_\varepsilon Y]\!] = [\![X]\!] \to [\![T_\varepsilon Y]\!]$$

$$[\![T_\varepsilon X]\!] = \bigcap_{R \in \mathcal{R}_\varepsilon} R \to R \times [\![X]\!]$$

where $\mathcal{R}_\varepsilon \subseteq \mathbb{P}(S \times S)$ is given by $\mathcal{R}_\varepsilon = \bigcap_{e \in \varepsilon} \mathcal{R}_e$ and for atomic effects e, $\mathcal{R}_e \subseteq \mathbb{P}(S \times S)$ is given by

$$\mathcal{R}_{r_\ell} = \{ R \mid (s, s') \in R \implies s\,\ell = s'\,\ell \}$$
$$\mathcal{R}_{w_\ell} = \{ R \mid (s, s') \in R \implies \forall n \in \mathbb{Z}.\, (s[\ell \mapsto n], s'[\ell \mapsto n]) \in R \}$$

Apart from the clause for computation types, this is a familiar-looking logical relation. To understand the interpretation of effect annotations, note that the first intersection is intersection of relations, whilst the second is an intersection of *sets* of relations. Then for each ε there is a set $\mathcal{R}_\varepsilon$ of relations on the state that computations of type $T_\varepsilon X$ have to preserve; the more possible effects occur in ε, the fewer relations are preserved.

Thus, for example, if ε is the empty set then $\mathcal{R}_\varepsilon$ is the empty intersection, i.e. *all* state relations. So $[\![T_\emptyset X]\!]$ relates two computations m and m' of type $[\![T(U(X))]\!]$ if for all state relations R and pre-states s, s' related by R, $m\, s$ and $m'\, s'$ yield post-states related by R and values related by $[\![X]\!]$, which is just what one would expect the definition of observational purity to be from the discussion in Section 1.2. A little more calculation shows that, if $\mathcal{L} = \{\mathbf{x}, \mathbf{y}\}$ then a state relation R is in $[\![T_{\{w_x, w_y, r_y\}}(\text{unit})]\!]$, the interpretation of commands not reading $\mathbf{x}$, just when it (is either empty or) factors as $R_{\mathbf{x}} \times \Delta$ with $R_{\mathbf{x}} \supseteq \Delta$, which again matches the observation in the introduction. What is going on is even clearer if one rephrases the RHS of the implication in the definition of $\mathcal{R}_{r_\ell}$ as

$$([\![\text{read}(\ell)]\!]\, ()\, s, [\![\text{read}(\ell)]\!]\, ()\, s') \in R \times [\![\text{int}]\!]$$

and that of $\mathcal{R}_{w_\ell}$ as saying

$$([\![\text{write}(\ell, V)]\!]\, ()\, s, [\![\text{write}(\ell, V')]\!]\, ()\, s') \in R \times [\![\text{unit}]\!]$$

for all V, V' such that $([\![V]\!]\, (), [\![V']\!]\, ()) \in [\![\text{int}]\!]$. The usual 'logical' relational interpretation of a type can be understood as 'preserving all the relations that are preserved by all the operations on the type' and the above shows how the semantics of our refined types really does extend the usual notion: the refined type is a subtype with only a subset of the original operations and thus will preserve all relations that are preserved by that smaller set of operations.

We also extend the relational interpretation of refined types to refined contexts in the natural way:

$$[\![\Theta]\!] \subseteq [\![U(\Theta)]\!] \times [\![U(\Theta)]\!]$$
$$[\![x_1 : X_1, \ldots, x_n : X_n]\!] = [\![X_1]\!] \times \cdots \times [\![X_n]\!]$$

Lemma 5. *For any Θ, X and ε, all of $[\![\Theta]\!]$, $[\![X]\!]$ and $[\![T_\varepsilon X]\!]$ are partial equivalence relations.*   □

The following sanity check says that the interpretation of a refined type with the top effect annotation everywhere is just equality on the interpretation of its erasure:

Lemma 6. *For all A, $[\![G(A)]\!] = \Delta_{[\![A]\!]}$.*   □

The following establishes semantic soundness for our subtyping relation:

Lemma 7. *If $X \leq Y$ then $[\![X]\!] \subseteq [\![Y]\!]$, and similarly for computation types.*   □

And we can then show a 'fundamental theorem' establishing the soundness of the effect analysis itself:

Theorem 1

1. If $\Theta \vdash V : X$, $(\rho, \rho') \in [\![\Theta]\!]$ then

$$([\![U(\Theta) \vdash V : U(X)]\!]\, \rho, [\![U(\Theta) \vdash V : U(X)]\!]\, \rho') \in [\![X]\!]$$

2. *If* $\Theta \vdash M : T_\varepsilon X$, $(\rho, \rho') \in [\![\Theta]\!]$ *then*

$$([\![U(\Theta) \vdash M : T(U(X))]\!] \rho, [\![U(\Theta) \vdash M : T(U(X))]\!] \rho') \in [\![T_\varepsilon X]\!] \qquad \Box$$

Because we have used standard technology (logical relations, PERs), the pattern of what we have to prove here is obvious and the definitions are all set up so that the proofs go through smoothly. Had we defined the semantics of effects in some more special-purpose way (e.g. trying to work directly with the property of being uniformly either constant or the identity), it could have been rather less clear how to make everything extend smoothly to higher-order and how to deal with combining effects in the let-rule.

2.4 Basic Equations

Before looking at effect-dependent equivalences, we note that the semantics validates all the usual equations of the computational metalanguage, including congruence laws and β and η laws for products, function spaces, booleans and the computation type constructor. We show some of these rules in Figure 4. Note that the correctness of the basic congruence laws subsumes Theorem 1 and that, rather subtly, we have made the reflexivity PER rule invertible. This is sound because our effect annotations are purely descriptive (or *extrinsic* in Reynolds's terminology [17]) whereas the simple types are more conventionally prescriptive (which Reynolds calls *intrinsic*). We actually regard the rules of Figure 3 as abbreviations for a subset of the equational judgements of Figure 4; thus we can allow the refined type of the conclusion of interesting equational rules (e.g. the dead computation rule, to be presented shortly) to be different from (in particular, have a smaller effect than) the refined types in the assumptions. In practical terms, this is important for allowing inferred effects to be improved locally as transformations are performed, rather than having to periodically reanalyse the whole program to obtain the best results.

3 Using Effect Information

More interesting equivalences are predicated on the effect information. The *read-set* of an effect ε is denoted $\mathrm{rds}(\varepsilon)$ and defined as $\{\ell \in \mathcal{L} \mid \mathbf{r}_\ell \in \varepsilon\}$. Likewise, the *write-set* of an effect ε is denoted $\mathrm{wrs}(\varepsilon)$ and defined as $\{\ell \in \mathcal{L} \mid \mathbf{w}_\ell \in \varepsilon\}$. The set of locations mentioned in an effect is $\mathrm{locs}(\varepsilon) = \mathrm{rds}(\varepsilon) \cup \mathrm{wrs}(\varepsilon)$. We make use of these definitions in refined side-conditions for the effect-dependent equivalences, presented in Figure 5.

The **Dead Computation** transformation allows the removal of a computation producing an unused value, provided the effect of that computation is at most reading (if the computation could write the store then its removal would generally be unsound, as that write could be observed by the rest of the computation).

The **Duplicated Computation** transformation allows two evaluations of the same computation to be replaced by one, provided that the observable reads and observable writes of the computation are disjoint. Intuitively, the locations that

PER rules (+ similar for computations):

$$\frac{\Theta \vdash V : X}{\Theta \vdash V = V : X} \qquad \frac{\Theta \vdash V = V' : X}{\Theta \vdash V' = V : X} \qquad \frac{\Theta \vdash V = V' : X \quad \Theta \vdash V' = V'' : X}{\Theta \vdash V = V'' : X}$$

$$\frac{\Theta \vdash V = V' : X \quad X \leq X'}{\Theta \vdash V = V' : X'}$$

Congruence rules (extract):

$$\frac{\Theta \vdash V_1 = V_1' : \text{int} \quad \Theta \vdash V_2 = V_2' : \text{int}}{\Theta \vdash (V_1 + V_2) = (V_1' + V_2') : \text{int}} \qquad \frac{\Theta \vdash V = V' : X_1 \times X_2}{\Theta \vdash \pi_i V = \pi_i V' : X_i}$$

$$\frac{\Theta, x : X \vdash M = M' : T_\varepsilon Y}{\Theta \vdash (\lambda x : U(X).M) = (\lambda x : U(X).M') : X \to T_\varepsilon Y}$$

β rules (extract):

$$\frac{\Theta, x : X \vdash M : T_\varepsilon Y \quad \Theta \vdash V : X}{\Theta \vdash (\lambda x : U(X).M) V = M[V/x] : T_\varepsilon Y} \qquad \frac{\Theta \vdash V : X \quad \Theta, x : X \vdash M : T_\varepsilon Y}{\Theta \vdash \text{let } x \Leftarrow \text{val } V \text{ in } M = M[V/x] : T_\varepsilon Y}$$

η rules (extract):

$$\frac{\Theta \vdash V : X \to T_\varepsilon Y}{\Theta \vdash V = (\lambda x : U(X).V\,x) : X \to T_\varepsilon Y} \qquad \frac{\Theta \vdash M : T_\varepsilon X}{\Theta \vdash (\text{let } x \Leftarrow M \text{ in val } x) = M : T_\varepsilon X}$$

Commuting conversions:

$$\frac{\Theta \vdash M : T_{\varepsilon_1} Y \quad \Theta, y : Y \vdash N : T_{\varepsilon_2} X \quad \Theta, x : X \vdash P : T_{\varepsilon_3} Z}{\Theta \vdash \text{let } x \Leftarrow (\text{let } y \Leftarrow M \text{ in } N) \text{ in } P = \text{let } y \Leftarrow M \text{ in let } x \Leftarrow N \text{ in } P : T_{\varepsilon_1 \cup \varepsilon_2 \cup \varepsilon_3} Z}$$

Fig. 4. Effect-independent equivalences

may be read on the second evaluation were not written during the first one, so will have the same values. Hence the actual values written during the second evaluation will be the same as were written during the first evaluation. Thus both the final state and the computed value after the second evaluation will be the same (equivalent) to the state and value after the first evaluation.

The **Commuting Computations** transformation allows the order of two value-independent computations to be swapped provided that their write sets are disjoint and neither may read a location that the other may write.

The **Pure Lambda Hoist** transformation allows a computation to be hoisted out of a lambda abstraction (so it is performed once, rather than every time the function is applied) provided that it is observably pure (and, of course, that it does not depend on the function argument). This is not only useful, but also interesting as an example of a transformation we did *not* manage to prove sound in our earlier [6] work.

Dead Computation:

$$\frac{\Theta \vdash M : T_\varepsilon X \quad \Theta \vdash N : T_{\varepsilon'} Y}{\Theta \vdash \mathtt{let}\ x \Leftarrow M\ \mathtt{in}\ N = N : T_{\varepsilon'} Y} \; x \notin \Theta, \mathrm{wrs}(\varepsilon) = \emptyset$$

Duplicated Computation:

$$\frac{\Theta \vdash M : T_\varepsilon X \quad \Theta, x : X, y : X \vdash N : T_{\varepsilon'} Y}{\Theta \vdash \begin{array}{l} \mathtt{let}\ x \Leftarrow M\ \mathtt{in}\ \mathtt{let}\ y \Leftarrow M\ \mathtt{in}\ N \\ = \mathtt{let}\ x \Leftarrow M\ \mathtt{in}\ N[x/y] \end{array} : T_{\varepsilon \cup \varepsilon'} Y} \; \mathrm{rds}(\varepsilon) \cap \mathrm{wrs}(\varepsilon) = \emptyset$$

Commuting Computations:

$$\frac{\Theta \vdash M_1 : T_{\varepsilon_1} X_1 \quad \Theta \vdash M_2 : T_{\varepsilon_2} X_2 \quad \Theta, x_1 : X_1, x_2 : X_2 \vdash N : T_{\varepsilon'} Y}{\Theta \vdash \begin{array}{l} \mathtt{let}\ x_1 \Leftarrow M_1\ \mathtt{in}\ \mathtt{let}\ x_2 \Leftarrow M_2\ \mathtt{in}\ N \\ = \mathtt{let}\ x_2 \Leftarrow M_2\ \mathtt{in}\ \mathtt{let}\ x_1 \Leftarrow M_1\ \mathtt{in}\ N \end{array} : T_{\varepsilon_1 \cup \varepsilon_2 \cup \varepsilon'} Y} \; \begin{array}{l} \mathrm{rds}(\varepsilon_1) \cap \mathrm{wrs}(\varepsilon_2) = \emptyset \\ \mathrm{wrs}(\varepsilon_1) \cap \mathrm{rds}(\varepsilon_2) = \emptyset \\ \mathrm{wrs}(\varepsilon_1) \cap \mathrm{wrs}(\varepsilon_2) = \emptyset \end{array}$$

Pure Lambda Hoist:

$$\frac{\Theta \vdash M : T_{\{\}} Z \quad \Theta, x : X, y : Z \vdash N : T_\varepsilon Y}{\Theta \vdash \begin{array}{l} \mathtt{val}\ (\lambda x : U(X).\mathtt{let}\ y \Leftarrow M\ \mathtt{in}\ N) \\ = \mathtt{let}\ y \Leftarrow M\ \mathtt{in}\ \mathtt{val}\ (\lambda x : U(X).N) \end{array} : T_{\{\}} (X \to T_\varepsilon Y)}$$

Fig. 5. Effect-dependent equivalences

The following Lemma states that a computation with effect ε cannot change the state of locations outside $\mathrm{wrs}(\varepsilon)$. We write $s =_L s'$ if for all $\ell \in L, s(\ell) = s'(\ell)$.

Lemma 8 (No writes). *Suppose* $\Theta \vdash M : T_\varepsilon X$ *and* $(\rho, \rho) \in \llbracket \Theta \rrbracket$. *If* $\llbracket \Theta \vdash M : T_\varepsilon X \rrbracket \rho\, s_0 = (s_1, x)$ *then* $s_0 =_{\mathcal{L} \backslash \mathrm{wrs}(\varepsilon)} s_1$.

Proof. Define a relation $R = \{(s, s) \mid s =_{\mathcal{L} \backslash \mathrm{wrs}(\varepsilon)} s_0\}$. It is easy to see that $R \in \mathcal{R}_\varepsilon$, and clearly $(s_0, s_0) \in R$. Then applying Theorem 1 to M and $(\rho, \rho) \in \llbracket \Theta \rrbracket$ we can deduce that $(s_1, s_1) \in R$, so $s_1 =_{\mathcal{L} \backslash \mathrm{wrs}(\varepsilon)} s_0$. □

Dually, running a computation with effect ε on states that differ only outside $\mathrm{rds}(\varepsilon)$ makes an identical change to each state:

Lemma 9 (No reads). *Suppose* $\Theta \vdash M : T_\varepsilon X$ *and* $(\rho, \rho') \in \llbracket \Theta \rrbracket$. *Let* s_0 *and* s_0' *be two states such that* $s_0 =_{\mathrm{rds}(\varepsilon)} s_0'$. *If* $\llbracket \Theta \vdash M : T_\varepsilon X \rrbracket \rho\, s_0 = (s_1, x)$ *and* $\llbracket \Theta \vdash M : T_\varepsilon X \rrbracket \rho'\, s_0' = (s_1', x')$ *then* $(x, x') \in \llbracket X \rrbracket$ *and for all* $\ell \in \mathcal{L}$, *either* $s_1(\ell) = s_1'(\ell)$ *(locations are updated, identically), or* $s_1(\ell) = s_0(\ell)$ *and* $s_1'(\ell) = s_0'(\ell)$ *(locations are left unchanged).*

Proof. Define a relation $R = \{(s, s') \mid \forall \ell \in \mathcal{L}, s\,\ell = s'\,\ell \vee (s\,\ell = s_0\,\ell \wedge s'\,\ell = s_0'\,\ell)\}$. It is straightforward to check that $R \in \mathcal{R}_\varepsilon$, and that $(s_0, s_0') \in R$. Then applying Theorem 1 to M and $(\rho, \rho') \in \llbracket \Theta \rrbracket$ we can deduce that $(s_1, s_1') \in R$ and $(x, x') \in \llbracket X \rrbracket$ and the result follows immediately. □

If $U(\Theta) \vdash V : U(X)$ and $U(\Theta) \vdash V' : U(X)$ then write $\Theta \models V = V' : X$ to mean that for all $(\rho, \rho') \in \llbracket \Theta \rrbracket$

$$([\![U(\Theta) \vdash V : U(X)]\!] \, \rho, [\![U(\Theta) \vdash V' : U(X)]\!] \, \rho') \in \llbracket X \rrbracket$$

and similarly for computations.

Theorem 2. *All of the equations shown in Figures 4 and 5 are soundly modelled in the semantics:*

- *If $\Theta \vdash V = V' : X$ then $\Theta \models V = V' : X$.*
- *If $\Theta \vdash M = M' : T_\varepsilon X$ then $\Theta \models M = M' : T_\varepsilon X$.*

Proof. We present proofs for the equivalences in Figure 5.

Dead computation. If we let $\Gamma = U(\Theta)$, $A = U(X)$ and $B = U(Y)$ and $(\rho, \rho') \in \llbracket \Theta \rrbracket$ then we have to show

$$([\![\Gamma \vdash \mathtt{let}\ x \Leftarrow M \ \mathtt{in}\ N : TB]\!] \, \rho, \ [\![\Gamma \vdash N : TB]\!] \, \rho') \in \llbracket T_{\varepsilon'} Y \rrbracket$$

Pick $R \in \mathcal{R}_{\varepsilon'}$ and $(s, s') \in R$, and let $(s_1, x) = [\![\Gamma \vdash M : TA]\!] \, \rho \, s$. As $\llbracket \Theta \rrbracket$ is a PER we know $(\rho, \rho) \in \llbracket \Theta \rrbracket$, and because $\mathrm{wrs}(\varepsilon) = \emptyset$ we can apply Lemma 8 to deduce that $s_1 = s$. Hence

$$[\![\Gamma \vdash \mathtt{let}\ x \Leftarrow M \ \mathtt{in}\ N : TB]\!] \, \rho \, s = [\![\Gamma \vdash N : TB]\!] \, \rho \, s$$

and by assumption on N

$$([\![\Gamma \vdash N : TB]\!] \, \rho \, s, [\![\Gamma \vdash N : TB]\!] \, \rho' \, s') \in R \times \llbracket Y \rrbracket$$

so we're done.

Pure lambda hoist. Define $\Gamma = U(\Theta)$, $A = U(X)$, $B = U(Y)$, $C = U(Z)$. Pick $(\rho, \rho') \in \llbracket \Theta \rrbracket$, $R \in \mathcal{R}_{\{\}}$ and $(s, s') \in R$ (note that R is actually unconstrained in this case). Then

$$\begin{aligned} &[\![\Gamma \vdash \mathtt{val}\ (\lambda x : A.\mathtt{let}\ y \Leftarrow M \ \mathtt{in}\ N) : T(A \to TB)]\!] \, \rho \, s \\ &= (s, \lambda x \in \llbracket A \rrbracket.[\![\Gamma, x : A \vdash \mathtt{let}\ y \Leftarrow M \ \mathtt{in}\ N : TB]\!] \, (\rho, x)) \end{aligned}$$

and

$$\begin{aligned} &[\![\Gamma \vdash \mathtt{let}\ y \Leftarrow M \ \mathtt{in}\ \mathtt{val}\ (\lambda x : A.N) : T(A \to TB)]\!] \, \rho', s' \\ &= (s'', \lambda x' \in \llbracket A \rrbracket.[\![\Gamma, x : A, y : C \vdash N : TB]\!] \, (\rho', x', y')) \end{aligned}$$

where

$$(s'', y') = [\![\Gamma \vdash M : TC]\!] \, \rho' \, s'$$

Now, as M doesn't write, Lemma 8 entails $s'' = s'$ and hence $(s, s'') \in R$. Thus it remains to show that the two functions are in $\llbracket X \to T_\varepsilon Y \rrbracket$. So assume $(x, x') \in \llbracket X \rrbracket$, we have now to show

$$\begin{aligned} ([\![\Gamma, x : A \vdash \mathtt{let}\ y \Leftarrow M \ \mathtt{in}\ N : TB]\!] \, (\rho, x), \\ [\![\Gamma, x : A, y : C \vdash N : TB]\!] \, (\rho', x', y')) \end{aligned} \in \llbracket T_\varepsilon Y \rrbracket$$

So pick $R_2 \in \mathcal{R}_\varepsilon$, $(s_2, s_2') \in R_2$ and calculate

$$[\![\Gamma, x{:}A \vdash \mathtt{let}\ y \Leftarrow M\ \mathtt{in}\ N : TB]\!]\,(\rho, x)\,s_2 = [\![\Gamma, x{:}A, y{:}C \vdash N : TB]\!]\,(\rho, x, y_2)\,s_3$$

where (as $x \notin fv(M)$)

$$(s_3, y_2) = [\![\Gamma \vdash M : TC]\!]\,\rho\,s_2$$

By Lemma 8, $s_3 = s_2$, so $(s_3, s_2') \in R_2$. As M preserves all relations, it preserves $\{(s_2, s')\}$, so $(y_2, y') \in [\![Z]\!]$, which implies

$$((\rho, x, y_2), (\rho', x', y')) \in [\![\Theta, x : X, y : Z]\!]$$

so we're done by assumption that N preserves R_2.

Duplicated computation. Let $\Gamma = U(\Theta)$, $A = U(X)$, $B = U(Y)$ and $(\rho, \rho') \in [\![\Theta]\!]$. Because $[\![\Theta]\!]$ is a PER, we also have $(\rho, \rho) \in [\![\Theta]\!]$ and $(\rho', \rho') \in [\![\Theta]\!]$. Pick $R \in \mathcal{R}_{\varepsilon \cup \varepsilon'}$ and $(s_0, s_0') \in R$. We need to show

$$\begin{pmatrix} [\![\Gamma \vdash \mathtt{let}\ x \Leftarrow M; y \Leftarrow M\ \mathtt{in}\ N : TB]\!]\,\rho\,s_0, \\ [\![\Gamma \vdash \mathtt{let}\ x \Leftarrow M\ \mathtt{in}\ N[x/y] : TB]\!]\,\rho'\,s_0' \end{pmatrix} \in R \times [\![Y]\!]$$

Let

$$(s_1, x) = [\![\Gamma \vdash M : TA]\!]\,\rho\,s_0$$
$$(s_1', x') = [\![\Gamma \vdash M : TA]\!]\,\rho'\,s_0'$$
$$(s_2, y) = [\![\Gamma \vdash M : TA]\!]\,\rho\,s_1.$$

By Lemma 8 we can deduce $s_1 =_{\mathcal{L} \setminus \mathrm{wrs}(\varepsilon)} s_0$. We can use this fact as assumption to Lemma 9 starting in states s_1 and s_0, since $\mathrm{rds}(\varepsilon) \cap \mathrm{wrs}(\varepsilon) = \emptyset$, to obtain $(y, x) \in [\![X]\!]$ and for all $\ell \in \mathcal{L}$, either $s_2(\ell) = s_1(\ell)$, or $s_2(\ell) = s_1(\ell)$ and $s_1(\ell) = s_0(\ell)$. Hence $s_2 = s_1$; in other words, M behaves idempotently.

Expanding the semantics,

$$[\![\Gamma \vdash \mathtt{let}\ x \Leftarrow M; y \Leftarrow M\ \mathtt{in}\ N : TB]\!]\,\rho\,s_0 = [\![\Gamma' \vdash N : TB]\!]\,(\rho, x, y)\,s_2$$
$$[\![\Gamma \vdash \mathtt{let}\ x \Leftarrow M\ \mathtt{in}\ N[x/y] : TB]\!]\,\rho'\,s_0' = [\![\Gamma' \vdash N : TB]\!]\,(\rho', x', x')\,s_1'$$

where $\Gamma' = \Gamma, x : A, y : A$.

Since $R \in \mathcal{R}_{\varepsilon \cup \varepsilon'}$ we must have $R \in \mathcal{R}_\varepsilon$. Therefore M preserves R, so we can deduce that $(x, x') \in [\![X]\!]$ and $(s_1, s_1') \in R$, so $(s_2, s_1') \in R$. By transitivity we have that $(y, x') \in [\![X]\!]$. Hence $((\rho, x, y), (\rho', x', x')) \in [\![\Gamma']\!]$. Finally, because $R \in \mathcal{R}_{\varepsilon'}$, we know that N preserves R, from which we obtain the desired result.

Commuting computations. Let $\Gamma = U(\Theta)$, $A_i = U(X_i)$ and $B = U(Y)$. Pick $(\rho, \rho') \in [\![\Theta]\!]$, $R \in \mathcal{R}_{\varepsilon_1 \cup \varepsilon_2 \cup \varepsilon'}$, $(s_0, s_0') \in R$. Let

$$(s_1, x_1) = [\![\Gamma \vdash M_1 : TA_1]\!]\,\rho\,s_0 \quad \text{and} \quad (s_2, x_2) = [\![\Gamma \vdash M_2 : TA_2]\!]\,\rho\,s_1$$
$$(s_1', x_2') = [\![\Gamma \vdash M_2 : TA_2]\!]\,\rho'\,s_0' \quad \text{and} \quad (s_2', x_1') = [\![\Gamma \vdash M_1 : TA_1]\!]\,\rho'\,s_1'.$$

By the definition of $\mathcal{R}_{\varepsilon_1 \cup \varepsilon_2}$ for reading we know (1) that $s_0 =_{\mathrm{rds}(\varepsilon_1) \cup \mathrm{rds}(\varepsilon_2)} s_0'$. By four applications of Lemma 8, we have

$$s_1 =_{\mathcal{L} \setminus \mathrm{wrs}(\varepsilon_1)} s_0 \quad (2) \qquad s_2 =_{\mathcal{L} \setminus \mathrm{wrs}(\varepsilon_2)} s_1 \quad (3)$$
$$s_1' =_{\mathcal{L} \setminus \mathrm{wrs}(\varepsilon_2)} s_0' \quad (4) \qquad s_2' =_{\mathcal{L} \setminus \mathrm{wrs}(\varepsilon_1)} s_1' \quad (5)$$

From (1), (4) and the first side-condition on the rule, we have $s_0' =_{\mathrm{rds}(\varepsilon_1)} s_1'$. We can use this as assumption to apply Lemma 9 to M_1 starting in states s_0 and s_1' with corresponding environments ρ and ρ', to get $(x_1, x_1') \in [\![X_1]\!]$ and

$$\forall \ell \in \mathcal{L}, s_1(\ell) = s_2'(\ell) \vee (s_1(\ell) = s_0(\ell) \wedge s_2'(\ell) = s_1'(\ell)) \tag{6}$$

From (1), (2) and the second side-condition on the rule, we have $s_0' =_{\mathrm{rds}(\varepsilon_2)} s_1$. We can use this as assumption to apply Lemma 9 to M_2 starting in states s_1 and s_0' with corresponding environments ρ and ρ', to get $(x_2, x_2') \in [\![X_2]\!]$ and

$$\forall \ell \in \mathcal{L}, s_2(\ell) = s_1'(\ell) \vee (s_2(\ell) = s_1(\ell) \wedge s_1'(\ell) = s_0'(\ell)) \tag{7}$$

We now show that for all $\ell \in \mathcal{L}$ either $\ell \in \mathrm{wrs}(\varepsilon_1 \cup \varepsilon_2)$ and $s_2(\ell) = s_2'(\ell)$, or $s_2(\ell) = s_0(\ell)$ and $s_2'(\ell) = s_0'(\ell)$. In other words, there is some state change Δ with $\mathrm{dom}(\Delta) \subseteq \mathrm{wrs}(\varepsilon_1 \cup \varepsilon_2)$ such that $s_2 = s_0[\Delta]$ and $s_2' = s_0'[\Delta]$.

First suppose $\ell \notin \mathrm{wrs}(\varepsilon_1 \cup \varepsilon_2)$. By (2) and (3) we have $s_2(\ell) = s_0(\ell)$, and by (4) and (5) we have $s_2'(\ell) = s_0'(\ell)$ so we've shown the right hand disjunct.

Now suppose $\ell \in \mathrm{wrs}(\varepsilon_1)$. Therefore $\ell \notin \mathrm{wrs}(\varepsilon_2)$ by the third side-condition on the rule. By (6) either $s_1(\ell) = s_2'(\ell)$ ($= s_2(\ell)$ by (3)), or $s_1(\ell) = s_0(\ell)$ ($= s_2(\ell)$ by (3)) and $s_2'(\ell) = s_1'(\ell)$ ($= s_0'(\ell)$ by (4)) which is the disjunction above. Similar reasoning applies if $\ell \in \mathrm{wrs}(\varepsilon_2)$.

Since $(s_0, s_0') \in R$ we can show that $(s_2, s_2') \in R$ by induction on the size of $\mathrm{dom}(\Delta)$, using the definition of $\mathcal{R}_{\mathbf{w}_\ell}$ for each $\ell \in \mathrm{dom}(\Delta)$.

Now, expanding the semantics,

$$[\![\Gamma \vdash \mathtt{let}\, x_1 \Leftarrow M_1; x_2 \Leftarrow M_2 \,\mathtt{in}\, N : TB]\!]\, \rho\, s_0 = [\![\Gamma' \vdash N : TB]\!]\, (\rho, x_1, x_2)\, s_2$$
$$[\![\Gamma \vdash \mathtt{let}\, x_2 \Leftarrow M_2; x_1 \Leftarrow M_1 \,\mathtt{in}\, N : TB]\!]\, \rho'\, s_0' = [\![\Gamma' \vdash N : TB]\!]\, (\rho', x_1', x_2')\, s_2'$$

where $\Gamma' = \Gamma, x_1 : A_1, x_2 : A_2$. We have $((\rho, x_1, x_2), (\rho', x_1', x_2')) \in [\![\Gamma']\!]$. Finally, because $R \in \mathcal{R}_{\varepsilon'}$, we know that N preserves R starting in states s_2 and s_2', from which we obtain the desired result. $\qquad\square$

To make the link between relatedness and contextual equivalence, we have to say something just a little more sophisticated than 'related terms are contextually equivalent', as we also have to restrict the set of contexts. Write $(\Theta \vdash T_\varepsilon X)^\top$ for the set of all ground contexts $C[-]$ whose holes $-$ are typable as $\Theta \vdash - : T_\varepsilon X$ in the extended language. Then write $(\Theta \models T_\varepsilon X)^\top$ for the set of all contexts with a hole typeable as $U\Theta \vdash - : T(UX)$ in the base language such that

$$\forall M, M'. \Theta \models M = M' : T_\varepsilon X \implies [\![\vdash C[M] : T(\mathtt{bool})]\!] = [\![\vdash C[M'] : T(\mathtt{bool})]\!]$$

Then Theorem 2 plus adequacy implies that whenever $\Theta \vdash M = M' : T_\varepsilon X$, then for all $C[-]$ in $(\Theta \models T_\varepsilon X)^\top$ and for all s_0, s_1

$$\langle s_0, C[M] \rangle \Downarrow \langle s_1, \mathit{true} \rangle \iff \langle s_0, C[M'] \rangle \Downarrow \langle s_1, \mathit{true} \rangle.$$

and by the congruence rules, $(\Theta \vdash T_\varepsilon X)^\top \subseteq (\Theta \models T_\varepsilon X)^\top$.

The equations above also imply some effect-dependent type isomorphisms, proved by defining contexts transforming typed terms in both directions and showing that both compositions rewrite to the identity. For example

$$X \times Y \to T_\varepsilon Z \;\cong\; X \to T_{\{\}}(Y \to T_\varepsilon Z)$$

follows from $\beta\eta$ rules and the pure lambda hoist equation. However, there are valid contextual equivalences and isomorphisms that do not follow from the semantics. For example

$$(1 \to T_{\mathtt{w_x}}\mathtt{bool}) \to T_{\{\}}\mathtt{bool} \;\cong\; 1 \to T_{\{\}}\mathtt{bool}$$

does not hold in the model because of the presence of the non-definable 'snap-back' [7] function $\lambda g.\lambda s.\, let\ (s', b) = g()\, s\ in\ (s, b)$.

4   Discussion

We have shown how an extensional interpretation of read and write effects may be given using a non-standard form of relational parametricity over a standard semantics, and how that semantics may be used to justify program transformations. This contrasts with more common intensional approaches, based on traces in an instrumented semantics, which fail to decouple program properties from a particular syntactic system for establishing them and are not well-suited to reasoning about equivalences. We have also verified the interesting results of Sections 2.3 and 3 using the Coq proof assistant; the script is available via the first author's homepage.

The general relational approach that we are using here has been demonstrated to work well in both denotational and operational settings. Denotational approaches to the semantics of analysis properties using directly the obvious "factors through" style of definition (e.g. saying a computation is observationally pure if its denotation factors through that of val) can easily raise unpleasant questions of definability if one tries to recast them in an operational framework.

In this paper we have concentrated on an extremely simple effect system, so as to make the methodology as clear as possible. Working with domains instead of sets, to allow recursion, is straightforward. With Buchlovsky, we have also successfully applied just the same techniques to reason about transformations justified by an effect analysis for exceptions. Looking at the set of all relations preserved by a subset of the operations on a monad really does seem to be the 'right' way of understanding effect systems (and seems not unrelated to the algebraic view of effects being developed by Plotkin and Power [15]). We are confident the idea extends to a wide class of effect analyses (and more general notions of refinement type), and are currently working on applying it to region-based encapsulation of state effects in the presence of dynamic allocation. This is a challenging problem; despite much work on monadic encapsulation (and on region-based memory management [19]) since the introduction of runST in Haskell [10], some of it incorrect and most of it rather complex, previous work mostly addresses simple syntactic type soundness, rather than equations [12], though the region calculus has been given a relation-based semantics [2] and studied using bisimulation [9]. Parametric logical relations have previously been used for establishing particular equivalences involving encapsulated state [16,7] and even provide a complete characterization of contextual equivalence for a language with integer store [14]. However, a combination of those constructions with our notion of refined types that is suitably generic and also expressive enough to validate, for example, interesting cases of the duplicated computations equation, has so far proved elusive.[2]

One interesting application of effect analyses is in assertion checking for imperative languages. Assertions are typically boolean expressions in the same language as is being checked and make use of side-effecting operations such as mutation in computing their results. Yet it is important that these side-effects do not affect the behaviour of the program being specified: assertions should be observationally pure. Naumann uses simulation relations to capture a notion of observational purity for boolean-valued expressions that allows mutation of encapsulated state [13].

PER-based accounts of dependency and information flow [1,18] are closely related to the present work; as a referee observed, observable notions of reading and writing have a natural connection with confidentiality and integrity.

Apart from the lines of future work implicit in the above, it would be interesting to try to use our approach to capture some general relationship between effect systems and their intuitive duals, capability/permission systems.

References

1. M. Abadi, A. Banerjee, N. Heintze, and J. G. Riecke. A core calculus of dependency. In *26th Symposium on Principles of Programming Languages (POPL)*, 1999.
2. A. Banerjee, N. Heintze, and J. Riecke. Region analysis and the polymorphic lambda calculus. In *Proceedings of the 14th IEEE Symposium on Logic in Computer Science (LICS)*, 1999.
3. N. Benton. Simple relational correctness proofs for static analyses and program transformations. In *Proceedings of the 31st ACM Symposium on Principles of Programming Languages (POPL)*, January 2004. Revised version available from http://research.microsoft.com/~nick/publications.htm.
4. N. Benton. Semantics of program analyses and transformations. Lecture Notes for the PAT Summer School, Copenhagen, June 2005.
5. N. Benton, J. Hughes, and E. Moggi. Monads and effects. In G. Barthe, P. Dybjer, L. Pinto, and J. Saraiva, editors, *Applied Semantics, Advanced Lectures*, volume 2395 of *Lecture Notes in Computer Science*. Springer-Verlag, 2002.
6. N. Benton and A. Kennedy. Monads, effects and transformations. In *3rd International Workshop on Higher Order Operational Techniques in Semantics (HOOTS), Paris*, volume 26 of *Electronic Notes in Theoretical Computer Science*. Elsevier, September 1999.

---

[2] This is not *quite* the same problem as in region-based memory management. We want to reason about encapsulated state being non-observable to the rest of the program, but that does not necessarily mean it may safely be deallocated.

7. N. Benton and B. Leperchey. Relational reasoning in a nominal semantics for storage. In *Proc. 7th International Conference on Typed Lambda Calculi and Applications (TLCA)*, volume 3461 of *Lecture Notes in Computer Science*, 2005.

8. D. K. Gifford and J. M. Lucassen. Integrating functional and imperative programming. In *ACM Conference on LISP and Functional Programming*, Cambridge, Massachusetts, August 1986.

9. S. Helsen. Bisimilarity for the region calculus. *Higher-Order and Symbolic Computation*, 17(4), 2004.

10. S. Peyton Jones and J. Launchbury. State in Haskell. *Lisp and Symbolic Computation*, 8(4), 1995.

11. J. M. Lucassen and D. K. Gifford. Polymorphic effect systems. In *Conference Record of the 15th Annual ACM Symposium on Principles of Programming Languages (POPL)*, 1988.

12. E. Moggi and A. Sabry. Monadic encapsulation of effects: A revised approach (extended version). *Journal of Functional Programming*, 11(6), 2001.

13. D. Naumann. Observational purity and encapsulation. *Theoretical Computer Science*, To appear.

14. A. M. Pitts and I. D. B. Stark. Operational reasoning for functions with local state. In *Higher Order Operational Techniques in Semantics*. CUP, 1998.

15. G. D. Plotkin and J. Power. Notions of computation determine monads. In *Foundations of Software Science and Computation Structures, Proceedings of FOSSACS '02*, volume 2303 of *Lecture Notes in Computer Science*. Springer-Verlag, 2002.

16. U. S. Reddy and H. Yang. Correctness of data representations involving heap data structures. *Science of Computer Programming*, 50(1–3):129–160, March 2004.

17. J. C. Reynolds. The meaning of types – from intrinsic to extrinsic semantics. Technical Report BRICS RS-00-32, BRICS, University of Aarhus, December 2000.

18. A. Sabelfeld and D. Sands. A PER model of secure information flow in sequential programs. *Higher-Order and Symbolic Computation*, 14(1):59–91, March 2001.

19. M. Tofte and J.-P. Talpin. Region-based memory management. *Information and Computation*, 132(2):109–176, 1997.

20. A. Tolmach. Optimizing ML using a hierarchy of monadic types. In *Proceedings of the Workshop on Types in Compilation (TIC)*, volume 1473 of *Lecture Notes in Computer Science*. Springer-Verlag, 1998.

21. P. Wadler and P. Thiemann. The marriage of effects and monads. *ACM Trans. Comput. Logic*, 4(1):1–32, 2003.

A Fine-Grained Join Point Model
for More Reusable Aspects

Hidehiko Masuhara[1], Yusuke Endoh[2,*], and Akinori Yonezawa[2]

[1] Graduate School of Arts and Sciences, University of Tokyo
masuhara@acm.org
[2] Department of Computer Science, University of Tokyo
{mame, yonezawa}@yl.is.s.u-tokyo.ac.jp

Abstract. We propose a new join point model for aspect-oriented programming (AOP) languages. In most AOP languages including AspectJ, a join point is a time interval of an action in execution. While those languages are widely accepted, they have problems in aspects reusability, and awkwardness when designing advanced features such as tracematches. Our proposed join point model, namely the point-in-time join point model redefines join points as the moments both at the beginning and end of actions. Those finer-grained join points enable us to design AOP languages with better reusability and flexibility of aspects. In this paper, we designed an AspectJ-like language based on the point-in-time model. We also give a denotational semantics of a simplified language in a continuation passing style, and demonstrate that we can straightforwardly model advanced language features such as exception handling and `cflow` pointcuts.

1 Introduction

Aspect-oriented programming (AOP) is a programming paradigm that addresses problems of crosscutting concerns[11, 15], such as exception handling, security mechanisms and coordinations among modules. Since implementations of crosscutting concerns without AOP have to involve with many modules, AOP improves maintainability of programs by making those concerns into separate modules.

One of the fundamental language mechanisms in AOP is the *pointcut and advice* mechanism, which can be found in many AOP languages including AspectJ[15]. As previous studies have shown, design of pointcut language and selection of join points are key design factors of the pointcut and advice mechanisms in terms of expressiveness, reusability and robustness of advice declarations [4,14,16–18, 21].

A pointcut serves as an abstraction of join points in the following senses:

– It can give a name to a set of join points (e.g., by means of *named pointcuts* in AspectJ).

---

* Currently with Toshiba Corp.

N. Kobayashi (Ed.): APLAS 2006, LNCS 4279, pp. 131–147, 2006.

- Differences among join points, such as join point kinds and parameter positions, can be subsumed. For example, when we define a logging aspect that records the first argument to runCommand method and the second argument to debug, different parameter positions are subsumed by the next pointcut:

```
pointcut userInput(String s):
    (call(* Toplevel.runCommand(String)) && args(s))
 || (call(* Debugger.debug(int,String)) && args(*,s));
```

- It can separate concrete specifications of interested join points from advice declarations (e.g., by means of *abstract pointcuts* and *aspect inheritance* in AspectJ). In other words, we can parameterize interested join points in an advice declaration.

There have been several studies on advanced pointcut primitives for accurately and concisely abstracting join points[4, 16, 17, 21].

In order to allow pointcuts to accurately abstract join points, the pointcut and advice mechanisms should also have a rich set of join points. If an interested event is not a join point, there is not way to advise it at all. Several studies have investigated to introduce new kinds of join points, such as loops[14], conditional branches[18], and local variable accesses[19] into AspectJ-like languages. In other words, the more kinds of join points the pointcut and advice mechanism has, the more opportunities advice declarations can be applied to.

This paper focuses on a language with finer grained join points for improving reusability of advice declarations. The join point model can be compared with traditional join point model in AspectJ-like languages as follows:

- In the join point model in AspectJ-like languages, a join point represents duration of an event, such as a call to a method until its termination. We call this model the *region-in-time* model because a join point corresponds to a region on a time line.
- In our proposing join point model, a join point represents an instant of an event, such as the beginning of a method call and the termination of a method call. We call this model the *point-in-time* model because a join point corresponds to a point on a time line.

The contributions of the paper are:

- We demonstrate that the point-in-time join point model can improve reusability of advice.
- We present an experimental AOP language called PitJ based on the point-in-time model. PitJ's advice is as expressive as AspectJ's in most typical use cases even though the advice mechanism in PitJ is simpler than the one in AspectJ-like languages.
- We give a formal semantics of the point-in-time model by using a small functional AOP language called Pitλ. Thanks to affinity with continuation passing style, the semantics gives a concise model with advanced features such as exception handling.

```
1 aspect ConsoleLogging {
2   pointcut userInput(): call(String *.readLine());
3   after() returning(String s): userInput() {
4     Log.add(s);
5   }
6 }
```

Fig. 1. Logging aspect for the console version

2   Reusability Problem of Region-in-Time Join Point Model

Although languages that are based on the region-in-time join point model are designed to be reusable, there are situations where aspects are not as reusable as they seem to be. This section explains such situations, and argues that this is common problem to the region-in-time join point model.

In order to clarify the problem, this section uses a crosscutting concern that is to log user's input received by the following two versions of base program:

a console version that receives user input from the console.

a hybrid version, evolved from the console version, that receives user input from both the console and GUI components.

2.1   Logging Aspect for the Console Version

Figure 1 shows a logging aspect for the console version in AspectJ[15]. We assume that the base program receives user input as return values of `readLine` method in several classes.

Line 2 declares a pointcut `userInput` that matches any join point that represents a call to `readLine` method. Lines 3–5 declare advice to log the input. `after() returning(String s)` is an advice modifier of the advice declaration that specifies to run the advice body *after* the action of the matched join points with binding the return value from the join point to variable `s`. The body of the advice, which is at line 4, records the value.

It is possible to declare a generic aspect in order to subsume changes of join points to be logged in different versions. For example, Figure 2 shows a generic logging aspect that uses abstract pointcut `userInput` in an advice declaration, and a concrete logging aspect for the console version that concretizes `userInput` into `call(String *.readLine())`.

The generic logging aspect is reusable to log user's input from environment variables by changing `userInput()` pointcut in `ConsoleLogging` in Figure 2 to `call(String *.readLine()) || call(String System.getenv(String))`. Note that we do not need to modify the generic logging aspect.

```
1 abstract aspect UserInputLogging {
2   abstract pointcut userInput();
3   after() returning(String s): userInput() {
4     Log.add(s);
5   }
6 }


7 aspect ConsoleLogging extends UserInputLogging {
8   pointcut userInput(): call(String *.readLine());
9 }
```

Fig. 2. Generic logging aspect and its application to the console version

```
1 aspect HybridLogging extends UserInputLogging {
2   pointcut userInput(): call(String *.readLine());
3   pointcut userInput2(String s):
4     call(String *.onSubmit(String)) && args(s);
5   before(String s): userInput2(s) {
6     Log.add(s);
7   }
8 }
```

Fig. 3. Logging aspect for the hybrid version

2.2 Modifying the Aspect to the Hybrid Version

The generic logging aspect is not reusable when the base program changes its programming style. In other words, pointcuts no longer can subsume changes in certain kinds of programming style.

Consider a hybrid version of the base program that receives user input from GUI components as well as from the console. The version uses the GUI framework which calls onSubmit (String) method on a listener object in the base program with the string *as an argument* when a user inputs a string via GUI interface.

Since UserInputLogging in Figure 2 can only log return values, we have to define a different pointcut and advice declaration as shown in Figure 3.

Making the logging aspect for hybrid version reusable is tricky and awkward. Since single pointcut and advice can not subsume differences between return values and arguments, we have to define a pair of pointcuts and advice declarations. In order to avoid duplication in advice bodies, we need to define an auxiliary method and let advice bodies call the method. The resulted aspect is shown in Figure 4.

Some might argue that it is possible to reuse UserInputLogging aspect in Figure 4 by finding join points that always run before calls to onSubmit. However, such join points can not always be found, especially when advice declarations take parameters from join points. Moreover, such a compromise usually

```
 1 abstract aspect UserInputLogging2 {
 2    abstract pointcut userInputAsReturnValue();
 3    abstract pointcut userInputAsArgument(String s);
 4    after() returning(String s): userInputAsReturnValue() {
 5       log(s);
 6    }
 7    before(String s): userInputAsArgument(s) {
 8       log(s);
 9    }
10    void log(String s) {
11       Log.add(s);
12    }
13 }
```

Fig. 4. Generic logging aspect that can log for both return values and arguments

makes aspects fragile because the pointcuts *indirectly* specify join points that the aspects are actually interested in.

2.3   Awkwardness in Advanced Pointcuts

Some advanced pointcuts require to distinguish beginnings and ends of actions as different events. However, since region-in-time model does not distinguish them as different join points, the resulted languages have to introduce mechanisms to not only identifying join points but also mechanisms to specify their beginnings and ends.

For example, the *trace maching* mechanism is one of the useful extensions to AOP languages that enables advice run based on the history of events[1]. The code below shows an example of a tracematch that logs query calls performed only after completion of a login call.

```
1 tracematch() {
2    sym login after returning: call(* login(User,..));
3    sym query before: call(* query(Query));
4    login query+        // any query after login
5    { Log.add(...); }   // shall be logged
6 }
```

The description of the tracematch consists of two parts, namely declarations of the symbols and a piece of code with a trace pattern. Line 2 and 3 declare symbols login and query as the end of a login call and the beginning of a query call, respectively. Then line 4 specify the trace pattern of those events in a regular expression of declared symbols.

One might first think that using named pointcuts instead of symbols could simplify the language without losing expressiveness. However, it is not possible as the named pointcuts can merely specify the join points and lack the information whether the programmer is interested in either the beginnings or the ends of the join points.

2.4 Analysis of the Problem

By generalizing the above problem, we argue that pointcuts in the region-in-time join point model can not subsume differences between the beginnings of actions and the ends of actions.

Such a difference is not unique to the logging concern, but can also be seen in many cases. For example, following differences can not be subsumed by pointcuts in the region-in-time join point model:

- a polling style program that waits for events by calling a method and an event driven style program that receives events by being called by a system,
- a method that reports an error by returning a special value and a method that does by an exception, and
- a direct style program in which caller performs rest of the computation and continuation-passing style in which the rest of computation is specified by function parameters.

Our claim is that the problem roots from the design of join point model in which a join point represents a region-in-time, or a time interval during program execution. For example, in AspectJ, a call join point represents a region-in-time while invoking the method, executing the body of the method and returning from the method. This design in turn requires advice modifiers which indicate either the beginnings or the ends of the join points that are selected by pointcut.

3   Point-in-Time Join Point Model

3.1   Overview

We propose a new join point model, called *point-in-time join point model*, and design an experimental AOP language, called *PitJ*. PitJ differs from AspectJ-like languages in the following ways:

- A join point represents a point-in-time (or an instant of program execution) rather than a region-in-time (or an interval). Consequently, there are no such notions like "beginning of a join point" or "end of a join point".
- There are new kinds of join points that represent terminations of actions. For example, a return from methods is an independent join point, which we call *a reception*[1] *join point*, from a call join point. Similarly, an exceptional return is *a failure join point*. Table 1 lists the join points in PitJ along with respective ones in AspectJ.

---

[1] Older versions of AspectJ[15] have reception join points for representing different actions.

PitJ	AspectJ
call / reception / failure	method call
execution / return / throw	method execution
get / success_get / failure_get	field reference
set / success_set / failure_set	field assignment

Table 1. Join points in PitJ and AspectJ

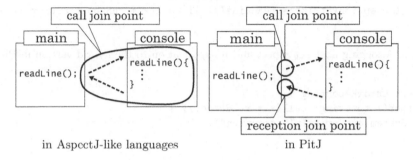

in AspectJ-like languages   in PitJ

Fig. 5. Join points in languages based on region-in-time and point-in-time models

- There are new pointcut constructs that match those new kinds of join points. For example, `reception(m)` is a pointcut that selects any reception join point that returns from the method `m`.
- Advice declarations no longer take modifiers like `before` and `after` to specify timing of execution.

Figure 5 illustrate the difference between the point-in-time join point model and region-in-time one.

Figure 6 shows example aspect definitions in PitJ. The generic aspect (lines 1–6) is not different from the one in AspectJ expect that the advice does not take a modifier (line 3). `HybridLogging` aspect concretizes the pointcut by using reception and call pointcut primitives (lines 9–10). When `readLine` returns to the base program, a reception join point is created and matches the `userInput`. The return value is bound to `s` by `args` pointcut. When `onSubmit` method is called, a call join point matches the pointcut with binding the argument to `s`.

As we see in Figure 6, differences in the timing of advice execution as well as the way of passing parameters can be subsumed by pointcuts with the point-in-time join point model. This ability allows us to define more reusable aspect libraries by using abstract pointcuts because users of the library can fully control the join points to apply aspect.

We verified the reusability problem which is effectively solved by the point-in-time join point model by case study with some realistic applications, aTrack[2] and AJHotDraw[20]. The details of the case study are presented in the other literature[13].

```
1 abstract aspect UserInputLogging {
2    abstract pointcut userInput(String s);
3    advice(String s) : userInput(s) {
4       Log.add(s);
5    }
6 }

7 aspect HybridLogging extends UserInputLogging {
8    pointcut userInput(String s): args(s) &&
9       (reception(String *.readLine()) || call(* *.onSubmit(String)));
10 }
```

Fig. 6. A logging abstract aspect and its application to the hybrid vertion in PitJ

```
1 aspect ErrorReporting {
2    after() throwing: call(* *.readLine()) {
3       System.out.println("exception");
4    }
5 }
```

Fig. 7. An aspect to capture exceptions in AspectJ

3.2   Exception Handling

In AspectJ, advice declarations have to distinguish exceptions by using a special advice modifier `after() throwing`. It specifies to run the advice body when interested join points terminate by throwing exception. For example, a sample aspect in Figure 7 prints a message when an uncaught exception is thrown from `readLine`. Similar to the discussion on the `before` and `after` advice, termination by throwing an exception and normal termination can not be captured by single advice declartion[2].

In PitJ, 'termination by throwing an exception' is regarded as an independent failure join point. Figure 8 is an equivalent to the one in Figure 7. A pointcut `failure` matches a failure join point which represents a point-in-time at the termination of a specified method by throwing an exception.

3.3   Around-like Advice

One of the fundamental questions to PitJ is, by simplifying advice modifiers, whether it is expressive enough to implement around advice in AspectJ, which has powerful mechanisms. We analyzed that around advice in AspectJ has four abilities:

1. replace the parameters to the join point with new ones,

---

[2] It is possible to capture them by using `after` advice, which however can not access to return values or exception objects.

```
1 aspect ErrorReporting {
2   advice(): failure(* *.readLine()) {
3     System.out.println("exception");
4   }
5 }
```

Fig. 8. An aspect to capture exceptions in PitJ

2. replace the return values to the caller of the join point,
3. go back to the caller without executing the join point, and
4. execute the join point more then once.

In PitJ, the abilities 1 and 2 can be simulated by treating a return value of an advice body as a new value. For example, consider an advice declaration:

```
advice(String s): args(s) && (reception(* *.readLine())
                          || call(* *.onSubmit(String)) {
  return s.replaceAll("<", "&lt;").replaceAll(">", "&gt;");
}
```

This advice sanitizes user input by replacing unsafe characters with escape sequences. When an advice body ends without **return**, the value in the join points remains unchanged.

For the ability 3, we introduce a new construct **skip**. When it is evaluated in a call join point, jump occurs to the subsequent reception join point with no execution between the two join points. Nothing happens when evaluated in a reception and failure join points. For example, consider an advice declaration:

```
advice(): call(* *.readLine()) { skip "dummy"; }
```

With the advice, even if `readLine()` is evaluated, it immediately returns "dummy" without reading any string from a console.

For the ability 4, a special function **proceed** is added. It executes the action until the subsequent reception one, and then returns the result. For example, consider an advice declaration:

```
advice(): call(* *.readLine()) {
  skip(proceed() + proceed());
}
```

With this advice, the method `readLine` receives two lines at once, concatenates them, and returns it.

We introduced the construct **skip** so that advice declarations can dynamically control how to **proceed**. An alternative design would be to introduce a different kind of advice that does not proceed to original join points even if it does not evaluate **skip**. We need further programming experience to compare those alternatives in terms of program readability.

3.4   More Advanced Features

Some existing AOP systems including AspectJ provides some context sensitive pointcuts. They don't always match specific kinds of join points. Instead, they judge whether a join point is in a specific context. PitJ has `cflow` pointcut, which is a kind of context sensitive pointcuts. It identifies join points based on whether they occur in the dynamic context during a region-in-time between a specified call join point and the subsequent reception one. For example, `cflow(call(* *.onSubmit(String)))` specifies any join point that occurs between when a `onSubmit` method is called and when it returns.

In addition, we are considering the integration of trace sensitive aspects [9, 10, 21] which use execution trace, or history of occured join points, to judge whether to perform additional computation, We expect that our finer grained join points enhance its effectiveness and robustness.

3.5   Design Considerations of Pointcut Primitives

The design of the pointcuts in PitJ is chosen among several alternatives. In fact, we examined the following three designs, which have different advantages and disadvantages:

1. Provide a primitive for each kind of join point, similar to the pointcuts in AspectJ. While it makes each pointcut description simple, it requires many pointcut primitives. This is our current design.
2. Provide a set of primitives that discriminates kinds of events (e.g., call and execution) and a set of primitives taht discriminates timing relative to an event (e.g., entry and exit). For example, `call(* *.readLine())` matches both beginnings and ends of `readLine` calls, and `call(* *.readLine()) && exit()` matches only ends of `readLine` calls. It requires a smaller set of pointcut primitives, but often makes each pointcut description longer.
3. Provide a set of primitive that identifies join points that represent beginnings of events, in addition to `cflow`-like pointcuts that create pointcuts that identify ends and failures of events from a given pointcut. For example, `call(* *.readLine())` matches begginings of `readLine` calls and `cont(call(* *.readLine()))` matches ends of `readLine` calls. Though this design might be more powerful than the above two designs, it is not certain whether we can define a clear semantics.

We chose the first design because its simplicity and affinity with AspectJ. No design is, however, clearly better than others. More programming experiences will give us better insight to discuss about the right design.

4   Formal Semantics

We present a formal semantics of Pitλ, which is a simplified version of PitJ. Pitλ simplifies PitJ by using a lambda-calculus as a base language, and by supporting

Syntax:

(Expression) $e ::=$	x	(IDENTIFIER)
	$\mid$ **fun** $x \to e$	(FUNCTION)
	$\mid$ $e\ e$	(APPLICATION)

Semantic algebras:
numbers Int, booleans $Bool$, identifiers Ide

$v \in Val = Int + Bool + Fun$	(VALUES)
$\rho \in Env = Ide \to Val$	(ENVIRONMENTS)
$\kappa \in Ctn = Val \to Ans$	(CONTINUATIONS)
$f \in Fun = Ctn \to Ctn$	(FUNCTIONS)
$Ans = Val_\perp$	(ANSWERS)

Valuation function for the expressions:

$$\mathcal{E} : \text{Expression} \to Env \to Ctn \to Ans$$
$$\mathcal{E}[\![x]\!]\ \rho\ \kappa = \kappa\ (\rho\ x)$$
$$\mathcal{E}[\![\textbf{fun}\ x \to e]\!]\ \rho\ \kappa = \kappa\ (inFun(\lambda\kappa'v.\ \mathcal{E}[\![e]\!]\ ([v\ /\ x]\rho)\ \kappa'))$$
$$\mathcal{E}[\![e_0\ e_1]\!]\ \rho\ \kappa = \mathcal{E}[\![e_0]\!]\ \rho\ (\lambda Fun(f).\ \mathcal{E}[\![e_1]\!]\ \rho\ (\lambda v.f\ \kappa\ v))$$

Fig. 9. Syntax and semantics of the base language

only call, reception and failure join points. The semantics contributes to clarify the detailed behavior of the program especially when integrated with other advanced features such as exception handling and context sensitive pointcuts. It also helps to compare expressiveness of the point-in-time join point model against the region-in-time one.

4.1 Base Language

Figure 9 shows the syntax of the base language and its denotational semantics in a continuation passing style (CPS). We use untyped lambda-calculus as the base language. The semantics follows the style of Danvy and Filinski[8].

4.2 Syntax and Semantics of Pitλ_0

We begin with Pitλ_0, which is a core part of Pitλ that has only call and reception join points. Syntactically, it uses the same expressions to the base language, and has pointcuts and a list of advice as shown in Figure 10.

We give a semantics of Pitλ_0 by modifying the semantics of the base language in Section 4.1.

First, we define additional semantic algebras. An event ϵ is either call or reception with a function name and a join point θ is a pair of an event and an argument:

$$\epsilon ::= \textsf{call}(x) \mid \textsf{reception}(x) \qquad (Evt)$$
$$\theta ::= (\epsilon, v) \qquad (Jp)$$

(Expression) $e ::=$	x	(IDENTIFIER)
	$\mid$ **fun** $x \to e$	(FUNCTION)
	$\mid$ $e\ e$	(APPLICATION)

(Pointcut) $p ::= \text{call}(x) \mid \text{reception}(x) \mid \text{args}(x) \mid p\ \&\&\ p \mid p\ \mid\mid\ p$

(Advice) $a ::= \cdot \mid \text{advice} : p \to e;\ a$

Fig. 10. Pitλ_0 syntax

$$\mathcal{P} : \text{Pointcut} \to Env \to Jp \to (Env \cup \{False\})$$

$$\mathcal{P}[\![\text{call}(x)]\!]\ \rho\ (\text{call}(x'), v) = \begin{cases} \rho & \text{if } x = x' \text{ or } x = * \\ False & \text{otherwise} \end{cases}$$

$$\mathcal{P}[\![\text{reception}(x)]\!]\ \rho\ (\text{reception}(x'), v) = \begin{cases} \rho & \text{if } x = x' \text{ or } x = * \\ False & \text{otherwise} \end{cases}$$

$$\mathcal{P}[\![\text{args}(x)]\!]\ \rho\ (\epsilon, v) = [v\ /\ x]\rho$$

$$\mathcal{P}[\![p_0\ \&\&\ p_1]\!]\ \rho\ \theta = \begin{cases} \mathcal{P}[\![p_1]\!]\ \rho'\ \theta & \text{if } \mathcal{P}[\![p_0]\!]\ \rho\ \theta = \rho' \\ False & \text{otherwise} \end{cases}$$

$$\mathcal{P}[\![p_0\ \mid\mid\ p_1]\!]\ \rho\ \theta = \begin{cases} \rho' & \text{if } \mathcal{P}[\![p_0]\!]\ \rho\ \theta = \rho' \\ \mathcal{P}[\![p_1]\!]\ \rho\ \theta & \text{otherwise} \end{cases}$$

Fig. 11. Semantics of pointcuts

Additionally, we define an auxiliary function σ that extracts a signature (or a name) from an expression.

$$\sigma : \text{Expression} \to \text{IDENTIFIER}$$

$$\sigma(e) = \begin{cases} e & \text{if } e \text{ is IDENTIFIER} \\ \$ & \text{otherwise} \end{cases}$$

If it receives an IDENTIFIER, the argument itself is returned. Otherwise, it returns the dummy signature $\$$. For example, $\sigma(x)$ is x, and $\sigma(\text{fun } x \to x)$ is $\$$.

The semantics of the pointcuts is a function $\mathcal{P}$ shown in Figure 11. $\mathcal{P}[\![p]\!]\ \rho_{empty}\ \theta$ tests whether the pointcut p and the current join point θ match. If they do, it returns an environment that binds a variable to a value by args pointcut. Otherwise, it returns $False$.

We then define the semantic function $\mathcal{A}$ for lists of advice declarations (Figure 12), which receives an advice list, an event and a continuation. When the pointcut of the first advice matches a join point, it returns a continuation that evaluates the advice body and then evaluates the rest of the advice list. Otherwise, it returns a continuation that evaluates the rest of the advice list. At the end of the list, it continues to the original computation.

We finally define the semantic function of the expression. In the section, the semantics of IDENTIFIER and FUNCTION remain unchanged. The semantics of APPLICATION in Pitλ_0 is defined by inserting application to $\mathcal{A}$ at appropriate

$$\mathcal{A} : Advices \rightarrow Evt \rightarrow Ctn \rightarrow Ctn$$

$$\mathcal{A}[\![\mathbf{advice} : p \rightarrow e; a']\!] \, \epsilon \, \kappa \, v = \begin{cases} \mathcal{E}[\![e]\!] \, \rho' \, (\mathcal{A}[\![a']\!] \, \epsilon \, \kappa) & \text{if } \mathcal{P}[\![p]\!] \, \rho_{empty} \, (\epsilon, v) = \rho' \\ \mathcal{A}[\![a']\!] \, \epsilon \, \kappa \, v & \text{otherwise} \end{cases}$$

$$\mathcal{A}[\![\, \cdot \,]\!] \, \epsilon \, \kappa \, v = \kappa \, v$$

Fig. 12. Semantics of advice

$$\mathcal{E} : Expression \rightarrow Env \rightarrow Ctn \rightarrow Ans$$

$$\mathcal{E}[\![x]\!] \, \rho \, \kappa = \kappa \, (\rho \, x)$$

$$\mathcal{E}[\![\mathbf{fun} \; x \rightarrow e]\!] \, \rho \, \kappa = \kappa \, (inFun(\lambda\kappa'v. \, \mathcal{E}[\![e]\!] \, ([v \, / \, x]\rho) \, \kappa'))$$

$$\mathcal{E}[\![e_0 \, e_1]\!] \, \rho \, \kappa = \mathcal{E}[\![e_0]\!] \, \rho \, (\lambda Fun(f). \, \mathcal{E}[\![e_1]\!] \, \rho \, (\lambda v.$$
$$\mathcal{A}[\![a_0]\!] \, \mathsf{call}(\sigma(e_0))(f \, (\mathcal{A}[\![a_0]\!] \, \mathsf{reception}(\sigma(e_0)) \, \kappa)) \, v))$$

Fig. 13. Semantics of expressions

positions. The original semantics of APPLICATION is as follows:

$$\mathcal{E}[\![e_0 \, e_1]\!] \, \rho \, \kappa = \mathcal{E}[\![e_0]\!] \, \rho \, (\lambda Fun(f). \, \mathcal{E}[\![e_1]\!] \, \rho \, (\lambda v. \; \boxed{f \, \kappa} \; v))$$

The shadowed part $f \, \kappa$ is a continuation that executes the function body and passes the result to the subsequent continuation κ. The application to the continuation $f \, \kappa \, v$, therefore, corresponds to a call join point. By replacing the continuation with $\mathcal{A}[\![a]\!] \, \mathsf{call}(x) \, (f \, \kappa)$, we can run applicable advice at function calls:

$$\mathcal{E}[\![e_0 \, e_1]\!] \, \rho \, \kappa = \mathcal{E}[\![e_0]\!] \, \rho \, (\lambda Fun(f). \, \mathcal{E}[\![e_1]\!] \, \rho \, (\lambda v.\mathcal{A}[\![a_0]\!] \, \mathsf{call}(\sigma(e_0)) \, (f \, \kappa) \, v))$$

where a_0 is the globally defined list of all advice declarations.

Similarly a reception of a return value from a function application can be found by η-expanding[3] as follows:

$$\mathcal{E}[\![e_0 \, e_1]\!] \, \rho \, \kappa = \mathcal{E}[\![e_0]\!] \, \rho \, (\lambda Fun(f). \mathcal{E}[\![e_1]\!] \, \rho \, (\lambda v.f \, (\lambda v'.\boxed{\kappa \, v'}) \, v))$$

Therefore, advice application at reception join point can be achieved by replacing κ with $\mathcal{A}[\![a]\!] \, \mathsf{reception}(x) \, \kappa$.

Figure 13 shows the final semantics for the expression with call and reception join points. As we have seen, advice application is taken into the semantic function in a systematic way: given a continuation κ that represents a join point, substitute with $\mathcal{A}[\![a]\!] \, \epsilon \, \kappa$. In the next section, we will see advanced features can also be incorporated in the same ways.

---

[3] This η-expansion prevents *tail-call elimination*. It fits the facts that defining an advice whose pointcut specifies a reception join point makes tail-call elimination impossible.

(Expression) $e ::= \dots$	
$\mid$ **try** e **with** $x \to e$	(TRY)
$\mid$ **raise** e	(RAISE)
(Pointcut) $p ::= \dots \mid$ **failure** (x)	

Fig. 14. Additional constructs for exception handling

5   Advanced Features with Pitλ

With the aid of the clarified semantics, we are now able to discuss advanced language features with the point-in-time model. Thus far, we investigated several advanced features by defining an extended language called Pitλ_1. The investigated features include exception handling, context sensitive pointcuts (i.e., `cflow`-like pointcut) and around advice. Due to the space limitation, we only present the exception handling mechanism below. The other features are explained in the other literatures[12, 13].

5.1   Exception Handling

In AspectJ, advice declarations have to distinguish exceptions by using a special advice modifier (as described in Subsection 3.2). It not only complicates the problem in reusability, but also makes the semantics awkward. This is because we have to pay attention to all combinations of advice modifiers and pointcuts. In fact, some existing formalizations[22, 23] gave a slightly different semantic equation to each kind of advice declarations. Meanwhile, the point-in-time join point model has no advice modifiers, which makes the semantics simpler.

Figure 14 shows additional constructs for exception handling: TRY and RAISE as the expression, and `failure` as the pointcut. For the sake of simplicity, we don't introduce the special values which represent an exception; an arbitrary value can be raised. For example, (`fun` x $\to$ `raise` x) 1 raises the value 1 as an exception. `try` ((`fun` x $\to$ `raise` x) 1) $+ 2$ `with` x $\to$ x$+ 3$ is evaluated normally to the value 4. But, with `advice` : `failure`(*) `&&` `args`(x) $\to$ x $*$ 2, it is evaluated to the value 5.

We first give a standard denotational semantics to these constructs. In preparation for it, we introduce a continuation which represents current exception handler to the semantics algebra *Fun* and the semantic functions $\mathcal{A}$ and $\mathcal{E}$:

$$f \in Fun = Ctn \to Ctn \to Ctn$$

$$\mathcal{E} : \text{Expression} \to Env \to Ctn \to Ctn \to Ans$$

$$\mathcal{E}[\![x]\!] \, \rho \, \kappa_h \, \kappa = \kappa \, (\rho \, x)$$

$$\mathcal{E}[\![\textbf{fun } x \to e]\!] \, \rho \, \kappa_h \, \kappa = \kappa \, (inFun(\lambda \kappa_h{}' \kappa' v.$$
$$\mathcal{E}[\![e]\!] \, ([v \, / \, x]\rho) \, \kappa_h{}' \, \kappa'))$$

$$\mathcal{E}[\![e_0 \, e_1]\!] \, \rho \, \kappa_h \, \kappa = \mathcal{E}[\![e_0]\!] \, \rho \, \kappa_h \, (\lambda Fun(f). \, \mathcal{E}[\![e_1]\!] \, \rho \, \kappa_h \, (\lambda v.$$
$$\mathcal{A}[\![a]\!] \, \text{call}(\sigma(e_0)) \, \kappa_h \, (f \, \kappa_h \, (\mathcal{A}[\![a]\!] \, \text{reception}(\sigma(e_0)) \, \kappa_h \, \kappa)) \, v))$$

(a) Pointcuts (`failure` only):

$$\mathcal{P}[\![\texttt{failure}(x)]\!]\, \rho\, (\texttt{failure}(x'), v) = \begin{cases} \rho & \text{if } x = x' \text{ or } x = * \\ \text{False} & \text{otherwise} \end{cases}$$

(b) Advices:

$$\mathcal{A} : \text{Advices} \to \text{Evt} \to \boxed{\text{Ctn} \to} \text{Ctn} \to \text{Ctn}$$

$$\mathcal{A}[\![\texttt{advice} : p \to e; a']\!]\, \epsilon\, \kappa_h\, \kappa\, v = \begin{cases} \mathcal{E}[\![e]\!]\, \rho'\, (\mathcal{A}[\![a']\!]\, \epsilon\, \kappa_h\, \kappa) & \text{if } \mathcal{P}[\![p]\!]\, \rho_{empty}\, (\epsilon, v) = \rho' \\ \mathcal{A}[\![a']\!]\, \epsilon\, \kappa_h\, \kappa\, v & \text{otherwise} \end{cases}$$

$$\mathcal{A}[\![\,\cdot\,]\!]\, \epsilon\, \kappa_h\, \kappa\, v = \kappa\, v$$

(c) Expressions (APPLICATION, TRY and RAISE only):

$$\mathcal{E}[\![e_0\ e_1]\!] \rho \kappa_h \kappa = \mathcal{E}[\![e_0]\!]\, \rho\, \kappa_h\, (\lambda Fun(f).\, \mathcal{E}[\![e_1]\!]\, \rho\, \kappa_h\, (\lambda v.$$
$$\mathcal{A}[\![a]\!]\, \texttt{call}(\sigma(e_0))\, \kappa_h$$
$$(f\, (\mathcal{A}[\![a]\!]\, \texttt{failure}(\sigma(e_0))\, \kappa_h\, \kappa_h)(\mathcal{A}[\![a]\!]\, \texttt{reception}(\sigma(e_0))\, \kappa_h\, \kappa))\, v))$$
$$\mathcal{E}[\![\texttt{try}\ e_0\ \texttt{with}\ x \to e_1]\!]\, \rho\, \kappa_h\, \kappa = \mathcal{E}[\![e_0]\!]\, \rho\, (\lambda v.\, \mathcal{E}[\![e_1]\!]\, ([v\,/\,x]\rho)\, \kappa_h\, \kappa)\, \kappa$$
$$\mathcal{E}[\![\texttt{raise}\ e]\!]\, \rho\, \kappa_h\, \kappa = \mathcal{E}[\![e]\!]\, \rho\, \kappa_h\, \kappa_h$$

Fig. 15. Semantics of Pitλ_1 with exception handling

The new definition of $\mathcal{A}$ is in Figure 15-(b). This modification, adding the shadowed parts, is mechanical since additional continuations are dealt with only by the additional constructs. After that, we can define a semantics of the TRY and the RAISE as Figure 15-(c).

Now, we define the semantics of a failure join point by modifying the original semantics. The failure is added to the events Evt:

$$\epsilon ::= \ldots \mid \texttt{failure}(x)$$

and the semantics of the `failure` pointcuts is defined as Figure 15-(a).

Then, look the semantics of APPLICATION. From the first argument κ_h in $f\ \kappa_h\ \ldots$, show up the application form by η-expansion.

$$\mathcal{E}[\![e_0\ e_1]\!]\, \rho\, \kappa_h\, \kappa = \mathcal{E}[\![e_0]\!]\, \rho\, \kappa_h\, (\lambda Fun(f).\, \mathcal{E}[\![e_1]\!]\, \rho\, \kappa_h\, (\lambda v.$$
$$\mathcal{A}[\![a]\!]\, \texttt{call}(\sigma(e_0))\, \kappa_h$$
$$(f\, (\lambda v.\, \kappa_h\, v)(\mathcal{A}[\![a]\!]\, \texttt{reception}(\sigma(e_0))\, \kappa_h\, \kappa))\, v))$$

This continuation κ_h corresponds to a failure join point. We therefore define the semantics of APPLICATION as Figure 15-(c), in a similar way to call and reception.

The above semantics clarifies the detailed behavior of the aspect mechanism with exception handling. For example, consider that an exception is to be thrown in an advice body, which runs at a call join point. It is not obvious whether other advice declarations matching the same join point shall be executed in this case. With the above semantics, we can easily tell that no declaration will be executed.

This is because the semantics of APPLICATION passes κ_h to the semantic $\mathcal{A}$ in order to execute advice at a call join point, like $\mathcal{A}[\![a]\!] \, \mathsf{call}(name) \, \kappa_h \, \ldots$, which means that the exception handler of the advice execution is the same one to the one of the function application.

6   Related Work

As far as we know, practical AOP languages with pointcut and advice, including AspectJ[15], AspectWerkz[3] and JBoss AOP[6], are all based on the region-in-time model. Therefore, the reusability problem in Section 2 is common to those languages even though they have mechanisms for aspect reuse.

A few formal studies[5, 9, 22] treat beginning and end of an event as different join points. However, motivations behind those studies are different from ours. MinAML[22] is a low-level language that serves as a target of translation from a high-level AOP language. Douence and Teboul's work[9] focuses on identifying calling contexts from execution history. Brichau et al.[5] attempt to provide a language model that generalizes many AOP languages.

Including the region-in-time and point-in-time models, previous formal studies focus on different properties of aspect-oriented languages. Aspect SandBox (ASB)[23] focuses on formalizing behavior of pointcut matching and advice execution by using denotational semantics. Since ASB is based on the region-in-time model, the semantics of advice execution has to have a rule for each advice modifier. MiniMAO$_1$[7] focuses on type soundness of **around** advice, based on ClassicJava style semantics. It is also based on the region-in-time model.

7   Conclusion

We proposed an experimental new join point model. The model treats ends of actions, such as returns from methods, as different join points from beginnings of actions. In PitJ, ends of actions can be captured solely by pointcuts, rather than advice modifiers. This makes advice declaration more reusable. Even with simplified advice mechanism, PitJ is as expressive as AspectJ in typical use cases.

We also gave a formal semantics of Pitλ, which simplified from PitJ. It is a denotational semantics in a continuation passing style, and symmetrically represents beginnings and ends of actions as join points. With the aid of the semantics, we investigated integration of advanced language features with the point-in-time join point model.

Our future work includes the following topics. We will integrate more advanced features, such as `dflow` pointcut[17], first-class continuation and tail-call elimination. We will also plan to implement compiler for PitJ languages.

Acknowledgments. We would like to thank Kenichi Asai, the members of the Principles of Programming Languages Group at University of Tokyo, the members of the Kumiki Project and the anonymous reviewers for their careful proof-reading and valuable comments. An earlier version of the paper was presented at the FOAL'06 workshop. We appreciate the comments from the workshop attendees, especially from Gregor Kiczales, Gary Leavens and Mira Mezini.

References

1. Allan, C., et al.: Adding trace matching with free variables to AspectJ. In: OOP-SLA'05. (2005) 345–364
2. Bodkin, R., Almaer, D., Laddad, R.: aTrack: an enterprise bug tracking system using AOP. Demonstration at AOSD'04. (2004)
3. Bonér, J.: What are the Key Issues for Commercial AOP use: How Does AspectWerkz Address Them? In: AOSD'04. (2004) 5–6 Invited Industry Paper.
4. Brichau, J., Meuter, W.D., De Volder, K.: Jumping aspects. In: Workshop on Aspects and Dimensions of Concerns at ECOOP'00. (2000)
5. Brichau, J., et al.: An initial metamodel for aspect-oriented programming languages. AOSD-Europe-VUB-12, Vrije Universiteit Brussel. (2006)
6. Burke, B., Brok, A.: Aspect-oriented programming and JBoss. Published on The O'Reilly Network (2003) http://www.oreillynet.com/pub/a/onjava/2003/05/28/aop_jboss.html.
7. Clifton, C., Leavens, G.T.: MiniMAO: Investigating the semantics of proceed. In: FOAL'05. (2005)
8. Danvy, O., Filinski, A.: Abstracting control. In: LFP '90. (1990) 151–160
9. Douence, R., Teboul, L.: A pointcut language for control-flow. In: GPCE'04. (2004)
10. Douence, R., Fritz, T., Loriant, N., Menaud, J.M., Ségura-Devillechaise, M., Südholt, M.: An expressive aspect language for system applications with Arachne. In: AOSD'05. (2005) 27–38
11. Elrad, T., Filman, R.E., Bader, A.: Aspect-oriented programming. Communications of the ACM 44(10) (2001) 29–32
12. Endoh, Y., Masuhara, H., Yonezawa, A.: Continuation join points. In: FOAL'06. (2006) 1–10
13. Endoh, Y.: Continuation join points. Master's thesis, Department of Computer Science, University of Tokyo (2006) Revised version is available at http://www.graco.c.u-tokyo.ac.jp/ppp/projects/pit/.
14. Harbulot, B., Gurd, J.R.: A join point for loops in AspectJ. In: AOSD'06. (2006) 63–74
15. Kiczales, G., Hilsdale, E., Hugunin, J., Kersten, M., Palm, J., Griswold, W.G.: An overview of AspectJ. In: ECOOP'01, LNCS 2072. (2001) 327–353
16. Kiczales, G.: The fun has just begun. Keynote Speech at AOSD'03. (2003)
17. Masuhara, H., Kawauchi, K.: Dataflow pointcut in aspect-oriented programming. In: APLAS'03, LNCS 2895. (2003) 105–121
18. Rajan, H., Sullivan, K.: Aspect language features for concern coverage profiling. In: AOSD'05. 181–191
19. Usui, Y., Chiba, S.: Bugdel: An aspect-oriented debugging system. In: Proceedings of The First Asian Workshop on AOSD. (2005) 790–795
20. van Deursen, A., Marin, M., Moonen, L.: AJHotDraw: A showcase for refactoring to aspects. In: LATE'05. (2005)
21. Walker, R.J., Murphy, G.C.: Implicit context: Easing software evolution and reuse. In: FSE-8. ACM SIGSOFT Software Engineering Notes 25(6). (2000) 69–78
22. Walker, D., Zdancewic, S., Ligatti, J.: A theory of aspects. In: ICFP'03. (2003)
23. Wand, M., Kiczales, G., Dutchyn, C.: A semantics for advice and dynamic join points in aspect-oriented programming. In: FOAL'02. (2002) 1–8

Automatic Testing of Higher Order Functions

Pieter Koopman and Rinus Plasmeijer

Nijmegen Institute for Computer and Information Science, The Netherlands
{pieter, rinus}@cs.ru.nl

Abstract. This paper tackles a problem often overlooked in functional programming community: that of testing. Fully automatic test tools like Quickcheck and G∀ST can test first order functions successfully. Higher order functions, HOFs, are an essential and distinguishing part of functional languages. Testing HOFs automatically is still troublesome since it requires the generation of functions as test argument for the HOF to be tested. Also the functions that are the result of the higher order function needs to be identified. If a counter example is found, the generated and resulting functions should be printed, but that is impossible in most functional programming languages. Yet, bugs in HOFs do occur and are usually more subtle due to the high abstraction level.

In this paper we present an effective and efficient technique to test higher order functions by using intermediate data types. Such a data type mimics and controls the structure of the function to be generated. A simple additional function transforms this data structure to the function needed. We use a continuation based parser library as main example of the tests. Our automatic testing method for HOFs reveals errors in the library that was used for a couple of years without problems.

1 Introduction

Automatic test tools for functional languages are able to generate test cases, execute the associated tests and derive a verdict from the test results. Basically a predicate of the form $\forall x \in X : P(x)$ is replaced by a function P :: X → Bool. The predicate is tested by evaluating the function P for a large number of elements of type X. In Quickcheck these elements are generated in pseudo random order by a user defined instance of a type class. G∀ST has a generic algorithm that is able to generate elements of any type in a systematic way [6]. The user can specify any other algorithm if the generic algorithm is inappropriate.

The advantages of this automatic testing is that it is cheap and fast. Moreover, the real code is tested. A inherent limitation of testing is that a proof by exhaustive testing is only possible for finite types (due to generation algorithm used, Quickcheck is not able to determine when all elements are tested and never detects that a property is proven by exhaustive testing). A formal proof of a property gives more confidence, but usually works on a model of the program instead of the program itself and requires (much) user guidance. Hence, both formal proofs and testing have their own value. It is at least useful to do a quick automatic test of some property before investing much effort in a formal proof.

N. Kobayashi (Ed.): APLAS 2006, LNCS 4279, pp. 148–164, 2006.

The generation of elements of a type works well for (first order) data structures. Testing properties of HOFs requires functions as test argument and hence the generation of functions by the test system. The possibilities to generate functions are rather limited. In Quickcheck functions of type A → B are generated by transforming elements of type A to an integer by a user defined instance of the class coarbitrary. This integer is used to select an element of type B. A multi-argument function of type A → B → C is transformed to a function B → C by providing a pseudo randomly generated element of type A. In this way all information of all arguments is encoded in a single integer. This approach is not powerful enough for more complex functions, and has as drawback that it is impossible to print these functions in a decent way. G∀ST used the same approach with the difference that functions can be derived using a generic algorithm. Using an extensional representation of functions, by providing explicit input-output pairs, is unsuited for large data types since it is usually impossible to determine the arguments that will occur.

In this paper we show how functions of the desired form can be generated systematically. The key step is to represent such a function by its abstract syntax tree, AST. This AST is represented as algebraic data type. Its instances can be generated automatically by G∀ST in the usual way. It is simple to transform the AST to the desired function. An additional advantage of using a data type as AST is that this can be printed in a generic way as well, while printing functions is impossible in functional languages like Haskell and Clean.

We illustrate this technique with a full fleshed parser combinator library. In [4] we introduced a library of efficient parser combinators. Using this library it is possible to write concise, efficient, recursive descent parsers. The parsers can be ambiguous if that is desired. Basically there are two ingredients that makes the constructed parsers efficient. First, the user can limit the amount of backtracking by a special version of the choice combinator that only yields a single result. Second, the implementation of the combinators uses continuations instead of intermediate data structures. Especially when parsed objects are processed in a number of steps before a final parse result is produced, continuation based parsers are faster than a straight forward implementation of parsers.

The price to be paid for using continuations instead of intermediate data structures, is that the implementation of the combinator becomes more complicated. Each parser has three continuations, and some of these continuations have their own continuation arguments. The parser combinators manipulate these continuations in a rather tricky way. However, the use of the combinators is independent of their implementation, and is not different for a library with a simple implementation using intermediate data types. The published combinators are tested manually by the authors and checked by many users of the library. Much to our surprise last year some errors in the library were found.

After improving the combinators we wanted to obtain more confidence in the correctness of the library. Manual testing by a number of typical examples was clearly insufficient. Using the techniques described here it was possible to test this library automatically. During these test an additional error was found.

It turns out that a similar representation of functions by data types is used at different places in the literature. The technique is called *defunctionalisation*, and the function transforming the data type is usually called *apply*. This technique was introduced by Reynolds [9], and repopularized by Danvy [3]. Using defunctionalisation for generating functions and testing is new.

In the next section we will illustrate testing equality of functions with simple examples. Section 3 introduces the basic techniques for generating functions as arguments. We will apply this in the well-known example of monads by testing the monadic laws. The main example treated in this paper is the testing of a library of advanced parser combinators. Finally there is a conclusion.

2   Functions as Result of Higher Order Functions

Testing higher order functions that yield functions as results is relatively easy. The test system has to verify whether the correct function is produced. In most functional programming languages it is impossible to look inside functions (LISP is an exception). Hence it is impossible to decide if this function is the desired one by inspecting the function directly.

More importantly, for functions we are usually not interested in the exact definition of the function, but in its behavior. Any definition will do, if it produces the right function result to the given parameters. This implies that even if it would be possible to look inside a function directly, this would not help us. We are interested in the input/output behavior of the function instead of the algorithm it uses.

Changing the function to be tested in such a way that it delivers a data structure instead of a function is an unattractive option: we want to test the software as it is and this does not solve the problem of testing the behavior instead of the actual definition.

Testing functions for equal input output relations is relative easy. As example we consider the function isAlpha and the function isUpperOrLower defined as

```
isUpperOrLower :: Char → Bool
isUpperOrLower c = isUpper c || isLower c
```

Using G∀ST the equivalence of the functions isAlpha and isUpperOrLower can be tested by stating a property stating that $\forall c . isAlpha\ c = isUpperOrLower\ c$. In Clean this property reads:

```
propEq :: Char → Bool
propEq c = isAlpha c == isUpperOrLower c
```

Testing this in G∀ST is done by executing Start = test propEq. G∀ST *proves* this property by exhaustive testing: the function propEq is evaluated for all possible characters. Since the number of characters is finite (and small), G∀ST is able to test it for all possible arguments and to yield *Proof* rather than *Pass* (the latter indicates a successful test for all arguments used).

In section 7 we show how this approach is used to compare parsers by applying them to various inputs and comparing the results.

3   Functions as Argument of Higher Order Functions

Testing properties over higher order functions that have functions as arguments is a harder problem. In these properties there is a universal quantification over functions. This implies that the test system must supply appropriate functions as argument.

A typical example of a property over higher order functions is:

$$\forall f, g : (x \rightarrow y) \, . \, \forall l : [x] \, . \, map \; f \; (map \; g \; l) = map \; (f \circ g) \; l.$$

For any test we need to choose concrete types for x and y. Choosing small finite types like Bool or Char usually give good test results. The Clean version of this property where all types are Char is:

```
propMap :: (Char → Char) (Char → Char) [Char] → Bool
propMap f g l = map f (map g l) == map (f o g) l
```

Former versions of G∀ST where able to generate functions. The generated function of type X → Y converts the argument x to an index in a list of values ys of type Y: λx . ys !! (toIndex x rem length ys). For simple functions (like f and g in propMap) this is adequate, but not for more complex functions (like continuation parsers). Moreover, in the generic framework the generation of values and the index function needs to be coupled. This slows down the generation of ordinary values considerably. For these reasons the existing generation of function algorithm was removed from G∀ST.

Another serious problem is that the code of a given function cannot be shown. This implies that if an counterexample would be found by G∀ST, it can only print the argument f and g as <function>.

As a solution for the problem of generating functions and printing them we propose to use a tailor made data structure that exactly determines the functions that are needed in a particular test context. Instances of this data structure can be generated by the default generic algorithm used in G∀ST. Since the data type determines the needed functions exactly, the conversion from a generated instance of the data type to the corresponding function is easy.

As example we will show how the property for the map function can be tested. Apart from the library functions toUpper and toLower we will use the function shift in the tests. The function shift shifts any character n places in the ascii table. It is defined as:

```
shift :: Int Char → Char
shift n c = toChar (abs (fromChar c + n) rem 256)
```

A data type representing all functions that we want to be generated as test argument and the corresponding conversion function are defined as:

```
:: Fun = Shift Int | ToUpper | ToLower

class apply s t :: apply s → t
instance apply Fun (Char → Char)
where apply (Shift n) = shift n
```

```
apply ToUpper  = toUpper
apply ToLower  = toLower
```

We will use the class apply for any transformation of a data type, s, to the corresponding function of type, t, in this paper. Using a type class instead of a set of functions with different names is that ons can use apply always if a transformation is needed. The disadvantage is that we have to provide additional type information in some circumstances to resolve the overloading.

Now we are able to test the property for the map function. Instances of the type Fun are generated by the generic generation algorithm. Instances of this data type are converted to functions by applying apply to them. In propMap2 we reuse propMap, the needed functions are obtained from the type Fun. Finally, there is a Start-function initiating the testing.

```
propMap2 :: Fun Fun [Char] → Bool
propMap2 f g l = propMap (apply f) (apply g) l
```

```
Start = test propMap2
```

This property passes any number of tests. In the next section we will show how this principle can be applied to continuation parsers. In order to obtain more complex parsers, the data type to represent functions will be recursive.

4   Testing Monads

Monads [10] are well-known higher order functions that can be used as a programming pattern to handle state in a functional programming language. The advantage of handling state in a program by a monad is that it is much easier to change the type of this state without having a significant impact on parts of the program using this state.

As a bare minimum a monad contains just the function unit to convert a value to a monad containg this value, and the operator $\gg=$ (called *bind*) to pass the state between two state manipulating functions. Such a monad is defined by the type constructor class Monad:

```
class Monad m
where unit :: a → (m a)
      (>>=) infixl 1 :: (m a) (a → (m b)) → (m b)
```

A typical example of the use of monads is found in the expression unit $3 \gg=$ λa.unit (a+a) $\gg=\lambda$b.unit (2*a*(b+1)). The subexpression unit 3 constructs the initial state containing the value 3. Next, the subexpression λa.unit (a+a) retrieves this value from the state and stores the new value 6 (computed by a+a where a=3). Finally, λb.unit (2*a*(b+1)) retrieves the current value, 6, from the state, binds it to b and stores the value 42. Note that in the computation of the last value both the first and second value of the state are used.

This expression allows the use of many implementations of the monad without changes. A typical example is a state where the value is stored in a list[1].

```
instance Monad []
where unit a = [a]
      (>>=) m f = [e \\ l ← m, e ← f l]
```

As an alternative monad implementation we introduce a state monad that count the number of changes of its state in an integer that is silently passed from one monad state to the next.

```
:: CountMonad a = CM (Int → (a, Int))
```

```
instance Monad CountMonad
where unit a = CM λx.(a,x+1)
      (>>=) (CM m) f = CM (λx. let (a,y) = m x; (CM g) = f a in g y)
```

Based on category theory one imposes the following laws on their behavior:

$$\forall a, f . unit\, a \ggg f = f\; a \tag{1}$$

$$\forall m, a . m \ggg \lambda.unit\, a = m \tag{2}$$

$$\forall m, f, g . m \ggg (\lambda x . f\, x \ggg g) = (m \ggg f) \ggg g \tag{3}$$

We want to use these laws in order to test whether the given implementations of the type class Monad are correct. The first step is to express the laws in G∀ST:

```
leftUnit :: a (a →m b) → Bool | Monad m & == (m b)
leftUnit a f = (unit a >>= f) == f a
```

```
rightUnit :: (m b) a → Bool | Monad m & == (m b)
rightUnit m a = (m >>= λa.unit a) == m
```

```
associative :: (m a) (a →m a) (a →m a) → Bool | Monad m & == (m a)
associative m f g = (m >>= (λx.f x >>= g)) == ((m >>= f) >>= g)
```

The type restrictions Monad m & == (m b) states that m must be in the type class Monad and the equality must be defined for elements of type b.

This leaves the task to generate monads of type m a and functions of type a → m a. We use the approach outline above, we define a data type representing the necessary functions and instances of apply for the transformations needed. In order to avoid a tricky game with type variables and restrictions on them, we restrict us to monads containing integers. The data types used are:

```
:: M = Unit Expr | Bind M M
:: Expr = Var | Const Int | Plus Expr Expr | Times Expr Expr
```

Generation of instances of these types can be derived from the generic algoritm:

derive ggen Expr, M

---

[1] Usually one define more operators for monads. These operators enable also states with other numbers of values than exactly one as in this simple example.

The instances of `apply` are:

```
instance apply M (Int → (m Int)) | Monad m where apply m = applyM m
applyM :: M → (Int → (m Int)) | Monad m
applyM (Unit e) = λx.unit (apply e x)
applyM (Bind f g) = λx.applyM f x >>= applyM g

instance apply Expr (Int → Int)
where    apply (Const i)  = λx.i
         apply Var        = λx.x
         apply (Plus n m) = λx.apply n x+apply m x
         apply (Times n m) = λx.apply n x*apply m x
```

In order to test whether the law *leftUnit* holds for monads of type list we define:

```
testLeftUnit :: Int M → Bool
testLeftUnit i m = leftUnit i f
where f :: (Int → [Int])
      f = apply m
```

Similar properties are specified for the other laws. Testing show that the monad [] passes these tests. In order to test the state monad `CountMonad` we have to change the property of f in `testLeftUnit` to Int → CountMonad Int. Moreover we provide an instance of equality for `CountMonad`:

```
instance == (CountMonad x) | == x
where (==) (CM f) (CM g) = a == b && n == m
      where (a,n) = f i; (b,m) = g i; i=0
```

The properties *leftUnit* and *rightUnit* does not hold for the count monad: the additional `unit` is counted and spoils the equality. G∀ST report counterexamples of *leftUnit* for values like 0 and `unit` x. When we exclude the hidden counter from the equality for `CountMonad` (by defining (==) (CM f) (CM g) = a == b), the property passes any number of tests. This shows that the `CountMonad` behaves as a decent monad apart from its hidden counter. Although this result in itself might not be new or surprising, the ability to determine it by automatically generated test cases is new.

5   Background: Continuation Based Parser Combinators

In order to make this paper self contained we repeat the most important parser combinators from [4]. In the continuation parser library [4] each continuation parser has four arguments:

1. The success continuation which determines what will be done if the current parser succeeds. This function gets the result of the current parser, the other continuations and the remaining input as its arguments.
2. The XOR-continuation is a function that tells what has to be done if only a single result of the parser is needed.
3. The OR-continuation determines the behavior when all possible results of the parser are needed.

4. The list of symbols to be parsed. In this paper these symbols will be characters, but also lists of more complex tokens can be parsed.

The result of a parser is a list of tuples containing the remaining input and the results of parsing the input until this point. This is reflected in the types:

```
:: Parser s r  := [s] → ParsResult s r
:: ParsResult s r := [(([s],r)]

:: CParser s r t:=(SucCont s r t) (XorCont s t) (AltCont s t) → Parser s t
:: SucCont s r t:=r (XorCont s t) (AltCont s t) → Parser s t
:: XorCont s t  :=(AltCont s t) → ParsResult s t
:: AltCont s t  :=ParsResult s t
```

As an example the type of the continuation parser ast = symbol '*', that succeeds if the first character in the input is *, is CParser Char Char a. Expanding this type to basic types yields:

```
ast::((Char→([([Char],a)]↦[([Char],a)])↦[([Char],a)]↦Char↦[([Char],a)])
    → ([([Char],a)]↦[([Char],a)]) → [([Char],a)] → [Char] → [([Char],a)])
```

This complicated type indicates that testing for first order properties is inadequate. The definition of the parser combinator symbol is:

```
symbol :: s → CParser s s t | = s
symbol s = psymbol
where psymbol sc xc ac [x:ss] | x = s = sc s xc ac ss
      psymbol sc xc ac _          = xc ac
```

The function begin turns a continuation parser into a standard parser by providing appropriate initial continuations. The parser takes a list of tokens as arguments and produces a list of successes. Each success is a tuple containing the remaining input tokens and the parse result.

```
begin :: (CParser s t t) → Parser s t
begin p = p (λx xc ac ss . [(ss,x):xc ac]) id []
```

The result of applying begin ast to the input ['*abc'] will be [(['abc'],'*')], while applying it to the input ['abc'] yields the empty list of results.

The concatenation of two parsers, p <&> q, requires that the parser q is applied to the rest of the input left by the parser p. This is done by inserting q in the success continuation of p. The result of p is given as the first argument to q.

```
(<&>) infixr 6 :: (CParser s u t) (u→ CParser s v t) → CParser s v t
(<&>) p q = λsc . p (λt . q t sc)
```

There are several variants of the operator <&>: the operator <& yields only the result of p, &> yields only the result of q, <:&> constructs a list with the result of p as head and the result of q as tail, <++> appends the results of p and q, <!&> removes the XOR-alternatives if p succeeds.

The construct p <|> q indicates that we want all results of p and all results of q. This is achieved by putting q in the alternative continuation ac of p.

```
(<|>) infixr 4 :: (CParser s r t) (CParser s r t) → CParser s r t
(<|>) p q
= λ sc xc ac ss .p (λx xc1.sc x id) id (q (λx xc1.sc x id) xc ac ss) ss
```

The operator `<!>` yields only the result of q if p has no results. This is done by putting q in the XOR-continuation xc of p. The success continuation of p takes care of removing q if p succeeds.

```
(<!>) infixr 4 :: (CParser s r t) (CParser s r t) → CParser s r t
(<!>) p q = λ sc xc ac ss
            .p (λx xc2.sc x id) (λ_.q (λx xc3.sc x id) xc ac ss) ac ss
```

The combinator `<@` applies the function f to the items recognized by parser p.

```
(<@) infixl 5 :: (CParser s r t) (r → u) → CParser s u t
(<@) p f = λ sc . p (sc o f)
```

The operator `<*>` mimics the Kleene star: it repeats parser p as often as possible. The results of all applications of p are collected in a list. It behaves like:

```
<*> :: (CParser s r t) → CParser s [r] t
<*> p = (p <&> λr . <*> p <@ λrs . [r:rs]) <!> yield []
```

For efficiency reasons the actual implementation used is different.

6   Testing Basic Combinators

The parser combinator library contains a number of basic combinators for tasks like recognizing symbols in the input and yielding specific values. As an example we consider the parser combinator `symbol :: s → CParser s s t | == s` that should recognize the given symbol s in the input. A desirable property of `symbol` is that it yields a single success when the input list starts with the given symbol. For characters as input tokens, this can be specified in G∀ST as:

```
propSymbol :: Char [Char] → Bool
propSymbol c l = begin (symbol c) [c:l] == [(l,c)]
```

Using `begin` (`symbol c`) instead of `symbol c` in the test makes it possible to compare parse results (lists of tuples), instead of comparing higher order functions.

The property `propSymbol` can be tested directly by G∀ST by applying the function `test` to the property in the `Start`-function. The result of the test is that it passes any number of tests. When we restrict the input to, for instance, lists of two characters such a property can even be proven. The property for inputs of exactly two character reads:

```
propSymbol2 :: Char Char → Bool
propSymbol2 c d = begin (symbol c) [c,d] == [([d],c)]
```

Within a split second G∀ST proves this property by executing all possible tests. All measurements in this paper are done on a fairly moderate PC running the latest windows XP, Clean 2.1.1 and G∀ST 0.5.1.

Although this kind of property states clearly the intended semantics of the basic parser combinators and the associated tests are useful, this does not capture the signaled problems with the combinator library.

7 Testing Parser Combinators

For parser combinators that compose continuation parsers, one can specify properties in the way just explained. For example the result of applying p <|> q to some input is equal to the concatenation of results from p to the same input and applying q to that input. Stated as property for G∀ST this is:

```
propOR p q input = begin (p <|> q) input == begin p input ++ begin q input
```

The generation of continuation parsers needed as arguments p and q is again done with a data type and a corresponding instance of apply. The type P is a recursive data type that represents parsers that consumes lists of characters and yield a character as result.

```
:: P = Fail           // basic operator: fails for any input
   | Yield  Sym        // basic operator: yields the specified symbol for any input
   | Symbol Sym        // basic operator: recognize the specified symbol, see above
   | Or P P            // concatenation of the successes of both parsers
   | XOr P P           // successes of second parser if first parser fails
```

```
:: Sym = Char Char // Symbols are just constructor Char and a character
```

The generation of instances of these data types is straightforward. The default generic generation algorithm ggen of G∀ST is used for the data type P representing the structure of the parser. For the type Sym we use only the characters 'a' and 'b' in order to limit the number of characters used in the tests. This increases the number of more complicated parses used in a finite number of tests.

```
derive ggen P
ggen {|Sym|} n r = [Char 'a', Char 'b']
```

The instance of apply that transforms elements of type P to the corresponding continuation parsers is straightforward:

```
instance apply P (CParser Char Char Char)
where
    apply Fail            = fail
    apply (Yield (Char c))  = yield c
    apply (Symbol (Char c)) = symbol c
    apply (Or p q)          = apply p <|> apply q
    apply (XOr p q)         = apply p <!> apply q
```

The property to test the parser combinator <|> using the type P becomes:

```
propOR :: P P [Char] → Bool
propOR x y chars = begin (p <|> q) chars == begin p chars ++ begin q chars
where p = apply x; q = apply y
```

Since the continuation parsers x and y are now represented by instances of the data type P, printing them by the generic mechanism of G∀ST reveals the structure of the combinator parsers used in the actual test clearly. If desired we can make a tailored instance of genShow {|P|} that prints the data type exactly as the functions generated by apply, instead of deriving the default behavior.

Testing such a property in G∀ST is quick. Testing this property for the first 1000 combinations of arguments takes only half a second.

In the same spirit we can test the other combinators in the original combinator library. For instance the xor-combinator, `<!>`, only applies the second parser if the first one fails. This is expressed by the property `propXOR`:

```
propXOR :: P P [Char] → Bool
propXOR x y chars
    | isEmpty (begin p chars)
        = begin (p <!> q) chars == begin q chars
        = begin (p <!> q) chars == begin p chars
where p = apply x; q = apply y
```

Testing this property reveals the problems with the original parser combinator library. One of the counterexamples found is for (`Or (Yield (Char 'b')) Fail`) as the value of `x`, (`Yield (Char 'a')`) for `y`, and the empty input `[]`. The problem is that `begin ((yield 'b' <|> fail) <!> yield 'a') []` produces the result `['ba']` instead of the desired result `['b']`. This is equivalent to the reported error that initiates this research. Since this is a unusual combination of parser combinators its in not strange that this issue was not discovered during manual tests and ordinary use of the library.

7.1   Repetition of Parsers

The parsers generated and tested above do not contain the repetition operators `<*>`. Although it is easy to add the desired constructors to the type `P` and the function `apply`, certain instances of the generated parsers can cause serious problems. For example, the parser `<*> (yield 'a')` will produce an infinite list of 'a's without consuming input.

We only want to incorporate parsers containing proper applications of the operator `<*>` in our tests. This implies that we either have to prevent that parsers causing problems (by designing a more sophisticated data type), or we have to prevent that they are actually used in the tests (by a precondition in the property). Both solutions are feasible, but the selection of parsers that behave well is somewhat simpler and will be used here. Selection of well behaving parsers is done by inspection of the corresponding data structure and the operator ⟹ from G∀ST.

First we add appropriate clauses to the type `P` and the function `apply`. Since we have now a repetition it is more convenient to generate a parser that yields the list of all generated and recognized characters, than a parser yielding a single characters as we used above.

```
:: P = Fail | Yield Sym | Symbol Sym | Or P P | XOr P P | AND P P | Star P

instance apply P (CParser Char [Char] [Char])
where apply Fail             = fail
      apply (Yield (Char c))  = yield [c]
      apply (Symbol (Char c)) = symbol c <@ (λc=[c])
```

```
apply (Or  p q)        = apply p <|> apply q
apply (XOr p q)        = apply p <!> apply q
apply (AND  p q)       = apply p <++> apply q
apply (Star p)         = (<*> (apply p)) <@ flatten
```

Generated parsers will not cause problems if they are *finite*. A parser is finite if it does not contain the parser combinators `<*>`:

```
finite :: P → Bool
finite (Or   p q) = finite p && finite q
finite (XOr  p q) = finite p && finite q
finite (AND  p q) = finite p && finite q
finite (Star p)   = False
finite other      = True
```

Parsers that need to *consume* input in order to produce a result are also safe.

```
consuming :: P → Bool
consuming (Symbol c) = True
consuming (Or   p q) = consuming p && consuming q
consuming (XOr  p q) = consuming p && consuming q
consuming (AND  p q) = consuming p && consuming q
consuming (Star p)   = consuming p
consuming other      = False
```

These predicates allow us to define a class of parsers that will not produce infinite results without consuming input as:

```
notInfiniteNonConsuming :: P → Bool
notInfiniteNonConsuming (Star p) = consuming p
notInfiniteNonConsuming p = consuming p || finite p
```

Experiments show that a little less than 8% of the generated parsers will be rejected by this predicate. Using this predicate the property for the parser combinator `<!>` can be reformulated for parsers with repetition as:

```
propXOR2 :: P P [Char] → Property
propXOR2 x y chars
 = notInfiniteNonConsuming x && notInfiniteNonConsuming y
    ⟹ case begin p chars of
       [] = begin (p <!> q) chars == begin q chars
       _  = begin (p <!> q) chars == begin p chars
where p = apply x; q = apply y
```

Despite the fact that there are more different parsers generated, this property produces a counterexample indicating an error as test case 202 (the actual number depends on the pseudo random streams used in the test data generation).

8   Input Generation

Apart from controlling the functions used in the properties over HOFs, it is possible to control the generation of ordinary types used in properties over HOFs.

In our running example of parser combinators we used the type [Char] as input for the parsers. G∀ST will generate list of characters containing all 98 printable characters from the empty list to longer and longer lists. Although the test introduced above appear to be effective they can be improved. The parsers are generated in such a way that only the characters 'a' and 'b' will be accepted (by the definition of **ggen** {|Sym|}). This implies that about 98% of the input symbols will be rejected by each instance of the parser combinator **symbol**. This can be improved by generating lists of characters with a limited number of characters. Without changing the instance for **ggen** {|Char|} in the library this can be achieved by the introduction of an additional data type and a user defined instance of **ggen**.

```
:: InputList = Input [Char]
```

```
ggen {|InputList|} n r = map Input l
where l = [[] : [[c:t] \\ (c,t) ← diag2 ['a'..'c'] l]]
```

The character 'c' is included to ensure that there are input symbols that need to be reject by any consuming parser. In each use we have to remove the constructor Input from the generated input. For example:

```
propXORInput :: P P InputList → Property
propXORInput x y (Input chars)
  = notInfiniteNonConsuming x && notInfiniteNonConsuming y
    ⟹ case begin p chars of
        [] = begin (p <!> q) chars == begin q chars
        _  = begin (p <!> q) chars == begin p chars
where p = apply x; q = apply y
```

This test appears indeed to be more effective. For this property G∀ST founds 319 counterexamples in the first 10,000 tests. Using **propXOR** 'only' 136 counterexamples are found in this number of tests. For this property this does not matter much, one counterexample is enough to invalidate a property. In general this indicates that this algorithm yields more effective tests.

8.1   Generating Inputs That Should Be Accepted

In order to test whether a parser accepts the inputs it should accept, it is sufficient to use only inputs that should be accepted by the tested parser. Since we have the parsers available as data structure, it is not difficult to generate such inputs. The function PtoInput produces a list of inputs to be accepted by the parser corresponding to the given data structure of type P.

```
PtoInput :: P → [[Char]]
PtoInput Fail              = []
PtoInput (Yield (Char c))  = [[]]
PtoInput (Symbol (Char c)) = [[c]]
PtoInput (Or p q)          = removeDup (PtoInput p ++ PtoInput q)
PtoInput (XOr p q)         = removeDup (PtoInput p ++ PtoInput q)
PtoInput (AND  p q)        = [i++j \\ i←PtoInput p, j←PtoInput q]
```

```
PtoInput (Star p)                = take maxIter l
     where l = [[] : [ i++t \\ (i,t) ← diag2 (PtoInput p) l]]

maxIter = 10
```

The only point of interest are the repetition constructors `Star`. Here the inputs are limited to `maxIter` repetitions of the input corresponding to the argument of the repetition operator. There are two reasons for this.

First, if the parser handles inputs up to `maxIter` repetitions correctly for some decent value of `maxIter`, it is highly likely that all higher number of repetitions will be handled correctly. Test corresponding to more repetitions of the same input will not be very effective. In fact, also a much smaller value of `maxIter`, like 2 or 3, can be used.

Second, strange parsers and long inputs can produce enormous amounts of results. This is time and space consuming, but not a very effective test. As example we consider the parser `<+>` (`symbol 'a' <|> symbol 'a'`). Each symbol `'a'` will be recognized in two different ways. If this parser is applied to a list of n characters `'a'`, the result will be a list of 2^n identical parse results. In order to keep testing effective we either have to remove these kind of parsers, or prevent very large inputs for such a parser. Since we do want to exclude this kind of parsers, we have chosen to limit the size of the associated inputs.

As example of the use of the generation of inputs that have to be accepted we use again the property for `<!>` combinator:

```
propXOR3 :: P P → Property
propXOR3 x y = propXOR2 x y For PtoInput (XOr x y)
```

For the first 10,000 test cases we find now 916 counterexamples. This indicates that testing with inputs that should be accepted is even more effective as testing with pseudo random input constructed by the type `InputList`.

9   Direct Testing of Complete Parsers

Above we have shown how individual parser combinators are tested effectively. This requires that at least one property is stated for each parser combinator. In this section we will show that we can also test a large set of parser combinators in one go. The idea is to construct a very simple direct parser. Given an instance of the type `P` and an input, this parser should produce all desired results.

Given a grammar and an input, it is easy to determine what the result of the parser described in section 7.1 should be:

```
results :: P [Char] → [([Char],[Char])]
results Fail                  chars = []
results (Yield (Char c))  chars = [(chars,[c])]
results (Symbol (Char c)) [d:r] | c == d = [(r,[c])]
results (Symbol (Char c)) chars = []
results (Or p q)              chars = results p chars ++ results q chars
results (XOr p q)             chars = case results p chars of
```

```
                              [] = results q chars
                              r  = r
results (AND  p q)            chars
= [(c3,r1++r2) \\ (c2,r1)←results p chars, (c3,r2)←results q c2]
results (Star p)              chars = repeatP p [(chars,[])]

repeatP p res
   = case [(c2,r1++r2) \\ (c1,r1) ← res, (c2,r2) ← results p c1] of
       [] = res
       r  = repeatP p r
```

This simple parser is less efficient that the parser combinator library and less flexible, but for the set of constructors defined by the type P it yields the list of all recognized tokens.

Using this function it is possible to state a property that has to hold for any parser that corresponds to an instance of P: the result of transform p to a parser and applying it to an input i should be identical to results p i. That is:

```
propPI :: P [Char] → Property
propPI p i = notInfiniteNonConsuming p ⟹ results p i = begin (apply p) i
```

Also here we can limit the inputs to the character lists that should be accepted by the parser:

```
propP :: P → Property
propP p = notInfiniteNonConsuming p ⟹ (propPI p For PtoInput p)
```

This general property finds counterexamples corresponding to the reported problem in the original version of the library quickly. Since this property is more general it is not surprising that this property needs somewhat more tests to find a counterexample. After 279 test G∀ST reports the counterexample (XOr (Or (Yield (Char 'a')) (Symbol (Char 'a'))) (Yield (Char 'a'))) []. This is basically the same error as reported above. G∀ST needs less than one second to find this error.

After repairing this error we tested to library again with PropP. To our surprise an additional counterexample was found within 2 seconds. G∀ST reports: Counterexample found after 791 tests: (Star (Or (Symbol (Char 'a')) (Symbol (Char 'a')))) ['a']. The error is caused by an erroneous optimization in the parser combinator <*>. It appears that the parser <*> (symbol 'a' <|> symbol 'a') yields only one result for the input repeat n 'a', instead of the desired 2^n identical results.

After correction of this error no new issues were found in an additional 30,000 tests. This takes 2.4 seconds. In order to verify the error detecting capacity of this approach we made, by hand, 25 mutants of the library that are approved by the type system. Testing these incorrect libraries revealed counterexamples for each of these libraries within 2 seconds.

The final set of parser combinators can be found in the appendix.

10   Conclusion

Test systems like Quickcheck and G∀ST are very suited to test properties over first order functions [2,5]. Testing higher order functions was troublesome, since they have functions instead of data types as argument and result. The functions yielded by a higher order function are tested by supplying arguments until a data type is obtained. Until now test systems were able to generate functions as test argument in a primitive and unguided way. In this paper we have shown that the functions needed as argument can be generated by defining a data type representing the grammar for the desired functions, and a simple function that transforms this data type to the corresponding function. This is a reinvention of ideas similar to Reynolds defunctionalisation from 1972.

By using this technique for a library of parser combinators the test system has found a reported error as well as an until now unknown error. Since the errors occur for unusual combinations of parser combinators it is not strange that the errors were not discovered during manual testing and ordinary use of the library. Also 25 errors injected deliberately in order investigate the power of automatic testing are found within seconds. This indicates that this way of automatic testing is effective and efficient. Developing appropriate properties and associated data types takes time. Developing data types and the required instances can be done nearly systematically, as soon as the required functions are known. The efficient execution of the automatic tests themselves makes it possible to execute them frequently during the development of programs.

Our approach can be used in any situation where higher order functions needs to be tested, or even where systematically generated functions are needed. In this paper we have show the application of this approach to simple properties over map (see section 3), more advanced monad laws (see section 4), and an parser library as large example.

Acknowledgement. We thank Erik Zuurbier and Arjen van Weelden for indicating problems with the parser library initiating this research. Oliver Danvy pointed out the relation of our intermediate data types and defunctionalisation. Various anonymous referees provided useful feedback to improve this paper.

References

1. A. Alimarine, R. Plasmeijer. *A Generic Programming Extension for Clean.* IFL2001, LNCS 2312, pp.168–185, 2001.
2. K. Claessen, J. Hughes. *QuickCheck: A lightweight Tool for Random Testing of Haskell Programs.* ICFP, ACM, pp 268–279, 2000.
3. Olivier Danvy and Lasse R. Nielsen. *Defunctionalization at Work.* PPDP '01 Proceedings, 2001, pp 162–174.
4. Pieter Koopman and Rinus Plasmeijer: *Efficient Combinator Parsers* In Hammond, Davie and Clack: Proc. IFL'98, LNCS 1595, pp. 120–136. 1999
5. Pieter Koopman, Artem Alimarine, Jan Tretmans and Rinus Plasmeijer: *Gast: Generic Automated Software Testing*, Peña: IFL'02, LNCS 2670, pp 84–100, 2002.

6. P. Koopman and R. Plasmeijer. Generic Generation of Elements of Types. In *Sixth Symposium on Trends in Functional Programming (TFP2005)*, 2005.
7. Grant Malcom. *Algebraic Data Types and Program Transformations*, Thesis, 1990.
8. Rinus Plasmeijer and Marko van Eekelen: *Concurrent Clean Language Report (version 2.1.1)*, 2005. www.cs.ru.nl/~clean.
9. John C. Reynolds. *Definitional interpreters for higher-order programming languages*. Higher-Order and Symbolic Computation, 11(4):363-397, 1998. Reprinted from the proceedings of the 25th ACM National Conference (1972).
10. Philip Wadler. *Monads for functional programming* In J. Jeuring and E. Meijer, *Advanced Functional Programming*, LNCS 925, 1995.

A   Improved Parser Combinator Definitions

This appendix contains the changed and tested version of the parser combinators. The types used are unchanged. The most important change is that the role of the OR-continuation and the XOR-continuation is swapped in order to get the behavior both or-combinators correctly. The basic operators `fail`, `yield` and `symbol` are basically unchanged. The definitions are slightly changed in order to reflect the change in role of the continuations xc and ac.

```
symbol :: s → CParser s s t | == s
symbol s = psymbol
where psymbol sc xc ac [x:ss] | x == s = sc s xc [] ss
      psymbol sc xc ac _                = xc ac
```

Both choice combinators also reflect the change of role of the continuations. The combinator `<|>` inserts the second parser in the continuation of p with alternatives that are always taken. The `<!>` operator inserts q in the other continuation and changes the the other or-combinator such that it checks for results.

```
(<|>) infixr 4 :: (CParser s r t) (CParser s r t) → CParser s r t
(<|>) p q = λsc xc ac ss = p sc (λac3 = q sc xc ac3 ss) ac ss

(<!>) infixr 4 :: (CParser s r t) (CParser s r t) → CParser s r t
(<!>) p q = λsc xc ac ss
 = p sc (λac2 = if (isEmpty ac2) (xc []) ac2) (q sc xc ac ss) ss
```

The and-combinator for the composition of parsers is now:

```
(<&>) infixr 6 :: (CParser s u t) (u → CParser s v t) → CParser s v t
(<&>) p q = λsc xc ac ss → p (λt xc1 ac1 → q t sc xc1 ac) xc ac ss
```

The definition of all variants of this operator (like `<&`, `&>`, and `<++>`) is not changed.

From the repeat operators `<*>` and `<+>` we removed the error by deleting the erroneous optimization in ClistP.

```
<*> :: (CParser s r t) → CParser s [r] t
<*> p = ClistP p []

ClistP :: (CParser s r t) [r] → CParser s [r] t
ClistP p l = (p <!&> λr → ClistP p [r:l]) <!> yield (reverse l)
```

Event Driven Software Quality

Jens Palsberg

UCLA Computer Science Department
University of California, Los Angeles, USA
palsberg@ucla.edu
http://www.cs.ucla.edu/~palsberg

Event-driven programming has found pervasive acceptance, from high-performance servers to embedded systems, as an efficient method for interacting with a complex world. The fastest research Web servers are event-driven, as is the most common operating system for sensor nodes.

An event-driven program handles concurrent logical tasks using a cooperative, application-level scheduler. The application developer separates each logical task into event handlers; the scheduler runs multiple handlers in an interleaved fashion. Unfortunately, the loose coupling of the event handlers obscures the program's control flow and makes dependencies hard to express and detect, leading to subtle bugs. As a result, event-driven programs can be difficult to understand, making them hard to debug, maintain, extend, and validate.

This talk presents recent approaches to event-driven software quality based on static analysis and testing, along with some open problems. We will discuss progress on how to avoid buffer overflow in TCP servers, stack overflow and missed deadlines in microcontrollers, and rapid battery drain in sensor networks. Our work is part of the Event Driven Software Quality project at UCLA, which is aimed at building the next generation of language and tool support for event-driven programming.

Jens Palsberg is a Professor and Vice Chair of Computer Science at UCLA. His research interests span the areas of compilers, embedded systems, programming languages, software engineering, and information security. He has authored over 80 technical papers, co-authored the book Object-Oriented Type Systems, and co-authored the 2002 revision of Appel's textbook on Modern Compiler Implementation in Java. He is the recipient of National Science Foundation CAREER and ITR awards, a Purdue University Faculty Scholar award, an IBM Faculty Award, and an Okawa Foundation research award. Dr. Palsberg's research has also been supported by DARPA, Intel, and British Telecom. Dr. Palsberg is an associate editor of ACM Transactions of Programming Languages and Systems, a member of the editorial board of Information and Computation, and a former member of the editorial board of IEEE Transactions on Software Engineering. He is serving as the secretary/treasurer of ACM SIGBED, Special Interest Group on Embedded Systems, and he has served as the general chair of the ACM Symposium on Principles of Programming Languages.

N. Kobayashi (Ed.): APLAS 2006, LNCS 4279, p. 165, 2006.

Widening Polyhedra with Landmarks

Axel Simon and Andy King

Computing Laboratory, University of Kent, Canterbury, UK
{a.simon, a.m.king}@kent.ac.uk

Abstract. The abstract domain of polyhedra is sufficiently expressive to be deployed in verification. One consequence of the richness of this domain is that long, possibly infinite, sequences of polyhedra can arise in the analysis of loops. Widening and narrowing have been proposed to infer a single polyhedron that summarises such a sequence of polyhedra. Motivated by precision losses encountered in verification, we explain how the classic widening/narrowing approach can be refined by an improved extrapolation strategy. The insight is to record inequalities that are thus far found to be unsatisfiable in the analysis of a loop. These so-called landmarks hint at the amount of widening necessary to reach stability. This extrapolation strategy, which refines widening with thresholds, can infer post-fixpoints that are precise enough not to require narrowing. Unlike previous techniques, our approach interacts well with other domains, is fully automatic, conceptually simple and precise on complex loops.

1 Introduction

In the last decade, the focus of static analysis has shifted from program optimisations towards program verification [5]. In this context, the abstract domain of polyhedra [2,10] has attracted much interest due to its expressiveness, as have sub-classes of polyhedra [18,19,21,22] that solve specific analysis tasks more efficiently. However, an inherent problem in polyhedral analysis is the ability to finitely reason about loops. Since the values of variables may differ in each iteration, each iterate may well be described by a different polyhedron. In order to quickly analyse a large or potentially infinite number of iterations, special acceleration techniques are required. One such acceleration framework is provided by the widening/narrowing approach to abstract interpretation [9,10].

1.1 A Primer on Widening/Narrowing

In order to illustrate the widening/narrowing approach on the domain of polyhedra and to discuss the implications of applying narrowing in an actual analyser, consider the control flow graph of `for (i=0; i<100; i++) {/*empty*/}`:

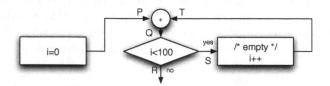

N. Kobayashi (Ed.): APLAS 2006, LNCS 4279, pp. 166–182, 2006.

The analysis amounts to characterising the values that can arise on the edges of the control flow graph. To this end, each edge is decorated with a polyhedron describing the relationships between the values of the variables on that edge. Given that the program contains only a single variable i, the polyhedra P, Q, R, S, T coincide with intervals over the reals. In the example, the polyhedron $P = \{i \in \mathbb{R} \mid 0 \leq i \leq 0\}$ describes the value of i at the beginning of the program. The +-node joins the polyhedra P and T to obtain $Q = P \sqcup T$. This join corresponds to the smallest convex polyhedron that includes the set of points $P \cup T$. Due to the integrality of i, the polyhedra that characterise the two outcomes of the test $i < 100$ are $R = Q \sqcap \{i \in \mathbb{R} \mid i \geq 100\}$ and $S = Q \sqcap \{i \in \mathbb{R} \mid i \leq 99\}$ where $\sqcap = \cap$ denotes the intersection of two polyhedra. The last polyhedron T is characterised by the affine map $T = \{i + 1 \mid i \in S\}$.

A solution of these equations can be found by applying Jacobi iteration [8], which calculates new polyhedra $P_{j+1}, Q_{j+1}, R_{j+1}, S_{j+1}, T_{j+1}$ from the polyhedra of the previous iteration P_j, Q_j, R_j, S_j, T_j. To ensure rapid convergence, a widening point must be inserted into the Q, S, T cycle. Widening at Q amounts to replacing the equation for Q with $Q_{j+1} = Q_j \nabla (P_j \sqcup T_j)$ where ∇ is a widening operator that removes unstable bounds [9]. The possible values of i are given below where $\bot$ denotes the empty set; the updated entries are shown in bold:

j	P_j	Q_j	R_j	S_j	T_j
1	$[0,0]$	$\bot$	$\bot$	$\bot$	$\bot$
2	$[0,0]$	$[\mathbf{0,0}]$	$\bot$	$\bot$	$\bot$
3	$[0,0]$	$[0,0]$	$\bot$	$[\mathbf{0,0}]$	$\bot$
4	$[0,0]$	$[0,0]$	$\bot$	$[0,0]$	$[\mathbf{1,1}]$
5	$[0,0]$	$[\mathbf{0,\infty}]$	$\bot$	$[0,0]$	$[1,1]$

j	P_j	Q_j	R_j	S_j	T_j
6	$[0,0]$	$[0,\infty]$	$[\mathbf{100,\infty}]$	$[\mathbf{0,99}]$	$[1,1]$
7	$[0,0]$	$[0,\infty]$	$[100,\infty]$	$[0,99]$	$[\mathbf{1,100}]$
8	$[0,0]$	$[0,\infty]$	$[100,\infty]$	$[0,99]$	$[1,100]$
1'	$[0,0]$	$[\mathbf{0,100}]$	$[100,\infty]$	$[0,99]$	$[1,100]$
2'	$[0,0]$	$[0,100]$	$[\mathbf{100,100}]$	$[0,99]$	$[1,100]$

In iteration 5, the output of the +-node is $P_4 \sqcup T_4 = [0,1]$. The widening operator compares $P_4 \sqcup T_4$ against $Q_4 = [0,0]$ and removes the unstable upper bound, yielding $Q_5 = [0,\infty]$. Stability is reached in iteration 8. The calculated post-fixpoint is now refined. This is realised by replacing widening with narrowing, i.e. $Q_{j+1} = Q_j \triangle (P_j \sqcup T_j)$. For polyhedra, it is sufficient to put $\triangle = \sqcap$ and to bound the number of iterations [9, page 290]. Hence, let $Q_{j+1} = Q_j \sqcap (P_j \sqcup T_j)$ which yields a refined state 1' and a further refinement 2' which, in this case, coincides with the least fixpoint of the original equations.

1.2 The Limitations of Narrowing

To illustrate one drawback of narrowing, consider a re-analysis of the above example where the widening is applied on S rather than on Q. In particular, let $S_{j+1} = S_j \nabla (Q_i \sqcap \{i \in \mathbb{R} \mid i \leq 99\})$. The analyses differ after the first 4 iterations:

j	P_j	Q_j	R_j	S_j	T_j	j	P_j	Q_j	R_j	S_j	T_j
5	$[0,0]$	$[0,1]$	$\bot$	$[0,0]$	$[1,1]$	10	$[0,0]$	$[0,\infty]$	$[100,\infty]$	$[0,\infty]$	$[1,\infty]$
6	$[0,0]$	$[0,1]$	$\bot$	$[\mathbf{0,\infty}]$	$[1,1]$	1'	$[0,0]$	$[0,\infty]$	$[100,\infty]$	$[\mathbf{0,99}]$	$[1,\infty]$
7	$[0,0]$	$[0,1]$	$\bot$	$[0,\infty]$	$[\mathbf{1,\infty}]$	2'	$[0,0]$	$[0,\infty]$	$[100,\infty]$	$[0,99]$	$[\mathbf{1,100}]$
8	$[0,0]$	$[\mathbf{0,\infty}]$	$\bot$	$[0,\infty]$	$[1,\infty]$	3'	$[0,0]$	$[\mathbf{0,100}]$	$[100,\infty]$	$[0,99]$	$[1,100]$
9	$[0,0]$	$[0,\infty]$	$[\mathbf{100,\infty}]$	$[0,\infty]$	$[1,\infty]$	4'	$[0,0]$	$[0,100]$	$[\mathbf{100,100}]$	$[0,99]$	$[1,100]$

In the first analysis, only the polyhedra Q and R are larger before narrowing commences. In the second analysis, S and T are also larger before narrowing. To illustrate the impact of this in the context of verification, suppose /*empty*/ is replaced by b = array[i] where array has 100 elements. To avoid an avalanche of false warning messages it is common practise to intersect S with the legal range of the index i [5], in this case $0 \leq i \leq 99$, yielding the polyhedron S', and thereafter use S' instead of S. Moreover, since the out-of-bounds check amounts to the subsumption test $S \not\subseteq S'$, it is straightforward to perform the check during fixpoint calculation; the test could be postponed until a fixpoint is reached, but this would require S' to be recalculated unnecessarily. However, this technique does not combine well with narrowing since a warning is issued if S is nominated for widening rather than Q, i.e. the placement of the widening point can determine whether a warning is issued or not.

Another implication of reducing a post-fixpoint with narrowing relates to domain interaction. Assume that the array above is embedded into a C structure declared as struct { int[100] array; int* p } s; and that the loop body is changed to b = s.array[i]. Consider again the second analysis in which S is widened to $[0, \infty]$ so that the upper bound of the array index i is lost. In this case, a points-to analysis [17,23] would generate a spurious l-value flow from s.p to b. Once narrowing infers $0 \leq i < 100$ it is desirable to remove this spurious flow. Alas, points-to analyses are typically formulated in terms of either closure operations [17] or union-find algorithms [23], none of which support the removal of flow information. Thus, even if narrowing can recover precision in one domain, the knock-on precision loss induced in other domains may be irrecoverable.

Furthermore, narrowing on polyhedra [9] cannot recover precision if the loop invariant is expressed as a disequality [5]. For instance, narrowing has no effect if the loop invariant in the example is changed from i<100 to the equivalent i!=100. Since it is unrealistic to modify the program under test, a substitute for narrowing is required to analyse programs with disequalities as loop conditions.

1.3   Our Contribution to Widening/Narrowing

Rather than recovering inequalities through narrowing that were widened away, our contribution is to use unsatisfiable inequalities as oracles to guide the fixpoint acceleration. Specifically, we propose widening with landmarks, which records inequalities that were found to be unsatisfiable in two consecutive iterates. We then extrapolate to the first iterate that makes any of these inequalities satisfiable. If this extrapolation is not a fixpoint, we continue until no unsatisfiable inequalities remain, at which point standard widening is applied [1,14]. The rationale for observing unsatisfiable inequalities is that the transition from unsatisfiable to satisfiable indicates a change in the behaviour of a program. Widening with landmarks is similar in spirit to widening with thresholds [5]. In this related approach, the value of an unstable variable is extrapolated to the next threshold from a set of user-supplied values. Rather than guiding widening with thresholds on individual variables, our approach automatically extracts linear inequalities from the program which bound the degree of extrapolation.

After introducing notation for polyhedra manipulation, Section 3 presents a worked example of a string buffer analysis that conveys the ideas behind widening with landmarks. Sections 4 and 5 formalise the notion of landmarks which are used in Section 6 to define an extrapolation strategy. Section 7 comments on our implementation and explains how widening with landmarks can be added to an existing analysis. We discuss related work in Section 8 and conclude in Section 9.

2 Preliminaries

Let $x = \langle x_1, \ldots x_n \rangle$ denote an ordered set of variables, let Lin denote the set of linear expressions of the form $a \cdot x$ where $a \in \mathbb{Z}^n$ and let $Ineq$ denote the set of linear inequalities $a \cdot x \leq c$ where $c \in \mathbb{Z}$. Moreover, let e.g. $6x_3 \leq x_1 + 5$ abbreviate $\langle -1, 0, 6, 0, \ldots 0 \rangle \cdot x \leq 5$ and let e.g. $x_2 = 7$ abbreviate the two opposing inequalities $7 \leq x_2$ and $x_2 \leq 7$. Each inequality $a \cdot x \leq c \in Ineq$ induces a half-space $[\![a \cdot x \leq c]\!] = \{x \in \mathbb{R}^n \mid a \cdot x \leq c\}$. Each finite set of inequalities $I = \{\iota_1, \ldots \iota_m\} \subseteq Ineq$ induces a closed, convex polyhedron $[\![I]\!] = \bigcap_{i=1}^{m} [\![\iota_i]\!]$. Let $Poly = \{[\![I]\!] \mid I \subseteq Ineq, |I| \in \mathbb{N}\}$ denote the set of all (finitely generated) polyhedra. Given two polyhedra $P_i = [\![I_i]\!]$, $i = 1, 2$, define $P_1 \sqcap P_2 = [\![I_1 \cup I_2]\!]$ and let $P_1 \sqsubseteq P_2$ iff $[\![I_1]\!] \subseteq [\![I_2]\!]$. Let $P_1 \sqcup P_2 = \sqcap \{P \in Poly \mid P_1 \sqsubseteq P \wedge P_2 \sqsubseteq P\}$; equivalently let $P_1 \sqcup P_2 = cl(hull(P_1 \cup P_2))$ where cl denotes topological closure and $hull$ is the convex hull operation on sets of points [10]. A set of inequalities $I \subseteq Ineq$ is said to be unsatisfiable if $[\![I]\!] = \emptyset$, otherwise it is satisfiable. The lattice $\langle Poly, \sqsubseteq, \sqcap, \sqcup \rangle$ contains infinite ascending chains $P_1 \sqsubseteq P_2 \sqsubseteq P_3 \ldots$ so that standard Kleene iteration [9] may not converge onto a fixpoint in finite time. To guarantee convergence, widening operators $\nabla : Poly \times Poly \to Poly$ have been proposed for $Poly$ which are required to satisfy the following properties [10]:

1. $\forall x, y \in Poly . x \sqsubseteq x \nabla y$
2. $\forall x, y \in Poly . y \sqsubseteq x \nabla y$
3. for all increasing chains $x_0 \sqsubseteq x_1 \sqsubseteq \ldots$, the increasing chain defined by $y_0 = x_0$ and $y_{i+1} = y_i \nabla x_{i+1}$ is ultimately stable.

Besides the standard lattice operations, we introduce a family of projection operators $\exists_{x_i} : Poly \to Poly$ such that $\exists_{x_i}(Q) = \{\langle x_1, \ldots, x_{i-1}, x, x_{i+1}, \ldots x_n \rangle \mid \langle x_1, \ldots x_n \rangle \in Q, x \in \mathbb{R}\}$. Intuitively, $\exists_{x_i}(Q)$ removes any information pertaining to x_i from the polyhedron $Q \in Poly$. This is useful to model assignment, e.g. $\exists_{x_i}(Q) \sqcap [\![\{x_i = 42\}]\!]$ updates the value of x_i to 42. Finally, in order to find the minimum value of an expression $a \cdot x$ such that $x \in P$, we introduce the operation min : $Lin \times Poly \to (\mathbb{Z} \cup \{-\infty\})$. To this end, let $C = \{c \in \mathbb{Z} \mid P \sqcap [\![\{a \cdot x \leq c\}]\!] \neq \emptyset\}$, that is, C contains all constants c such that the half-space defined by $a \cdot x \leq c$ intersects with P, and define

$$\min(a \cdot x, P) = \begin{cases} \min(C) & \text{if } \min(C) \text{ exists} \\ -\infty & \text{otherwise.} \end{cases}$$

Observe that $\min(a \cdot x, P)$ can be realised with Simplex: if there exists $y \in \mathbb{R}^n$ that minimises the expression $a \cdot y$ over P, then put $\min(a \cdot x, P) = \lceil a \cdot y \rceil$, otherwise put $\min(a \cdot x, P) = -\infty$.

3   Worked Example from String Buffer Analysis

In this section we explain the ideas behind widening with landmarks in the context of an example drawn from string buffer analysis. Consider the following loop which is naturally produced by a C compiler translating `while (*s) s++;`.

```
char s[32] = "the string";
int i = 0;
while (true) {
  c = s[i];
  if (c==0) break;
  i = i+1;
};
```

The task is to check that the string buffer `s` is only accessed within bounds. This program is challenging for automatic verification because the loop invariant is always satisfied and the extra exit condition within the loop does not mention the loop counter `i`. In C, a string is merely an array of bytes, in this case `s` is an array of 32 bytes. The string literal initialises the first ten characters whilst the eleventh position is set to 0 (the NUL character). The analysis of this function follows the ideas of [11,20,25] in representing only the position of the first NUL character, thereby ignoring the content of `"the string"`. Thus, a single variable per array suffices to express the relevant information. Specifically, let n represent the index of the NUL position in `s`. The control flow graph of the string buffer example is decorated with polyhedra P, Q, R, S, T, U as follows:

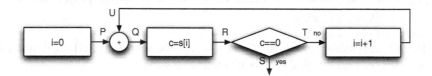

The initial values of the program variables is described by $P = [\![\{i = 0, n = 10\}]\!]$. The merge of this polyhedron and the polyhedron on the back edge, U, defines $Q = P \sqcup U$. To verify that the array access `s[i]` is within bounds, we compute $Q' = Q \sqcap [\![\{0 \le i \le 31\}]\!]$ and issue a warning if $Q' \ne Q$. The analysis continues under the premise that the access was within bounds and hence R is defined in terms of Q' rather than Q as follows:

$$R = (\exists_c(Q') \sqcap [\![\{i \le n - 1, 1 \le c \le 255\}]\!])$$
$$\sqcup (\exists_c(Q') \sqcap [\![\{i = n, c = 0\}]\!])$$
$$\sqcup (\exists_c(Q') \sqcap [\![\{n + 1 \le i, 0 \le c \le 255\}]\!])$$

The projection operator $\exists_c$ removes all information pertaining to c in Q' so that c can be updated. Since the contents of `s` are ignored in our model, the new value of c only depends on the relationship between the index i and n which describes the position of the *first* NUL character. The value of c is restricted to $[1, 255]$ if $i < n$, it is set to 0 if $i = n$ and to $[0, 255]$ if $i > n$. Note that this model is valid for platforms where the C `char` type is unsigned. The last three equations that comprise the system are given by the following:

$$S = R \sqcap [\![\{c = 0\}]\!]$$
$$T = (R \sqcap [\![\{c \leq -1\}]\!]) \sqcup (R \sqcap [\![\{c \geq 1\}]\!])$$
$$U = \{\langle n, i+1, c \rangle \mid \langle n, i, c \rangle \in T\}$$

The affine transformation in the last equation defining U assumes that the variables in the polyhedron are ordered as in the sequence n, i, c.

3.1 Applying the Widening/Narrowing Approach

As before, we solve these equations iteratively, nominating Q as the widening point to ensure convergence in the cycle Q, R, T, U. Thus, when the equations are reinterpreted iteratively, the equation Q is replaced with $Q_{j+1} = Q_j \nabla (P_j \sqcup U_j)$. Applying the standard widening/narrowing approach results in the iterates shown in Figure 1. Again, we apply widening when Q is evaluated the third time, so that widening is applied on Q_9 and $P_9 \sqcup U_9$ to obtain Q_{10}. The resulting polyhedron $Q_{10} = [\![\{0 \leq i\}]\!]$ is intersected with the verification condition to yield $Q'_{10} - [\![\{0 \leq i \leq 31\}]\!]$, thereby raising a warning since $Q_{10} \neq Q'_{10}$. Before proceeding to the evaluation of R_{11}, observe that $\exists_c(Q'_j) = Q'_j$ in all iterations j since P_j does not constrain c and consequently neither does $Q_j = U_j \sqcup P_j$. Given that Q'_{10} allows i to take on any value in $[0, 31]$, the three cases in the definition of R that are guarded by $i \leq n-1$, $i = n$ and $n+1 \leq i$ all contribute to the result R_{11}. This result is depicted as the grey region in Figure 1 which shows the relationship between i and c. The three regions whose join form the polyhedron R_{11} are marked with two rectangles and a small cross for the $c = 0$ case. Observe that applying narrowing, that is, replacing $Q_{j+1} = Q_j \nabla (U_j \sqcup P_j)$ with $Q_{j+1} = Q_j \triangle (U_j \sqcup P_j)$, yields another iterate $1'$ in which the value of i ranges over $[0, 32]$ which still violates the array bound check since $Q'_{1'} \neq Q_{1'}$ where $Q'_{1'} = Q_{1'} \sqcap \{0 \leq i \leq 31\}$ corresponds to $Q_{1'}$ restricted to valid array indices.

3.2 The Rationale Behind Landmarks

Now consider the same fixpoint calculation using widening with landmarks as shown in Figure 2. We omit the first nine iterates before widening is applied since they coincide with those given in Figure 1. While landmarks are gathered throughout the fixpoint calculation, we focus on the calculation of the polyhedron R as this gives rise to the only landmarks that are of relevance in this example. The three graphs in Figure 2 depict the relation between i and c in the polyhedra R_3, R_7, R_{11}, which are the three iterates in which R_j changes. The polyhedron R_3 is derived from $\exists_c(Q'_3) = Q'_3 = [\![\{0 \leq i \leq 0\}]\!]$. During this computation, Q'_3 is intersected with $[\![\{i \leq n-1, 1 \leq c \leq 255\}]\!]$, $[\![\{n \leq i \leq n, 0 \leq c \leq 0\}]\!]$ and $[\![\{n+1 \leq i, 0 \leq c \leq 255\}]\!]$ which represent three different behaviours of the program.

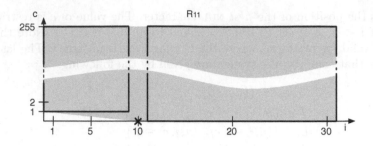

j	Q_j	R_j	S_j	T_j	U_j
1	$\perp$	$\perp$	$\perp$	$\perp$	$\perp$
2	$\{0 \le i \le 0\}$	$\perp$	$\perp$	$\perp$	$\perp$
3	$\{0 \le i \le 0\}$	$\left\{\begin{array}{l}0 \le i \le 0, \\ 1 \le c \le 255\end{array}\right\}$	$\perp$	$\perp$	$\perp$
4	$\{0 \le i \le 0\}$	$\left\{\begin{array}{l}0 \le i \le 0, \\ 1 \le c \le 255\end{array}\right\}$	$\perp$	$\left\{\begin{array}{l}0 \le i \le 0, \\ 1 \le c \le 255\end{array}\right\}$	$\perp$
5	$\{0 \le i \le 0\}$	$\left\{\begin{array}{l}0 \le i \le 0, \\ 1 \le c \le 255\end{array}\right\}$	$\perp$	$\left\{\begin{array}{l}0 \le i \le 0, \\ 1 \le c \le 255\end{array}\right\}$	$\left\{\begin{array}{l}1 \le i \le 1, \\ 1 \le c \le 255\end{array}\right\}$
6	$\{0 \le i \le 1\}$	$\left\{\begin{array}{l}0 \le i \le 0, \\ 1 \le c \le 255\end{array}\right\}$	$\perp$	$\left\{\begin{array}{l}0 \le i \le 0, \\ 1 \le c \le 255\end{array}\right\}$	$\left\{\begin{array}{l}1 \le i \le 1, \\ 1 \le c \le 255\end{array}\right\}$
7	$\{0 \le i \le 1\}$	$\left\{\begin{array}{l}0 \le i \le 1, \\ 1 \le c \le 255\end{array}\right\}$	$\perp$	$\left\{\begin{array}{l}0 \le i \le 0, \\ 1 \le c \le 255\end{array}\right\}$	$\left\{\begin{array}{l}1 \le i \le 1, \\ 1 \le c \le 255\end{array}\right\}$
8	$\{0 \le i \le 1\}$	$\left\{\begin{array}{l}0 \le i \le 1, \\ 1 \le c \le 255\end{array}\right\}$	$\perp$	$\left\{\begin{array}{l}0 \le i \le 1, \\ 1 \le c \le 255\end{array}\right\}$	$\left\{\begin{array}{l}1 \le i \le 1, \\ 1 \le c \le 255\end{array}\right\}$
9	$\{0 \le i \le 1\}$	$\left\{\begin{array}{l}0 \le i \le 1, \\ 1 \le c \le 255\end{array}\right\}$	$\perp$	$\left\{\begin{array}{l}0 \le i \le 1, \\ 1 \le c \le 255\end{array}\right\}$	$\left\{\begin{array}{l}1 \le i \le 2, \\ 1 \le c \le 255\end{array}\right\}$
10	$\{0 \le i\}$	$\left\{\begin{array}{l}0 \le i \le 1, \\ 1 \le c \le 255\end{array}\right\}$	$\perp$	$\left\{\begin{array}{l}0 \le i \le 1, \\ 1 \le c \le 255\end{array}\right\}$	$\left\{\begin{array}{l}1 \le i \le 2, \\ 1 \le c \le 255\end{array}\right\}$
11	$\{0 \le i\}$	$\left\{\begin{array}{l}0 \le i \le 31, \\ 0 \le c \le 255, \\ -i - 10c \le -10\end{array}\right\}$	$\perp$	$\left\{\begin{array}{l}0 \le i \le 1, \\ 1 \le c \le 255\end{array}\right\}$	$\left\{\begin{array}{l}1 \le i \le 2, \\ 1 \le c \le 255\end{array}\right\}$
12	$\{0 \le i\}$	$\left\{\begin{array}{l}0 \le i \le 31, \\ 0 \le c \le 255, \\ -i - 10c \le -10\end{array}\right\}$	$\left\{\begin{array}{l}10 \le i, \\ i \le 31, \\ 0 \le c \le 0\end{array}\right\}$	$\left\{\begin{array}{l}0 \le i \le 31, \\ 1 \le c \le 255\end{array}\right\}$	$\left\{\begin{array}{l}1 \le i \le 2, \\ 1 \le c \le 255\end{array}\right\}$
13	$\{0 \le i\}$	$\left\{\begin{array}{l}0 \le i \le 31, \\ 0 \le c \le 255, \\ -i - 10c \le -10\end{array}\right\}$	$\left\{\begin{array}{l}10 \le i, \\ i \le 31, \\ 0 \le c \le 0\end{array}\right\}$	$\left\{\begin{array}{l}0 \le i \le 31, \\ 1 \le c \le 255\end{array}\right\}$	$\left\{\begin{array}{l}1 \le i \le 32, \\ 1 \le c \le 255\end{array}\right\}$
14	$\{0 \le i\}$	$\left\{\begin{array}{l}0 \le i \le 31, \\ 0 \le c \le 255, \\ -i - 10c \le -10\end{array}\right\}$	$\left\{\begin{array}{l}10 \le i, \\ i \le 31, \\ 0 \le c \le 0\end{array}\right\}$	$\left\{\begin{array}{l}0 \le i \le 31, \\ 1 \le c \le 255\end{array}\right\}$	$\left\{\begin{array}{l}1 \le i \le 32, \\ 1 \le c \le 255\end{array}\right\}$
1'	$\{0 \le i \le 32\}$	$\left\{\begin{array}{l}0 \le i \le 31, \\ 0 \le c \le 255, \\ -i - 10c \le -10\end{array}\right\}$	$\left\{\begin{array}{l}10 \le i, \\ i \le 31, \\ 0 \le c \le 0\end{array}\right\}$	$\left\{\begin{array}{l}0 \le i \le 31, \\ 1 \le c \le 255\end{array}\right\}$	$\left\{\begin{array}{l}1 \le i \le 31, \\ 1 \le c \le 255\end{array}\right\}$

Fig. 1. Fixpoint calculation of the string loop. A polyhedron $[\![S]\!]$ is abbreviated to S and $\perp$ denotes an unsatisfiable set of inequalities. The column P_j is omitted since $P_j = [\![\{0 \le i \le 0\}]\!]$ for all iterations j. Further we omit $10 \le n \le 10$ from all polyhedra.

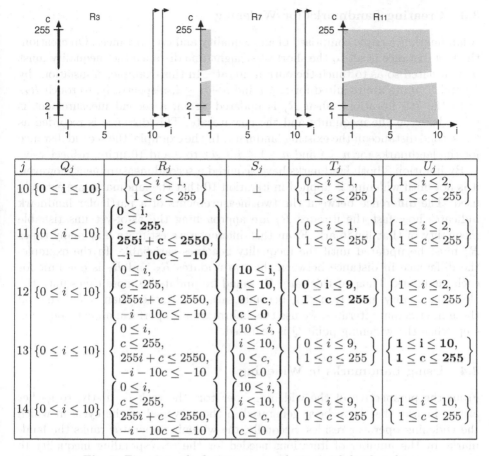

Fig. 2. Fixpoint calculation using widening with landmarks

As the fixpoint calculation progresses, polyhedra grow and new behaviours are incrementally enabled. A behaviour can only change from being disabled to being enabled when one of its constituent inequalities makes the transition from unsatisfiable to satisfiable. A fixpoint may exist in which not all behaviours of a program are enabled, that is, there are behaviours that contain unsatisfiable inequalities. The rationale for widening with landmarks is to find these fixpoints by systematically considering the inequalities that prevent a behaviour from being enabled. These inequalities are exactly those inequalities in the semantic equations that are unsatisfiable in the context of the current iterate. In the example, the last two behaviours contain the inequalities $n \leq i$ (arising from $i = n$) and $n + 1 \leq i$ that are responsible for enabling the second and third behaviour. These inequalities are unsatisfiable in Q'_3 and are therefore stored as landmarks. The leftmost graph in Figure 2 indicates the position of the two inequalities $n \leq i$ and $n + 1 \leq i$ which define the landmarks we record for R_3.

3.3 Creating Landmarks for Widening

A landmark is a triple comprised of an inequality and two distances. On creation, the first distance is set to the shortest straight-line distance the inequality must be translated so as to touch the current iterate. In this example, translations by 10 and 11 units are required for $n \leq i$ and $n + 1 \leq i$, respectively, to touch R_3.

In the 7th iteration, when R_j is updated again, a second measurement is taken between the inequality and the new iterate. This distance is recorded as the second distance in the existing landmark. In the example, the second distance for the landmarks for $n \leq i$ and $n + 1 \leq i$ is set to 9 and 10 units, respectively.

By iteration 8 both landmarks have acquired a second measurement, however, it is not until widening is applied in iteration 10 that the landmarks are actually used. The difference between the two measurements of a particular landmark indicates how fast the iterates R_j are approaching the as-of-yet unsatisfiable inequality of that landmark. From this difference we estimate how many times R_j must be updated until the inequality becomes satisfiable. In the example, the difference in distance between the two updates R_3 and R_7 is one unit for each landmark. Thus, at this rate, R_j would be updated 9 more times until the closer inequality, namely $n \leq i$, becomes satisfied. Rather than calculating all these intermediate iterates, we use this information to perform an extrapolation step when the widening point Q is revisited.

3.4 Using Landmarks in Widening

From the perspective of the widening operator, the task is, firstly, to gather all landmarks that have been generated in the traversal of the cycle in which the widening operator resides. Secondly, the widening operator ranks the landmarks by the number of iterations needed for the corresponding inequality to become satisfied. Thirdly, the landmark with the smallest rank determines the amount of extrapolation the widening operator applies. In the example, recall that the unsatisfiable inequality $n \leq i$ in R_7 would become satisfiable after 9 more updates of R whereas the other unsatisfiable inequality $n + 1 \leq i$ becomes satisfiable after 10 updates. Hence, $n \leq i$ constitutes the nearest inequality and, rather than applying widening when calculating $Q_{10} = Q_9 \nabla (P_9 \sqcup U_9)$, extrapolation is performed. Specifically, the changes between $Q_9 = [\![\{0 \leq i \leq 1\}]\!]$ and $P_9 \sqcup U_9 = [\![\{0 \leq i \leq 2\}]\!]$ are extrapolated 9 times to yield $Q_{10} = [\![\{0 \leq i \leq 10\}]\!]$. The new value of Q_{10} forces a re-evaluation of R, yielding R_{11}, as shown in Figure 2. In the next iteration, the semantic equation for T yields $[\![\{0 \leq i, 1 \leq c \leq 255, 255i + c \leq 2550\}]\!]$. Since i and c are known to be integral, this polyhedron can be refined [16] to the entry T_{12} as shown in the table. A final iteration leads to a fixpoint.

Note that it is possible to apply extrapolation as soon as a single landmark acquires its second measurement. However, to ensure that the state is extrapolated only to the point where the first additional behaviour becomes enabled, the extrapolation step should be deferred until all landmarks have acquired their

---

Listing 1. Adding or tightening a landmark: $updateLandmark(P, \iota, L)$

Require: $P \in Poly, \iota \in Ineq, L \subseteq Lin \times \mathbb{Z} \times (\mathbb{Z} \cup \{\infty\})$
1:   $e \le c \leftarrow \iota$
2:   $c' \leftarrow \min(P, e)$
3:   **if** $c < c'$ **then**   /* $P \sqcap [\![\{\iota\}]\!]$ is empty */
4:     $dist \leftarrow c' - c$ /* calculate the distance between P and $[\![\{\iota\}]\!]$ */
5:     **if** $\exists dist_c, dist_p \, . \, \langle e, dist_c, dist_p \rangle \in L$ **then**
6:       **return** $(L \setminus \{\langle e, dist_c, dist_p \rangle\}) \cup \{\langle e, \min(dist, dist_c), dist_p \rangle\}$
7:     **else**
8:       **return** $L \cup \{\langle e, dist, \infty \rangle\}$
9:     **end if**
10: **end if**
11: **return** L

---

second value. In practise, this means that no extrapolation is performed if a new landmark was created in the last iteration. Note that new landmarks cannot be added indefinitely as there is at most one landmark for each inequality that occurs in the semantic equations which are, in turn, finite.

The following sections formalise these ideas by presenting algorithms for gathering landmarks and performing extrapolation using landmarks.

4 Acquiring Landmarks

This section formalises the intuition behind widening with landmarks by giving a more algorithmic description on how landmarks are acquired. Listing 1 presents the algorithm $updateLandmark$ which is invoked whenever a polyhedron P is intersected with an inequality ι that arises from a semantic equation. In line 2, the distance between ι and P is measured by calculating $c' = \min(P, e)$. Intuitively, $e \le c'$ is a parallel translation of ι that has a minimal intersection with P. Line 3 compares the relative location of ι and its translation, thereby ensuring that lines 4 to 9 are only executed if ι is unsatisfiable and, thus, can yield a landmark. If ι is indeed unsatisfiable, line 4 calculates its distance to P.

Given this distance, line 5 determines if a landmark is to be updated or created. An update occurs whenever different semantic equations contain the same unsatisfiable inequality. In this case line 6 ensures that the smaller distance is stored in the landmark. The rationale for storing the distance to the closer inequality is that a landmark for the inequality that is further away can be gathered later. In particular, if extrapolation to the nearer inequality does not lead to a fixpoint, the nearer inequality is satisfiable in the extrapolated space and cannot induce a new landmark. At this point the inequality that is further away can become a landmark. Hence, tracking distances to closer inequalities ensures that all landmarks are considered in turn.

When creating a new landmark, line 8 sets the second distance to infinity which indicates that this new landmark is not yet ready to be used in extrapolation. The next section details how the acquired landmarks are manipulated.

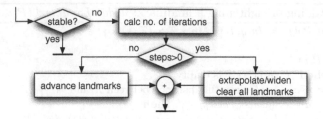

Fig. 3. Operations performed at a widening point

Listing 2. Advance a landmark: $advanceLandmarks(L)$

Require: $L \subseteq Lin \times \mathbb{Z} \times (\mathbb{Z} \cup \{\infty\})$
1: $L' \leftarrow \{\langle e, dist_c, dist_c \rangle \mid \langle e, dist_c, dist_p \rangle \in L\}$
2: **return** L'

---

5   Using Landmarks at a Widening Point

The semantic equations of the program induce cyclic dependencies between the
states at each program point. A widening point must be inserted into each cycle to
ensure that the fixpoint computation eventually stabilises. In case of nested cycles,
a fixpoint is calculated on each inner cycle before moving on to the containing cycle
[6]. Figure 3 schematically shows the actions taken when a semantic equation at a
widening point is evaluated. If stability has not yet been achieved, all landmarks
gathered in the current cycle (excluding those in inner cycles) are passed to the algorithm *calcIterations* which estimates the number of times the cycle needs to be
traversed until a state is reached at which the first as-of-yet unsatisfiable inequality becomes satisfiable. This count is denoted as *steps* in Figure 3. Two special
values are distinguished: 0 and ∞. A value of zero indicates that new landmarks
were created during the last traversal of the cycle. In this case, the left branch
of Figure 3 is taken and the algorithm *advanceLandmarks*, which is presented in
Listing 2, is called. Normal fixpoint computation is then resumed, allowing landmarks to acquire a second measurement. The call to *advanceLandmarks* stores the
calculated distance in the third element of each landmark, thereby ensuring that
this value is not lost when *updateLandmark* updates the second element of the
landmark tuple during the next iteration.

The right branch of Figure 3 is selected whenever *calcIterations* returns a
non-zero value for *steps* which indicates that all landmarks have acquired two
measurements. This is the propitious moment for extrapolation as only now
can all landmarks participate in predicting the number of cycles until the first
as-of-yet unsatisfiable inequality is reached. In order to show how this number is derived, consider Listing 3. The algorithm *calcIterations* calculates an
estimate of the number of iterations necessary to satisfy the nearest landmark
stored in *steps*. This variable is initially set to ∞ which is the value returned
if no landmarks have been gathered. An infinite value in *steps* indicates that

---

Listing 3. Calculate distance $calcIterations(L)$

Require: $L \subseteq Lin \times \mathbb{Z} \times (\mathbb{Z} \cup \{\infty\})$
1: $steps \leftarrow \infty$ /* indicate that normal widening should be applied */
2: **for** $\langle e, dist_c, dist_p \rangle \in L$ **do**
3:    **if** $dist_p = \infty$ **then**
4:       $steps \leftarrow 0$
5:    **else if** $dist_p > dist_c$ **then**
6:       $steps \leftarrow \min(steps, \lceil dist_c / (dist_p - dist_c) \rceil)$ /* assume $\min(\infty, n) = n$ */
7:    **end if**
8: **end for**
9: **return** $steps$

---

widening, rather than extrapolation, has to be applied. Otherwise, the loop in lines 2–8 examines each landmark in turn. For any landmark with two measurements, i.e. those for which $dist_p \neq \infty$, line 6 calculates after how many steps the unsatisfiable inequality that gave rise to the landmark $\langle e, dist_c, dist_p \rangle$ becomes satisfiable. Specifically, $dist_p - dist_c$ represents the distance traversed during one iteration. Given that $dist_c$ is the distance between the boundary of the unsatisfiable inequality and the polyhedron in that iteration, the algorithm computes $\lceil dist_c / (dist_p - dist_c) \rceil$ as an estimate of the number of iterations required to make the inequality satisfiable. This number is stored in $steps$ unless another landmark has already been encountered that can be reached in fewer iterations.

The next section presents an algorithm that extrapolates the change between two iterates by a given number of steps. It thereby completes the suite of algorithms necessary to realise widening with landmarks.

6   Extrapolation Operator for Polyhedra

In contrast to standard widening which removes inequalities that are unstable, extrapolation by a finite number of steps merely relaxes inequalities until the next landmark is reached. Listing 4 presents a simple extrapolation algorithm that performs this relaxation based on two iterates, namely P_1 and P_2. This extrapolation is applied by replacing any semantic equation of the form $Q_{i+1} = Q_i \nabla R_i$ with $Q_{i+1} = extrapolate(Q_i, R_i, steps)$ where $steps = calcIterations(L)$ and L is the set of landmarks relevant to this widening point. Thus the first argument to $extrapolate$, namely P_1, corresponds to the previous iterate Q_i, while P_2 corresponds to R_i. Line 2 calculates the join P of both, P_1 and P_2, which forms the basis for extrapolating the polyhedron P_1. Specifically, bounds of P_1 that are not preserved in the join are extrapolated. The loop in lines 7–15 implements this strategy which resembles the original widening on polyhedra [10] which can be defined as $E_{res} = \{\iota_i \mid P \sqsubseteq [\![\{\iota_i\}]\!]\}$ where $\iota_1, \ldots \iota_n$ is a non-redundant set of inequalities such that $[\![\{\iota_1, \ldots \iota_n\}]\!] = P_1$, c.f. [1]. Note that this widening can be inaccurate if the dimensionality of P_1 is smaller than that of $P = P_1 \sqcup P_2$; other inequalities from P can be added to E_{res} to remedy this [1,14] but we omit this additional step for brevity. The entailment check $P \sqsubseteq [\![\{\iota_i\}]\!]$ for $\iota_i \equiv e \leq c$ is implemented

---

Listing 4. Extrapolate changes $extrapolate(P_1, P_2, steps)$

Require: $P_1, P_2 \in Poly, steps \in \mathbb{N} \cup \{\infty\}$

1: $[\![\iota_1, \ldots \iota_n]\!] \leftarrow P_1$ /* $\iota_1, \ldots \iota_n$ is a non-redundant description of P_1 */
2: $P \leftarrow P_1 \sqcup P_2$
3: **if** $steps = 0$ **then**
4:     **return** P
5: **else**
6:     $Eres \leftarrow \emptyset$
7:     **for** $i = 1, \ldots n$ **do**
8:         $e \leq c \leftarrow \iota_i$
9:         $c' \leftarrow \min(P, e)$
10:        **if** $c' \leq c$ **then**
11:           $Eres \leftarrow Eres \cup \{e \leq c\}$ /* since $P \sqsubseteq [\![\iota_i]\!]$ */
12:        **else if** $steps \neq \infty$ **then**
13:           $Eres \leftarrow Eres \cup \{e \leq (c + (c' - c)steps)\}$
14:        **end if**
15:     **end for**
16:     **return** $[\![Eres]\!]$
17: **end if**

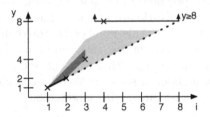

Fig. 4. Illustrating non-linear growth

in line 9 by calculating the smallest c' such that $P \sqsubseteq [\![\{e \leq c'\}]\!]$. In the case that $c' \leq c$, the entailment holds and line 11 adds the inequality to the result set. In the case that the entailment does not hold, the inequality is discarded whenever $steps = \infty$. In this case *extrapolate* reduces to a simple widening. If $steps$ is finite, line 13 translates the inequality, thereby anticipating the change that is likely to occur during the next $steps$ loop iterations.

The presented algorithm performs a linear translation of inequalities. Since array accesses are typically linear, this approach is well suited for verifying that indices fall within bounds. However, a non-linear relationship such as that arising in the C loop int i=1; for(int y=1; y<8; y=y*2) i++; is not amenable to linear extrapolation and thus leads to a loss of precision. The loop creates successive values for i, y that correspond to the points $\langle 1, 1 \rangle$, $\langle 2, 2 \rangle$, $\langle 3, 4 \rangle$ and, finally, at the exit of the loop, the point $\langle 4, 8 \rangle$. These are indicated as crosses in Figure 4. The best polyhedral approximation of these points restricted by the loop invariant $y < 8$ is shown in dark grey. However, extrapolating the first two iterates, namely the polyhedron $\{\langle 1, 1 \rangle\}$ and the polyhedron that additionally contains $\langle 2, 2 \rangle$, predicts that the shown landmark $y \geq 8$ becomes satisfiable after

7 additional loop iterations. The extrapolation results in the state depicted as a dashed line; continuing the fixpoint calculation leads to the light grey area as loop invariant which is a coarser approximation than the optimal polyhedron.

7   Implementation

We have implemented widening with landmarks in a verifier for C programs that combines numeric analysis with points-to analysis. The verifier is geared towards string buffer analysis in that it implements the tracking of NUL positions [20]. One obstacle in a polyhedral analysis is the complexity of the polyhedral operations. To support a large number of variables, we chose the two-variable-per-inequality (TVPI) domain [22] which can only represent inequalities with at most two non-zero variables per inequality. The underlying idea in this domain is to calculate a closure of the TVPI inequalities. A closure step eliminates a from any two (appropriately scaled) inequalities $ax_i + bx_j \leq c$ and $-ax_i + dx_k \leq e$ to obtain $bx_j + dx_k \leq c + e$ which is then added to the closure. A closed system makes it possible to implement all polyhedral operations efficiently on sets of planar polyhedra. For example, the convex hull operation on planar polyhedra runs in $O(n \log n)$ where n is the number of inequalities in the planar polyhedron [22]. Another advantage is the availability of algorithms to shrink each planar polyhedron around the integral grid [16]. This is not only useful to improve precision when analysing integer variables (as necessary in T_{12} of Figure 2) but also limits the size of coefficients of inequalities. Otherwise, inequalities with excessively large coefficients have to be removed to ensure progress [21], a step that is impossible in the TVPI domain since closure could re-introduce these inequalities.

   Implementing widening with landmarks requires two modifications to an existing analysis, namely modifying the intersection operation to gather landmarks and replacing widening operators by extrapolation operations that evaluate the acquired landmarks. When it comes to gathering landmarks, note that the TVPI domain implements intersection of a polyhedron P and a set of inequalities $\{\iota_1, \ldots \iota_n\}$ by computing $(\ldots((P \sqcap \{\iota_1\}) \sqcap \{\iota_2\}) \ldots) \sqcap \{\iota_n\}$ since a cheap incremental closure can be applied after adding a single inequality. Adding inequalities one-by-one makes it possible to intersperse calls to *updateLandmark* for landmark acquisition. While it may seem that calculating $\min(e, P)$ in line 2 of Listing 1 incurs a performance penalty, it turns out that running this linear program can actually improve memory performance of a domain. Consider the semantic equation of R from Section 3 whose calculation requires three copies of the input polyhedron $\exists_c(Q')$ which are then intersected with inequalities expressing three different behaviours. During the fixpoint calculation, many behaviours are disabled. A consequence of this is that a polyhedron will be copied, only for the copy to become unsatisfiable when intersected with an inequality that expresses such a disabled behaviour. Observe that in this case the test on line 3 of *updateLandmark* succeeds and a landmark is added. A better strategy is to call *updateLandmark* without copying the original input polyhedron and, only if no new landmarks arise, an actual copy of the input polyhedron is needed further

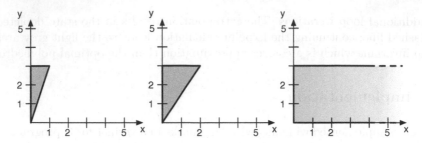

Fig. 5. Improved widening from polytopes to polyhedra

processing. This strategy avoids copying polyhedra that are shortly after abandoned when they turn unsatisfiable. Note that this refinement can be applied to many semantic equations, in particular, to those that model conditionals which, in our application, make up the majority of all intersection operations.

8   Related Work

Although the foundations of widening and narrowing were laid three decades ago [7], the value of widening was largely unappreciated until comparatively recently [9]. In the last decade there has been a resurgence of interest in applying polyhedral analysis and, specifically, polyhedral widenings [1,3,4]. The original widening operator in [10] discards linear relationships that result from joining the state of the previous loop iteration with the current loop iteration. This causes a loss of precision, especially when widening is applied in each loop iteration. The so-called revised widening [14] remedies this by adding additional inequalities from the join. Benoy [3] showed that the two widenings coincide whenever widening is postponed until the dimensionality of the iterates has stabilised.

Besson et al. [4] present widenings that are especially precise when widening polytopes into polyhedra. For instance, the iterates shown in Figure 5 feature an inequality with changing coefficients that standard widening would remove. Instead, this inequality is widened to $y \geq 0$, thereby retaining a lower bound on y. Extending our extrapolation function to include inequalities with changing coefficients is an interesting research question. Bagnara et al. [1] combine the techniques of Besson et al. and other widenings with extrapolation strategies that delay widening. More closely related is work on extrapolation using information from the analysed equation system. For instance, widening with thresholds [5] uses a sequence of user-specified values (thresholds) on individual variables up to which the state space is extrapolated in sequence. Halbwachs et al. [15] deduce thresholds automatically from guards in the semantic equations. However, they observe redundant inequalities rather than unsatisfiable inequalities, thereby possibly extrapolating to thresholds where no fixpoint can exist, such as redundant inequalities that express verification conditions. The restriction of inferring thresholds on single variables is lifted by lookahead widening which uses standard widening and narrowing operators and thereby is able to find bounds that are expressed with more than one variable [12]. It uses a pilot polyhedron on which widening and narrowing is performed alongside a main polyhedron. Once the pilot value has stabilised after narrowing, it is promoted to become the main value. By using the main value to evaluate effects in other domains, the problems of domain interaction as discussed in Section 1 do not occur. Furthermore, by discarding behaviours that are enabled after widening but are disabled with respect to the main value, their approach is able to find fixpoints in which not all behaviours are enabled, such as the one in the example on string buffers. While their approach solves essentially the same problem as widening with landmarks, the analysis operates on two polyhedra instead of one.

Further afield is the technique of counterexample-driven refinement that has recently been adapted to polyhedral analysis [13]. This approach is in some sense orthogonal to narrowing that refines a single fixpoint. In counterexample-driven refinement, the fixpoint computation is repeatedly restarted, guided by a backwards analysis from the point of a false warning to some widening point. Finally, it has been shown that widening and narrowing can be avoided altogether in a relational analysis if the semantic equations are affine [24]. Incredibly, for this restricted class of equations, least fixpoints can be found in polynomial time.

9   Conclusion

Motivated by shortcomings encountered in narrowing polyhedra, this paper proposes an extrapolation technique called widening with landmarks. The idea is to reason about unsatisfiable inequalities to guide the extrapolation process. This tactic is sensitive to invariants that are not obvious from the loop condition.

Acknowledgements. We would like to thank Denis Gopan for useful discussions on lookahead widening. This work was supported by EPSRC project EP/C015517.

References

1. R. Bagnara, P. Hill, E. Ricci, and E. Zaffanella. Precise Widening Operators for Convex Polyhedra. *Science of Computer Programming*, 58(1–2):28–56, 2005.
2. R. Bagnara, P. M. Hill, and E. Zaffanella. Not necessarily closed convex polyhedra and the double desciption method. *Formal Asp. Comput.*, 17(2):222–257, 2005.
3. P. M. Benoy. *Polyhedral Domains for Abstract Interpretation in Logic Programming*. PhD thesis, Computing Lab., Univ. of Kent, Canterbury, UK, January 2002.
4. F. Besson, T. P. Jensen, and J.-P. Talpin. Polyhedral Analysis for Synchronous Languages. In *SAS*, number 1694 in LNCS, pages 51–68, Venice, Italy, 1999.
5. B. Blanchet, P. Cousot, R. Cousot, J. Feret, L. Mauborgne, A. Mine, D. Monniaux, and X. Rival. Design and Implementation of a Special-Purpose Static Program Analyzer for Safety-Critical Real-Time Embedded Software. In *The Essence of Computation: Complexity, Analysis, Transformation*, number 2566 in LNCS, pages 85–108. Springer Verlag, 2002.
6. F. Bourdoncle. Efficient Chaotic Iteration Strategies with Widenings. In *International Conference on Formal Methods in Programming and their Applications*, volume 735 of *LNCS*, pages 128–141. Springer Verlag, 1993.

7. P. Cousot and R. Cousot. Static Determination of Dynamic Properties of Programs. In *Second International Symposium on Programming*, pages 106–130. Dunod, Paris, France, 1976.

8. P. Cousot and R. Cousot. Abstract Interpretation and Application to Logic Programs. *Journal of Logic Programming*, 13(2–3):103–179, 1992.

9. P. Cousot and R. Cousot. Comparing the Galois Connection and Widening/Narrowing Approaches to Abstract Interpretation. In M. Bruynooghe and M. Wirsing, editors, *International Symposium on Programming Language Implementation and Logic Programming*, volume 631 of *LNCS*, pages 269–295. Springer-Verlag, 1992.

10. P. Cousot and N. Halbwachs. Automatic Discovery of Linear Constraints among Variables of a Program. In *Symposium on Principles of Programming Languages*, pages 84–97, Tucson, Arizona, 1978. ACM Press.

11. N. Dor, M. Rodeh, and M. Sagiv. Cleanness Checking of String Manipulations in C Programs via Integer Analysis. In P. Cousot, editor, *Static Analysis Symposium*, number 2126 in LNCS, pages 194–212, Paris, France, 2001. Springer-Verlag.

12. D. Gopan and T. Reps. Lookahead Widening. In *CAV*, volume 4144. Springer, 2006. To appear.

13. B. S. Gulavani and S. K. Rajamani. Counterexample Driven Refinement for Abstract Interpretation. In *TACAS*, volume 3920 of *LNCS*, pages 474–488. Springer, April 2006.

14. N. Halbwachs. *Détermination Automatique de Relations Linéaires Vérifiées par les Variables d'un Programme*. Thèse de 3ème cicle d'informatique, Université scientifique et médicale de Grenoble, Grenoble, France, March 1979.

15. N. Halbwachs, Y.-E. Proy, and P. Roumanoff. Verification of Real-Time Systems using Linear Relation Analysis. *Formal Methods in System Design*, 11(2):157–185, August 1997.

16. W. Harvey. Computing Two-Dimensional Integer Hulls. *SIAM Journal on Computing*, 28(6):2285–2299, 1999.

17. N. Heintze and O. Tardieu. Ultra-fast Aliasing Analysis using CLA: A Million Lines of C Code in a Second. In *SIGPLAN Conference on Programming Language Design and Implementation*, pages 254–263, 2001.

18. A. Miné. The Octagon Abstract Domain. In *Eighth Working Conference on Reverse Engineering*, pages 310–319. IEEE Computer Society, 2001.

19. S. Sankaranarayanan, M. Colón, H. B. Sipma, and Z. Manna. Efficient Strongly Relational Polyhedral Analysis. In *VMCAI*, pages 111–125, 2006.

20. A. Simon and A. King. Analyzing String Buffers in C. In *Algebraic Methodology and Software Technology*, number 2422 in LNCS, pages 365–379. Springer, 2002.

21. A. Simon and A. King. Exploiting Sparsity in Polyhedral Analysis. In C. Hankin and I. Siveroni, editors, *Static Analysis Symposium*, number 3672 in LNCS, pages 336–351. Springer Verlag, September 2005.

22. A. Simon, A. King, and J. M. Howe. Two Variables per Linear Inequality as an Abstract Domain. In M. Leuschel, editor, *Logic Based Program Development and Transformation*, number 2664 in LNCS, pages 71–89. Springer, September 2002.

23. B. Steensgaard. Points-to Analysis in Almost Linear Time. In *Symposium on the Principles of Progamming Languages*, pages 32–41, 1996.

24. Z. Su and D. Wagner. A Class of Polynomially Solvable Range Constraints for Interval Analysis without Widenings. *Theor. Comput. Sci.*, 345(1):122–138, 2005.

25. D. Wagner. *Static analysis and computer security: New techniques for software assurance*. PhD thesis, University of California at Berkeley, December 2000.

Comparing Completeness Properties of Static Analyses and Their Logics

David A. Schmidt[*]

Kansas State University, Manhattan, Kansas, USA
schmidt@cis.ksu.edu.

Abstract. Static analyses calculate abstract states, and their logics validate properties of the abstract states. We place into perspective the variety of forwards, backwards, functional, and logical completeness used in abstract-interpretation-based static analysis by giving examples and by proving equivalences, implications, and independences. We expose two fundamental Galois connections that underlie the logics for static analyses and reveal a new completeness variant, *O-completeness*. We also show that the key concept underlying logical completeness is *covering*, which we use to relate the various forms of completeness.

When we use a static analysis, like data-flow analysis or model checking, to validate a program for correctness or code improvement, we must carefully define the domain of properties the analysis can calculate so that it includes both the goal properties we seek to validate as well as intermediate properties that lead to the goals. Say we try to validate $\{?\}y := -y; x := y + 1\{isPositive(x)\}$; our analysis requires properties like *isNegative* to calculate a sound precondition: $\{isNegative(y)\}$ y $:= -$y $\{isPositive(y)\}$ x $:= y + 1$ $\{isPositive(x)\}$. But, is the analysis *complete* — as expressive as possible? If we can express the properties, *isNonNegative* and *isNonPositive*, then a complete analysis calculates the weakest precondition: $\{isNonPositive(y)\}$ y $:= -$y; x $:= y + 1$ $\{isPositive(x)\}$.

The example suggests that "completeness" is a property of both static analyses as well as logics. Thanks to Cousot and Cousot [6,7,8,11], we have a well-defined notion of *functional completeness*: it is when a static analysis's abstract state-transition function precisely mimics the concrete state-transition function, modulo the Galois connection between concrete and abstract domains.

Giacobazzi, Ranzato, and Scozzari [17] showed how to refine an abstract interpretation to synthesize functionally complete transition functions; Giacobazzi and Quintarelli [16] showed that there are, in fact, two, independent notions of functional completeness — *forwards* and *backwards*. Cousot and Cousot [11] applied functional completeness to define the *logical completeness* of a logic that judges abstract values as compared to the logic that judges the concrete values. Recently, Ranzato and Tapparo [23,24] applied Giacobazzi, et al.'s refinement techniques to build logically complete abstract logics.

The present paper's contribution is to place into perspective the variants of forwards, backwards, functional, and logical completeness by giving examples

---

[*] Supported by NSF ITR-0086154 and ITR-0326577.

N. Kobayashi (Ed.): APLAS 2006, LNCS 4279, pp. 183–199, 2006.

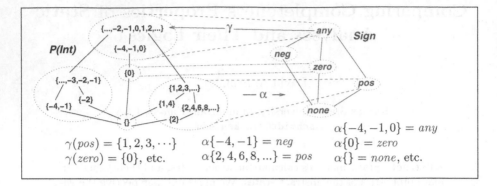

Fig. 1. Galois connection for signs; equivalence classes circled

and by proving equivalences, implications, and independences. By exposing two fundamental Galois connections that underlie logics for abstract values, we reveal yet another completeness variant, *O-logical-completeness*. We also show that the key concept underlying logical completeness notions is *covering*, which we use to relate the various forms of completeness.

1   Galois Connections and Functional Completeness

We use Galois connections to abstract concrete data into properties. A *Galois connection* [8,15] between two partially ordered sets, $(C, \subseteq)$ and $(A, \sqsubseteq)$, written $C\langle\alpha,\gamma\rangle A$, is a pair of functions, $\alpha : C \to A$ and $\gamma : A \to C$, such that for all $c \in C$ and $a \in A$,
$$c \subseteq \gamma(a) \text{ iff } \alpha(c) \sqsubseteq a.$$

The adjunction is equivalently defined by requiring that α and γ are monotone maps such that $id_{C \to C} \sqsubseteq \gamma \circ \alpha$ and $\alpha \circ \gamma \sqsubseteq id_{A \to A}$.

C is the *concrete domain* and A is the *abstract domain*. γ's adjoint, α, is uniquely defined as $\alpha(c) = \sqcap\{a \mid c \subseteq \gamma(a)\}$ and α's adjoint must be $\gamma(a) = \cup\{c \mid \alpha(c) \sqsubseteq a\}$[15]. γ is an *upper adjoint* of a Galois connection iff it preserves meets: $\gamma(\sqcap T) = \cap_{a \in T}\gamma(a)$, for all $T \subseteq A$. Similarly, α is a *lower adjoint* iff it preserves joins: $\alpha(\cup S) = \sqcup_{c \in S}\alpha(c)$, for all $S \subseteq C$ [15].

Figure 1 displays the classic Galois connection that abstracts sets of integers to their signs [8]. (In the Figure, C is $\mathcal{P}(Int)$ and A is $Sign$.)Each $S \in \mathcal{P}(Int)$ is abstracted to $\alpha(S) \in Sign$. Values like *pos* and *any* can be read as primitive logical propositions (*isPositive* and *true*, respectively) or they can be used as abstract arguments and answers to static-analysis functions (e.g. $succ^\sharp(zero) = pos$). The Galois connection is *overapproximating* because $S \subseteq \gamma(\alpha(S))$, for all $S \in \mathcal{P}(C)$.

The following little-known result [21] exposes the inner structure of Galois connections:[1] *There is a Galois connection between $(C, \subseteq)$ and $(A, \sqsubseteq)$ iff*

---

[1] In this paper, definitions and previously proved results are embedded into the text narrative. New results and new variations of known results are stated as Propositions, Theorems, and Corollaries. Due to lack of space, some proofs are omitted but can be found in the paper's accompanying technical report [28].

1. C is partitioned into equivalence classes, each class, p, having a unique maximal element, $max(p)$; A is partitioned into equivalence classes, each class, q, having a unique minimal element, $min(q)$; the subposet of maximal elements in C is order-isomorphic to the subposet of minimal elements in A.
2. For all $c, c' \in C$, if $c \subseteq c'$, then $max([c]_\alpha) \subseteq max([c']_\alpha)$, where $[c]_\alpha$ is c's equivalence class.
3. For all $a, a' \in A$, if $a \sqsubseteq a'$, then $min([a]_\gamma) \sqsubseteq min([a']_\gamma)$, where $[a]_\gamma$ is a's equivalence class.

Figure 1 illustrates the internal structure: α and γ partition their domains into equivalence classes, where the images of the two functions are order-isomorphic. Each concrete equivalence class "droops" from its canonical (maximal) element, and each abstract class "floats" from its canonical (minimal) element. In Figure 1, α is onto (hence, γ is one-one), making $Sign$'s equivalence classes singletons. The concrete domain's canonical elements are $\emptyset$, $\{\cdots, -2 - 1\}$, $\{0\}$ $\{1, 2, 3, \cdots\}$, and Int. (This is γ's image; α's image is $Sign$.) When α is onto, the Galois connection is characterized by $\gamma \circ \alpha$, a closure map [8,17].

1.1   The Internal Logic Defined by a Galois Connection

For Galois connection, $C\langle \alpha, \gamma \rangle A$, say that $c \in C$ has property $a \in A$, written $c \models a$, iff $c \subseteq \gamma(a)$ (equivalently, iff $\alpha(c) \sqsubseteq a$). Read the elements of A as assertions in a logic with conjunction, because $c \models a_1 \sqcap_A a_2$ iff $c \models a_1$ and $c \models a_2$. This is because γ preserves $\sqcap_A$ as $\cap_C$.

Other connectives might be present (e.g., disjunction), but this is not the case for $Sign$ in Figure 1, e.g., $\{0\} \models neg \sqcup pos$, but $\{0\} \not\models neg$ and $\{0\} \not\models pos$, because γ fails to preserve $\sqcup$. We will see that such "γ-preservations" lead to one notion of completeness and that there is a dual notion of "α preservation."

1.2   Sound Abstract Transformers

For Galois connection, $C\langle \alpha, \gamma \rangle A$, a state-transition function, $f : C \to C$, can be approximated: We say that a monotonic $f^\sharp : A \to A$ is sound for $f : C \to C$ iff $\alpha \circ f \sqsubseteq_{C \to A} f^\sharp \circ \alpha$, or equivalently, iff $f \circ \gamma \sqsubseteq_{A \to C} \gamma \circ f^\sharp$. That is, when $\alpha(c) = a$, $f^\sharp(a)$ computes an answer that is weaker (with respect to $\sqsubseteq_A$) than the name of $f(c)$'s α-equivalence class:

$$
\begin{array}{ccc}
c & \xrightarrow{\ f\ } f(c) & \xrightarrow{\ \alpha\ } \alpha(\, f(c)\,) \\
\alpha \downarrow & & \sqcap\sqcap \\
\alpha(\, c\,) & \xrightarrow{\quad f^\sharp \quad} & f^\sharp(\, \alpha(\, c\,))
\end{array}
$$

This makes $f^\sharp$ an overapproximation of f: $f(c) \subseteq \gamma(f^\sharp(\alpha(c)))$. The map, $f^\sharp_{best} = \alpha \circ f \circ \gamma$, is the "best" abstraction of f in the sense that $f^\sharp_{best}$ is sound for f and $f^\sharp_{best} \sqsubseteq_{A \to A} f^\sharp$ for all sound $f^\sharp$ [8] — it is the best one can do with f, α, and γ.

For $Sign$ in Figure 1, the transformer, $succ^* : \mathcal{P}(Int) \to \mathcal{P}(Int)$ is soundly abstracted by $succ^\sharp_0(a) = any$, whereas the best abstract transformer is $succ^\sharp_{best} = \alpha \circ succ^* \circ \gamma$, where $succ^\sharp_{best}(zero) = succ^\sharp_{best}(pos) = pos$. (For $f : C \to C$, define $f^* : \mathcal{P}(C) \to \mathcal{P}(C)$ as $f^*(S) = \{f(c) \mid c \in S\}$. Thus, for $succ(n) = n + 1$, we have $succ^*(S) = \{n + 1 \mid n \in S\}$.)

1.3   Complete Abstract Transformers

When the inclusions that define soundness are strengthened into equalities, this defines *functional completeness*: for $f : C \to C$ and $f^\sharp : A \to A$,

- $f^\sharp$ is *backwards (B(α)-) complete for f* iff $\alpha \circ f = f^\sharp \circ \alpha$ [8,17]. That is, α is a homomorphism that preserves f as $f^\sharp$.
- $f^\sharp$ is *forwards (F(γ)-) complete for f* iff $f \circ \gamma = \gamma \circ f^\sharp$ [16]. That is, γ is a homomorphism that preserves $f^\sharp$ as f.

We say that $f^\sharp$ is B- (respectively, F-) complete when the α (resp. γ) is clear from the context. The two completeness notions are *not* equivalent [16], and the distinctions are subtle: For $c, c' \in C$, write $c \sim_\alpha c'$ iff $\alpha(c) = \alpha(c')$.

- There exists a B-complete $f^\sharp$ for f iff for all $c, c' \in C$, $c \sim_\alpha c'$ implies $f(c) \sim_\alpha f(c')$. In this case, we say that f *itself* is B-complete.

For B-complete $f^\sharp$, $f^\sharp(a)$ computes the α-*equivalence class* of $f(c)$, for every $c \in \gamma(a)$, but the specific value within the equivalence class is lost. If $f^\sharp$ is B-complete for f, then so is $f^\sharp_{best} = \alpha \circ f \circ \gamma$. So, f itself is B-complete iff $\alpha \circ f = f^\sharp_{best} \circ \alpha$. If α is onto and there is a B-complete $f^\sharp$ for f, then it is $f^\sharp_{best}$ [17].

- There exists an F-complete $f^\sharp$ for f iff for all $c \in \gamma[A]$, $f(c) \in \gamma[A]$.[2] In this case, we say that f *itself* is F-complete [16].

For F-complete $f^\sharp$, $f^\sharp(a)$ computes the *concrete value of f applied to the canonical element*, $\gamma(a) \in C$ — it computes $\gamma(f^\sharp(a))$ — but the values and even the *equivalence-class names* of the noncanonical elements in C are lost. If $f^\sharp$ is F-complete for f, so is $f^\sharp_{best}$; f itself is F-complete iff $f \circ \gamma = \gamma \circ f^\sharp_{best}$. If γ is 1-1 and there is an F-complete $f^\sharp$ for f, then it is $f^\sharp_{best}$ [16].

The existence of a B- and an F-complete $f^\sharp$ for f depend solely on the Galois connection and f itself. Figure 2 graphs the behaviors of a B-complete and an F-complete $f : C \to C$ on the equivalence classes of C induced by a Galois connection.

Based on Figures 1 and 2, we can readily verify some *Sign*-completeness properties: *square** is B-complete but not F-complete; *negate** is both B- and F-complete; *succ** is neither;[3] and *enum** is F-complete but not B-complete, where $enum(n) = if\ (n\ mod\ 2 = 0)\ then\ (n\ div\ 2)\ else\ (n\ div(-2))$.

When α is not onto (that is, γ is not 1-1), there can be multiple abstract transformers $f^\sharp$ that are F-complete for f:

Proposition 1. $f \circ \gamma = \gamma \circ f^\sharp$ *iff, for all* $a \in A$, *(i)* $f(\gamma(a)) \in \gamma[A]$, *and (ii)* $f^\sharp_{best}(a) \sim_\gamma f^\sharp(a)$.

Proposition 2. $\alpha \circ f = f^\sharp \circ \alpha$ *iff, (i) for all* $c, c' \in C$, $c \sim_\alpha c'$ *implies* $f(c) \sim_\alpha f(c')$, *and (ii) for all* $a \in \alpha[C]$, $f^\sharp_{best}(a) = f^\sharp(a)$.

---

[2] Please recall, for function $f : C \to C$ and set $S \subseteq C$, that $f[S]$ denotes $\{f(s) \mid s \in S\}$.
[3] Where $square(n) = n * n$ and $negate(n) = -n$ and $succ(n) = n + 1$.

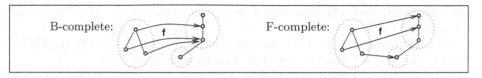

Fig. 2. Behavior of a B-complete and an F-complete $f : C \rightarrow C$

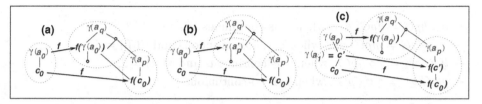

Fig. 3. Incompleteness (a) and its forwards (b) and backwards (c) refinements

Say that $f : C \rightarrow C$ is not itself F-complete (see Figure 3(a)); to make it so, we must ensure that f maps C-canonical arguments to C-canonical answers. To do this, for each $c \in \gamma[A]$ (that is, $c = \gamma(a_0)$), where $f(c) \notin \gamma[A]$, we make a new equivalence class, $\downarrow f(c) \cap [f(c)]_\alpha$, in C whose maximal, canonical element is $f(c) = \gamma(a_p')$, where a_p' is a new A-element.[4] If we close the canonical elements under $\cap$ (making even more new equivalence classes) and repeat until convergence, then f becomes F-complete. This is the *F-complete-shell construction* [16,23] — it adds elements by computing "forwards" from f. See Figure 3(b).

For example, since $square^*$ is not F-complete for $Sign$, we systematically add to $Sign$ new values that represent the canonical elements, $\{1, 4, 9, \cdots\}$, $\{1, 16, 81, \cdots\}$, $\{1, 256, 6561, \cdots\}$, ...; this time, the procedure does not finitely converge.

Dually, if $f : C \rightarrow C$ is not B-complete, we must make f map α-related arguments to α-related answers. We can either split equivalence classes in f's domain (the *B-complete shell construction* [17]) or merge equivalence classes in f's range (the *B-complete-core construction* [17]).

Consider the former, and say there is some $c_0 \in C$ such that $f(c_0) \not\sim_\alpha f(max[c_0]_\alpha)$. We compute the set, $[c_0]_\alpha \cap f^{-1}([f(c_0)]_\alpha)$, and we select the maximal elements, c', from this set as the canonical elements of new equivalence classes, $\downarrow c' \cap [c']_\alpha$. If we close under $\cap$ and repeat until convergence, then f becomes B-complete.[5] The B-complete shell construction adds elements by computing "backwards" from f. See Figure 3(c).

For example, $succ^*$ is not B-complete for $Sign$, because $succ^*\{-1, -2, ...\} \not\sim_\alpha succ^*\{-2\}$: the former maps into Int's equivalence class, and the latter maps into the class of negative ints. $[\{-2\}]_\alpha \cap f^{-1}[succ^*\{-2\}]_\alpha$ collects all nonempty sets of negative numbers less than -1; the maximal set in this collection is $\{-2, -3, \cdots\}$, and this set becomes the canonical element of a new equivalence class. We repeat

---

[4] Recall, for $c \in C$, that $\downarrow c = \{c' \in C \mid c' \subseteq c\}$.

[5] f must be chain continuous for the technique to converge correctly [16].

the refinements and add these new canonical elements: $\{-i, -(i+1), ...\}$ and $\{-i\}$, for all $i > 1$.

The shell constructions show that the match between $f : C \to C$ and Galois connection $\alpha\langle C, A\rangle\gamma$ must be "perfect" to achieve completeness.

The fixed point operators are well behaved with respect to completeness: Say that when $f^\sharp$ is B- (resp., F-)complete for f, then $G^\sharp(f^\sharp)$ is B- (F-)complete for $G(f)$. We have

- $\alpha \circ lfpG = lfpG^\sharp \circ \alpha$, when α is continuous
- $\alpha \circ gfpG = gfpG^\sharp \circ \alpha$, when α is co-continuous and $\alpha(\top) = \top$
- $lfpG \circ \gamma = \gamma \circ lfpG^\sharp$, when γ is continuous and $\gamma(\bot) = \bot$
- $gfpG \circ \gamma = \gamma \circ lfpG^\sharp$, when γ is co-continuous.

See Cousot and Cousot [8] and Ranzato and Tapparo [25] for elaboration.

2 Program Logics

A *logic for* C consists of a set of assertions, $\mathcal{L}$, and a judgement relation, $\models \subseteq C \times \mathcal{L}$; we write $c \models \phi$ when (c, ϕ) is in the relation. For example, a $\models$ based on Figure 1 might give us $\{2, 4, 6\} \models even$ and $\{4\} \models any$.

Section 1.1 noted that a Galois connection defines an "internal logic," where $\mathcal{L} = A$ and for all $c \in C$, $c \models a$ iff $c \subseteq \gamma(a)$ (iff $\alpha(c) \sqsubseteq a$). But most program logics are extensions of A, and given a Galois connection, $\mathcal{P}(D)\langle\alpha, \gamma\rangle A$ — *the concrete domain is a powerset* — we obtain this *inductively defined logic*:

1. an inductively defined set of assertions,

$$\mathcal{L} \ni \phi ::= a \mid op_i(\phi_j)_{0<j\leq ar(i)}, \text{ for } i \in I$$

   where op_i has arity $ar(i) \geq 0$, for every $i \in I$.
2. an inductively defined interpretation, $[\![\cdot]\!] : \mathcal{L} \to \mathcal{P}(D)$:

$$[\![a]\!] = \gamma(a)$$
$$[\![op_i(\phi_j)_{0<j\leq ar(i)}]\!] = g_i([\![\phi_j]\!])_{0<j\leq ar(i)}, \text{ where } g_i : \mathcal{P}(D)^{ar(i)} \to \mathcal{P}(D).$$

For $S \in \mathcal{P}(D)$, define $S \models \phi$ iff $S \subseteq [\![\phi]\!]$. See the example in Figure 4. Using Figures 4 and 1 and one-variable assignment programs, we can validate, for example, the precondition assertion, $\{-2, -4, 0\} \models [x := -x; x := x + 1]pos$.

The logic defines program correctness and transformation properties, and when we wish to validate a precondition assertion like $S_0 \models [f]\phi$ (or a postcondition assertion like $f^*(S_0) \models \phi$) via a static analysis, we use $f^\sharp : A \to A$ to approximate $f^* : \mathcal{P}(D) \to \mathcal{P}(D)$ and we use $a_0 \in A$ to approximate S_0. We then attempt to validate $a_0 \models [f^\sharp]\phi$ (resp., $f^\sharp(a_0) \models^A \phi$):

Given Galois connection, $\mathcal{P}(D)\langle\alpha,\gamma\rangle A$, define $\mathcal{L}$ as follows:

$$a \in Prim = A \text{ (the primitive assertions)}$$
$$\mathcal{L} \ni \phi ::= a \mid \phi_1 \wedge \phi_2 \mid \phi_1 \vee \phi_2 \mid [f]\phi$$

$$[\![\,\cdot\,]\!] : \mathcal{L} \to \mathcal{P}(D)$$

$[\![a]\!] = \gamma(a)$ $[\![[f]\phi]\!] = \widetilde{pre}_f[\![\phi]\!]$

$[\![\phi_1 \wedge \phi_2]\!] = [\![\phi_1]\!] \cap [\![\phi_2]\!]$ where $\widetilde{pre}_f(S) = \{c \in D \mid f(c) \subseteq S\}$

$[\![\phi_1 \vee \phi_2]\!] = [\![\phi_1]\!] \cup [\![\phi_2]\!]$ and $f : D \to \mathcal{P}(D)$ is a state-transition function

Fig. 4. An inductively defined precondition logic

- For $\mathcal{P}(D)\langle\alpha,\gamma\rangle A$, a judgement relation, $\models^A \subseteq A \times \mathcal{L}$, is γ-*sound* for $\models \subseteq \mathcal{P}(D) \times \mathcal{L}$ iff for all $a \in A$ and $\phi \in \mathcal{L}$, $a \models^A \phi$ implies $\gamma(a) \models \phi$.

For example, a γ-sound $\models^A$ might validate that $neg \models^A [\mathrm{x} := -\mathrm{x}; \mathrm{x} := \mathrm{x} + 1] pos$.

Define $[\![\phi]\!]^A = \{a \mid a \models^A \phi\}$. Since γ is monotonic, it is natural to demand that $\models^A$ be *downclosed*: $a_0 \sqsubseteq_A a_1$ and $a_1 \models^A \phi$ imply $a_0 \models^A \phi$. Downclosure is central to soundness — here is a second definition of soundness that shows why:

- For $\mathcal{P}(D)\langle\alpha,\gamma\rangle A$, $\models^A \subseteq A \times \mathcal{L}$ is α-*sound* for $\models \subseteq \mathcal{P}(D) \times \mathcal{L}$ iff for all $S \in \mathcal{P}(D)$ and $\phi \in \mathcal{L}$, $\alpha(S) \models^A \phi$ implies $S \models \phi$.

Proposition 3. *If $\models^A$ is downclosed, then $\models^A$ is γ-sound for $\models$ iff $\models^A$ is α-sound for $\models$.*

Hereafter, we speak only of "soundness" and omit γ (resp., α).

Let $(\mathcal{P}_\downarrow(A), \subseteq)$ define the complete lattice of downclosed subsets of A, ordered by subset inclusion, and for $\gamma : A \to \mathcal{P}(D)$, define $\overline{\gamma} : \mathcal{P}_\downarrow(A) \to \mathcal{P}(D)$ as $\overline{\gamma}(T) = \gamma^*(T)$, that is, $\cup_{a \in T} \gamma(a)$.[6] Here is yet another equivalent definition of soundness, stated in terms of $\overline{\gamma}$, $[\![\,\cdot\,]\!] : \mathcal{L} \to \mathcal{P}(D)$, and $[\![\,\cdot\,]\!]^A : \mathcal{L} \to \mathcal{P}_\downarrow(A)$:

- $[\![\,\cdot\,]\!]^A$ *is sound for* $[\![\,\cdot\,]\!]$ iff $\overline{\gamma}[\![\phi]\!]^A \subseteq [\![\phi]\!]$, for all $\phi \in \mathcal{L}$.

This definition suggests an adjunction using $\overline{\gamma}$; there are *two* possible ones:

Proposition 4. *For $\mathcal{P}(D)$, $\mathcal{P}_\downarrow(A)$, and $\gamma : A \to \mathcal{P}(D)$,*

1. *$\mathcal{P}(D)\langle\overline{\alpha_o},\overline{\gamma}\rangle\mathcal{P}_\downarrow(A)$ is a Galois connection, where $\overline{\alpha_o}(S) = \bigcap\{T \mid S \subseteq \overline{\gamma}(T)\} = \downarrow\{\alpha\{c\} \mid c \in S\}$, where $\downarrow T = \{a \mid \text{ exists } a' \in T \text{ such that } a \sqsubseteq a'\}$.*
2. *$\mathcal{P}(D)^{op}\langle\overline{\alpha_u},\overline{\gamma}\rangle\mathcal{P}_\downarrow(A)^{op}$ is a Galois connection, where $\overline{\alpha_u}(S) = \bigcup\{T \mid \overline{\gamma}(T) \subseteq S\} = \{a \mid \gamma(a) \subseteq S\}$, where $(P, \sqsubseteq_P)^{op}$ is $(P, \sqsupseteq_P)$.*

---

[6] $\mathcal{P}_\downarrow(A)$ is in fact the *disjunctive completion* of A [8,9], often used to lift a γ that does not preserve $\sqcup_A$ into a $\overline{\gamma}$ that preserves $\cup_{\mathcal{P}_\downarrow(A)}$, in effect adding disjunction to $\mathcal{P}_\downarrow(A)$'s internal logic.

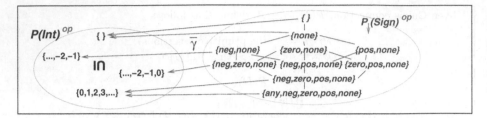

Fig. 5. Dualized disjunctive completion of Galois connection of signs

The one and the same $\overline{\gamma}$ is the upper adjoint of both Galois connections because $\overline{\gamma}$ preserves *both* meets (intersections) *and* joins (unions) in $\mathcal{P}_{\downarrow}(A)$.[7]

Why two Galois connections? The one in Proposition 4(2) defines an underapproximation such that when we *define* $[\![\phi]\!]^A = \overline{\alpha_u}[\![\phi]\!]$, we underapproximate the concrete logic. The Galois connection in Proposition 4(1) can be used to overapproximate transforms, $f^* : \mathcal{P}(D) \to \mathcal{P}(D)$, by $f^{\sharp} : \mathcal{P}_{\downarrow}(A) \to \mathcal{P}_{\downarrow}(A)$. But the logical interpretation, $[\![\phi]\!]^A = \overline{\alpha_o}[\![\phi]\!]$, is sound *iff*, for all $\phi \in \mathcal{L}$, $\overline{\gamma}(\overline{\alpha_o}[\![\phi]\!]) = [\![\phi]\!]$.

Figure 5 shows the completion of *Sign* to $\mathcal{P}_{\downarrow}(Sign)^{op}$. Here, $\overline{\alpha_u}$ is not onto, which becomes significant later. Proposition 4 justifies the following:

Proposition 5. *For $\phi \in \mathcal{L}$, the following are equivalent:*

1. $[\![\cdot]\!]^A$ *is sound for* $[\![\cdot]\!]$, *that is,* $\overline{\gamma}[\![\phi]\!]^A \subseteq [\![\phi]\!]$, *that is,* $[\![\phi]\!]^A \subseteq \overline{\alpha_u}[\![\phi]\!]$.
2. $T \subseteq [\![\phi]\!]^A$ *implies* $\overline{\gamma}(T) \subseteq [\![\phi]\!]$, *for all* $T \in \mathcal{P}_{\downarrow}(A)$.
3. $\overline{\alpha_o}(S) \subseteq [\![\phi]\!]^A$ *implies* $S \subseteq [\![\phi]\!]$, *for all* $S \in \mathcal{P}(D)$.
4. $[\![\phi]\!] \subseteq S$ *implies* $[\![\phi]\!]^A \subseteq \overline{\alpha_u}(S)$, *for all* $S \in \mathcal{P}(D)$.

Proof. It is easy to prove Item *1* equivalent to each of *2*, *3*, and *4*. Here is the equivalence of *1* and *3*:

1 implies 3: Assume $\overline{\alpha_o}(S) \subseteq [\![\phi]\!]^A$. By the definition of Galois connection, $S \subseteq \overline{\gamma}[\![\phi]\!]^A$. By *1*, $S \subseteq \phi$.

3 implies 1: By the definition of the Galois connection, $\overline{\alpha_o}(\overline{\gamma}[\![\phi]\!]^A) \subseteq [\![\phi]\!]^A$. Using *3* (set $S = \overline{\gamma}[\![\phi]\!]^A$), we have $\overline{\gamma}[\![\phi]\!]^A \subseteq [\![\phi]\!]$.   □

The three adjunction maps, $\overline{\gamma}$, $\overline{\alpha_o}$, and $\overline{\alpha_u}$, give us three ways to define soundness. Items *3.* and *4.* in the Proposition justify the slogan that one "overapproximates the model" and "underapproximates the logic" for sound static analysis.

Finally, we note that a soundness assertion of the form, "$\overline{\alpha_o}[\![\phi]\!] \subseteq [\![\phi]\!]^A$" is faulty, because $[\![\phi]\!] \subseteq \overline{\gamma}(\overline{\alpha_o}[\![\phi]\!])$.

3   Logical Completeness

In symbolic logic, one formal system, $\mathcal{A}$, is $\mathcal{L}$-sound for another formal system, $\mathcal{C}$, iff every property $\phi \in \mathcal{L}$ that is validated in $\mathcal{A}$ can be validated in $\mathcal{C}$. When

---

[7] If we use $\mathcal{P}(A)$ instead, we find that $\overline{\gamma} : \mathcal{P}(A) \to \mathcal{P}(D)$ does not preserve meets.

the converse holds true as well, then $\mathcal{A}$ is $\mathcal{L}$-complete for $\mathcal{C}$. In like fashion, we might strengthen each of the implications in Items 2-4 in Proposition 5 into equivalences: For $[\![\cdot]\!] : \mathcal{L} \to \mathcal{P}(D)$ and $[\![\cdot]\!]^A : \mathcal{L} \to \mathcal{P}_\downarrow(A)$, we define these properties:

- *best preservation:* for all $\phi \in \mathcal{L}$ and $T \in \mathcal{P}_\downarrow(A)$, $T \subseteq [\![\phi]\!]^A$ iff $\overline{\gamma}(T) \subseteq [\![\phi]\!]$.
- *strong preservation:* for all $\phi \in \mathcal{L}$ and $S \in \mathcal{P}(D)$, $S \subseteq [\![\phi]\!]$ iff $\overline{\alpha_o}(S) \subseteq [\![\phi]\!]^A$.
- *lower preservation:* for all $\phi \in \mathcal{L}$ and $S \in \mathcal{P}(D)$, $[\![\phi]\!] \subseteq S$ iff $[\![\phi]\!]^A \subseteq \overline{\alpha_u}(S)$.

In particular, strong preservation asserts for all $c \in D$, $\{c\} \models \phi$ iff there exists some $a_0 \in A^8$ such that $c \in \gamma(a_0)$ and $a_0 \models^A \phi$ — every c that "makes ϕ hold" can be validated by $\models^A$ (and a_0). In contrast, best preservation states that $a \models^A \phi$ iff for all $c \in \gamma(a)$, $\{c\} \models \phi$ — every a that "makes ϕ hold" can be validated by $\models^A$. We soon see that lower-preservation is equivalent, surprisingly, to strong preservation.

The obvious question to ask is, "What is the relationship between the above logical preservation properties and functional completeness?" Working from the Galois connection, $\mathcal{P}(D)^{op}\langle\overline{\alpha_u}, \overline{\gamma}\rangle \mathcal{P}_\downarrow(A)^{op}$, and the functions, $[\![\cdot]\!] : \mathcal{L} \to \mathcal{P}(D)$ and $[\![\cdot]\!]^A : \mathcal{L} \to \mathcal{P}_\downarrow(A)$, we calculate these definitions of functional completeness:[9]

- $[\![\cdot]\!]^A$ is $B(\overline{\alpha_u})$-*complete for* $[\![\cdot]\!]$ iff $\overline{\alpha_u}[\![\phi]\!] = [\![\phi]\!]^A$
- [25] $[\![\cdot]\!]^A$ is $F(\overline{\gamma})$-*complete for* $[\![\cdot]\!]$ iff $[\![\phi]\!] = \overline{\gamma}[\![\phi]\!]^A$

This strengthens into equalities the subset inclusions in Item 1, Proposition 5. As before, we use the terms, "B-complete" and "F-complete," as abbreviations for $B(\overline{\alpha_u})$-complete and $F(\overline{\gamma})$-complete, respectively.

The relationships within this soup of definitions go as follows:

Theorem 6. *For* $\mathcal{P}(D)\langle\alpha, \gamma\rangle A$, $[\![\cdot]\!] : \mathcal{L} \to \mathcal{P}(D)$, *and* $[\![\cdot]\!]^A : \mathcal{L} \to \mathcal{P}_\downarrow(A)$,

- *B-complete iff best preservation*
- *F-complete iff strong preservation iff lower preservation*

Proof. The results follow from application of the definitions and the properties of Galois connections. Here is the proof that F-completeness is equivalent to lower preservation; thanks to Proposition 5, we need only prove the following:

(i) F-completeness and $[\![\phi]\!]^A \subseteq \overline{\alpha_u}(S)$ imply $[\![\phi]\!] \subseteq S$: Assume $[\![\phi]\!]^A \subseteq \overline{\alpha_u}(S)$; then, $\overline{\gamma}[\![\phi]\!]^A \subseteq \overline{\gamma}(\overline{\alpha_u}(S)) \subseteq S$, by definition of Galois connection. By F-completeness, $\overline{\gamma}[\![\phi]\!]^A = [\![\phi]\!] \subseteq S$.

(ii) Lower preservation implies $[\![\phi]\!] \subseteq \overline{\gamma}[\![\phi]\!]^A$: By definition of Galois connection, $[\![\phi]\!]^A \subseteq \overline{\alpha_u}(\overline{\gamma}[\![\phi]\!]^A)$. By lower preservation (what was proved in *(i)*, where we set $S = \overline{\gamma}[\![\phi]\!]^A$), we have the result.   □

B- and F-completeness are *independent*, as shown by Figure 6. The first diagram shows how F-completeness holds yet B-completeness fails when there are distinct

---

[8] Indeed, the a_0 is $\overline{\alpha_o}\{c\}$.

[9] We use implicitly the identity Galois connection on arguments from $\mathcal{L}$.

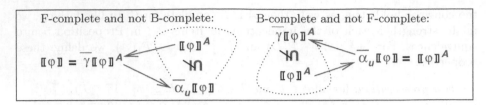

Fig. 6. Independence of F- and B-completeness of interpretation functions

assertions in $\mathcal{P}_{\downarrow}(A)$ that concretize to the same set. For example, say that $a \models^A \phi_1 \lor \phi_2$ *iff* $a \models^A \phi_1$ *or* $a \models^A \phi_2$ (cf. Figure 4). Consider $[\![neg \lor zero \lor pos]\!]^A$ and $[\![any \lor neg \lor zero \lor pos]\!]^A$, which denote different sets in $\mathcal{P}_{\downarrow}(Sign)^{op}$ but both concretize to *Int*. This is F-complete but not B-complete.

The absence of B-completeness in an abstract logic is a famous trouble spot, e.g., we are asked to validate *any* $\models^A$ *neg* $\lor$ *zero* $\lor$ *pos* — the above definition fails to do so, and a *focus* or *materialization* operation [14,26] must be employed to decompose *any* into a set of covering cases, such as $\{neg, zero, pos\}$ (because $\gamma(any) \subseteq \gamma(neg) \cup \gamma(zero) \cup \gamma(pos)$), and a proof-by-cases analysis is undertaken.[10]

The second diagram shows that F-completeness can fail when there is some $[\![\phi]\!]$ that cannot be exactly expressed in $\mathcal{P}_{\downarrow}(A)$. For example, without altering *Sign*, add to $\mathcal{L}$ the new assertion, *equals1*, such that $[\![equals1]\!] = \{1\}$, and define $[\![equals1]\!]^A = \overline{\alpha_u}[\![equals1]\!] = \{none\}$. F-completeness fails. The absence of F-completeness produces spurious counterexamples, e.g., a static analysis of

```
x:= 1; if x=1 then safe() else error()
```

using *Sign* announces that error() is reachable. This false counterexample is eliminated by *counterexample guided abstraction refinement* [2,3,27]), which adds new values to *Sign* (in this case, *one*), moving towards F-completeness [16].

In the previous section, we noted that the set inclusion, $\overline{\alpha_o}[\![\phi]\!] \subseteq [\![\phi]\!]^A$, does not guarantee soundness. Nonetheless, starting from Galois connection, $\mathcal{P}(D)\langle\overline{\alpha_o}, \overline{\gamma}\rangle\mathcal{P}_{\downarrow}(A)$, we define yet one more variant of functional completeness:

$$[\![\cdot]\!]^A \text{ is } B(\overline{\alpha_o})\text{-complete for } [\![\cdot]\!] \text{ iff } \overline{\alpha_o}[\![\phi]\!] = [\![\phi]\!]^A.$$

For clarity, we use *O-complete* as a synonym for $B(\overline{\alpha_o})$-complete. O-completeness is again independent from F-completeness, but with the concept of a *covering*, we can make many connections:

- For $[\![\cdot]\!] : \mathcal{L} \to \mathcal{P}(D)$ and $\overline{\gamma} : Q \to \mathcal{P}(D)$, $\overline{\gamma}$ *covers* $[\![\cdot]\!]$ iff for all $\phi \in \mathcal{L}$, $[\![\phi]\!] \in \overline{\gamma}[Q]$.
- For $[\![\cdot]\!]^A : \mathcal{L} \to \mathcal{P}_{\downarrow}(A)$ and $\overline{\alpha} : P \to \mathcal{P}_{\downarrow}(A)$, $\overline{\alpha}$ *covers* $[\![\cdot]\!]^A$ iff for all $\phi \in \mathcal{L}$, $[\![\phi]\!]^A \in \overline{\alpha}[P]$.

---

[10] In theory, the redundant elements in A can be removed by applying the backwards-complete-core construction, closing the sets in $\mathcal{P}_{\downarrow}(A)$ under join.

Proposition 7. *Let $\overline{\alpha}$, $\overline{\gamma}$ be the adjoints of a Galois connection. Then,*

- $\overline{\gamma}$ *covers* $[\![\cdot]\!]$ *iff* $\overline{\gamma}(\overline{\alpha}[\![\phi]\!]) = [\![\phi]\!]$ *for all* $\phi \in \mathcal{L}$
- $\overline{\alpha}$ *covers* $[\![\cdot]\!]^{A}$ *iff* $\overline{\alpha}(\overline{\gamma}[\![\phi]\!]^{A}) = [\![\phi]\!]^{A}$ *for all* $\phi \in \mathcal{L}$.

Proof. The results hold because each equivalence class in $\mathcal{P}(D)$ (resp., $\mathcal{P}_{\downarrow}(A)$) holds exactly one value that lies in the image of $\overline{\gamma}[\mathcal{P}_{\downarrow}(A)]$ (resp., $\overline{\alpha}[\mathcal{P}(D)]$).   □

Propositions 1, 2, and 7 characterize completeness:

Theorem 8. *Let $\overline{\alpha}$, $\overline{\gamma}$ be the adjoints of a Galois connection:*

- $[\![\cdot]\!]^{A}$ *is $F(\overline{\gamma})$-complete for $[\![\cdot]\!]$ iff $\overline{\gamma}$ covers $[\![\cdot]\!]$ and $[\![\phi]\!]^{A} \sim_{\overline{\gamma}} \overline{\alpha}[\![\phi]\!]$, for all $\phi \in \mathcal{L}$.*
- $[\![\cdot]\!]^{A}$ *is $B(\overline{\alpha})$-complete for $[\![\cdot]\!]$ iff $\overline{\alpha}$ covers $[\![\cdot]\!]^{A}$ and $[\![\phi]\!]^{A} \sim_{\overline{\gamma}} \overline{\alpha}[\![\phi]\!]$, for all $\phi \in \mathcal{L}$.*

Proof. The first result is a direct translation of Proposition 1, where $[\![\cdot]\!]^{\sharp}_{best} = \overline{\alpha} \circ [\![\cdot]\!] \circ id_{\mathcal{L}}$, that is $[\![\phi]\!]^{\sharp}_{best} = \overline{\alpha}[\![\phi]\!]$, for $\phi \in \mathcal{L}$.

The second result follows less directly. In Proposition 2, Clause *(i)* becomes $\phi = \phi'$ implies $[\![\phi]\!] = [\![\phi']\!]$, so only Clause *(ii)* remains: show $\overline{\alpha}[\![\phi]\!] = [\![\phi]\!]^{A}$ iff $\overline{\alpha}$ covers $[\![\cdot]\!]^{A}$ and $[\![\phi]\!]^{A} \sim_{\overline{\gamma}} \overline{\alpha}[\![\phi]\!]$. The if-part is immediate; for the only-if-part, $\overline{\alpha}$ covers $[\![\cdot]\!]^{A}$, because $\overline{\alpha}[\![\phi]\!] = [\![\phi]\!]^{A}$ implies that $\overline{\alpha}(\overline{\gamma}[\![\phi]\!]^{A}) = \overline{\alpha}[\![\phi]\!] = [\![\phi]\!]^{A}$ (cf. the proof of Prop. 7). Next, $\overline{\gamma}[\![\phi]\!]^{A} = \overline{\gamma}(\overline{\alpha}[\![\phi]\!])$ by applying $\overline{\gamma}$.   □

Both forms of completeness require the same, best equivalence-class precision and vary *only on the covering properties of $\overline{\alpha}$ and $\overline{\gamma}$.*

Corollary 9

- *If $[\![\cdot]\!]^{A}$ is F-complete for $[\![\cdot]\!]$ and $\overline{\alpha_u}$ covers $[\![\cdot]\!]^{A}$, then $[\![\cdot]\!]^{A}$ is B-complete.*
- *If $[\![\cdot]\!]^{A}$ is B-complete for $[\![\cdot]\!]$ and $\overline{\gamma}$ covers $[\![\cdot]\!]$, then $[\![\cdot]\!]^{A}$ is F-complete.*
- *If $[\![\cdot]\!]^{A}$ is F-complete for $[\![\cdot]\!]$ and $\overline{\alpha_o}$ covers $[\![\cdot]\!]^{A}$, then $[\![\cdot]\!]^{A}$ is O-complete.*
- *If $[\![\cdot]\!]^{A}$ is O-complete for $[\![\cdot]\!]$ and $\overline{\gamma}$ covers $[\![\cdot]\!]$, then $[\![\cdot]\!]^{A}$ is sound and F-complete.*

The Corollary explains why Ranzato and Tapparo, who work exclusively with onto $\overline{\alpha}$ functions, gravitate to proving F-completeness results [23,24,25].

4   Inductively Defined Abstract Logics

Given $[\![\cdot]\!] : \mathcal{L} \to \mathcal{P}(D)$, we can define $[\![\cdot]\!]^{A} : \mathcal{L} \to \mathcal{P}_{\downarrow}(A)$ to be $[\![\phi]\!]^{A} = \overline{\alpha_u}[\![\phi]\!]$, and consequently, $a \models^{A} \phi$ iff $\gamma(a) \subseteq [\![\phi]\!]$, but this definition is not inductively defined and is unlikely to be finitely computable. Assuming that $\mathcal{L}$ is defined inductively, we denote its inductive abstract interpretation as $[\![\cdot]\!]^{A}_{ind} : \mathcal{L} \to \mathcal{P}_{\downarrow}(A)$ and define it as

$$[\![op_i(\phi_j)_{0 < j \leq ar(i)}]\!]^{A}_{ind} = g_i^{\sharp}([\![\phi_i]\!]^{A}_{ind})_{0 < i \leq ar(i)}$$

where $g_i^{\sharp} : \mathcal{P}_{\downarrow}(A) \to \mathcal{P}_{\downarrow}(A)$ is sound for $g_i : \mathcal{P}(D) \to \mathcal{P}(D)$.

For example, based on Figure 4, we might define

$$[a]_{ind}^A = \overline{\alpha_u}(\gamma(a)) \qquad\qquad [\phi_1 \vee \phi_2]_{ind}^A = [\phi_1]_{ind}^A \cup_{\mathcal{P}_\downarrow(A)} [\phi_2]_{ind}^A$$
$$[\phi_1 \wedge \phi_2]_{ind}^A = [\phi_1]_{ind}^A \cap_{\mathcal{P}_\downarrow(A)} [\phi_2]_{ind}^A \qquad [[f]\phi]_{ind}^A = \widetilde{pre}_{f^\sharp}[\phi]_{ind}^A$$

It is well known that such a $[\cdot]_{ind}^A$ is sound for $[\![\cdot]\!]$ and also that, for all g_i and $g_i^\sharp$, if each $g_i^\sharp$ is B-complete (respectively, F-complete) for g_i, then $[\cdot]_{ind}^A$ is B-complete (F-complete) for $[\![\cdot]\!]$. Because the fixed-point operators are well behaved, we can easily add recursively defined operators to the logic [11,25].

For a logic with operators, op_i, and interpretations, g_i, we define each $g_{i\ best}^\sharp = \overline{\alpha_u} \circ g_i \circ \overline{\gamma}^{ar(i)} : \mathcal{P}_\downarrow(A)^{ar(i)} \to \mathcal{P}_\downarrow(A)$ so that

$$[op_i(\phi_j)_{0<j\leq ar(i)}]_{best}^A = g_{i\ best}^\sharp([\phi_j]_{best}^A)_{0<j\leq ar(i)}$$

Call this inductively defined interpretation, $[\cdot]_{best}^A$.

Corollary 10. $[\cdot]_{best}^A$ is F-complete for $[\![\cdot]\!]$ iff $\overline{\gamma}$ covers $[\![\cdot]\!]$.

Corollary 11. If $\overline{\gamma}$ covers $[\![\cdot]\!]$, then $[\cdot]_{best}^A$ is B-complete for $[\![\cdot]\!]$.

So, there is one crucial abstract interpretation where F-completeness implies B-completeness. No dual result is known where B-completeness implies F-completeness. Indeed, it is always the case that $\overline{\alpha_u}$ covers $[\cdot]_{best}^A$, so there is no relation between the B-completeness of $[\cdot]_{best}^A$ and $\overline{\alpha_u}$-covering.

5   Applications

5.1 $\mathcal{L} = A$

A standard static analysis computes on A-values and also uses them as the assertions of a correctness or transformation logic.

Given $C\langle \alpha, \gamma \rangle A$, use the Galois connection's internal logic: $\mathcal{L} = A$, and $c \models a$ iff $c \subseteq \gamma(a)$. Although the abstract judgement, $a' \models^A a$ iff $\gamma(a') \subseteq \gamma(a)$, would be best, one typically settles for its computable variant, $a' \models^A a$ iff $a' \sqsubseteq a$, that is, $[a]^A = \downarrow a$. This makes $[\cdot]^A$ F($\overline{\gamma}$)-complete (and sound!) for $[\![\cdot]\!]$. But $[\cdot]^A$ might not be O-complete nor B-complete:

Proposition 12. For all $a \in A$, $\overline{\alpha_o}(\gamma(a)) \subseteq \downarrow a \subseteq \overline{\alpha_u}(\gamma(a))$. But when α is onto, the second inclusion is an equality.

Say that $f(c_0) \models a_p$ holds, and we try to show this by validating $f_{best}^\sharp(a_0)) \models^A a_p$, where $a_0 = \alpha(c_0)$, but we fail. Since $f_{best}^\sharp(a_0) \sqsubseteq a_p$ iff $f(\gamma(a_0)) \subseteq \gamma(a_p)$, we must adjust either a_p or a_0; see Figure 3(a).

Perhaps we "weaken" a_p by making $f(\gamma(a_0))$ itself into a new canonical element, i.e., A gets the new element, a_p', such that $\gamma(a_p') = f(\gamma(a_0))$. This makes $f_{best}^\sharp(a_0) \models^A a_p'$ hold as well as $f_{best}^\sharp(a_0) \models^A a_p \sqcup a_p'$. This is an F-refinement step; see Figure 3(b).

Or we "strengthen" a_0 to a new element, a_1: Let c' be a maximal element from the set, $f^{-1}[\gamma(a_p)]_\alpha \cap [\gamma(a_0)]_\alpha$ and define $\gamma(a_1) = c'$. Now, $\alpha(c_0) = a_1$, and $f_{best}^\sharp(a_1) \models^A a_p$ holds. This is a B-refinement step; see Figure 3(c).

5.2 Partition Domains

An abstract domain used in model checking is the *partition domain* [3,23,24]:
Let D and A be discretely ordered sets, and let $\delta : D \to A$ be an onto function;
δ defines the equivalence relation, $c \sim_\delta c'$ iff $\delta(c) = \delta(c')$, and it partitions D,
where A are the partition names. Define $\gamma : A \to \mathcal{P}(D)$ as $\gamma(a) = \delta^{-1}(a)$. *There
is no Galois connection.* The logic looks like Figure 4 but includes negation:

$$[\![\neg\phi]\!] = \sim [\![\phi]\!]$$

($\sim$ is set complement.) As usual, $\{c\} \models \phi$ iff $c \in [\![\phi]\!]$.

From γ, we define $\overline{\gamma}$, $\overline{\alpha_o}$, and $\overline{\alpha_u}$. Since $\mathcal{P}(A)$ is a Boolean lattice and $\overline{\gamma}$ is 1-1,
we have that $\overline{\gamma}$ preserves $\cup$, $\cap$, and $\sim$. In addition, $[\![\cdot]\!]^A$, defined as

$$[\![a]\!]^A = \overline{\alpha_u}(\gamma(a)) \qquad [\![\phi_1 \wedge \phi_2]\!]^A = [\![\phi_1]\!]^A \cap [\![\phi_2]\!]^A$$
$$[\![\neg\phi]\!]^A = \sim [\![\phi]\!]^A \qquad [\![\phi_1 \vee \phi_2]\!]^A = [\![\phi_1]\!]^A \cup [\![\phi_2]\!]^A$$

is F($\overline{\gamma}$)-complete and equals $[\![\cdot]\!]^A_{best}$. Since both $\overline{\alpha_u}$ and $\overline{\alpha_o}$ cover $[\![\cdot]\!]^A$, the logic
is also B- and O-complete.

The usual application of a partition domain is to model checking, and the
usual model-checking logic includes the modality, $[f]\phi$, for $f : D \to \mathcal{P}(D)$ (cf.
Figure 4), which is abstracted by a sound $f^\sharp : A \to \mathcal{P}(A)$ as follows:

$$[\![[f]\phi]\!]^A = \widetilde{pre}_{f^\sharp_{best}} [\![\phi]\!]^A, \quad \text{where } \widetilde{pre}_{f^\sharp}(T) = \{a' \mid f^\sharp(a') \subseteq T\}.$$

We know that $\widetilde{pre}_{f^\sharp_{best}} = (\widetilde{pre}_f)^\sharp_{best} = \overline{\alpha_u} \circ \widetilde{pre}_f \circ \overline{\gamma}$ [29]. The definition is sound
but might not be complete.

The following holds for *all* abstract domains (not just partition domains):

Theorem 13. *For* $\widetilde{pre}_f : \mathcal{P}(D) \to \mathcal{P}(D)$, $f : D \to \mathcal{P}(D)$, *and* $f^* : \mathcal{P}(D) \to \mathcal{P}(D)$, *defined as* $f^*(S) = \cup_{c \in S} f(c)$,

1. $\widetilde{pre}_f$ *is* F($\overline{\gamma}$)-*complete iff* f^* *is* B($\overline{\alpha_o}$)-*complete.*
2. $\widetilde{pre}_f$ *is* B($\overline{\alpha_u}$)-*complete iff* f^* *is* F($\overline{\gamma}$)-*complete.*

Proof. We first prove 2. For the if-part, assume f^* is F-complete; we must
show $\overline{\alpha_u}(\widetilde{pre}_f(S)) \subseteq (\overline{\alpha_u} \circ \widetilde{pre}_f \circ \overline{\gamma})(\overline{\alpha_u}(S))$. When we expand the definitions
in the subset inclusion, we learn that we must assume $f^*[\gamma(a)] \subseteq S$ and prove
$f^*(\gamma(a)) \subseteq \overline{\gamma}(\overline{\alpha_u}(S))$. The assumption expands to $\overline{\gamma}(\overline{\alpha_u}(f^*(\gamma(a))) \subseteq \overline{\gamma}(\overline{\alpha_u}(S))$.
Now, its left-hand side equals $\overline{\gamma}(\overline{\alpha_u}(f^*(\overline{\gamma}(\downarrow a))))$. Since f^* is F-complete, this
equals $f^*(\gamma(a))$ and gives the result.

For the only-if-part, we must show for all $S \in \overline{\gamma}[\mathcal{P}_\downarrow(A)]$ that $f^*(S) \in \overline{\gamma}[\mathcal{P}_\downarrow(A)]$,
that is, $f^*(\overline{\gamma}(\overline{\alpha_u}(S))) \subseteq (\overline{\gamma} \circ \overline{\alpha_u} \circ f^*)(\overline{\gamma}(\overline{\alpha_u}(S)))$. Now, $f^*(\overline{\gamma}(\overline{\alpha_u}(S))) = f^*(\cup_{a \in \overline{\alpha_u}(S)})$.
By the B-completeness of $\widetilde{pre}_f$, which can be stated as, for all S, $f^*(\gamma(a)) \subseteq S$
iff $f^*(\gamma(a)) \subseteq \gamma(\overline{\alpha_u}(S))$, we can instantiate $S = f^*(\overline{\gamma}(\overline{\alpha_u}(S)))$, and we have that
$f^*(\gamma(a)) \subseteq (\overline{\gamma} \circ \overline{\alpha_u})(f^*(\overline{\gamma}(\overline{\alpha_u}(S))))$; the left-hand side equals $\cup_{a \in \overline{\alpha_u}(S)} f^*(\gamma(a))$.
Since f^* preserves unions, the result follows.

We next prove *1*. For the if-part, we must show that $\widetilde{pre}_f(\overline{\gamma}(T)) = (\overline{\gamma} \circ \overline{\alpha_u} \circ \widetilde{pre}_f \circ \overline{\gamma})(T)$. When we expand the definitions in the equation, we discover that we must prove $\cup\{S \mid f^*(S) \subseteq \overline{\gamma}(T)\} \subseteq \cup\{\gamma(a) \mid f^*(\gamma(a)) \subseteq \overline{\gamma}(T)\}$. (Soundness gives us the $\supseteq$ inclusion.)

So, for arbitrary S_0, assume that $f^*(S_0) \subseteq \overline{\gamma}(T)$. Since f^* is B-complete, we have that $f^*(S_0) \sim_{\overline{\alpha_o}} f^*(\overline{\gamma}(\overline{\alpha_o}(S_0)))$. We also have $S_0 \subseteq \overline{\gamma}(\overline{\alpha_o}(S_0))$. Since $f^*(S_0) \subseteq \overline{\gamma}(T)$, and the latter is a maximal point in its equivalence class, we have that $f^*(\overline{\gamma}(\overline{\alpha_o}(S_0))) \subseteq \overline{\gamma}(T)$ as well, implying that $\overline{\gamma}(\overline{\alpha_o}(S_0))$ lies in the goal set, $\{\gamma(a) \mid f^*(\gamma(a)) \subseteq \overline{\gamma}(T)\}$.

For the only-if-part, we must show $\overline{\alpha_o}(f^*(\overline{\gamma}(\overline{\alpha_o}(S)))) \subseteq \overline{\alpha_o}(f^*(S))$ for all $S \in \mathcal{P}(D)$. First consider the set, $G_S = \widetilde{pre}_f(\overline{\gamma}(\overline{\alpha_o}(f^*(S))))$; we have that $S \subseteq G_S$, because $f^*(S) \subseteq \overline{\gamma}(\overline{\alpha_o}(f^*(S)))$ and $\widetilde{pre}_f(f^*(S)) \supseteq S$. Since $\widetilde{pre}_f$ is F-complete, we have $G_S \in \overline{\gamma}[\mathcal{P}_\downarrow(A)]$, and we also have $\overline{\gamma}(\overline{\alpha_o}(S)) \subseteq G_S$.

This implies $f^*(\overline{\gamma}(\overline{\alpha_o}(S))) \subseteq \overline{\gamma}(\overline{\alpha_o}(f^*(S)))$, by the definition of $\widetilde{pre}_f$. We apply $\overline{\alpha_o}$ and obtain $(\overline{\alpha_o} \circ f^* \circ \overline{\gamma} \circ \overline{\alpha_o})(S) \subseteq (\overline{\alpha_o} \circ \overline{\gamma} \circ \overline{\alpha_o} \circ f^*)(S) = \overline{\alpha_o}(f^*(S))$, which is the result. $\square$

Giacobazzi and Quintarelli [16] (and Mastroeni [20]) show how to apply the F-complete shell construction to additive (continuous) f to achieve Item *1* above.

Recall that $pre_f(S) = \sim \widetilde{pre}_f(\sim S)$ [19]; When pre_f is not F-complete, Ranzato and Tapparo apply the F-complete-shell construction to pre_f [23]. The resulting abstract domain is still partitioned and its $\overline{\gamma}$ preserves $\sim$, so the equivalence, $\sim pre_f(\sim S) = \widetilde{pre}_f(S)$, yields F-completeness for $\widetilde{pre}_f$, too. $\overline{\gamma}$ is 1-1 as well (it preserves $\sim$), meaning $\overline{\alpha_o}$ is onto, giving B-completeness.

5.3   Predicate Abstraction

When an abstract domain is generated from a set, A, of assertions for variables within a program (e.g., x>y, ¬(y=0), ...), it is called a *predicate abstraction* [1,2,18,27]. The resulting static analysis annotates program points with sets of predicates that hold true at the program points.

We begin with the concrete state set, D, predicate set, A, and judgement relation, $\models \subseteq D \times A$. Think of A as a "subbasis" for domain generation. We generate the Galois connection, $\mathcal{P}(D)\langle \alpha, \gamma \rangle \mathcal{P}(A)^{op}$, where $\alpha(S) = \{a \mid S \models a\}$ (it maps S to all the predicates that hold true for S) and $\gamma(T) = \cap_{a \in T}\{c \mid c \models a\}$. (To understand γ, read $T \in \mathcal{P}(A)^{op}$ as $\bigwedge_{a \in T} a$.) The Galois connection is overapproximating, so $f^\sharp : \mathcal{P}(A)^{op} \to \mathcal{P}(A)^{op}$ computes sound postconditions for $f^* : \mathcal{P}(D) \to \mathcal{P}(D)$. The logical assertions are conjunctions,

$$\mathcal{L} \ni \phi ::= \bigwedge T, \text{ where } T \in \mathcal{P}(A)$$

interpreted by $\mathcal{P}(A)$'s internal logic: for $c \in D$, $\{c\} \models \bigwedge T$ iff $c \in \gamma(T)$.

The definition of the abstract judgement is crucial: if it is merely $T \models^A \bigwedge T'$ iff $T' \subseteq T$, then we have F($\overline{\gamma}$)-completeness but likely lose B($\overline{\alpha_u}$)-completeness, because it is possible that $a_1 \neq a_2$ and $\gamma\{a_1\} \subseteq \gamma\{a_2\}$, e.g., $\gamma\{x>2\} \subseteq \gamma\{x>0\}$ but x>2 $\not\models^A$ x>0. For this reason, implementations typically employ theorem provers that enforce $T \models^A \phi$ *iff* $T \Rightarrow \phi$ (that is, the prover uses T to deduce ϕ).

A second situation where completeness can fail is the calculation of imprecise postconditions. Suppose that we fail to prove $f^\sharp(a_0) \models \phi$. As we know from Section 5.1, we can either weaken ϕ or strengthen a_0. The latter is usually chosen, and we know that the B-complete refinement of f^* corresponds to the F-complete refinement of $\widetilde{pre}_f$ (Theorem 13 and [16]). This is the standard predicate-abstraction refinement strategy [2,27].

Disjunctive Predicate Abstraction: We can add disjunction to the predicate-abstraction domain by constructing the disjunctive completion of $\mathcal{P}(A)^{op}$. The elements of $\mathcal{P}_\downarrow(\mathcal{P}(A)^{op})$ are downclosed sets of sets of A-elements. Read such a $\overline{T} \in \mathcal{P}_\downarrow(\mathcal{P}(A)^{op})$ as the disjunctive normal form (DNF), $\bigvee_{T \in \overline{T}}(\bigwedge_{a \in T} a)$.

This coincides with the definition of $\overline{\gamma} : \mathcal{P}_\downarrow(\mathcal{P}(A)^{op}) \to \mathcal{P}(D)$, which is $\overline{\gamma}(\overline{T}) = \bigcup_{T \in \overline{T}} \gamma(T) = \bigcup_{T \in \overline{T}}(\bigcap_{a \in T} \gamma(a))$. Since the sets are downclosed (here, closed under superset), both union (disjunction) and intersection (conjunction) operations *automatically normalize to DNF*.[11]

Disjunctive completion gives us the Galois connection, $\mathcal{P}(D)\langle\overline{\alpha_o}, \overline{\gamma}\rangle\mathcal{P}_\downarrow(\mathcal{P}(A)^{op})$, completing the "basis" elements from $\mathcal{P}(A)^{op}$ to DNF elements [2]. The Galois connection supports this logic and its two interpretations:

$$\phi ::= a \mid \bigwedge_{i>0} \phi_i \mid \bigvee_{i>0} \phi_i$$

$$[\![a]\!] = \gamma\{a\} \qquad\qquad [\![a]\!]^A = \{T \in \mathcal{P}(A)^{op} \mid T \Rightarrow a\}$$
$$[\![\bigwedge_{i\geq0} \phi_i]\!] = \bigcap_{i\geq0} [\![\phi_i]\!] \qquad\qquad [\![\bigwedge_{i>0} \phi_i]\!]^A = \bigcap_{i>0} [\![\phi_i]\!]^A$$
$$[\![\bigvee_{i\geq0} \phi_i]\!] = \bigcup_{i\geq0} [\![\phi_i]\!] \qquad\qquad [\![\bigvee_{i>0} \phi_i]\!]^A = \bigcup_{i>0} [\![\phi_i]\!]^A$$

We have F($\overline{\gamma}$)-completeness, but B($\overline{\alpha_u}$)-completeness typically fails for disjunction, for the reasons given above.

6 Related Work

As noted in the Introduction, Galois-connection-based functional completeness was defined by Cousot [6] and Cousot and Cousot [8]. Mycroft [22] was perhaps the first to use B-completeness to define logical completeness; at the same time, Clarke, Grumberg, and Long [4] defined "exactness," stated in terms of homomorphisms, $h : D \to A$: $h(c) \models^A \phi$ iff $c \models \phi$, which is strong preservation.

Abstractions of state-transition systems led both Cleaveland, Iyer, and Yankevich [5] and Dams, Gerth, and Grumberg [13] to define an "optimal" abstract transition system as one that proves the most sound logical properties of a concrete system. Their definitions are not Galois-connection based but use the definition of strong preservation and yield strong preservation when Galois-connections are present.

Cousot and Cousot [10] formalized B-functional completeness and showed that it is preserved in inductively defined interpretations; they applied the results to proving logical B-completeness of a family of temporal logics and showing that B-completeness is preserved by fixed-point operators [11].

---

[11] An implementation of DNF will likely employ the normalization law, $S \wedge (\bigvee_i T_i) \Leftrightarrow \bigvee_i (S \wedge T_i)$, instead of using downclosed sets of sets.

Giacobazzi, Ranzato, and Scozzari [17] defined an iterative method for abstract-domain completion so that transfer functions are B-complete. Giacobazzi and Quintarelli [16] introduced F-completeness, defined its completion method, and used it to formalize counter-example-guided-abstraction refinement [3].

A thorough study of logical F-completeness (strong preservation) has been undertaken by Ranzato and Tapparo: for the class of partition domains, they showed that the minimal refinement of a partition domain to possess all sound properties of its corresponding concrete domain is iterative F-completion [23]. They also showed that the Paige-Tarjan algorithm for constructing a minimal bisimular abstract-transition system is an instance of F-completion [24]. Finally, they formalized strong preservation as logical F-completeness and showed that F-completeness is preserved by fixed-point operators [25]. The present paper was inspired by their work.

Finally, in his thesis [12], Dams proposed yet one more variant of logical completeness — *Dams's strong preservation* is defined as follows:

$$\text{for all } c \in D \text{ and } a \in A, \ c \in \gamma(a) \text{ iff (for all } \phi, \ a \models^A \phi \text{ iff } c \models \phi).$$

For *sets* A and D, onto $\delta : D \to A$, and $\gamma(a) = \delta^{-1}$, Dams's strong preservation implies *both* strong and best preservation.

Acknowledgements. I am grateful for discussions with Dennis Dams, Roberto Giacobazzi, Michael Huth, Isabella Mastroeni, Kedar Namjoshi, Francesco Ranzato, and Francesco Tapparo. Anindya Banerjee and the referees gave helpful suggestions for improving the paper.

References

1. T. Ball, A. Podelski, and S.K. Rajamani. Boolean and cartesian abstractions for model checking C programs. In *TACAS'01*, pages 268–283. LNCS 2031, 2001.
2. T. Ball, A. Podelski, and S.K. Rajamani. Relative completeness of abstraction refinement for software model checking. In *TACAS'02*, pages 158–172. Springer LNCS 2280, 2002.
3. E.M. Clarke, O. Grumberg, S. Jha, Y. Lu, and H. Veith. Counterexample-guided abstraction refinement. In *CAV'00*, pages 154–169. Springer LNCS 1855, 2000.
4. E.M. Clarke, O. Grumberg, and D.E. Long. Model checking and abstraction. *ACM Transactions on Programming Languages and Systems*, 16(5):1512–1542, 1994.
5. R. Cleaveland, P. Iyer, and D. Yankelevich. Optimality in abstractions of model checking. In *Proc. SAS'95*. Springer LNCS 983, 1995.
6. P. Cousot. *Méthodes itératives de construction et d'approximation de points fixes d'opérateurs monotones sur un treillis, analyse sémantique de programmes*. PhD thesis, University of Grenoble, 1978.
7. P. Cousot and R. Cousot. Abstract interpretation: a unified lattice model for static analysis of programs. In *Proc. 4th ACM Symp. POPL*, pages 238–252, 1977.
8. P. Cousot and R. Cousot. Systematic design of program analysis frameworks. In *Proc. 6th ACM Symp. POPL*, pages 269–282, 1979.
9. P. Cousot and R. Cousot. Higher-order abstract interpretation. In *Proceedings IEEE Int. Conf. Computer Lang.*, 1994.

10. P. Cousot and R. Cousot. Compositional and inductive semantic definitions in fixpoint, equational, constraint, closure-condition, rule-based and game theoretic form. In *Proc. CAV'95*, pages 293–308. Springer LNCS 939, 1995.
11. P. Cousot and R. Cousot. Temporal abstract interpretation. In *Proc. 27th ACM Symp. on Principles of Programming Languages*, pages 12–25. ACM Press, 2000.
12. D. Dams. *Abstract interpretation and partition refinement for model checking*. PhD thesis, Technische Universiteit Eindhoven, The Netherlands, 1996.
13. D. Dams, R. Gerth, and O. Grumberg. Abstract interpretation of reactive systems. *ACM Trans. Prog. Lang. Systems*, 19:253–291, 1997.
14. D. Dams and K. Namjoshi. The existence of finite abstractions for branching time model checking. In *Proc. IEEE Symp. LICS'04*, pages 335–344, 2004.
15. B.A. Davey and H.A Priestley. *Introduction to Lattices and Order, 2d ed.* Cambridge Univ. Press, 2002.
16. R. Giacobazzi and E. Quintarelli. Incompleteness, counterexamples, and refinements in abstract model checking. In *SAS'01*, pages 356–373. LNCS 2126, 2001.
17. R. Giacobazzi, F. Ranzato, and F. Scozzari. Making abstract interpretations complete. *J. ACM*, 47:361–416, 2000.
18. S. Graf and H. Saidi. Verifying invariants using theorem proving. In *Proc. CAV'96*, Springer LNCS 1102, 1996.
19. C. Loiseaux, S. Graf, J. Sifakis, A. Bouajjani, and S. Bensalem. Property preserving abstractions for verification of concurrent systems. *Formal Methods in System Design*, 6:1–36, 1995.
20. I. Mastroeni. *Abstract non-interference: an abstract-intepretation-based approach to secure information flow*. PhD thesis, University of Verona, IT, 2006.
21. A. Melton, G. Strecker, and D. Schmidt. Galois connections and computer science applications. In *Category Theory and Computer Programming*, pages 299–312. Springer LNCS 240, 1985.
22. A. Mycroft. Completeness and predicate-based abstract interpretation. In *Proc. ACM Symp. Partial Evaluation (PEPM'93)*, pages 179–185, 1993.
23. F. Ranzato and F. Tapparo. Strong preservation as completeness in abstract interpretation. In *Proc. ESOP*, LNCS 2986, pages 18–32. Springer, 2004.
24. F. Ranzato and F. Tapparo. An abstract interpretation-based refinement algorithm for strong preservation. In *TACAS'05*, LNCS 3440, pages 140–156. Springer, 2005.
25. F. Ranzato and F. Tapparo. Strong preservation of temporal fixpoint-based operators by abstract interpretation. In *Proc. Conf. VMCAI'06*, LNCS 3855, pages 332–347. Springer Verlag, 2006.
26. M. Sagiv, T. Reps, and R. Wilhelm. Parametric shape analysis via 3-valued logic. *ACM TOPLAS*, 24:217–298, 2002.
27. H. Saidi. Model checking guided abstraction and analysis. In *Proc. SAS'00*, pages 377–396. Springer LNCS 1824, 2000.
28. D.A. Schmidt. Comparing completeness properties of static analyses and their logics. Technical Report 06-03, Kansas State University, 2006.
29. D.A. Schmidt. Underapproximating predicate transformers. In *Proc. SAS'06*, LNCS. Springer, 2006.

Polymorphism, Subtyping, Whole Program Analysis and Accurate Data Types in Usage Analysis

Tobias Gedell[1], Jörgen Gustavsson[2], and Josef Svenningsson[1]

[1] Department of Computing Science,
Chalmers University of Technology and Göteborg University
{gedell, josefs}@cs.chalmers.se
[2] Spotfire, Inc.

Abstract. There are a number of choices to be made in the design of a type based usage analysis. Some of these are: Should the analysis be monomorphic or have some degree of polymorphism? What about subtyping? How should the analysis deal with user defined algebraic data types? Should it be a whole program analysis?

Several researchers have speculated that these features are important but there has been a lack of empirical evidence. In this paper we present a systematic evaluation of each of these features in the context of a full scale implementation of a usage analysis for Haskell.

Our measurements show that all features increase the precision. It is, however, not necessary to have them all to obtain an acceptable precision.

1 Introduction

In this article we study the impact of polymorphism, subtyping, whole program analysis and accurate data types on type based *usage analysis*. Usage analysis is an analysis for lazy functional languages that aims to predict whether an argument of a function is used at most once. The information can be used to reduce some of the costly overhead associated with call-by-need and perform various optimizing program transformations. The focus of this paper is however solely on improving the precision of usage analysis, not on its uses.

Polymorphism. Polymorphism is the primary mechanism for increasing the precision of a type based analysis and achieving a degree of context sensitivity.

Previous work by Peyton Jones and Wansbrough has indicated that polymorphism is important for usage analyses. Convinced that polymorphism could be dispensed with they made a full scale implementation of a completely monomorphic usage analysis. However, it turned out that it was "almost useless in practice" [WPJ99]. They drew the conclusion that the reason was the lack of polymorphism. In the end they implemented an improved analysis with a simple form of polymorphism that also incorporated other improvements [Wan02]. The resulting analysis gave a reasonable precision but there is no evidence that polymorphism was the crucial feature.

N. Kobayashi (Ed.): APLAS 2006, LNCS 4279, pp. 200–216, 2006.

Studies of other program analyses have come to a different conclusion about polymorphism. On example is points-to analysis for C for which several studies have shown that monomorphic analyses [FFA00, HT01, FRD00, Das00, DLFR01] give adequate precision for the purpose of an optimizing compiler [DLFR01]. Moreover, extending these analyses with polymorphism seem to have only a moderate effect [FFA00, DLFR01].

Point-to analysis may not be directly relevant for usage analysis but it still begs the question of how much polymorphism really can contribute to the precision of an analysis. One of the goals of this paper has been to shed some light on this question.

Subtyping. Another important feature in type based analysis is subtyping. It provides a mechanism for approximating a type by a less informative super type. This gives a form of context sensitivity since a type may have different super types at different call sites. It also provides a mechanism for combining two types, such as the types of the branches of an if expression, by a common super type. Thus, the effects of subtyping and polymorphism overlap.

This raises a number of questions. Does it suffice with only polymorphism or only subtyping? How much is gained by having the combination?

Whole program analysis. Another issue that also concerns context sensitivity is whole program analysis versus modular program analysis. A modular analysis which considers each module in isolation must make a worst case assumption about the context in which it appears.

This will clearly degrade the precision of the analysis. But how much? Is whole program analysis a crucial feature? And how does it interact with the choice of monomorphism versus polymorphism?

Data types. Another important design choice in a type based analysis is how to deal with user defined data types. The intuitive and accurate approach may require that the number of annotations on a type is exponential in the size of the type definitions of the analyzed program. The common solution to the problem is to limit the number of annotations on a type in some way, which can lead to loss of precision. The question is how big the loss is in practice.

Contributions. In order to evaluate the above features, we have implemented a range of usage analyses:

- With different degrees of polymorphism (Section 3)
- With and without subtyping (Section 4)
- Using different treatments of data types (Section 5)
- As whole program analyses and as modular analyses (Section 6)

All analyses have been implemented in the GHC compiler and have been measured with GHC's optimizing program transformations both enabled and disabled. We present figures summarizing (the arithmetic mean of) the effectiveness of each of the different features. More detailed figures for each of the programs we've analyzed can be found in the first authors licentiate thesis [Ged06].

We have not measured every combination of the above features. Instead we have started with a very precise analysis and successively turned off various features to see how much precision is lost. The initial analysis is the most precise in all but one aspect. It doesn't use whole program analysis. Our reason for that is that we wanted to stay close to how we would have implemented the analysis in GHC. Since GHC supports separate compilation so does our base line analysis.

Our systematic evaluation shows that each of these features has a significant impact on the precision of the analysis. Especially, it is clear that some kind of context sensitivity is needed through polymorphism or subtyping. Our results also show that the different features partly overlap. The combined effect of polymorphism and subtyping is for example not very dramatic although each one of them has a large effect on the accuracy. Another example is that whole program analysis is more important for monomorphic analysis than polymorphic analysis.

2   Usage Analysis

Implementations of lazy functional languages maintain sharing of evaluation by updating. For example, the evaluation of

$$(\lambda x.x + x)\,(1 + 2)$$

proceeds as follows. First, a closure for $1 + 2$ is built in the heap and a reference to the closure is passed to the abstraction. Second, to evaluate $x + x$ the value of x is required. Thus, the closure is fetched from the heap and evaluated. Third, the closure is updated (i.e., overwritten) with the result so that when the value of x is required again, the expression needs not be recomputed.

The same mechanism is used to implement lazy data structures such as potentially infinite lists.

The sharing of evaluation is crucial for the efficiency of lazy languages. However, it also carries a substantial overhead which is often not needed. For example, if we evaluate

$$(\lambda x.x + 1)\,(1 + 2)$$

then the update of the closure is unnecessary because the argument is only used once.

The aim of usage analysis is to detect such cases. The output of the analysis is an annotated program. Each point in the program that allocates a closure in the heap is annotated with 1 if the closure that is created at that point is always used at most once. It is annotated with ω if the closure is possibly used more than once or if the analysis cannot ensure that the closure is used at most once.

The annotations allow a compiler to generate code where the closures are not updated and thus effectively turning call-by-need into call-by-name. Usage analysis also enables a number of program transformations [PJPS96, PJM99].

Usage analysis has been studied by a number of researchers [LGH+92, Mar93, TWM95, Fax95, Gus98, WPJ99, WPJ00, GS00, Wan02].

2.1   Measuring the Effectiveness

We measured the effectiveness of the analyses by running them on the programs from the *nofib* suite [Par93] which is a benchmarking suite designed to evaluate the Glasgow Haskell Compiler (GHC). We excluded the toy programs and ran our analysis on the programs classified in the category *real* but had to exclude the following three programs: *HMMS* did not compile with GHC on our test system, *ebnf2ps* is dependent on a version of Happy that we could not get to work with our version of GHC, and *veritas* because many analyses ran out of memory when analyzing it.

Despite the name of the category, the average size of the programs is unfortunately quite small, ranging from 74 to 2,391 lines of code, libraries excluded.

The notion of effectiveness. When measuring the effectiveness it is natural to do so by modifying the runtime system of GHC. The runtime system is modified to collect the data needed to compute the effectiveness during a program's execution.

The easiest way is to count how many created closures that are only used once and how many of those closures that were detected by the analysis. This can be implemented by adding three counters to the runtime system: one that is incremented as soon as an updatable closure is created, one that is incremented each time a closure is used a second time, and one that is incremented as soon as a closure annotated with 1 is created. With these counters one can compute an effectiveness of an analysis:

$$\frac{closures\ annotated\ with\ 1}{created\ closures\ -\ closures\ used\ twice}$$

This is the metric used by Wansbrough [Wan02].

A drawback of this approach is that it does not take into account that each program point can only have one annotation – if any of the closures allocated at a program point is used more than once, that program point has to be annotated with ω for the analysis to be sound. Thus, any program point which has some closures used more than once and some used at most once would make even a perfect analysis get less than a 100 percent effectiveness. And such program points are common.

What we would like to do is to compute the effectiveness by measuring the proportion of *program points* that are correctly annotated instead of the proportion of *updates* that are avoided. We, therefore, modified the run time system to compute the best possible annotations which are consistent with the observed run time behavior. I.e., if all the closures allocated at a specific program point is used at most once during the execution, that program point could be annotated with 1 otherwise ω. We did this by, for each closure, keeping track of at which program point it was created. When a closure is used a second time we add its program point to the set of program points that need to be annotated with ω. We were careful to exclude dead code i.e. code that was not executed in the executions such as parts of imported libraries which were not used. It is important to note that this way of measuring is still based on running the program on a particular input and a perfect analysis may still get an effectiveness which is less than 100 percent.

Wansbrough's and our metrics differ also at another crucial point. The former metric depends very much on how many times each program point that allocates closures is executed. If a single program point allocates a majority of all closures, the computed effectiveness will depend very much on whether that single program point was correctly annotated by the analysis. In contrast, the effectiveness computed with the latter measurement will hardly be affected by one conservative annotation.

We think that our metric is more informative and have, therefore, used it for all our measurements.

Optimizing program transformations. Our implementation is based on GHC which is a state of the art Haskell implementation. The specific version of GHC we have used is 5.04.3. GHC parses the programs and translates them into the intermediate language Core, which is essentially System F [PJPS96]. When GHC is run with optimizations turned on (i.e. given the flag -O), it performs aggressive program transformation on Core before it is translated further. We inserted our analyses after GHC's program transformations just before the translation to lower level representations.

We ran the analysis with GHC's program transforming optimizations both enabled and disabled. The latter gives us a measure of the effectiveness of an analysis on code prior to program transformations. This is relevant because usage information can be used to guide the program transformations themselves.

2.2 Implementation

Actually implementing all the analyses we report on in this paper would have been a daunting task. To get around this problem we used the following trick: The only analysis we actually implemented was the most precise analysis, with polymorphism, polymorphic recursion, subtyping and whole program analysis. This analysis generated constraints, in the form of Constraint Abstractions [GS01]. These constraints have enough structure preserved from the original program to enable us to identify precisely where we can change them to correspond to a lesser precise analysis. We implemented several transformations on our constraints which effectively removed polymorphism, polymorphic recursion, subtyping, whole program analysis and which mimicked various ways of handling data types, respectively.

Although this trick helped us greatly in performing the measurements it had an unfortunate drawback. The transformed constraints, although semantically equivalent to a less precise analysis, was very remote from what an actual analysis would have generated. Several of our translations produced constraints that were very hard for the constraint solver. Therefore, any timings that we might have reported on would have been highly misleading. This is the reason why we have chosen to exclude them from this paper.

3 Polymorphism

We start by evaluating usage polymorphism. To see why it can be a useful feature, consider the function that adds up three integers.[1]

$$plus3\ x\ y\ z = x + y + z$$

Which usage type should we give to this function? Since the function uses all its arguments just once, it seems reasonable to give it the following type.

$$Int^1 \rightarrow Int^1 \rightarrow Int^1 \rightarrow Int^\omega$$

The annotations on the type express that all three arguments are used just once by the function and that the result may be used several times. However, this type is not correct. The problem is that the function may be partially applied:

$$map\ (plus3\ (1 + 2)\ (3 + 4))\ xs$$

If xs has at least two elements then $plus3\ (1 + 2)\ (3 + 4)$ is used more than once. As a consequence, so is also $(1 + 2)$ and $(3 + 4)$.

To express that functions may be used several times we need to annotate also function arrows. A possible type for $plus3$ could be:

$$Int^\omega \rightarrow^\omega Int^\omega \rightarrow^\omega Int^1 \rightarrow^\omega Int^\omega$$

The function arrows are annotated with ω which indicates that $plus3$ and its partial applications may be used several times. The price we pay is that the first and the second argument are given the type Int^ω. This type is sound but it is clearly not a good one for call sites where $plus3$ is not partially applied. What is needed is a mechanism for separating call sites with different usage.

The solution to the problem is to give the function a usage polymorphic type:

$$\forall\ u_0\ u_1\ u_2\ u_3\ |\ u_2 \leq u_0, u_3 \leq u_0, u_3 \leq u_1.Int^{u_0} \rightarrow^\omega Int^{u_1} \rightarrow^{u_2} Int^1 \rightarrow^{u_3} Int^\omega$$

The type is annotated with usage variables and the type schema contains a set of constraints which restrict how the annotations can be instantiated. A constraint $u \leq u'$ simply specifies that the values instantiated for u must be smaller than or equal to the values instantiated for u' where we have the ordering that $1 < \omega$. This form of polymorphism is usually referred to as constrained polymorphism or bounded polymorphism.

In our example, $u_2 \leq u_0$ enforces that if a partial application of $plus3$ to one argument is used more than once then that first argument is also used more than once. Similarly, $u_3 \leq u_0$ and $u_3 \leq u_1$ makes sure that if we partially apply $plus3$ to two arguments and use it more than once then both these arguments are used more than once.

---

[1] This example is due to Wansbrough and Peyton Jones [WPJ00].

3.1   Degrees of Polymorphism

There are many different forms of parametric polymorphism. In this paper we consider three different systems where usage generalization takes place at let-bindings.

- An analysis with monomorphic recursion in the style of ML. Intuitively, this gives the effect of a monomorphic analysis where all non-recursive calls have been unwound.
- An analysis with polymorphic recursion [Myc84, Hen93, DHM95]. Intuitively, this gives the effect of the previous analysis where recursion has been (infinitely) unwound.
- An analysis where the form of type schemas are restricted so that generalized usage variables may not be constrained. A consequence of the restriction is that an implementation need not instantiate (i.e., copy) a potentially large constraint set whenever the type is instantiated. Wansbrough and Peyton Jones [WPJ00] suggested this in the context of usage analysis and called it *simple usage polymorphism*.

With simple usage polymorphism it is not possible to give *plus3* the type

$$\forall u_0 \, u_1 \, u_2 \, u_3 \mid u_2 \leq u_0, u_3 \leq u_0, u_3 \leq u_1 . Int^{u_0} \to^\omega Int^{u_1} \to^{u_2} Int^1 \to^{u_3} Int^\omega$$

because the generalized variables u_0, u_1, u_2, u_3 are all constrained. Instead we can give it the type

$$\forall u . Int^u \to^\omega Int^u \to^u Int^1 \to^u Int^\omega$$

where we have unified the generalized variables into one. This type is clearly worse but it gives a degree of context sensitivity. An alternative is to give it a monomorphic type. For example

$$Int^\omega \to^\omega Int^1 \to^\omega Int^1 \to^1 Int^\omega.$$

These types are incomparable and an implementation needs to make a heuristic choice. We use the heuristic proposed by Wansbrough [Wan02] to generalize the types of all exported functions and give local functions monomorphic types.

The analyses include usage subtyping; use an aggressive treatment of algebraic data types and are compatible with separate compilation (i.e., we analyze the modules of the program one by one in the same order as GHC). We discuss and evaluate all these features later on.

3.2   Evaluation

The results are shown in Figure 1, which shows the average effectiveness of each analysis.

The most striking observation is that the results are very different depending on whether GHC's optimizing program transformations are turned on or off.

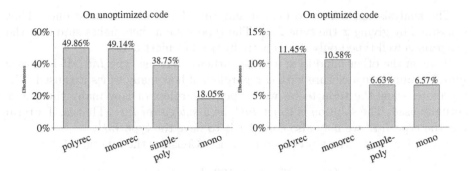

Fig. 1. Measurements of polymorphism

The effectiveness is much lower with program transformations turned on. While we have yet to make any detailed studies of this phenomenon we here suggest some possible explanations. Firstly, one possible contributor to this phenomenon is GHC's aggressive inliner [PJM99]. There is no need to create closures for the arguments of inlined function calls and thus many targets for the analysis disappears. The net effect is that the proportion of difficult cases (such as closures in data structures and calls to unknown functions) increases which reduces the effectiveness.

Another explanation is strictness analysis [Myc82]. Strictness analysis can decide that the argument of a function is guaranteed to be used at least once (in any terminating computation). In those cases there is no need to suspend the evaluation of that argument. If an argument is used exactly once then it is a target for both strictness and usage analysis. When the strictness analysis (as part of GHC's program transformation) is run first it removes some easy targets.

Our measurements also show that the polymorphic analyses are significantly better than the monomorphic one. Polymorphic recursion turns out to have hardly any effect compared to monomorphic recursion. Simple polymorphism comes half way on unoptimized code – it is significantly better than monomorphism but significantly worse than constrained polymorphism, which shows that it can serve as a good compromise. This is, however, not the case for optimized code.

The largest surprise to us was that the accuracy of the monomorphic analysis is relatively good. This seems to contradict the results reported by Wansbrough and Peyton Jones [WPJ00] who implemented and evaluated the monomorphic analysis from [WPJ99]. They found that the analysis was almost useless in practice and concluded that it was the lack of polymorphism that caused the poor results. We do not have a satisfactory explanation for this discrepancy.

4 Subtyping

Consider the following code fragment.

$$\text{let } x =^u 1 + 2 \text{ in } \ldots$$

Here u is the usage annotation associated with the closure for $1 + 2$.

The analysis can take u to be 1 if and only if x is used at most once. That is assured by giving x the type Int^1. The type system then makes sure that the program is well typed only if x is actually used at most once.

If we on the other hand take u to be ω then x has the type Int^ω. It is always sound to annotate a closure with ω regardless of how many times it is used. We, therefore, want the term to be well typed regardless of how many times x is actually used. The solution is to let Int^ω be a *subtype* of Int^1. That is, if a term has the type Int^ω we may also consider it to have the type Int^1.

Subtyping makes the system more precise. Consider the function f.

$$f\, x\, y\ =\ \textbf{if}\, x * x > 100\, \textbf{then}\, x\, \textbf{else}\, y$$

It seems reasonable that we should be able to give it, for example, the type

$$Int^\omega \rightarrow^\omega Int^1 \rightarrow^\omega Int^1.$$

This type expresses that if the result of the function is used at most once then the second argument is used only once. The first argument is, however, used at least twice regardless of how many times the result is used.

To derive this type we must have usage subtyping. Otherwise, the types of the branches of the conditional would be incompatible – x has type Int^ω and y has the type Int^1. With subtyping we can consider x to have the type Int^1.

Without subtyping x and y has to have the same type and the type of the function must be

$$Int^\omega \rightarrow^\omega Int^\omega \rightarrow^\omega Int^\omega$$

which puts unnecessary demands on y.

Subtyping can also give a degree of context sensitivity. Consider, for example, the following program.

$$\begin{aligned}
&\textbf{let}\ f\, x = x + 1\\
&\qquad a = 1 + 2\\
&\qquad b = 3 + 4\\
&\textbf{in}\ \ f\, a + f\, b + b
\end{aligned}$$

Here, b is used several times and is given the type Int^ω. Without subtyping nor polymorphism we would have to give a the same type and the two call sites would pollute each other.

When subtyping is combined with polymorphism it naturally leads to constrained polymorphism. Note, however, that subtyping is not the only source of inequality constraints in a usage analysis. Inequality constraints are also used for the correct treatment of partial application (see Section 3) and data structures. Thus, we use constrained polymorphism also in the systems without subtyping.

4.1   Evaluation

We have evaluated two systems without subtyping – a polymorphicly recursive and a monomorphic analysis. Both analyses use an aggressive treatment of data

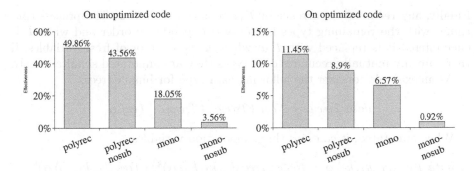

Fig. 2. Measurements of subtyping

types and are compatible with separate compilation. Figure 2 shows the average effectiveness of each analysis. We have included the system with polymorphic recursion and subtyping and the monomorphic system with subtyping from Section 3 for an easy comparison.

The results show that the accuracy of the monomorphic system without subtyping is poor. The precision is dramatically improved if we add subtyping or polymorphism. Our explanation is that both polymorphism and subtyping gives a degree of context sensitivity which is crucial.

The polymorphic system without subtyping is in principle incomparable to the monomorphic system with subtyping. However, in practice the polymorphic system outperforms the monomorphic one. The difference is much smaller when the analyses are run on optimized code which is consistent with our earlier observation that context sensitivity becomes less important because of inlining.

The combination of subtyping and polymorphism has a moderate but significant effect when compared to polymorphic analysis without subtyping. The effect is relatively larger on optimized code. The explanation we can provide is that the proportion of hard cases - which requires the combination – is larger because the optimizer has already dealt with many simple cases.

5   Algebraic Data Types

An important issue is how to deal with data structures such as lists and user defined data types. In this section we evaluate some different approaches.

Let us first consider the obvious method. The process starts with the user defined data types which only depend on predefined types. Suppose T is such a type.

$$data\ T\ \alpha = C_1\ \tau\ |\ \dots\ |\ C_n\ \tau$$

The types on the right hand side are annotated with fresh usage variables. If there are any recursive occurrences they are ignored. The type is then parameterized on these usage variables, u.

$$data\ T\ u\ \alpha = C_1\ \tau_1'\ |\ \dots\ |\ C_n\ \tau_n'$$

Finally, any recursive occurrence of T is replaced with $T\ \boldsymbol{u}$. The process continues with the remaining types in the type dependency order and when T is encountered it is replaced with $T\ \boldsymbol{u}'$ where $\boldsymbol{u}'$ is a vector of fresh variables. If there are any mutually recursive data types they are annotated simultaneously.

As an example consider the following data type for binary trees:

$$data\ Tree\ \alpha = Node\ (Tree\ \alpha)\ (Tree\ \alpha)\ |\ Leaf\ \alpha$$

When annotated, it contains three annotation variables:

$$data\ Tree\ \langle k_0, k_1, k_2\rangle\ \alpha = Node\ (Tree\ \langle k_0, k_1, k_2\rangle\ \alpha)^{k_0}\ (Tree\ \langle k_0, k_1, k_2\rangle\ \alpha)^{k_1}$$
$$|\ Leaf\ \alpha^{k_2}$$

This approach is simple and accurate and we used it in all the analyses in the previous sections. The net effect is equivalent to a method where all non-recursive occurrences in a type are first unwound. As a result the number of annotation variables can grow exponentially. An example of this is the following data type:

$$data\ T_0\ \langle k_0\rangle\ = C\ Int^{k_0}$$
$$data\ T_1\ \langle k_0, k_1, k_2, k_3\rangle = C'\ (T_0\ \langle k_1\rangle)^{k_0}\ |\ C''\ (T_0\ \langle k_3\rangle)^{k_2}$$
$$\dots$$
$$data\ T_n\ \langle k_0, \dots, k_m\rangle = C'_n\ (T_{n-1}\ \langle\dots\rangle)^{k_0}\ |\ C''_n\ (T_{n-1}\ \langle\dots\rangle)^{k_{m/2}}$$

Here T_n will contain $O(2^n)$ usage variables.

In practice, the number of required variables sometimes grows very large. The largest number we have encountered was a type in the Glasgow Haskell Compiler which required over two million usage annotations. As a consequence a single subtyping step leads to over two million inequality constraints and our implementation simply could not deal with all those constraints. This problem was the reason for why we had to exclude the program veritas from our study. It is clear that an alternative is needed and we tried two different ones.

The first approach was to put a limit on the number of usage variables which are used to annotate a type. If the limit is exceeded then we simply use each variable several times on the right hand side of the type. We do not try to do anything clever and when we exceed the limit we simply recycle the variables in a round robin manner. This approach leads to ad-hoc spurious behavior of the analysis when the limit is exceeded but maintains good accuracy for small types. We tried this approach with a limit of 100, 10 and 1.

The second approach was to simply annotate all types on the right hand side with only ω. The effect is that information is lost when something is inserted into a data structure – the analysis simply assumes the worst about its usage. Intuitively this can be thought of as a special case of the approach above where the limit is zero.

All the analyses used for measuring the treatment of data types have subtyping and polymorphic recursion and are compatible with separate compilation.

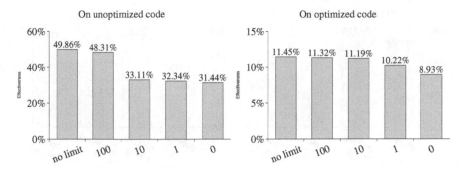

Fig. 3. Measurements of treatments of data types

5.1 Evaluation

The average effectiveness of each analysis is shown in Figure 3.

The results are quite different for optimized and unoptimized code. In the case of unoptimized code there is a clear loss in precision when we limit the number of annotation variables. The loss is quite small when the limit is 100 but quite dramatic when the limit is only 10. Going further and annotating with only one or no variables has a smaller effect.

The situation is different for optimized code. Here there is only a small difference when the number of variables are limited to 100 or 10. But there is a noticeable effect when one or no variables are used.

We believe that this effect stems from Haskell's class system. When Haskell programs are translated into Core each class context is translated to a so called dictionary parameter. A dictionary is simply a record of the functions in an instance of a class. Large classes leads to large records of functions which are passed around at run time. When the number of annotations are limited, it substantially degrades the precision for these records. Presumably, most dictionaries require more than 10 variables but less than 100 which explains the effect for unoptimized code.

These records are often eliminated by GHC's program transformations which tries to specialize functions for each particular instance [Jon94, Aug93]. Thus, in optimized code there are not so many large types which explains why the effect of limiting the number of variables to 10 is quite small.

6 Whole Program Analysis

So far all the analyses have been compatible with separate compilation. In this section we consider whole program analysis.

Suppose that f is an exported library function where the closure created for x' is annotated with u.

$$f\ x = \mathbf{let}\ x' =^u x + 1\ \mathbf{in}\ \lambda y.x' + y$$

In the setting of separate compilation we have to decide which value u should take without knowledge of how f is called. In the worst case, f is applied to one

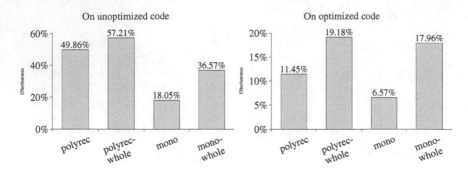

Fig. 4. Measurements of whole program analysis

argument and the resulting function is applied repeatedly. The closure of x' is then used repeatedly so we must assume the worst and let u be equal to ω. We can then give f the type

$$Int^1 \rightarrow^\omega Int^1 \rightarrow^\omega Int^\omega$$

With separate compilation we must make sure that the types of exported functions are general enough to be applicable in all contexts. That is, it must still be possible to annotate the remaining modules such that the resulting program is well typed. Luckily, this is always possible if we ensure that the types of all exported functions have an instance where the positive (covariant) positions in the type are annotated with ω. In the type of f this is reflected in that the function arrows and the resulting integer are annotated with ω. Wansbrough and Peyton Jones [WPJ00] calls this process pessimization. Further discussion can be found in Wansbrough's thesis [Wan02].

In the setting of whole program analysis this process in unnecessary which improves the result of the analysis. We have chosen to evaluate the effect on two analyses, the polymorphicly recursive analysis with subtyping and the monomorphic analysis with subtyping. Both analyses use the aggressive treatment of data types.

6.1 Evaluation

The average effectiveness for each analysis is shown in Figure 4. They show that whole program analysis improves both analyses significantly on both unoptimized and optimized code.

The effect is greater for the monomorphic analysis. The explanation is that the inaccuracies that are introduced by the pessimization, needed for separate compilation, spreads further in the monomorphic analysis due to the lack of context sensitivity. One can think of pessimization as simulating the worst possible calling context which then spreads to all call sites.

An interesting observation is that there is only a small difference between the polymorphic and the monomorphic whole program analysis for optimized code. The combination of aggressive inlining and whole program analysis almost cancels out the effect of polymorphism.

7   Related Work

The usage analyses in this paper build on the type based analyses in[TWM95, Gus98, WPJ99, WPJ00, GS00, Wan02]. The use of polymorphism in usage analysis was first sketched in [TWM95] and was developed further in [GS00] and [WPJ00, Wan02] where simple polymorphism was proposed. Usage subtyping was introduced in [Gus98, WPJ99]. The method for dealing with data types was suggested independently by Wansbrough [Wan02] and ourselves [Ged03]. The method for dealing with separate compilation is due to Wansbrough and Peyton Jones [WPJ99].

The measurements of Wansbrough and Peyton Jones on their monomorphic analysis with subtyping and a limited treatment of data types showed that is was "almost useless in practice". Wansbrough later made thorough measurements of the precision of simple usage polymorphism with some different treatments of data types in [Wan02]. He concludes that the accuracy of the simple usage polymorphism with a good treatment of data types is reasonable which is consistent with our findings. He also compares the accuracy with a monomorphic usage analysis but the comparison is incomplete – the monomorphic analysis only has a very coarse treatment of data types.

Foster et al [FFA00] evaluate the effect of polymorphism and monomorphism on Steensgaard's equality based points-to analysis [Ste96] as well as Andersen's inclusion based points-to analysis [And94]. Their results show that the inclusion based analysis is substantially better than the unification based. Adding polymorphism to the equality based analysis also has a substantial effect but adding polymorphism to the inclusion based analysis gives only a small improvement.

There are clear analogies between Steensgaard's equality based analysis and usage analysis without subtyping. Andersen's inclusion based analysis relates to usage analysis with subtyping. Given these relationships, our results are consistent with the results of Foster et al with one exception – the combination of polymorphism and subtyping has a significant effect in our setting. However, when we apply aggressive program transformations prior to the analysis and run it in whole program analysis mode then our results coincide.

8   Conclusions

We have performed a systematic evaluation of the impact on the accuracy of four dimensions in the design space of a type based usage analyses for Haskell. We evaluated

- different degrees of polymorphism: polymorphic recursion, monomorphic recursion, simple polymorphism and monomorphism,
- subtyping versus no subtyping,

– different treatments of user defined types, and
– whole program analysis versus analysis compatible with separate compilation.

Our results show that all of these features individually have a significant effect on the accuracy. A striking outcome was that the results depended very much on whether the analyzed programs were first subject to aggressively optimizing program transformations. A topic for future work would be to investigate how much each optimization affects the analysis result.

Our evaluation of polymorphism and subtyping showed that the polymorphic analyses clearly outperform their monomorphic counterparts. The effect was larger when the analyses did not incorporate subtyping. This is not surprising given that subtyping gives a degree of context sensitivity and, thus, partially overlaps with polymorphism. Polymorphic recursion turned out to give very little when compared to monomorphic recursion. For unoptimized code, simple polymorphism (where variables in types schemas cannot be constrained) was shown to lie in between monomorphism and constrained polymorphism.

The measurements also showed that the treatment of data types is important. The effectiveness of the different alternatives turned out to depend on whether the code was optimized or not. We believe that the explanation is coupled to the implementation of Haskell's class system and, thus, that this observation might be rather Haskell specific.

Whole program analysis turned out to have a rather large impact. The effect was greater for monomorphic analysis. The reason is that the conservative assumptions, that have to be made in the setting of separate compilation, have larger impact due to the lack of context sensitivity in monomorphic analysis. In fact, the whole program monomorphic analysis with subtyping was almost as good as the whole program polymorphic analysis with subtyping on optimized programs.

Finally we note that the effectiveness of even the most precise analysis seems quite poor. For unoptimized code the best figure is 57% and for optimized code the top effectiveness is a poor 19%. Is this because we have used an imprecise measure or because of fundamental limitations of the form of usage analysis used in this paper? We leave this question for future investigation.

References

[And94]   L. O. Andersen. *Program Analysis and Specialization for the C Programming Language*. PhD thesis, DIKU, University of Copenhagen, May 1994. (DIKU report 94/19).

[Aug93]   Lennart Augustsson. Implementing haskell overloading. In *Functional Programming Languages and Computer Architecture*, pages 65–73, 1993.

[Das00]   Manuvir Das. Unification-based pointer analysis with directional assignments. In *PLDI'00*, pages 35–46. ACM Press, June 2000.

[DHM95]   D. Dussart, F. Henglein, and C. Mossin. Polymorphic recursion and subtype qualifications: Polymorphic binding-time analysis in polynomial time. In *SAS'95*, September 1995.

[DLFR01]   Manuvir Das, Ben Liblit, Manuel Fähndrich, and Jakob Rehof. Estimating the impact of scalable pointer analysis on optimization. In *SAS'01*. Springer LNCS 2126, 2001.

[Fax95]   Karl-Filip Faxén. Optimizing lazy functional programs using flow inference. In *Proc. of SAS'95*, pages 136–153. Springer-Verlag, LNCS 983, September 1995.

[FFA00]   Jeffrey S. Foster, Manuel Fähndrich, and Alexander Aiken. Polymorphic versus monomorphic flow-insensitive points-to analysis for c. In *SAS'00*, pages 175–198, 2000.

[FRD00]   Manuel Fähndrich, Jakob Rehof, and Manuvir Das. Scalable Context-Sensitive Flow Analysis using Instantiation Constraints. In *PLDI'00*, Vancouver B.C., Canada, June 2000.

[Ged03]   Tobias Gedell. A Case Study on the Scalability of a Constraint Solving Algorithm: Polymorphic Usage Analysis with Subtyping. Master thesis, October 2003.

[Ged06]   Tobias Gedell. Static analysis and deductive verification of programs. Licentiate thesis, 2006.

[GS00]   Jörgen Gustavsson and Josef Svenningsson. A usage analysis with bounded usage polymorphism and subtyping. In Markus Mohnen and Pieter W. M. Koopman, editors, *IFL*, volume 2011 of *Lecture Notes in Computer Science*, pages 140–157. Springer, 2000.

[GS01]   Jörgen Gustavsson and Josef Svenningsson. Constraint abstractions. In *PADO II*, pages 63–83. Springer Verlag LNCS 2053, 2001.

[Gus98]   Jörgen Gustavsson. A type based sharing analysis for update avoidance and optimisation. In *ICFP*, pages 39–50. ACM, SIGPLAN Notices 34(1), 1998.

[Hen93]   Fritz Henglein. Type inference with polymorphic recursion. *ACM Transactions on Programming Languages and Systems*, 15(2):253–289, April 1993.

[HT01]   Nevin Heintze and Olivier Tardieu. Ultra-fast aliasing analysis using CLA: A million lines of C code in a second. In *PLDI'01*, pages 254–263. ACM-Press, June 2001.

[Jon94]   Mark P. Jones. Dictionary-free overloading by partial evaluation. In *Partial Evaluation and Semantics-Based Program Manipulation, Orlando, Florida, June 1994 (Technical Report 94/9, Department of Computer Science, University of Melbourne)*, pages 107–117, 1994.

[LGH+92]   J. Launchbury, A. Gill, J. Hughes, S. Marlow, S. L. Peyton Jones, and P. Wadler. Avoiding Unnecessary Updates. In J. Launchbury and P. M. Sansom, editors, *Functional Programming*, Workshops in Computing, Glasgow, 1992. Springer.

[Mar93]   S. Marlow. Update Avoidance Analysis by Abstract Interpretation. In *Proc. 1993 Glasgow Workshop on Functional Programming*, Workshops in Computing. Springer–Verlag, 1993.

[Myc82]   Alan Mycroft. *Abstract Interpretation and Optimizing Transformations for Applicative Programs*. PhD thesis, University of Edinburg, 1982.

[Myc84]   Alan Mycroft. Polymorphic Type Schemes and Recursive Definitions. In *Proceedings 6th International Symposium on Programming, Lecture Notes in Computer Science*, Toulouse, July 1984. Springer Verlag.

[Par93]   W. Partain. The nofib benchmark suite of haskell programs, 1993.

[PJM99]   S. Peyton Jones and S. Marlow. Secrets of the Glasgow Haskell compiler inliner. In *Workshop on Implementing Declarative Languages*, 1999.

[PJPS96]   S. Peyton Jones, W. Partain, and A. Santos. Let-floating: moving bindings
            to give faster programs. In *Proc. of ICFP'96*, pages 1–12. ACM, SIGPLAN
            Notices 31(6), May 1996.
[Ste96]   B. Steensgaard. Points-to analysis in almost linear time. In *POPL'96*,
            pages 32–41. ACM Press, January 1996.
[TWM95]   D. N. Turner, P. Wadler, and C. Mossin. Once upon a type. In *Proc. of
            FPCA*, La Jolla, 1995. ACM Press, ISBN 0-89791-7.
[Wan02]   Keith Wansbrough. *Simple Polymorphic Usage Analysis*. PhD thesis, Com-
            puter Laboratory, Cambridge University, England, March 2002.
[WPJ99]   Keith Wansbrough and Simon Peyton Jones. Once Upon a Polymorphic
            Type. In *Proc. of POPL'99*. ACM Press, January 1999.
[WPJ00]   Keith Wansbrough and Simon Peyton Jones. Simple Usage Polymorphism.
            In *ACM SIGPLAN Workshop on Types in Compilation*. Springer-Verlag,
            September 2000.

A Modal Language for the Safety of Mobile Values

Sungwoo Park

Pohang University of Science and Technology, Republic of Korea
gla@postech.ac.kr

Abstract. In the context of distributed computations, local resources give rise to an issue not found in stand-alone computations: the safety of mobile code. One approach to the safety of mobile code is to build a modal type system with the modality □ that corresponds to necessity of modal logic. We argue that the modality □ is not expressive enough for safe communications in distributed computations, in particular for the safety of mobile values. We present a modal language which focuses on the safety of mobile values rather than the safety of mobile code. The safety of mobile values is achieved with a new modality ⊡ which expresses that given code evaluates to a mobile value. We demonstrate the use of the modality ⊡ with a communication construct for remote procedure calls.

1   Introduction

A distributed computation is a cooperative process taking place in a network of nodes. Each node is capable of performing a stand-alone computation and also communicating with other nodes to distribute and collect code and data. Thus a distributed computation has the potential to make productive use of all the nodes in the network simultaneously.

Usually a distributed computation assumes a heterogeneous group of nodes with different *local resources*. A local resource can be either a permanent/physical object available at a particular node (*e.g.*, printer, database) or an ephemeral/semantic object created during a stand-alone computation (*e.g.*, heap cell, abstract data type). Local resources are accessed via their references (*e.g.*, handle for a database file, pointer to a heap cell).

Local resources, however, give rise to an issue not found in stand-alone computations: the safety of *mobile code*, or in our terminology, the safety of *mobile terms* where a term represents a piece of code. In essence, a node cannot access remote resources in the same way that it accesses its own local resources, but it may receive mobile terms in which references to remote resources are exposed. Therefore the safety of mobile terms is achieved by supporting direct access to remote resources (*e.g.*, remote file access, remote memory access), as in Obliq [1], by transmitting copies of local resources along with mobile terms, as in Facile [2], by preventing references to remote resources from being dereferenced, as in Mobile UNITY [3], or by allowing all of these methods, as in λdist [4]. Our paper focuses on the third case where we reject mobile terms containing references to remote resources.

One approach to the safety of mobile terms is to build a modal type system with the modality □ [5,6,7,8] which is based on a spatial interpretation of necessity of modal logic such as S4 and S5. The basic idea is that a value of modal type □A contains a

N. Kobayashi (Ed.): APLAS 2006, LNCS 4279, pp. 217–233, 2006.

mobile term that can be evaluated at any node. By requiring that a mobile term be from a value of type □A, we ensure its safety without recourse to runtime checks.

A type system augmented with the modality □ is not, however, expressive enough for safe communications of *values*, *i.e.*, the safety of *mobile values*. In other words, we cannot rely solely on modal types □A to verify that a value communicated from one node to another is mobile (*e.g.*, when a remote procedure call returns, or when a value is written to a channel). The reason is that in general, a value of type □A contains *not a mobile value but a mobile term*. The evaluation of such a mobile term (with the intention of obtaining a mobile value) may result in a value that is not necessarily mobile because of references to local resources created during the evaluation.

As an example, consider a term of type int -> int in an ML-like language:

```
let
   val new_reference = ref 0
   val f = fn x => x + !new_reference
in
   f
end
```

The above term can be evaluated at any node and thus may be used in building a mobile term of type □(int -> int). The resultant value f, however, is not mobile because it accesses a local resource new_reference. In contrast, the following term, also of type int -> int, cannot be used in building a mobile term of type □(int -> int), but the resultant value is mobile because it does not access any local resource:

```
let
   val v = !some_existing_reference
   val f = fn x => x + v
in
   f
end
```

Hence the modality □ is irrelevant to the safety of mobile values, which should now be verified by programmers themselves.

This paper investigates a new modality ◘ which expresses that a given term evaluates to a mobile value. The basic idea is that a term contained in a value of modal type ◘A evaluates to a value that is valid at any node. For example, the first term above cannot be used in building a term of type ◘(int -> int), but the second term above may be used in building such a term. To obtain a value to be communicated to other nodes, we evaluate a term contained in a value of type ◘A. In this way, we achieve the safety of mobile values.

While the mobility of a term is independent of the mobility of the value to which it evaluates, the modality □ is weaker than the modality ◘ in that we can emulate □ with ◘. For example, we may define □A as ◘(unit -> A), in which case we check the mobility of a term M of type A by checking the mobility of a value fn _ => M of type unit -> A. Thus ◘ is inherently more expressive than □, and the use of ◘ practically eliminates the need for □. The converse is not the case, however: we cannot emulate ⊡ with □ because the modality ⊡ requires at least a distinction between terms and values, which is not provided by the type system for the modality □.

Since the modality □ is inadequate for ensuring the safety of mobile values, safe communications are restricted to mobile terms if the underlying type system uses only □. Such a restriction leads to an unusual implementation of common communication constructs in distributed computations. For example, in λ_{rpc} by Jia and Walker [7] and *Lambda 5* by Murphy *et al.* [8], a remote procedure call returns a mobile term (instead of a mobile value) which the caller node needs to further evaluate in order to obtain the final result of the remote procedure call. By focusing on mobile values rather than mobile terms, the modality ⊡ avoids such anomalies and gives a faithful implementation of common communication constructs.

In Sections 2 and 3, we develop a call-by-value language $\lambda_{\boxdot}$ with mutable references and the modality ⊡. We choose mutable references as a representative example of local resources; other kinds of local resources can be treated in an analogous way. We formulate its type system in the natural deduction style by giving introduction and elimination rules for each connective and modality. The modality ⊡ requires us to introduce a typing judgment differentiating values from terms. The type system takes into account *primitive types* (such as boolean values and integers) for which mobility is an inherent property.

In Section 4, we develop $\lambda_{\boxdot}$ into $\lambda_{\boxdot}^N$ which has a *network operational semantics* and is thus capable of modeling distributed computations. We demonstrate the use of modal types with a communication construct for remote procedure calls. The safety of mobile terms and mobile values is shown by type safety of $\lambda_{\boxdot}^N$, *i.e.*, its progress and type preservation properties.

Section 5 compares $\lambda_{\boxdot}^N$ with other modal languages for distributed computations. Section 6 concludes with future work. Due to space limitations, we refer the reader to our technical report [9] for details of all proofs.

2   Call-by-Value Language λ with Mutable References

This section reviews the type system of λ, a typical call-by-value language with mutable references, in the context of distributed computations. Figure 1 shows the definition of λ.

The syntax of λ uses metavariables A, B, C for types and M, N for terms. () is an expression of type **unit**, which we include as an example of a primitive type. $\lambda x : A.\,M$ and $M\,M'$ are a λ-abstraction and a λ-application, respectively. **ref** M allocates a fresh reference, $!M$ dereferences an existing reference, and $M := M'$ assigns a new value to a reference; a location l, of type **ref** A, is a value for a reference.

A variable x with binding $x : A$ is assumed to hold a value because λ uses the call-by-value strategy. We use a typing judgment $\Gamma \mid \Psi \vdash M : A$ to mean that term M has type A under typing context Γ and store typing Ψ; a store typing judgment $\Psi \vdash \psi$ **okay** means that store ψ conforms to store typing Ψ.

The operational semantics of λ uses a reduction judgment $M \mid \psi \longrightarrow M' \mid \psi'$ to mean that term M with store ψ reduces to term M' with store ψ' where $\psi = \psi'$ is allowed. A β-reduction judgment $M \longrightarrow_\beta M'$ uses a capture-avoiding substitution $[V/x]M$ defined in a standard way. We write $\phi[\![M]\!]$ for a term obtained by filling the hole [] in an

$$
\begin{array}{lllll}
\text{type} & A & ::= & \text{unit} \mid A \to A \mid \text{ref } A \\
\text{term} & M & ::= & () \mid x \mid \lambda x{:}A.\,M \mid M\,M \mid \text{ref } M \mid !M \mid M := M \mid l \\
\text{value} & V & ::= & () \mid \lambda x{:}A.\,M \mid l \\
\text{typing context} & \Gamma & ::= & \cdot \mid \Gamma, x : A \\
\text{store typing} & \Psi & ::= & \cdot \mid \Psi, l \mapsto A \\
\text{store} & \psi & ::= & \cdot \mid \psi, l \mapsto V
\end{array}
$$

$$
\dfrac{}{\Gamma \mid \Psi \vdash () : \text{unit}} \ \text{Unit}
$$

$$
\dfrac{x : A \in \Gamma}{\Gamma \mid \Psi \vdash x : A} \ \text{Var}
\qquad
\dfrac{\Gamma, x : A \mid \Psi \vdash M : B}{\Gamma \mid \Psi \vdash \lambda x{:}A.\,M : A \to B} \ {\to}\text{I}
\qquad
\dfrac{\Gamma \mid \Psi \vdash M : A \to B \quad \Gamma \mid \Psi \vdash N : A}{\Gamma \mid \Psi \vdash M\,N : B} \ {\to}\text{E}
$$

$$
\dfrac{\Gamma \mid \Psi \vdash M : A}{\Gamma \mid \Psi \vdash \text{ref } M : \text{ref } A} \ \text{Ref}
\qquad
\dfrac{\Gamma \mid \Psi \vdash M : \text{ref } A}{\Gamma \mid \Psi \vdash !M : A} \ \text{Deref}
\qquad
\dfrac{\Gamma \mid \Psi \vdash M : \text{ref } A \quad \Gamma \mid \Psi \vdash N : A}{\Gamma \mid \Psi \vdash M := N : \text{unit}} \ \text{Assign}
$$

$$
\dfrac{\Psi(l) = A}{\Gamma \mid \Psi \vdash l : \text{ref } A} \ \text{Loc}
\qquad
\dfrac{dom(\Psi) = dom(\psi) \quad \cdot \mid \Psi \vdash \psi(l) : \Psi(l) \ \text{for every } l \in dom(\psi)}{\Psi \vdash \psi \ \text{okay}} \ \text{Store}
$$

$$
(\lambda x{:}A.\,M)\,V \ \longrightarrow_\beta \ [V/x]M
$$

$$
\text{evaluation context} \quad \phi \quad ::= \quad [\,] \mid \phi\,M \mid V\,\phi \mid \text{ref } \phi \mid !\phi \mid \phi := M \mid V := \phi
$$

$$
\dfrac{M \longrightarrow_\beta M'}{\phi[\![M]\!] \mid \psi \longrightarrow \phi[\![M']\!] \mid \psi} \ Red_\beta
\qquad
\dfrac{l \notin dom(\psi)}{\phi[\![\text{ref } V]\!] \mid \psi \longrightarrow \phi[\![l]\!] \mid \psi, l \mapsto V} \ Ref
$$

$$
\dfrac{\psi(l) = V}{\phi[\![!l]\!] \mid \psi \longrightarrow \phi[\![V]\!] \mid \psi} \ Deref
\qquad
\dfrac{}{\phi[\![l := V]\!] \mid \psi \longrightarrow \phi[\![()]\!] \mid [l \mapsto V]\psi} \ Assign
$$

Fig. 1. Definition of the language λ

evaluation context ϕ with M. $[l \mapsto V]\psi$ replaces $l \mapsto V'$ in ψ by $l \mapsto V$; we write $\psi(l)$ and $\Psi(l)$ for the value and the type to which l is mapped under ψ and Ψ, respectively.

In the context of distributed computations, $x : A$ in a typing context Γ means that variable x holds a value of type A that is valid at a hypothetical node where typechecking takes place, which we call the *current node* throughout the paper. Then a typing judgment $\Gamma \mid \Psi \vdash M : A$ means that if both typing context Γ and store typing Ψ are satisfied, the evaluation of term M at the current node returns a value V of type A. It does not, however, tell us if M is a mobile term that can be evaluated at other nodes. More importantly, it does not tell us if V is a mobile value that is valid at other nodes. Therefore the above type system is not expressive enough for the safety of mobile terms and mobile values in distributed computations.

$\lambda_\square$ extends λ with the modality $\square$ which is concerned with *where we can use the result of evaluating a given term*. We call $\lambda_\square$ a *modal language* because of its use of the modality $\square$ in the type system. Although its type system addresses the safety of mobile values, $\lambda_\square$ is still a language for stand-alone computations in which no communications between nodes actually take place. The modality $\square$ does not originate from modal logic, but the type system of $\lambda_\square$ reuses typing judgments for necessity of modal logic by Pfenning and Davies [10].

3 Modal Language $\lambda_\square$

The idea behind the modality $\square$ is two-fold. First, if a term M is well-typed under an empty typing context and an empty store typing, *i.e.*, $\cdot \mid \cdot \vdash M : A$, we can evaluate it at any node. Intuitively M is valid at any node, or *globally valid*, because its evaluation depends on no existing local resources. As a special case, if a value V satisfies $\cdot \mid \cdot \vdash V : A$, it is globally valid because it does not contain references (to local resources). Second the typing judgment $\Gamma \mid \Psi \vdash M : A$ of λ is unable to express the property that the value to which term M evaluates is globally valid. Therefore we need an additional typing judgment for the type system of $\lambda_\square$ so as to express such properties of terms.

In order to indicate that a variable stores a globally valid value, we introduce a *global typing context* Δ. Γ is now called a *local typing context*.

$$
\begin{aligned}
\text{global typing context} \quad &\Delta \quad ::= \quad \cdot \mid \Delta, x \sim A \\
\text{local typing context} \quad &\Gamma \quad ::= \quad \cdot \mid \Gamma, x : A
\end{aligned}
$$

A binding $x \sim A$ in Δ means that variable x holds a globally valid value of type A; hence a global typing context does not affect the mobility of a term being typechecked.

We use a typing judgment $\Delta; \Gamma \mid \Psi \vdash M : A$ to mean that under global typing context Δ, local typing context Γ, and store typing Ψ, term M evaluates to a value of type A valid at the current node; it may be viewed as a typing judgment for λ where a typing context is split into Δ and Γ. We introduce a new form of typing judgment $\Delta; \Gamma \mid \Psi \vdash M \sim A$ to mean that M evaluates to a globally valid value of type A (which is also valid at the current node). By the definition of these typing judgments, the following typing rules hold independently of the syntax of $\lambda_\square$:

$$
\frac{x \sim A \in \Delta}{\Delta; \Gamma \mid \Psi \vdash x \sim A} \text{ GVar} \qquad \frac{x \sim A \in \Delta}{\Delta; \Gamma \mid \Psi \vdash x : A} \text{ GVar}' \qquad \frac{\Delta; \cdot \mid \cdot \vdash V : A}{\Delta; \Gamma \mid \Psi \vdash V \sim A} \text{ GVal}
$$

The rule GVar′ says that a globally valid variable x in $x \sim A$ is valid at the current node. The rule GVal conforms to the definition of the new typing judgment: the premise check if V is globally valid, in which case the conclusion holds because V is already a value.

The type system of $\lambda_\square$ classifies types into three kinds: *primitive types P*, *potentially global types G*, and *local types L*. A primitive type is one for which mobility is an inherent property. For example, (), of type unit, is atomic and cannot contain references to local resources. Therefore values of type unit are always globally valid, which implies that unit is a primitive type. Formally we define primitive types as follows:

Definition 1. *P is a primitive type if and only if $\Delta; \Gamma \mid \Psi \vdash V : P$ implies $\Delta; \cdot \mid \cdot \vdash V : P$.*

By the definition of primitive types, $\Delta; \Gamma \mid \Psi \vdash M : P$ semantically implies $\Delta; \Gamma \mid \Psi \vdash M \sim P$. In order to relieve the programmer of the burden of explicitly expressing mobility for primitive types, $\lambda_\square$ provides a separate typing rule for primitive types:

$$
\frac{\Delta; \Gamma \mid \Psi \vdash M : P}{\Delta; \Gamma \mid \Psi \vdash M \sim P} \text{ Prim} \sim
$$

In contrast to primitive types, a local type L has no globally valid values associated with it. For example, locations, of type ref A, can never be globally valid, which implies that ref A is a local type. Thus $\Delta; \Gamma \mid \Psi \vdash M \sim L$ never holds. (See Proposition 2.) A value of a potentially global type may or may not be globally valid depending on whether it contains references to local resources. For example, a function type $A \to B$ is a potentially global type.

$\lambda_\square$ introduces two new terms box M and letbox $x = M$ in N:

$$\text{term} \quad M \quad ::= \quad \cdots \mid \text{box } M \mid \text{letbox } x = M \text{ in } M$$
$$\text{value} \quad V \quad ::= \quad \cdots \mid \text{box } M$$

box M has a modal type $\square A$, and expects M to evaluate to a globally valid value. letbox $x = M$ in N expects M to evaluate to box M'; then it evaluates M' before substituting the resultant value for x in N. The β-reduction rule for the modality $\square$ uses a capture-avoiding substitution $[V/x]M$ extended in a standard way.

$$\text{letbox } x = \text{box } V \text{ in } M \quad \longrightarrow_\beta \quad [V/x]M$$
$$\text{evaluation context} \quad \phi \quad ::= \quad \cdots \mid \text{letbox } x = \phi \text{ in } M \mid \text{letbox } x = \text{box } \phi \text{ in } M$$

box M corresponds to the introduction rule for the modality $\square$. Note that in letbox $x = M$ in N, the type of M does not determine the form of the typing judgment for the whole term. That is, regardless of the type of M, there are two possibilities for where the result of evaluating N is valid: at the current node and at any node. Therefore $\square$ has one introduction rule and two elimination rules:

$$\frac{\Delta; \Gamma \mid \Psi \vdash M \sim A}{\Delta; \Gamma \mid \Psi \vdash \text{box } M : \square A} \; \square\text{I} \qquad \frac{\Delta; \Gamma \mid \Psi \vdash M : \square A \quad \Delta, x \sim A; \Gamma \mid \Psi \vdash N : C}{\Delta; \Gamma \mid \Psi \vdash \text{letbox } x = M \text{ in } N : C} \; \square\text{E}$$

$$\frac{\Delta; \Gamma \vdash M : \square A \quad \Delta, x \sim A; \Gamma \mid \Psi \vdash N \sim C}{\Delta; \Gamma \mid \Psi \vdash \text{letbox } x = M \text{ in } N \sim C} \; \square\text{E}'$$

Figure 2 summarizes the definition of $\lambda_\square$. The operational semantics of $\lambda_\square$ uses the same reduction judgment $M \mid \psi \longrightarrow M' \mid \psi'$ as in λ. Proposition 3 confirms that $\Delta; \Gamma \mid \Psi \vdash M \sim A$ is stronger than $\Delta; \Gamma \mid \Psi \vdash M : A$.

Proposition 2. *If no variables are bound to local types in Δ, then $\Delta; \Gamma \mid \Psi \vdash M \sim L$ is not derivable. That is, if $\Delta; \Gamma \mid \Psi \vdash M \sim A$, then A is not a local type.*

Proposition 3. *The rule* $\dfrac{\Delta; \Gamma \mid \Psi \vdash M \sim A}{\Delta; \Gamma \mid \Psi \vdash M : A}$ Global *is admissible.*

3.1 Example

We illustrate the use of the modality $\square$ by rewriting in $\lambda_\square$ the two examples in Introduction. We assume a primitive type int for integers and an infix operator $+$ for adding two integers. We encode a modal type $\square A$ as $\square(\text{unit} \to A)$, and check the mobility of a *term* M of type A by checking the mobility of a *value* $\lambda\_: \text{unit}. M$ of type unit $\to A$ where $\_$ denotes a fresh variable.

The first example is written in $\lambda_\square$ as follows:

$$M_1 = (\lambda r : \text{ref int}. \lambda x : \text{int}. x + !r) \text{ (ref 0)}$$

We cannot use M_1 to build a term of type $\square(\text{int} \to \text{int})$ because there is no typing derivation of $\Delta; \Gamma \mid \Psi \vdash M_1 \sim \text{int} \to \text{int}$:

$$\frac{\dfrac{\textit{(no typing rule applicable)}}{\Delta; \Gamma \mid \Psi \vdash (\lambda r : \text{ref int}. \lambda x : \text{int}. x + !r) \text{ (ref 0)} \sim \text{int} \to \text{int}}}{\Delta; \Gamma \mid \Psi \vdash \text{box } (\lambda r : \text{ref int}. \lambda x : \text{int}. x + !r) \text{ (ref 0)} : \square(\text{int} \to \text{int})} \; \square\text{I}$$

type	A	$::=$	$P \mid G \mid L$
primitive type	P	$::=$	unit
potentially global type	G	$::=$	$A \to A \mid \Box A$
local type	L	$::=$	ref A
term	M	$::=$	$\cdots \mid \text{box } M \mid \text{letbox } x = M \text{ in } M$
value	V	$::=$	$\cdots \mid \text{box } M$
global typing context	Δ	$::=$	$\cdot \mid \Delta, x \sim A$
local typing context	Γ	$::=$	$\cdot \mid \Gamma, x : A$

$$\frac{x \sim A \in \Delta}{\Delta; \Gamma \mid \Psi \vdash x \sim A} \ \text{GVar} \qquad \frac{x \sim A \in \Delta}{\Delta; \Gamma \mid \Psi \vdash x : A} \ \text{GVar}'$$

$$\frac{\Delta; \Gamma \mid \Psi \vdash M \sim A}{\Delta; \Gamma \mid \Psi \vdash \text{box } M : \Box A} \ \Box\text{I} \qquad \frac{\Delta; \Gamma \mid \Psi \vdash M : \Box A \quad \Delta, x \sim A; \Gamma \mid \Psi \vdash N : C}{\Delta; \Gamma \mid \Psi \vdash \text{letbox } x = M \text{ in } N : C} \ \Box\text{E}$$

$$\frac{\Delta; \Gamma \mid \Psi \vdash M : \Box A \quad \Delta, x \sim A; \Gamma \mid \Psi \vdash N \sim C}{\Delta; \Gamma \mid \Psi \vdash \text{letbox } x = M \text{ in } N \sim C} \ \Box\text{E}'$$

$$\frac{\Delta; \Gamma \mid \Psi \vdash M : P}{\Delta; \Gamma \mid \Psi \vdash M \sim P} \ \text{Prim}\sim \qquad \frac{\Delta; \cdot \mid \cdot \vdash V : A}{\Delta; \Gamma \mid \Psi \vdash V \sim A} \ \text{GVal}$$

$$\text{letbox } x = \text{box } V \text{ in } M \quad \longrightarrow_\beta \quad [V/x]M$$

$$\text{evaluation context} \quad \phi \quad ::= \quad \cdots \mid \text{letbox } x = \phi \text{ in } M \mid \text{letbox } x = \text{box } \phi \text{ in } M$$

Fig. 2. Definition of the modal language $\lambda_\Box$

M_1 itself, however, is mobile because $\lambda_- : \text{unit}$. M_1 is mobile:

$$\frac{\vdots}{\dfrac{\Delta; \cdot \mid \cdot \vdash \lambda_- : \text{unit}. \ (\lambda r : \text{ref int}. \ \lambda x : \text{int}. \ x + !r) \ (\text{ref } 0) : \text{unit} \to (\text{int} \to \text{int})}{\Delta; \Gamma \mid \Psi \vdash \lambda_- : \text{unit}. \ (\lambda r : \text{ref int}. \ \lambda x : \text{int}. \ x + !r) \ (\text{ref } 0) \sim \text{unit} \to (\text{int} \to \text{int})}} \ \text{GVal}$$

The second example is written in $\lambda_\Box$ as follows where variable r is bound to an existing reference of type ref int:

$$M_2 = \text{letbox } v = \text{box } !r \text{ in } \lambda x : \text{int}. \ x + v$$

We can use M_2 to build a term of type $\Box(\text{int} \to \text{int})$:

$$\cfrac{\cfrac{\cfrac{\cfrac{\Delta; \Gamma, r : \text{ref int} \mid \Psi \vdash r : \text{ref int}}{\Delta; \Gamma, r : \text{ref int} \mid \Psi \vdash !r : \text{int}} \ \text{Deref}}{\cfrac{\Delta; \Gamma, r : \text{ref int} \mid \Psi \vdash !r \sim \text{int}}{\Delta; \Gamma, r : \text{ref int} \mid \Psi \vdash \text{box } !r : \Box \text{int}}} \ \Box\text{I}}{\Delta; \Gamma, r : \text{ref int} \mid \Psi \vdash \text{letbox } v = \text{box } !r \text{ in } \lambda x : \text{int}. \ x + v \sim \text{int} \to \text{int}}}{\Delta; \Gamma, r : \text{ref int} \mid \Psi \vdash \text{box letbox } v = \text{box } !r \text{ in } \lambda x : \text{int}. \ x + v : \Box(\text{int} \to \text{int})} \ \Box\text{I}$$

with the right branch:

$$\cfrac{\cfrac{\vdots}{\cfrac{\Delta, v \sim \text{int}; x : \text{int} \mid \cdot \vdash x + v : \text{int}}{\Delta, v \sim \text{int}; \cdot \mid \cdot \vdash \lambda x : \text{int}. \ x + v : \text{int} \to \text{int}} \ \to\text{I}}}{\Delta, v \sim \text{int}; \Gamma, r : \text{ref int} \mid \Psi \vdash \lambda x : \text{int}. \ x + v \sim \text{int} \to \text{int}} \ \text{GVal}$$

M_2 itself, however, is not mobile because $\lambda_- : \text{unit}$. M_2 is not mobile:

$$\frac{\textit{(impossible to typecheck because of r)}}{\dfrac{\Delta; \cdot \mid \cdot \vdash \lambda_- : \text{unit}. \ \text{letbox } v = \text{box } !r \text{ in } \lambda x : \text{int}. \ x + v : \text{unit} \to (\text{int} \to \text{int})}{\Delta; \Gamma, r : \text{ref int} \mid \Psi \vdash \lambda_- : \text{unit}. \ \text{letbox } v = \text{box } !r \text{ in } \lambda x : \text{int}. \ x + v \sim \text{unit} \to (\text{int} \to \text{int})}} \ \text{GVal}$$

A more straightforward but less satisfactory translation of the second example uses a λ-application instead of a letbox construct:

$$M_2' = (\lambda v : \text{int.} \ \lambda x : \text{int.} \ x + v) \ (!r)$$

M_2' is operationally equivalent to M_2, but cannot be used in building a term of type $\Box(\text{int} \rightarrow \text{int})$:

$$\cfrac{\cfrac{(\textit{no typing rule applicable})}{\Delta; \Gamma, r : \text{ref int} \mid \Psi \vdash (\lambda v : \text{int.} \ \lambda x : \text{int.} \ x + v) \ (!r) \sim \text{int} \rightarrow \text{int}}}{\Delta; \Gamma, r : \text{ref int} \mid \Psi \vdash \text{box} \ (\lambda v : \text{int.} \ \lambda x : \text{int.} \ x + v) \ (!r) : \Box(\text{int} \rightarrow \text{int})} \ \Box\text{I}$$

The reason why box M_2' fails to have type $\Box(\text{int} \rightarrow \text{int})$ is that the type of $\lambda v : \text{int.} \ \lambda x : \text{int.} \ x + v$, namely int $\rightarrow$ (int $\rightarrow$ int), fails to express that a mobile value of type int $\rightarrow$ int is returned. In fact, the inner λ-abstraction $\lambda x : \text{int.} \ x + v$ cannot be a mobile value anyway, since a binding $v \sim \text{int}$ is not added to a global typing context.

We could introduce a new type $A \ \boxdot\!\!\rightarrow B$ for those λ-abstractions taking a value of type A and returning a mobile value of type B. The typing rules for the new connective $\boxdot\!\!\rightarrow$ are given as follows:

$$\cfrac{\Delta; \Gamma, x : A \mid \Psi \vdash M \sim B}{\Delta; \Gamma \mid \Psi \vdash \lambda x : A. \ M : A \ \boxdot\!\!\rightarrow B} \ \rightarrow\text{I}_\Box \qquad \cfrac{\Delta; \Gamma \mid \Psi \vdash M : A \ \boxdot\!\!\rightarrow B \quad \Delta; \Gamma \mid \Psi \vdash N : A}{\Delta; \Gamma \mid \Psi \vdash M \ N \sim B} \ \rightarrow\text{E}_\Box$$

Although the new connective $\boxdot\!\!\rightarrow$ allows more flexibility in programming, we decide not to include it in the definition of $\lambda_\Box$ because a simple encoding of $A \ \boxdot\!\!\rightarrow B$ as $A \rightarrow \Box B$ suffices. For example, we can eliminate the rule $\rightarrow\text{I}_\Box$ by translating $\lambda x : A. \ M : A \ \boxdot\!\!\rightarrow B$ into $\lambda x : A. \ \text{box} \ M : A \rightarrow \Box B$ and the rule $\rightarrow\text{E}_\Box$ by translating $M \ N$ into letbox $v = M \ N$ in v.

3.2   Type Safety of $\lambda_\Box$

The proof of type safety of $\lambda_\Box$ is routine except for the formulation of the substitution theorem (Theorem 4). In the second clause of the substitution theorem, $\Delta; \cdot \mid \cdot \vdash V : A$ proves that V is a globally valid value of type A, which we substitute for variable x in term M. Corollary 5 follows from the definition of primitive types as given in Definition 1.

Theorem 4   (Substitution)
   If $\Delta; \Gamma \mid \Psi \vdash V : A$ and $\Delta; \Gamma, x : A \mid \Psi \vdash M : C$, then $\Delta; \Gamma \mid \Psi \vdash [V/x]M : C$.
   If $\Delta; \Gamma \mid \Psi \vdash V : A$ and $\Delta; \Gamma, x : A \mid \Psi \vdash M \sim C$, then $\Delta; \Gamma \mid \Psi \vdash [V/x]M \sim C$.
   If $\Delta; \cdot \mid \cdot \vdash V : A$ and $\Delta, x \sim A; \Gamma \mid \Psi \vdash M : C$, then $\Delta; \Gamma \mid \Psi \vdash [V/x]M : C$.
   If $\Delta; \cdot \mid \cdot \vdash V : A$ and $\Delta, x \sim A; \Gamma \mid \Psi \vdash M \sim C$, then $\Delta; \Gamma \mid \Psi \vdash [V/x]M \sim C$.

Corollary 5
   If $\Delta; \Gamma \mid \Psi \vdash V : P$ and $\Delta, x \sim P; \Gamma \mid \Psi \vdash M : C$, then $\Delta; \Gamma \mid \Psi \vdash [V/x]M : C$.
   If $\Delta; \Gamma \mid \Psi \vdash V : P$ and $\Delta, x \sim P; \Gamma \mid \Psi \vdash M \sim C$, then $\Delta; \Gamma \mid \Psi \vdash [V/x]M \sim C$.

Theorem 6   (Progress). *Suppose that term M satisfies $\cdot; \cdot \mid \Psi \vdash M : A$ or $\cdot; \cdot \mid \Psi \vdash M \sim A$ for some store typing Ψ and type A. Then either:*
   (1) M is a value, or
   (2) for any store ψ such that $\Psi \vdash \psi$ okay, there exist some term M' and store ψ' such that $M \mid \psi \longrightarrow M' \mid \psi'$.

Theorem 7 (Type preservation)

Suppose $\begin{cases} \cdot;\cdot \mid \Psi \vdash M : A \\ \Psi \vdash \psi \text{ okay} \\ M \mid \psi \longrightarrow M' \mid \psi' \end{cases}$.

Then there exists a store typing Ψ' *such that* $\begin{cases} \cdot;\cdot \mid \Psi' \vdash M' : A \\ \Psi \subset \Psi' \\ \Psi' \vdash \psi' \text{ okay} \end{cases}$.

Suppose $\begin{cases} \cdot;\cdot \mid \Psi \vdash M \sim A \\ \Psi \vdash \psi \text{ okay} \\ M \mid \psi \longrightarrow M' \mid \psi' \end{cases}$.

Then there exists a store typing Ψ' *such that* $\begin{cases} \cdot;\cdot \mid \Psi' \vdash M' \sim A \\ \Psi \subset \Psi' \\ \Psi' \vdash \psi' \text{ okay} \end{cases}$.

3.3 Logic for $\lambda_\Box$

The type system for modal types $\Box A$ is unusual in that it differentiates values (*i.e.*, terms in weak head normal form) from ordinary terms, as shown in the rule GVal. This differentiation implies that the logic corresponding to the modality $\Box$ via the Curry-Howard isomorphism requires a judgment that inspects not only hypotheses in a proof but also the proof structure itself (*e.g.*, inferences rules used in the proof). Thus the modality $\Box$ sets itself apart from other modalities and is not found in any other logic.

In the pure fragment of $\lambda_\Box$ without primitive types and local types, the modality $\Box$ shows similarities with modal possibility $\Diamond$ and lax modality $\bigcirc$ in [10]. Specifically a proof-theoretic analysis of $\Box$ gives rise to a new form of substitution $\langle M/x \rangle N$ which is defined inductively on the structure of the term being substituted (*i.e.*, M) instead of the term being substituted into (*i.e.*, N). Let us interpret a β-reduction rule as the reduction of a typing derivation in which an introduction rule is followed by a corresponding elimination rule. For example, the β-reduction rule for the connective $\rightarrow$ may be seen as the reduction of the following typing derivation in the pure λ-calculus (where we omit store typings):

$$\dfrac{\dfrac{\Gamma, x : A \vdash M : B}{\Gamma \vdash \lambda x{:}A.\, M : A \rightarrow B} \rightarrow \text{I} \quad \Gamma \vdash N : A}{\Gamma \vdash (\lambda x{:}A.\, M)\, N : B} \rightarrow \text{E} \qquad \longrightarrow_\beta \qquad \Gamma \vdash [N/x]M : B$$

Likewise we obtain a β-reduction rule for $\Box$ from the reduction of a typing derivation in which the introduction rule $\Box$I is followed by the elimination rule $\Box$E or $\Box$E' (where we omit store typings):

$$\dfrac{\dfrac{\Delta; \Gamma \vdash M \sim A}{\Delta; \Gamma \vdash \text{box } M : \Box A} \,\Box\text{I} \quad \Delta, x \sim A; \Gamma \vdash N : C}{\Delta; \Gamma \vdash \text{letbox } x = \text{box } M \text{ in } N : C} \,\Box\text{E} \qquad \longrightarrow_\beta \qquad \Delta; \Gamma \vdash \langle M/x \rangle N : C$$

To see why $\langle M/x \rangle N$ is defined inductively on the structure of M, observe that the reduction of letbox $x = $ box M in N requires an analysis of M instead of N. The reason is that only a value can be substituted for x, but M may not be a value; therefore we have to analyze M to decide how to transform the whole term so that x is eventually replaced by a value. Conceptually N should be replicated at those places within M where the evaluation of M is finished, so that M and N are evaluated exactly once and in that order. If M is already a value V, we reduce the whole term to $[V/x]N$. Thus we are led to define $\langle M/x \rangle N$ as follows:

$$\langle V/x \rangle N \;=\; [V/x]N$$
$$\langle \text{letbox } x' = M' \text{ in } M''/x \rangle N \;=\; \text{letbox } x' = M' \text{ in } \langle M''/x \rangle N$$

Note that we *cannot* define $\langle M_1\, M_2/x \rangle N$ because without primitive types and the rule Prim$\sim$, there is no typing derivation of $\Delta; \Gamma \vdash M_1\, M_2 \sim A$ and thus box $M_1\, M_2$ cannot be well-typed.

In the presence of primitive types, the β-reduction

$$\text{letbox } x = \text{box } M \text{ in } N \longrightarrow_\beta \langle M/x \rangle N$$

is no longer valid because letbox $x = $ box M in N may typecheck while $\langle M/x \rangle N$ is undefined. For example, $M = M_1\, M_2$ of type unit satisfies $\Delta; \Gamma \vdash M \sim$ unit by the rule Prim$\sim$, but $\langle M_1\, M_2/x \rangle N$ is undefined. Intuitively the rule Prim$\sim$ disguises an unanalyzable term of a primitive type as an analyzable term. Thus, in order to reduce letbox $x = $ box M in N, the operational semantics of $\lambda_\square$ is forced to reduce M into a value V first, instead of analyzing M to transform the whole term. Then an ordinary substitution $[V/x]N$ suffices for the reduction of letbox $x = $ box M in N.

We close this section with a brief discussion of the properties of the modality $\square$.

- $\square A \rightarrow A$ $\hspace{5cm} \lambda x\!:\!\square A.\, \text{letbox } y = x \text{ in } y$
  A mobile value is a special case of an ordinary term.
- $\square A \rightarrow \square\square A$ $\hspace{4.3cm} \lambda x\!:\!\square A.\, \text{letbox } y = x \text{ in box box } y$
  A mobile value itself is mobile.
- $\square(A \rightarrow B) \rightarrow \square A \nrightarrow \square B$
  A mobile λ-abstraction does not necessarily return a mobile value.

4 $\lambda_\square^N$ with a Network Operational Semantics

While the type system of $\lambda_\square$ is appropriate for understanding the role of the modality $\square$, it is not expressive enough for distributed computations which may generate terms whose type is determined by *remote nodes*. For example, a future construct [11] initiates a stand-alone computation at a remote node and returns a pointer to the remote node; then the type of the pointer is determined by the term being evaluated at the remote node.

This section extends the type system of $\lambda_\square$ so that we can typecheck such terms, and also develop a network operational semantics to model distributed computations. We refer to the resultant language as $\lambda_\square^N$. We incorporate a communication construct for remote procedure calls into $\lambda_\square$ so as to allow communications between nodes to actually take place. Type safety of $\lambda_\square^N$ ensures the safety of mobile terms and mobile values.

4.1 Extended Type System and Network Operational Semantics

We represent the state of a network with a *configuration* π which records term M and store ψ associated with each node γ. A *configuration typing* Π records the type of the term being evaluated at each node. We assume that no node appears more than once in π, and consider Π as an unordered set. As a new term, γ serves as a reference to a node.

$$
\begin{array}{llll}
\text{term} & M & ::= & \cdots \mid \gamma & \text{(node reference)} \\
\text{configuration} & \pi & ::= & \cdot \mid \pi, \{M \mid \psi @ \gamma\} \\
\text{configuration typing} & \Pi & ::= & \cdot \mid \Pi, \gamma \sim A & (A \neq L)
\end{array}
$$

- $\{M \mid \psi @ \gamma\}$ in π means that node γ is currently evaluating term M with store ψ.
- $\gamma \sim A$ in Π means that the term at node γ evaluates to a value of type A. For the sake of simplicity, we require that every term in a network evaluates to a globally valid value.

The extended type system is formulated with a *configuration typing judgment* $\Pi \vdash \pi$ okay which means that configuration π has configuration typing Π. In order to be able to typecheck a node reference γ (which is a term), we include a configuration typing Π in each typing judgment: $\Delta; \Gamma \mid \Psi \mid \Pi \vdash M : A$, $\Delta; \Gamma \mid \Psi \mid \Pi \vdash M \sim A$, and $\Psi \mid \Pi \vdash \psi$ okay. The rules for the extended type system are derived from (and given the same name as) the previous rules by including a configuration typing in every typing judgment. We need two additional typing rules Node and Node' for node references; the rule Conf may be regarded as the definition of the configuration typing judgment.

$$
\frac{\gamma \sim A \in \Pi}{\Delta; \Gamma \mid \Psi \mid \Pi \vdash \gamma \sim A} \text{ Node} \qquad \frac{\gamma \sim A \in \Pi}{\Delta; \Gamma \mid \Psi \mid \Pi \vdash \gamma : A} \text{ Node'}
$$

$$
\frac{dom(\Pi) = dom(\pi) \quad \begin{array}{c} \gamma \sim A \in \Pi \\ \Psi \mid \Pi \vdash \psi \text{ okay} \\ \cdot; \cdot \mid \Psi \mid \Pi \vdash M \sim A \end{array} \quad \text{for every } \{M \mid \psi @ \gamma\} \in \pi}{\Pi \vdash \pi \text{ okay}} \text{ Conf}
$$

The network operational semantics is formulated with a *configuration reduction judgment* $\pi \Longrightarrow \pi'$, which means that configuration π reduces (or evolves) to configuration π'. We provide two rules for the configuration reduction judgment:

$$
\frac{M \mid \psi \longrightarrow M' \mid \psi'}{\pi, \{M \mid \psi @ \gamma\} \Longrightarrow \pi, \{M' \mid \psi' @ \gamma\}} \text{ Red}
$$

$$
\frac{}{\pi, \{\phi[\![\gamma']\!] \mid \psi @ \gamma\}, \{V \mid \psi' @ \gamma'\} \Longrightarrow \pi, \{\phi[\![V]\!] \mid \psi @ \gamma\}, \{V \mid \psi' @ \gamma'\}} \text{ Sync}
$$

The rule *Red* says that stand-alone computations at individual nodes are part of a distributed computation. In the rule *Sync*, a node reference γ' suspends the stand-alone computation at node γ until it is replaced by a mobile value V through a synchronization operation with node γ'. That is, node reference γ' is *not* a value, but reduces to a mobile value (which is globally valid) only after node γ' has finished evaluating a term. Note that a configuration reduction is non-deterministic because the rule *Red* can choose an arbitrary node γ from a given configuration.

4.2 Communication Construct for Remote Procedure Calls

The network operational semantics becomes interesting only with communication constructs; without communication constructs, all nodes perform stand-alone computations independently of each other, and type safety holds trivially.

In designing communication constructs, we could begin with an existing modal logic, such as S4 and S5, and adhere to a spatial interpretation of the modalities in it. Then there arise a few logically motivated primitive operations, with which we can implement various communication constructs. This approach is appealing because of the strong logical foundation underlying communication constructs as well as the pleasant correspondence between modal logic and distributed computations.

A strict adherence to a spatial interpretation of modal logic, however, sacrifices flexibility in programming. For example, all previous work on modal languages for distributed computations [6,7,8] builds on the idea of using modal types $\Box A$ for mobile *terms* that may be evaluated at any node in the network, which is a typical spatial interpretation of the modality $\Box$. As modal types $\Box A$ do not ensure the safety of mobile values and safe communications are thus restricted to mobile terms, it is difficult to give a faithful implementation of those communication constructs (such as remote procedure calls, future constructs, and communication channels) that expect or return mobile values.

Since it is not concerned with "how" to transmit mobile values between nodes, the modality $\Box$ itself does not specify a principle for the design of communication constructs in $\lambda_\Box^N$. Instead we have to design each communication construct individually by exploiting node references γ in conjunction with the rule *Sync*. We do not believe that our approach is *ad hoc*, since not every communication construct can be given a logical interpretation anyway (*e.g.*, communication channels). In fact, even λ_{rpc} [7] and *Lambda 5* [8], both of which are based on a spatial interpretation of modal logic S5, introduce primitive operations which are logically "motivated," but do not actually have their counterparts in S5.

As an illustration, we develop a communication construct for remote procedure calls. We use the natural deduction style by giving introduction and elimination rules for it. (Thus our communication construct is also logically motivated to a certain extent.) We can use the same idea to develop similar communication constructs, such as future constructs, that transmit both mobile terms and mobile values.

A remote procedure call transmits a mobile term M to a remote node γ to initiate a stand-alone computation, and then waits for the result of evaluating M. In order to ensure the safety of the remote procedure call, M needs to satisfy the following two conditions:

- M itself is globally valid so that the evaluation of M at node γ is safe.
- M evaluates to a globally valid value so that the result of the remote procedure call is valid.

We can test if M satisfies the two conditions by typechecking box box M:

- Typechecking the outer box construct tests if box M evaluates to a globally valid value, in which case M is also globally valid because box M is already a value.
- Typechecking the inner box construct tests if M evaluates to a globally valid value.

Thus, under typing contexts Δ and Γ and store typing Ψ, we have to prove $\Delta; \cdot \mid \cdot \vdash M \sim A$:

$$\frac{\dfrac{\dfrac{\Delta; \cdot \mid \cdot \vdash M \sim A}{\Delta; \cdot \mid \cdot \vdash \text{box } M : \Box A} \ \Box\text{I}}{\Delta; \Gamma \mid \Psi \vdash \text{box } M \sim \Box A} \ \text{GVal}}{\Delta; \Gamma \mid \Psi \vdash \text{box box } M : \Box\Box A} \ \Box\text{I}$$

We do not, however, use a term box box M of type $\Box\Box A$ for a remote procedure call because there is no way to tell whether such a term is intended for a remote procedure call or just for creating a globally valid value. Instead we introduce a new modality $\Box^2$ specifically designed for remote procedure calls. As far as the type system is concerned, we may think of $\Box^2 A$ as an abbreviation of $\Box\Box A$. We use box^2 M and letbox^2 $x = M$ in N for the introduction and elimination rules for $\Box^2$, respectively:

$$
\begin{array}{lllll}
\text{potentially global type} & G & ::= & \cdots \mid \Box^2 A \\
\text{term} & M & ::= & \cdots \mid \text{box}^2\, M \mid \text{letbox}^2\, x = M \text{ in } M \\
\text{value} & V & ::= & \cdots \mid \text{box}^2\, M
\end{array}
$$

$$\frac{\Delta; \cdot \mid \cdot \vdash M \sim A}{\Delta; \Gamma \mid \Psi \vdash \text{box}^2\, M : \Box^2 A} \ \Box^2\text{I} \qquad \frac{\Delta; \Gamma \mid \Psi \vdash M : \Box^2 A \quad \Delta, x \sim A; \Gamma \mid \Psi \vdash N : C}{\Delta; \Gamma \mid \Psi \vdash \text{letbox}^2\, x = M \text{ in } N : C} \ \Box^2\text{E}$$

$$\frac{\Delta; \Gamma \mid \Psi \vdash M : \Box^2 A \quad \Delta, x \sim A; \Gamma \mid \Psi \vdash N \sim C}{\Delta; \Gamma \mid \Psi \vdash \text{letbox}^2\, x = M \text{ in } N \sim C} \ \Box^2\text{E}'$$

In the rules $\Box^2\text{E}$ and $\Box^2\text{E}'$, it helps to think of letbox^2 $x = M$ in N as letbox $x' = M$ in letbox $x = x'$ in N where x' is a fresh variable.

As for the operational semantics, $\Box^2 A$ diverges from $\Box\Box A$. letbox^2 $x = M$ in N at node γ expects M to evaluate to box^2 M'; then it makes a remote procedure call by starting an evaluation of M' at a fresh node γ' and replacing M' by a node reference γ'. When the remote procedure call returns a (globally valid) mobile value V, we replace node reference γ' by V, and then reduce letbox^2 $x = $ box^2 V in N to $[V/x]N$.

$$\text{letbox}^2\, x = \text{box}^2\, V \text{ in } M \quad \longrightarrow_\beta \quad [V/x]M$$

$$\text{evaluation context} \quad \phi \quad ::= \quad \cdots \mid \text{letbox}^2\, x = \phi \text{ in } M \mid \text{letbox}^2\, x = \text{box}^2\, [] \text{ in } M$$

$$\frac{M \neq \gamma' \quad \text{fresh node reference } \gamma'}{\pi, \left\{\phi[\![\text{letbox}^2\, x = \text{box}^2\, M \text{ in } N]\!] \mid \psi @ \gamma\right\} \Longrightarrow \atop \pi, \left\{\phi[\![\text{letbox}^2\, x = \text{box}^2\, \gamma' \text{ in } N]\!] \mid \psi @ \gamma\right\}, \{M \mid \cdot @ \gamma'\}} \ \text{RPC}$$

In the extended definition of evaluation contexts, an important restriction is that the hole in letbox^2 $x = $ box^2 $[]$ in M can be filled only with a node reference. For example, (letbox^2 $x = $ box^2 $[]$ in $M)[\![\gamma]\!]$ is allowed, but (letbox^2 $x = $ box^2 $[]$ in $M)[\![N]\!]$ is not allowed. Without this restriction, letbox^2 $x = $ box^2 N in M reduces to letbox^2 $x = $ box^2 N' in M without making a remote procedure call, if N reduces to N'. Note also that letbox^2 $x = $ box^2 γ' in M does not reduce to $[\gamma'/x]M$ because node reference γ' is not a value.

Independently of the modality $\Box^2$, the modality $\Box$ is still useful for creating arguments to remote procedure calls. That is, we use $\Box$ to compose mobile terms for remote procedure calls, and $\boxdot^2$ to transmit them to remote nodes. For example, the following term makes a remote procedure call to add two integers n_1 and n_2, both of which are bound to variables x_1 and x_2 via letbox constructs:

$$\mathsf{letbox}\ x_1 = \mathsf{box}\ n_1\ \mathsf{in}\ \mathsf{letbox}\ x_2 = \mathsf{box}\ n_2\ \mathsf{in}\ \mathsf{letbox}^2\ v = \mathsf{box}^2\ x_1 + x_2\ \mathsf{in}\ v$$

4.3   Type Safety of $\lambda_{\boxdot}^N$

Type safety of $\lambda_{\boxdot}^N$ consists of *configuration progress* (Theorem 9) and *configuration typing preservation* (Theorem 11). Proofs of Theorems 9 and 11 use type safety for stand-alone computations in $\lambda_{\boxdot}^N$ (Theorems 8 and 10).

Theorem 8 (Progress). *Suppose that term M satisfies $\cdot; \cdot \mid \Psi \mid \Pi \vdash M : A$ or $\cdot; \cdot \mid \Psi \mid \Pi \vdash M \sim A$ for some store typing Ψ, configuration typing Π, and type A. Then one of the following holds:*

(1) M is a value,

(2) $M = \phi[\![\gamma]\!]$,

(3) $M = \phi[\![\mathsf{letbox}^2\ x = \mathsf{box}^2\ M'\ \mathsf{in}\ N]\!]$,

(4) for any store ψ such that $\Psi \mid \Pi \vdash \psi$ okay, there exist some term M' and store ψ' such that $M \mid \psi \longrightarrow M' \mid \psi'$.

Theorem 9 (Configuration progress). *Suppose $\Pi \vdash \pi$ okay. Then either:*

(1) π consists only of
$$\{V \mid \psi\ @\ \gamma\},$$
$$\{\phi[\![\gamma']\!] \mid \psi\ @\ \gamma\},$$
$$\{\phi[\![\mathsf{letbox}^2\ x = \mathsf{box}^2\ \gamma'\ \mathsf{in}\ N]\!] \mid \psi\ @\ \gamma\},\ or$$
(2) there exists π' such that $\pi \Longrightarrow \pi'$.

Theorem 10 (Type preservation)

Suppose $\begin{cases} \cdot; \cdot \mid \Psi \mid \Pi \vdash M : A \\ \Psi \mid \Pi \vdash \psi\ \mathsf{okay} \\ M \mid \psi \longrightarrow M' \mid \psi' \end{cases}$.

Then there exists a store typing Ψ' such that $\begin{cases} \cdot; \cdot \mid \Psi' \mid \Pi \vdash M' : A \\ \Psi \subset \Psi' \\ \Psi' \mid \Pi \vdash \psi'\ \mathsf{okay} \end{cases}$.

Suppose $\begin{cases} \cdot; \cdot \mid \Psi \mid \Pi \vdash M \sim A \\ \Psi \mid \Pi \vdash \psi\ \mathsf{okay} \\ M \mid \psi \longrightarrow M' \mid \psi' \end{cases}$.

Then there exists a store typing Ψ' such that $\begin{cases} \cdot; \cdot \mid \Psi' \mid \Pi \vdash M' \sim A \\ \Psi \subset \Psi' \\ \Psi' \mid \Pi \vdash \psi'\ \mathsf{okay} \end{cases}$.

Theorem 11 (Configuration typing preservation)

Suppose $\begin{cases} \Pi \vdash \pi\ \mathsf{okay} \\ \pi \Longrightarrow \pi' \end{cases}$.

Then there exists a configuration typing Π' such that $\begin{cases} \Pi \subset \Pi' \\ \Pi' \vdash \pi'\ \mathsf{okay} \end{cases}$.

Type safety of $\lambda_{\square}^{N}$ implies that mobile terms and mobile values are both safe to use: well-typed terms never go wrong even in the presence of mobile terms and mobile values.

5 Related Work

Borghuis and Feijs [5] present a typed λ-calculus *MTSN* (Modal Type System for Networks) which assumes stationary services (*i.e.*, stationary code) and mobile data. An indexed modal type $\square^{\omega}(A \rightarrow B)$ represents services transforming data of type A into data of type B at node ω. MTSN is a task description language rather than a programming language, since services are all "black boxes" whose inner workings are unknown. For example, terms of type *tex* $\rightarrow$ *dvi* all describe procedures to convert *tex* files to *dvi* files. Thus reduction on terms is tantamount to simplifying procedures to achieve a certain task.

Jia and Walker [7] present a modal language λ_{rpc} which is based on hybrid logic [12] as every typing judgment explicitly specifies the current node where typechecking takes place. The modalities $\square$ and $\diamond$ are used for mobile terms that can be evaluated at any node and at a certain node, respectively.

Murphy *et al.* [8] present a modal language *Lambda 5* which addresses both code mobility and resource locality. It is based on modal logic S5 where all judgments are relativized to nodes, as in Simpson [13]. A value of type $\square A$ contains a mobile term that can be evaluated at any node, and a value of type $\diamond A$ contains a *label*, a reference to a local resource. A label may appear at remote nodes, but the type system guarantees that it is dereferenced only at the node where it is valid.

λ_{rpc} and *Lambda 5* are fundamentally different from $\lambda_{\square}^{N}$ in their use of modal types $\square A$ for remote procedure calls. In both languages, a remote procedure call, by the pull construct in λ_{rpc} and by the fetch construct in *Lambda 5*, is given a specific node where the evaluation is to occur, and therefore *does not expect a term contained in a value of type $\square A$*. Instead it expects just a term of type $\square A$, which itself may not be mobile but eventually produces a mobile term valid at any node including the caller node. The resultant mobile term is delivered to (*i.e.*, pulled or fetched by) the caller node, which needs to further evaluate it to obtain a value. As such, both languages do not address the issue of value mobility. In contrast, a remote procedure call in $\lambda_{\square}^{N}$ transmits a term *contained* in a value of type $\square^2 A$ and relies on the modality $\square^2$ to directly return a mobile value.

Moody [6] presents a system which is based on modal logic S4. The modality $\square$ is used for mobile terms that can be evaluated at any node, and the modality $\diamond$ is used for terms located at some node. As in λ_{rpc} and *Lambda 5*, remote procedure calls use modal types $\square A$ to transmit mobile terms to unknown remote nodes. Moody's system uses the elimination rules for the modalities $\square$ and $\diamond$ to send mobile terms to remote nodes, and does not provide a separate construct for remote procedure calls.

Liblit and Aiken [14] give a type-theoretic analysis of pointers in distributed computations. Their type systems distinguish between global pointers (for global address space) and local pointers (for local address space), and deal with safety and performance issues with global pointer dereferencing. While the use of type qualifiers gives a powerful type inference system for minimizing the number of global pointers, their language focuses on distributed data rather than mobile code, and it is not obvious whether their type systems can be extended to include mobile code.

6   Conclusion and Future Work

We present a modal language $\lambda_\boxdot^N$ for distributed computations which ensure the safety of both mobile terms and mobile values with a single modality $\boxdot$. The modality $\boxdot$ is more expressive than the necessity modality $\square$ from modal logic, and enables us to achieve a more faithful implementation of common communication constructs. $\boxdot$ is, however, useful in $\lambda_\boxdot^N$ only because the unit of communication includes values. That is, if the unit of communication was just terms and did not include values, $\square$ would be enough and $\boxdot$ would be unnecessary.

A drawback of $\lambda_\boxdot^N$ is that references to local resources cannot be transmitted to remote nodes. As an example, consider a location l of type ref A at node γ. Node γ wishes to share l among all its child nodes, *e.g.*, those nodes created by remote procedure calls. No child node, however, even knows the existence of l because references to local resources cannot escape their host nodes.

To overcome this drawback, we are currently investigating another modality $\diamond$ which is similar to the modality $\diamond$ of λ_{rpc} [7], *but focuses on values rather than terms*. The idea is that term M in dia M of type $\diamond A$ evaluates to a value valid at a certain node that is unknown to the type system but known to the runtime system. The modality $\diamond$ makes it possible for mobile terms to contain references to remote resources, thereby allowing more flexibility in programming for distributed computations.

References

1. Cardelli, L.:   A language with distributed scope.   In: Proceedings of the 22nd ACM SIGPLAN-SIGACT Symposium on Principles of Programming Languages, ACM Press (1995) 286–297
2. Knabe, F.C.: Language Support for Mobile Agents. PhD thesis, Department of Computer Science, Carnegie Mellon University (1995)
3. Mascolo, C., Picco, G.P., Roman, G.C.: A fine-grained model for code mobility. In: Proceedings of the 7th European Software Engineering Conference held jointly with the 7th ACM SIGSOFT International Symposium on Foundations of Software Engineering, Springer-Verlag (1999) 39–56
4. Sekiguchi, T., Yonezawa, A.: A calculus with code mobility. In: FMOODS '97: Proceeding of the IFIP TC6 WG6.1 International Workshop on Formal Methods for Open Object-based Distributed Systems, Chapman & Hall, Ltd. (1997) 21–36
5. Borghuis, T., Feijs, L.: A constructive logic for services and information flow in computer networks. The Computer Journal **43**(4) (2000) 275–289
6. Moody, J.: Modal logic as a basis for distributed computation. Technical Report CMU-CS-03-194, Carnegie Mellon University (2003)
7. Jia, L., Walker, D.: Modal proofs as distributed programs (extended abstract). In Schmidt, D., ed.: Proceedings of the European Symposium on Programming, LNCS 2986, Springer (2004) 219–233

8. Murphy, VII, T., Crary, K., Harper, R., Pfenning, F.: A symmetric modal lambda calculus for distributed computing. In: Proceedings of the 19th IEEE Symposium on Logic in Computer Science (LICS 2004), IEEE Press (2004)
9. Park, S.: A modal language for the safety of mobile values. Technical Report POSTECH-CSE-06-001, Department of Computer Science and Engineering, Pohang University of Science and Technology (2006)
10. Pfenning, F., Davies, R.: A judgmental reconstruction of modal logic. Mathematical Structures in Computer Science 11(4) (2001) 511–540
11. Halstead, Jr., R.H.: Multilisp: a language for concurrent symbolic computation. ACM Transactions on Programming Languages and Systems 7(4) (1985) 501–538
12. Braüner, T.: Natural deduction for hybrid logic. Journal of Logic and Computation 14(3) (2004) 329–353
13. Simpson, A.K.: The Proof Theory and Semantics of Intuitionistic Modal Logic. PhD thesis, Department of Philosophy, University of Edinburgh (1994)
14. Liblit, B., Aiken, A.: Type systems for distributed data structures. In: Proceedings of the 27th ACM SIGPLAN-SIGACT symposium on Principles of programming languages, ACM Press (2000) 199–213

An Analysis for Proving Temporal Properties of Biological Systems

Roberta Gori and Francesca Levi

Department of Computer Science, University of Pisa, Italy

Abstract. This paper concerns the application of formal methods to biological systems, modeled specifically in BioAmbients [34], a variant of the Mobile Ambients [4] calculus. Following the semantic-based approach of abstract interpretation, we define a new static analysis that computes an abstract transition system. Our analysis has two main advantages with respect to the analyses appearing in literature: (i) it is able to address *temporal* properties which are more general than *invariant* properties; (ii) it supports, by means of a particular *labeling discipline*, the validation of systems where several copies of an ambient may appear.

1 Introduction

Nowadays one of the great challenges for computer science is to understand whether models, originally developed for describing systems of interacting components, can be applied for modeling and analyzing biological systems. This very promising and recent application to systems biology could offer biologists very useful simulation and verification tools that could replace expensive experiments in vitro or guide the experiments by making predictions on their possible results.

Among the many formalisms that have been successfully applied to biology there are traditional specification languages for concurrent and reactive systems [25,20,19], and process calculi, designed for modeling distributed and mobile systems. Process calculi turned out to be very appropriate for describing both the molecular and biochemical aspect, as pioneered by the application of stochastic π-calculus [35,33]. New process calculi have also been proposed in order to faithfully model biological structures such as compartments, membranes and hierarchy, which play a key role in the organization of biomolecular systems. Recent proposals are BioAmbients [34], Beta-Binders [32], and Brane calculi [2].

BioAmbients (BA) is a variant of a very popular calculus for mobile processes, the Mobile Ambients calculus (MA)[4], based on the key concept of *ambient*. An ambient represents a bounded location where computation happens; ambients are organized into a hierarchy, that can be dynamically modified as a consequence of an ambient movement or dissolution. For better modeling basic biological concepts, minor modifications are introduced in BA with respect to standard MA. Ambients are nameless; the primitive for opening is replaced by a primitive of merge, which realizes the fusion of two ambients; capabilities have corresponding co-capabilities; new primitives for communication and choice are introduced.

N. Kobayashi (Ed.): APLAS 2006, LNCS 4279, pp. 234–252, 2006.

A great advantage of the BA calculus is that the variety of formal verification techniques, proposed for MA in the last few years, can be naturally adapted. In particular, due to the intrinsic complexity of biological systems, *static analysis* techniques appear very promising, and can be applied to infer information on the possible behavior of biological systems that cannot be handled by simulation tools [35,33] or by automatic verification techniques [23,24].

Static analyses define safe and computable approximations of the (run-time) behavior of a system, and they have been typically applied in the MA setting (see [27,18,14,21,15,26,11]) for verifying security properties, specifically for proving *invariant* properties. To this aim, they collect information about the reachable states by reporting approximate descriptions of the possible nesting of ambients and processes. This information can be exploited to show that certain events *will not happen* in *each* state of the system; for example, that an ambient *will never* end up inside another one; and similarly, that an interaction between two ambients *will never* take place.

As expected, some of these techniques [27,14,11,21,15] were successfully translated to the BA calculus (see [29,28,30,31,15]). Nonetheless, we believe that *temporal* properties, much more general than invariant properties, should be addressed in order to reason on real biological systems. Examples of interesting temporal properties could be: for each path of computation "after A interacts with B than it does not interact with C anymore"; for each path of computation " event A may happen only after event B". Such properties could help biologists to better understand both the *spatial* and *temporal* evolution of complex biological systems, such as pathways and networks of proteins, as already pointed out in [5,23,24,1].

As an example, we consider a typical specification of an enzymatic reaction, following the approach proposed in [34] based on ambient movements,

$$[M]^{mol} \mid \ldots \mid [M]^{mol} \mid [E]^e \ldots \mid [E]^e \tag{1}$$
$$M ::= \textbf{in}\, m.\, \textbf{out}\, n.\, P \quad E ::= \textbf{rec}\, Y.\, \overline{\textbf{in}}\, m.\, \overline{\textbf{out}}\, n.\, Y$$

The system (1) describes an (irreversible) enzymatic reaction; the enzyme and its substrate are modeled by ambients, labeled[1] e and *mol*, resp.. Processes M and E realize the reaction in this way: the binding is modeled as entry of the substrate ambient inside the enzyme ambient; symmetrically, the release of product P is modeled as ambient exit.

In the reaction described in (1), for *any* ambient *mol*, the binding with an ambient e is a *necessary* for the release of product P. Even this very simple property, however, cannot be captured by standard reachability analyses for BA / MA [27,18,11,14,21,29,28,30,31]. In fact, these proposals predict the possible contents of ambients, at any evolution step, and can just conclude that any ambient *mol* may reside both at top-level and inside an ambient e. In order to infer that the former event is a so called *necessary check-point* for the latter, information about the possible moves of the system is needed.

It is clear that the validation of such properties requires *more powerful analyses* able to observe the possible evolution of a system , i.e., to compute an

---

[1] In BA labels are attached to ambients as comments, in that ambients are nameless.

approximation of the transition system. However, the approaches proposed in literature, specifically [27,18,11,21,29,28,30,31], would be not adequate for deriving an abstract transition system relevant for typical biological systems. This is because they do not support techniques for accurately handling systems where *multiple occurrences* of objects, e.g. ambients and capabilities, may appear. Based on the previous motivations we propose a new analysis for BA following the *abstract interpretation* [7,8] approach, specifically by refining the approach of [21]. More in details, we enhance the structure of the abstract states, then we derive an abstract transition system (by abstracting each transition step).

First of all, we introduce *occurrence counting information* in the style of the reachability analysis of [16], which records in the abstract states information about the number of occurrences of ambients and capabilities that may appear in *any* location. Note that this idea is not completely new (see [26,13,15]), while in [21,18] a less precise information is tracked since the number of objects, which may occur in the *whole* system, is taken into account. Occurrence counting information is essential for reasoning about the firing of capabilities and for achieving detailed information about the possible sequences of moves (which are very important for establishing temporal properties such as check-points). For example, in the case of system (1) it is necessary for distinguishing process E, modeling the expected behavior of the enzyme, from an anomalous process such as $E ::= \text{rec}Y.(\overline{\text{in}}\,m.\,\overline{\text{out}}\,n.\,Y \mid \overline{\text{in}}\,m)$; in this case indeed the enzyme may bind with two distinct molecules, at the time.

Moreover, for handling systems, such as (1), where multiple occurrences of ambients appear we adopt a special *labeling discipline* for ambients, both in the concrete and in the abstract semantics. Labels are profitably exploited for distinguishing different occurrences of ambients, and for establishing temporal properties which hold for all the copies of an ambient appearing in a system. This feature is relevant in the context of biological systems, which typically contain hundred of copies of a given protein.

Our abstract transition system is a safe over-approximation in the sense of [6,10], and thus preserves the properties of a fragment of CTL, ∀-CTL without eventually. In this paper, however, we focus on the validation of systems where multiple occurrences of ambients may appear (such as (1)), for which the standard interpretation of ∀-CTL seems not adequate. Hence, in the complete version of this paper [17] we introduce a simple class of temporal properties and corresponding validation methods (both in the concrete and in the abstract case) which exploit the labels of ambients in order to deal with multiple copies of ambients. The logic supports the specification of interesting temporal properties of pathways (including check-points) which hold precisely for *any* occurrence of an ambient; for example in (1) for any copy of ambient *mol*.

For a lack of of space, we omit the formal definition of the temporal logic, and we describe in an informal way the validation of the check-point property for system (1). We refer the reader to [17] also for more complex and interesting examples and properties.

2   Syntax and Semantics

For a lack of space, we consider a simplified version of BA [34] without communication primitives; the analysis can easily be extended to the full calculus.

In the style of [27,11,21] we adopt labels and we treat α-conversion in a particular way, based on a given partition of names. In particular, we consider a set $\mathcal{N}$ (ranged over by $n, m, h, k, \ldots$) of *channel names* such that $\mathcal{N} = \uplus_i \mathcal{N}_i$, $i \in \{1, \ldots, \omega\}$, where $\uplus$ denotes disjoint union and each $\mathcal{N}_i$ is an infinite set. We also consider an infinite set of recursion variables $\mathcal{V}$ (ranged over by $X, Y, Z, \ldots$). For ambients, we consider an infinite set of *ambients names* $\mathcal{N}_a$ (ranged over by $a, b, c, \ldots$), such that $\mathcal{N}_a \cap \mathcal{N} = \emptyset$ and $\top \in \mathcal{N}_a$, where $\top$ is a distinct symbol used to denote the outermost ambient. Moreover, we consider an infinite set $\widehat{\mathcal{L}}$ of *run-time labels* (ranged over by $\Psi, \Gamma, \Delta, \ldots$), and of *ambients labels* $\mathcal{L}_a = \{(a, \Psi) \mid a \in \mathcal{N}_a \text{ and } \Psi \in \widehat{\mathcal{L}}\}$ (ranged over by $A, B \ldots$). An ambient label $A = (a, \Psi)$ shows the name of the ambient a (denoted by $(A)_1$ using the standard notation for projection) and the run-time label of the ambient Ψ (denoted by $(A)_2$).

The syntax of (labeled) *processes* is defined in Table 1. The constructs for inactivity, parallel composition, restriction are standard. Operator $\mathtt{rec}X. P$ defines a recursive process (which is more convenient than standard replication $!P$). Specific to the ambient calculi, are the ambient construct, $[P]^A$, the capability prefix $M. P$, where M is an action or co-action[2], and the derived capability choice primitive $\Sigma_{i \in I} M_i. P_i$. Specifically, process $\lfloor P \rfloor^A$ defines an ambient (labeled) A where process P runs.

For processes we adopt standard syntactical conventions. We often omit the trailing 0, and we assume that parallel composition has the least syntactic precedence. The operator $(\nu n)P$ acts as static binder for channel name n, and defines the standard notions of free and bound names of a process; similarly, $\mathtt{rec}X. P$ is a binder for X with scope P. In the following, we consider only processes that are closed on recursion variables, e.g. they have no free recursion variables. As usual, we also identify processes which are α-convertible, meaning that they can be made syntactically equals by a change of bound names. In the style of [11,21] we, however, discipline α-conversion by assuming that a bound name m can be replaced only with a name n provided that $n, m \in \mathcal{N}_i$.

We stress that labels are introduced for the specification of the analysis, and do not modify the standard behavior of processes. Specifically, they are designed for handling systems where multiple occurrences of ambients may appear, and for proving temporal properties for *any* occurrence of an ambient. In this sense, given an ambient labeled (a, Ψ): the name a is shared by all the occurrences; by contrast, the run-time label Ψ is used for distinguishing the occurrences of ambients named a. For these purposes, it is necessary to consider *well-labeled processes*, where ambients related to the same name are distinguished by means of distinct run-time labels.

---

[2] For coactions the notation of Safe Ambients [22] is used in place of the standard one.

Table 1. BioAmbients Processes and Reduction Rules

		P,Q::=	(*processes*)
		0	inactivity
M,N::=	(*capabilities*)	$(\nu n)\,P$	restriction
in n	enter	$P \mid Q$	parallel composition
$\overline{\text{in}}\,n$	co-enter	X	recursion variable
out n	exit	$\text{rec}X.\,P$	recursive process
$\overline{\text{out}}\,n$	co-exit	$[P]^A$	ambient
merge n	merge	$M.\,P$	capability prefix
$\overline{\text{merge}}\,n$	co-merge	$\Sigma_{i \in I} M_i.\,P_i$	capability choice

$$[+\text{in}\,m.\,P \mid Q]^A \mid [+\overline{\text{in}}\,m.\,R \mid S]^B \to_\emptyset [[P \mid Q]^A \mid R \mid S]^B \qquad \text{(In)}$$

$$[[+\text{out}\,m.\,P \mid Q]^A \mid +\overline{\text{out}}\,mR \mid S]^B \to_\emptyset [P \mid Q]^A \mid [R \mid S]^B \qquad \text{(Out)}$$

$$[+\text{merge}\,m.\,P \mid Q]^A \mid [+\overline{\text{merge}}\,m.\,R \mid S]^B \to_\emptyset [P \mid Q \mid R \mid S]^A \qquad \text{(Merge)}$$

$$(L = \mathcal{L}_a(P\eta) \quad \mathcal{L}_a(P) \cap L = \emptyset) \Rightarrow \text{rec}X.\,P \to_L P[\text{rec}X.\,P\eta / X] \qquad \text{(Rec)}$$

$$P \to_L Q \Rightarrow (\nu n)\,P \to_L (\nu n)\,Q \qquad \text{(Res)}$$

$$(\mathcal{L}_a(R) \cap \mathcal{L}_a(Q\eta) = \emptyset \quad dom(\eta) = L \quad P \to_L Q) \Rightarrow P \mid R \to_{\eta(L)} Q\eta \mid R \quad \text{(Par)}$$

$$(P \to_L Q \quad A \notin \mathcal{L}_a(Q\eta) \quad dom(\eta) = L) \Rightarrow [P]^A \to_{\eta(L)} [Q\eta]^A \qquad \text{(Amb)}$$

$$(P' \to_L Q' \quad P \equiv P' \quad Q' \equiv Q) \Rightarrow P \to_L Q \qquad \text{(Cong)}$$

Definition 1 (Well-labeled). *A process P is* well-labeled *iff whenever two ambients $[Q]^A$ and $[R]^B$ appear, such that $(A)_1 = (B)_1$, then $(A)_2 \neq (B)_2$.*

In the following, we use $\mathcal{L}_a(P)$ and $\mathcal{N}_a(P)$ for denoting the set of the ambients labels and names appearing in process P, resp.. We also adopt a standard notion of *relabeling*, by using injective functions $\eta : \mathcal{L}_a \to \mathcal{L}_a$, such that for each $A \in dom(\eta)$, $(A)_1 = (\eta(A))_1$ (this guarantees that the name of an ambient is not modified). We also use $P\eta$ for the application of η to process P.

Reduction Semantics. The semantics of BA is given in the form of a reduction relation. Minor modifications are needed with respect to the standard definition [34] for preserving the condition of well-labeling; specifically, for handling the new copies of ambients (related to a given name) which may be produced, by the unfolding of recursion. A very simple *labeling discipline* is used: each ambient maintains its label, as the computation proceeds, and the new copies of ambients introduced by the move are relabeled with fresh labels (in particular run-time labels).

Formally, this is realized (see the rules of Table 1) by considering reduction arrows $\to_L$, where $L \subseteq \mathcal{L}_a$ is the set of fresh ambients labels, introduced by the move. The reduction axioms (In), (Out) and (Merge) model the movement of an ambient, in or out, of another ambient and the merge of two ambients. They differ from those of MA mainly because ambients are nameless, because actions have corresponding coactions and because the primitive *merge* replaces the standard primitive of opening. For compacting the presentation, we adopt a special notation for capability prefix and capability choice, by writing $+M.P$ both for $M.P$ and for $\Sigma_{i \in I} M_i . Q_i$, where $M = M_i$ and $P = Q_i$ for $i \in I$.

Moreover, the unfolding of recursion is modeled as a reduction rule, e.g. (Rec). Here a relabeled version of the recursive process, e.g. $\mathrm{rec}X. P\eta$, is introduced, and the information about the fresh labels $\mathcal{L}_a(P\eta)$ is recorded accordingly. The inference rules (Res), (Par), (Amb) and (Cong) are standard; they handle reductions in contexts and permit to apply structural congruence, e.g. relation $\equiv$. Structural congruence is defined in a standard way (we therefore refer the reader to [34]). Notice that, in case of (Par) and (Amb), the fresh labels are updated (if needed) in order to guarantee well-labeling.

In the following, we say that a process P is *active* if either $P = \Sigma_{i \in I} M_i . Q_i$, $P = M.Q$ or $P = \mathrm{rec}X.P$. Moreover, we use $\mathcal{P}$ and $\mathcal{AP}$ to denote the set of (well-labeled) processes and active processes, resp.. We also say that a context C is *enabling* whenever the hole does not appear under a capability prefix or a recursion; also we say that an ambient, labeled A, is *enabled* in P whenever $P \equiv C[[Q]^A]$ for some enabling context C. With $\mathrm{amb}(P), \mathrm{amb}(P, a) \subseteq \mathcal{L}_a$ we denote the labels of the ambients and of the ambients named a, that are enabled in process P.

The transition system. Let $\mathcal{T} = \{P \rightarrow P' \mid P, P' \in \mathcal{P}\}$ be the set of transitions, and, let $Ts = \{(Ss, Ss_0, Ts) \mid Ss, Ss_0 \in \wp(\mathcal{P}),$ and $Ts \in \wp(\mathcal{T})\}$ be the set of transition systems[3]. The *concrete domain* is $\mathcal{A} = \langle Ts, \subseteq \rangle$, where $\subseteq$ is defined component-wise. Given $P \in \mathcal{P}$, we define $\mathfrak{S}[\![P]\!]$, as the *transition system* obtained from the initial process P by considering the transitive closure of the $\rightarrow$ reduction relation.

3   The Abstraction

The analysis computes an abstract transition system, which is derived, by abstracting processes into abstract states and reduction steps into abstract transitions. The abstract domain includes a notion of ordering, expressing precision of approximations, and is related to the concrete one through a Galois connection [7,8].

The abstraction is *parametric* with respect to the choice of *abstract names* and *labels*. Given an abstract partition of channel names $\mathcal{N}$, $\mathcal{N} = \uplus_i \mathcal{N}_i^\circ$, $i \in \{1, \ldots, h\}$, such that, for each $n, m \in \mathcal{N}_i$ we have $n, m \in \mathcal{N}_j^\circ$, we consider *abstract channel names* $\mathcal{N}^\circ = \mathcal{N}_{/\cong}$ where $\cong$ is the corresponding equivalence relation. Analogously, we consider *abstract ambient names* $\mathcal{N}_a^\circ = \mathcal{N}_{a/\cong}$ by adopting an equivalence relation $\cong$ over $\mathcal{N}_a$. We also consider an infinite set of *run-time labels* $\widehat{\mathcal{L}}^\circ = \widehat{\mathcal{L}} \cup \{\infty\}$ (ranged over by $\overline{\Psi}, \overline{\Delta}, \ldots$), and we define the *abstract ambients labels* $\mathcal{L}_a^\circ = \{(a^\circ, \overline{\Psi}) \mid a^\circ \in \mathcal{N}_a^\circ$ and $\overline{\Psi} \in \widehat{\mathcal{L}}^\circ\}$.

In the following, we consider also *abstract processes* which are obtained by replacing standard names and labels with their abstract versions; we also use $\mathcal{P}^\circ$

---

[3] The usual notion is generalized by allowing sets of initial states; also we remove the information about the fresh labels related to a reduction step.

and $\mathcal{AP}^\circ$ for denoting the set of abstract and active abstract processes, resp.. According to the notation for meta-variables of Section 2, we use $-^\circ$ to denote the abstraction of a label, name or process $-$.

It is worth stressing that the abstract ambients labels $\widehat{\mathcal{L}}^\circ$ are infinite (in that there is no a priori abstraction of run-time labels). In the concrete semantics distinct run-time labels are used precisely to distinguish the occurrences of ambients with the same name. Since the concrete labeling discipline is obviously not effective (e.g. infinite run-time labels may be generated), here we adopt a different approach and we define a framework where: (i) the run-time labels can be approximated, by merging together the information related to distinct run-time labels; (ii) the run-time labels of ambients *may vary*, as the computation proceeds (provided that the information is properly recorded in the corresponding abstract transition). In the analysis we apply these concepts in order to implement a particular *labeling discipline* which guarantees that, for any abstract ambient name $a^\circ \in \mathcal{N}_a{}^\circ$, at most max_{a° distinct run-time labels $\widehat{\mathcal{L}}^\circ$ can be generated. The bound imposed by parameter max_{a° is guaranteed by means of the special run-time label ∞.

Abstract states. Abstract states are designed to represent approximate information about processes. In the style of [16] an *abstract state* reports: (i) the abstract labels of the ambients that may appear; and (ii) for each one of them, a set of *configurations* describing the possible contents of the related ambients. In details, a configuration contains both the *abstract labels* of the ambients and the *active abstract processes* which may appear at top-level, and the number of their occurrences. For representing occurrence counting information, we adopt $\mathcal{M} = \{0, 1, [0 - \omega], [1 - \omega]\}$. Each $\mathbf{m} \in \mathcal{M}$ denotes a *multiplicity*: 0 and 1 indicate zero and exactly one, resp.; the intervals $[1 - \omega]$ and $[0 - \omega]$ indicate at least one and zero or more, resp..

Example 1. We consider the following process,

$$[M]^{(mol,\Psi_1)} \mid \ldots \mid [M]^{(mol,\Psi_{h-1})} \mid [E]^{(e,\Delta_1)} \mid \ldots \mid [E]^{(e,\Delta_{k-1})} \mid$$
$$[\overline{out}\, n.\, E \mid [out\, n.\, P]^{(mol,\Psi_h)}]^{(e,\Delta_k)}$$

which is derived from a (well-labeled) version of the system (1) described in the Introduction, after an ambient named *mol* (with run-time label Ψ_h) has moved inside an ambient named e (with run-time label Δ_k).

We assume here that the abstract names and ambient names are defined by the equivalence classes $\mathcal{N}^\circ = \{n, m\}$, and $\mathcal{N}_a^\circ = \mathcal{N}_a$. The following abstract states define safe approximations of the previous process,

$S_{1,1}^\circ = \{(\top, C_{0,1}^\circ)\} \bigcup_{i \in \{1,\ldots,h-1\}} \{(D_i^\circ, C_{1,1}^\circ)\} \bigcup_{i \in \{1,\ldots,k-1\}} \{(F_i^\circ, C_{2,1}^\circ), (D_h^\circ, C_{1,2}^\circ), (F_k^\circ, C_{2,2}^\circ)\}$

$C_{0,1}^\circ = \{(D_1^\circ, 1), \ldots, (D_{h-1}^\circ, 1), (F_1^\circ, 1), \ldots, (F_k^\circ, 1)\}$ $C_{1,1}^\circ = \{(M^\circ, 1)\}$ $C_{2,1}^\circ = \{(E^\circ, 1)\}$

$E^\circ ::= \mathbf{rec}Y.\, \overline{in}\, m^\circ.\, \overline{out}\, m^\circ.\, Y$ $M^\circ ::= in\, m^\circ.\, out\, m^\circ.\, P^\circ$

$C_{1,2}^\circ = \{(out\, m^\circ.\, P^\circ, 1)\}$ $C_{2,2}^\circ = \{(\overline{out}\, m^\circ.\, E^\circ, 1), (D_h^\circ, 1)\}$

$S_{1,2}^\circ = \{(\top, C_{0,2}^\circ), (A_1^\circ, C_{1,1}^\circ), (B_1^\circ, C_{2,1}^\circ), (A_2^\circ, C_{1,2}^\circ), (B_2^\circ, C_{2,3}^\circ)\}$

$C_{0,2}^\circ = \{(A_1^\circ, [1 - \omega]), (B_1^\circ, [1 - \omega]), (B_2^\circ, 1)\}$ $C_{2,3}^\circ = \{(\overline{out}\, m^\circ.\, E^\circ, 1), (A_2^\circ, 1)\}$

$S_{1,3}^\circ = \{(\top, C_{0,3}^\circ), (A_3^\circ, C_{1,1}^\circ), (A_3^\circ, C_{1,2}^\circ), (B_3^\circ, C_{2,1}^\circ), (B_3^\circ, C_{2,4}^\circ)\}$
$C_{0,3}^\circ = \{(A_3^\circ, [1-\omega]), (B_3^\circ, [1-\omega])\}$ $C_{2,4}^\circ = \{(\overline{\text{out}}\, m^\circ. E^\circ, 1), (A_3^\circ, 1)\}$

$S_{1,4}^\circ = \{(\top, C_{0,3}^\circ), (A_3^\circ, C_1^\circ), (B_3^\circ, C_2^\circ)\}$ $C_1^\circ = \{(\text{out}\, m^\circ. P^\circ, [0-\omega]), (M^\circ, [0-\omega])\}$
$C_2^\circ = \{(\overline{\text{out}}\, m^\circ. E^\circ, [0-\omega]), (A_3^\circ, [0-\omega]), (E^\circ, [0-\omega])\}$

State $S_{1,1}^\circ$ is the *best approximation* and does not introduce any approximation on ambient labels (to simplify the presentation we use $\top = (\top, \Lambda)$, $D_i^\circ = (mol, \Psi_i)$ and $F_i^\circ = (e, \Delta_i)$). In particular, configuration $C_{0,1}^\circ$ for the special symbol $\top$ reports information about the processes running at top-level; it reveals the presence of *exactly one* ambient labeled D_i°, with $i \in \{1, h-1\}$, and labeled F_i° with $i \in \{1, k\}$. Configuration $C_{1,1}^\circ$ describes the ambients named *mol* and labeled D_i° for $i \in \{1, h-1\}$, showing that they contain *exactly* one process abstracted by M°. By contrast, configuration $C_{1,2}^\circ$ describes the ambient named *mol* and labeled D_h°, i.e., the ambient *mol* residing inside ambient e. It shows that it contains *exactly one* process abstracted by $\text{out}\, m^\circ. P^\circ$. Analogously, the configurations $C_{2,1}^\circ$ and $C_{2,2}^\circ$ describe the possible contents of the ambients named e. In particular, configuration $C_{2,2}^\circ$ describes the occurrence labeled F_k°, which contains *exactly one* ambient named *mol* and labeled D_h°, and a process $\overline{\text{out}}\, m^\circ. E^\circ$.

The states $S_{1,2}^\circ$, $S_{1,3}^\circ$, $S_{1,3}^\circ$ describe *safe approximations* of state $S_{1,1}^\circ$ and illustrate the approximation of ambients labels. Intuitively, distinct run-time labels, related to the same name, can be represented by a single abstract label, provided that coherent information about the corresponding configurations and multiplicities is reported.

As an example, in state $S_{1,2}^\circ$ the labels are approximated by using a simple partitioning criteria: the occurrences of ambients with the same name, described by the same configuration, are identified (by adopting abstract labels $A_i^\circ = (mol, \Lambda_i)$ and $B_i^\circ = (e, \Phi_i)$). More in details, the labels $D_1^\circ, \ldots, D_{h-1}^\circ$, for name *mol*, are represented by label A_1°, while label D_h° is represented by A_2°; analogously, the labels $F_1^\circ, \ldots, F_{k-1}^\circ$, for name e, are represented by label B_1°, and label F_k° is represented by B_2°. The related configurations are updated by modifying the multiplicities accordingly; for example configuration $C_{0,2}^\circ$ shows that $[1-\omega]$ ambients labeled A_1° and B_1°, and exactly one ambient labeled B_2° may appear at top-level.

Notice that label A_1° describes all the occurrences of *mol*, which are running at top-level and are described by configuration $C_{1,1}^\circ$; instead, label A_2° identifies the occurrence of *mol*, residing inside the enzyme and is described by configuration $C_{1,2}^\circ$. Notice that the interpretation of configuration $C_{1,1}^\circ$ is that, *any* ambient named *mol* labeled A_1° contains *exactly* one process abstracted by M°. In this sense, the counting of occurrences is local, being $[1-\omega]$ the global number of occurrences of processes M°.

State $S_{1,3}^\circ$ introduces a further approximation, where all occurrences of ambients (named) *mol* and e are represented by the same abstract labels A_3° and B_3°, resp. Labels A_3° and B_3°, however, are related to a set of configurations; for example, A_3° for *mol* is related to configurations $C_{1,1}^\circ$ and $C_{1,2}^\circ$. The

Table 2. Occurrence Counting

$+^\circ$	0	1	$[1-\omega]\,[0-\omega]$		$-^\circ$	1
0	0	1	$[1-\omega]\,[0-\omega]$		0	0
1	1	$[1-\omega]\,[1-\omega]$	$[1-\omega]\,[1-\omega]\,[1-\omega]$		1	0
$[1-\omega]\,[1-\omega]$ $[0-\omega]\,[0-\omega]$	$[1-\omega]\,[1-\omega]$ $[0-\omega]\,[0-\omega]$	$[1-\omega]\,[1-\omega]$ $[1-\omega]\,[1-\omega]$	$[1-\omega]\,[1-\omega]$ $[0-\omega]\,[0-\omega]$		$[1-\omega]\,[0-\omega]$ $[0-\omega]\,[0-\omega]$	$[1-\omega]\,[0-\omega]$ $[0-\omega]\,[0-\omega]$

interpretation is that the contents of *any* ambient *mol* may be described *either* by $C_{1,1}^\circ$ or by $C_{1,2}^\circ$.

Finally, in state $S_{1,4}^\circ$ the configurations of a given label are merged into a single one, e.g. configuration C_1° for ambients *mol* and C_2° for ambients *e*. The loss of precision is clear; for example, configuration C_1° says that any ambient *mol* may contain, at the same time, process $out\, m^\circ.\,P^\circ$ and process M°.   □

Let $\widehat{\mathcal{PL}} = \mathcal{L}_a{}^\circ \cup \mathcal{AP}^\circ$ (ranged over by e) be the set of abstract ambients labels and abstract active processes, and let $\mathcal{E} = \widehat{\mathcal{PL}} \times \mathcal{M}$.

Definition 2 (Configurations and Abstract States). *A configuration C is a subset of $\mathcal{E}$ such that: (i) if $(e,\mathsf{m}), (e,\mathsf{m}') \in C^\circ$, then $\mathsf{m} = \mathsf{m}'$; and (ii) for each $(e,\mathsf{m}) \in C^\circ$, $\mathsf{m} \neq 0$. An abstract state S° is a set of pairs (A°, C°), where C° is a configuration and $A^\circ \in \mathcal{L}_a{}^\circ$ is an ambient label.*

In the following, we use $\mathcal{S}^\circ$ and $\mathcal{C}^\circ$ for the set of abstract states and configurations, resp. Given $S \in \mathcal{S}^\circ$, we also use $\mathsf{amb}(S^\circ) = \{A^\circ \mid (A^\circ, C^\circ) \in S^\circ\}$ and $\mathsf{amb}(S^\circ, a^\circ) = \{A^\circ \mid (A^\circ, C^\circ) \in S^\circ, (A^\circ)_1 = a^\circ\}$ for denoting the ambients labels described by a configuration. Notice that in configurations, no pair $(e, 0)$ can appear, recording explicitly that there are no occurrences of element e. However, we may write $(e, 0) \in C^\circ$ in place of $(e, \mathsf{m}) \notin C^\circ$ for any $\mathsf{m} \in \mathcal{M}$ for convenience.

In order to define the information order on abstract states, we assume that the domain $\mathcal{M}$ of multiplicity comes equipped with the expected (information) order $\leq_m$ and with the set of operations $+^\circ$ and $-^\circ$, reported in Table 2. Moreover, we introduce for configurations a derived ordering and an operator $\cup^+$ that realizes their union,

1. $C_1^\circ \leq^c C_2^\circ$ iff, for each $(e, \mathsf{m}) \in C_1^\circ$ there exists $(e, \mathsf{m}') \in C_2^\circ$ such that $\mathsf{m} \leq_m \mathsf{m}'$;
2. $C_1^\circ \cup^+ C_2^\circ = \{(e, \mathsf{m}) \mid (e, \mathsf{m}_i) \in C_i^\circ, \text{ for each } i \in \{1, 2\}, \mathsf{m} = \mathsf{m}_1 +^\circ \mathsf{m}_2\}$.

The ordering over states is rather complex due to the possible approximation of run-time labels (as illustrated in Ex. 1). For merging ambients labels we adopt *approximation functions* $\sigma : \mathcal{L}_a{}^\circ \rightarrow \mathcal{L}_a{}^\circ$, such that for any $A^\circ \in dom(\sigma)$, $(A^\circ)_1 = (\sigma(A^\circ))_1$. The application of an approximation function to a configuration is defined as follows, $C^\circ \sigma = \bigcup^+_{\{(e,\mathsf{m}) \in C^\circ\}} \{(e\sigma, \mathsf{m})\}$.

Definition 3 (Order on States). *Let $S_1^\circ, S_2^\circ \in \mathcal{S}^\circ$ and σ be an approximation function. We say that $S_1^\circ \sqsubseteq_\sigma S_2^\circ$ iff, for each $(A^\circ, C_1^\circ) \in S_1^\circ$, there exists $(\sigma(A^\circ), C_2^\circ) \in S_2^\circ$ such that $C_1^\circ \sigma \leq^c C_2^\circ$. Moreover, we say that $S_1^\circ \sqsubseteq^\circ S_2^\circ$ iff there exists an approximation function σ such that $S_1^\circ \sqsubseteq_\sigma S_2^\circ$.*

Table 3. Abstract Translation Function

DRes°	$\eta°((\nu n°)P°)$	$= \eta°(P°)$
DAmb°	$\eta°([P°]^{A°})$	$= (\{(A°, 1)\}, \delta°(A°, P°))$
DZero°	$\eta°(0)$	$= (\emptyset, \emptyset)$
DPar°	$\eta°(P_1 \mid P_2)$	$= (C_1° \cup^+ C_2°, S_1° \cup° S_2°) \quad \eta°(P_i) = (C_i°, S_i°) \text{ for } i \in \{1,2\}$
DRec°	$\eta°(recX.\,P°)$	$= (\{(recX.\,P°, 1)\}, \emptyset)$
DPref°	$\eta°(M.\,P°)$	$= (\{(M.\,P°, 1)\}, \emptyset)$
DSum°	$\eta°(\Sigma_{i \in I} M_i°.\,P_i°)$	$= (\{(\Sigma_{i \in I} M_i°.\,P_i°, 1)\}, \emptyset)$

Abstract Transition Systems. The abstract labeling disciple requires the possibility that the labels (specifically the run-time labels) of ambients *can vary*, as the computation proceeds. For tracking the possible evolution of the run-time labels, we expand the information reported by standard transitions, by exploiting *evolution relations* $\mathcal{R}° \subseteq (\mathcal{L}_a° \cup \{\bot\}) \times (\mathcal{L}_a° \cup \{\bot\})$, such that for each $A° \in \mathcal{L}_a°$, if $(A°, B°) \in \mathcal{R}°$, $(A°)_1 = (B°)_1$. Intuitively, $(A°, B°) \in \mathcal{R}°$ says that label $A°$ has been replaced by label $B°$; $(A°, \bot) \in \mathcal{R}°$ says that all the ambients labeled $A°$ disappear; $(\bot, A°) \in \mathcal{R}°$ says that $A°$ is the label of a new enabled ambient.

Hence, we consider *abstract transitions* $T° = \{S_1° \mapsto_{\mathcal{R}°} S_2° \mid S_1°, S_2° \in \mathcal{S}°$ and $dom(\mathcal{R}°) = \mathrm{amb}(S_1°)$ and $cod(\mathcal{R}°) = \mathrm{amb}(S_2°)\}$. In the ordering on transitions we guarantee by means of approximation functions that: (i) the source and target state are approximated; (ii) the approximation over states is consistent with the information reported by the corresponding evolution relations.

Definition 4 (Order on Transitions). *Let* $S_{1,1}° \mapsto_{\mathcal{R}_1°} S_{1,2}°, S_{2,1}° \mapsto_{\mathcal{R}_2°} S_{2,2}° \in T°$, *and* σ_1, σ_2 *be approximation functions. We say that* $S_{1,1}° \mapsto_{\mathcal{R}_1°} S_{1,2}° \sqsubseteq_{(\sigma_1, \sigma_2)} S_{2,1}° \mapsto_{\mathcal{R}_2°} S_{2,2}°$ *iff:* (1) $S_{1,1}° \sqsubseteq_{\sigma_1} S_{2,1}°$ *and* $S_{1,2}° \sqsubseteq_{\sigma_2} S_{2,2}°$; (2) *for each* $A° \in \mathrm{amb}(S_{1,1}°)$: (i) *if* $\mathcal{R}_1°(A°) = \bot$, *then* $\mathcal{R}_2°(\sigma_1(A°)) = \bot$; *or* (ii) $\sigma_2(\mathcal{R}_1°(A°)) \subseteq \mathcal{R}_2°(\sigma_1(A°))$; *and* $\sigma_2(\mathcal{R}_1°(\bot)) \subseteq \mathcal{R}_2°(\bot)$.

Based on Def. 3 and 4 it is immediate to derive a corresponding order $\subseteq°$ on *abstract transition systems* $Ts° = \{(Ss°, S_0°, Ts°) \mid Ss° \in \wp(\mathcal{S}°), S_0° \in \mathcal{S}°$ and $Ts° \in \wp(T°)\}$. Consequently, we define the *abstract domain* $\mathcal{A}° = (Ts°, \subseteq°)$.

Galois Connection. A Galois connection formalizes the notion of *safe approximation* of an abstract transition system, e.g the relation between the concrete and the abstract domain.

First of all, we define the *abstraction* of a process, by introducing a *translation function* that given the label of the enclosing ambient, reports the most precise abstract state, e.g. its best approximation. Formally, we define $\delta° : (\mathcal{L}_a° \times \mathcal{P}°) \to \mathcal{S}°$ as follows

$$\delta°(A°, P°) = \{(A°, C°)\} \cup S° \quad \text{where} \quad \eta°(P°) = (C°, S°).$$

The auxiliary function function $\eta° : \mathcal{P}° \to (\mathcal{C}° \times \mathcal{S}°)$ is reported in Table 3 and computes: (i) an abstract configuration $C°$ reporting both the active processes and the labels of the ambients occurring at top-level, and their multiplicities; (ii) an abstract state $S°$ describing the internal ambients. In the following we use $\alpha^\circ(P)$ for denoting the best approximation of process P with respect to the enclosing ambient $\top$, e.g. $\alpha^\circ(P) = \delta^\circ(\top, P^\circ)$.

Analogously, we introduce the *abstraction* of concrete transitions, e.g. $P \to P'$. For this, we define an evolution relation $\mathcal{R}^\circ$, expressing how the labels of the enabled ambients (specifically their run-time labels) vary.

Given $P \to P' \in \mathcal{T}$, we define[4] $\alpha^\circ(P \to P') = \alpha^\circ(P) \mapsto_{\mathcal{R}^\circ}^\circ \alpha^\circ(P')$ where

$$\mathcal{R}^\circ = \mathrm{id}(\mathrm{amb}(P) \cap \mathrm{amb}(P')) \cup (\{\bot\}, \mathrm{amb}(P') \setminus \mathrm{amb}(P)) \cup (\mathrm{amb}(P) \setminus \mathrm{amb}(P'), \{\bot\}),$$

using $(L, L') = \{(A, B) \mid A \in L, B \in L'\}$ and $\mathrm{id}(L) = (L, L)$, for $L, L' \subseteq \mathcal{L}_a$.

Relation $\mathcal{R}$ reflects the concrete labeling discipline; no pair (A, B) with $A \neq B$ could actually appear given that all the ambients maintain their labels; by contrast, $\mathcal{R}$ records the labels of the new enabled ambients.

The following abstraction and concretization functions between the concrete and abstract domain are derived in the obvious way.

Definition 5. *Let $Ss, Ss_0 \in \wp(\mathcal{P})$, $Ss^\circ \in \wp(\mathcal{S}^\circ)$, $S_0^\circ \in \mathcal{S}^\circ$, $Ts \in \wp(\mathcal{T})$ and $Ts^\circ \in \wp(\mathcal{T}^\circ)$. We define $\alpha^\circ : \mathcal{A} \to \mathcal{A}^\circ$ and $\gamma^\circ : \mathcal{A}^\circ \to \mathcal{A}$, where*

$$\alpha^\circ((Ss, Ss_0, Ts)) = (\bigcup_{P \in Ss}\{\alpha^\circ(P)\}, \bigcup_{P \in Ss_0}\{\alpha^\circ(P)\}, \bigcup_{P_1 \to P_2 \in Ts}\{\alpha^\circ(P_1 \to P_2)\});$$
$$\gamma^\circ((Ss^\circ, S_0^\circ, Ts^\circ)) = (\bigcup_{\{P \mid \{\alpha^\circ(P)\} \subseteq^\circ Ss^\circ\}}\{P\}, \bigcup_{\{P \mid \{\alpha^\circ(P)\} \subseteq^\circ S_0^\circ\}}\{P\},$$
$$\bigcup_{\{P_1 \to P_2 \mid \{\alpha^\circ(P_1 \to P_2)\} \subseteq^\circ Ts^\circ\}}\{P_1 \to P_2\}).$$

Theorem 1. *The pair $(\alpha^\circ, \gamma^\circ)$ is a Galois connection between $\langle \mathcal{A}, \subseteq \rangle$ and $\langle \mathcal{A}^\circ, \subseteq^\circ \rangle$.*

Abstract semantics. The analysis defines *abstract transitions* which approximate the unfolding of recursion, the movements of ambients, in and out, and the merge of two ambients. The most critical part (w.r.t the similar proposals in [21,16]) concerns the treatment of ambients labels. Our *labeling discipline* is based on the idea of using a one-to-one correspondence between labels and configurations; meaning that the same abstract label is used to represent ambients with the same name that exhibit the same behavior (e.g. which are described by the same configuration). In order to reduce the complexity, however, we use, for each ambient name a°, at most max_{a° distinct run-time labels. Whenever more than max_{a° labels are needed, we approximate by describing all the occurrences related to name a° and their configurations by means of the special label (a°, ∞).

For implementing the labeling discipline we introduce *normalized states* and a related notion of normalization, by means of approximation functions.

Definition 6 (Normalized States). *A state $S^\circ \in \mathcal{S}^\circ$ is normalized iff, for each $a^\circ \in \mathcal{N}_a^\circ$, and $A^\circ, B^\circ \in \mathrm{amb}(S^\circ, a^\circ)$,*
1. *if $(A^\circ, C_1^\circ), (B^\circ, C_1^\circ) \in S^\circ$, then $A^\circ = B^\circ$;*
2. *if $(A^\circ, C_1^\circ), (B^\circ, C_2^\circ) \in S^\circ$ then $(B^\circ)_2 = (A^\circ)_2$ implies $(B^\circ)_2 = (A^\circ)_2 = \infty$;*
3. *either $\mathrm{amb}(S^\circ, a^\circ) = \{(a^\circ, \infty)\}$ or $\mathrm{amb}(S^\circ, a^\circ) = \{(a^\circ, \Phi_i)\}_{i \in \{1, \ldots, n\}}$, where $n \leq max_{a^\circ}$.*

Conditions (1) and (2) impose, for each ambient name a°, a one-to-one correspondence between configurations and run-time labels different from ∞; condition (3) explains the meaning of parameter max_{a°. In this way, in a normalized

---

[4] $\mathcal{R}^\circ$ is obtained from $\mathcal{R}$ by replacing the ambient labels by their abstract versions.

state: *either* at most n (with $n \leq max_{a^\circ}$) distinct run-time labels Φ_i appear, each related to a different configuration, *or* the special label ∞ describes all the copies and a set of configurations.

Definition 7 (Normalization). *An approximation function σ is a normalization for a state S° iff $S^\circ\sigma$[5] is a normalized state. Moreover, σ is a minimal normalization for S° iff, for each normalization σ' for S°, $S^\circ\sigma \subseteq^\circ S^\circ\sigma'$. We also use $\mathcal{M}(S^\circ)$ to denote the set of minimal normalizations for S°.*

The transition rules are reported in Table 4 and use the following auxiliary notions. For simplicity we use $\mathbf{new}(A^\circ)$ to generate a fresh label with the same name of A°, e.g. $(\mathbf{new}(A^\circ))_1 = (A^\circ)_1$. Moreover, we introduce operators: over configurations for removing one occurrence of an object e (and similarly for a set of objects); and, over states for replacing a pair (A°, C°) with a pair (A_1°, C_1°) such that $(A_1^\circ)_1 = (A^\circ)_1$. In the definition, we adopt $\mathcal{O}_{S^\circ}(e)$ reporting the (global) number of occurrences of object e in the abstract state S°,

$$C^\circ\backslash^\circ e = C^\circ \setminus \{(e,\mathtt{m})\} \cup \{(e,\mathtt{m}-^\circ 1)\} \qquad C^\circ\backslash^\circ PL^\circ = C^\circ\backslash^\circ_{e\in PL^\circ} e.$$

$$S^\circ[^{(A_1^\circ,C_1^\circ)}/_{(A^\circ,C^\circ)}] = \begin{cases} (S^\circ[^{A_1^\circ}/_{A^\circ}]) \setminus \{(A^\circ,C^\circ)\} \cup \{(A_1^\circ,C_1^\circ)\} & \text{if } \mathcal{O}_{S^\circ}(A^\circ) = 1 \\ (S^\circ[^{A_1^\circ}/_{A^\circ}]) \cup \{(A_1^\circ,C_1^\circ)\} & \text{otherwise} \end{cases}$$

$$S^\circ[^{A_1^\circ}/_{A^\circ}] = \bigcup_{(D^\circ,C^\circ)\in S^\circ}(D^\circ,C_1^\circ), \text{ where } C_1^\circ = \begin{cases} (C^\circ\backslash^\circ A^\circ) \cup^+ (A_1^\circ,1) & \text{if } (A^\circ,m) \in C^\circ \\ C^\circ & \text{otherwise} \end{cases}$$

As expected the effect of the operators depends on the multiplicity of the objects; for example, the pair (A°, C°) is not removed whenever more than one occurrence of A° appears.

The rules $\mathbf{Rec}^\circ$, $\mathbf{In}^\circ$, $\mathbf{Out}^\circ$, $\mathbf{Merge}^\circ$ are similar. As an example, we comment $\mathbf{In}^\circ$, which models the movement of an ambient labeled A_1° inside an ambient labeled A_2°. It can be applied whenever they may be siblings, meaning that they may reside, at the same time, inside an ambient (labeled A_3°) and that they offer the right action or coaction. Formally: (i) a configuration C_3° for A_3° contains *both* A_1° and A_2°; (ii) configurations C_1° and C_2° for A_1° and A_2° contain capabilities $\mathbf{in}\, M^\circ$ and $\overline{\mathbf{in}}\, M^\circ$, resp..

The rule is based on the following intuition: (1) we generate fresh labels for describing the instance of ambients labeled A_1°, A_2° A_3° involved in the movement (e.g. $\mathbf{new}(A_i^\circ)$ for $i \in \{1,2,3\}$); (2) we design new configurations representing the variation of their contents, due to the movement. In particular,

1. $C_{1,1}^\circ$ describes the local process of ambient $\mathbf{new}(A_1^\circ)$; it is obtained from configuration C_1°, by adding the translation of the continuation and by removing the executed process (according to their multiplicities);
2. $C_{2,1}^\circ$ describes the contents of ambient $\mathbf{new}(A_2^\circ)$ similarly as in case 1, in addition an ambient $\mathbf{new}(A_1^\circ)$ is introduced in C_2°;
3. $C_{3,1}^\circ$ describes the contents of ambient $\mathbf{new}(A_3^\circ)$; it is obtained from C_3° taking into account that an ambient A_1° has moved into another location.

---

[5] With an abuse of notation $S^\circ\sigma = \{((\sigma(A^\circ), C^\circ\sigma) \mid (A^\circ, C^\circ) \in S^\circ\}$.

Table 4. Abstract Transitions

Rec°
$$\frac{(A^\circ, C^\circ) \in S^\circ \qquad (T^\circ, \mathtt{m}) \in C^\circ \qquad T^\circ = \mathbf{rec}X.\,P^\circ}{S^\circ \mapsto^\circ_{\mathcal{R}^\circ \sigma} S_0^\circ \sigma}$$

$S_1^\circ = S^\circ[^{(\mathbf{new}(A^\circ),\,C_1^\circ)}/_{(A^\circ,C^\circ)}]$
$C_1^\circ = (C^\circ \backslash^\circ T^\circ) \cup^+ C_2^\circ \quad \eta^\circ(P^\circ[T^\circ/X]) = (C_2^\circ, S_2^\circ) \quad \mathcal{R}^\circ = \mathcal{R}_1^\circ \cup \{(A^\circ, \mathbf{new}(A^\circ))\}$

In°
$$\frac{\begin{array}{lll} (A_1^\circ, C_1^\circ) \in S^\circ & (T^\circ, \mathtt{m}_1) \in C_1^\circ & T^\circ = +\mathbf{in}\, m^\circ.\,P^\circ \\ (A_2^\circ, C_2^\circ) \in S^\circ & (T'^\circ, \mathtt{m}_2) \in C_2^\circ & T'^\circ = +\overline{\mathbf{in}}\, m^\circ.\,Q^\circ \\ (A_3^\circ, C_3^\circ) \in S^\circ & (A_1^\circ, \mathtt{m}_3), (A_2^\circ, \mathtt{m}_4) \in C_3^\circ & A_1^\circ = A_2^\circ \to \mathtt{m}_3 = \mathtt{m}_4 >_m 1 \end{array}}{S^\circ \mapsto^\circ_{\mathcal{R}^\circ \sigma} S_0^\circ \sigma}$$

$S_1^\circ = S^\circ[^{(\mathbf{new}(A_i^\circ),\,C_{i,1}^\circ)}/_{(A_i^\circ,C_i^\circ)}]_{i \in \{1,2,3\}} \qquad S_2^\circ = S_{1,2}^\circ \cup S_{2,2}^\circ$
$C_{1,1}^\circ = (C_1^\circ \backslash^\circ T^\circ) \cup^+ C_{1,2}^\circ \quad \eta^\circ(P^\circ) = (C_{1,2}^\circ, S_{1,2}^\circ)$
$C_{3,1}^\circ = C_3^\circ \backslash^\circ \{A_1^\circ\} \quad C_{2,1}^\circ = (C_2^\circ \backslash^\circ T'^\circ) \cup^+ C_{2,2}^\circ \cup^+ \{(\mathbf{new}(A_1^\circ), 1)\}$
$\eta^\circ(Q^\circ) = (C_{2,2}^\circ, S_{2,2}^\circ) \quad \mathcal{R}^\circ = \mathcal{R}_1^\circ \cup \{(A_i^\circ, \mathbf{new}(A_i^\circ))\}_{i \in \{1,2,3\}}$

Out°
$$\frac{\begin{array}{llll} (A_1^\circ, C_1^\circ) \in S^\circ & (T^\circ, \mathtt{m}_1) \in C_1^\circ & T^\circ = +\mathbf{out}\, m^\circ P^\circ & \\ (A_2^\circ, C_2^\circ) \in S^\circ & (T'^\circ, \mathtt{m}_2) \in C_2^\circ & T'^\circ = +\overline{\mathbf{out}}\, m^\circ.\,Q^\circ & (A_1^\circ, \mathtt{m}_3) \in C_2^\circ \\ (A_3^\circ, C_3^\circ) \in S^\circ & (A_2^\circ, \mathtt{m}_4) \in C_3^\circ & & \end{array}}{S^\circ \mapsto^\circ_{\mathcal{R}^\circ \sigma} S_0^\circ \sigma}$$

$S_1^\circ = S^\circ[^{(\mathbf{new}(A_i^\circ),\,C_{i,1}^\circ)}/_{(A_i^\circ,C_i^\circ)}]_{i \in \{1,2,3\}} \qquad S_2^\circ = S_{1,2}^\circ \cup S_{2,2}^\circ$
$C_{1,1}^\circ = (C_1^\circ \backslash^\circ T^\circ) \cup^+ C_{1,2}^\circ \quad \eta^\circ(P^\circ) = (C_{1,2}^\circ, S_{1,2}^\circ)$
$C_{2,1}^\circ = (C_2^\circ \backslash^\circ \{T'^\circ, A_1^\circ\} \quad \eta^\circ(Q^\circ) = (C_{2,2}^\circ, S_{2,2}^\circ)$
$C_{3,1}^\circ = C_3^\circ \cup^+ \{(\mathbf{new}(A_1^\circ), 1)\} \quad \mathcal{R}^\circ = \mathcal{R}_1^\circ \cup \{(A_i^\circ, \mathbf{new}(A_i^\circ))\}_{i \in \{1,2,3\}}$

Merge°
$$\frac{\begin{array}{lll} (A_1^\circ, C_1^\circ) \in S^\circ & (T^\circ, \mathtt{m}_1) \in C_1^\circ & T^\circ = +\mathbf{merge}\, m^\circ P^\circ \\ (A_2^\circ, C_2^\circ) \in S^\circ & (T'^\circ, \mathtt{m}_2) \in C_2^\circ & T'^\circ = +\overline{\mathbf{merge}}\, m^\circ.\,Q^\circ \\ (A_3^\circ, C_3^\circ) \in S^\circ & (A_1^\circ, \mathtt{m}_3)(A_2^\circ, \mathtt{m}_4) \in C_3^\circ & A_1^\circ = A_2^\circ \to \mathtt{m}_3 = \mathtt{m}_4 >_m 1 \end{array}}{S^\circ \mapsto^\circ_{\mathcal{R}^\circ \sigma} S_0^\circ \sigma}$$

$S_1^\circ = S^\circ[^{(\mathbf{new}(A_i^\circ),\,C_{i,1}^\circ)}/_{(A_i^\circ,C_i^\circ)}]_{i \in \{1,2,3\}} \qquad S_2^\circ = S_{1,2}^\circ \cup S_{2,2}^\circ$
$C_{1,1}^\circ = (C_1^\circ \backslash^\circ T^\circ) \cup^+ C_{1,2}^\circ \cup^+ C_{2,2}^\circ \quad \eta^\circ(P^\circ) = (C_{1,2}^\circ, S_{1,2}^\circ) \quad \eta^\circ(Q^\circ) = (C_{2,2}^\circ, S_{2,2}^\circ)$
$C_{3,1}^\circ = C_3^\circ \backslash^\circ \{A_1^\circ, A_2^\circ\} \cup^+ \{(\mathbf{new}(A_1^\circ), 1)\} \quad \mathcal{R}^\circ = \mathcal{R}_1^\circ \cup \{(A_i^\circ, \mathbf{new}(A_i^\circ))\}_{i \in \{1,3\}} \cup \{(A_2^\circ, \bot)\}$

Common Part
$S_0^\circ = S_1^\circ \cup S_2^\circ \quad \sigma \in \mathcal{M}(S_0^\circ) \quad \mathcal{R}_1^\circ = \{(B^\circ, B^\circ) \mid B^\circ \in \mathbf{amb}(S^\circ) \cap \mathbf{amb}(S_0^\circ)\} \cup \{(\bot, \mathbf{amb}(S_2^\circ))\}$

The resulting state is $S_0^\circ = S_1^\circ \cup S_2^\circ$ where: (i) $S_2^\circ = S_{1,2}^\circ \cup S_{2,2}^\circ$ records the configurations describing the new ambients introduced by the move; (ii) S_1° is obtained from state S° by replacing (A_i°, C_i°) with $(\mathbf{new}(A_i^\circ), C_{i,1}^\circ)$, for $i \in \{1, 2, 3\}$. Finally, state S_0° is normalized (by means of a normalization function σ) in order to guarantee that the labels are properly merged according to the labeling discipline. The evolution relation R° tracks the variation of labels: (i) label A_i° is replaced by $\mathbf{new}(A_i^\circ)$ for $i \in \{1, 3\}$; (ii) all the other ambients appearing in S° remain unchanged; (iii) the translation of the new processes may introduce new ambients labels. Notice, however, that the effect of the normalization function has to be properly propagated also to relation R°. To this aim, we define $R^\circ \sigma$ in the obvious way, e.g. $R^\circ \sigma = \{(A^\circ, \sigma(B^\circ)) \mid (A^\circ, B^\circ) \in R^\circ\}$.

The abstract semantics computes the *abstract transition system* starting from a normalized version of the abstraction of the process. Given a process $P \in \mathcal{P}$ and $\sigma \in \mathcal{M}(\alpha^\circ(P))$, we define $\mathfrak{S}^\circ[\![P]\!]$, as the transition system obtained from the initial process $\alpha^\circ(P)\sigma$ by considering the transitive closure of $\mapsto^\circ_{\mathcal{R}^\circ}$.

Theorem 2 (Safeness). *Let $P \in \mathcal{P}$ be a process, then $\alpha^\circ(\mathfrak{S}[\![P]\!]) \subseteq {}^\circ\mathfrak{S}^\circ[\![P]\!]$.*

4   An Example

We consider the (well-labeled) system (1) illustrated in the Introduction and we present (in an informal way) the validation of the check-point property.

$$SYS ::= [M]^{(mol,\Psi_1)} \mid \ldots \mid [M]^{(mol,\Psi_h)} \mid [E]^{(e,\Delta_1)} \mid \ldots \mid [E]^{(e,\Delta_k)}$$
$$E ::= \mathbf{rec}\, Y.\overline{\mathbf{in}}\, m.\overline{\mathbf{out}}\, n.Y \quad M ::= \mathbf{in}\, m.\overline{\mathbf{out}}\, n.P$$

We assume the same abstraction of names and labels of Ex. 1, and that $max_{mol} = 6$ and $max_e = max_T = 0$. We obtain the abstract transition system of Fig.1[6], where we have an abstract transition $S_i^\circ \mapsto^\circ_{\mathcal{R}_{i,j}} S_j^\circ$ for each $\mathcal{R}_{i,j} = \mathcal{R}_{S_i^\circ,S_j^\circ} \cup \mathrm{id}(\mathrm{amb}(S_i^\circ))$ listed below.

$S_1^\circ = \{(\top, C_{0,1}^\circ), (A_1^\circ, C_{1,1}^\circ), (B_\infty^\circ, C_{2,1}^\circ)\}$ $S_2^\circ = \{(\top, C_{0,1}^\circ), (A_1^\circ, C_{1,1}^\circ), (B_\infty^\circ, C_{2,1}^\circ), (B_\infty^\circ, C_{2,2}^\circ)\}$
$S_3^\circ = \{(\top, C_{0,1}^\circ), (A_1^\circ, C_{1,1}^\circ), (A_2^\circ, C_{1,2}^\circ), (B_\infty^\circ, C_{2,1}^\circ), (B_\infty^\circ, C_{2,2}^\circ), (B_\infty^\circ, C_{2,3}^\circ)\}$
$S_4^\circ = \{(\top, C_{0,2}^\circ), (A_1^\circ, C_{1,1}^\circ), (A_2^\circ, C_{1,2}^\circ), (A_3^\circ, C_{1,3}^\circ)(B_\infty^\circ, C_{2,1}^\circ), (B_\infty^\circ, C_{2,2}^\circ), (B_\infty^\circ, C_{2,3}^\circ)\}$
$S_5^\circ = \{(\top, C_{0,3}^\circ), (A_1^\circ, C_{1,1}^\circ), (A_2^\circ, C_{1,2}^\circ), (A_3^\circ, C_{1,3}^\circ)(B_\infty^\circ, C_{2,1}^\circ), (B_\infty^\circ, C_{2,2}^\circ), (B_\infty^\circ, C_{2,3}^\circ)\}$

$C_{0,1}^\circ = \{(A_1^\circ, [0 - \omega]), (B_\infty^\circ, [0 - \omega])\}$ $C_{0,2}^\circ = \{(A_1^\circ, [0 - \omega]), (A_3^\circ, 1), (B_\infty^\circ, [0 - \omega])\}$
$C_{0,3}^\circ = \{(A_1^\circ, [0 - \omega]), (A_3^\circ, [0 - \omega]), (B_\infty^\circ, [0 - \omega])\}$
$C_{1,1}^\circ = \{(M^\circ, 1)\}$ $M^\circ ::= \mathbf{in}\, m^\circ.\overline{\mathbf{out}}\, m^\circ.P^\circ$ $C_{1,2}^\circ = \{(\overline{\mathbf{out}}\, m^\circ.P^\circ, 1)\}$ $C_{1,3}^\circ = \{(P^\circ, 1)\}$
$C_{2,1}^\circ = \{(E^\circ, 1)\}$ $C_{2,2}^\circ = \{(E_1^\circ, 1)\}$ $C_{2,3}^\circ = \{(E_2^\circ, 1), (A_2^\circ, 1)\}$
$E^\circ ::= \mathbf{rec}\, Y.\overline{\mathbf{in}}\, m^\circ.\overline{\mathbf{out}}\, m^\circ.Y$ $E_1^\circ = \overline{\mathbf{in}}\, m^\circ.\overline{\mathbf{out}}\, m^\circ.E^\circ$ $E_2^\circ = \overline{\mathbf{out}}\, m^\circ.E^\circ$

$\mathcal{R}_{S_1^\circ,S_2^\circ} = \mathcal{R}_{S_2^\circ,S_2^\circ} = \mathcal{R}_{S_3^\circ,S_3^\circ} = \mathcal{R}_{S_4^\circ,S_4^\circ} = \mathcal{R}_{S_5^\circ,S_5^\circ} = \emptyset$
$\mathcal{R}_{S_2^\circ,S_3^\circ} = \mathcal{R}_{S_3^\circ,S_3^\circ} = \mathcal{R}_{S_4^\circ,S_4^\circ} = \mathcal{R}_{S_5^\circ,S_5^\circ} = \{(A_1^\circ, A_2^\circ)\}$
$\mathcal{R}_{S_3^\circ,S_4^\circ} = \mathcal{R}_{S_4^\circ,S_5^\circ} = \mathcal{R}_{S_5^\circ,S_5^\circ} = \{(A_2^\circ, A_3^\circ)\}$

State S_1° is the normalization of the translation of SYS, obtained by identifying by means of the same abstract label the occurrences of ambients mol and e, described by the same configuration. Note that all the occurrences of ambients e are described by label $B_\infty = (e, \infty)$, since $max_e = 0$.

Transition $S_1^\circ \mapsto^\circ_{\mathcal{R}_{1,2}} S_2^\circ$ is obtained by rule **Rec°**, and models the unfolding of process E° inside an ambient e (labeled B_∞°). Due to normalization all the occurrences of ambients e are described by label B_∞°; however, a new configuration is added $C_{2,2}^\circ$ (containing the unfolded process E_1°). As a consequence, relation $\mathcal{R}_{1,2} = \mathrm{id}(\mathrm{amb}(S_1^\circ))$ shows that there is no variation of labels.

Transition $S_2^\circ \mapsto^\circ_{\mathcal{R}_{2,3}} S_3^\circ$ is derived by rule **In°** and models the movement of an ambient mol (labeled A_1°) inside an ambient e (labeled B_∞°). The involved

---

[6] For simplicity, we safely approximate $[1 - \omega]$ with $[0 - \omega]$.

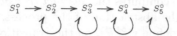

Fig. 1. The abstract transition system

ambient *mol* is represented by a fresh label A_2° and by a new configuration $C_{1,2}^\circ$ (containing the continuation of process M°). By contrast, the involved ambient e is still represented by label B_∞° (due to normalization) and by a new configuration $C_{2,3}^\circ$ (where an occurrence of ambient A_2° is added). The variation of labels is recorded accordingly in relation $\mathcal{R}_{2,3} = \{(B_\infty^\circ, B_\infty^\circ), (A_1^\circ, A_2^\circ), (A_1^\circ, A_1^\circ), (\top, \top)\}$.

Transition $S_3^\circ \mapsto_{\mathcal{R}_{3,4}} S_4^\circ$ (and analogously $S_4^\circ \mapsto_{\mathcal{R}_{4,5}} S_5^\circ$) is derived by rule **Out°** and models the movement of an ambient *mol* (labeled A_2°) out from an ambient e (labeled B_∞°). Similarly as in the case of **In°**, the involved ambient *mol* is modeled by a fresh label A_3° and by a new configuration $C_{1,3}^\circ$ (containing process P°). Relation $\mathcal{R}_{3,4} = \{(B_\infty^\circ, B_\infty^\circ), (A_2^\circ, A_2^\circ), (A_1^\circ, A_1^\circ), (\top, \top), (A_2^\circ, A_3^\circ)\}$ reports the variation of labels.

Finally, notice that loop-transitions are due to the presence of several copies of the molecule and enzyme ambients in SYS; they show that other occurrences may repeat one of the previous interactions.

The simple reaction modeled by SYS is characterized by a crucial property: for any ambient *mol*, the binding with an enzyme ambient is *necessary* for the release of product P. This requirement can be expressed more formally by saying that, for each ambient (named) *mol*: the presence inside an ambient e (denoted by $[mol]^e$) is a *necessary check-point* for the presence of process P running at top-level (denoted by $[P]^{mol}$). This property can be established by reasoning on the abstract transition system of SYS.

Intuitively, when just one copy of *mol* and e are in the system we should verify that: for each path (starting from the initial state) where there exists a state which *may satisfy* $[P]^{mol}$ there also exists a *previous* state which *must satisfy* $[mol]^e$. The validation of state formulas such as $[P]^{mol}$ and $[mol]^e$ is immediate and can be formalized by simple conditions related to the configurations describing the possible contents of ambients (named) *mol* and (named) e resp.. In the former case a state *may satisfy* $[P]^{mol}$ whenever there exists a configuration related to a label for name *mol*, which reports the possible presence of process P. In the latter case, instead, a state *must satisfy* $[mol]^e$, whenever each configuration related to a label for name e guarantees the presence of ambient *mol*. Given that the abstract transition system is a safe over-approximation of the concrete one this reasoning guarantees that the check-point property holds also for the concrete transition system.

When more than one copies of ambients *mol* and e comes into the picture we have to establish the previous property *for any* occurrence of ambient *mol*. To this aim, however, we can profitably exploit the labeling discipline in order to trace the possible evolution of each occurrence of ambient *mol*. Intuitively, we have to consider all the labels related to name *mol* appearing in the initial state; then, we have to observe their possible moves by taking into account each abstract transition and the possible variations of labels (reported by the evolution relation). We discuss the main steps of the validation.

We recall that all the ambients (named) mol appearing in the system are initially described by label A_1° (see state S_1°). Moreover, we observe that there are only two states which $may\ satisfy\ [P]^{mol}$, e.g. S_4° and S_5°. Both states say that the ambients mol labeled A_3° may contain process P, as reported by configuration $C_{1,3}^\circ$. Hence, we can restrict the attention to the paths from state S_1° to states S_4° and S_5°, by taking into account the corresponding evolution of label A_1°. For each, we have to guarantee that $either$ label A_1° cannot evolve into label A_3° or that there exists an intermediate state and a corresponding label which $must$ $satisfy\ [mol]^e$.

We begin by observing that state S_1° shows that there are no occurrence of ambient mol which satisfy $[mol]^e$. This is because all the occurrences of ambients e are described by label B_∞° and by configuration $C_{2,1}^\circ$, which does not contain ambients labeled A_1°. Hence, we have to consider the possible derivatives of label A_1° for each move.

In the move from S_1° to S_2° no variation of the labels related to name mol, e.g. A_1°, is reported. Therefore, we are left in considering again label A_1° in state S_2°. Analogously as in the case of S_1°, there are no occurrences of ambient mol which satisfy $[mol]^e$. As a consequence, we have still to consider the possible derivates of label A_1° for each move.

In the move from S_2° to S_3° pairs $(A_1^\circ, A_2^\circ), (A_1^\circ, A_1^\circ)$ appear in the evolution relation $\mathcal{R}_{2,3}$ showing a variation of label A_1°. This means that in state S_3° we have to consider $both$ labels A_1° and A_2°. For A_1° the same considerations used in states S_1° and S_2° hold; by contrast, the occurrences related to label A_2° satisfy property $[mol]^e$. In fact, all the occurrences related to A_2°, appearing in the system, $must$ reside inside an ambient named e (if any) labeled B_∞, described by configuration $C_{2,3}^\circ$. Therefore, we are left to consider again the possible evolution of label A_1°, for each move (label A_2° is not considered anymore because we have already established $[mol]^e$).

In the move from S_3° to S_4° we observe that, according to relation $\mathcal{R}_{3,4}$, label A_1° does not vary, thus we have to consider again label A_1°. Notice that S_4° is one of the critical states in that it reports the possibility for some occurrences of ambients mol (those related to label A_3) to satisfy $[P]^{mol}$. However, there is no violation of the check-point formula in that: label A_3 is an evolution of label A_2 for which we have already proved $[mol]^e$ in a previous state. For label A_1 in state S_4° it is enough to apply the same arguments used for state S_3°. This means that we have to continue by considering the possible images of label A_1° in state S_5°. For S_5° it is enough to apply an argument similar to that used for S_4°, by observing that label A_1° does not vary.

Note that, in the reasoning above, we have not considered loop-transitions. Since they model the same variations of labels, it is enough to repeat the same arguments applied before.

5 Conclusions and Related Works

Our analysis is much more informative and powerful with respect to the reachability analyses for BA/MA. This is obviously paid in terms of complexity (in the worst case, the analysis is double exponential in the size of the abstract process); by contrast, most of the existing proposals [27,11,14,21,29,28,30,31,15] are associated with polynomial time algorithms. Our approach, however, offers several possibilities for finding a balance between precision and computational cost. The abstraction is parametric, in the sense that one can choose *which part of the system he is interested in*: (i) by defining equivalence classes of names; and (ii) by properly choosing the parameters max_{a° for each abstract name a°. Moreover, in [17] we show that the *widening operators* [9] approach of abstract interpretation can suitably be applied also to our analysis, and we derive a weaker but more efficient (exponential) analysis. The widening is obtained by merging into a single configuration all the configurations related to a given name a° and run-time label ∞. This widening is still able to prove the checkpoint property for system (1) discussed in this paper.

A few related papers have to be mentioned. The reachability analyses of [26,14,15] compute very precise information about occurrence counting, and support the validation of interesting properties, such as mutual exclusion. The techniques of [26,15] could probably be extended in order to derive an abstract transition system, able to accurately describe multiple copies of ambients. It is not clear whether the validation of temporal properties, which hold for any occurrence of an ambient, can be formalized in this setting. In [13] an occurrence counting analysis has been used to infer temporal properties of π-calculus processes. [12] defines for MA a finite abstract model able to establish security properties by means of model checking techniques. The derived model, however, is not sufficiently precise for validating the examples illustrated in this paper.

References

1. R. Barbuti, S. Cataudella, A. Maggiolo-Schettini, P. Milazzo and A.Troina, *A Probabilistic Calculus for Molecular Systems*. Proc. of Workshop CS & P, Humboldt University, vol 202–216, 2004.
2. L. Cardelli. *Membrane Interactions*. Proc. of BioCONCUR '03, ENTCS, 2003.
3. L. Caires, L. Cardelli. *A Spatial Logic for Concurrency*. Information and Computation, 186, 194-235, 2003.
4. L. Cardelli and A.D. Gordon. *Mobile ambients*. TCS 240, 177–213, 2000.
5. N. Chabrier, Marc Chiaverini, Vincent Danosand F. Fages. *Modeling and querying biomolecular interaction networks*. Theoretical Computer Science 325(1), 25-44, 2004.
6. M. Clarke, O. Grumberg and E. Long. *Model Checking and Abstraction*. TOPLAS, 16(5), 1512-1542, 1994.
7. P. Cousot and R. Cousot. *Abstract Interpretation: A Unified Lattice Model for Static Analysis of Programs by Construction or Approximation of Fixpoints*. Proc. of POPL'77, 238–252, 1977.

8. P. Cousot and R. Cousot. *Systematic Design of Program Analysis Frameworks.* Proc. of POPL'79 , 269–282, 1979.

9. P. Cousot and R. Cousot. *Comparing the Galois Connection and Widening/ Narrowing Approaches to Abstract Interpretation.* Proc. of PLILP'92, LNCS 631, 269–295, 1992.

10. D. Dams, R. Gerth and O. Grumberg. *Abstract Interpretation of Reactive Systems.* TOPLAS, 19(2), 253-291, 1997.

11. P. Degano, F. Levi and C. Bodei. *Safe Ambients: Control Flow Analysis and Security.* Proc. of ASIAN '00, LNCS 1961, 199-214, 2000.

12. D. Distefano. *A Parametric Model for the Analysis of Mobile Ambients.* Proc. of APLAS' 05, LNCS 3780, 401–417, Springer Verlag, 2005.

13. J. Feret. *Occurrence Counting Analysis for the pi-calculus.* ENTCS 39, 2001.

14. J. Feret. *Abstract Interpretation-Based Static Analysis of Mobile Ambients.* Proc. of SAS'01, LNCS 2126, 412-430, Springer Verlag, 2001.

15. J. Feret. *Analysis of mobile systems by abstract interpretation.* PhD Thesis, 2005.

16. R.Gori and F. Levi. *A new occurrence Counting analysis for BioAmbients.* Proc. of APLAS '05, LNCS 3780, 381–400, 2005.

17. R.Gori and F. Levi. *An Analysis for proving Temporal Properties of Biological Systems (Extended Version).* Available at http://www.di.unipi.it/~ levifran/ papers.html, 2006.

18. R. R. Hansen and J. G. Jensen and F. Nielson and H. R.Nielson. *Abstract Interpretation of Mobile Ambients.* Proc. of SAS'99, LNCS 1694, 135-148, Springer-Verlag, 1999.

19. N. Kam, D. Harel, H. Kugler, R. Marelly, A. Pnueli, E.J.A. Hubbard and M.J. Stern. *Formal Modeling of C. elegans Development: A Scenario-Based Approach.* Proc. of CMSB' 03, LNCS 2602, 4-20, 2003.

20. R. Hofestadt and S.Thelen. *Quantitative modeling of biochemical networks.* Silico Biology, volume1, 39-53, 1998.

21. F. Levi and S. Maffeis. *On Abstract Interpretation of Mobile Ambients.* Information and Computation 188, 179–240, 2004.

22. F. Levi and D. Sangiorgi. *Mobile Safe Ambients.* TOPLAS, 25(1), 1–69. ACM Press, 2003.

23. R. Mardare and C. Priami. *Logical Analysis of Biological Systems.* Fundamenta Informaticae, 64, 271–285, 2005.

24. R. Mardare, O. Vagin, P. Quaglia and C. Priami. *Model Checking Biological Systems described using Ambient Calculus.* Proc. of CMSB'04, LNCS 3082, 85–103, 2005.

25. H.Matsuno, A.Doi, M.Nagasaki and S.Miyano. *Hybrid petri net representation of gene regulatory network.* Pacific Symposium on Biocomputing (5), 338-349, 2000.

26. F. Nielson and H.R. Nielson. *Shape analysis for mobile ambients.* Proc. of POPL'00, 142-154, ACM Press, 2000.

27. F. Nielson, H.R. Nielson, R.R. Hansen. *Validating firewalls using flow logics.* TCS, 283(2), 381-418, 2002.

28. F. Nielson, H.R. Nielson and H. Pilegaard. *Spatial Analysis of BioAmbients.* Proc. of SAS'04, LNCS 3148, pp. 69–83, Springer-Verlag, 2004.

29. F. Nielson, H.R. Nielson, C. Priami and D. Schuch da Rosa. *Control Flow Analysis for BioAmbients.* Proc. of BioCONCUR'03, ENTCS, 2003.

30. F. Nielson, H.R. Nielson, C. Priami and D. Schuch da Rosa. *Static Analysis for Systems Biology.* Proc. of the winter International Symposium on Information and Communication Technologies, 1–6, 2004.

31. H. Pilegaard, F. Nielson and H.R. Nielson. *Static Analysis of a Model of the LDL Degradation Pathway.* Proc. of CMSB'05, 2005.
32. C.Priami and P. Quaglia. *Beta binders for biological interactions.* Proc. of CMSB'04, LNCS 3082,20–33,2005
33. C. Priami, A. Regev, W. Silverman and E. Shapiro. *Application of a stochastic name-passing calculus to representation and simulation of molecular processes.* Information Processing Letters, 80 (1), 25–31, 2001.
34. A. Regev, E. M. Panina, W. Silverman, L. Cardelli and E. Shapiro. *BioAmbients: an Abstraction for Biological Compartments.* TCS, 325, 141–167, 2004.
35. A. Regev, W. Silverman and E. Shapiro. *Representation and Simulation of Biochemical Processes using the pi-calculus process algebra.* Proc. of the Pacific Symposium on Biocomputing 2001, 6, 459–470, 2001.

Computational Secrecy by Typing for the Pi Calculus

Martín Abadi[1,2], Ricardo Corin[1,3], and Cédric Fournet[1]

[1] Microsoft Research
[2] University of California, Santa Cruz
[3] University of Twente

Abstract. We define and study a distributed cryptographic implementation for an asynchronous pi calculus. At the source level, we adapt simple type systems designed for establishing formal secrecy properties. We show that those secrecy properties have counterparts in the implementation, not formally but at the level of bitstrings, and with respect to probabilistic polynomial-time active adversaries. We rely on compilation to a typed intermediate language with a fixed scheduling strategy. While we exploit interesting, previous theorems for that intermediate language, our result appears to be the first computational soundness theorem for a standard process calculus with mobile channels.

1   Introduction

In security, both attacks and defenses can operate at various levels of abstraction. For a distributed program, reasoning about security can be in terms of programming-language constructs and concepts, or in terms of their implementations. When those implementations use cryptography, the cryptographic primitives may be represented as black boxes, as specific functions on bitstrings, or even as computing processes with timing and power-consumption characteristics that an attacker may attempt to exploit. While programming abstractions for security can be helpful, they should ideally be mapped to concrete implementations that resist realistic low-level attacks.

In the last decade, a substantial research effort has started to address this problem (e.g., [1, 5, 7, 9, 11–13, 17, 19]). In this paper, we contribute to this line of work by investigating an implementation of a concurrent language with message passing and channel mobility. We treat cryptography both formally (in terms of symbolic expressions) and computationally (at the level of bitstrings, with resource-bounded adversaries).

Specifically, we define and study a distributed cryptographic implementation for an asynchronous pi calculus. At the source level, we adapt simple type systems designed for establishing formal secrecy properties. In particular, we rely on secrecy types for asymmetric communication, in the style of the local pi calculus [3, 18], and on the name-confinement guarantees implied by putting names into scoped groups [14]. We show that those secrecy properties have strong computational counterparts in the implementation, with respect to probabilistic polynomial-time active adversaries that operate on concrete bitstrings.

The implementation leverages Laud's recent results [17] on secrecy by typing in the context of a simulatable cryptographic library [9, 11, 12]. Laud has defined a restricted variant of the spi calculus [6] with a fixed scheduling strategy and without channel mobility (so with fixed, global communication ports). We use Laud's calculus as an

N. Kobayashi (Ed.): APLAS 2006, LNCS 4279, pp. 253–269, 2006.

intermediate language: we translate the pi calculus to his calculus, then rely on his use of the simulatable cryptographic library. Laud employs a type system for secrecy and proves its soundness with respect to the cryptographic library. We show that our translation is type-preserving. Then, via Laud's results, we obtain computational secrecy guarantees, as a soundness theorem for our pi calculus typings.

Related Work. The comparison of formal and computational cryptography is an active research field (e.g., [7, 11, 17, 19]); it has produced computational justifications for formal models of cryptographic operations and for classes of protocols that use formal cryptography. At a higher level, we have implementations of process calculi in terms of black-box, formal cryptography (e.g., [1, 4, 5]). It might be tempting to try to compose the results from those two efforts. For instance, one might imagine a translation from the pi calculus to Turing machines via the spi calculus. Unfortunately, this strategy is not viable at present, and may never be. First, compiling the pi calculus to the spi calculus while preserving security guarantees is difficult at best [1]. In addition, we lack a full computational interpretation for the pi or the spi calculus; in particular, the pi calculus features non-determinism and non-termination, which seem at odds with probabilistic polynomial-time computation. Type systems do help, as does a certain realism in setting goals—for instance, aiming to preserve only secrecy properties, and not necessarily all testing equivalences. Alternatively, one may alter the pi calculus to reflect implementation constraints; Adão and Fournet [8] thus designed a calculus with mobile names (but not mobile channels) and ad hoc communications primitives, and established the computational soundness of its implementation for observational equivalence. Other works also develop implementations of abstract security functions. In particular, Canetti and Krawczyk have considered the problem of implementing secure channels [13], without however a language framework.

Our main result appears to be the first computational soundness theorem for a standard process calculus with mobile channels. In fact, the literature does not seem to contain even a computational soundness theorem for CCS. Going beyond CCS, the main difficulties that we address pertain to channel scopes and mobility, which are central to the pi calculus. Secrecy by typing can be regarded as a discipline for that mobility.

Contents. Section 2 defines our source language. Section 3 presents a local type system. Section 4 explains the intermediate language. Section 5 describes a distributed implementation of the asynchronous pi calculus. Section 6 presents the computational secrecy result. Section 7 considers the addition of name groups. Section 8 concludes.

2   The Source Language

This section introduces our source process calculus, by giving its syntax and semantics. It also discusses secrecy, informally.

The syntax of the calculus appears in Figure 1. It assumes an infinite set of names and an infinite set of variables; a, b, c, k, s, and similar identifiers range over names, and x, y, and z range over variables. The syntax distinguishes a category of terms (data) and processes (programs). The terms are variables and names. The processes include constructs for communication, concurrency, and dynamic name creation, roughly those of the pi calculus, and a conditional. The calculus is polyadic, in the sense that messages

$M, N ::=$	terms	$P, Q ::=$	processes
x, y, z	variable	$\overline{M}\langle M_1, \ldots, M_n\rangle$	output
a, b, c, k, s	name	$M(x_1, \ldots, x_n).P$	input
		$!M(x_1, \ldots, x_n).P$	replicated input
		0	nil
		$P \mid Q$	parallel composition
		$(\nu a)P$	restriction
		if $M = N$ then P else Q	conditional

Fig. 1. Syntax of the process calculus

are tuples of terms, and asynchronous, in the sense that the output construct does not have a built-in acknowledgment. Inputs may be replicated by prefixing a "!". We write $!^=M(x_1, \ldots, x_n)$ when the replication is optional. As usual, we may omit an "*else*" clause when it consists of the nil process 0. The name a is bound in $(\nu a)P$. The variables $x_1, \ldots, x_n$ are bound in P in the process $M(x_1, \ldots, x_n).P$. We write $fn(P)$ for the set of names free in P. A process is closed if it has no free variables; it may have free names. We identify processes up to renaming of bound names and variables.

The semantics of our calculus is defined as usual for the asynchronous pi calculus. We write $P \rightarrow Q$ when P reduces to Q in a single reduction step. We write $P \equiv Q$ when P and Q are structurally equivalent. We also let $\approx$ represent weak observational congruence. These relations are defined only on closed processes; their definitions appear in the full version of this paper.

Concepts of Secrecy. In this formal setting, there are two different definitions of secrecy. (See [2] for some discussion and references.) According to the first definition, a process P preserves the secrecy of a piece of data M if P never publishes M, or anything that would permit the computation of M, even in interaction with an attacker. This kind of secrecy guarantee is common in the analysis of security protocols. It is particularly adequate and effective for dealing with the secrecy of fresh values that can be viewed as atomic, such as keys and nonces. Cardelli, Ghelli, and Gordon, and also Abadi and Blanchet, use versions of this definition in their work on secrecy by typing [3, 14]. Even though both Laud's type system and ours draw on those works, our computational results correspond to a stronger definition of secrecy. According to this second definition, a process $P(x)$ preserves the secrecy of the value of a variable x if an adversary cannot distinguish $P(M)$ from $P(N)$ for every M and N. This definition has the advantage of excluding partial or implicit flows of information.

3   A Local Type System for the Source Language

In this section we give a first type system for the source language. This type system enforces asymmetric communication in the sense of the local pi calculus [18].

Our type system is based upon that of Abadi and Blanchet [3], as is Laud's (so this section is partly a review, borrowing from previous papers). More precisely, we adapt a fragment of the original type system which excludes cryptography. In order to match Laud's intermediate type system, we also modify the subtyping relation, and restrict the typing rule for conditionals. Our types are defined by the grammar:

$$T ::= D^{\text{Secret}} \mid C^{\text{Secret}}[T_1, \ldots, T_n] \mid C^{\text{Public}}[T_1, \ldots, T_n] \mid \text{Public}$$

Type D^{Secret} is used for data intended to be kept secret, like message payloads of a protocol; $C^{\text{Secret}}[T_1, \ldots, T_n]$ is the type of a channel on which the adversary cannot communicate, and which carries n-tuples with components of types $T_1, \ldots, T_n$. On the other hand, $C^{\text{Public}}[T_1, \ldots, T_n]$ is the type of a channel on which the adversary may send (but not receive) messages; the channel may be intended to carry n-tuples with components of types $T_1, \ldots, T_n$, but the adversary may send any data it has on the channel. Finally, Public is the type of all public data. The subtyping relation is the least reflexive relation such that $C^{\text{Public}}[T_1, \ldots, T_n] \leq \text{Public}$.

The rules of the type system concern four judgments:

- $E \vdash \diamond$ means that E is a well-formed environment.
- $E \vdash M : T$ means that M is a term of type T in environment E.
- $E \vdash_\diamond M : S$ means that S is the set of possible "true" types of M in environment E.
- $E \vdash P$ says that the process P is well-typed in environment E.

The rules are as follows. The metavariable u ranges over both names and variables.

Well-formed environment:
$$\frac{}{\emptyset \vdash \diamond} \qquad \frac{E \vdash \diamond \quad u \notin dom(E)}{E, u : T \vdash \diamond}$$

Terms:
$$\frac{E \vdash \diamond \quad (u : T) \in E}{E \vdash u : T} \qquad \frac{E \vdash M : T \quad T \leq T'}{E \vdash M : T'}$$

Sets of types of terms:
$$\frac{E \vdash \diamond \quad (x : T) \in E}{E \vdash_\diamond x : \{T' \mid T' \leq T\}} \qquad \frac{E \vdash \diamond \quad (a : T) \in E}{E \vdash_\diamond a : \{T\}}$$

Processes:

$$\frac{E \vdash M : \text{Public} \quad \forall i \in \{1, \ldots, n\}, E \vdash M_i : \text{Public}}{E \vdash \overline{M}\langle M_1, \ldots, M_n \rangle} \qquad \text{(Output Public)}$$

$$\frac{E \vdash M : C^L[T_1, \ldots, T_n] \quad \forall i \in \{1, \ldots, n\}, E \vdash M_i : T_i}{E \vdash \overline{M}\langle M_1, \ldots, M_n \rangle} \qquad \text{(Output } C^L)$$

$$\frac{(a : \text{Public}) \in E \quad E, x_1 : \text{Public}, \ldots, x_n : \text{Public} \vdash P}{E \vdash != a(x_1, \ldots, x_n).P} \qquad \text{(Input Public)}$$

$$\frac{(a : C^{\text{Public}}[T_1, \ldots, T_m]) \in E \quad E, x_1 : \text{Public}, \ldots, x_n : \text{Public} \vdash P \quad E, x_1 : T_1, \ldots, x_m : T_m \vdash P \text{ if } m = n}{E \vdash != a(x_1, \ldots, x_n).P} \qquad \text{(Input } C^{\text{Public}})$$

$$\frac{(a : C^{\text{Secret}}[T_1, \ldots, T_n]) \in E \quad E, x_1 : T_1, \ldots, x_n : T_n \vdash P}{E \vdash != a(x_1, \ldots, x_n).P} \qquad \text{(Input } C^{\text{Secret}})$$

$$\frac{E \vdash \diamond}{E \vdash 0}\text{(Nil)} \qquad \frac{E \vdash P \quad E \vdash Q}{E \vdash P \mid Q}\text{(Parallel)} \qquad \frac{E, a : T \vdash P \quad T \neq D^{\text{Secret}}}{E \vdash (\nu a)P}\text{(Restriction)}$$

$$\frac{E \vdash_\diamond M : S_1 \quad E \vdash_\diamond N : S_2 \quad D^{\text{Secret}} \notin S_1 \cup S_2 \quad \text{if } S_1 \cap S_2 \neq \emptyset \text{ then } E \vdash P \quad E \vdash Q}{E \vdash \text{ if } M = N \text{ then } P \text{ else } Q}$$
$$\text{(Cond)}$$

The typing rules for output say that any public data can be sent on a public channel, and tuples with the expected types $T_1, \ldots, T_n$ can be sent on a channel of type

$C^L[T_1, \ldots, T_n]$, for $L \in \{\text{Public}, \text{Secret}\}$. Therefore, by subtyping, any public data can be sent on a channel of type $C^{\text{Public}}[T_1, \ldots, T_n]$. On the other hand, the attacker cannot have channels of type $C^{\text{Secret}}[T_1, \ldots, T_n]$. Therefore, we can guarantee that only tuples with types $T_1, \ldots, T_n$ can be sent on such channels. In the rules for input, the channel in question is required to be represented by a name a (not a variable), as in the local pi calculus. We distinguish three cases, considering the type of a.

- If a is of type Public, then the corresponding output must have been typed using (Output Public), so the input values are public. Rule (Input Public) treats this case.
- When a is of type $C^{\text{Public}}[T_1, \ldots, T_m]$, two cases arise. In the first case, the corresponding output has been typed using (Output Public) and subtyping. Then the input values are of type Public. In the second case, the corresponding output has been typed using (Output C^L). In this case, the input values have the expected types $T_1, \ldots, T_m$. Rule (Input C^{Public}) takes into account both cases, by checking that the process P executed after the input is well-typed in both.
- When a is of type $C^{\text{Secret}}[T_1, \ldots, T_n]$, it cannot be known by the attacker, and the corresponding output must have been typed using (Output C^L). The input values are therefore of the expected types $T_1, \ldots, T_n$.

Rule (Cond) exploits the idea that if two terms M and N cannot have the same type, then they are certainly different. In this case, the process *if $M = N$ then P else Q* may be well-typed without P being well-typed. To determine whether M and N may have the same type, we determine the set of possible types of M and N. If M is a variable x, and $(x : T) \in E$, then x may of course have type T. Because of subtyping, when $T = \text{Public}$, x may also be replaced at run-time with a name whose type is a subtype of T. Hence the possible types of x are $\{T' \mid T' \leq T\}$. When M is a name a, its only possible type is the type assigned to it in the environment. Rule (Cond) also has a condition that excludes any comparison of D^{Secret} terms. This condition simply rules out any flow of information from D^{Secret} values to the control flow of the process, which may be observable by the adversary. Finally, rule (Restriction) excludes the creation of names with type D^{Secret} (although not of names with secret-channel types). These two last conditions on rules (Cond) and (Restriction) are not present in the work of Abadi and Blanchet, but they are imposed to meet the requirements of payload secrecy (see Section 4).

An Example. We revisit and adapt an example from Abadi and Blanchet that concerns the following protocol in which A sends to B a secret s and B acknowledges it:

$$\begin{aligned}
&\text{Message 1. } A \to B : k, a \text{ on } b \\
&\text{Message 2. } B \to A : k, k' \text{ on } a \\
&\text{Message 3. } A \to B : s \text{ on } k' \\
&\text{Message 4. } B \to A : ack \text{ on } k
\end{aligned}$$

Here, a and b are channels with A and B as only receivers, respectively. Initially, A creates a secret channel k, and sends it along with the return channel a on b. In response, B sends k, as proof of origin, along with a new secret channel k'. Finally, A sends s on k', and B sends ack on k. The goal of this protocol is to guarantee the secrecy of s.

In our calculus, we may represent the principals of this protocol by the processes:

$$\begin{aligned}
A &= (\nu k)(\overline{b}\langle k, a \rangle \mid a(x, y).\textit{if } x = k \textit{ then } (\overline{y}\langle s \rangle) \mid k(z)) \\
B &= b(x, y).(\nu k')(\overline{y}\langle x, k' \rangle \mid k'(z).\overline{x}\langle ack \rangle)
\end{aligned}$$

As detailed below, we can assign types such that $A \mid B$ typechecks with type D^{Secret} for s. According to our main result (Theorem 1), this typing implies the computational secrecy of any value substituted for s. We let

$$
\begin{aligned}
E = \ &a : C^{\text{Public}}[C^{\text{Secret}}[\text{Public}], C^{\text{Secret}}[D^{\text{Secret}}]], \\
&b : C^{\text{Public}}[C^{\text{Secret}}[\text{Public}], C^{\text{Public}}[C^{\text{Secret}}[\text{Public}], C^{\text{Secret}}[D^{\text{Secret}}]]], \\
&s : D^{\text{Secret}}, \ ack : \text{Public}
\end{aligned}
$$

and obtain $E \vdash A \mid B$ as follows. In the typing of A, we choose $k : C^{\text{Secret}}[\text{Public}]$. The output $\overline{b}\langle k, a \rangle$ is then typed by rule (Output C^L). The input $a(x, y)$ is typed by rule (Input C^{Public}), and two cases arise:

- $x : \text{Public}, y : \text{Public}$. This case is vacuous by rule (Cond): in the test $x = k$, the two terms do not have common types.
- $x : C^{\text{Secret}}[\text{Public}], y : C^{\text{Secret}}[D^{\text{Secret}}]$. In this case, the output $\overline{y}\langle s \rangle$ is typed by (Output C^L). (The condition of (Cond) is fulfilled: $D^{\text{Secret}} \notin \{C^{\text{Secret}}[\text{Public}]\}$.) The remaining input $k(z)$ is easily typed by rule (Input C^{Secret}).

In process B, the input $b(x, y)$ is typed by (Input C^{Public}), and two similar cases arise.

4   The Intermediate Language

The models of Backes et al. and Laud are concerned with configurations of probabilistic polynomial-time Turing machines. The machines are connected at ports; two ports can be connected by a wire. Some of these machines represent honest parties; others are controlled by the adversary. At any given time, at most one machine is active.

The Idealized Cryptographic Library [9–12]. The cryptographic library provides an abstract view of cryptography, in the following sense. Each principal is associated with a deterministic machine P_i; this machine is connected to a concrete instance of the library M_i that runs all cryptographic algorithms on behalf of P_i and maintains a database that maps abstract handles to cryptographic representations. Instead of n concrete library machines M_i, one can connect a single idealized library TH_n, with the same ports, that maps abstract handles to shared, symbolic ("Dolev-Yao") representations. The main results of Backes et al. relate the security of two systems that use, respectively, the concrete and idealized versions of the library, under standard computational cryptographic assumptions. Hence, in order to prove the security of a system that uses the concrete version, it suffices to reason on a system that uses the idealized version.

Laud's Intermediate Language [17]. Laud's language can be used for programming each of the machines P_i, using processes that can send and receive messages and abstractly operate on message contents using library calls. Although the language is inspired by the spi calculus, its semantics is significantly different, as it reflects low-level implementation constraints of the cryptographic library. In particular:

- Communications occur on global, static, bidirectional channels, associated with the ports of the underlying machines. Some of these channels are intrinsically secure, but are used solely to code initialization and security specifications.

- The adversary controls the scheduling between machines, and all channels that represent an untrusted network. Hence, it can intercept all network traffic, and even disable the execution of a local process. (In contrast, a pi calculus context can read a replicated output message on a public channel, but cannot prevent other processes from reading it as well; see [8].)
- In other respects, the language is deterministic; in particular, parallel execution within a machine is supported by an interpreter that maintains a run-queue of input processes.
- The control flow of the machines is carefully restricted. When a machine is activated, it reads a single message from one of its input wires, it processes the message and runs for a bounded amount of time, it puts at most one message in one of its output wires, and yields.
- The usage of the library imposes some programming discipline, for instance to exclude encryption cycles [9] or the leakage of private keys.

We use the following grammar for Laud's language, with minor syntactic changes:

$v ::=$	values	$I ::=$	input process
x	variable	$c(x).Q$	input
n	integer constant	$!c(x).Q$	replicated input
$\perp$	failed computation	$I^* ::=$	sequence of inputs
$e ::=$	expressions	$I; I^*$	
v	value	0	
$\mathsf{gen\_nonce}()$	nonce generation	$Q ::=$	processes
$\mathsf{gen\_symenc\_key}(i)$	symmetric-key generation	I^*	input
$\mathsf{privenc}(e_k, e_t)$	symmetric-key encryption	$\overline{c}\langle e \rangle.I^*$	output
$\mathsf{privdec}(e_k, e_t)$	symmetric-key decryption	$\perp$	run-time failure
$\mathsf{keypair}()$	asymmetric-key generation	$let\ x = e\ in\ Q_1\ else\ Q_2$	
$\mathsf{pubkey}(e)$	asymmetric encryption key		let binding
$\mathsf{pubenc}(e_k, e_t)$	asymmetric-key encryption	$if\ e = e'\ then\ Q_1\ else\ Q_2$	
$\mathsf{pubdec}(e_k, e_t)$	asymmetric-key decryption		conditional
$\mathsf{store}(e)$	value storage		
$\mathsf{retrieve}(e)$	value retrieval (by handle)		
$\mathsf{list}(e_1, \ldots, e_n)$	list		
$\mathsf{list\_proj}(e_i, e)$	projection		

Expressions represent calls to the cryptographic library. These calls, when successful, return handles to new entries; otherwise they return $\perp$. Expression $\mathsf{gen\_nonce}()$ creates a fresh nonce. Expression $\mathsf{gen\_symenc\_key}(i)$ generates a symmetric key (where i is a key rank used to prevent cycles; see Section 7). Expression $\mathsf{keypair}()$ generates an asymmetric key pair and returns the private decryption key; $\mathsf{pubkey}(e)$ returns the associated encryption key. Expressions $\mathsf{privenc}(e_k, e_t)$, $\mathsf{privdec}(e_k, e_t)$, $\mathsf{pubenc}(e_k, e_t)$, and $\mathsf{pubdec}(e_k, e_t)$ provide encryptions and decryptions; decryption visibly fails if e_t is not a message encrypted under the key associated with e_k. Expressions $\mathsf{store}(e)$ and $\mathsf{retrieve}(e)$ store and retrieve data, to and from the library, respectively. Expression $\mathsf{list}(e_1, \ldots, e_n)$ constructs a list from n values; $\mathsf{list\_proj}(e_i, e)$ retrieves its ith value.

Input processes I represent passive threads, held in the interpreter run-queue. Processes Q represent threads activated by an input; they perform at most one output, and append input processes I^* to the run-queue. Processes for input, output, and conditional are similar to those of the source calculus. Process *let $x = e$ in Q_1 else Q_2* evaluates the expression e; if evaluation succeeds, then Q_1 runs with the result value substituted for x; otherwise, Q_2 runs. Process $\perp$ represents run-time failure, written II for "invalid input" in [17]. Intuitively, $\perp$ causes the current thread to abort, for instance after failing an evaluation or a test: the input process that triggered the thread is put back into the run-queue, and the rejected message is passed to the next input in the run-queue.

Next, we give the syntax for types for the intermediate language, as it is used in this paper. See [17] for further details, including the subtyping relation and the typing rules.

$$
\begin{array}{lll}
T ::= & & \text{intermediate types} \\
& \text{Public} & \text{public data} \\
& \text{SecData} & \text{secret data} \\
& \text{SNonce} & \text{secret nonce} \\
& \text{EK}[T] & \text{asymmetric encryption key} \\
& \text{DK}[T] & \text{asymmetric decryption key} \\
& \text{list}(T_1, \dots, T_n) & \text{list} \\
& \text{SK}^i[T] & \text{symmetric key} \\
& T_1 + T_2 & \text{sum}
\end{array}
$$

Type Public is the type for public data. Its counterpart for secret data is SecData. Type SNonce is the type for secret nonces. Type $\text{list}(T_1, \dots, T_n)$ is for lists. Types $\text{EK}[T]$ and $\text{DK}[T]$ are the types of public/private asymmetric keys for encrypting values of type T, while $\text{SK}^i[T]$ is the type of symmetric keys of order i for encrypting values of type T. The index i is used for avoiding encryption cycles. Finally, type $T_1 + T_2$ is the sum type of T_1 and T_2. Sum types play a role similar to the double typing of P in rule (Input C^{Public}) of Section 3.

Secrecy by Typing. A concrete configuration $C_n = \langle \text{S}, \text{H}, \text{A} \rangle$ consists of a concrete system S of $(\text{P}_i)_{i=1..n}$ machines connected to their library machines $(\text{M}_i)_{i=1..n}$, along with a user machine H connected to free ports of S, plus an adversary machine A that connects all the remaining unconnected ports. Let $(I_i)_{i=1..n}$ be intermediate-level input processes (hence, consisting of passive threads) used to program the machines P_i of S. Laud's results [17, Theorem 1, Corollary 2] say that if each I_i typechecks in some environment Γ, then C_n preserves secrecy of all data communicated by the user machine H to S. More precisely, Laud shows that in the configuration C_n, the system S preserves *payload secrecy* of all user data, in the sense defined by Backes and Pfitzmann within the simulatable cryptographic library [10]. Basically, a system S preserves payload secrecy if no adversary A, even if colluding with a user machine H, can distinguish an instance of S running with the user inputs provided by H from an instance of S where the inputs are converted to random values (and then replaced back), by a "scrambling" machine F that runs between S and H. Hence, the notion of payload secrecy can be regarded as a computational version of the second formal definition of secrecy described in Section 2.

5   A Distributed Implementation of the Source Language

In this section, we translate assemblies of pi calculus processes into intermediate-language input processes. A pi calculus process represents a concurrent system, but does not indicate the distribution of its subprocesses across machines.

For the source process $P = \prod_{i=1..n} P_i$, our implementation distributes the subprocesses P_i across the machines P_i, for each $i = 1..n$.

We first rearrange the source processes P_i into threads. We then give a compositional translation for the threads that run within each machine. Finally, we describe the top-level implementation and its initialization process.

Normal Forms for Source Processes. Source threads are processes that perform a series of name creations and tests, then yield a parallel composition of inputs and outputs. We use the following grammar:

$A ::=$		atomic processes	$T ::=$		threads
	$M(x_1, \ldots, x_n).T$	input		$(\nu n)T$	restriction
	$!M(x_1, \ldots, x_n).T$	replicated input		$if\ M = N\ then\ T\ else\ T'$	conditional
	$\overline{M}\langle M_1, \ldots, M_n \rangle$	output		$\prod_{i=1}^{n} A_i$	$(n \geq 0)$ atomic processes

For every source process P, we show that there exists a thread $T \approx P$, obtained from P by repeatedly applying the two rewriting steps below in all process contexts:

$$P \,|\, (\nu n)Q \rightsquigarrow (\nu n)(P \,|\, Q) \qquad \text{after renaming } n \text{ so that } n \notin fn(P) \qquad (1)$$

$$P \,|\, if\ M = N\ then\ Q\ else\ Q' \rightsquigarrow if\ M = N\ then\ P \,|\, Q\ else\ P \,|\, Q' \qquad (2)$$

Step (1) is a structural equivalence. Step (2) is an observational equivalence in all contexts. Both steps preserve source typing, and the rewriting always terminates. We let $\mathcal{T}(P)$ represent one such thread for P.

Machine Translation. The core of our translation maps channel-based communications to runs of a particular cryptographic protocol.

Informally, the machine run-queue contains one input process for every running atomic process of the source process. When a machine is proposed a message, the message is matched against the pending inputs in the run-queue. If the message is accepted by the translation of an input, then the message triggers the translation of a thread, which runs to completion, then returns one acknowledgment message and appends new input processes to the run-queue. If the message is accepted by the translation of an output, then the message simply triggers this pending output.

We translate a term M to a list of two elements: an encryption key and a nonce. We let $M^+ = \mathsf{list\_proj}(M, 1)$ and $M^c = \mathsf{list\_proj}(M, 2)$. We write $let\ x_1, \ldots, x_n = e\ in\ P$ to abbreviate $let\ l = e\ in\ let\ x_1 = \mathsf{list\_proj}(l, 1)\ in\ \ldots\ in\ let\ x_n = \mathsf{list\_proj}(l, n)$ $in\ P\ else\ \bot \ldots\ else\ \bot$ where l does not occur in P.

We translate processes as follows:

$$[\![\overline{M}\langle M_1, \ldots, M_n \rangle]\!] = cont(\_).\overline{net}\langle \mathsf{pubenc}(M^+, \mathsf{list}(M^c, M_1, \ldots, M_n)) \rangle$$

$$[\![!^{\scriptscriptstyle=}a(x_1, \ldots, x_n).P]\!] = !^{\scriptscriptstyle=}net(z).let\ a', x_1, \ldots, x_n = \mathsf{pubdec}(a^-, z)\ in$$
$$\qquad\qquad if\ a' = a^c\ then\ (\overline{ack}\langle\_\rangle.[\![P]\!])\ else\ \bot$$

$$[\![0]\!] = 0$$

$$[\![P \,|\, Q]\!] = [\![P]\!]; [\![Q]\!]$$

$$[\![(\nu a)P]\!] = let\ a^- = \mathsf{keypair}()\ in$$
$$\qquad\qquad (let\ a = \mathsf{list}(\mathsf{pubkey}(a^-), \mathsf{gen\_nonce}())\ in\ [\![P]\!]\ else\ 0)\ else\ 0$$

$$[\![if\ M = N\ then\ P\ else\ Q]\!] = if\ M = N\ then\ [\![P]\!]\ else\ [\![Q]\!]$$

We represent every output by an encryption followed by an output on a public channel *net*, and every input by the corresponding input and decryption. Specifically, we translate a local channel a to an asymmetric key pair (with public key a^+ and private key a^-) and a nonce a^c. The capability to receive on channel a is represented by having a^-, while the capability to send on channel a is represented by having both a^+ and a^c. The nonce a^c is necessary as well as the key a^+ because, under standard cryptographic assumptions, a^+ may be recovered from any message encrypted under a^+.

Every output is guarded by an input on channel *cont*. This guard ensures that our implementation sends one output at a time. Conversely, every successful input is acknowledged by an immediate output on channel *ack*, so that the environment knows that the message has been delivered and need not be proposed again—as required for functional correctness. (The symbol _ represents a fresh variable or a dummy value.) The translation of inputs is defined only for local channel names—not for variables, as in $x(y).P$; this condition ensures that every input translation is within the static scope of the corresponding decryption key.

Crucially, our implementation does not depend on typing information. In contrast to ordinary types, secrecy types need not be known to the implementor. They express relative secrecy properties that can be used for studying the behaviour of a system in the presence of an adversary, possibly with different typings for different adversaries.

Initialization of the Distributed Computation. Initialization deals with the free names of the source processes P_i for $i = 1..n$. We first group these names, as follows. Let $\widetilde{a}_i$ be the free names used for input in P_i. Let $\widetilde{a} = \cup \widetilde{a}_i$, $\widetilde{b}_i = fn(P_i) \setminus \widetilde{a}_i$, and $\widetilde{b} = \cup \widetilde{b}_i \setminus \widetilde{a}$. Informally, the names $\widetilde{b}$ represent data supplied by the attacker or the user.

We require that $\widetilde{a}_i \cap \widetilde{a}_j = \emptyset$ when $i \neq j$, thereby reflecting a requirement of the underlying cryptographic library: asymmetric decryption keys cannot be communicated. It is similar to the locality requirement of the local pi calculus. Otherwise, our typed translation would accommodate the distribution of private encryption keys as well.

Turning our attention to the knowledge of the adversary, we let $\widetilde{a}_{RW}$ represent names controlled by the adversary, such that $\widetilde{a}_{RW} \cap \widetilde{a} = \emptyset$, and let $\widetilde{a}_W \subseteq \widetilde{a}$ represent names made available to the adversary for output. We finally let $\widetilde{s}$ be $\widetilde{b} \setminus \widetilde{a}_{RW}$. These names represent user secrets.

We are basically interested in source processes that behave like $(\nu \widetilde{a})(\overline{export}\langle \widetilde{a}_W \rangle \mid import(\widetilde{a}_{RW}).(P_1 \mid \ldots \mid P_n)\{\widetilde{M}/\widetilde{s}\})$, where $\widetilde{M}$ are the secrets substituted for $\widetilde{s}$. In order to obtain a distributed program in the intermediate language, we use an additional machine P_0 for initialization. In particular, P_0 distributes the cryptographic materials associated with top-level restricted channels, using low-level secure communications.

We introduce syntactic sugar for polyadic communication in the intermediate language: we let $c(\widetilde{x}).P$ abbreviate $c(z).let\ \widetilde{x} = z\ in\ P$ and $\overline{c}\langle \widetilde{e} \rangle.P$ abbreviate $\overline{c}\langle list(\widetilde{e})\rangle.P$. We arrive at the following definition for the intermediate-level input processes I_0, I_1, $\ldots$, I_n initially hosted by the machines P_0, P_1, $\ldots$, P_n:

$$I_0 = (export_i\langle \widetilde{a}_i\rangle)_{i=1..n}.\overline{export}\langle \widetilde{a}_W \rangle.import(\widetilde{a}_{RW}).user(\widetilde{s}).(cont(\_).\overline{import}_i\langle \widetilde{b}_i\rangle)_{i=1..n}$$
$$I_i = cont(\_).[\![(\nu \widetilde{a}_i[\_])]\!]\ [\overline{export}_i\langle \widetilde{a}_i\rangle.import_i(\widetilde{b}_i).[\![T(P_i)]\!]] \qquad \text{for } i = 1..n$$

where $export_i$ and $import_i$ are low-level secure channels between P_0 and P_i, *user* is a low-level secure channel from the user H to P_0, *export* and *import* are low-level channels between P_0 and the adversary A, the context $[(\nu\tilde{a}_i)[\_]][\_]$ is the translation of the source context that binds the names $\tilde{a}_i$, and $(\_)_{i=1..n}$ abbreviates a sequence of actions for $i = 1, \dots, n$.

(Considering that initialization is part of the specification, rather than the implementation itself, we rely on low-level secure channels. We could perform most of the initialization on net, but we would still rely on some initial key distribution.)

In summary, our concrete distributed configuration $C_n = \langle S, H, A \rangle$ consists of a system S of $n + 1$ machines P_i that each runs the intermediate-language processes I_i defined above plus $n + 1$ library machines M_i that realize the cryptographic primitives, along with a user machine H and an adversary machine A.

Discussion. Our definition of the processes I_i for $i = 1..n$ does not depend on the origin of the imported values $\tilde{b}_i$. In other words, the implementation does not know a priori which values are controlled by the adversary. This origin is determined instead in the definition of I_0, by the multiplexing between values that come either from peer machines or from the adversary.

For simplicity, our implementation assumes that all communications are distributed—even if I_i includes matching inputs and outputs. We could also support (and typecheck) a sort of channels for machine-local communications, with an optimized implementation that does not rely on cryptography.

Our implementation is not meant to resist all attacks. Indeed, the adversary can affect the control flow of the program, for instance by replaying messages. Consider for example the source process $P = (\nu a)(\overline{a}\langle\rangle \mid a().a().\overline{adv}\langle s\rangle)$. According to the pi calculus semantics, P preserves the secrecy of s from a context that knows adv—in fact P behaves just like the inert process 0. With our implementation, the secrecy of s is broken if the adversary has the decryption key for adv: the adversary observes an opaque message on net (produced by evaluating $\mathsf{pubenc}(a^+, \mathsf{list}(a^c)))$ and it can forward that message twice to the machine that hosts the inputs on a, causing that machine to send back $\mathsf{pubenc}(adv^+, \mathsf{list}(adv^c, s))$, and eventually the adversary can extract s. Note, however, that the rules of Section 3 safely exclude any typing $E \vdash P$ that contains both $s : \mathsf{D}^{\mathsf{Secret}}$ and $adv : \mathsf{Public}$.

Functional Correctness. Although we are mainly interested in secrecy, it is also important to check that our implementation actually works. We therefore establish that our implementation is functional for one particular definition of the adversary that implements a reliable network.

To this end, we briefly recall the main notations used by Laud in the deterministic operational semantics of the intermediate language. Let $P_i[Q]$ represent the passive state of a local machine that implements the series of input processes Q, along with the state of the idealized cryptographic library. We write $(P_i[Q], \alpha) \longrightarrow\!\!\!\!\rightarrow (P_i'[Q'], \beta_\perp)$ for a series of computation steps from state $P_i[Q]$ to state $P_i'[Q']$. The message α represents an encoded input from the adversary. The outcome $\beta_\perp$ represents either an encoded output or $\perp$, which indicates either that the input was not accepted or that the input was accepted with no response. We omit the definition of encoded inputs and outputs, and simply write $((A))$ for an encoded message produced by P_i to send the source output A.

We state operational correspondences for inputs and outputs as follows. We let T, T', T'' range over parallel compositions of source inputs and outputs, and let A range over source outputs.

- If $T \mid A \to T'$ then $T \mid A \to P$ and $(\mathsf{P}_i[\![T]\!], net(\!(A)\!)) \longrightarrow\!\!\!\!\twoheadrightarrow (\mathsf{P}'_i[\![T'']\!]), ack)$ for some P and $(\nu \widetilde{a}')T'' \equiv \mathcal{T}(P)$. Otherwise, $(\mathsf{P}_i[\![T]\!], net(\!(A)\!)) \longrightarrow\!\!\!\!\twoheadrightarrow (\mathsf{P}'_i[\![T]\!], \bot)$.
- If T has an output, then $T \equiv A \mid T''$ and $(\mathsf{P}_i[\![T]\!], cont) \longrightarrow\!\!\!\!\twoheadrightarrow (\mathsf{P}'_i[\![T'']\!], net(\!(A)\!))$ for some A and T''. Otherwise, $(\mathsf{P}_i[\![T]\!], cont) \longrightarrow\!\!\!\!\twoheadrightarrow (\mathsf{P}'_i[\![T]\!], \bot)$.

These correspondences reflect an unknown, deterministic scheduling; they guarantee only that, if some threads in T may input A, then one of their implementations will input A, and similarly for outputs. In the first correspondence, $(\nu \widetilde{a}')$ represents the new restrictions in evaluation context; their translations create new keys recorded in the library, so the source restrictions are discarded in T''.

The proposition below relies on the cooperation of an adversary N that performs initialization, then repeatedly retrieves all pending outputs, stores them in a queue, and repeatedly attempts to deliver the pending outputs to each of the machines in turn. The proposition states that the implementation then follows one of the expected (finite or infinite) source traces.

Proposition 1 (Functional correctness). *Let the machines $(\mathsf{P}_i)_{i=0..n}$ implement the source processes $(P_i)_{i=1..n}$ with initialization parameters $\widetilde{a}, \widetilde{a}_{RW}, \widetilde{a}_W, \widetilde{s}$. Let S be the idealized system $((\mathsf{P}_i)_{i=0..n}, \mathsf{TH_n})$. Let $P = (\nu \widetilde{a}) \prod_{i=1..n} P_i$.*

There exist an adversary N, a user H, and source reductions $P \to^* P' \not\to$ (or $P \to^\ell P'$ for any $\ell \geq 0$) such that $P' \equiv (\nu \widetilde{a}') \prod_{i=1..n} P'_i$ and the configuration $(\mathsf{S}, \mathsf{H}, \mathsf{N})$ reaches a state such that the run-queue of every machine P_i of S contains the input processes $[\![\mathcal{T}(P'_i)]\!]$ for $i = 1..n$.

6   Computational Secrecy by Local Typing

We establish payload secrecy for the distributed implementation of arbitrary source processes. We translate types and type environments, then verify that source type derivations always yield valid type derivations in the intermediate language. The translation of types is as follows:

$$
\begin{aligned}
[\![\mathsf{D}^{\mathsf{Secret}}]\!]^t &= \mathsf{SecData} \\
[\![\mathsf{Public}]\!]^t &= \mathsf{Public} \\
[\![\mathsf{C}^{\mathsf{Secret}}[T_1, \dots, T_n]]\!]^t &= \mathsf{list}(\mathsf{EK}[\mathsf{list}(\mathsf{SNonce}, [\![T_1]\!]^t, \dots, [\![T_n]\!]^t)], \mathsf{SNonce}) \\
[\![\mathsf{C}^{\mathsf{Public}}[T_1, \dots, T_n]]\!]^t &= \mathsf{list}(\mathsf{EK}[\mathsf{list}(\mathsf{Public}, [\![T_1]\!]^t, \dots, [\![T_n]\!]^t)], \mathsf{Public})
\end{aligned}
$$

Hence, the translation of channel types follows our choice of communication protocol.

We lift our translation from types to environments. When translating the name binding for a, we bind two variables: a to the translated type, and a^- to the type of the corresponding private decryption key. We translate bindings as follows:

$$
\begin{aligned}
[\![x{:}T]\!]^t &= x{:}[\![T]\!]^t \\
[\![a{:}\mathsf{D}^{\mathsf{Secret}}]\!]^t &= a{:}[\![\mathsf{D}^{\mathsf{Secret}}]\!]^t \\
[\![a{:}\mathsf{Public}]\!]^t &= a{:}[\![\mathsf{Public}]\!]^t, a^-{:}[\![\mathsf{Public}]\!]^t \\
[\![a{:}\mathsf{C}^{\mathsf{Secret}}[T_1, \dots, T_n]]\!]^t &= a{:}[\![\mathsf{C}^{\mathsf{Secret}}[T_1, \dots, T_n]]\!]^t, a^-{:}\mathsf{DK}[\mathsf{list}(\mathsf{SNonce}, [\![T_1]\!]^t, \dots, [\![T_n]\!]^t)] \\
[\![a{:}\mathsf{C}^{\mathsf{Public}}[T_1, \dots, T_n]]\!]^t &= a{:}[\![\mathsf{C}^{\mathsf{Public}}[T_1, \dots, T_n]]\!]^t, a^-{:}\mathsf{DK}[\mathsf{list}(\mathsf{Public}, [\![T_1]\!]^t, \dots, [\![T_n]\!]^t)]
\end{aligned}
$$

We let Γ_0 be the intermediate-language environment that assigns types to the implementation channels net, ack, $cont$, $export$, $import$, and $export_i$, $import_i$, $user_i$ for $i = 1..n$ in such a way that $\Gamma_0 \vdash I_0$. (The definition of Γ_0 appears in the full version of this paper.) We let $[\![E]\!]^t$ be Γ_0 plus the translations of the bindings in E.

The next lemma states that source subtyping is preserved, and that all type derivations for source terms and processes yield type derivations in the intermediate language.

Lemma 1 (Type preservation)

1. *If $T \leq T'$ then $[\![T]\!]^t \leq [\![T']\!]^t$.*
2. *If $E \vdash M : T$ then $[\![E]\!]^t \vdash M : [\![T]\!]^t$.*
3. *If $E \vdash P$, then $[\![E]\!]^t \vdash [\![P]\!]$.*

We obtain:

Theorem 1. *Let $P = \prod_{i=1..n} P_i$. Let the machines $(\mathsf{P}_i)_{i=0..n}$ implement the source processes $(P_i)_{i=1..n}$ with initialization parameters $\tilde{a}, \tilde{a}_{RW}, \tilde{a}_W, \tilde{s}$.*

Let E be the source typing environment that contains

- *$(s : \mathrm{D}^{\mathrm{Secret}})$ for each $s \in \tilde{s}$;*
- *$(a : \mathrm{C}^{\mathrm{Secret}}[\tilde{T}])$ for each $a \in \tilde{a} \setminus \tilde{a}_W$;*
- *$(a : \mathrm{C}^{\mathrm{Public}}[\tilde{T}])$ for each $a \in \tilde{a}_W$;*
- *$(b : \mathrm{Public})$ for each $b \in \tilde{a}_{RW}$.*

If $E \vdash P$, then the concrete system $(\mathsf{P}_i, \mathsf{M}_i)_{i=0..n}$ preserves payload secrecy of $\tilde{s}$.

We illustrate the use of the theorem on the example of Section 3. We have established that $E \vdash A \,|\, B$. Let S be the system that includes machines $(\mathsf{P}_i)_{i=0,1,2}$ with initialization parameters $\tilde{a}_1 = \{a\}$, $\tilde{a}_2 = \{b\}$, $\tilde{a} = \{a, b\}$, $\tilde{b}_1 = \{b, s\}$, $\tilde{b}_2 = \{ack\}$, $\tilde{b} = \{ack, s\}$, $\tilde{a}_{RW} = \{ack\}$, $\tilde{a}_W = \{a, b\}$, and $\tilde{s} = \{s\}$, such that P_1 hosts the translation of A, P_2 hosts the translation of B, and P_0 runs the initialization process I_0:

$$I_0 = export_1(a).export_2(b).\overline{export}\langle a, b\rangle.import(ack).user(s).$$
$$cont(\_).\overline{import_1}\langle b, s\rangle.cont(\_).\overline{import_2}\langle ack\rangle$$

Since E meets the conditions of Theorem 1, system S preserves payload secrecy of s.

7 Types for Channel Groups

In this section, we supplement our type system with typing rules adapted from Cardelli et al. [14]. These rules are also designed to ensure formal secrecy by typing, but they concern symmetric communication channels, confined using scoped groups of names. Relying on this confinement discipline, we can implement channels using symmetric encryption, with computational secrecy guarantees.

Group Types in the Source Language. Group types embody static scoping policies in the pi calculus; they help control the dynamic extrusion of channels by partitioning them into named groups and statically controlling the scope of these groups. Groups can be dynamically created as part of the computation; they ensure that "channels of group G are forever secret outside the initial scope of (νG)" [14].

We extend the grammars for source processes and types accordingly:

$P, Q ::=$	processes	$T ::=$	types
$\ldots$	(see Section 2)	$\ldots$	(see Section 3)
$\overline{M}\langle M_1, \ldots, M_n \rangle_s$	output	$G[T_1, \ldots, T_n]$	channel in group G
$M(x_1, \ldots, x_n)_s.P$	input		
$!M(x_1, \ldots, x_n)_s.P$	replicated input		
$(\nu G)P$	group restriction		
$(\nu_s a : G[T_1, \ldots, T_n])P$	restriction		

We assume an infinite set of groups and let G, G' range over groups. The process $(\nu G)P$ binds G with scope P. We consider processes up to renaming of bound groups.

The other processes enable communication and restriction on names that belong to a group, much as the processes of Section 2, except for an additional "s" that indicates the usage of group names (so that we can select symmetric-key cryptography in the implementation). Restrictions also mention types, which are useful here for guiding the translation.

Operationally, group restrictions behave like name restrictions, with similar structural-equivalence rules and an additional context rule for reductions: $P \rightarrow P' \Rightarrow (\nu G)P \rightarrow (\nu G)P'$. Hence, group types do not play any dynamic role, and we can retrieve untyped source processes and the untyped semantics by type erasure [14, Section 3].

We supplement our type system with additional typing rules for groups:

$$\frac{E \vdash \diamond \quad G \notin dom(E)}{E, G \vdash \diamond} \qquad \frac{E \vdash \diamond \quad G \in dom(E) \quad u \notin dom(E) \quad E \vdash T_1, \ldots, E \vdash T_n}{E, u : G[T_1, \ldots, T_n] \vdash \diamond}$$

$$\frac{E \vdash M : G[T_1, \ldots, T_n] \quad E, x_1 : T_1, \ldots, x_n : T_n \vdash P}{E \vdash !=M(x_1, \ldots, x_n)_s.P} \text{ (Input } G)$$

$$\frac{E \vdash M : G[T_1, \ldots, T_n] \quad \forall i \in \{1, \ldots, n\}, E \vdash M_i : T_i}{E \vdash \overline{M}\langle M_1, \ldots, M_n \rangle_s} \text{ (Output } G)$$

$$\frac{E, G \vdash P}{E \vdash (\nu G)P} \text{ (Group Restriction)} \qquad \frac{E, a : G[T_1, \ldots, T_n] \vdash P}{E \vdash (\nu_s a : G[T_1, \ldots, T_n])P} \text{ (Restriction } G)$$

The well-formedness rules demand that all groups are recorded in E and group types are not mutually recursive. Thus, (Group Restriction) ensures that a restricted G never occurs in the type of a free variable.

The other rules are standard. In contrast with the rules for local channels, (Input G) enables inputs on any term with a group type.

An Example. Consider the processes:

$$A = (\nu_s d : G[D^{\text{Secret}}])(\overline{c}\langle d \rangle_s \mid \overline{d}\langle s_1 \rangle_s \mid \overline{d}\langle s_2 \rangle_s)$$
$$B = !c(z)_s.z(x_1)_s.z(x_2)_s$$

Here, c represents a private, long-term channel between A and B, and d represents a private channel for a session; A creates d in group G, sends it to B on c, and uses d to send secrets s_1 and s_2 to B.

We can assign types so that $(\nu G)(\nu_s c : G[G[D^{\text{Secret}}]])(A \mid B)$ typechecks, with s_1 and s_2 of type D^{Secret}.

Two Difficulties with Symmetric Encryption. Scoped group types are a good match for symmetric keys, with their limitations. We discuss two such standard limitations in the context of the intermediate language and the idealized cryptographic library.

- *Encryption cycles* may occur when the same symmetric keys are used both as encryption keys and within encrypted values. Cycles are potentially unsafe, and therefore excluded by standard computational definitions of secrecy [7]. In particular, cycles must be excluded in the cryptographic library [9], as follows: every secret symmetric-key encryption has an integer rank, k, and the idealized library checks that, for every encryption, (the symbolic representation of) the value to be encrypted includes only encryptions of a strictly lower rank.
- *Key compromises* may occur during the computation, but they are hard to model computationally. The cryptographic library simplifies the issue by requiring that any symmetric key that may eventually be leaked to the adversary be leaked before any encryption under the key becomes known by the adversary [9]. Laud's type system simplifies further, and excludes any leakage of symmetric keys by typing.

To address the second limitation, we extend the intermediate language, as follows. By convention, we use rank 0 to indicate a key that is (immediately) leaked to the adversary. We refine the rule (SK) for gen_symenc_key(k) [17]:

$$\frac{k \geq 0}{\text{gen\_symenc\_key}(k) : \text{SK}^k[T]} \text{ (SK)}$$

into two rules:

$$\frac{}{\text{gen\_symenc\_key}(0) : \text{Public}} \text{ (PSK)} \qquad \frac{k > 0}{\text{gen\_symenc\_key}(k) : \text{SK}^k[T]} \text{ (SK}')$$

The special typing rule for $k = 0$ is admissible[1]; indeed, Laud's system already supports symmetric keys of type Public received from the adversary.

Moreover, we assume that the library implementation of gen_symenc_key(k) detects $k = 0$ and then leaks the key to the adversary, using some additional port. Technically, we establish payload secrecy result for systems with this modification. However, it is straightforward to show that, if a system preserves payload secrecy while leaking some symmetric keys, then the same system without the leak also preserves payload secrecy. (If an adversary breaks payload secrecy for the system without the leak, then the same adversary breaks payload secrecy for the system with the leak—by just ignoring the extra input.) This latter system does not dynamically rely on the rank parameters k.

Distributed Implementation. We describe the distributed implementation of source processes with groups as an extension of the implementation of Section 5.

As a global, preliminary step, we partition the free groups of the source processes P_i for $i = 1, \ldots, n$ into public and private groups, we rename the restricted groups so that all groups are pairwise distinct, and we give a rank to every type: $\text{rank}(G[T_1, \ldots, T_n]) = 1 + \max_{i=1..n}(\text{rank}(T_i))$ when G is private or restricted; all other types have rank 0.

---

[1] P. Laud, private communication.

We extend the translations for types and processes as follows:

$$[\![G[T_1,\ldots,T_n]]\!]^t = \begin{cases} \text{Public} & \text{when } G \text{ public} \\ \text{SK}^{\text{rank}(G[T_1,\ldots,T_n])}[\text{list}([\![T_1]\!]^t,\ldots,[\![T_n]\!]^t)] & \text{otherwise} \end{cases}$$

$$[\![\overline{M}\langle M_1,\ldots,M_n\rangle_{\mathsf{s}}]\!] = cont(\_).\overline{net}\langle\mathsf{privenc}(M,\mathsf{list}(M_1,\ldots,M_n))\rangle$$

$$[\![!^{=}M(x_1,\ldots,x_n)_{\mathsf{s}}.P]\!] = !^{=}net(z).let\ x_1,\ldots,x_n = \mathsf{privdec}(M,z)\ in\ \overline{ack}\langle\_\rangle.[\![P]\!]$$

$$[\![(\nu G)P]\!] = [\![P]\!]$$

$$[\![(\nu_{\mathsf{s}}a:T)P]\!] = let\ a = \mathsf{gen\_symenc\_key}(\mathsf{rank}(T))\ in\ [\![P]\!]\ else\ 0$$

The translation of environment is extended to group-type bindings pointwise, and discards groups. As in Section 6, we show that our translation of processes is well-typed. Initialization applies unchanged: we exchange private-group names in $\widetilde{a} \setminus \widetilde{a}_W$ (just as names of type $C^{\text{Secret}}[T_1,\ldots,T_n]$) and public-group names in $\widetilde{a}_{RW}$.

Finally, we generalize Proposition 1, Lemma 1, and Theorem 1 to systems with both kinds of channel implementations, with the additional requirement that, in the top-level source environment, the types within public-group types be either Public or other public-group types. (We leave details for the full version of this paper.)

8 Conclusion

In summary, we obtain computational secrecy guarantees for an implementation of a standard process calculus with mobile channels. The guarantees apply to processes that conform to typing disciplines originally designed for establishing formal secrecy. It is pleasing that these typing disciplines have a strong, non-trivial computational meaning. One may also be able to extend these results to other secrecy requirements. Further, we expect that analogous results may be established for typing disciplines that enforce authenticity [16] (as already suggested by Laud) and authorization [15]. In addition, implementations such as the one considered in this paper can be hardened against many kinds of attacks, whether or not the corresponding security properties are captured in type systems. Unfortunately, however, some attractive extensions appear challenging. For instance, protection against traffic analysis may require expensive implementation strategies or changes in the source calculus [1, 8]. An interesting direction for further research is the development of high-level models and calculi that would be both convenient for programming and amenable to sound, efficient implementations.

Acknowledgments. Abadi's work was partly supported by the National Science Foundation under Grants CCR-0208800 and CCF-0524078. Corin's work was partly supported by an NWO travel grant 02-1979.

References

1. M. Abadi. Protection in programming-language translations. In *25th International Colloquium on Automata, Languages and Programming*, volume 1443 of *LNCS*, pages 868–883. Springer-Verlag, 1998.
2. M. Abadi. Security protocols and their properties. In F. Bauer and R. Steinbrueggen, editors, *Foundations of Secure Computation*, NATO Science Series, pages 39–60. IOS Press, 2000.

3. M. Abadi and B. Blanchet. Secrecy types for asymmetric communication. *Theoretical Computer Science*, 298(3):387–415, Apr. 2003.
4. M. Abadi, C. Fournet, and G. Gonthier. Authentication primitives and their compilation. In *27th ACM Symposium on Principles of Programming Languages*, pages 302–315, Jan. 2000.
5. M. Abadi, C. Fournet, and G. Gonthier. Secure implementation of channel abstractions. *Information and Computation*, 174(1):37–83, Apr. 2002.
6. M. Abadi and A. D. Gordon. A calculus for cryptographic protocols: The spi calculus. *Information and Computation*, 148(1):1–70, 1999.
7. M. Abadi and P. Rogaway. Reconciling two views of cryptography (the computational soundness of formal encryption). *Journal of Cryptology*, 15(2):103–127, 2002.
8. P. Adão and C. Fournet. Cryptographically sound implementations for communicating processes (extended abstract). In *33rd International Colloquium on Automata, Languages and Programming*, volume 4052 of *LNCS*, pages 83–94. Springer-Verlag, July 2006.
9. M. Backes and B. Pfitzmann. Symmetric encryption in a simulatable Dolev-Yao style cryptographic library. In *17th IEEE Computer Security Foundations Workshop*, pages 204–218, 2004.
10. M. Backes and B. Pfitzmann. Relating symbolic and cryptographic secrecy. In *IEEE Symposium on Security and Privacy*, pages 171–182, 2005.
11. M. Backes, B. Pfitzmann, and M. Waidner. A composable cryptographic library with nested operations. In *10th ACM Conference on Computer and Communications Security*, pages 220–230, 2003.
12. M. Backes, B. Pfitzmann, and M. Waidner. Symmetric authentication within a simulatable cryptographic library. *International Journal of Information Security*, 4(3):135–154, 2005.
13. R. Canetti and H. Krawczyk. Analysis of key-exchange protocols and their use for building secure channels. In *Encrocrypt 2001*, volume 2045 of *LNCS*. Springer-Verlag, 2001.
14. L. Cardelli, G. Ghelli, and A. D. Gordon. Secrecy and group creation. *Information and Computation*, 196(2):127–155, 2005.
15. C. Fournet, A. D. Gordon, and S. Maffeis. A type discipline for authorization policies. In *14th European Symposium on Programming*, volume 3444 of *LNCS*, pages 141–156. Springer, 2005.
16. A. D. Gordon and A. S. A. Jeffrey. Types and effects for asymmetric cryptographic protocols. *J. Computer Security*, 12(3/4):435–484, 2004.
17. P. Laud. Secrecy types for a simulatable cryptographic library. In *12th ACM Conference on Computer and Communications Security*, pages 26–35, 2005. Also Research Report IT-LU-O-162-050823, Cybernetica, Aug. 2005.
18. M. Merro and D. Sangiorgi. On asynchrony in name-passing calculi. In *25th International Colloquium on Automata, Languages and Programming*, volume 1443 of *LNCS*, pages 856–867. Springer-Verlag, 1998.
19. D. Micciancio and B. Warinschi. Soundness of formal encryption in the presence of active adversaries. In *1st Theory of Cryptography Conference (TCC)*, pages 133–151, 2004.

Scheme with Classes, Mixins, and Traits

Matthew Flatt[1], Robert Bruce Findler[2], and Matthias Felleisen[3]

[1] University of Utah
[2] University of Chicago
[3] Northeastern University

Abstract. The Scheme language report advocates language design as the composition of a small set of orthogonal constructs, instead of a large accumulation of features. In this paper, we demonstrate how such a design scales with the addition of a class system to Scheme. Specifically, the PLT Scheme class system is a collection of orthogonal linguistic constructs for creating classes in arbitrary lexical scopes and for manipulating them as first-class values. Due to the smooth integration of classes and the core language, programmers can express mixins and traits, two major recent innovations in the object-oriented world. The class system is implemented as a macro in terms of procedures and a record-type generator; the mixin and trait patterns, in turn, are naturally codified as macros over the class system.

1 Growing a Language

The Revised[5] Report on the Scheme programming language [20] starts with the famous proclamation that "[p]rogramming languages should be designed not by piling feature on top of feature, but by removing the weaknesses and restrictions that make additional features appear necessary." As a result, Scheme's core expression language consists of just six constructs: variables, constants, conditionals, assignments, procedures, and function applications. Its remaining constructs implement variable definitions and a few different forms of procedure parameter specifications. Everything else is defined as a function or macro.

PLT Scheme [25], a Scheme implementation intended for language experimentation, takes this maxim to the limit. It extends the core of Scheme with a few constructs, such as modules and generative structure definitions, and provides a highly expressive macro system. Over the past ten years, we have used this basis to conduct many language design experiments, including the development of an expressive and practical class system. We have designed and implemented four variants of the class system, and we have re-implemented DrScheme [13]—a substantial application of close to 200,000 lines of PLT Scheme code—in terms of this class system as many times.

Classes in PLT Scheme are first-class values, and the class system's scoping rules are consistent with Scheme's lexical scope and single namespace. Furthermore, the class system serves as a foundation for further macro-based explorations into class-like mechanisms, such as mixins and traits.

A mixin [11] is a class declaration parameterized over its superclass using `lambda`. Years of experience with these mixins shows that they are practical. Scoping rules for

N. Kobayashi (Ed.): APLAS 2006, LNCS 4279, pp. 270–289, 2006.

methods allow both flexibility and control in combining mixins, while explicit inheritance specifications ensure that unintentional collisions are flagged early.

In this setting, a trait [29] is a set of mixins. Although mixins and traits both represent extensions to a class, we distinguish traits from mixins, because traits provide fine-grained control over individual methods in the extension, unlike mixins.

Last but not least, objects instantiated by the class system are efficient in space and time, whether the class is written directly or instantiated through mixins and or traits. In particular, objects in our system consume a similar amount of space to a Smalltalk or Java object. Method calls have a cost similar to Smalltalk method calls or interface-based Java calls. In short, the class system is efficient as well as effective.

2 Classes

In PLT Scheme, a class expression denotes a first-class value, just like a lambda expression:

```
(class superclass-expr decl-or-expr*)
```

The *superclass-expr* determines the superclass for the new class. Each *decl-or-expr* is either a declaration related to methods, fields, and intialization arguments, or it is an expression that is evaluated each time that the class is instantiated. In other words, instead of a method-like constructor, a class has initialization expressions interleaved with field and method declarations. Figure 1 displays a simplified grammar for *decl-or-expr*.

By convention, class names end with %. The built-in root class is object%. Thus the following expression creates a class with public methods get-size, grow, and eat:

```
(class object%
  (init size)                 ; initialization argument
  (define current-size size)  ; field
  (super-new)                 ; superclass initialization
  (define/public (get-size)
    current-size)
  (define/public (grow amt)
    (set! current-size (+ amt current-size)))
  (define/public (eat other-fish)
    (grow (send other-fish get-size))))
```

The size initialization argument must be supplied via a named argument when instantiating the class through the new form:

```
(new (class object% (init size) ...) [size 10])
```

Of course, we can also name the class and its instance:

```
(define fish% (class object% (init size) ...))
(define charlie (new fish% [size 10]))
```

In the definition of fish%, current-size is a private field that starts out with the value of the size initialization argument. Initialization arguments like size are available

decl-or-expr ::=	(define *id expr*)	private field definition
	| (define/*method-spec* (*method-id id**)	method definition
	*expr**)	
	| (init *id-with-expr**)	initialization argument
	| (field *id-with-expr**)	public field
	| (inherit *method-id**)	inherit method, for direct access
	| *expr*	initialization expression
method-spec ::=	public	new method
	| override	override method
	| private	private method
id-with-expr ::=	*id*	without initial value or default
	| [*id expr*]	with initial value or default
expr ::=	(new *class-expr* [*id expr*]*)	object creation
	| (send *object-expr method-id expr**)	external method call
	| (*method-id expr**)	internal method call (in class)
	| this	object self-reference (in class)
	| (super *method-id expr**)	call overridden method (in class)
	| (super-new [*id expr*]*)	call super initialization (in class)
	| ...	all other Scheme expression forms

superclass-expr, *class-expr*, and *object-expr* are aliases for *expr*; *method-id* is an alias for *id*

Fig. 1. Simplified PLT Scheme class system grammar

only during class instantiation, so they cannot be referenced directly from a method. The current-size field, in contrast, is available to methods.

The (super-new) expression in fish% invokes the initialization of the superclass. In this case, the superclass is object%, which takes no initialization arguments and performs no work; super-new must be used, anyway, because a class must always invoke its superclass's initialization.

Initialization arguments, field declarations, and expressions such as (super-new) can appear in any order within a class, and they can be interleaved with method declarations. The relative order of expressions in the class determines the order of evaluation during instantiation. For example, if a field's initial value requires calling a method that works only after superclass initialization, then the field declaration is placed after the super-new call. Ordering field and initialization declarations in this way helps avoid imperative assignment. The relative order of method declarations makes no difference for evaluation, because methods are fully defined before a class is instantiated.

2.1 Methods

Each of the three define/public declarations in fish% introduces a new method. The declaration uses the same syntax as a Scheme function, but a method is not accessible as an independent function. A call to the grow method of a fish% object requires the send form:

```
(send charlie grow 6)
(send charlie get-size) ; ⇒ 16
```

Within `fish%`, self methods can be called like functions, because the method names are in scope. For example, the `eat` method within `fish%` directly invokes the `grow` method. Within a class, attempting to use a method name in any way other than a method call results in a syntax error.

In some cases, a class must call methods that are supplied by the superclass but not overridden. In that case, the class can use `send` with `this` to access the method:

```
(define hungry-fish% (class fish% (super-new)
                       (define/public (eat-more fish1 fish2)
                         (send this eat fish1)
                         (send this eat fish2))))
```

Alternately, the class can declare the existence of a method using `inherit`, which brings the method name into scope for a direct call:

```
(define hungry-fish% (class fish% (super-new)
                       (inherit eat)
                       (define/public (eat-more fish1 fish2)
                         (eat fish1) (eat fish2))))
```

With the `inherit` declaration, if `fish%` had not provided an `eat` method, an error would be signaled in the evaluation of the `class` form for `hungry-fish%`. In contrast, with (`send this ...`), an error would not be signaled until the `eat-more` method is called and the `send` form is evaluated. For this reason, `inherit` is preferred.

Another drawback of `send` is that it is less efficient than `inherit`. Invocation of a method via `send` involves finding a method in the target object's class at run time, making `send` comparable to an interface-based method call in Java. In contrast, `inherit`-based method invocations use an offset within the class's method table that is computed when the class is created.

To achieve performance similar to `inherit`-based method calls when invoking a method from outside the method's class, the programmer must use the `generic` form, which produces a class- and method-specific *generic method* to be invoked with `send-generic`:

```
(define get-fish-size (generic fish% get-size))
(send-generic charlie get-fish-size) ; ⇒ 16
(send-generic (new hungry-fish% [size 32]) get-fish-size) ; ⇒ 32
(send-generic (new object%) get-fish-size) ; Error: not a fish%
```

Roughly speaking, the form translates the class and the external method name to a location in the class's method table. As illustrated by the last example, sending through a generic method checks that its argument is an instance of the generic's class.

Whether a method is called directly within a `class`, through a generic method, or through `send`, method overriding works in the usual way:

```
(define picky-fish% (class fish% (super-new)
                      (define/override (grow amt)
                        ;; Doesn't eat all of its food
                        (super grow (* 3/4 amt)))))
(define daisy (new picky-fish% [size 20]))
(send daisy eat charlie) ; charlie's size is 16
(send daisy get-size) ; ⇒ 32
```

The *grow* method in `picky-fish%` is declared with `define/override` instead of `define/public`, because *grow* is meant as an overriding declaration. If *grow* had been declared with `define/public`, an error would have been signaled when evaluating the class expression, because `fish%` already supplies *grow*.

Using `define/override` also allows the invocation of the overridden method via a super call. For example, the *grow* implementation in `picky-fish%` uses super to delegate to the superclass implementation.

2.2 Initialization Arguments

Since `picky-fish%` declares no initialization arguments, any initialization values supplied in (new `picky-fish%` ...) are propagated to the superclass initialization, i.e., to `fish%`. A subclass can supply additional initialization arguments for its superclass in a super-new call, and such initialization arguments take precedence over arguments supplied to new. For example, the following `size-10-fish%` class always generates fish of size 10:

```
(define size-10-fish% (class fish% (super-new [size 10])))
(send (new size-10-fish%) get-size) ; ⇒ 10
```

In the case of `size-10-fish%`, supplying a `size` initialization argument with new would result in an initialization error; because the `size` in super-new takes precedence, a `size` supplied to new would have no target declaration.

An initialization argument is optional if the class form declares a default value. For example, the following `default-10-fish%` class accepts a `size` initialization argument, but its value defaults to 10 if no value is supplied on instantiation:

```
(define default-10-fish% (class fish%
                          (init [size 10])
                          (super-new [size size])))
(new default-10-fish%) ; ⇒ a fish of size 10
(new default-10-fish% [size 20]) ; ⇒ a fish of size 20
```

In this example, the super-new call propagates its own `size` value as the `size` initialization argument to the superclass.

2.3 Internal and External Names

The two uses of `size` in `default-10-fish%` expose the double life of class-member identifiers. When `size` is the first identifier of a bracketed pair in new or super-new, `size` is an *external name* that is symbolically matched to an initialization argument in a class. When `size` appears as an expression within `default-10-fish%`, `size` is an *internal name* that is lexically scoped. Similarly, a call to an inherited `eat` method uses `eat` as an internal name, whereas a send of `eat` uses `eat` as an external name.

The full syntax of the class form allows a programmer to specify distinct internal and external names for a class member. Since internal names are local, they can be α-renamed to avoid shadowing or conflicts. Such renaming is not frequently necessary, but workarounds in the absence of α-renaming can be especially cumbersome.

2.4   Interfaces

Interfaces are useful for checking that an object or a class implements a set of methods with a particular (implied) behavior. This use of interfaces is helpful even without a static type system (which is the main reason that Java has interfaces).

An interface in PLT Scheme is created using the `interface` form, which merely declares the method names required to implement the interface. An interface can extend other interfaces, which means that implementations of the interface automatically implement the extended interfaces.

```
(interface (superinterface-expr*) id*)
```

To declare that a class implements an interface, the `class*` form must be used instead of `class`:

```
(class* superclass-expr (interface-expr*) decl-or-expr*)
```

For example, instead of forcing all fish classes to be derived from `fish%`, we can define `fish-interface` and change the `fish%` class to declare that it implements `fish-interface`:

```
(define fish-interface (interface () get-size grow eat))
(define fish% (class* object% (fish-interface) ...))
```

If the definition of `fish%` does not include `get-size`, `grow`, and `eat` methods, then an error is signaled in the evaluation of the `class*` form, because implementing the `fish-interface` interface requires those methods.

The `is-a?` predicate accepts either a class or interface as its first argument and an object as its second argument. When given a class, `is-a?` checks whether the object is an instance of that class or a derived class. When given an interface, `is-a?` checks whether the object's class implements the interface. In addition, the `implementation?` predicate checks whether a given class implements a given interface.

2.5   Final, Augment, and Inner

As in Java, a method in a `class` form can be specified as *final*, which means that a subclass cannot override the method. A final method is declared using `public-final` or `override-final`, depending on whether the declaration is for a new method or an overriding implementation.

Between the extremes of allowing arbitrary overriding and disallowing overriding entirely, the class system also supports Beta-style *augmentable* methods [22]. A method declared with `pubment` is like `public`, but the method cannot be overridden in subclasses; it can be augmented only. A `pubment` method must explicitly invoke an augmentation (if any) using `inner`; a subclass augments the method using `augment`, instead of `override`.

In general, a method can switch between augment and override modes in a class derivation. The `augride` method specification indicates an augmentation to a method where the augmentation is itself overrideable in subclasses (though the superclass's implementation cannot be overridden). Similarly, `overment` overrides a method and makes the overriding implementation augmentable. Our earlier work [19] motivates and explains these extensions and their interleaving.

2.6   Controlling the Scope of External Names

As noted in Section 2.3, class members have both internal and external names. A member definition binds an internal name locally, and this binding can be locally α-renamed. External names, in contrast, have global scope by default, and a member definition does not bind an external name. Instead, a member definition refers to an existing binding for an external name, where the member name is bound to a *member key*; a class ultimately maps member keys to methods, fields, and initialization arguments.

Recall the `hungry-fish%` class expression:

```
(define hungry-fish% (class fish% ...
                       (inherit eat)
                       (define/public (eat-more fish1 fish2)
                         (eat fish1) (eat fish2))))
```

During its evaluation, the `hungry-fish%` and `fish%` classes refer to the same global binding of `eat`. At run time, calls to `eat` in `hungry-fish%` are matched with the `eat` method in `fish%` through the shared method key that is bound to `eat`.

The default binding for an external name is global, but a programmer can introduce an external-name binding with the `define-member-name` form.

```
(define-member-name id member-key-expr)
```

In particular, by using (`generate-member-key`) as the *member-key-expr*, an external name can be localized for a particular scope, because the generated member key is inaccessible outside the scope. In other words, `define-member-name` gives an external name a kind of package-private scope, but generalized from packages to arbitrary binding scopes in Scheme.

For example, the following `fish%` and `pond%` classes cooperate via a `get-depth` method that is only accessible to the cooperating classes:

```
(define-values (fish% pond%) ;; two mutually recursive classes
  (let () ; create a local definition scope
    (define-member-name get-depth (generate-member-key))
    (define fish%
      (class ... (define my-depth ...)
                 (define my-pond ...)
                 (define/public (dive amt)
                   (set! my-depth
                     (min (+ my-depth amt)
                          (send my-pond get-depth))))))
    (define pond%
      (class ... (define current-depth ...)
                 (define/public (get-depth) current-depth)))
    (values fish% pond%)))
```

External names are in a namespace that separates them from other Scheme names. This separate namespace is implicitly used for the method name in `send`, for initialization-argument names in `new`, or for the external name in a member definition. The special `member-name-key` provides access to the binding of an external name in an arbitrary expression position: (`member-name-key` *id*) form produces the member-key binding of *id* in the current scope.

A member-key value is primarily used on with a `define-member-name` form. Normally, then, `(member-name-key id)` captures the method key of *id* so that it can be communicated to a use of `define-member-name` in a different scope. This capability turns out to be useful for generalizing mixins (see Section 3.4).

2.7 Implementation of Classes

The `class` form is implemented in terms of a primitive `make-struct-type` procedure, which generates a data type that is distinct from all existing data types. The new data type's specification includes the number of slots that should be allocated for instances of the data type, plus properties for the data type. A class corresponds to a fresh data type with one slot for each field and with a property for the class's method table.

Most of the compile-time work for the `class` macro is in expanding the individual expressions and declarations in the method body, and ensuring that the declarations are locally consistent (e.g., no duplicate method declarations). Indeed, of the roughly 3,500 lines of Scheme code that implement the class system, 3/4 implement compile-time work (especially syntax checking to provide good error messages), and 1/4 of the lines implement run-time support.

The run-time representation of a class includes the method implementations—as procedures transformed to take an explicit `this` argument—and information about introduced methods and expected superclass methods. The run-time work of class creation mostly checks the consistency of the class extensions with a supplied superclass, closes the method implementations with specific methods for `super` calls, and closes method implementations with specific `vtable` indices for direct method calls.

3 Mixins

Since `class` is an expression form instead of a top-level declaration as in Smalltalk and Java, a `class` form can be nested inside any lexical scope, including `lambda`. The result is a *mixin*, i.e., a class extension that is parameterized with respect to its superclass [11].

For example, we can parameterize the `picky-fish%` class over its superclass to define `picky-mixin`:

```
(define (picky-mixin %)
  (class % (super-new)
    (define/override (grow amt) (super grow (* 3/4 amt)))))
(define picky-fish% (picky-mixin fish%))
```

Many small differences between Smalltalk-style classes and our classes contribute to the effective use of mixins. In particular, the use of `define/override` makes explicit that `picky-mixin` expects a class with a `grow` method. If `picky-mixin` is applied to a class without a `grow` method, an error is signaled as soon as `picky-mixin` is applied.

Similarly, a use of `inherit` enforces a "method existence" requirement when the mixin is applied:

```
(define (hungry-mixin %)
  (class % (super-new)
    (inherit eat)
    (define/public (eat-more fish1 fish2) (eat fish1) (eat fish2))))
```

The advantage of mixins is that we can easily combine them to create new classes whose implementation sharing does not fit into a single-inheritance hierarchy—without the ambiguities associated with multiple inheritance. Equipped with *picky-mixin* and *hungry-mixin*, creating a class for a hungry, yet picky fish is straightforward:

```
(define picky-hungry-fish% (hungry-mixin (picky-mixin fish%)))
```

The use of keyword initialization arguments is critical for the easy use of mixins. For example, *picky-mixin* and *hungry-mixin* can augment any class with suitable *eat* and *grow* methods, because they do not specify initialization arguments and add none in their super-new expressions:

```
(define person% (class object%
                  (init name age)
                  ...
                  (define/public (eat food) ...)
                  (define/public (grow amt) ...)))
(define child% (hungry-mixin (picky-mixin person%)))
(define oliver (new child% [name "Oliver"] [age 6]))
```

Finally, the use of external names for class members (instead of lexically scoped identifiers) makes mixin use convenient. Applying *picky-mixin* to *person%* works because the names *eat* and *grow* match, without any a priori declaration that *eat* and *grow* should be the same method in *fish%* and *person%*. This feature is a potential drawback when member names collide accidentally; some accidental collisions can be corrected by limiting the scope external names, as discussed in Section 2.6.

3.1   Mixins and Interfaces

Using `implementation?`, *picky-mixin* could require that its base class implements *grower-interface*, which could be implemented by both *fish%* and *person%*:

```
(define grower-interface (interface () grow))
(define (picky-mixin %)
  (unless (implementation? % grower-interface)
    (error "picky-mixin: not a grower-interface class"))
  (class % ...))
```

Another use of interfaces with a mixin is to tag classes generated by the mixin, so that instances of the mixin can be recognized. In other words, is-a? cannot work on a mixin represented as a function, but it can recognize an interface (somewhat like a *specialization interface* [21]) that is consistently implemented by the mixin. For example, classes generated by *picky-mixin* could be tagged with *picky-interface*, enabling the *is-picky?* predicate:

```
(define picky-interface (interface ()))
(define (picky-mixin %)
  (unless (implementation? % grower-interface)
    (error "picky-mixin: not a grower-interface class"))
  (class* % (picky-interface) ...))
(define (is-picky? o)
  (is-a? o picky-interface))
```

3.2 The Mixin Macro

To codify the `lambda-plus-class` pattern for implementing mixins, including the use of interfaces for the domain and range of the mixin, PLT Scheme's class system provides a `mixin` macro:

(mixin (*interface-expr**) (*interface-expr**) *decl-or-expr**)

The first set of *interface-expr*s determines the domain of the mixin, and the second set determines the range. That is, the expansion is a function that tests whether a given base class implements the first sequence of *interface-expr*s and produces a class that implements the second sequence of *interface-expr*s. Other requirements, such as the presence of `inherited` methods in the superclass, are then checked for the `class` expansion of the `mixin` form.

3.3 Mixins, Augment, and Inner

Mixins not only override methods and introduce public methods, they can also augment methods, introduce augment-only methods, add an overrideable augmentation, and add an augmentable override — all of the things that a class can do (see Section 2.5).

Bracha and Cook [11] observed that mixins alone can express both Smalltalk-style method overriding and Beta-style method augmenting, depending on the order of mixin composition. Their result, however, depends on choosing an order of composition; otherwise, the security benefits of Beta-style augmenting are lost (as we have observed [19] to be the case for gbeta). Our goal in adding `augment` and `inner` to the class system is to provide the same sort of security guarantees as Beta, which explains why we implement mixins in terms of classes, not classes in terms of mixins.

3.4 Parameterized Mixins

As noted in Section 2.6, external names can be bound with `define-member-name`. This facility allows a mixin to be generalized with respect to the methods that it defines and uses. For example, we can parameterize *hungry-mixin* with respect to the external member key for *eat*:

```
(define (make-hungry-mixin eat-method-key)
  (define-member-name eat eat-method-key)
  (mixin () () (super-new)
    (inherit eat)
    (define/public (eat-more x y) (eat x) (eat y))))
```

To obtain a particular hungry-mixin, we must apply this function to a member key that refers to a suitable `eat` method, which we can obtain using `member-name-key`:

```
((make-hungry-mixin (member-name-key eat))
 (class object% ... (define/public (eat x) 'yum)))
```

Above, we apply *hungry-mixin* to an anonymous class that provides *eat*, but we can also combine it with a class that provides *chomp*, instead:

```
((make-hungry-mixin (member-name-key chomp))
 (class object% ... (define/public (chomp x) 'yum)))
```

4   Traits

A *trait* [28, 29] is similar to a mixin, in that it encapsulates a set of methods to be added
to a class. A trait is different from a mixin in that its individual methods can be manipulated with trait operators such as sum (merge the methods of two traits), exclude
(remove a method from a trait), and alias (add a copy of a method with a new name;
do not redirect any calls to the old name). The practical difference between mixins and
traits is that two traits can be combined, even if they include a common method and
even if neither method can sensibly override the other. In that case, the programmer
must explicitly resolve the collision, usually by aliasing methods, excluding methods,
and merging a new trait that uses the aliases.

Suppose our fish% programmer wants to define two class extensions, spots and
stripes, each of which includes a get-color method. The fish's spot color should
not override the stripe color nor vice-versa; instead, a spots+stripes-fish% should
combine the two colors, which is not possible if spots and stripes are implemented
as plain mixins. If, however, spots and stripes are implemented as traits, they can be
combined. First, we alias get-color in each trait to a non-conflicting name. Second,
the get-color methods are removed from both and the traits with only aliases are
merged. Finally, the new trait is used to create a class that introduces its own get-color
method based on the two aliases, producing the desired spots+stripes extension.

4.1   Traits as Sets of Mixins

One natural approach to implementing traits in PLT Scheme is as a set of mixins, with
one mixin per trait method. For example, we might attempt to define the spots and
stripes traits as follows, using association lists to represent sets:

```
(define spots-trait
  (list (cons 'get-color
              (lambda (%) (class % (super-new)
                            (define/public (get-color) 'black))))))
(define stripes-trait
  (list (cons 'get-color
              (lambda (%) (class % (super-new)
                            (define/public (get-color) 'red))))))
```

A set representation, such as the above, allows sum and exclude as simple manipulations; unfortunately, it does not support the alias operator. Although a mixin can be
duplicated in the association list, the mixin has a fixed method name, e.g., get-color,
and mixins do not support a method-rename operation. To support alias, we must parameterize the mixins over the external method name in the same way that eat was
parameterized in Section 3.4.

4.2   Traits as Parameterized Mixins

To support the alias operation, *spots-trait* should be represented as:

```
(define spots-trait
  (list (cons (member-name-key get-color)
              (lambda (get-color-key %)
                (define-member-name get-color get-color-key)
                (class % (super-new)
                  (define/public (get-color) 'black)))))))
```

When the *get-color* method in *spots-trait* is aliased to *get-trait-color* and the *get-color* method is removed, the resulting trait is the same as

```
(list (cons (member-name-key get-trait-color)
            (lambda (get-color-key %)
              (define-member-name get-color get-color-key)
              (class % (super-new)
                (define/public (get-color) 'black)))))))
```

To apply a trait T to a class C and obtain a derived class, we use (apply-trait T C). The apply-trait function supplies each mixin of T the key for the mixin's method and a partial extension of C:

```
(define (apply-trait T C)
  (foldr (lambda (m %) ((cdr m) (car m) %)) C T))
```

Thus, when the trait above is combined with other traits and then applied to a class, the use of *get-color* becomes a reference to the external name *get-trait-color*.

4.3   Inherit and Super in Traits

This first implementation of traits supports alias, and it supports a trait method that calls itself, but it does not support trait methods that call each other. In particular, suppose that a spot-fish's market value depends on the color of its spots:

```
(define spots-trait
  (list (cons (member-name-key get-color) ...)
        (cons (member-name-key get-price)
              (lambda (get-price %) ...
                (class % ...
                  (define/public (get-price) ... (get-color) ...)))))))
```

In this case, the definition of *spots-trait* fails, because *get-color* is not in scope for the *get-price* mixin. Indeed, depending on the order of mixin application when the trait is applied to a class, the *get-color* method may not be available when *get-price* mixin is applied to the class. Therefore adding an (inherit *get-color*) declaration to the *get-price* mixin does not solve the problem.

One solution is to require the use of (send this *get-color*) in methods such as *get-price*. This change works because send always delays the method lookup until the method call is evaluated. The delayed lookup is more expensive than a direct call, however. Worse, it also delays checking whether a *get-color* method even exists.

A second, effective, and efficient solution is to change the encoding of traits. Specifically, we represent each method as a pair of mixins: one that introduces the method and one that implements it. When a trait is applied to a class, all of the method-introducing mixins are applied first. Then the method-implementing mixins can use inherit to directly access any introduced method.

```
(define spots-trait
  (list (list (local-member-name-key get-color)
              (lambda (get-color get-price %) ...
                (class % ...
                  (define/public (get-color) (void))))
              (lambda (get-color get-price %) ...
                (class % ...
                  (define/override (get-color) 'black))))
        (list (local-member-name-key get-price)
              (lambda (get-price get-color %) ...
                (class % ...
                  (define/public (get-price) (void))))
              (lambda (get-color get-price %) ...
                (class % ...
                  (inherit get-color)
                  (define/override (get-price)
                    ... (get-color) ...))))))
```

With this trait encoding, alias works as in the Squeak implementation of traits. It adds a new method with a new name, but it does not change any references to the old method.

In contrast to the Squeak implementation [28], we can easily support a rename operation for traits with a bit of additional external-name parameterizations. Indeed, our rename operation even works for references in inherit and send.

Properly supporting super calls within a trait requires relatively little work when each super call to a method appears in an overriding implementation for the same method. In that case, no method-introducing mixin is needed, since overriding implies that the method exists already in the superclass. Special care is required if a super call is allowed in a method other than an overriding implementation, and a cycle of mutually super-calling methods may require an indirection to prevent a super call from accessing an implementation in the trait instead of the base class. Fortunately, the trait-application operator can generate this indirection automatically.

4.4   The Trait Macro

The general-purpose trait pattern is clearly too complex for a programmer to use directly, but it is easily codified in a trait macro:

```
(trait (inherit id*)? (define/method-spec (id id*) expr*)*)
```

The ids in the optional inherit clause are available for direct reference in the method exprs, and they must be supplied either by other traits or the base class to which the trait is ultimately applied.

Using this form in conjunction with trait operators such as sum, exclude, alias, and apply-trait, we can implement spots-trait and stripes-trait as desired; see Figure 2.

```
(define spots-trait
  (trait
    (define/public (get-color) 'black)
    (define/public (get-price) ... (get-color) ...)))

(define stripes-trait
  (trait
    (define/public (get-color) 'red)))

(define spots+stripes-trait
  (sum (exclude (alias spots-trait get-color get-spots-color)
                get-color)
       (exclude (alias stripes-trait get-color get-stripes-color)
                get-color)
       (trait
         (inherit get-spots-color get-stripes-color)
         (define/public (get-color)
           ... (get-spots-color) ... (get-stripes-color) ...)))))
```

Fig. 2. An example use of full-fledged traits

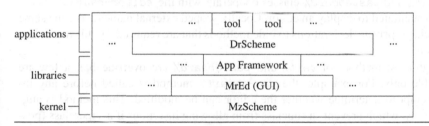

Fig. 3. PLT Scheme architecture

5 History and Experience

DrScheme is the most recognizable application that is built with PLT Scheme, and its implementation makes extensive use of the class system. Figure 3 shows how DrScheme fits into the architecture of PLT Scheme. *MzScheme* is the core compiler and run-time system, analogous to the JVM for Java. *MrEd* is the core GUI layer, analogous to AWT for Java. The *application framework* provides skeleton classes for typical kinds of GUI applications. Finally, DrScheme supports plug-in *tools* that extend the programming environment. (Ellipses in the figure represent other PLT libraries and applications.)

The language, kernel, and programming environment are sometimes difficult to distinguish, in part because they reinforce each other: MzScheme and MrEd were created as a platform to build DrScheme, and many programmers now choose PLT Scheme specifically because it is supported by DrScheme. Nevertheless, the distinctions are useful for understanding the uses of classes in DrScheme's implementation.

5.1   Current Uses of Classes

DrScheme employs classes primarily for its graphical interface, since the benefits of class-oriented programming are well understood for GUIs. In particular, the MrEd layer exports a class- and interface-based API for GUI programming, and it uses mixins internally to build most of the widget classes. The application framework layer exports a class-, interface-, and mixin-based API; the framework even includes classes with overrideable methods that act as mixins.

DrScheme's *editor* classes demonstrate many typical uses of classes and mixins. An editor represents the content of a window with interactive text and images:

Editors in MrEd. Every editor implements the `editor<%>` interface, which has two base implementations: the `text%` class for a text-oriented, line-based layout, and the `pasteboard%` class for a free-form, two-dimensional layout.

The `text%` and `pasteboard%` classes are derived from more primitive, private variants `wx-text%` and `wx-pasteboard%`. The `wx-` variants share a superclass that implements common behavior at the primitive level, but `text%` and `pasteboard%` also share behavior that cannot be implemented in the primitive layer. Instead of duplicating refinements of `wx-text%` and `wx-pasteboard%`, the common refinements are implemented once in an internal mixin, thus creating a single point of control for shared behavior in `text%` and `pasteboard%`.

The `text%` and `pasteboard%` classes cooperate with the `editor-canvas%` class, which is instantiated to display an editor. Locally scoped external names serve the same role as package-private declarations to hide methods that are required for this inter-class cooperation.

Although most methods of `text%` and `pasteboard%` are overrideable, a few are augmentable only. For example, the `can-insert?` method is called before any insertion attempt to determine whether the editor can be modified. This method is augmentable only, which prevents a subclass from allowing insertions if a superclass (possibly defined by a more primitive layer) must disallow insertions to preserve invariants.

Editors in the Framework. The application framework provides several editor mixins, such as an autosave mixin, a mixin to display editor state (such as the current line and column) into an information panel, and a mixin for chaining keymaps together. The framework also supplies nearly a dozen mixins that are specific to `text%`. The framework's top-level window class includes `get-editor%` and `get-canvas%` methods, so that a mixin for top-level windows can consistently extend the editor and canvas classes that are created for the window.

Certain editor and text mixins cooperate with a corresponding mixin for the display canvas. So far, we have mostly relied on naming conventions and run-time checks to help keep mixin applications in sync; we are considering implementing mixin layers [30] (via macros) for this purpose.

Editors in DrScheme. A tool that extends to the DrScheme programming environment is implemented as a unit [16]. DrScheme supplies each tool unit with functions to register mixin refinements of its editors. That is, tool implementors get the same convenient API as the DrScheme implementors for extending the environment, even though tools can be mixed and matched in a given installation.

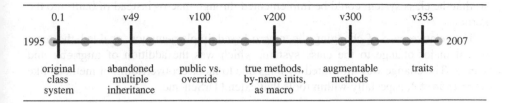

Fig. 4. PLT Scheme class system timeline

5.2 Language Evolution

Figure 4 shows how the class system in PLT Scheme has evolved over the project's 11-year history. To create the initial GUI base for DrScheme, we combined an embeddable Scheme system, libscheme [8], with a C++-based multi-platform GUI library, wxWindows [31]. We also added our own C++-based editor classes, which is why the GUI layer is called "MrEd." To make the C++ classes available in Scheme (for both class extension and instantiation), we extended libscheme with a built-in object system. As our changes to libscheme accumulated, we renamed it "MzScheme."

Our earliest design for classes included support for both mixins (as class plus lambda) and multiple inheritance of classes. We soon abandoned multiple inheritance, since it was rarely used, whereas mixins took hold early in our libraries.

For the first major re-design, we introduced the distinction between public methods and override methods. This avoided occasional confusion where a mixin application that was intended to introduce a method would instead override an existing method.

Through the first two major design stages, the class system implemented objects as records of closures, where a method is represented as a closure with this as a free variable. Such records are a typical way to represent objects in Scheme, and it worked well enough when objects were used in small quantities, such as objects for windows, buttons, and drawing pens. Over time, the addition of new kinds of snips to the editors, especially the nesting of text objects inside of editors, caused an overwhelming consumption of space and time.

The third major design abandoned methods as closures over this in favor of a more Smalltalk-like implementation where an object is a record of field values, plus a class-specific table of method procedures that accept an implicit this argument. This change eliminated performance problems related to the size of text objects in editors.

The third design also introduced by-name initialization arguments as an alternative to by-position arguments. As noted in Section 3, named initialization arguments complement mixin composition; in contrast, by-position arguments often force mixins to provide imperative initialization methods, since there is no simple way to distinguish optional initialization arguments for the mixin from initialization arguments intended for the superclass. In the current design, both forms of initialization arguments remain, but by-position arguments are used only in older libraries.

The first two implementations of classes were built into the language kernel. The implementation of the third design was greatly facilitated by MzScheme's switch from traditional Lisp macros to a modular macro system based on *syntax-case* [12, 15], so that the class system could be implemented through macros instead of built into the kernel.

The relative ease of changing the macro-based implementation enabled the most recent major change to the class system, which was the addition of augment and inner. The change was motivated by bugs due to incorrect overriding of methods like can-insert?, especially within tools that extend DrScheme.

5.3 Open Issues

The PLT Scheme class system has evolved in response to ever more stringent requirements for stability, performance, and expressiveness. The regularity of events in Figure 4 is surprising—the tick marks correspond to actual dates when changes became widely deployed to users—but they match the consistent growth of PLT Scheme. Predicting further change (and, apparently, its timing) is easier than predicting the specific nature of the change, but several open issues are likely to attract attention.

The class forms's distinction between initialization arguments and fields makes explicit that values used only for initialization need not be stored in the object. Nevertheless, initialization arguments often turn into fields, and there seems to be no advantage in forcing programmers to explicitly designate such conversions; merely referencing an initialization argument from a method should be enough to convert it to a field. Automatic conversion, however, requires expanding all subexpressions when expanding a class form, but the class form needs to expand sub-expressions differently for fields than for initialization arguments. In other words, our macro technology affects our language design (in much the same way that parsing and type-checking concerns sometimes influence the outcome of other language design decisions).

In a similar vein, the class system prohibits an internal reference to a method that is not in an application position (i.e., as a method call). Occasionally, we would like to pass a method as a first-class value to functionals such as map. In this case, the class macro could easily convert the method to a closure over this; we instead force programmers to wrap the method with a lambda so that the closure allocation is more apparent. We may reconsider this design decision.

The run-time cost of object instantiation is higher than it should be. For an object with two initialization arguments that are both converted to fields, the instantiation time is a factor of 20 slower than for a comparable PLT Scheme record. The difference is in gathering and finding initializations arguments by name (which accounts for a factor of 10) and copying saved initialization arguments into fields (remaining factor of 2). One possible solution is to provide a form for specializing new in much the same way that send-generic specializes send.

Like most class systems, the PLT Scheme system conflates implementation inheritance and interface inheritance. That is, a subclass automatically implements any interface that its superclass implements. We are in a good position to try detaching interface inheritance from subclassing, but we have not yet explored that possibility.

Finally, although we have designed a class system that supports mixins and traits as separate extensions, the class system itself includes many built-in features that seem orthogonal: initialization protocols, several method overriding and augmenting protocols, and both implementation and interface inheritance. Future work may uncover ways to remove weaknesses and restrictions, making our little pile of features even smaller.

6 Related Work on Classes in Scheme

Our approach of adding objects to Scheme closely resembles Friedman's [18] object-oriented style, but it also differs significantly from his work. The key difference concerns the instantiation of classes, which we separate from the macro expansion phase. Instead of specifying a class's method statically, we rely on a run-time computation to completely determine a class's shape. As a result, combining our `class` with `lambda` defines mixins that work on varieties of superclass shapes.

Historically, implementors of class systems for Scheme have used the message-passing metaphor literally, representing an object as a procedure that accepts a method-selecting symbol [1, 2]. More generally, Scheme programmers are often tempted to think of an object as a collection of closures, where `this` is built into each method's closure instead of passed as an (implicit) argument. Unfortunately, the cost of this per-object representation depends on the number of methods the object supports, instead of just the number of fields. In our experience, the extra overhead is bearable when classes are used sparingly, but it becomes overwhelming otherwise.

Finally, the CLOS approach to classes is relatively popular in Scheme, e.g., the Meroon library [26] or Barzilay's Swindle library [7]. In contrast to Smalltalk-style classes, where behaviors are added by changing a class or deriving a new subclass, behavioral extensions in CLOS are attached to *generic methods*. An advantage of this approach is that it provides a clear path for adding "methods" to existing data types, including primitive types like numbers and strings. Another advantage is that it generalizes well to multi-method dispatch, which can easily specialize an operation to a particular combination of classes. A major drawback is that it encourages an imperative programming style, where generic methods are mutated to add new class-specific implementations.

7 Related Work on Mixins and Traits

The terms *mixin* and *trait* have a somewhat troubled and intertwined history, making comparisons among "mixin" and "trait" systems potentially confusing. In this paper, we have committed to particular definitions of the terms, and in the following comparisons, we add a superscript (*, †, or ‡) to each use of a term that does not match our definition.

The term *mixin** originates with Flavors [23], which inspired the Common Lisp Object System (CLOS). In Flavors and CLOS, a mixin* is simply a class that is meant to be combined with other classes via multiple inheritance.

Bracha and Cook refined the definition of *mixin* to "a subclass definition that may be applied to different superclasses" [11]. As defined by Bracha and Cook, mixins subsume classes, and we took a similar approach in our previous model of mixins for Java [17]. Implementations, however, typically define mixins over a base language with classes, as in PLT Scheme and the Jam language [4]. In the same vein, Smaradagkis and

Batory implement mixins with C++ templates [30] in the spirit of our mix of class and lambda.

For his dissertation, Bracha used the term *mixin*[†] for a construct in his Jigsaw language [10], which included operations on mixins[†] such as sum and exclude. Ancona and Zucca explore a formal framework [5, 6] for mixins[†].

Schärli's *traits* [28, 29] are a form of mixin[†] in the sense of Bracha's dissertation. In particular, Fisher, Reppy, and Turon [14, 27] provide typed models of traits that closely resemble the typed mixin[†] models of Ancona and Zucca [5, 6]. Using the sense of *mixin* in Bracha and Cook (and PLT Scheme), however, fine-grained operations make traits qualitatively different from mixins. Our encodings of mixins and traits in Scheme illustrate the difference. In practice, Black et al. [9] note the importance of alias and exclude trait operations for the refactoring of the Smalltalk collection classes. Their experience suggests that mixins are less suited to this kind of refactoring job than traits, but additional experience with both is needed.

The Scala programming language [24] includes a typed trait[‡] construct, but it does not support any operation on traits[‡] other than inheritance and combination with a base class; in other words, the construct may well have been called a *mixin*. Indeed, since multiple Scala traits[‡] can be composed when they override the same method, and since the order of the composition determines the resulting pattern of super calls, a Scala trait[‡] closely resembles a PLT Scheme mixin (but with a static type system). The Fortress [3] language also includes a trait[‡] construct that is similar to Scala's. Again, Fortress's traits[‡] could be characterized as mixins, although the lack of method overriding in Fortress makes the difference nearly insignificant.

Acknowledgements. We thank our PLT colleagues and numerous anonymous users for coping with 11 years of changes to the class system. We wish to acknowledge the financial support of the National Science Foundation and Texas ATP through these years.

References

1. H. Abelson and G. J. Sussman. *Structure and Interpretation of Computer Programs.* MIT Press, 1984.
2. N. Adams and J. Rees. Object-oriented programming in Scheme. In *Proc. ACM Conference on Lisp and Functional Programming*, pages 277–288, 1988.
3. E. Allen, D. Chase, V. Luchangco, J.-W. Maessen, S. Ryu, G. L. S. Jr., and S. Tobin-Hochstadt. The Fortress language specification. 2006.
4. D. Ancona, G. Lagorio, and E. Zucca. Jam - designing a Java extension with mixins. *ACM Transactions on Computing Systems*, 25:641–712, Sept. 2003.
5. D. Ancona and E. Zucca. An algebraic approach to mixins and modularity. In M. Hanus and M. Rodríguez-Artalejo, editors, *Proc. Conference on Algebraic and Logic Programming*, volume 1139 of *Lecture Notes in Computer Science*, pages 179–193. Springer-Verlag, 1996.
6. D. Ancona and E. Zucca. A primitive calculus for module systems. In G. Nadathur, editor, *Proc. International Conference on Principles and Practice of Declarative Programming*, volume 1702 of *Lecture Notes in Computer Science*, pages 62–79. Springer-Verlag, 1999.
7. E. Barzilay. *Swindle*, 2002. http://www.barzilay.org/Swindle/.
8. Benson Jr., Brent W. libscheme: Scheme as a C library. In *Proc. USENIX Symposium on Very High Level Languages*, 1994.

9. A. P. Black, N. Schärli, and S. Ducasse. Applying traits to the Smalltalk collection hierarchy. In *Proc. ACM Conference on Object-Oriented Programming, Systems, Languages, and Applications*, pages 47–64, Oct. 2003.

10. G. Bracha. *The Programming Language Jigsaw: Mixins, Modularity and Multiple Inheritance*. Ph.D. thesis, Dept. of Computer Science, University of Utah, Mar. 1992.

11. G. Bracha and W. Cook. Mixin-based inheritance. In *Proc. Joint ACM Conf. on Object-Oriented Programming, Systems, Languages and Applications and the European Conference on Object-Oriented Programming*, Oct. 1990.

12. R. K. Dybvig, R. Hieb, and C. Bruggeman. Syntactic abstraction in Scheme. *Lisp and Symbolic Computation*, 5(4):295–326, 1993.

13. R. B. Findler, C. Flanagan, M. Flatt, S. Krishnamurthi, and M. Felleisen. DrScheme: A pedagogic programming environment for Scheme. In *Proc. International Symposium on Programming Languages: Implementations, Logics, and Programs*, pages 369–388, Sept. 1997.

14. K. Fisher and J. Reppy. A typed calculus of traits. In *Proc. ACM International Workshop on Foundations of Object-Oriented Languages*, 2004.

15. M. Flatt. Compilable and composable macros. In *Proc. ACM International Conference on Functional Programming*, Oct. 2002.

16. M. Flatt and M. Felleisen. Units: Cool modules for HOT languages. In *Proc. ACM Conference on Programming Language Design and Implementation*, pages 236–248, June 1998.

17. M. Flatt, S. Krishnamurthi, and M. Felleisen. Classes and mixins. In *Proc. ACM Symposium on Principles of Programming Languages*, pages 171–183, Jan. 1998.

18. D. P. Friedman. Object-oriented style (invited talk). In *International LISP Conference*, 2003.

19. D. Goldberg, R. B. Findler, and M. Flatt. Super and inner — together at last! In *Proc. ACM Conference on Object-Oriented Programming, Systems, Languages, and Applications*, pages 116–129, Oct. 2004.

20. R. Kelsey, W. Clinger, and J. Rees (Eds.). The revised[5] report on the algorithmic language Scheme. *ACM SIGPLAN Notices*, 33(9), Sept. 1998.

21. J. Lamping. Typing the specialization interface. In *Proc. ACM Conference on Object-Oriented Programming, Systems, Languages, and Applications*, pages 201–214, 1993.

22. O. Lehrmann Madsen, B. Møller-Pedersen, and K. Nygaard. *Object-oriented programming in the BETA programming language*. ACM Press/Addison-Wesley, 1993.

23. D. A. Moon. Object-oriented programming with Flavors. In *Proc. ACM Conference on Object-Oriented Programming, Systems, Languages, and Applications*, pages 1–8, Nov. 1986.

24. M. Odersky and M. Zenger. Scalable component abstractions. In *Proc. ACM Conference on Object-Oriented Programming, Systems, Languages, and Applications*, pages 41–57, 2005.

25. *PLT Scheme*, 2006. www.plt-scheme.org.

26. C. Queinnec. *Meroon V3: A Small, Efficient, and Enhanced Object System*, 1997.

27. J. Reppy and A. Turon. A foundation for trait-based metaprogramming. In *Proc. ACM International Workshop on Foundations of Object-Oriented Languages*, 2006.

28. N. Schärli. *Composing Classes from Behavioral Building Blocks*. PhD thesis, University of Berne, 2002.

29. N. Schärli, S. Ducasse, O. Nierstrasz, and A. P. Black. Traits: Composable units of behaviour. In *Proc. European Conference on Object-Oriented Programming*, volume 2743 of *Lecture Notes in Computer Science*, pages 248–274. Springer-Verlag, 2003.

30. Y. Smaragdakis and D. Batory. Implementing layered designs with mixin layers. In *Proc. European Conference on Object-Oriented Programming*, pages 550–570, 1998.

31. Smart, J. et al. wxWindows.
http://web.ukonline.co.uk/julian.smart/wxwin/.

Using Metadata Transformations to Integrate Class Extensions in an Existing Class Hierarchy

Markus Lumpe

Department of Computer Science
Iowa State University
Ames, IA 50011, USA
lumpe@cs.iastate.edu

Abstract. Class extensions provide a fine-grained mechanism to define incremental modifications to class-based systems when standard subclassing mechanisms are inappropriate. To control the impact of class extensions, the concept of *classboxes* has emerged that defines a new module system to restrict the visibility of class extensions to selected clients. However, the existing implementations of the classbox concept rely either on a "classbox-aware" virtual machine, an expensive runtime introspection of the method call stack to build the structure of a classbox, or both. In this paper we present an implementation technique that allows for the structure of a classbox to be constructed at compile-time by means of metadata transformations to rewire the inheritance graph of refined classes. These metadata transformations are language-neutral and more importantly preserve both the semantics of the classbox concept and the integrity of the underlying deployment units. As a result, metadata transformation provides a feasible approach to incorporate the classbox concept into programming environments that use a *virtual execution system*.

1   Introduction

It is generally accepted that the inheritance relationships supported by mainstream object-oriented and class-based languages are not powerful enough to express many useful forms of incremental modifications. To address this problem, several approaches have emerged (e.g., Smalltalk [10], CLOS [22], MultiJava [6], Scala [21], or AspectJ [13]) that focus on a particular technique: *class extensions*. A class extension is a method that is defined in a packaging unit other than the class it is applied to. The most common kinds[1] of class extensions are the *addition* of a new method and the *replacement* of an existing method, respectively.

However, a major obstacle when specifying class extension is that their embodied changes have global impact [2]. Moreover, even if a system allows for a modular specification of class extensions (e.g., MultiJava [6] or AspectJ [13]), it may not support multiple versions of a given class to coexist at the same time. To remedy these shortcomings, Bergel et al. [1, 2] have recently proposed *classboxes*, a new module system that defines a packaging and scoping mechanism for controlling the visibility of isolated

---

[1] Bracha and Lindstrom [3] have also presented a *hide* operator that renders a method of a class invisible to clients of that class.

N. Kobayashi (Ed.): APLAS 2006, LNCS 4279, pp. 290–306, 2006.

extensions to portions of class-based systems. Besides the "traditional" operation of *subclassing*, classboxes also support the *local refinement* of imported classes by adding or modifying their features without affecting the originating classbox. Consequently, the classbox concept provides an attractive and powerful framework to develop, maintain, and evolve large-scale software systems and can significantly reduce the risk for introducing design and implementation anomalies in those systems [2].

At present, there exist two implementations of classboxes in Smalltalk [2] and a restricted prototype in Java [1]. The first Smalltalk implementation relies on a modified, "classbox-aware" virtual machine in which a dedicated graph search algorithm implements local rebinding of methods. The second implementation uses a combination of bytecode manipulation and a reified method call stack to build the structure of a classbox. This technique is also applied in Classbox/J [1], an implementation of classboxes for the Java environment. In Classbox/J, a preprocessor translates each method redefinition into a `if` statement that uses a `ClassboxInfo` object to determine, which definition to call in the current context.

Common to all three implementations is that the integration of class extensions occurs at runtime by means of a specially-designed method lookup mechanism. This implementation scheme adds a significant execution overhead to redefined methods. For the Smalltalk implementations, for example, this overhead is generally in-between 25% to 60%, compared to the "normal" method lookup [2]. Similarly, the method lookup of redefined methods in Classbox/J is on average 22 times slower than the normal method lookup [1].

In this paper we present an alternative implementation strategy that uses *metadata transformations* to integrate class extensions into a given class hierarchy. More precisely, we present a "classbox-aware" dialect of C# that defines a minimal extension to the C# language in order to provide support for the classbox concept, and Rewire.NET, a metadata adapter that implements a *compile-time* mechansism to incorporate the local refinements defined in a classbox into their corresponding classes. This approach allows us to treat standard .NET assemblies as classboxes, that is, we can import classes originating form standard .NET assemblies into a newly defined classbox, apply some local refinements to those classes, and generate a classbox assembly that is backward-compatible with the standard .NET framework. As a result, we obtain a mechanism that supports the coexistence of non-classbox-aware and classbox-aware software artifacts in one system and therefore allows for phased and fine-grained software evolution approach.

Our approach to incorporate the classbox concept into the .NET framework uses *code instrumentation* [4, 5, 12, 14, 15] to *rewire* the inheritance graph of a class hierarchy in order to build the structure of a classbox. This approach preserves the original semantics of the classbox concept while moving the process of constructing the structure of a classbox from runtime to compile-time. Furthermore, the application of metadata transformations allows us to use the standard method lookup mechanism for redefined methods. No dynamic introspection of the method call stack is required.

A key aspect of our approach is that a growing number of modern programming systems compile program code into a platform-independent representation that is executed in a *virtual execution system*. The virtual execution system provides an *abstract machine* to execute *managed* code. The two most known virtual execution systems are the Java platform [16] and the Common Language Infrastructure (CLI) [20]. Common to both systems is that the concrete layout of classes is not specified. This decision rests with the implementation of the virtual execution machine or a corresponding just-in-time (JIT) compiler. Both, Java and the CLI use a combination of *Intermediate Language* (IL) bytecode and *metadata*. Metadata provides the means for *self-describing* units of deployment in these systems. Besides application-specific resources like images or custom attributes, metadata contains information to locate and load classes, lay out instances in memory, resolve method invocations, and enforce security constraints. In other words, it is metadata and not the IL code that defines the structure of classes and their underlying class hierarchies. Rewire.NET exploits this special relationship between IL-bytecode and metadata in order to bind class extensions defined in a given classbox to their corresponding classes at compile-time.

The rest of this paper is organized as follows: in Section 2, we describe the classbox programming model for the .NET framework. In Section 3 we present the architectural elements to map the classbox concept to the CLI. We discuss the implementation of Rewire.NET in Section 4 and provide a brief overlook of related work in Section 5. We conclude this paper in Section 6 with a summary of the presented work and outline future activities in this area.

2 Integration of the Classbox Model in the .NET Framework

2.1 Classbox Characteristics

The main characteristics of classboxes can be summarized as follows [2]:

- A classbox is an explicitly named unit of scoping in which classes (and their associated members) are defined. A class belongs to the classbox it is first *defined*, but it can be made visible to other classboxes by either *importing* or *extending* it.
- Any extension applied to a class is only visible to the classbox in which it occurs first and any classboxes that either explicitly or implicitly import the extended class. Hence, redefining a particular method of a class in a given classbox will not have an effect on the originating classbox.
- Class extensions are only locally visible. However, their embodied refinements extend to all collaborating classes within a given classbox, in particular to any subclasses that are either explicitly imported, extended, or implicitly imported.

There are four additional, yet critical aspects in the definition of the classbox semantics [1, 2] that need to be satisfied also, when adding support for the classbox concept to a new programming environment:

Implicit import. The import mechanism provided by languages like Java or C# is non-transitive, that is, a declaration namespace ns cannot export a class C, if C was imported rather than defined in ns. In contrast, the module concept defined by classboxes uses transitive import. More precisely, if a classbox cb explicitly imports a class C, then all of C's superclasses are *implicitly* imported into cb also. This not only allows for a local refinement of the explicitly imported class C, but also for a refinement of all other classes in the inheritance graph of C in cb.

Method extension. The decision, whether a method m is added or acts as replacement depends on its signature. That is, if a locally refined class C already defines a method with the same name and signature, then m replaces this method. Otherwise, m is added to C. Moreover, method replacement takes precedence in a *flattened* version of class C [2].

Identity of classes. A key element of the semantics of classboxes is that the identity of locally refined imported classes is preserved. By preserving the identity of a class C, existing clients of C can benefit from the extensions applied to C also.

Virtual methods. The classbox concept rest upon virtual methods and dynamic binding [1,2]. There are no provisions for non-virtual methods. In addition, the decision, whether a method m is added or replaced in a given class C that occurs locally refined in a classbox cb is based on the members defined by C and its superclasses. If a subclass of C, say class D, is also explicitly imported into cb, then D should benefit from the extensions applied to C. However, if D defines its own version of m, then this method may hide C's method m, effectively rendering parts of the class extensions applied to C invisible to clients of D. A "classbox-aware" compiler can detect this situation, but the classbox concept is blind for this behavior.

2.2 Dynamic Graph Search

Common to both the Smalltalk and the Java implementations of classboxes is a specially-designed method lookup mechanism that performs a dynamic search over a classbox graph in order to ensure that import takes precedence over inheritance [1,2]. More precisely, if a given method cannot be located in the current imported class, then rather than continuing with the superclass, the modified lookup tries to locate the required method in the provider classbox. Only if the requested method cannot be located in the provider classbox, then the search continues in the imported class' superclass. The effect of this method lookup mechanism is that local refinements to imported classes are *dynamically* linked into the corresponding class hierarchy. In other words, extending an imported class is an operation that is performed at *runtime*.

Consider, for example, Figure 1 in which we highlight the search for the method foo with respect to the class C. The lookup starts at point '1' and as class C neither implements nor has been extended with a corresponding method, the lookup continues in its superclass B (denoted by '2'), which occurs as an implicitly imported class in SampleClassbox. Again, the class B does not implement the foo method. Therefore, the search has to continue by inspecting its superclass. However, since we have defined an extension to class A (we use the rounded box as a graphical means to indicate that the class A has been extended with the method foo), the search terminates in the extension that defines the method foo (denoted by '3') rather than in the class A directly, as this is the first point along the search path that implements the method foo.

The reader should note that this special method lookup mechanism is required, because the structure of a classbox is not known until runtime in both the Smalltalk and

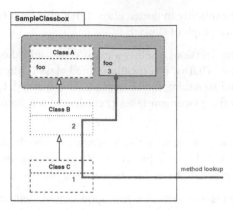

Fig. 1. Method lookup as search over the classbox graph

Java implementations. Moreover, even though extensions are bound dynamically into a class hierarchy, the classbox concept neither supports virtual classes [11] nor any form of "chameleon" objects that can change their structure based on the environment in which they are currently being used. Objects are instantiated with respect to a provider classbox that determines and finalizes the capabilities of that object. The dynamic graph search does not supersede the method layout, but amends it to build the structure of a given object's provider classbox at runtime.

2.3 Classbox-Aware C#

To ally the classbox concept with the .NET framework, we define a "classbox-aware" dialect of C#[2]. In previous work, we already explored a technique to amend the C# language with the classbox concept [17]. However, even though we were able to define a conceptual approach for the integration of the classbox concept in the .NET framework, the resulting language extensions could not be properly type-checked. Furthermore, the use of the *Metadata Unmanaged API* [19] turned out to be unsuitable for the purpose of manipulating .NET assemblies, as this API does not provide access to IL-bytecode, which is essential for a comprehensive solution. The language model proposed in this work not only follows closely the one proposed by Bergel et. al [2], but also allows for a proper type checking of the specified class extensions:

Class Import. To explicitly import a class, we use the *alias* form of the C# using-directive [7, §16.4.1]. An alias for a type is a user-defined name that is only available within the namespace body that introduces it. However, in contrast to standard C#, the *using-alias-directive* in classbox-aware C# creates an "empty" subclass with the same name for each explicitly imported class in the importing classbox. This approach not only enables the local refinement of the explicitly imported class, but publishes the explicitly imported class to clients of the importing classbox as it had been defined in the importing classbox itself. The introduction of a new subclass does not

---

[2] We are currently experimenting with the open-source Mono compiler in order to define a frontend for classbox-aware C# [17].

```
using System;

namespace TraceAndColorCB
{
  using System.Drawing;

  using Point = PointHierarchyCB.Point include
  {
    private Color color;
    public Color Color { get{ return color; } set{ color = value; } }
    public void MoveBy( int dx, int dy )
    {
      Console.WriteLine( "MoveBy: {0}, {1}", new object[] { dx, dy } );
      base.MoveBy( dx, dy );
    }
  }

  using LinearBPoint = PointHierarchyCB.LinearBPoint;
}
```

Listing 1. Classbox `TraceAndColorCB` in classbox-aware C#

preserve the identity of classes as required by the classbox model. To restore it, we apply
Rewire.NET to the assemblies constituting the physical structure of the corresponding
classbox.

Subclassing. Subclassing is represented by the standard class building mechanisms.
The available C# language abstractions suffice to specify this operation. A subclass
introduces a new type name in the defining classbox. This type name must be unique.
However, the classbox concept allows for the coexistence of both the new subclass and
implicitly imported classes with identical names in the same classbox.

Class Extension. We use the modified *alias* form of the C# using-directive and add
an include-clause to specify the local refinements to an imported class. The members of the local refinements are specified in a *class-body* [7, §17.1.3]. All methods
and properties are implicitly marked virtual. If the extended class already defines a
member with the same name and signature, then this member becomes overridden (i.e.,
replaced). Otherwise, the extension is added to the class. Extending an imported class
results in a new subclass with the same name in the importing classbox. As in the case
of class import, we have to use Rewire.NET to restore the class identity.

A classbox in the .NET framework has a *logical* and a *physical* structure. These
concepts do not change the underlying semantics of the classbox model, but provide us
with the means to separate the program interface from the implementation of a classbox.
The logical structure of a classbox defines a namespace to specify the *import* of classes,
the introduction of *subclasses*, and the *extension* of classes. The physical structure of a
classbox, on the other hand, identifies the assemblies that contain the executable code
that is specified by the logical structure of a classbox.

To illustrate the new language abstractions, consider the specification of the classbox
`TraceAndColorCB`, as shown in Listing 1. The namespace `TraceAndColorCB`
defines the logical structure of the classbox `TraceAndColorCB` in which we explicitly import the classes `Point` and `LinearBPoint`, both originating from classbox
`PointHierarchyCB`. In `TraceAndColorCB`, we extend class `Point` with the

```
using System;

namespace TraceAndColorCB
{
  using System.Drawing;

  public class Point : PointHierarchyCB.Point
  {
    private Color color;
    public Point( int ix, int iy ) : base( ix, iy ) {}
    public virtual Color Color { get{ return color; } set{ color = value; } }
    public override void MoveBy( int dx, int dy )
    {
      Console.WriteLine( "MoveBy: {0}, {1}", new object[] { dx, dy } );
      base.MoveBy( dx, dy );
    }
  }

  public class LinearBPoint : PointHierarchyCB.LinearBPoint
  {
    public LinearBPoint( int ix, int iy, int ibound ) : base( ix, iy, ibound ) {}
  }
}
```

Listing 2. Classbox `TraceAndColorCB` in standard C#

property `Color` (utilizing a private instance variable `color`) and the method `MoveBy` that defines a tracing facility to monitor invocations of `MoveBy`. The method `MoveBy` overrides (i.e., replaces) an exiting method in class `Point`. It defines also an access to the original behavior through a `base`-call. The property `Color`, on the other hand, is new and therefore added to the refined class `Point` in classbox `TraceAndColorCB`. The class `LinearBPoint`, which defines a non-constant linear upper bound for point objects, is an indirect subclass of class `Point` (i.e., in `PointHierarchyCB` the class `LinearBPoint` is derived from `BoundedPoint` that is a direct subclass of `Point`). Therefore, the local refinements defined for class `Point` impact class `LinearBPoint` also, that is, it possesses now a property `Color` and a method `MoveBy` with a tracing facility in `TraceAndColorCB`.

The classbox-aware C#-compiler translates the specification of this classbox into an internal representation that corresponds to the standard C#-code shown in Listing 2. Each explicitly imported class results in a new class definition in which the imported class becomes the direct supertype. Moreover, in order to preserve all constructors defined by class `Point` and `LinearBPoint`, we add corresponding "empty" constructors to the new class definitions. This approach prevents the automatic insertion of a *default*-constructor that would render the original constructors invisible.

The result of compiling the classbox `TraceAndColorCB` is the assembly `Trace-AndColorCB.dll` that together with `PointHierarchyCB.dll` (i.e., the assembly defining the classbox `PointHierarchyCB`) constitute a *provisional* physical structure of the classbox `TraceAndColorCB`. In the provisional structure, the identity of imported classes has not yet been established. To restore the identity of imported classes, we have to rewire the inheritance graph of the classes `Point` and `LinearBPoint` by using Rewire.NET. The result is the final physical structure of the classbox `TraceAndColorCB`.

3   Building the Structure of a Classbox at Compile-Time

3.1   Metadata Type Declarations

Each CLI-enabled language has to define a language-appropriate scheme to represent types and members in metadata. At the core of every CLI-enabled programming language is a set of built-in data types compliant with the Common Type System (CTS), mechanisms to combine them to construct new types, and a facility to assign names to new types to seamlessly integrate them in the CLI [20]. The CLI uses an implementation-dependent declarative encoding mechanism to represent metadata information, called *metadata token*. A metadata token is a scoped typed identifier of a metadata object and is represented as a **read-only** index into a corresponding metadata table.

New types are introduced via metadata type declarations [20]. TYPEDEF tokens encode the name of a type, its declaration namespace, the super type (index into TYPEDEF or TYPEREF table), an index into the FIELD table that marks the first of a continuous run of field definitions owned by this type, and an index into the METHODDEF table that marks the first of a continuous run of method definitions owned by this type. In addition, a given assembly can refer to types defined in another module or assembly. These references are encoded by TYPEREF, MEMBERREF, and ASSEMBLYREF tokens, respectively. A TYPEREF token encodes the resolution scope (e.g., index into ASSEMBLYREF table), the name of the type, and its declaration namespace. MEMBER-REF tokens are references used for both fields and methods of a class defined in another assembly. MEMBERREF tokens encode the type that owns the member, the member's name, and its signature. Finally, ASSEMBLYREF is a metadata token, which encodes the information that uniquely identifies another assembly on which the current assembly is depending. ASSEMBLYREF tokens not only encode the name to the referenced assembly, but also its version, which enables a deployment mechanism that allows for multiple versions of assemblies with the same name to coexist on the one system.

Metadata is organized in tables, whose rows start with index 1. Metadata may contain unreachable rows, but an index into a table must denote a valid row in that table. The indices into the metadata tables create a static dependency or *link* graph. The CLI loader imports the metadata into its own in-memory data structures, which can be browsed via *Reflection* services. Both the metadata in an assembly and the corresponding in-memory runtime structures are immutable. However, they provide fast and direct access to required type information.

3.2   Changing the Metadata

To move the process of creating the structure of a classbox from runtime to compile-time, we take advantage of the separation of metadata and IL-bytecode. Both, the import of a class and extending an imported class trigger the creation of a new subclass with the same name as outlined in Section 2.3. However, subclassing is an operation that breaks the connection to former clients [9]. To restore this connection and to enable a former clients of the extended class to benefit from the local refinements, we have to redirect the supertype edge of any direct explicitly or implicitly imported subclass of a refined class to the newly created class in the current classbox.

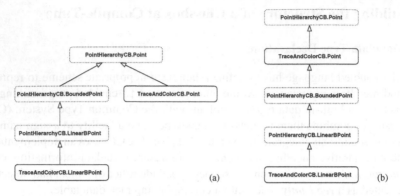

Fig. 2. Inheritance graph in classbox `TraceAndColorCB` before and after flattening

Consider again the classbox `TraceAndColorCB`. This classbox explicitly imports the classes `Point` and `LinearBPoint` from `PointHierarchyCB`. As a result, we create two new subclasses with the same name in `TraceAndColorCB`. The resulting inheritance graph is shown in Figure 2(a) (explicitly imported classes are marked with a solid rounded box, whereas implicitly imported types are marked with a dotted rounded box).

A name of a type in CLI consists of two elements: a *typename* and a *namespace*. Therefore, when we introduce the new subclasses for explicitly imported types, we create a new name in which the namespace component identifies the importing classbox. The scheme allows for the coexistence of different versions of a class in the same classbox, since it is always possible to distinguish them by using their namespace name. In the provisional structure of classbox `TraceAndColorCB`, the class `TraceAndColorCB.Point` is not in the inheritance graph of class `TraceAndColorCB.LinearBPoint`. As a consequence, the class `TraceAndColorCB.LinearBPoint` does not yet benefit from the local refinements applied to the class `TraceAndColorCB.Point`, as required by the classbox model. To change this, we have to make `TraceAndColorCB.Point` a direct supertype of class `PointHierarchyCB.BoundedPoint`. To accomplish this, we change the TYPEDEF metadata token defining the class `PointHierarchyCB.BoundedPoint` in the metadata of the assembly `PointHierarchyCB.dll`. More precisely, we need rewire the *Extends* column of `PointHierarchyCB.BoundedPoint`'s TYPEDEF metadata token to point to the TYPEDEF metadata token defining class `TraceAndColorCB.Point` in assembly `TraceAndColorCB.dll`. We proceed by performing the following instructions:

1. Create a new version of `PointHierarchyCB.dll` and name this assembly `PointHierarchyCB(TraceAndColorCB).dll`, where the name `TraceAndColorCB` firmly associates this new assembly with the classbox `TraceAndColorCB` to *disambiguate* multiple rewired versions of the `PointHierarchyCB` classbox.

2. Add an ASSEMBLYREF token for `TraceAndColorCB` to the metadata of `PointHierarchyCB(TraceAndColorCB).dll`.

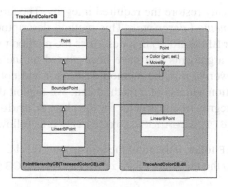

Fig. 3. Structure of classbox `TraceAndColorCB`

3. Add a `TYPEREF` token for `TraceAndColorCB.Point` to the metadata of `Po-
   intHierarchyCB(TraceAndColorCB).dll`.
4. Set the *Extends* column of the `TYPEDEF` token for class `PointHierarchyCB.-
   BoundedPoint` to point to the newly added `TYPEREF` token in `PointHierar-
   chyCB(TraceAndColorCB).dll`.

The result of this transformation is a *flattened* classbox that publishes two classes:
`Point` and `LinearBPoint`, whose inheritance graph is shown in Figure 2(b). The
metadata manipulations do not affect existing clients of `PointHierarchyCB`, since
we create a new version for this assembly, before applying the transformations. Moreover, in contrast to Classbox/J, we do not need access to the original source code to create to structure of a classbox. The logical structure of classbox `TraceAndColorCB`
is defined by the static link graph in metadata of its corresponding physical representation, that is, the assemblies `TraceAndColorCB.dll` and `PointHierarchy-
CB(TraceAndColorCB).dll`, as shown in Figure 3.

3.3   Restoring Constructor Integrity

The rewiring process outlined in the previous section manipulates metadata, but not
the IL-bytecode. The process preserves the integrity of metadata, that is, all indices to
tables in metadata denote a valid row. Unfortunately, changing the *Extends* column of
the `TYPEDEF` token describing class `BoundedPoint` does not preserve the integrity
of the IL-bytecode in `PointHierarchyCB(TraceAndColorCB).dll`.

In order to initialize a new object being created for a given class, the constructor for that class always calls its *statically known* superclass constructor first. In the
original assembly `PointHierarchyCB.dll`, this statically known superclass constructor is `PointHierarchyCB.Point::.ctor`. The situation in the assembly
`PointHierarchyCB(TraceAndColorCB).dll` is different, however, as we
have changed the supertype of the class `BoundedPoint` to `TraceAndColorCB.-
Point`. It is, therefore, not correct to call `PointHierarchyCB.Point::.ctor`.
As a consequence, the IL-bytecode for the constructor of the class `BoundedPoint`
loses its integrity, since object initialization cannot *skip* classes.

We can, however, easily restore the required integrity. The target of a static method call is indicated by a *method descriptor*. This method descriptor is a metadata token (either METHODDEF or MEMBEREF) that describes the method to call and the number, type, and order of the arguments that have been placed on the stack to be passed to that method. In other words, it is the method descriptor and not the IL-bytecode that determines the destination address of a method call. We exploit this fact, to restore the broken IL-bytecode integrity of constructor for the class BoundedPoint in assembly PointHierarchyCB(TraceAndColorCB).dll, as follows:

1. Add a MEMBEREF token indicating the constructor for the class TraceAndColorCB.Point to the metadata of PointHierarchyCB(TraceAndColorCB).dll.
2. Construct, using the new MEMBEREF token, a new method descriptor for TraceAndColorCB.Point::.ctor.
3. Use the *Relative Virtual Address* (i.e., the *RVA* column) of the METHODDEF token describing the constructor for the class BoundedPoint to locate the method descriptor for PointHierarchyCB.Point::.ctor and replace it with the descriptor built in the previous step.

Using these instructions, the integrity of the constructor for the class BoundedPoint in assembly PointHierarchyCB(TraceAndColorCB).dll is restored. As a result, we have obtained the final physical structure of the classbox TraceAndColorCB. The assemblies PointHierarchyCB(TraceAndColorCB).dll and TraceAndColorCB.dll are standard .NET assemblies and pass verification. Thus, we can use them like any other non-classbox-aware assembly. The structure of the classbox TraceAndColorCB is imprinted in the metadata of the underlying assemblies. Moreover, by moving the process of building the structure of a classbox from run-time to compile-time we recover the standard method lookup mechanism for redefined methods and therefore, eliminate the execution overhead formerly associated with class extensions.

3.4 Evaluation of the Rewiring Technique

A major benefit of our solution is that we can use the standard method lookup mechanism for redefined methods. As a result, there is no measurable difference in the execution time of both plain and redefined methods.

While the size of the IL-bytecode remains the same, the size of the metadata grows due to the rewiring process. The amount of change underlies several varying factors. First, the metadata is not located at the end of the .text section. In this case, we cannot recycle the old metadata and therefore create a new image of the metadata at the end of the .text section, which effectively renders the old metadata into garbage. The second factor influencing the growth of metadata is associated with the amount of "reusable" rows. The rewiring process takes a very conservative approach, as it only adds new rows to the metadata, if no appropriate row exists. All byte-indexed data (i.e., strings, blob data, and UTF-16 strings) cannot be reused, as this may break indices from IL-bytecode into the corresponding heaps. When a new row is needed, then this row is always added to the end of its corresponding table or heap.

To illustrate the the change in size, consider, for example, the rewiring process of `PointHierarchyCB.dll`. The required transformations require 168 additional bytes of metadata. Unfortunately, the resulting size of the new metadata exceeds the available free space at the end of the `.text` section. Therefore, we are required to enlarge it by one unit of size *SectionAlignment*, which is 4K. However, the numbers for the two system assemblies `System.Drawing.dll` and `System.Windows.Forms.-dll` indicate that the overhead for placing the metadata at the end of the `.text` section may reach a threshold at which it cannot be ignored anymore. In these two assemblies, the size of the metadata amounts to almost half of their total size. We plan, therefore, to explore alternative approaches in future work that will allow us to reorder the `.text` section data, so that the space occupied by the old metadata can be reclaimed.

One of the key features of the classbox concept is that multiple versions of a class can coexist in the same classbox or application. Our rewiring technique preserves this property of classboxes by adding a *target classbox tag* to the originating namespace names of all explicitly imported types[3]. For example, the namespace name `PointHierarchyCB` in classbox `TraceAndColorCB` is changed to `TraceAndColorCB:PointHierarchyCB`, an identifier that cannot be defined in C#. The effect of this tag is twofold. First, in C# the visibility of a superclass cannot be more restrictive than the one of any of its subclasses. As a consequence, even implicitly imported types possess public visibility in a provider classbox. The target classbox tag eliminates this problem completely, as it renders all implicit imported types invisible. Secondly, the target classbox tag *disambiguates* multiple versions of the same class. For example, a client can safely use both classboxes `PointHierarchyCB` and `TraceAndColorCB`, even though all provided classes occur multiple times either explicitly imported, implicitly imported or both in the client space. Therefore, different versions of a class can coexist and be unequivocally identified in the same declaration space.

4   Rewire.NET

Rewire.NET is a .NET component, written in C#, that accepts as input a *rewiring specification* that lists the target classbox, the referenced assemblies, and all explicitly imported classes. Rewire.NET analyzes the provisional physical structure of the target classbox and performs the necessary transformations to produce a final physical structure of the target classbox. The implementation of Rewire.NET has one subsystem for the representation of assemblies, called `CLI`. The `CLI` subsystem is a namespace that defines a collection of classes that provide an object-oriented interface to read, alter, and write .NET assemblies (cf., Figure 4).

4.1   The CLI Subsystem

Several methods and tools have been proposed to perform assembly introspection. The .NET framework already provides the `System.Reflection` API, which can be used

---

[3] We have omitted these tags in the above explanation of the rewiring technique to preserve readability.

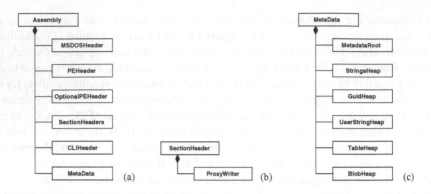

Fig. 4. CLI.Assembly, CLI.SectionHeader, and CLI.MetaData

for this purpose. Using the services provided by this API, we are able to programmatically obtain the metadata contained in an assembly. Unfortunately, this API lacks the ability to access IL-bytecode. However, as outlined in Section 3.3, we need access to the IL-bytecode in order to restore the integrity of a constructor, whose class was subject to a supertype change. We face a similar problem with the *Metadata Unmanaged API* [19] that can be used by a compiler to query the metadata of a host assembly and emit the correspondingly updated information into a new version of the host assembly.

A framework that provides access to both metadata and IL-bytecode is the *Runtime Assembly Instrumentation Library* (RAIL) [4]. RAIL closes the gap between the reflection capabilities in the .NET framework and its support for code emission. RAIL offers an object-oriented interface for an easy manipulation of assemblies, modules, classes, and even IL-bytecode. Nevertheless, RAIL cannot be used for the implementation of Rewire.NET, as this API does not allow for the manipulation of type references. RAIL treats type references (i.e., TYPEREF metadata tokens) as read-only pointers to members defined outside the current assembly being instrumented.

The CLI API addresses these shortcomings. The primary purpose of this API is to provide an object-oriented view of an assembly with a symmetric support for reading and writing Portable Executable files. In addition, the CLI API defines mechanisms to manipulate the metadata of an assembly and to fetch the IL-bytecode. It does, however, not define any IL-bytecode manipulation capabilities, except for the update of method descriptors. We can use the Reflection.Emit API or RAIL for IL-bytecode instrumentation.

At the center of the CLI API is the class Assembly, which is composed from the core elements of the extended Portable Executable file format, as shown in Figure 4(a). The class Assembly represents an in-memory image of a Portable Executable file. It provides access to the structure of the runtime file format of an assembly. The class Assembly defines both a Read and a Write method to load an assembly into memory and to create a new PE image, respectively. However, rather than retaining the contents of all native PE sections in memory, the Read method constructs a ProxyWriter object and associates it with its corresponding section data (cf., Figure 4(b)). The class ProxyWriter defines a method FetchILMethod to acquire the IL-bytecode associated with a given Relative Virtual Address (RVA), a method

`Update` that takes a byte array and a RVA to change the byte sequence starting at RVA in the associated section data, and a method `Copy` that writes the associated section data to a new Portable Executable file.

The class `MetaData`, as shown in Figure 4(c), represents the logical format of metadata. It provides access to all metadata stream heaps. These stream heaps are structured as tables and provide an index-based access to rows. Furthermore, each heap defines an `Add` method to append a new row to a table. Stream heaps do not allow for the removal of a row. Deleting a row may destroy the integrity of metadata. However, stream heaps may contain *garbage*, that is, rows that are not indexed by either metadata or IL-bytecode.

4.2   Rewire.NET

Rewire.NET is a *Console Application* that reads the rewiring specification that is generated by the classbox-aware C# compiler while compiling a classbox. The format of the rewiring specification is given below:

Specification ::= { *Definition* }*
Definition   ::= **R** # *ReferencedAssemblyFileName* | **T** # *ClassboxAssemblyFileName* |
                    I # *ExplicitlyImportedClass* | **N** # *ClassboxName*

We have added support for the generation of a rewiring specification to the open source C#-compiler of the Mono project [23, version 1.1.8.3]. At compile-time, the modified C#-compiler generates a list regarding all explicitly referenced assemblies, all explicitly imported classes, and all extended imported classes. For example, consider again the classbox `TraceAndColorCB`. The specification for building the final physical structure of this classbox is given below:

```
N # TraceAndColorCB
T # TraceAndColorCB.dll
R # PointHierarchyCB.dll
I # PointHierarchyCB.Point
I # PointHierarchyCB.LinearBPoint
```

After reading the rewiring specification, the rewiring process proceeds in two phases. In the first phase, we identify (i) all classes, whose super type is in the set of explicitly imported classes and register these classes for update, (ii) build a list of all assemblies for which we need to create a new version, and (iii) add the required target classbox tags. For example, in the case of the classbox `TraceAndColorCB`, we need to update the class `BoundedPoint` originating from `PointHierarchyCB`, have to create a new version of the assembly `PointHierarchyCB.dll`, and add the classbox tag `TraceAndColorCB:` to the namespace name `PointHierarchyCB`. In the second phase, we perform the actual metadata transformations. First, we create the required new assembly versions. Next, we add the required new `ASSEMBLYREF` metadata tokens to their respective assemblies. Adding the new `ASSEMBLYREF` tokens first simplifies the next step, as these new `ASSEMBLYREF` tokens are required for the update of the super type information. In the final step in this phase, we update the super type information and restore the integrity of the constructors of all classes marked for update.

Both phases take place in memory. To create the actual images of the updated assemblies, we have to call the their `Write` method. Metadata must be stored in the text section (i.e., the .text section). The Write method places the new metadata at the end of the text section. If necessary, the text section is enlarged to accommodate the new metadata. It is in general not possible to reclaim the space occupied by the old metadata, as there are no requirements to place metadata at the end of the text section. However, by placing the new metadata at the end of the text section, we can recycle the space occupied by metadata in future updates.

5   Related Work

Code instrumentation has been a subject of intense research in the last decade. Code instrumentation focuses on three primary purposes: introspection, optimization, and security. By using code instrumentation we can, for example, detect any places in compiled code, where this code accesses the local file system and insert an additional authentication layer. To edit *fully-linked* executables, Larus and Schnarr [15] have proposed the *Executable Editing Library* (EEL). EEL is a framework for building tools to analyze and modify executable (i.e., compiled) code. EEL provides an object-oriented architecture- and system-independent set of abstractions (i.e., C++ class hierarchies) to read, analyze, and modify executable code. These abstractions are very similar to those found in a compiler, as the purpose of both EEL and a compiler is to manipulate programs.

Code instrumentation frameworks that target the Java platform are *Binary Component Adaptation* (BCA) [12] and *Javassist* [5], which allow for an *on-the-fly* code instrumentation of binary Java components. Both frameworks use a customizable class loader to rewrite and/or reflect on binary components before (or while) they are loaded. The rewriting process does not require source code access and guarantees release-to-release compatibility.

RAIL [4] is the first general purpose code instrumentation library for the .NET platform. RAIL supports structural [8] as well as behavioral reflection [18]. The abstractions provided by RAIL allow for both low- and high-level modifications of assemblies. RAIL enables the modification of assemblies at class level (e.g., substitution of classes, members, and member access). RAIL does not, however, allow for the manipulation of references to external types.

Lafferty and Cahill [14] have presented Weave.NET, a load-time weaver for the .NET framework that allows aspects and components written in different languages to be freely intermixed. Weave.NET relies on the Common Language Infrastructure and XML to specify aspect bindings. By using CLI, Weave.NET provides a language-independent aspect-oriented programming model.

6   Conclusion and Future Work

In this paper, we have presented an approach to seamlessly incorporate the classbox concept into the .NET framework. Classboxes provide a feasible solution to the problem of controlling the visibility of change in object-oriented systems without breaking existing applications, as they allow for strictly limiting both the scope and the impact of any modifications. Consequently, classboxes can significantly reduce the risk for introducing design and implementation anomalies due to the need to adapt a software system to changing requirements [2].

We replaced the dynamic integration of class extensions at runtime by a static, *compile-time*-based approach. Our approach not only eliminates the runtime overhead that is associated with the construction of the classbox structure, but allows us also to treat standard .NET assemblies as classboxes. The key method underlying the integration of the classbox concept in the .NET framework is *metadata manipulation*. Using this code instrumentation method we can restructure the inheritance graph of a class hierarchy in order to incorporate local refinements (i.e., class extensions) into the behavior of explicitly imported classes. Hence, by using the metadata concept of the underlying Common Language Infrastructure (CLI), classboxes can be seamlessly integrated into the .NET environment without the need to modify the underlying runtime infrastructure.

The re-wiring process requires the originating assemblies to be copied. This appears to be a drawback of our implementation. However, the new versions of these assemblies play a major role in a compile-time-based approach to integrate extensions into a existing class hierarchy. The .NET framework uses a strong version control mechanism as each assembly is assigned a unique version number. In our implementation, we utilize this mechanism to distinguish between different classboxes. An extension to an imported class triggers the creation of new versions of referenced assemblies that contain types the imported class is depending upon. These new assemblies are bound to a particular classbox. The result is a physical and logical structure the captures precisely the defined classbox and does not affect previously defined classboxes. As a consequence, this structure can be deployed independently.

In this work, we have used a rather conservative approach to manipulate metadata. However, metadata transformation allow for a variety of manipulations of the structure of classes. We plan, therefore, to explore more aggressive class restructuring techniques in the future in order to enrich the classbox concept. In addition, we plan to apply the rewiring technique to Classbox/J. However, since Java platform uses a different deployment mechanism (usually based on JAR-files) that lacks a strong association between deployment unit, version, and package name, the physical structure of a classbox cannot span across multiple physical units as in the .NET framework. Future work on the classbox concept will include, therefore, the exploration of an alternative packaging mechanism to represent the physical structure of a classbox in which the classes of a classbox are grouped in one physical deployment unit.

Acknowledgements. We would like Alexandre Bergel, Andre Lokasari, Hua Ming, Jean-Guy Schneider, and the anonymous reviewers for their valuable discussions.

References

1. Alexandre Bergel, Stéphane Ducasse, and Oscar Nierstrasz. Classbox/J: Controlling the Scope of Change in Java. In *Proceedings OOPSLA '05*, volume 40 of *ACM SIGPLAN Notices*, pages 177–189, San Diego, USA, October 2005.
2. Alexandre Bergel, Stéphane Ducasse, Oscar Nierstrasz, and Roel Wuyts. Classboxes: Controlling Visibility of Class Extensions. *Journal of Computer Languages, Systems & Structures*, 31(3–4):107–126, May 2005.

3. Gilad Bracha and Gary Lindstrom. Modularity Meets Inheritance. In *Proceedings of the International Conference on Computer Languages*, pages 282–290. IEEE Computer Society, April 1992.
4. Bruno Cabral, Paulo Marques, and Luís Silva. RAIL: Code Instrumentation for .NET. In Lorie M. Liebrock, editor, *Proccedings of Symposium On Applied Computing (SAC'05)*, pages 1282–1287. ACM Press, March 2005.
5. Shigeru Chiba. Load-Time Structural Reflection in Java. In Elisa Bertino, editor, *Proceedings ECOOP 2000*, LNCS 1850, pages 313–336, Cannes, France, June 2000. Springer.
6. Curtis Clifton, Gary T. Leavens, Craig Chambers, and Todd Millstein. MultiJava: Modular Open Classes and Symmetric Multiple Dispatch for Java. In *Proceedings OOPSLA 2000*, volume 35 of *ACM SIGPLAN Notices*, pages 130–146, October 2000.
7. European Computer Machinery Association. *Standard ECMA-334: C# Language Specification*, third edition, June 2005.
8. Jacques Ferber. Computational Reflection in Class based Object-Oriented Languages. In *Proceedings OOPSLA '89*, pages 317–326. ACM Press, October 1989.
9. Robert Bruce Findler and Matthew Flatt. Modular Object-Oriented Programming with Units and Mixins. In *Proceedings of the ACM SIGPLAN International Conference on Functional Programming (ICFP '98)*, volume 34, pages 94–104, 1998.
10. Adele Goldberg and David Robson. *Smalltalk-80: The Language*. Addison-Wesley, September 1989.
11. Atsushi Igarashi and Benjamin Pierce. Foundations for Virtual Types. In Rachid Guerraoui, editor, *Proceedings ECOOP '99*, LNCS 1628, pages 161–185. Springer, June 1999.
12. Ralph Keller and Urs Hölzle. Binary Component Adaptation. In Eric Jul, editor, *Proceedings ECOOP'98*, LNCS 1445, pages 307–329, Brussels, Belgium, July 1998. Springer.
13. Grégor Kiczales, Erik Hilsdale, Jim Hugunin, Mik Kersten, Jeffrey Palm, and William G. Griswold. An Overview of AspectJ. In Jørgen Lindskov Knudsen, editor, *Proceedings ECOOP 2001*, LNCS 2072, pages 327–355, Budapest, Hungary, June 2001. Springer.
14. Donal Lafferty and Vinny Cahill. Language-Independent Aspect-Oriented Programming. In *Proceedings OOPSLA 2003*, pages 1–12. ACM Press, October 2003.
15. James R. Larus Larus and Eric Schnarr. EEL: Machine-Independent Executable Editing. In *Proceedings of the ACM SIGPLAN'95 Conference on Programming Language Design and Implementation (PLDI)*, pages 291–300, La Jolla, California, June 1995.
16. Tim Lindholm and Frank Yellin. *The Java Virtual Machine Specification*. The Java Series. Addison-Wesley, September 1996.
17. Markus Lumpe and Jean-Guy Schneider. On the Integration of Classboxes into C#. In Welf Löwe and Mario Südholt, editors, *Proceedings of the 5th International Symposium on Software Composition (SC 2006)*, LNCS 4089, pages 307–322, Vienna, Austria, March 2006. Springer.
18. Jacques Malenfant, Christophe Dony, and Pierre Cointe. Behavioral Reflection in a Prototype-Based Language. In A. Yonezawa and B. Smith, editors, *Proceedings of International Workshop on Reflection and Meta-Level Architectures*, pages 143–153, Tokyo, Japan, November 1992.
19. Microsoft Corporation. *Metadata Unmanaged API*, 2002.
20. James S. Miller and Susann Ragsdale. *The Common Language Infrastructure Annotated Standard*. Microsoft .NET Development Series. Addison-Wesley, 2003.
21. Martin Odersky, Philippe Altherr, Vincent Cremet, Burak Emir, Sebastian Maneth, Stéphane Micheloud, Nikolay Mihaylov, Michel Scinz, Erik Stenmanm, and Matthias Zenger. An Overview of the Scala Programming Language. Technical Report IC/2004/64, École Polytechnique Fédérale de Lausanne, School of Computer and Communication Sciences, 2004.
22. Guy L. Steele. *Common Lisp the Language*. Digital Press, Thinking Machines, Inc., 2nd edition, 1990.
23. The Mono Project. http://www.mono-project.com/Main_Page.

Combining Offline and Online Optimizations: Register Allocation and Method Inlining

Hiroshi Yamauchi and Jan Vitek

Department of Computer Sciences, Purdue University
{yamauchi, jv}@cs.purdue.edu

Abstract. Fast dynamic compilers trade code quality for short compilation time in order to balance application performance and startup time. This paper investigates the interplay of two of the most effective optimizations, register allocation and method inlining for such compilers. We present a bytecode representation which supports offline global register allocation, is suitable for fast code generation and verification, and yet is backward compatible with standard Java bytecode.

1 Introduction

Programming environments that support dynamic loading of platform-independent code must provide supports for efficient execution and find a good balance between responsiveness (shorter delays due to compilation) and performance (optimized compilation). Thus, most commercial Java Virtual Machines (JVM) include several execution engines. Typically, there is an interpreter or a *fast compiler* for initial executions of all code, and a profile-guided optimizing compiler for performance-critical code.

Improving the quality of the code of a fast compiler has the following benefits. It raises the performance of short-running and medium length applications that exit before the expensive optimizing compiler fully kicks in. It also benefits long-running applications with improved startup performance and responsiveness (due to less eager optimizing compilation). One way to achieve this is to shift some of the burden to an offline compiler. The main question is what optimizations are profitable when performed offline and are either guaranteed to be safe or can be easily validated online.

We investigate the combination of offline analysis with online optimizations for the two most important Java optimizations [12]: register allocation and method inlining, targeted for a fast compiler. The first challenge we are faced with is the choice of intermediate representation (IR). Java bytecode was designed for compactness, portability, and verifiability and not for encoding offline program optimizations. We build on the previous work [16,18,17,2,9,11,10] and propose a simplified form of the Java bytecode augmented with annotations that support offline register allocation in an architecture independent way. We call it SimpleIR (or SIR). A SIR program is valid Java bytecode and can thus be verified and used in any JVM. We then evaluate offline register allocation heuristics [2,10]

N. Kobayashi (Ed.): APLAS 2006, LNCS 4279, pp. 307–322, 2006.

and propose novel heuristics. Another challenge is that performing method inlining offline is not always effective because of separate compilation (e.g., dynamic class loading over network and dynamic bytecode generation), architecture independence (e.g., platform-dependent (standard) library modules), and access restriction (e.g., inter-class inlining of methods that access private fields). Thus, we ask the question: can we combine offline register allocation with online method inlining? The contributions of this paper are as follows:

- **Backward-compatible IR for offline register allocation:** *We propose a simplified form of Java bytecode with annotations which supports encoding offline register allocation, fast code generation and verification, and backward compatibility.*
- **Evaluation of offline register allocation heuristics:** *We directly compare two previously known register allocation heuristics and two new heuristics.*
- **Register allocation merging technique:** *which quickly and effectively computes register allocation for inlined methods based on offline register allocation for individual methods.*
- **Empirical evaluation:** *We have implemented our techniques in a compiler and report on performance results and compilation times for different scenarios.*

2 Intermediate Representations

Alternative intermediate code representations have been explored in the literature. They can be categorized into three groups according to their level of abstraction and conceptual distance from the original format. The first category is annotated bytecode using the existing features of Java bytecode format. This approach is backward compatibile as any JVM can run the code by simply ignoring the annotations. The work of Krintz et al. [11], Azevedo et al. [2], and Pominville et al. [14] are some examples. The second category can be described as optimization-oriented high-level representations. These representations do not necessarily bear any resemblance to Java bytecodes. An example is SafeTSA [1] which is a type safe static single assignment based representation. The last category is that of fully optimized low-level architecture dependent representations with certain safety annotations, such as the typed assembly language (TAL) [13].

2.1 An IR for Offline Register Allocation

We propose an IR for offline register allocation which is a simplified form of the Java bytecode (called SIR). We motivate our design choices and contrast them with previous results.

Backward compatibility with Java. SIR is a subset of Java bytecode and thus backwards compatibile. This is important: Any JVM can run SIR code with the expected semantics. Existing tools can be used to analyze, compile, and transform SIR code. This is in contrast to [1,18] which proposes an incompatible register-based bytecode or a SSA form. Offline register allocation results are encoded in annotations following [2,9,10,11].

Local variables as virtual registers. We follow Shaylor [16] who suggested mapping local variables in the Java bytecode to (virtual) registers. In contrast, [2,9,10] suggest using a separate annotation stream. Directly mapping locals to registers has the advantage that no verification is needed. Other formats must ensure that annotations are consistent. Any additional verification effort will increase the (online) compilation time and thus reduce the usefulness of offline optimizations.

Cumulative register allocation. We refer to local variables as *virtual registers* since they are candidates for physical registers. We adopt a *cumulative* register allocation strategy, following [2,10]. That means that the allocation decision for K physical registers is computed on top of the decision for $K - 1$ registers by adding an additional mapping from the Kth register to some locals that were previously not allocated to registers. It produces a 'priority list' of locals variables. Cumulative allocation aims to support an arbitrary number of physical registers while trying to minimize the degradation in allocation quality when the number of available registers is unknown offline. [9] doesn't discuss how registers are allocated. [11] simply encode the static counts of variable occurrences as hints. [16] limits allocation to the first nine local variables.

Register tables. We store our register allocation annotations in a *register table* which associates local variables with their *scores* in decreasing order, in the form $\{(l_1, s_1), (l_2, s_2), ...\}$. Scores indicate the desirability of allocating a given variable to a physical register. In our implementation, these scores are weighted reference counts of variables (count 10^d in a loop of depth d). The fast compiler takes as many local variables as the available physical registers on the target architecture from the top of the register table and assigns them to the physical registers. There is a separate table for each of integers, object references, longs, floats, and doubles. A register table bears some similarity to a *stack map* that is used to store the types of local variables at different program points for fast bytecode verification [15]. Register tables tend to be smaller than the parallel register annotations of [2,9,10] (space overheads of more than 30% have been reported).

Simplified control and data flow. In SIR, subroutines (the `jsr` and `ret` instructions to implement `finally` clauses) of the Java bytecode are disallowed. Subroutines are notorious for making code analysis, optimization and verification slower and more complex. Furthermore, the operand stack must be empty at basic block boundaries, in order to achieve single-pass code generation. For example, if a loop head is only reachable from the backward edge, a single-pass code generator (like ours) cannot know the height of the evaluation stack without a second pass. SIR requires the evaluation stack to be empty between core operations (such as arithmetic operations, method calls, and so on). Operands must always be loaded from local variables and the result stored to a local variable. That essentially means that we treat bytecode as a three-address IR, following [16]. When a method is called, the arguments reside in the first part of the local variables array. For backward compatibility, we treat these locals specially. We do not consider them to be virtual registers and exclude them from the register table. We insert a sequence of moves (loads and stores) at the method entry to copy arguments to local variables. Furthermore, we restrict local variable to hold only one type for the entire method. That simplifies the mapping local variables to physical registers.

Verification. It is easy to verify whether the bytecode is SIR, and that check can be performed in a single pass. It is simply a matter of making sure that restricted instructions (e.g., `jsr`, `ret`, `swap`) do not appear, that the local variables are not used to hold more than one type and that they match the type of the register table, that there is a store (or a `pop`) after each instruction that produces a value, and that the evaluation stack is empty at branch instructions. Our compiler performs the checks during the code generation in a single pass. We do not verify the scores in register tables because the correctness of the scores does not affect the safety of the code. However, incorrect scores may influence the performance.

3   Offline Register Allocation

3.1   Cumulative Assignments

We formulate offline register allocation in terms of *cumulative register assignment* where an assignment for K physical registers is reused for $K + 1$ registers by adding an assignment for the $(K + 1)th$ register without changes for the first K registers. There are two benefits of cumulative assignments: architecture independence as any number of physical registers can be matched to the top K virtual registers. Second, cumulative assignments are more space efficient than an alternative approach where separate assignments for each possible value of K are stored in the IR. Cumulative allocation can be viewed as a packing problem where an ordered list of containers (virtual registers) and items (live ranges of data values) must be packed into as few containers as possible and as densely toward the first container as possible, so that interfering items (data values whose live ranges overlap) will not be put in the same container.

A fast compiler can use cumulative assignment as follows. If K physical registers are available, the top K virtual registers in the register table will be mapped to physical registers. Several scratch registers have to be reserved for loading and spilling the virtual registers that are not assigned to physical registers and for micro operations hidden in the bytecode. The drawback of a cumulative register assignment is that a cumulative assignment may not be optimal for any K .

There are two potentially conflicting goals in cumulative allocation: minimizing the number of virtual registers in an assignment and maximizing density in terms of the packing problem (the sum of the score of the variables that are mapped to physical registers). There may be a situation where obtaining the highest density possible in the first virtual registers leads to requiring an extra register to assign to all variables. Conversely, minimizing the number of virtual registers needed to assign to all variables may cause lower density in the first virtual registers.

```
mov c, 1
add a, c, c
add b, a, 2
add d, b, 1
call m(d)
ret d
```

(a) Code

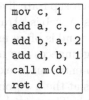

(b) Interference graph

K	Assignment	Score
1	(v0 ↦c,d)	6
2	(v0 ↦c,d), (v1 ↦a)	8
3	(v0 ↦c,d), (v1 ↦a), (v2 ↦b)	10

(c) Cumulative register assignment

K	Assignment	Score
1	(v0 ↦c,d)	6
2	(v0 ↦a,d), (v1 ↦c, b)	10

(d) Traditional assignment

Fig. 1. An example of register allocation. (a) is the code. (b) is the interference graph for the code. (c) is the (cumulative) offline register allocation result generated by offline allocator IGC. (d) is the normal non-cumulative register allocation result generated by traditional allocator GC.

3.2   Example

Figure 1 illustrates cumulative allocation. The code is in register transfer form for the example. The interference graph shows the presence of interference between the variables as edges between nodes. The fraction on the side of each node is the ratio of the score (weighted reference count) to the current degree (the number of edges) of the node. Cumulative allocation results are in Figure 1 (c). Each row represents the result with one additional register on top of the previous row. Three virtual registers are needed in total. The allocation result for row K includes the results for the rows 0 to $K - 1$. The 'score' column shows the sum of the scores (weighted reference counts) of the virtual registers assigned in each row. We see that with one register ($K = 1$), variables c and d are assigned to virtual register v0. The combined score for c and d is 6 because c and d appear in the code six times in total. With two registers ($K = 2$), that assignment is extended with v1 assigned to a and the combined score is, thus, 8. Finally, with three registers ($K = 3$), all variables are assigned to virtual registers with the combined score 10. Figure 1 (d) shows the result of non-cumulative allocation. The differences are that in the non-cumulative case, the mappings for different numbers of registers do not completely intersect, which means that one cannot encode assignments for all possible numbers of K in one mapping. Furthermore, the non-cumulative allocator only needs two registers to assign to all the variables in this example.

4   Offline Register Allocation Heuristics

Offline register allocation heuristics assign virtual registers to live ranges of data, called *webs*. The live ranges are not identical to variables since multiple definitions of the same variable can be renamed and each separate live range of the variable can be assigned to different virtual registers. A web is a transitive closure of def-use chains that share a definition or use point and is often used as the target of register allocation in order to avoid inserting unnecessary moves between registers. A web corresponds to a consecutive multi-entry multi-exit control flow range which starts at the definition points and ends at the use points. We assign virtual registers to webs in offline register allocation. The actual offline register allocation consists of finding webs, computing the interference graph of the webs, making an ordered list of the sets of non-interfering webs based on one of the offline register allocation heuristics described later in this section, and renaming the local variables in the original bytecode so that the webs in the same set are assigned to the same local variable number in the order (local variable 1 is assigned to the first web set in the list, local variable 2 is assigned to the second, and so on, ignoring locals used to pass arguments).

Some of the heuristics described below are based on the optimistic allocator [4], which repeats allocation whenever a spill occurs and the interference graph changes. This repetitive part is omitted in the the heuristics because spilling is handled by the online compiler.

4.1   Linear Packing (LP)

Webs are sorted into a list in non-increasing order of scores (weighted reference counts). By linear-scanning over the list, we merge together the webs that are consecutive in the list and do not interfere with each other. At the end, we obtain a list of web sets where consecutive web sets interfere with each other. We sort the list according to the combined scores of the web sets. The ith virtual register is assigned to the ith web set in the list. This heuristic has a $O(n \log n)$ time complexity where n is the number of webs (due to sorting).

4.2   Greedy Packing (GP)

This heuristic is equivalent to that of Azevedo et al. [2] and Sites [19]. As with LP, webs are sorted into a list in non-increasing order of scores. We iterate the following process until all webs are picked: Keep picking the web with the highest score in the list that does not interfere with the already picked webs in this iteration, until there are no more such web left in the list. Each iteration produces a set of webs. Eventually, we obtain a list of web sets. We sort the list according to the combined scores of the web sets. The ith virtual register is assigned to the ith web set in the list. This heuristic has a quadratic time complexity in the number of webs.

4.3   Exact Graph Coloring (EGC)

This heuristic is based on the optimistic graph coloring allocator. We merge webs by performing a binary search for the minimum number of virtual registers needed to assign to all webs, using the optimistic graph coloring allocator. We obtain a set of web sets, each of which is to be assigned to the same virtual register. We sort the set into a list of web sets according to the combined scores of the web sets. The ith register is assigned to the ith web set in the list. Even with the binary search technique, this heuristic may have to run the underlying graph coloring allocator many times and may take a relatively long time. The heuristic of Jones et al. [10] based on [6,3] seems comparable to EGC.

4.4   Incremental Graph Coloring (IGC)

This heuristic is also based on the optimistic graph coloring allocator. We merge webs by incrementally running the optimistic graph coloring allocator for only one register at each iteration. After each iteration, we remove the allocated webs out of the interference graph. We obtain a list of web sets in the end. We sort the list according to the combined scores of the web sets. The ith register is assigned to the ith web set in the list.

To compare the cumulative register allocation heuristics above with a traditional non-cumulative register allocation heuristic, we also include the traditional optimistic graph coloring allocator in the measurements, which we call GC.

5   Method Inlining and Register Table Merging

Register Table Merging (RTM) is a technique used to perform online method inlining by reusing offline register assignments for individual methods. It is similar to the merge sort algorithm and described as follows. We have a register table for each method computed offline. These tables contain virtual registers sorted in the order of non-increasing scores. When we inline method B (callee) into another method A (caller), we combine the register tables of A and B into a single register table using the following algorithm.

First, we multiply the scores of the virtual registers in B's register table by 10^{depth} where **depth** is the loop nesting depth of the inlining site in A. We then repeat the following process until we reach the end of either A's or B's register table: we pick the virtual register with the higher score between A's top register and B's top register and append it to the register table of the combined method. After the above loop, if there are some registers left either in A's or B's register table, the remaining registers are appended to the combined table. The combined register table is already sorted and the virtual registers are renamed. We update the combined method body with the new register names to obtain the final combined method body. RTM has a time complexity of $O(a + b)$ where a and b are the size of A's and B's register table, respectively. The algorithm is described in Figure 2.

Figure 3 shows an example of RTM. Suppose that there is an inlining site where a method (callee) is inlined in another method (caller). The inlining site is in a nested loop (the loop depth is 2). The caller and the callee have the register tables shown in Figure 3 (a) and (b), respectively. These register tables are computed offline. The merging result is shown in Figure 3 (c). This table shows the list of virtual registers of the combined method, their scores, and the

---

Input:
a (virtual register array sorted by score for method A (caller))
b (virtual register array sorted by score for method B (callee))
depth (loop nest depth of the inlining site in A)

Output:
c (virtual registers for combined method)

```
map := make a hash map
ia := 0, ib := 0, ic := 0
while   ia < a.length and ib < b.length
    if   a[ia].score ≥ b[ib].score * 10^depth
            c[ic] := make a new virtual register with score: a[ia].score
            put (a[ia], c[ic]) into map
            ia := ia + 1, ic := ic + 1
    else
            c[ic] := make a new virtual register with score: b[ib].score * 10^depth
            put (b[ib], c[ic]) into map
            ia := ia + 1, ib := ib + 1
if   ia < a.length
    for   i := ia to a.length-1
        c[ic] := make a new virtual register
                    with score: a[i].score
        put (a[ia], c[ic]) into map
        ia := ia + 1, ic := ic + 1
if   ib < b.length
    for   i := ib to b.length-1
        c[ic] := make a new virtual register with score: b[i].score * 10^depth
        put (b[ib], c[ic]) into map
        ib := ib + 1, ic := ic + 1
update virtual registers in the combined method body using map
```

Fig. 2. Inlining and Register Table Merging

mapping from the two register sets of the caller and the callee to the merged register set of the combined method.

This merging algorithm, of course, does not in general give as good register allocation results as redoing full-scale register allocation *after* method inlining. However, our goal is to achieve non-optimal but acceptable level of allocation quality for fast compilers in exchange for short online compilation time. We will see below how this algorithm performs in comparison with results from doing a full-scale register allocation after method inlining.

Performing some optimizations (e.g., constant propagation) after method inlining in order to further optimize the combined method is optional because we focus on fast compilers and additional data flow analysis and optimizations would increase compilation time considerably for fast compilers.

regs	v-registers	score
1	v0	1001
2	v1	800
3	v2	753
4	v3	3

(a) Caller's register table

regs	v-registers	score	old v-reg
1	v0	1100	v0'
2	v1	1001	v0
3	v2	1000	v1'
4	v3	800	v1
5	v4	753	v2
6	v5	500	v2'
7	v6	3	v3

(c) Merged register table

regs	v-registers	score
1	v0'	11
2	v1'	10
3	v2'	5

(b) Callee's register table

Fig. 3. An example of register table merging. (a), (b), and (c) show the register allocation result for a caller method, a callee method, the combined method after the callee method is inlined in the caller method, respectively, provided that the inlining site is in a nested loop.

6   Experimental Results

We compare the four different compilation scenarios shown in Figure 4. The first is online allocation (referred to as ONR) where the register allocation is performed without annotations. The second scenario is offline register allocation (OFR) where an offline compiler computes register tables and a fast compiler performs allocation using them. The third scenario is online register allocation with method inlining (ONRI), the same as ONR except that the compiler inlines methods *before* applying register allocation. The last scenario is offline register allocation with method inlining (OFRI), the same as OFR except that the fast compiler performs online method inlining with RTM. In addition, we also consider the baseline scenario where the compiler does not perform any optimizations and generates code that literally emulates the evaluation stack and the local variables, as in a typical fast compiler.

The objectives of the measurements are to evaluate the offline scenarios versus the online scenarios in terms of code size, performance, compilation time, and to compare the four offline register allocation heuristics. We only consider compilers that use one intermediate representation (i.e., Java bytecode which includes SIR) because we are focusing on fast compilers, rather than optimizing compilers that can afford to build other intermediate representations.

The experimental environment is the following. We use the SimpleJIT compiler in the Ovm virtual machine framework [20] on a 1.33 Ghz PowerPC G4 processor with 2 GB of RAM, running Mac OS X. We use the code from Ovm and SPECjvm98 [7] for measurements.

6.1   Code Size

We measure the space overhead of SIR versus bytecode. There are two sources of space overhead, additional loads and stores and register tables. Figure 5 shows

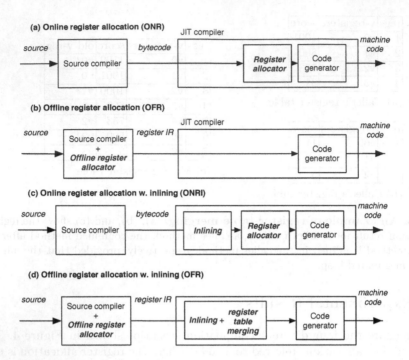

Fig. 4. The four compile scenarios: in (a) and (c) register allocation (and method inlining in (c)) is performed online by the fast compiler; in (b) and (d) register allocation is performed offline, the online compiler uses the register assignments to generate code (and inlining in (d))

(Kbytes)	Total	Ovm	SPECjvm98
# classes	3,317	2,767	550
Original	8,854	7,291	1,563
LP	10,568(19.4%)	8,472(16.2%)	2,095(34.0%)
GP	10,434(17.8%)	8,374(14.9%)	2,059(31.7%)
EGC	10,435(17.9%)	8,375(14.9%)	2,060(31.8%)
IGC	10,423(17.7%)	8,366(14.8%)	2,056(31.5%)

Fig. 5. The code size overhead of SimpleIR

the space overhead in terms of the class file size for each of the offline register allocation heuristics. The overall space overhead is 15-34% (18-20% overall). Previous work reports overheads of 100% [2] and 31% [10].

6.2   Offline Translation Time

We measure the time for offline translator to convert Java bytecode into SIR. This involves: (a) Eliminating subroutines (by duplicating the subroutine body for each subroutine call site), (b) Inserting loads and stores to make the

(sec)	Total	Ovm	SPECjvm98
# classes	3,317	2,767	550
LP	629	395	234
GP	676	426	250
EGC	948	541	407
IGC	668	437	230

Fig. 6. The offline bytecode translation time

evaluation stack empty between core instructions and at basic block boundaries, (c) Introducing extra local variables to let local variables have only one consistent type for the entire method, (d) Performing several simple dataflow optimizations such as constant propagation, copy propagation, and dead code elimination, (e) Applying one of the offline register allocation heuristics (including liveness analysis needed), (f) Computing register tables, and (g) Writing the converted code into class files.

Figure 6 shows the offline translation time for the four different offline allocation heuristics. EGC takes the longest translation time because it needs to iterate the graph coloring heuristic to find the minimal number of virtual registers. LP is the fastest overall due to its simplicity. The two other heuristics came relatively close.

6.3   Performance

Next, we measure the execution time of the seven benchmarks of SPECjvm98 to evaluate the steady-state performance of the generated code. The PowerPC G4 processor has 32 32-bit general purpose registers (GPR) and 32 64-bit floating point registers (FPR). We use 15 GPRs for the register allocation of the integer and reference type virtual registers (local variables) and 13 FPRs for the float and double type virtual registers. We do not assign registers for *long* typed virtual registers. The rest of the registers are used for argument and scratch uses. To share a single set of physical registers (e.g., GPRs) for multiple virtual register sets (e.g., integer and reference virtual registers), we merge two register tables into one register table before assigning virtual registers to physical registers.

The method inlining heuristics we use is the following. We inline all methods (callees) that are private, static, or final, and whose bytecode size is less than or equal to 27 bytes. The maximum inlining depth is 5. The maximum caller code size is 240 bytes. We do not attempt to perform devirtualization or inlining of non-final virtual methods.

The results for the two online scenarios (ONR and ONRI) and the eight offline scenarios (OFR and OFRI for each of LP, GP, EGC, and IGC) are shown in Figure 7. They are the averages of nine runs. For the online scenarios, we used the standard optimistic graph coloring allocator GC. The rightmost bars show the geometric means over the seven benchmarks. Method inlining contributes about a 10% overall performance gain. As expected, with or without method inlining, the online scenarios ONR and ONRI result in the best overall performance.

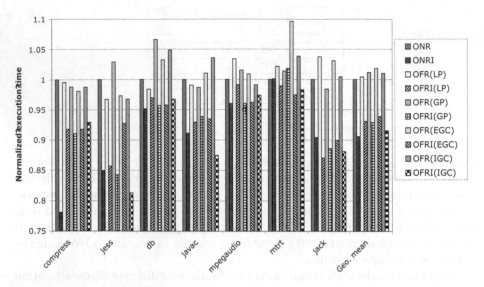

Fig. 7. The normalized SPECjvm98 execution time (steady state performance) of the two online scenarios and the eight offline scenarios

However, the quality difference between the (online) traditional register allocation, which needs the fixed number of registers, and the (offline) cumulative register allocation, which does not, turns out to be small. Second, the quality difference between register allocation *after* inlining (ONRI) and register allocation *before* inlining (OFRI), that is the phase ordering problem between register allocation and method inlining, is also small due to RTM.

Comparing the four heuristics (new heuristics LP and IGC, and GP and EGC from the previous work), we can derive the following observations. First, without inlining, LP overall performs the best. This is surprising because of LP's simplicity, and may imply that, without inlining, we have a sufficient number of physical registers for many methods (i.e., small methods), and that the quality differences among the heuristics do not stand out. This is actually supported by Figure 8, which shows the overall SPECjvm98 results with varying numbers of registers used for allocation. LP perform worse than the other heuristics with fewer registers. Second, with inlining, IGC achieves the best overall results. This implies that IGC, with sufficient registers, tends to work better for large methods that are produced after inlining. Third, unexpectedly, EGC do not work well. However, EGC seems to work well in some cases with fewer registers, as indicated in Figure 8.

We also compare the four major scenarios: the baseline compilation, the online register allocation (ONR and ONRI), the offline register allocation (OFR and OFRI with IGC), and the optimizing compilation. The baseline compilation does not perform any optimizations and the optimizing compilation performs the highest level of optimizations. Figure 9 shows the results. The online or offline scenarios achieve about 2.5 times lower performance than the optimizing scenario whereas the baseline compilation is about 5 times lower.

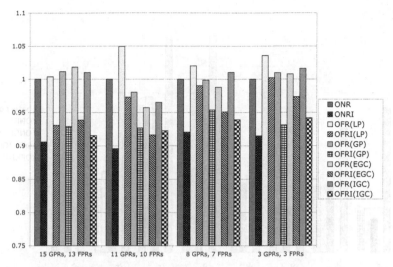

Fig. 8. The SPECjvm98 geometric means with varying numbers of allocated registers

6.4 Compilation Time

We measure the online compilation time in an ahead-of-time compilation setting. This is not what we advocate since a fast compiler is ideally invoked in a just-in-time manner, but simply a mechanism we use to evaluate the compilation time in this paper.

Figure 10 shows the compilation time results. The compilation times are in milliseconds and shown with the relative lengths compared to the baseline compilation time (in parentheses) and with the ratio of compilation time to the sum of the compilation time and the execution time for SPECjvm98 (in square brackets). The baseline compilation and the offline scenario compilations scans the input bytecode once for code generation. The offline scenarios, in addition, need to parse the register table annotations from the class files, merge the register tables (e.g., integer and reference tables) before code generation, and perform the light-weight code verification to check that the input bytecode complies with SIR during code generation. Without inlining, the four heuristics have the compilation overhead of about -9 to 78% (20-25% on the average) from the baseline. The compilation overhead is higher for SPECjvm98 (72-78%) because there are some large methods whose register table tends to be large. With inlining, the compilation time is 1.8-3.2 times (2.2-2.34 on the average) longer than the baseline. SPECjvm98 needs up to a 3.2 times longer compilation time with inlining. The online scenario compilation time includes the time to perform control flow graph construction, optional inlining (if ONRI), liveness analysis, the traditional graph coloring allocation (GC), and code generation. The overall online scenario compilation time is longer than the baseline scenario by a factor of 15.9 (19.3 with inlining). We believe that the offline scenario compilations achieve high cost-performance considering the compilation time overhead and the performance gain, compared to the online compilations.

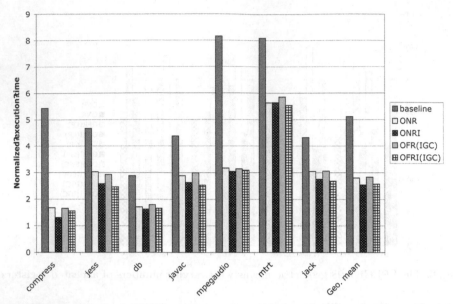

Fig. 9. The normalized SPECjvm98 execution time (steady state performance) of the baseline scenario, the two online scenarios, the two offline scenarios (**IGC**), and the scenario with the optimizing compiler. The bars are normalized against the optimizing scenario.

(msec)	Total	Ovm	SPECjvm98
# of methods	9523	6761	2762
baseline	6880 (1.00)	4526 (1.00)	2354 (1.00) [0.004]
ONR	71984(15.90)	27014(5.97)	44970(19.10) [0.136]
ONRI	87153(19.25)	33768(7.46)	53385(22.67) [0.170]
OFR(LP)	8242 (1.20)	4136 (0.91)	4106 (1.74) [0.014]
OFRI(LP)	16082 (2.34)	8644 (1.91)	7438 (3.16) [0.028]
OFR(GP)	8504 (1.24)	4553 (1.01)	3951 (1.68) [0.014]
OFRI(GP)	15159 (2.20)	8202 (1.81)	6957 (2.96) [0.025]
OFR(EGC)	8431 (1.23)	4233 (0.94)	4198 (1.78) [0.014]
OFRI(EGC)	15567 (2.26)	8367 (1.85)	7200 (3.06) [0.026]
OFR(IGC)	8288 (1.20)	4231 (0.93)	4057 (1.72) [0.013]
OFRI(IGC)	15363 (2.23)	8162 (1.80)	7201 (3.06) [0.027]

Fig. 10. The online compilation time

7   Related Work

Sites [19] used a simple packing heuristic equivalent to GP on Pascal U-Code. Gupta et al. [8] and Callahan et al. [5] proposed compositional graph coloring register allocation heuristics. The interference graph of a procedure is decomposed into subgraphs. Subgraphs are colored separately and are combined into a single graph. These two approaches are analogous to register table merging in our work in the sense that subparts of programs are register-allocated separately and the allocation results are combined together. However, these two approaches are different from our work because their approaches are for online register allocation where the number of available colors is known at allocation time.

8   Conclusions

We investigated the interplay of two of the most effective optimizations in object-oriented programs: register allocation and inlining in a combination of offline and online compilation, for fast dynamic compilers. With offline register allocation heuristics, SIR, and RTM, we achieved performance very close to that of the online allocation scenarios, with significantly shorter online compilation time. Compared to the baseline compilation, the offline scenarios achieved good cost-performance with about 80% (99% with inlining) better performance, 20% of code size overhead, and 25% (a factor of 2.3 with inlining) online compilation overhead on the average for our benchmark set.

References

1. Wolfram Amme, Nial Dalton, Jeffrey von Ronne, and Michael Franz. SafeTSA: A type safe and referentially secure mobile-code representation based on static single assignment form. In *Conference on Programming Language Design and Implementation (PLDI)*, 2001.
2. Ana Azevedo, Alex Nicolau, and Joe Hummel. Java annotation-aware just-in-time (AJIT) compilation system. In *Java Grande Conference*, 1999.
3. D. Bernstein, M. Golumbic, y. Mansour, R. Pinter, D. Goldin, H. Krawczyk, and I. Nahshon. Spill code minimization techniques for optimizing compliers. In *Conference on Programming language design and implementation (PLDI)*, 1989.
4. Preston Briggs, Keith D. Cooper, and Linda Torczon. Improvements to graph coloring register allocatoion. *Transaction on Programming Languages and Systems*, 1994.
5. David Callahan and Brian Koblenz. Register allocation via hierarchical graph coloring. In *Conference on Programming language design and implementation (PLDI)*, 1991.
6. G.J. Chaitin, M.A. Auslander, A.K. Chandra, J. Cocke, M.E. Hopkins, and P.W. Markstein. Register allocation via coloring. *Journal of Computer Languages*, 6:47–57, 1981.
7. Standard Performance Evaluation Corporation. SPECjvm98, 1998.
8. Rajiv Gupta, Mary Lou Soffa, and Tim Steele. Register allocation via clique separators. In *Conference on Programming language design and implementation (PLDI)*, 1989.
9. Joseph Hummel, Ana Azevedo, David Kolson, and Alexandru Nicolau. Annotating the Java bytecodes in support of optimization. *Concurrency: Practice and Experience*, 9(11):1003–1016, 1997.

10. Joel Jones and Samuel Kamin. Annotating Java class files with virtual registers for performance. *Concurrency: Practice and Experience*, 12(6):389–406, 2000.
11. Chandra Krintz and Brad Calder. Using annotations to reduce dynamic optimization time. In *Conference on Programming language design and implementation (PLDI)*, 2001.
12. Han Lee, Daniel von Dincklage, Amer Diwan, and J. Eliot B. Moss. Understanding the behavior of compiler optimizations. Technical Report Technical Report CU-CS-978-04, University of Colorado at Boulder, 2004.
13. Greg Morrisett, David Walker, Karl Crary, and Neal Glew. From system f to typed assembly language. In *Symposium on Principles of Programming Languages (POPL)*, 1998.
14. Patrice Pominville, Feng Qian, Raja Vallée-Rai, Laurie Hendren, and Clark Verbrugge. A framework for optimizing java using attributes. In *Compiler Construction (CC)*, 2001.
15. E. Rose and K. H. Rose. Lightweight bytecode verification. In *Workshop "Formal Underpinnings of the Java Paradigm"*, 1998.
16. Nik Shaylor. A just-in-time compiler for memory-constrained low-power devices. In *Java Virtual Machine Research and Technology Symposium (JVM)*, 2002.
17. Nik Shaylor, Douglas N. Simon, and William R. Bush. A Java virtual machine architecture for very small devices. In *Conference on Language, compiler, and tool for embedded systems, (LCTES)*, 2003.
18. Yunhe Shi, David Gregg, Andrew Beatty, and M. Anton Ertl. Virtual machine showdown: stack versus registers. In *Conference on Virtual execution environments (VEE)*, 2005.
19. R. L. Sites. Machine-independent register allocation. In *Symposium on Programming Language Design and Implementation*, 1979.
20. Purdue University. The ovm virtual machine framework.

A Localized Tracing Scheme
Applied to Garbage Collection

Yannis Chicha* and Stephen M. Watt

Department of Computer Science
University of Western Ontario
London Canada N6A 5B7

Abstract. We present a method to visit all nodes in a forest of data structures while taking into account object placement. We call the technique a *Localized Tracing Scheme* as it improves locality of reference during object tracing activity. The method organizes the heap into regions and uses trace queues to defer and group tracing of remote objects. The principle of localized tracing reduces memory traffic and can be used as an optimization to improve performance at several levels of the memory hierarchy. The method is applicable to a wide range of uniprocessor garbage collection algorithms as well as to shared memory multiprocessor collectors. Experiments with a mark-and-sweep collector show performance improvements up to 75% at the virtual memory level.

1 Introduction

Many algorithms require visiting all objects in a forest of data structures in a systematic manner. When there are no algorithmic constraints on the visiting order, we are free to choose any strategy to optimize system performance. This paper examines an optimization of object tracing to improve performance in a memory hierarchy. The basic idea is to delay the tracing of non-local objects and to handle them all together on a region-by-region basis. We call this a *localized tracing scheme* (LTS).

An LTS organizes its visit of the heap based partly on the graph of objects and partly on the location of objects. A consequence is that LTS can be memory hierarchy friendly, which means we are able to optimize visits of objects at different levels of the memory hierarchy, including cache, virtual memory and network. At one level, LTS can be used to reduce paging and keep object tracing in main memory as much as possible. At another level, as on-chip cache memory increases in size, LTS may be used to minimize traffic between cache and main memory. LTS may also be used in modern portable devices, where relatively large and slow flash memory cards extend the smaller and faster device memory.

Our LTS technique is based on dividing the heap into *regions* with a *trace queue* associated to each region to hold a list of objects to visit. Trace queues are the origin of the performance improvements displayed by the LTS. They are used to delay the tracing of remote objects, allowing tracing to concentrate on

---

* Present address: Teradyne SAS, 3 chemin de la Dhuy, 38240 Meylan, France.

N. Kobayashi (Ed.): APLAS 2006, LNCS 4279, pp. 323–339, 2006.

local objects. This enhances locality of reference by relying on object location, rather than object connectivity, to order tracing. The sizes of regions and trace queues are determined by the level of the memory hierarchy that we wish to optimize. For example, to obtain a cache-conscious algorithm, a region and the trace queues should be small enough to fit entirely in cache.

This idea may be applied to memory management, where reachable objects must be visited as part of garbage collection. Uniprocessor garbage collection is mature and offers satisfactory performance for many applications. In fact, garbage collection is now an integral part of the run-time for popular programming languages, such as Java and C#, which serve as the delivery platform for widely used applications. Improvements in garbage collection technology can therefore have impact on a broad user base.

We note that adding LTS to an existing collector is a relatively easy operation. This consideration is important in practice, where vendors are reluctant to make significant modifications to products' memory management for fear of introducing bugs. We have found it to be straightforward to modify two garbage collectors to use LTS, that of the Aldor programming language [1,2] run-time support and that of the Maple computer algebra system [3].

The impact of localizing tracing depends on the garbage collection method in use: Mark-and-sweep collectors first visit all live objects, marking them, and then sweep the memory area to recover unused space. Optimization of memory traffic during the *sweep* phase has been considered by Boehm [4]. We observe that memory hierarchy traffic can also be improved during the *mark* phase using LTS. Since objects do not move in memory with mark-and-sweep, the benefits of LTS are similar at each GC occurrence. Improvements of the overall GC time decrease when few objects are live. In this case, the mark phase is short and optimizations have a small impact.

Stop-and-copy garbage collectors can move objects to new locations at each GC occurrence. To do this, they must visit all live objects. Generational collectors [5] also use tracing because each generation is handled by a copying or mark-and-sweep collection algorithm. In these cases the tracing may be performed using LTS.

The rest of this paper is organized as follows. Section 2 describes a family of localized tracing algorithms. Section 3 gives an example to illustrate the LTS. Section 4 presents an informal proof of correctness for this algorithm. Section 5 details our experiments and results with the GC for the Aldor run-time environment. Section 6 explores advantages and drawbacks of the LTS in a multiprocessor environment. Section 7 discusses related work in various garbage collection settings. Section 8 suggests directions for future work and concludes the paper.

2   The Localized Tracing Scheme

2.1   Depth-First Tracing

We start by considering the usual recursive object tracing scheme. This will be useful for comparison with our local tracing algorithm.

```
main()
    for each root r { trace(r) }

trace(p)
    o := object to which p points
    if isMarked(o), return.
    mark o
    for each valid pointer p' in o  { trace(p') }
```

The operation mark has its meaning specified by context. For example, a mark-and-sweep collector simply sets a bit corresponding to the object, while a copying collector moves this same object to a "live area." In any case, the only property we rely upon is that it is possible to test whether an object is marked using isMarked. We use this to ensure termination of the LTS process. It does not add to the principal idea of the optimization we propose. Instead, we focus on how objects are visited.

We observe that the algorithm presented above uses a depth-first traversal. While elegant, there are two problems with this technique:

The first problem is that recursion can be very deep and the associated overhead of stack activity can be expensive (allocation/deallocation of stack frames, context saving, *etc.*) This can be addressed with a combination of tail recursion, explicit stack management and pointer reversal. Pointer reversal temporarily modifies the heap, however, which creates problems in multi-threaded environments.

The second problem is that the topology of the graph of objects has a direct influence on traffic within the memory hierarchy. A traditional tracing algorithm does not take advantage of the relative locations of objects in the heap, possibly resulting in very bad locality of reference. For example, a page may be brought from disk to main memory to visit only one object even if other live objects are made accessible.

In this paper we demonstrate the possibility of improving on *both* aspects by transforming the depth-first tracing process into a "semi-breadth-first" one.

2.2   A Family of Tracing Algorithms

The principal idea behind our tracing technique is to defer visiting objects that lie outside a working set by maintaining queues of deferred pointers in fast memory (cache for example). When a queue becomes full, the deferred visits are made, altering the working set in a controlled fashion. This idea to localize the tracing process can be applied with minimal, localized modification to existing trace-based garbage collectors.

The deferred trace queues can be managed in a number of ways:

– One may keep all deferred object pointers in a common list, allowing or disallowing duplicates. When the list becomes full, it is analyzed to determine how to alter the working set. This has the advantage that the memory of the global queue is fully used, but the cost of the analysis may outweigh the benefit of making the optimal choice of working set alteration.

– One may associate a sub-queue to each range of addresses (heap region), with the number of ranges and size of sub-queues being parameters. Deferred object pointers are added to the appropriate sub-queue, either allowing or disallowing duplicates. When a queue is full, the associated region is added to the working set and visits are made. This has the advantage that deferring visits is fast, but the disadvantage is the deferred trace queue as a whole may be largely empty. This may be addressed by dynamically adjusting the size of the sub-queues based on use.

We have identified six strategies: { common list, static sub-queues, dynamic sub-queues} × { duplicate pointers allowed, not allowed }. We would expect the sub-queue strategies to be best when the far memory (RAM or secondary storage) speed is within a few orders of magnitude of that of the close memory (cache or RAM). Beyond this, we would expect the common list strategy to yield better results because here it is more important to avoid remote memory references.

Note that performing the deferred visits to one region may cause the trace queue of a second region to fill. At this point, starting to trace in the second region may cause the queue for the first region to fill. If both regions' deferred trace queues are nearly full and there are too many mutually referencing pages, local memory access can be lost. This situation degenerates to the usual handling of tracing, but with additional overhead. The problem may be avoided by taking one additional action: before performing the deferred marks on a region, the trace queue could be flushed to local store in the region itself or in a shared pool. This saved queue could then be substantially larger than the per-region queue maintained in fast memory.

2.3   Algorithm

We present a tracing algorithm where trace queues are associated with each heap region. This is the static sub-queues allowing duplicates strategy, described above. To allow fast access to these queues, they are contained in one contiguous area that we choose to be small enough to be maintained in fast memory.

Each region contains objects that will be marked and scanned. The difference from a regular tracing process is that scanning an object can reveal pointers *inside* the region currently collected or *outside*. If the pointer is to an object in the region, the object is visited recursively. When it points to another region of the heap, it means that following this pointer would not be optimal for the working set (or cache) behavior. In this case, we simply place this pointer in a trace queue for later examination. We thus maintain the working set for as long as possible, and reduce the number of cache misses or page faults.

When the process for a region is completed, we proceed to another region. The policy to determine the order in which regions are visited is implementation- or even application-dependent. It is likely, however, that choosing a region with a full or close to full trace queue will improve performance. A simple solution, avoiding the complexity of choosing the most populated queue, is to use a round-robin mechanism, and visit regions one by one. This is what we describe here.

In the initial step of the algorithm, roots are entirely dispatched into the different trace queues as if those pointers originated from an "external" region. Once the roots have all been recorded, the actual tracing begins. The complete algorithm is as follows:

```
mainTrace()
    initialRootsScan() -- initialize the trace queues
    while not all queues are empty
        { Q := choose a non-empty trace queue ; emptyQueue Q }

initialRootsScan()
    for each root r
        { Q := get trace queue for region where r points; enqueue(Q,r) }

emptyQueue(Q)
    while Q is not empty { p := dequeue Q ; followRef p }

followRef(p)
    o := object pointed to by p
    if (not isMarked(o)) { mark o ; trace o }

trace(o)
    for each valid pointer p in o
        if (p points to the same region as o)
            followRef(p)
        else
            { Q:= get trace queue for region where p points; enqueue(Q,p) }
```

In the above, **enqueue** and **dequeue** are operations that add and remove elements from the trace queues.

2.4 Algorithm with Finite-Size Queues

We describe the static sub-queues strategy. In this scenario, it is required that a limit is placed on the size of the queues. We thus need to handle the problem of untimely full queues. In particular, when we visit a region and need to enqueue a pointer into a full queue, something must be discarded from the current working set to make room to work with the region with the full queue. Several strategies can be adopted:

− Empty the queue and deal with the pointer.
− Deal with the pointer first and then empty the queue.
− Empty a percentage of the queue and insert the pointer in the queue.
− Dump the queue to a reserved part of the region.

The *first* strategy is likely to be the safest, because the first action is to remove a pointer from the queue so it is not full anymore, thus allowing a new pointer to be enqueued. A situation where we need to add a new pointer to this queue can occur if, for example, the first visited object holds a pointer to a region which also has a full queue. In this case, this region is chosen to be visited and the first pointer may be to an object holding a pointer to the region we just visited. The *second* strategy allows following the new pointer first, thus removing the need to keep its information on the stack, but it is likely to become too costly in the case described above. The *third* strategy may be chosen when the working set is not entirely filled by pages of the current region. In this case, a certain number of pages can be brought into memory without dismantling the current working set. The *last* strategy may work in practice. In principle, however, the same problem must be considered in case the dump area overflows.

For simplicity, we choose to empty the queue first and then deal with the new pointer. The resulting algorithm is the same as that for unbounded queues, shown in Section 2.3, but with the calls to `enqueue` replaced by calls to `enqueueRef`, defined as follows

```
enqueueRef(Q, p)
  if (not full(Q)) enqueue(Q,p)
  else { emptyQueue(Q) ; followRef p }
```

3   Example

This section presents an example of the behavior of our algorithm. We follow the LTS process step by step.

1. First, the roots are copied into the trace queues. See Figure 1(a). (In GC, these are typically taken from registers, stack and intial static data area.)
2. Once the initial phase is completed, we see that two pointers have been recorded in the trace queue Q_1. We dequeue the first pointer and mark (using black coloring) the corresponding object. This object holds a pointer to another object in the same region R_1. We continue tracing along this path to mark the other object. See Figure 1(b).
3. We now use the second pointer recorded in Q_1. The object it points to is marked and scanned, and is found to hold a pointer to an object in R_2. This pointer is recorded in Q_2, as shown in Figure 1(c). Once this is done, we see that Q_1 is empty for now, so we continue the process with Q_2.
4. We retrieve each pointer of Q_2 and mark the objects, as we did for Q_1. We see in Figure 1(d) that Q_1 has been updated because an object in R_2 was pointing to R_1. Similarly, a pointer is also added to Q_3. Once Q_2 is empty, we visit Q_3.
5. Q_3 is visited and all reachable objects are marked. It is now empty, and we continue with Q_1. Once Q_1 has been visited, all queues are empty, and the tracing process is thus over, as shown in Figure 1(e).

We see that these trace queues act in a manner similar to entry items in a distributed garbage collection environment. Each pointer included in the queue indicates that an object of the region is reachable. All objects identified as live in a given phase of the LTS (depending on the graph of objects, there may be several phases) will be visited before starting the visit of another region, thus improving locality of treatment.

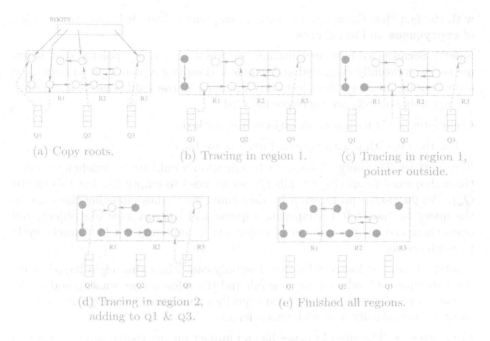

(a) Copy roots.

(b) Tracing in region 1.

(c) Tracing in region 1, pointer outside.

(d) Tracing in region 2, adding to Q1 & Q3.

(e) Finished all regions.

Fig. 1. Local Tracing Scheme example

Another comparison can be made: our trace queues are simply remembered sets that are used to keep track of cross-boundary pointers. Note that trace queues may contain pointers to objects either marked (black, in the usual terminology), being marked (gray) or not yet traced (white), exactly like remembered sets.

4   Correctness of LTS

We provide an informal proof that LTS algorithm rephrases a regular GC mark phase algorithm. We first show correctness with the assumption that trace queues have infinite size (*i.e.* we can never reach a state where queue is full). Later we treat the case of finite queues.

The LTS algorithm has two phases: initial root scan and trace phase. The code for the initial root scan is a simple recording of the roots. We show the trace phase is correct: that it is *safe* (marks all live objects), *complete* (does not mark any garbage) and *terminates*.

Termination: The number of times `trace` is called is bounded by the number of calls to `mark`, which is in turn bounded by the number of objects. After the initial root scan, `enqueue` is called only from `trace`, so the number of calls to `enqueue` is also bounded. The depth of recursion (through `followRef`) for a call to `trace` is limited by the bound on the number of calls to `trace`. Therefore any call to `trace` terminates, and so does any call to `followRef`. This, together with the fact that the number of calls to enqueue is bounded, gives termination of emptyQueue and mainTrace.

Safety: Because we have termination, we know that every pointer that is enqueued is eventually dequeued and handled. Handling a pointer to an unmarked object entails marking the object and enqueuing all the valid pointers it contains. All reachable objects are therefore handled.

Completeness: Only reachable objects are marked.

For the algorithm with bounded queues, we have:

Termination: The only obstacle to termination would be to indefinitely cycle through queues (emptying Q_a fills Q_b, so we need to empty Q_b, but this re-fills Q_a). We guarantee progression by dequeuing *first* (thus changing the state of the queue to "non-full"). Emptying a queue will treat at least one object, and since there are a finite number of objects it is impossible to indefinitely cycle through queues.

Safety: There is no loss of reference. The only case where this might happen with fixed size queues is when a queue is full and the reference we want to add to the queue is lost. However, the algorithm specifies that once the full queue has been emptied, we actually deal with this reference.

Completeness: The size of queues has no impact on the visited objects. We still start from the roots, in the same way the non-LTS algorithm does. Garbage is still guaranteed to be found.

5 Experiments and Results

5.1 The Test Environment

We implemented and tested LTS using the garbage collector of the Aldor language environment as a test harness. To support multi-language programming, the Aldor implementation employs a conservative mark-and-sweep GC. We compared the performance of various LTS-based mark phases with that of the usual depth-first mark phase. Our experiments have focused on improving paging performance, but we also made preliminary tests with cache-conscious configurations.

Finding appropriate standard benchmarks for garbage collection algorithms is quite difficult. We found that GC benchmarks are quite rare and macrobenchmarks usually focus on applications with modest memory footprint, e.g. 20-30MB (see [6] and [7]). In particular, we did not find any standard benchmark using heaps larger than the normal size of physical memory. In order to permit careful study of LTS, we therefore constructed a set of micro-benchmarks. Each of these tested a particular kind of memory use. This allows greater understanding of the range of possible behaviours of LTS than macro-benchmarks would provide. In this context, we built a test suite that uses small programs by today's standards of desktop machines but that helps us confirm that the LTS is indeed an appropriate solution for large applications. Note that our tests are obviously not designed to represent real-life programs; rather, we have tuned them to exercise specific situations to help us better understand the limits of the LTS.

The precise nature of any improvement from LTS will of course depend on the relative speeds and sizes of the relevant two levels of the memory hierarchy. We expect the qualitative aspects to remain the same, however. Our tests were conducted with a 500 MHz Pentium III, with a UDMA66 hard disk and running Redhat Linux 7.1 (kernel 2.4.2). We were interested in testing our algorithm in an environment with a heap larger than physical memory. Since testing very large programs is time-consuming, we simulated the situation by working with programs using heaps of up to 178MB while limiting the amount of main memory available to the operating system to 32 MB. A preliminary form of these results was presented in [8].

5.2   The Benchmarks

Test 1: Fit in RAM (6MB used/32MB primary memory) The graph of objects fits entirely in RAM. There is no possibility of swapping so we expect no gain from LTS. This test allows us to quantify the overhead due to the extra management of regions.

Test 2: Linear structure (90MB used/32MB primary memory) Memory is filled with a linked list of large objects, with the links of the list in ascending address order. Here we observe paging, but the LTS does not change the order in which objects are visited. This test thus also allows us to quantify the LTS overhead.

Test 3: Parallel list creation (90MB used/32MB primary memory) Memory is filled with multiple parallel linked lists. Each list spans several consecutive regions and has its links in reverse memory order. All lists are pointed to by arrays in the first region. Depth first tracing would access objects in multiple regions for the first list, then the same regions again for the second list, *etc.* LTS should avoid this.

Test 4: Parallel list creation and use (178MB used/32MB primary memory) This test represents a more general memory situation. As before, lists are pointed to by arrays in the first region. Once all lists are created, a mutator loop is started. First, lists are swapped to allow the order of marking to be different from the original structure. Then, pointers to some lists are dropped, creating garbage. Finally, new parallel lists are created to re-populate the arrays. This is closer to a "real" application.

Test 5: Pointers everywhere! (178MB used/32MB primary memory) Here the arrays pointing to the lists are spread throughout the heap rather than being restricted to the first region.

Test 6: Cons-reversed lists (178MB used/32MB primary memory) Test 4 is modified to create lists linked in ascending memory order.

Test 7: Mixed-order lists (178MB used/32MB primary memory) Similar to Test 6, but only every second list is in ascending memory order. The others are in reverse memory order. The arrays pointing to the lists are still located at the beginning of the heap. This mixed order shows the behavior of the LTS in the presence of data structures that are accessible from different regions.

Test 8: Mixed-order lists with pointers everywhere (178MB used/32MB primary memory) This test is a combination of Test 5 and Test 7. Arrays are spread all over the heap while some lists are in reversed order and others are not. We hope to observe the behavior of the algorithm in presence of a graph of objects evolving in a less obvious manner than previous tests.

The details of the object sizes is as follows: Test 1 (Fit in RAM) used 600 linked lists, each of length 100. Test 2 (Linear structure) used 50 lists, each of length 15,000. All other tests used 3000 lists, each of length 500. The leaf objects contained in the lists were of three sizes: 16, 52 or 100 bytes.

5.3   Test Results

The timing results for the tests are displayed in Figure 2. For each set of parameters, the ratio of LTS to Non-LTS times is given. Tests were run three times each and the numbers shown here are the averages. We observed very little variation in the results (as can be expected because these tests are not random).

The table displays the test number as the header of each column. The row labels have the following meaning:

- *Non-LTS* corresponds to the results obtained with a regular tracing algorithm.
- *LTS-XX-YY* shows the results using the LTS with a region size of XX MB and a total size for the trace queues of YY KB. For example, LTS-4-512 corresponds to a test with a region size of 4MB and trace queues of 512KB.
- *Total app time* is the total application time, including the time taken by the Non-LTS GC.

We make the following observations:

Test 1: Fit in RAM This test illustrates a situation where there is no benefit in enhancing locality of reference. We measure that the overhead of maintaining the queues is about 25%. However, we note that this is for a total application time of 1 second, and the actual overhead is low in absolute terms. Also note that this overhead disappears if the GC is configured to use the LTS only when it can be beneficial.

Test 2: Linear structure This test measures the other case for which the LTS approach is not well suited: With a single linked list, there are very few cross-region pointers and we see the basic LTS overhead. We see that by choosing carefully the size of the region and the queues, this overhead can be brought down to a reasonable level (15%).

	Test 1	Test 2	Test 3	Test 4
Non-LTS Marking	0.297	53	274	1222
LTS-4-256	0.366 *(1.23)*	62 *(1.17)*	127 *(0.46)*	322 *(0.26)*
LTS-4-512	0.366 *(1.23)*	65 *(1.23)*	128 *(0.47)*	317 *(0.26)*
LTS-4-1024	0.366 *(1.23)*	61 *(1.15)*	131 *(0.48)*	312 *(0.25)*
LTS-8-256	0.371 *(1.25)*	68 *(1.28)*	131 *(0.48)*	326 *(0.27)*
LTS-8-512	0.371 *(1.25)*	72 *(1.36)*	145 *(0.53)*	352 *(0.29)*
LTS-8-1024	0.372 *(1.25)*	69 *(1.30)*	141 *(0.51)*	344 *(0.28)*
LTS-16-256	0.371 *(1.25)*	83 *(1.57)*	139 *(0.51)*	338 *(0.28)*
LTS-16-512	0.371 *(1.25)*	75 *(1.41)*	141 *(0.51)*	350 *(0.29)*
LTS-16-1024	0.371 *(1.25)*	80 *(1.51)*	141 *(0.51)*	355 *(0.29)*
Total app time	1.000	108	404	1923

	Test 5	Test 6	Test 7	Test 8
Non-LTS Marking	1831	1217	1263	1869
LTS-4-256	755 *(0.41)*	341 *(0.28)*	352 *(0.28)*	1296 *(0.69)*
LTS-4-512	958 *(0.52)*	342 *(0.28)*	336 *(0.27)*	1311 *(0.70)*
LTS-4-1024	1061 *(0.58)*	347 *(0.28)*	350 *(0.28)*	1426 *(0.76)*
LTS-8-256	1145 *(0.62)*	363 *(0.30)*	329 *(0.26)*	1321 *(0.71)*
LTS-8-512	1025 *(0.56)*	358 *(0.29)*	332 *(0.26)*	1385 *(0.74)*
LTS-8-1024	1039 *(0.57)*	361 *(0.30)*	322 *(0.25)*	1434 *(0.77)*
LTS-16-256	872 *(0.48)*	368 *(0.30)*	338 *(0.27)*	1163 *(0.62)*
LTS-16-512	921 *(0.50)*	381 *(0.31)*	353 *(0.28)*	1144 *(0.61)*
LTS-16-1024	994 *(0.54)*	376 *(0.31)*	360 *(0.28)*	1156 *(0.62)*
Total app time	3038	1697	1946	3051

Fig. 2. Marking times (in seconds) for different parameters. The LTS/Non-LTS ratio is shown in parentheses.

Test 3: Parallel list creation This is the first test where we can observe the advantage of using the LTS. As explained before, lists in this example are created in parallel, resulting in many cross-region pointers. Following one list across several pages, then re-visiting the same pages for a second list, *etc.*, is very inefficient. LTS cuts the marking time by half and the total application time by a third.

Tests 4, 6, and 7: These tests give significant results: the structure of the lists in memory (from beginning to end, or end to beginning, or mixed) does not seem to influence the behavior of the tracing process. Here we see up to 75% improvement in marking time and a 50% improvement in total time.

Tests 5 and 8: Although speedups are less spectacular, they are still quite interesting: between 38% and 59% for *Test 5* and between 23% and 39% for *Test 8*. These results can be explained by the fact that "roots" (i.e the arrays that hold the lists) are scattered in memory. Instead of gathering all of them in the same set of pages, the GC has to swap extra pages in to reach these special objects.

5.4   Discussion

We observe a loss of performance for applications smaller than main memory or in which there are only a few objects with cross-region pointers. Although the overhead can be up to about half, it mostly concerns small applications which tend to be very fast anyway. For larger problems, however, speedups can be substantial, up to 75%.

Our algorithm performs better when swap space is involved. Small programs that fit in RAM do not need LTS. In fact, as emphasized by our experiments, our modifications will generate some overhead due to unnecessary actions such as tests to figure out if two objects are in the same region.

We propose a solution to avoid this overhead: we add a test before starting the tracing process. If the size of the heap is smaller than main memory, then LTS is not used. If the heap is larger than main memory, we activate the LTS. Alternatively, if paging statistics are available they may be used to trigger LTS.

At another level, it is also possible to activate LTS in a cache-oriented configuration when the heap is smaller than main memory. Further experiments are required to understand the merits of such an approach.

There are two parameters that can be tuned to control the behaviour of the LTS: the size of regions and the size of trace queues. The main issue is the choice of the optimal size of "window of collection" (or "region"). A region should be large enough to avoid the need for large trace queues and small enough both to avoid thrashing and to keep a reasonable working set. Obviously, there is no one best choice, as the size of a region largely depends on the nature of the applications. In our experiments, we found that region sizes of 4MB gave the best results most of the time, but this is not always the case (see for example *Test 7* and *8*). The second parameter is the size of the trace queues and this is dependent on the size of a region.

6   Multiprocessor LTS

The LTS organizes the heap in such a manner that parallelization becomes natural. The heap is divided into regions that can each be mapped to a thread or a processor. In this section, we discuss various aspects of using the LTS in a multiprocessor environment.

It is straightforward to assign regions to be handled independently and in parallel by threads on separate processors. Each thread can scan a group of regions repeatedly and update the different trace queues. Although performance is likely to improve due to the parallel nature of processing, the organization of the memory hierarchy can be more complex in a multiprocessor, so specific working set considerations will be architecture-dependent. The single processor LTS optimization controls the working set to reduce inefficiencies within the memory hierarchy during tracing. A shared memory multiprocessor version should strive to preserve this essential characteristic.

When the LTS is configured to improve cache behavior, its multiprocessor performance should also be improved. This results from a useful property of certain multiprocessor environments: While the heap may be common to all processing units, there is usually at least one level of per-processor cache. When several processors are used, each of them will use its cache while accessing objects. An advantage of the LTS is that cache consistency is maintained very simply by the assignment of a range of regions to each processor. A given processor will never visit an object in a region assigned to another one (except in the case of work stealing as described below, but in this case the region can be reassigned to another processor).

The only synchronization required is to manage accesses to trace queues and to identify termination. A simple idea to discover termination is to maintain a counter of threads going to sleep when no more work is available. If a thread adds a pointer to a queue, it wakes up the thread associated to that region. Termination occurs when the last thread goes to sleep. If a thread appears to be the last one going to sleep, it synchronously checks the counter and the queues to make sure no reference has been left behind.

A final issue is that of load balancing among processors. It is likely that regions will be unequally populated. One region may hold a large number of objects, while others contain no or few objects. In this case, some processors will starve due to the lack of work. Endo [9] proposed a solution in the form of "work stealing"[10]. In this case, each thread maintains a "work queue" containing pointers that the thread should examine next. Once it is empty, there are two possibilities: Either the thread goes to sleep until something has been put in its queue or the thread helps other threads by "stealing" pointers from their queues and inserting them into its own queue.

If work-stealing is used naïvely, the parallel version of the LTS reverts to Endo's technique where several processors scan a single region, involving a synchronization mechanism to access objects. This can be avoided by making regions small enough to assign several regions to one processor. In this case, regions – instead of pointers – can be stolen. This requires a simple locking mechanism at the level of regions rather than objects. We believe this coarser-grained approach could lead to a significant improvement over Endo's results in some cases.

7   Related Work

This section presents garbage collection techniques – both in uniprocessor and multiprocessor contexts – that we can relate to the LTS.

Although it is more generally applicable, we have presented LTS primarily in the context of mark-and-sweep (M&S) collectors. Some have argued that with recent advances in GC technology, M&S is no longer important. We feel otherwise. Boehm [11] and Zorn [12] argue that stop-and-copy collectors do not necessarily perform better than M&S. Particularly, Zorn compares both techniques in a generational setting and concludes that M&S typically uses 20% less memory than stop-and-copy, but was only 3%-6% slower on the problems he tested. While a copying collector apparently improves locality over time, these analyses show that this factor is not sufficient to clearly improve performance.

From another perspective, it is increasingly common to use hybrid techniques to combine the attractive features of various methods; M&S collectors figure prominently in this setting. Finally, in some settings, *e.g.* with heavy use of non-GC aware foreign libraries, conservative M&S is the only viable option.

Generational algorithms divide the heap into "regions" (called generations) to reduce to a minimum the work done by the collector at each call. Because each collection of the nursery is focused in a small area of memory, a side-effect of this organization is to localize data treatment thus reducing page faults and possibly cache misses. Collecting the old generation often involves collecting the entire heap. This is sometimes done with M&S and sometimes with other techniques. In either case, the LTS can be used in the same way as with non-generational algorithms. We would then benefit from the use of generations *and* of an improved trace process for the collection of old generations when large heaps are collected.

The observation that collecting the old generation is disruptive has been previously made in MOS [13]. This incremental GC precisely defines the memory block to examine at each call of the collector for the old generation. It is claimed that this allows a more suitable solution for real-time applications, for example. While the LTS does not solve the problem of real-time applications, we believe it proposes a simple, useful technique to reduce the time spent in collecting the old generation.

Attardi's CMM [14] proposes a heap organization similar to the LTS but for a different purpose. In CMM, each region of the heap is associated with a specific memory management scheme. This allows potential use of a different GC for each sub-heap. Consequences for paging and caching behaviors were not considered. The point of view proposed by the LTS could be used to CMM's advantage. The natural technique used by CMM is to allow collectors to follow pointers even in other sub-heaps to possibly discover live objects in the current sub-heap. Such out-of-sub-heap pointers could be buffered in trace queues to preserve the working set of the collector, which is the job of the LTS.

In [15], Boehm studies a technique to improve caching behavior during tracing of a mark-and-sweep garbage collection. It relies on a standard hardware feature (which can be found on Intel and AMD platforms, as well as HP RISC machines) to pre-fetch "child" objects into the cache when an object is examined. When the object is required by the tracing process, it is already in cache. In comparison, the LTS improves another aspect of tracing. Instead of importing objects before they are needed, it keeps objects in cache as much as possible to increase the probability they will be available in case they are needed. It is likely that both techniques could be combined.

Boehm [15] also mentions an improvement of the sweep phase that uses a bitmap to mark dirty pages (*i.e.* containing live objects). When sweeping memory, the GC checks the bitmap before examining a page in detail to rebuild its free list of fixed-sized objects. If the bit is not set, the page can be reclaimed as a whole. The LTS provides a simple solution to store the bitmap: it may be placed in the trace queues. In addition to storing pointers, we maintain a bitmap of pages in the same memory area. This is useful because trace queues are designed to fit in main memory (or cache), which also allows fast access to the bitmap. The overhead is of 1 bit per page, that is 512 bytes for a region of 16MB. Preliminary experiments showed up to 55% improvement with the Aldor compiler.

The idea of optimizing paging access during garbage collection was mentioned in [16]. The original objective was to improve performance when collecting the old generation in a generational garbage collector. The principle was to partition the heap into sections called buckets that are similar to regions in the LTS. As mentioned in the paper, limiting the trace activity to one card at a time is also a solution to avoid paging. This may have the drawback of maintaining book-keeping information (incoming out-of-card pointers) for a possibly long time.

Hertz *et al* [17] propose an alternative solution to control paging access. Their garbage collector is a generational collector using "book-marking" to keep pages in main memory as much as possible. The proposed mechanism is quite precise as it associates actions to swapped-out pages. This technique requires modifications of low-level layers to gain control over the paging system. The LTS takes a different approach. Although less precise, the solution proposed by the LTS is simple to put in place and does not require low-level modification of a virtual machine or operating system: The idea behind LTS is to keep working with the same set of objects as long as possible. This means corresponding pages will stay in faster memory for long periods. The LTS approach does not rely on interfaces that (if available) will differ by operating system and memory hierarchy level.

Multiprocessor parallel collectors do not benefit from the same attention as concurrent GCs. However, several techniques were studied: [9] and [18], for example. An advantage offered by the LTS compared to the parallel collector described by Endo *et al* in [9] is that there is no need for synchronization at the object level. Even though Endo proposed an optimization to access these objects, a synchronization mechanism is still required. This can lead to a costly marking process (although this aspect is not the only issue, as observed in the paper). Instead of asking each processor to trace a given data structure from beginning to the end, the LTS limits the activity of each processor to regions of memory. If a structure steps over a frontier, the rest of its tracing is handled by another processor. This removes the need for complex synchronization at this level.

We also note that, as mentioned in Section 6, the LTS offers a simple organization of the heap suitable for a parallel configuration. The advantage is that uniprocessor and multiprocessor environments requiring mark-and-sweep could use the same memory management technique with very little modification, *and* receive interesting performance optimization.

8   Conclusions and Future Directions

In this paper we described what we have called a "Localized Tracing Scheme," a technique to improve performance of tracing activities such as those used in garbage collectors. The LTS localizes the tracing process by dividing memory into regions and deferring out-of-region tracing. The idea of deferred pointer queues is simple to implement and can be readily added to existing collectors.

LTS limits the working set to a region of the heap rather than the entire heap. If a region can fit largely or entirely in cache, cache misses are reduced. In the same way, if the region is smaller than available RAM, thrashing due to page faults diminishes. Consequently, optimizations can be made at different levels of the memory hierarchy: cache, virtual memory and network.

We have tested this strategy in the context of the Aldor garbage collector, using a suite of specific micro-benchmarks to observe the behaviour of the LTS in practice. We obtained up to 75% improvement with a configuration oriented towards virtual memory optimization.

Finally, we presented how LTS can function in a multiprocessor context. We observed two axes: (i) independently of any optimization, the organization of the heap in regions results in a natural setting for parallel garbage collections, and (ii) parallel GCs in multiprocessor environments may be improved at cache and virtual memory levels.

We are interested in a number of directions suggested by LTS. First, it has become a practice in scientific computing to deduce and optimize hardware-related parameters through dynamic tuning of algorithms. This may be a useful approach to determine the best sizes for memory regions and deferred pointer queues. Second, GC implementations often maintain an explicit tracing stack, rather than relying on functional recursion. It would be interesting to study different ways of combining deferred pointer queues and the explicit tracing stack. Third, it would be useful to better understand the performance trade-offs arising in different strategies to flush full queues. Fourth, with multi-core processors becoming the norm for personal computing, a full implementation of the multiprocessor LTS would be of practical interest. Finally, the LTS was developed for the Aldor language for computations in computer algebra, which are typically very demanding in dynamic memory use. It would be useful to implement LTS in a more mainstream environment, such as the MMTk [19], allowing direct comparisons over a wider range of common benchmarks and experiments in conjunction with other memory management strategies.

References

1. Watt, S.M.: Aldor. In Grabmeier, J., Kaltofen, E., Weispfenning, V., eds.: Handbook of Computer Algebra, Springer Verlag (2003) 265–270
2. Aldor.org: Aldor user guide. http://www.aldor.org/AldorUserGuide (2003)
3. Maplesoft: Maple User Manual, Maplesoft, a division of Waterloo Maple Inc. (2005)
4. Boehm, H.J., Weiser, M.: Garbage collection in an uncooperative environment. Software Practice and Experience 18 (1988) 807–820
5. Lieberman, H., Hewitt, C.E.: A real-time garbage collector based on the lifetimes of objects. Comm. ACM 26(6) (1983) 419–429. Also report TM–184, Laboratory for Computer Science, MIT, Cambridge, MA, July 1980.
6. Boehm, H.J.: GCBench. http://www.hpl.hp.com/personal/Hans_Boehm/gc/gc_bench

7. Grunwald, D., Zorn, B.: Malloc benchmarks. `ftp://ftp.cs.colorado.edu/pub/cs/misc/MallocStudy`
8. Chicha, Y.: Practical Aspects of Interacting Garbage Collectors. Ph.D. Thesis, University of Western Ontario (2002)
9. Endo, T., Taura, K., Yonezawa, A.: A scalable mark-sweep garbage collector on large-scale shared-memory machines. In: Proc. High Performance Computing and Networking (SC'97). (1997)
10. Burton, F.W., Sleep, M.R.: Executing functional programs on a virtual tree of processors. In: Proc. the 1981 Conference on Functional Programming Languages and Computer Architecture. (1981) 187–194
11. Boehm, H.J.: Mark-and-sweep vs. copying collection and asymptotic complexity. `http://www.hpl.hp.com/personal/Hans_Boehm/gc/complexity.html`
12. Zorn, B.: Comparing mark-and-sweep and stop-and-copy garbage collection. In: Proc. 1990 ACM Symposium on Lisp and Functional Programming. (1990)
13. Hudson, R.L., Moss, J.E.B.: Incremental garbage collection for mature objects. In: IWMM'92 Proceedings. (1992)
14. Attardi, G., Flagella, T.: A customisable memory management framework. Proc. USENIX C++ Conference, Cambridge, MA. (1994)
15. Boehm, H.J.: Reducing garbage collector cache misses. In: ISMM 2000 Proc. Second International Symposium on Memory Management. (2000)
16. Demers, A., Weiser, M., Hayes, B., Bobrow, D.G., Shenker, S.: Combining generational and conservative garbage collection: Framework and implementations. In: Proc. ACM Symposium on Principles of Programming Languages, San Francisco, California, ACM Press (1990) 261–269.
17. Hertz, M., Feng, Y., Berger, E.D.: Garbage collection without paging. In: Proc. SIGPLAN 2005 Conference on Programming Languages Design and Implementation, Chicago, IL, ACM Press (2005)
18. Taura, K., Yonezawa, A.: An effective garbage collection strategy for parallel programming languages on large scale distributed-memory machines. In: ACM Symposium on Principles and Practice of Parallel Programming. (1997) 264–275
19. Blackburn, S.M., Cheng, P., McKinley, K.S.: Oil and water? high performance garbage collection in Java with MMTk. In: ICSE 2004, 26th International Conference on Software Engineering, Edinburgh (2004)

A Pushdown Machine for Recursive XML Processing*

Keisuke Nakano[1] and Shin-Cheng Mu[2]

[1] Department of Mathematical Informatics, University of Tokyo, Japan
ksk@mist.i.u-tokyo.ac.jp
[2] Institute of Information Science, Academia Sinica, Taiwan
scm@iis.sinica.edu.tw

Abstract. XML transformations are most naturally defined as recursive functions on trees. A naive implementation, however, would load the entire input XML tree into memory before processing. In contrast, programs in stream processing style minimise memory usage since it may release the memory occupied by the processed prefix of the input, but they are harder to write because the programmer is left with the burden to maintain a state. In this paper, we propose a model for XML stream processing and show that all programs written in a particular style of recursive functions on XML trees, the *macro forest transducer*, can be automatically translated to our stream processors. The stream processor is declarative in style, but can be implemented efficiently by a pushdown machine. We thus get the best of both worlds — program clarity, and efficiency in execution.

1 Introduction

Since an XML document has a tree-like structure, it is natural to define XML transformations as recursive functions over trees. Several XML-oriented languages, such as XSLT [34], *fxt* [3], XDuce [11] and CDuce [2], allow the programmer to define mutual recursive functions over forests. As an example, consider the program in Figure 1. Let $\sigma\langle f_1\rangle f_2$ denote a forest where the head is a σ-labelled tree whose children constitute the forest f_1, and the tail is a sibling forest f_2. The empty forest is denoted by ϵ and is usually omitted when enclosed in other trees. The function $Main$ in Figure 1 scans through the input tree and reverses the order of all subtrees under nodes labelled r by calling the function Rev. For example, the input tree $a\langle r\langle b\langle c\langle\rangle d\langle\rangle\rangle e\langle\rangle\rangle f\langle\rangle\rangle$ is transformed into $a\langle r\langle e\langle\rangle b\langle d\langle\rangle c\langle\rangle\rangle\rangle f\langle\rangle\rangle$.

A naive way to execute functions defined in this style is to load the entire forest into memory, so that we have convenient access to the children and siblings for each node. The input stream of tokens, also called *XML events*, is parsed to build the corresponding forest, which is then transformed by the function, before the resulting forest is unparsed to an XML stream. Loading the entire tree into memory is not preferable when we have to process large input. However,

---

* Partially supported by *Comprehensive Development of e-Society Foundation Software* of the Ministry of Education, Culture, Sports, Science and Technology, Japan.

$$
\begin{array}{ll}
Main(\epsilon) = \epsilon & Rev(\epsilon,\ y) = y \\
Main(\mathbf{r}\langle x_1\rangle x_2) = \mathbf{r}\langle rev(x_1, \epsilon)\rangle(Main(x_2)) & Rev(\sigma\langle x_1\rangle x_2,\ y) = Rev(x_2,\ \sigma\langle Rev\ x_1\ \epsilon\rangle\ y) \\
Main(\sigma\langle x_1\rangle x_2) = \sigma\langle main\ x_1\rangle(Main(x_2)) \quad \text{if } \sigma \neq \mathbf{r} &
\end{array}
$$

Fig. 1. A functional program reversing the subtrees under nodes labelled $\mathbf{r}$

many XML transformation languages such as XSLT, *fxt*, XDuce and CDuce are actually implemented this way.

To optimise space usage, the programmer may switch to programming style (e.g SAX [32]). The stream processor reads XML events one by one, and the programmer defines respectively what to do when it encounters a start tag `<σ>`, an end tag `</σ>`, or end of stream `$`. Consider performing the same task given the input `<a><r><b><c></c><d></d></b><e> </e></r><f></f></a>`. Upon reading the first event `<a>`, we can output `<a>` immediately. The next event `<r>` is also copied to the output. After that, no output event will be produced for a while, because there is no way for the processor to know what to output before the closing tag `</r>` is read. Between `<r>` and `</r>`, the computer reads the input and stores a reversed stream in some environment[1]. While stream processing saves memory usage, it is much harder to program in this style.

Can we write a recursive function on forests and have it automatically transformed to a program in the stream processing style, thereby achieve both clarity and memory efficiency? In this paper, we present a model for an XML stream processor, and shows how to automatically derive XML stream processors from a very expressive class of recursive functions on forests.

We have made two main contributions. Firstly, we propose a model for XML stream processing which is declarative in nature but has an efficient implementation. The environment can be represented uniformly by a partially evaluated stream, called a *temporary expression*. Secondly, we present a method to derive a stream processor from any function definable in terms of the *macro forest transducer* (mft), proposed by Perst and Seidl [26]. The derivation, which can be seen as a special case of program fusion [30], works by fusing the mft with an XML parser recast as a *top-down tree transducer* (tdtt). The fusion is similar Engelfriet and Vogler's method of composing a (finitary) tdtt and a *macro tree transducer* [6]. but we have a proof that the method works for our tdtt with a infinite number of states.

This paper summaries our work. Interested readers are also referred to the full version [22] available online, which contains the proof of the main theorem and more discussions.

2   XML and the Macro Forest Transducer

For simplicity, we deal with a simplified model of XML with only element nodes, and assume that the input XML is well-formed.

---

[1] An 'environment' is a state storing information needed to carry out the computation. We use the term 'environment' to avoid confusion with mft states.

Let Σ be an alphabet. A Σ-*forest* (also called a Σ-hedge [18]), is defined by

$$f ::= \sigma\langle f\rangle f \mid \epsilon,$$

where $\sigma \in \Sigma$ and ϵ denotes the empty forest. We denote by $\mathcal{F}_\Sigma$ the set of Σ-forests. A Σ-forest $a\langle b\langle\epsilon\rangle c\langle\epsilon\rangle\epsilon\rangle\epsilon$ with $\Sigma = \{a, b, c\}$ represents the XML fragment `<a><b></b><c></c></a>`. The concatenation of two forests $f_1, f_2 \in \mathcal{F}_\Sigma$ is written $f_1 f_2$. The symbol ϵ, being the unit of concatenation, is often omitted.

The Σ-*events*, written $\Sigma_{<>}$, is defined by $\Sigma_{<>} = \{$`<`σ`>` $\mid \sigma \in \Sigma\} \cup \{$`</`$\sigma$`>` $\mid \sigma \in \Sigma\}$. An XML stream is a sequence of Σ-*events*. We denote by $\Sigma_{<>}^\circ$ the set of well-formed sequences of Σ-events and denote by ε the empty sequence. The symbol $\$$ denotes the end of an (input) XML stream, which is also regarded as an event. We write $\Sigma_{<>\$}$ for $\Sigma_{<>} \cup \{\$\}$.

Let Σ be an alphabet. The *streaming* of a forest is the function $\lfloor\_\rfloor :$ $\mathcal{F}_\Sigma \to \Sigma_{<>}^\circ$ defined by $\lfloor\sigma\langle f_1\rangle f_2\rfloor =$ `<`σ`>` $\lfloor f_1\rfloor$ `</`σ`>` $\lfloor f_2\rfloor$ and $\lfloor\epsilon\rfloor = \varepsilon$. For example, $\lfloor a\langle b\langle\rangle c\langle\rangle\rangle\rfloor =$ `<a><b></b><c></c></a>`.

The *macro forest transducer* (mft) was proposed by Perst and Seidl [26] as an extension to the *macro tree transducer* (mtt) [6] by taking concatenation as a basic operator. Functional programmers can think of an mft as a recursive function mapping a forest (and some accumulating parameters) to a forest, with certain restriction on their shapes — the pattern on the forest extracts only the label, the children and the sibling of the first tree; the accumulating parameters cannot be pattern-matched; each function call is passed either the children or the sibling. We do not propose using the mft as a programming language, but as an intermediate language. It was shown that mft is in fact rather expressive [17]. In particular, XPath expressions can be converted to a computation model weaker than mfts [21]. More discussions will be given in Section 6.

In the convention of mft, a function is called a *state* and its arity is called its *rank*. Let us write $\mathbb{N}$ and $\mathbb{N}^+$ for the set of non-negative integers including and excluding 0, respectively.

Definition 1. A *macro forest transducer* is a tuple $M = (Q, \Sigma, \Delta, in, R)$, where

- Q is a finite set of ranked states, the rank of a state given by a function $rank : Q \to \mathbb{N}^+$,
- Σ and Δ are alphabets with $Q \cap (\Sigma \cup \Delta) = \emptyset$, called the *input alphabet* and the *output alphabet*, respectively,
- $in \in Q$ is the initial ranked state,
- R is a set of rules partitioned by $R = \bigcup_{q \in Q} R_q$. For each $q \in Q$, R_q consists of rules of the form $q(pat, y_1, \ldots, y_n) \to rhs$, where $n = rank(q) - 1$ and
  - pat is either ϵ or $\sigma\langle x_1\rangle x_2$ for some $\sigma \in \Sigma$,
  - rhs ranges over expressions defined by

  $$rhs ::= q'(x_i, rhs, \ldots, rhs) \mid \epsilon \mid \delta\langle rhs\rangle \mid y_j \mid rhs \ rhs$$

  with $q' \in Q$, $\delta \in \Delta$, $i = 1, 2$ and $j = 1, \ldots, n$. Additionally, no variable x_i occurs in rhs when $pat = \epsilon$.

Perst and Seidl's mft, designed for type checking, can be non-deterministic. Since our focus is on program transformation, our mft's are deterministic and total. That is, for each q and σ there is exactly one such rule $q(\sigma\langle x_1\rangle x_2, \dots) \to rhs$. We will denote its right-hand side by $rhs^{q,\sigma}$. Similarly $rhs^{q,\epsilon}$ stands for the right-hand side rhs of the unique rule $q(\epsilon, \dots) \to rhs$. If a rule for state q and pattern p is missing, we assume that there is an implicit rule $q(p, \dots) \to \epsilon$. The semantics of mft's is given by translating every state into a function [26]:

Definition 2. Let $M = (Q, \Sigma, \Delta, in, R)$ be an mft. The semantics of a states $q \in Q$ is given by the function $[\![q]\!] : \mathcal{F}_\Sigma \times (\mathcal{F}_\Delta)^n \to \mathcal{F}_\Delta$ where $n = rank(q) - 1$. Each $[\![q]\!]$ is defined by:

- $[\![q]\!](\sigma\langle\omega_1\rangle\omega_2, \varphi_1, \dots, \varphi_n) = [\![rhs^{q,\sigma}]\!]_\rho$ where $\rho(x_i) = \omega_i$ for $i = 1, 2$ and $\rho(y_j) = \varphi_j$ for $j = 1, \dots, n$,
- $[\![q]\!](\epsilon, \varphi_1, \dots, \varphi_n) = [\![rhs^{q,\epsilon}]\!]_\rho$ where $\rho(y_j) = \varphi_j$ for $j = 1, \dots, n$,

where $[\![\_]\!]_\rho$ evaluates the right-hand side with respect to the environment ρ:

$$[\![q'(x_i, rhs_1, \dots, rhs_{n'})]\!]_\rho = [\![q']\!](\rho(x_i), [\![rhs_1]\!]_\rho, \dots, [\![rhs_{n'}]\!]_\rho),$$
$$[\![\epsilon]\!]_\rho = \epsilon, \qquad\qquad [\![\delta\langle rhs\rangle]\!]_\rho = \delta\langle[\![rhs]\!]_\rho\rangle,$$
$$[\![y_j]\!]_\rho = \rho(y_j), \qquad\qquad [\![rhs\ rhs']\!]_\rho = [\![rhs]\!]_\rho[\![rhs']\!]_\rho.$$

Definition 3. The transformation induced by an mft $M = (Q, \Sigma, \Delta, in, R)$ is the function $\tau_M : \mathcal{F}_\Sigma \to \mathcal{F}_\Delta$ defined by $\tau_M(f) = [\![in]\!](f, \epsilon, \dots, \epsilon)$.

Example 1. Let $Q = \{Main, Rev\}$, Σ some alphabet containing r and R the rules in Figure 1 (replacing = by $\to$), then $M_{rev} = (Q, \Sigma, \Sigma, Main, R)$ is an mft.

Example 2. The mft $M_{htm} = (Q, \Sigma, \Delta, Main, R)$ defined below reads an XML document consisting of a title and several paragraphs with some keywords. The output is a (simplified) HTML document where the **para** tag is converted to **p** and **key** tag to **em**. Furthermore, before the **ps** tag we dump the list of keywords we collect so far. Text data is denoted by a node with no children.

$Q = \{Main, Title, InArticle, Key2Em, AllKeys, Copy\}$,

$\Sigma = \Delta = $ (some alphabet containing English words and the XML/HTML tags below),

$R = \{$ $Main(\mathtt{article}\langle x_1\rangle x_2) \to \mathtt{html}\langle\mathtt{head}\langle Title(x_1)\rangle\mathtt{body}\langle InArticle(x_1, \epsilon)\rangle\rangle\epsilon$,

$\qquad Title(\mathtt{title}\langle x_1\rangle x_2) \to \mathtt{title}\langle Copy(x_1)\rangle$,

$\qquad InArticle(\mathtt{title}\langle x_1\rangle x_2, y_1) \to \mathtt{h1}\langle Copy(x_1)\rangle InArticle(x_2, y_1)$,

$\qquad InArticle(\mathtt{para}\langle x_1\rangle x_2, y_1) \to \mathtt{p}\langle Key2Em(x_1)\rangle InArticle(x_2, y_1\ AllKeys(x_1))$,

$\qquad InArticle(\mathtt{ps}\langle x_1\rangle x_2, y_1) \to \mathtt{h2}\langle\mathtt{Index}\langle\rangle\rangle\ \mathtt{ul}\langle y_1\rangle\ \mathtt{h2}\langle\mathtt{Postscript}\langle\rangle\rangle\ Copy(x_1)$,

$\qquad Key2Em(\mathtt{key}\langle x_1\rangle x_2) \to \mathtt{em}\langle Copy(x_1)\rangle\ Key2Em(x_2)$,

$\qquad Key2Em(\sigma\langle x_1\rangle x_2) \to \sigma\langle Key2Em(x_1)\rangle\ Key2Em(x_2)\ (\sigma \neq \mathtt{key}), Key2Em(\epsilon) \to \epsilon$,

$\qquad AllKeys(\mathtt{key}\langle x_1\rangle x_2) \to \mathtt{li}\langle Copy(x_1)\rangle AllKeys(x_2)$,

$\qquad AllKeys(\sigma\langle x_1\rangle x_2) \to AllKeys(x_1)AllKeys(x_2)\ (\sigma \neq \mathtt{key}), \qquad AllKeys(\epsilon) \to \epsilon$,

$\qquad Copy(\sigma\langle x_1\rangle x_2) \to \sigma\langle Copy(x_1)\rangle Copy(x_2)\ (\sigma \in \Sigma), \qquad\qquad Copy(\epsilon) \to \epsilon\ \}$

3   XML Stream Processors and Its Derivation

A *temporary expression* is a partially computed stream of XML events. An XML stream processor (xsp) defines how to rewrite a temporary expression upon reading each input event.

Definition 4. An *XML stream processor* is a tuple $S = (Q, \Sigma, \Delta, in, R)$, where

- Q is a (possibly infinite) set of ranked states, the rank for each state given by $rank : Q \to \mathbb{N}$,
- Σ and Δ are (finite) alphabets with $Q \cap (\Sigma \cup \Delta) = \emptyset$, called the *input alphabet* and the *output alphabet*, respectively,
- $in \in Q$ is the initial state,
- $R = \{q(y_1, \ldots, y_n) \xrightarrow{\chi} rhs \mid q \in Q, \chi \in \Sigma_{<>\$}\}$ is a set of rules, where $n = rank(q)$ and rhs ranges over expressions defined by

$$rhs ::= q'(rhs, \ldots, rhs) \mid \varepsilon \mid \texttt{<}\delta\texttt{>}rhs\texttt{</}\delta\texttt{>} \mid y_j \mid rhs \ rhs$$

where $q' \in Q$, $\delta \in \Delta$ and $j = 1, \ldots, n$. Additionally, the pattern $q'(\ldots)$ does not occur in rhs for any $q' \in Q$ when $\chi = \$$.

3.1   Semantics of XML Stream Processors

The semantics of an xsp is defined by translating every rule of the xsp into a transition for temporary expressions.

Definition 5. *Let* $S = (Q, \Sigma, \Delta, in, R)$ *be an xsp. A temporary expression for* S*, denoted by* Tmp_S*, is defined by* $E ::= \varepsilon \mid \texttt{<}\delta\texttt{>}E \mid \texttt{</}\delta\texttt{>}E \mid q(E, \ldots, E)E.$

Definition 6. Let $S = (Q, \Sigma, \Delta, in, R)$ be an xsp and $s \in \Sigma_{<>}^\circ$. The *transition* over Tmp_S for an input Σ-event is a function $\langle\!\langle \_\_, \_\_ \rangle\!\rangle : Tmp_S \times \Sigma_{<>\$} \to Tmp_S$ defined by

- $\langle\!\langle \varepsilon, \chi \rangle\!\rangle = \varepsilon,$
- $\langle\!\langle \texttt{<}\delta\texttt{>}e, \chi \rangle\!\rangle = \texttt{<}\delta\texttt{>}\langle\!\langle e, \chi \rangle\!\rangle$ where $\delta \in \Delta,$
- $\langle\!\langle \texttt{</}\delta\texttt{>}e, \chi \rangle\!\rangle = \texttt{</}\delta\texttt{>}\langle\!\langle e, \chi \rangle\!\rangle$ where $\delta \in \Delta,$
- $\langle\!\langle q(e_1, \ldots, e_n)e, \chi \rangle\!\rangle = (rhs[y_j := \langle\!\langle e_j, \chi \rangle\!\rangle]_{j=1,\ldots,n})\langle\!\langle e, \chi \rangle\!\rangle$ where $(q(y_1, \ldots, y_n) \xrightarrow{\chi} rhs) \in R$ with $q \in Q$ and $\chi \in \Sigma_{<>\$}.$

The initial temporary expression is $in(\varepsilon, \ldots, \varepsilon)$. An xsp reads the input stream of events and updates the temporary expression with the transition $\langle\!\langle \_\_, \_\_ \rangle\!\rangle$. The end of stream is marked by $\$$. Let $\chi_1 \chi_2 \ldots \chi_k$ be the input stream with each $\chi_j \in \Sigma_{<>}$. The final expression is $\langle\!\langle \langle\!\langle \ldots \langle\!\langle \langle\!\langle in(\varepsilon, \ldots, \varepsilon), \chi_1 \rangle\!\rangle, \chi_2 \rangle\!\rangle, \ldots, \chi_k \rangle\!\rangle, \$ \rangle\!\rangle$. Note that the final temporary expression is always in $\Delta_{<>}^\circ$, since, by Definition 4, the right-hand side of a $(q, \$)$-rule does not contain any unevaluated state $q'(\ldots)$.

Definition 7. The transformation induced by an xsp $S = (Q, \Sigma, \Delta, in, R)$ is the function $\tau_S : \Sigma_{<>}^\circ \to \Delta_{<>}^\circ$ defined by $\tau_S(s) = \theta_S(in(\varepsilon, \ldots, \varepsilon), s\$)$ where, for $e \in Tmp_S$,

$$\theta_S(e, \varepsilon) = e, \qquad\qquad \theta_S(e, \chi s) = \theta_S(\langle\!\langle e, \chi \rangle\!\rangle, s).$$

The induced transformation defines declaratively what the output stream is, given the input stream. The very reason we program in the stream processing style, however, is to be able to print out a prefix of the output stream while reading the input. That is, we would like to 'squeeze' some part of the result from after each event read. This will be described in Section 4.3.

3.2 Deriving Stream Processors from Macro Forest Transducers

Given an mft $M = (Q, \Sigma, \Delta, in, R)$, a stream x, and a function $Parse :: \Sigma_{<>}^{\circ} \rightarrow \mathcal{F}_\Sigma$ parsing a stream of events into a forest, the expression $\lfloor \llbracket in \rrbracket (Parse(x), \epsilon, \ldots, \epsilon) \rfloor$ yields a $\Delta_{<>}^{\circ}$ stream. If we can fuse the three functions, $\lfloor \_ \rfloor$, $\llbracket in \rrbracket$, and $Parse$ into one, we may have a stream processor. Fusing $\lfloor \_ \rfloor$ and $\llbracket in \rrbracket$ is a relatively easy task. The interesting step is fusing them with the parser. An XML parser can be written as a *top-down tree transducer* (tdtt) with an (countably-)infinite number of states

$Parse[1] \; (\texttt{<}\sigma\texttt{>}s) = \sigma\langle Parse[1] \; s\rangle(Parse[2] \; s), \quad Parse[1] \; (\texttt{</}\sigma\texttt{>}s) = \epsilon,$

$Parse[i] \; (\texttt{<}\sigma\texttt{>}s) = Parse[i+1] \; s \; i > 1), \qquad Parse[i] \; (\texttt{</}\sigma\texttt{>}s) = Parse[i-1] \; s \quad (i > 1),$

$Parse[i] \; (\texttt{\$}) = \epsilon.$

for every $\sigma \in \Sigma$. Note that we do not need a forest transducer for parsing. The forest is constructed without using forest concatenation. Therefore, although it returns a forest, *Parse* is still technically a tree transducer where the forest is represented by a binary tree. Multiple traversals of s is in fact avoided in the implementation, to be discussed in Section 4. We will also talk about a more typical way to specify the parser, and its effects, in Section 6.

Some previous work [24,21,25] talked about fusing a tree transducer for parsing with a transformation, but not one as expressive as an mft. More details are given in Section 7. Engelfriet and Vogler [6] described how to fuse a *finitary* tdtt and a *macro tree transducer* (mtt). Their method, however, does not apply directly to our application because *Parse* has a infinite number of states. Our derivation from an mft to an xsp, to be presented in this section and proved in the full paper [22], is basically Engelfriet and Vogler's transducer fusion extended to mft's and specialised to one particular infinitary tdtt, *Parse*. The readers are not required to have knowledge of their method.

For a rationale behind the derivation, consider mft $M = (Q, \Sigma, \Delta, in, R)$. For every state $q \in Q$, we introduce in the derived xsp a set of states $\{q[i] \mid i \in \mathbb{N}^+\}$. Imagine that we are building forests as we read the input stream of events. With each start tag, the forest construction descends by one level. The state $q[1]$ performs the task that the state q in the mft is supposed to do. The number 1 indicates that the current forest will be its input. The states $q[i]$ for $i > 1$, on the other hand, represent 'suspended' states which will take effect $i - 1$ levels *above* the forest currently being built. The number i denotes the number of end tags expected. When an end tag is read, the number decrease by one, until the number reaches 1 and the state gets activated. When a start tag is read, the number shall increase by one because there is one more start tag to be matched.

Definition 8. Let $M = (Q, \Sigma, \Delta, in, R)$ be an mft. We define an xsp $\mathcal{SP}(M) = (Q', \Sigma, \Delta, in', R')$ where

- $Q' = \{q[i] \mid q \in Q, i \in \mathbb{N}^+\}$ where $rank(q[i]) = rank(q) - 1$,
- $in' = in[1] \in Q'$,
- R' contains rules introduced by the following three cases:
  xsp-(1). for all $q \in Q$ and $\sigma \in \Sigma$, we introduce

$$q[1](y_1, \ldots, y_n) \xrightarrow{\text{<}\sigma\text{>}} \mathcal{A}(rhs^{q,\sigma}),$$

  xsp-(2). for all $q \in Q$, $\sigma \in \Sigma$ and $i \in \mathbb{N}^+$, we introduce:

$$q[1](y_1, \ldots, y_n) \xrightarrow{\text{</}\sigma\text{>}} \mathcal{A}(rhs^{q,\epsilon}),$$

$$q[i](y_1, \ldots, y_n) \xrightarrow{\$} \mathcal{A}(rhs^{q,\epsilon}),$$

  xsp-(3). for all $q \in Q$, $\sigma \in \Sigma$ and $i > 1$, we introduce:

$$q[i](y_1, \ldots, y_n) \xrightarrow{\text{<}\sigma\text{>}} q[i+1](y_1, \ldots, y_n),$$

$$q[i](y_1, \ldots, y_n) \xrightarrow{\text{</}\sigma\text{>}} q[i-1](y_1, \ldots, y_n).$$

The translation $\mathcal{A}$ is defined by:

$$\mathcal{A}(q(x_i, rhs_1, \ldots, rhs_n)) = q[i](\mathcal{A}(rhs_1), \ldots, \mathcal{A}(rhs_{n'})),$$

$$\mathcal{A}(\epsilon) = \varepsilon, \qquad\qquad\qquad \mathcal{A}(\delta\langle rhs \rangle) = \text{<}\delta\text{>}\mathcal{A}(rhs)\text{</}\delta\text{>},$$

$$\mathcal{A}(y_j) = y_j, \qquad\qquad\qquad \mathcal{A}(rhs\ rhs') = \mathcal{A}(rhs)\ \mathcal{A}(rhs'),$$

where $q \in Q$, $n = rank(q)$, $\delta \in \Delta$, $i \in \{1, 2\}$ and $j \in \{1, \ldots, n\}$.

Note that among the three cases of rule introduction, **xsp-(1)** covers the situation when the state and the input symbols are $(q[1], \text{<}\sigma\text{>})$; **xsp-(2)** covers $(q[1], \text{</}\sigma\text{>})$ and $(q[i], \$)$ for $i \in \mathbb{N}^+$; and **xsp-(3)** covers $(q[i], \text{<}\sigma\text{>})$ and $(q[i], \text{</}\sigma\text{>})$ for $i > 1$. Therefore, the derived xsp $\mathcal{SP}(M)$ is total if M is. For the examples below, we define a predicate testing whether the state and the input symbols is in the **xsp-(2)** case: $\epsilon_\Sigma(i, \chi) = (i = 1 \wedge \chi = \text{</}\sigma\text{>}) \vee \chi = \$$, with $\sigma \in \Sigma$. The following theorem, stating the correctness of the derivation, is proved in the full version of this paper [22].

Theorem 1. Let $M = (Q, \Sigma, \Delta, in, R)$ be an mft. Then $\tau_{\mathcal{SP}(M)}(\lfloor f \rfloor) = \lfloor \tau_M(f) \rfloor$ for every $f \in \mathcal{F}_\Sigma$.

Example 3. Apply the derivation to EXAMPLE 1, we get $\mathcal{SP}(M_{rev}) = (Q', \Sigma, \Sigma, Main[1], R')$, where $Q' = \{q[i] \mid q \in \{Main, Rev\}, i \in \mathbb{N}^+\}$ and the set R' is:

$\{Main[1]() \xrightarrow{\text{<r>}} \text{<r>}\ Rev[1](\varepsilon)\ \text{</r>}\ Main[2](),$

$Main[1]() \xrightarrow{\text{<}\sigma\text{>}} \text{<}\sigma\text{>}\ Main[1]()\ \text{</}\sigma\text{>}\ Main[2]()$ $\quad Rev[1](y_1) \xrightarrow{\text{<}\sigma\text{>}} Rev[2](\text{<}\sigma\text{>}\ Rev[1](\varepsilon)\ \text{</}\sigma\text{>}\ y_1)$
$\quad (\sigma \neq \text{r}),$ $\qquad\qquad\qquad\qquad\qquad\qquad\qquad (\sigma \in \Sigma),$

$Main[i]() \xrightarrow{\text{<}\sigma\text{>}} Main[i+1]()$ $\quad (\sigma \in \Sigma,\ i > 1),$ $\quad Rev[i](y_1) \xrightarrow{\text{<}\sigma\text{>}} Rev[i+1](y_1)$ $\quad (\sigma \in \Sigma,\ i > 1),$

$Main[i]() \xrightarrow{\text{</}\sigma\text{>}} Main[i-1]()$ $\quad (\sigma \in \Sigma,\ i > 1),$ $\quad Rev[i](y_1) \xrightarrow{\text{</}\sigma\text{>}} Rev[i-1](y_1)$ $\quad (\sigma \in \Sigma,\ i > 1),$

$Main[i]() \xrightarrow{\chi} \varepsilon$ $\quad (\text{if } \epsilon_\Sigma(i, \chi)),$ $\qquad\qquad Rev[i](y_1) \xrightarrow{\chi} y_1$ $\quad (\text{if } \epsilon_\Sigma(i, \chi))\ \}.$

Figure 2(a) shows a sample run when the input is `<a><r><b><c></c><d></d><e>``</e></r><f></f></a>$`.

Example 4. The xsp derived from EXAMPLE 2 is $\mathcal{SP}(M_{htm}) = (Q', \Sigma, \Delta, Main[1], R')$, where $Q' = \{q[i] \mid q \in Q, i \in \mathbb{N}^+\}$ and R' is shown in Figure 2(b).

4 Pushdown XML Stream Processor

The semantics given in Section 3 implies a direct implementation of xsp performing term rewriting each time an event is read. However, an xsp derived from an mft follows a more regular evaluation pattern which resembles a stack. In this section, we present an efficient implementation of the xsp's derived from mft's.

4.1 Summary of Behavior

Let us look at an example first. Consider the sample run of the xsp $\mathcal{SP}(M_{rev})$ in Figure 2, when event `<c>` is read. We abbreviate Rev to r and $Main$ to m. The prefix `<a><r>` has been 'squeezed' to the output. We need only to keep a suffix of the temporary expression in memory:

$$e_{before} = r[2](\texttt{<b>}r[1](\varepsilon)\texttt{</b>})\texttt{</r>}m[3]()\texttt{</a>}m[4]().$$

After `<c>` is read, the expression gets updated to

$$e_{after} = r[3](\texttt{<b>}r[2](\texttt{<c>}r[1](\varepsilon)\texttt{</c>})\texttt{</b>})\texttt{</r>}m[4]()\texttt{</a>}m[5]().$$

We shall present a data structure such that the update can be efficient.

We represent a temporary expression by a pair of a *main output stream* and a *pushdown*, as shown in Figure 3. The left and right parts in the figure correspond to temporary expressions e_{before} and e_{after}, respectively. Consider e_{before}. Separating the evaluated and unevaluated segments, it can be partitioned into five parts: $r[2](\ldots)$, `</r>`, $m[3]()$, `</a>` and $m[4]()$. If we abstract away the unevaluated parts and replace them with *holes* $[\ ]_{\nu_i}$ using a physical address ν_i, we obtain the main output stream $[\ ]_{\nu_1}\texttt{</r>}[\ ]_{\nu_2}\texttt{</a>}[\ ]_{\nu_3}$.

The pushdown is a stack of sets, each set consisting of *state frames*. A state frame is a pair of a state $q(\ldots)$ and a hole address ν, denoted by $q(\ldots)/\nu$. The state may have a number of arguments, represented by a sequence in a way similar to the main output stream. In the pushdown representation, every state $q[i]$ appears in the i-th set from the top. Therefore the index i need not be stored in the representation. Since all states in e_{before} have distinct indexes, the pushdown contains only singleton sets, which need not be true in general.

Only the states with index 1 gets expanded. In our representation, that means we only need to update the top of the pushdown. Upon reading `<c>`, the rule of $r[1]$ that gets triggered is $r[1](\varepsilon) \xrightarrow{\texttt{<c>}} r[2](\texttt{<σ>}\ r[1](\varepsilon)\ \texttt{</σ>}\ \varepsilon)$. That corresponds to popping the set $\{r(\varepsilon)/\nu_4\}$ (representing $r[1](\varepsilon)$ in e_{before}), and pushing two sets $\{r(\varepsilon)/\nu_5\}$ (representing $r[1](\varepsilon)$ in e_{after}) and $\{r(\texttt{<c>}\ [\ ]_{\nu_5}\ \texttt{</c>})/\nu_6\}$

$Main[1]()\ \xrightarrow{\texttt{<a>}}\ $ `<a>`$Main[1]()$`</a>`$Main[2]()$

$\xrightarrow{\texttt{<r>}}\ $ `<a><r>`$Rev[1](\varepsilon)$`</r>`$Main[2]()$`</a>`$Main[3]()$

$\xrightarrow{\texttt{}}\ $ `<a><r>`$Rev[2]($`<b>`$Rev[1](\varepsilon)$`</b>`$)$`</r>`$Main[3]()$`</a>`$Main[4]()$

$\xrightarrow{\texttt{<c>}}\ $ `<a><r>`$Rev[3]($`<b>`$Rev[2]($`<c>`$Rev[1](\varepsilon)$`</c>`$)$`</b>`$)$`</r>`$Main[4]()$`</a>`$Main[5]()$

$\xrightarrow{\texttt{</c>}}\ $ `<a><r>`$Rev[2]($`<b>`$Rev[1]($`<c></c>`$)$`</b>`$)$`</r>`$Main[3]()$`</a>`$Main[4]()$

$\xrightarrow{\texttt{<d>}}\ $ `<a><r>`$Rev[3]($`<b>`$Rev[2]($`<d>`$Rev[1](\varepsilon)$`</d><c></c>`$)$`</b>`$)$`</r>`$Main[4]()$`</a>`$Main[5]()$

$\xrightarrow{\texttt{</d>}}\ $ `<a><r>`$Rev[2]($`<b>`$Rev[1]($`<d></d><c></c>`$)$`</b>`$)$`</r>`$Main[3]()$`</a>`$Main[4]()$

$\xrightarrow{\texttt{}}\ $ `<a><r>`$Rev[1]($`<b><d></d><c></c></b>`$)$`</r>`$Main[2]()$`</a>`$Main[3]()$

$\xrightarrow{\texttt{<e>}}\ $ `<a><r>`$Rev[2]($`<e>`$Rev[1](\varepsilon)$`</e><b><d></d><c></c></b>`$)$`</r>`$Main[3]()$`</a>`$Main[4]()$

$\xrightarrow{\texttt{</e>}}\ $ `<a><r>`$Rev[1]($`<e></e><b><d></d><c></c></b>`$)$`</r>`$Main[2]()$`</a>`$Main[3]()$

$\xrightarrow{\texttt{</r>}}\ $ `<a><r><e></e><b><d></d><c></c></b></r>`$Main[1]()$`</a>`$Main[2]()$

$\xrightarrow{\texttt{<f>}}\ $ `<a><r><e></e><b><d></d><c></c></b></r><f>`$Main[1]()$`</f>`$Main[2]()$`</a>`$Main[3]()$

$\xrightarrow{\texttt{</f>}}\ $ `<a><r><e></e><b><d></d><c></c></b></r><f></f>`$Main[1]()$`</a>`$Main[2]()$

$\xrightarrow{\texttt{</a>}}\ $ `<a><r><e></e><b><d></d><c></c></b></r><f></f></a>`$Main[1]()$

$\xrightarrow{\texttt{\$}}\ $ `<a><r><e></e><b><d></d><c></c></b></r><f></f></a>`

(a)

$R' = \{\ Main[1]()\ \xrightarrow{\texttt{<article>}}\ $ `<html> <head>` $Title[1]()$ `</head> <body>` $InArticle[1](\varepsilon)$ `</body> </html>`,

$Title[1]()\ \xrightarrow{\texttt{<title>}}\ $ `<title>` $Copy[1]()$ `</title>`,

$InArticle[1](y_1)\ \xrightarrow{\texttt{<title>}}\ $ `<h1>` $Copy[1]()$ `</h1>` $InArticle[2](y_1)$,

$InArticle[1](y_1)\ \xrightarrow{\texttt{<para>}}\ $ `<p>` $Key2Em[1]()$ `</p>` $InArticle[2](y_1\ AllKeys[1]())$,

$InArticle[1](y_1)\ \xrightarrow{\texttt{<ps>}}\ $ `<h2>Index</h2><ul>`y_1`</ul><h2>Postscript</h2>` $Copy[1]()$,

$Key2Em[1]()\ \xrightarrow{\texttt{<key>}}\ $ `<em>` $Copy[1]()$ `</em>` $Key2Em[2]()$,

$Key2Em[1]()\ \xrightarrow{\texttt{<}\sigma\texttt{>}}\ $ `<`σ`>` $Key2Em[1]()$ `</`σ`>` $Key2Em[2]()$ $(\sigma \neq \texttt{key})$,

$AllKeys[1]()\ \xrightarrow{\texttt{<key>}}\ $ `<li>` $Copy[1]()$ `</li>` $AllKeys[2]()$,

$AllKeys[1]()\ \xrightarrow{\texttt{<}\sigma\texttt{>}}\ $ $AllKeys[1]()AllKeys[2]()$ $(\sigma \neq \texttt{key})$,

$Copy[1]()\ \xrightarrow{\texttt{<}\sigma\texttt{>}}\ $ `<`σ`>` $Copy[1]()$ `</`σ`>` $Copy[2]()$ $(\sigma \in \Sigma)$,

$q[i]()\ \xrightarrow{\texttt{<}\sigma\texttt{>}}\ q[i+1]()$ $(\sigma \in \Sigma,\ i > 1,\ q \neq InArticle)$,

$q[i]()\ \xrightarrow{\texttt{</}\sigma\texttt{>}}\ q[i-1]()$ $(\sigma \in \Sigma,\ i > 1,\ q \neq InArticle)$,

$q[i]()\ \xrightarrow{\chi}\ \varepsilon$ (if $\epsilon_\Sigma(i, \chi)$),

$InArticle[i](y_1)\ \xrightarrow{\texttt{<}\sigma\texttt{>}}\ InArticle[i+1](y_1)$ $(\sigma \in \Sigma,\ i > 1)$,

$InArticle[i](y_1)\ \xrightarrow{\texttt{</}\sigma\texttt{>}}\ InArticle[i-1](y_1)$ $(\sigma \in \Sigma,\ i > 1)$,

$InArticle[i](y_1)\ \xrightarrow{\chi}\ \varepsilon$ $((\chi, i) \in \Sigma_\epsilon)\ \}$.

(b)

Fig. 2. Stream processing induced by $\mathcal{SP}(M_{rev})$ and $\mathcal{SP}(M_{htm})$

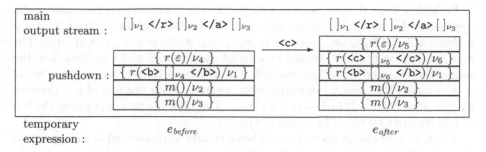

Fig. 3. Pushdown representation for temporary expressions and its updating

(representing $r[2](<\sigma> \ldots </\sigma>)$ in e_{after}). Now that ν_4 is expanded, all occurrences of $[\,]_{\nu_4}$ in the pushdown should be filled with $[\,]_{\nu_6}$. Since two items are pushed, all other sets in the pushdown descend for one level. This corresponds to updating all states $q[i]$ $(i > 1)$ to $q[i + 1]$ at the same time.

4.2   Pushdown Representation and Its Updating

Let $M = (Q, \Sigma, \Delta, in, R)$ be an mft. An *output stream* s for M is defined by

$$m ::= \varepsilon \mid <\delta> m \mid </\delta> m \mid [\,]_\nu \, m,$$

where $\delta \in \Delta$, and $[\,]_\nu$ is a hole whose physical address is ν. We denote the set of output streams by $\mathcal{S}_M$. A *state frame* has the form $q(m_1, \ldots, m_n)/\nu$ where ν is a hole address, $q \in Q$, $n = rank(q)$, and $m_i \in \mathcal{S}_M$ $(i = 1, \ldots, n)$.

A *pushdown* is a mapping from a positive number, representing the depth, to a set of state frames. Furthermore, each hole address ν occurs on the right-hand side of $/$ in a pushdown at most once. The empty pushdown is denoted by $\emptyset$. Given a set of state frames Ψ, we denote by $\{1 \mapsto \Psi, \ldots\}$ a pushdown p such that $p(1) = \Psi$. Two pushdowns p_1 and p_2 can be merged by $p_1 \oplus p_2 = \{d \mapsto p_1(d) \uplus p_2(d)\}_{d \in \mathbb{N}^+}$.[2]

Definition 9. Let $M = (Q, \Sigma, \Delta, in, R)$ be an mft. A *pushdown representation* $pd(e)$ for $e \in Tmp_{\mathcal{SP}(M)}$ is a pair $\langle m, p \rangle$ of a *main output stream* m and a *pushdown* p defined by

$$pd(\varepsilon) = \langle \varepsilon, \emptyset \rangle, \qquad pd(<\delta> e) = \langle <\delta> m, p \rangle, \qquad pd(</\delta> e) = \langle </\delta> m, p \rangle,$$
$$pd(q[i](e_1, \ldots, e_n)\, e) = \langle [\,]_\nu \, m, \{i \mapsto \{q(m_1, \ldots, m_n)/\nu\}\} \oplus p_1 \oplus \cdots \oplus p_n \oplus p \rangle,$$

where $\langle m, p \rangle = pd(e)$, $\langle m_i, p_i \rangle = pd(e_i)$ and ν is a fresh address. Denote the set of pushdown representations for temporary expressions in $Tmp_{\mathcal{SP}(M)}$ by Pdr_M.

From a pushdown representation, we can recover the temporary expression by filling every hole according to the corresponding state frame in the pushdown.

---

[2] For any $d \in \mathbb{N}^+$, $p_1(d)$ and $p_2(d)$ are disjoint because hole addresses are unique.

We define several operations to manipulate the pushdown representation. An *application* for a hole $[\ ]_\nu$ in an output stream m with another output stream u is denoted by $m@_\nu u$, i.e., when $m = m_1[\ ]_\nu m_2$, we have $m@_\nu u = m_1 u m_2$. The hole application can be extended to a set of state frames and a pushdown in the same way, denoted by $\Psi@_\nu u$ and $p@_\nu u$. Let p be a pushdown and Ψ a set of state frames. The pushdown obtained by pushing Ψ on the top of p is denoted by $p \ll \Psi = \{1 \mapsto \Psi\} \cup \{d \mapsto p(d-1)\}_{d>1}$. The dual operation popping the top of p is denoted by $\rhd p = \{d \mapsto p(d+1)\}_{d \in \mathbb{N}^+}$.

The hole application operation can be efficiently implemented in the sense that the execution time is independent of the size of main output streams and pushdowns. Experimental implementation introduced in Section 5 uses doubly-linked cyclic lists to represent output streams, so we can implement hole application, concatenation and squeeze efficiently.

4.3   Pushdown Machines for Macro Forest Transducers

For a given mft M, we introduce a pushdown machine in stream processing style which simulates the behavior of the xsp $\mathcal{SP}(M)$. Since the semantics of an xsp is specified by a transition $\langle\!\langle \_\_\,, \_\_ \rangle\!\rangle$ on temporary expressions, we construct the pushdown machine as a transition on pushdown representations. In the following definition, the function pd° extends pd by one extra case, $pd^\circ(y_i) = y_i$ for $i \in \mathbb{N}^+$. Therefore pd° can be applied to the right-hand side of rules in an xsp.

Definition 10. Let $M = (Q, \Sigma, \Delta, in, R)$ be an mft. The *pushdown machine for M*, denoted by $\mathcal{PD}(M)$, is a function $\langle\!\langle \_\_\,, \_\_ \rangle\!\rangle : Pdr_M \times \Sigma_{<>\$} \to Pdr_M$. For a pushdown representation $\langle m, p \rangle \in Pdr_M$ and input event $\chi \in \Sigma_{<>\$}$, a new pushdown representation $\langle\!\langle \langle m, p \rangle, \chi \rangle\!\rangle$ is given as follows:

- $\langle\!\langle \langle m, p \rangle, \texttt{<}\sigma\texttt{>} \rangle\!\rangle = \Phi_\sigma(m, (\rhd p) \ll \emptyset \ll \emptyset, p(1))$, where function Φ_σ is defined by

$$\Phi_\sigma(m, p, \emptyset) = \langle m, p \rangle$$
$$\Phi_\sigma(m, p, \{q(m_1, \ldots, m_n)/\nu\} \uplus \Psi) = \Phi_\sigma(m@_\nu m', p@_\nu m' \oplus p', \Psi@_\nu m')$$

  with $\langle m', p' \rangle = pd^\circ(\mathcal{A}(rhs^{q,\sigma}))[y_j := m_j]_{j=1,\ldots,n}$.
- $\langle\!\langle \langle m, p \rangle, \texttt{</}\sigma\texttt{>} \rangle\!\rangle = \Phi_\epsilon(m, \rhd p, p(1))$, where the function Φ_ϵ is defined by

$$\Phi_\epsilon(m, p, \emptyset) = \langle m, p \rangle$$
$$\Phi_\epsilon(m, p, \{q(m_1, \ldots, m_n)/\nu\} \uplus \Psi) = \Phi_\epsilon(m@_\nu m', p@_\nu m' \oplus p', \Psi@_\nu m')$$

  with $\langle m', p' \rangle = pd^\circ(\mathcal{A}(rhs^{q,\epsilon}))[y_j := m_j]_{j=1,\ldots,n}$.
- $\langle\!\langle \langle m, p \rangle, \$ \rangle\!\rangle = \Phi_\epsilon(m, \emptyset, \bigcup_{d \in \mathbb{N}^+} p(d))$, where Φ_ϵ is as in the case $\chi = \texttt{</}\sigma\texttt{>}$.

For an mft $M = (Q, \Sigma, \Delta, in, R)$, the initial pushdown representation of $\mathcal{PD}(M)$ is $\langle [\ ]_{\nu_0}, \{1 \mapsto \{in(\varepsilon, \ldots, \varepsilon)/\nu_0\}\} \rangle$ with address ν_0. It corresponds to the initial state of an xsp $\mathcal{SP}(M)$, that is, $in[1](\varepsilon, \ldots, \varepsilon)$. For a pushdown machine $P = \mathcal{PD}(M)$, the transformation $\tau_P : \Sigma_{<>}^\circ \to \Delta_{<>}^\circ$ induced by P a defined in a way similar to $\tau_{\mathcal{SP}(M)}$, that is, $\tau_P(s) = \zeta_P(\langle [\ ]_{\nu_0}, \{1 \mapsto \{in(\varepsilon, \ldots, \varepsilon)/\nu_0\}\} \rangle, s\$)$, where $\zeta_P(\langle m, p \rangle, \varepsilon) = m$ and $\zeta_P(\langle m, p \rangle, \chi s) = \zeta_P(\langle\!\langle \langle m, p \rangle, \chi \rangle\!\rangle, s)$ for a pushdown representation $\langle m, p \rangle$.

For an mft M, the behaviour of $\mathcal{PD}(M)$ on pushdown representations mirrors that of $\mathcal{SP}(M)$ on temporary expressions. Consider the case when a start tag `<σ>` is read. In the xsp $\mathcal{SP}(M)$, every state $q[i]$ $(i > 1)$ is rewritten into $q[i+1]$. In the pushdown machine $\mathcal{PD}(M)$, the corresponding state frame $q(\dots)/\nu$ in the i-th set of the pushdown descends by one level because we perform one pop and two pushes on the pushdown. In $\mathcal{SP}(M)$, every state $q[1]$ is rewritten by $\mathcal{A}(rhs^{q,\sigma})$. In the pushdown machine $\mathcal{PD}(M)$, for each corresponding state frame $q(\dots)/\nu$ in the top set of the pushdown, the hole $[\ ]_\nu$ is filled according to $\mathcal{A}(rhs^{q,\sigma})$. Since a computation of $pd^\circ(\mathcal{A}(rhs^{q,\sigma}))$ is invoked, the state $q[1]$ in $\mathcal{A}(rhs^{q,\sigma})$ is put as an element of the top set of the pushdown and $q[2]$ in $\mathcal{A}(rhs^{q,\sigma})$ is put as an element of the second set from the top.

Consider the case when an end tag `</σ>` is read. In the xsp $\mathcal{SP}(M)$, every state $q[i]$ $(i > 1)$ is rewritten to $q[i-1]$. The corresponding state frame $q(\dots)/\nu$ in the i-th set of the pushdown ascends by one level after popping. In the xsp $\mathcal{SP}(M)$, every state $q[1]$ is replaced according to $\mathcal{A}(rhs^{q,\epsilon})$. In the pushdown machine $\mathcal{PD}(M)$, for the corresponding state frame $q(\dots)/\nu$ in the top set of the pushdown, the hole $[\ ]_\nu$ is filled according to $\mathcal{A}(rhs^{q,\epsilon})$.

After reading \$, the pushdown must be empty since $\mathcal{A}(rhs^{q,\epsilon})$ contains no pattern $q[i](\dots)$ and all state frames in the previous pushdown is consumed by $\Phi_\epsilon(s, \emptyset, \bigcup_{d \in \mathbb{N}^+} p(d))$. Therefore the final output stream has no holes.

Since every transition on pushdown representations corresponds to a transition on temporary expressions, we can see that $\tau_{\mathcal{PD}(M)}(s) = \tau_{\mathcal{SP}(M)}(s)$ for every mft M and every input stream s. From THEOREM 1, we have $\tau_{\mathcal{PD}(M)}(\lfloor f \rfloor) = \lfloor \tau_M(f) \rfloor$ for every input forest f for M, which shows the equivalence of the original mft and the derived pushdown machine.

The above definition of τ_P for a pushdown machine P can be made more efficient by *squeezing*, that is, printing out the prefix, up to the first hole, of the main output stream. We define the following function sqz for output streams:

$$sqz(\varepsilon) = (\varepsilon, \varepsilon), \qquad\qquad\qquad sqz([\ ]_\nu\ m) = (\varepsilon, [\ ]_\nu\ m),$$
$$sqz(<\delta>\ m) = (<\delta>\ m', m''), \qquad sqz(</\delta>\ m) = (</\delta>\ m', m''),$$

where $(m', m'') = sqz(m)$. We can then redefine ζ_P with sqz as follows:

$$\zeta_P(\langle m, p \rangle, \varepsilon) = m,$$
$$\zeta_P(\langle m, p \rangle, \chi s) = m'\ \zeta_P(\langle\langle m'', p \rangle, \chi \rangle, s) \text{ where } (m', m'') = sqz(\langle\langle m, p \rangle, \chi \rangle).$$

Some variables do not occur in the right-hand side. For example, consider a rule $q(pat, y_1) \to \epsilon$ and the corresponding xsp rule $q[1](y_1) \xrightarrow{\chi} \varepsilon$. When the top set of the pushdown contains $q(m_1)/\nu$, the occurrence of $[\ ]_\nu$ will be filled with ε. To avoid ineffective updating, all hole addresses contained in m_1 should be discarded if the hole does not occur in other positions. Some variables may occur more than once. For example, consider the rule $q(pat, y_1) \to y_1\ y_1$. and the corresponding xsp rule $q[1](y_1) \xrightarrow{\chi} y_1\ y_1$. If we use doubly-linked cyclic lists to represent main output streams, a hole $[\ ]_\nu$ may occur twice. When the hole $[\ ]_\nu$ is required to be filled, we cannot replace both occurrence of ν with the same doubly-linked list. Therefore, we mark the state frame to remember that it appears twice.

Table 1. Benchmarking results

input size	1MB	4MB	16MB	64MB	256MB
pushdown xsp	0.49sec / 1.10MB	1.19sec / 1.10MB	3.85sec / 1.10MB	15.2sec / 1.10MB	84.6sec / 1.10MB
direct impl. mft	0.52sec / 4.87MB	1.39sec / 16.7MB	4.92sec / 62.1MB	20.2sec / 250MB	588sec / 415MB
xsltproc	0.79sec / 8.73MB	3.51sec / 33.2MB	19.4sec / 129MB	162sec / 462MB	n/a
saxon	3.12sec / 24.5MB	5.40sec / 36.5MB	13.1sec / 94.4MB	43.7sec / 289MB	n/a

(execution time / max. memory usage)

(a) For transformation M_{rev}

input size	4MB	64MB
pushdown xsp	1.26sec / 3.93MB	17.1sec / 49.8MB
direct impl. mft	1.25sec / 15.9MB	17.7sec / 233MB

(execution time / max. memory usage)

(b) For transformation M_{htm}

input size	4MB	64MB
pushdown xsp	1.60sec / 11.6MB	24.8sec / 170MB
direct impl. mft	1.40sec / 16.6MB	20.4sec / 249MB

(execution time / max. memory usage)

(c) For transformation M_{frev}

5   Benchmarking Results

We use the random sample generator XMark [33] to produce sample XML documents of sizes 1MB, 4MB, 16MB, 64MB and 256MB. A document contains a sequence of `item` nodes, each having a list of children about a dozen lines long.

The first task is to reverse the order of subtrees under `item`. The pushdown machine automatically derived from the mft M_{rev}, shown as the entry **pushdown xsp** in Table 1, is implemented in Objective Caml, with extensions to handle text nodes. The entry **direct impl. mft** is the program in Figure 1 implemented as mutual recursive functions in Objective Caml. The entry **xsltproc** is one of the fastest XSLT processors bundled with `libxslt` [31] 1.1.11, written in C, while **saxon** [13] 8.7.3 is one of the fastest XSLT processors in Java. All entries apart from **pushdown xsp** build the entire forest in memory before the transformation. The experiments were conducted on a 1.33 GHz PowerBook G4 with 768 MB of memory. Table 1(a) compares the total execution time and maximum memory size in seconds and megabytes.

As we expected, **pushdown xsp** uses the smallest heap. That it also outperforms the two XSLT processors may be due to the overhead of the latter maintaining full-fledged XML data, including e.g., namespace URI, number of children. For a fairer comparison, we added the entry **direct impl. mft**. The entry **pushdown xsp** is slightly faster than **direct impl. mft** because it incurs less garbage collection, and saves the overhead of building the trees. We expect that xsp will also deliver competitive speed even after scaling to full XML.

For other transformations, we compared only **pushdown xsp** and **direct impl. mft** for random inputs of 4MB and 64MB. Table 1(b) shows the results for transformation M_{htm} in EXAMPLE 2. This result also indicates a small heap residency of **pushdown xsp** with elapsed time similar to **direct impl. mft**. Table 1(c) shows results for full reversal M_{frev}, which will be discussed later.

6   Discussion

Comparison with Lazy Evaluation. Many of our readers wondered: "Can we not just use lazy evaluation?" Consider the program *unparse* (*trans* (*parse input*)) in a non-strict language, where the function *parse* builds the tree lazily upon the demand of the forest-to-forest transformation *trans*. When the program is run by a lazy evaluator, do we get the desired space behaviour? We run a number of experiments in Haskell. The parser in Section 3.2 shares the input stream s and causes a space leak. Instead we use a definition of *parse* that returns a pair of the tree and the unprocessed tail of the stream, such that the input stream can be freed after being used. However, its space behaviour is compiler-dependent, due to a space leak of when returning pairs, addressed by Wadler [29]. The fix he proposed is actually implemented in both NHC98 [23] and GHC [7], but is fragile in presence of other valuable optimisations of GHC [12].

EXAMPLE 2 shows a problem more intrinsic to the nature of lazy evaluation. The list of keywords appears very late and remain unevaluated until it is finally output. This is in fact what we expect of lazy evaluation. However, the thunk contains a reference to the beginning of the input stream, which means that the entire input stream will reside in memory. Put it in a wider context, we recall Wadler's claim [29] that we need a parallel evaluator to avoid certain classes of space leaks. Our xsp implementation, which evaluates all the states $q[1]$ indexed 1, can actually be seen as a parallel evaluator specialised for XML processing.

Streaming for Existing XML Transformation Languages. It has been shown how to convert XPath expressions into attributed tree transducers [21], which is weaker than mfts. Can we convert functions defined in languages such as XSLT [34], *fxt* [3], XDuce [11], or CDuce [2], into mft's?

TL [17] is like mft, but supports pattern matching by *monadic second-order logic* (MSO) formulae. Each TL rule has the form $q(\phi, y_1, \ldots, y_n) \rightarrow rhs$, where ϕ is an MSO formula. When q is called, the nodes satisfying ϕ is passed as it argument. Maneth et al. showed that most practical TL programs use only MSO formulae that does not select ancestor nodes, and such programs can be represented by a deterministic mft. It implies that XSLT programs using only forward XPath expressions can be expressed as mft's.

XDuce and CDuce support regular expression pattern [10]. The following *tail-capturing* XDuce program can be captured by an mft:

```
fun mkTelList (val e as (Name,Addr,Tel?)*) =
    match o with name[val n], addr[val a], tel[val t], val rest
               -> name[n], tel[t], mkTelList (rest)
             | name[val n], addr[val a], val rest -> mkTelList (rest)
             | () -> ()
```

$$MkTelList(\text{name}\langle x_1 \rangle x_2) \qquad Name(\text{addr}\langle x_1 \rangle x_2, y_1) \rightarrow NameAddr(x_2, y_1)$$
$$\rightarrow Name(x_2, \text{name}\langle Val(x_1) \rangle) \qquad NameAddr(\text{tel}\langle x_1 \rangle x_2, y_1) \rightarrow y_1 \text{ tel}\langle Val(x_1) \rangle\ MkTelList(x_2)$$
$$MkTelList(\epsilon) \rightarrow \epsilon \qquad NameAddr(\text{name}\langle x_1 \rangle x_2, y_1) \rightarrow Name(x_2, \text{name}\langle Val(x_1) \rangle)$$
$$NameAddr(\epsilon, y_1) \rightarrow y_1$$

Here we extend mft's to handle text data, and *Val* is the identity function for text. This mft is total if inputs are restricted to the type `(Name,Addr,Tel?)*` specified by the original XDuce program. Hosoya and Pierce [10] talked about how to convert non-tail-capturing patterns into tail-capturing equivalents. It will be among our future work to see how this approach works in general.

The mft can be extended to handle other datatypes. For example, we can extend the right-hand side with booleans, boolean operators, and conditional branches: $rhs ::= \ldots \mid true \mid false \mid if(rhs, rhs, rhs)$, and correspondingly extend the xsp with some extra rules [21]: $if(true, e_1, e_2) \rightarrow e_1$ and $if(false, e_1, e_2) \rightarrow e_2$. Some extra care is needed to ensure that if is always in the top set of a pushdown. With booleans and conditionals we can express transformations including the invite/visit iteration with XPath expressions in XTiSP [19].

Limitation. The goal of xsp is to ensure that the input stream does not reside in memory. On the other hand, the space occupied by temporary result of the computation is a separate issue related to the nature of the computation performed. Certain transformations are *inherently memory inefficient* [25]. For example, if we replace the two rules of M_{rev} for $\mathtt{r}\langle x_1 \rangle x_2$ and $\sigma\langle x_1 \rangle x_2$ with a single rule: $Main(\sigma\langle x_1 \rangle x_2) \rightarrow Rev(x_2, \sigma\langle Rev(x_1, \epsilon) \rangle)$, the mft (call it M_{frev}) reverses the subtrees for all nodes. The derived xsp still efficiently consumes the input stream, but the temporary expression grows linearly. Every SAX-like stream processing program has the same problem. As a trial experiment, Table 1(c) compares M_{frev} and a program **direct impl. mft** which simply loads the tree and performs the full reverse. The result shows that our implementation does not carry too much overhead even for this inherently inefficient transformation.

Memory used by the xsp's in this paper are all minimum for the desired computation, which is not true in general and remains a future work to analyse.

7   Conclusion and Related Work

We have presented a method to automatically derive an XML stream processor from a program expressed as a macro forest transducer. The XML stream processor has an efficient implementation based on a pushdown machine. The framework presented in this paper will be the core of the next release of XTiSP [19]. We believe that the mft is expressive enough that we can transform most practical programs written in existing XML processing languages [11,2,34] to mft, in order to streamlise them.

Most of the work devoted to automatic derivation of XML stream processors from declarative programs focus on query languages, such as XPath [1,5,8,9] and a subset of XQuery [16]. They are not expressive enough to describe some useful transformation such as the structure-preserving transformation renaming all the labels a to b. The key idea of our framework was presented in the first author's previous work [21,25], based on the composition of (stack-)attributed tree transducers (att) [20]. All programs definable in the XML transformation language XTiSP [21,19] can be translated into att's, which are less expressive than mft's [6,26]. Our result in this paper is therefore stronger. The formalisation here helps to produce the next version of XTiSP that is both correct and efficient.

Kodama, Suenaga, Kobayashi and Yonezawa [15] studied *ordered-linear typed* programs and how to buffer the input and process the buffered tree. In a subsequent paper [28], they tried to derive stream processors by automatically detecting which input should be buffered. The restrictions imposed by ordered linear type may not always be preferred for stream processing. In EXAMPLE 2, where one argument is shared by two functional calls, our stream processor still consumes the input as its tokens are read. An ordered linear typeable alternative would keep a copy of the input in memory until it is pattern-matched.

Kiselyov [14] proposed defining XML transformation using a function `foldts` over rose trees. and actions `fup`, `fdown` and `fhere`. This programming style is not flexible enough and many function closures are created. STX [4] is a template-based XML transformation language that operates on stream of SAX [32] events. While the programmers can define XML transformation as well as XSLT [34], they have to explicitly manipulate the environment. TransformX by Scherzinger and Kemper [27] provides a framework for syntax-directed transformations of XML streams, using attribute grammar on the type schema for inputs. However, we must still keep in mind which information should be buffered before and after reading each subtree in the input.

Acknowledgment. The authors wish to express their gratitude to Zhenjiang Hu and Giuseppe Castagna for their comments and advice on earlier drafts.

References

1. M. Altinel and M. J. Franklin. Efficient filtering of XML documents for selective dissemination of information. *International Journal on Very Large Data Bases*, pages 53–64, 2000.
2. V. Benzaken, G. Castagna, and A. Frisch. CDuce: an XML-centric general-purpose language. In *Proceedings of the 8th International Conference of Functional Programming*, pages 51–63, 2003.
3. A. Berlea and H. Seidl. fxt – a transformation language for XML documents. *Journal of Computing and Information Technology*, 10(1):19–35, 2002.
4. P. Cimprich, O. Becker, C. Nentwich, M. K. H. Jiroušek, P. Brown, M. Batsis, T. Kaiser, P. Hlavnička, N. Matsakis, C. Dolph, and N. Wiechmann. Streaming transformations for XML (STX) version 1.0. http://stx.sourceforge.net/.
5. Y. Diao and M. J. Franklin. High-performance XML filtering: An overview of YFilter. In *IEEE Data Engineering Bulletin*, volume 26(1), pages 41–48, 2003.
6. J. Engelfriet and H. Vogler. Macro tree transducers. *Journal of Computer and System Sciences*, 31(1):71–146, 1985.
7. The Glasgow Haskell Compiler. http://www.haskell.org/ghc/.
8. T. J. Green, A. Gupta, G. Miklau, M. Onizuka, and D. Suciu. Processing XML streams with deterministic automata and stream indexes. *ACM Transactions on Database Systems*, 29(4):752–788, 2004.
9. A. K. Gupta and D. Suciu. Stream processing of XPath queries with predicates. In *Proceedings of the 2003 ACM SIGMOD International Conference on Management of Data*, pages 419–430, 2003.
10. H. Hosoya and B. C. Pierce. Regular expression pattern matching for XML. *Journal of Functional Programming*, 13(6):961–1004, Novermber 2003.
11. H. Hosoya and B. C. Pierce. XDuce: A statically typed XML processing language. *ACM Transactions on Internet Technology*, 3(2):117–148, 2003.
12. S. P. Jones. Space usage. Glasgow Haskell Users Mailing List, http://www.haskell.org/pipermail/glasgow-haskell-users/2004-August/007023.html, 17th August 2004.

13. M. Kay. SAXON: The XSLT and XQuery processor. http://saxon.sourceforge.net/.
14. O. Kiselyov. A better XML parser through functional programming. In *4th International Symposium on Practical Aspects of Declarative Languages*, volume 2257 of *Lecture Notes in Computer Science*, pages 209–224, 2002.
15. K. Kodama, K. Suenaga, N. Kobayashi, and A. Yonezawa. Translation of tree-processing programs into stream-processing programs based on ordered linear type. In *The 2nd ASIAN Symposium on Programming Languages and Systems*, volume 3302 of *Lecture Notes in Computer Science*, pages 41–56, 2004.
16. B. Ludäscher, P. Mukhopadhyay, and Y. Papakonstantinou. A transducer-based XML query processor. In *Proceedings of 28th International Conference on Very Large Data Bases*, pages 227–238, 2002.
17. S. Maneth, A. Berlea, T. Perst, and H. Seidl. XML type checking with macro tree transducers. In *Proceedings of 24th ACM SIGMOD-SIGACT-SIGART Symposium on Principles of Database Systems*, pages 283–294, 2005.
18. M. Murata. Extended path expressions of XML. In *Proceedings of the 20th ACM Symp. on Principles of Database Systems*, pages 153–166, 2001.
19. K. Nakano. XTiSP: XML transformation language intended for stream processing. http://xtisp.org/.
20. K. Nakano. Composing stack-attributed transducers. Technical Report METR-2004-01, Department of Mathematical Informatics, University of Tokyo, 2004.
21. K. Nakano. An implementation scheme for XML transformation lauguages through derivation of stream processors. In *The 2nd ASIAN Symposium on Programming Languages and Systems*, volume 3302 of *Lecture Notes in Computer Science*, pages 74–90, 2004.
22. K. Nakano and S.-C. Mu. A pushdown machine for recursive XML processing (full version). http://www.ipl.t.u-tokyo.ac.jp/~ksk/en/?Publication.
23. The nhc98 compiler. http://www.haskell.org/nhc98/.
24. S. Nishimura. Fusion with stacks and accumulating prameters. In *the 2004 ACM SIGPLAN Workshop on Partial Evaluation and Semantics-based Program Manipulation*, pages 101–112, 2004.
25. S. Nishimura and K. Nakano. XML stream transformer generation through program composition and dependency analysis. *Science of Computer Programming*, 54:257–290, 2005.
26. T. Perst and H. Seidl. Macro forest transducers. *Information Processing Letters*, 89:141–149, 2004.
27. S. Scherzinger and A. Kemper. Syntax-directed transformations of XML streams. In *Workshop on Programming Language Technologies for XML*, pages 75–86, 2005.
28. K. Suenaga, N. Kobayashi, and A. Yonezawa. Extension of type-based approach to generation of stream processing programs by automatic insertion of buffering primitives. In *International workshop on Logic-based Program Synthesis and Transformation*, 2005. To appear.
29. P. Wadler. Fixing a space leak with a garbage collector. *Software Practice and Experience*, 17(9):595–608, September 1987.
30. P. Wadler. Deforestation: Transforming programs to eliminate trees. In *Proceedings of the European Symposium on Programming*, volume 300 of *Lecture Notes in Computer Science*, pages 344–358, 1988.
31. libxslt: the XSLT C library for Gnome. http://xmlsoft.org/XSLT/.
32. SAX: the simple API for XML. http://www.saxproject.org/.
33. XMark: an XML benchmark project. http://www.xml-benchmark.org/.
34. XSL transformations (XSLT). http://www.w3c.org/TR/xslt/.

XML Validation for Context-Free Grammars

Yasuhiko Minamide[1] and Akihiko Tozawa[2]

[1] Department of Computer Science
University of Tsukuba
[2] IBM Research,
Tokyo Research Laboratory, IBM Japan, ltd.

Abstract. String expression analysis conservatively approximates the possible string values generated by a program. We consider the validation of a context-free grammar obtained by the analysis against XML schemas and develop two algorithms for deciding inclusion $L(G_1) \subseteq L(G_2)$ where G_1 is a context-free grammar and G_2 is either an XML-grammar or a regular hedge grammar. The algorithms for XML-grammars and regular hedge grammars have exponential and doubly exponential time complexity, respectively. We have incorporated the algorithms into the PHP string analyzer and validated several publicly available PHP programs against the XHTML DTD. The experiments show that both of the algorithms are efficient in practice although they have exponential complexity.

1 Introduction

String expression analysis conservatively approximates the possible string values generated by a program [CMS03b]. Minamide adopted context-free grammars as a foundation of string expression analysis and developed a string analyzer for PHP [Min05]. We consider the validation of a context-free grammar obtained by the analysis against XML schemas and develop two algorithms for deciding inclusion $L(G_1) \subseteq L(G_2)$ where G_1 is a context-free grammar and G_2 is either an XML-grammar or a regular hedge grammar, which are subclasses of context-free grammars theoretically corresponding to XML schema languages such as Document Type Definition (DTD) and RELAX NG [CM01].

To simplify the discussion on XML validation, we consider languages over a paired alphabet. Context-free languages with parentheses or paired alphabets were studied extensively in the 1960s and 1970s [McN67, Knu67, Tak75]. Let A be a base alphabet. Then, we introduce a paired alphabet consisting of two sets $\acute{A}$ and $\grave{A}$:

$$\acute{A} = \{\, \acute{a} \mid a \in A \,\} \qquad \grave{A} = \{\, \grave{a} \mid a \in A \,\}$$

where $\acute{A}$ and $\grave{A}$ correspond to the set of start tags and the set of end tags, respectively. We consider that $\acute{a}$ and $\grave{a}$ match. We write Σ for $\acute{A} \cup \grave{A}$. This notation is based on Takahashi's work on context-free grammars [Tak75].

The fundamental notion on a string over a paired alphabet is whether it is balanced. For example, $\acute{a}\grave{b}\grave{b}\acute{c}\grave{c}\grave{a}$ and $\acute{a}\grave{a}\grave{b}\grave{b}$ are balanced, but $\acute{a}\grave{b}$ and $\acute{a}\grave{b}\grave{b}$ are not.

N. Kobayashi (Ed.): APLAS 2006, LNCS 4279, pp. 357–373, 2006.

This notion of balanced strings corresponds to well-formed documents in XML. We call the set of all balanced strings $B(\Sigma)$ the Dyck set over Σ.

As a balanced subclass of context-free languages, Berstel and Boasson proposed XML-grammars modeling DTDs and studied their formal properties [BB02]. An XML-grammar consists of a set of terminals $\Sigma = \acute{A} \cup \grave{A}$, a set of nonterminals V in one-to-one correspondence with base alphabet A, a start nonterminal S, and a set of productions. For each $a \in A$, there must be a unique production of the following form:

$$X_a \rightarrow \acute{a} R_a \grave{a}$$

where X_a is the nonterminal corresponding to a and R_a is a regular expression over V.

Example 1. Consider the following DTD, taken from [BB02].

```
<!DOCTYPE a [
  <!ELEMENT a ((a|b),(a|b)) >
  <!ELEMENT b (b)* >
]>
```

This DTD can be represented by an XML-grammar with the following productions:

$$X_a \rightarrow \acute{a}(X_a|X_b)(X_a|X_b)\grave{a}$$
$$X_b \rightarrow \acute{b}X_b^*\grave{b}$$

where X_a and X_b are the nonterminals corresponding to a and b, respectively, and X_a is the start symbol.

In this formal setting, validating a context-free grammar against a DTD corresponds to checking $L(G) \subseteq L(G_{\mathsf{xml}})$ for a context-free grammar G and an XML-grammar G_{xml}. To develop an algorithm checking this inclusion, we exploit locality in DTDs and XML-grammars. They have locality in the sense that they can only describe a relation between an element and its children as can be seen in the definition of XML-grammars. The algorithm has exponential time complexity and is presented in Section 4.

There is a larger class of grammars called *regular hedge grammars* corresponding to regular tree languages over unranked alphabets [Mur99]. The class of regular hedge grammars can be formulated as an extension of XML-grammars where each production has the following form:

$$X \rightarrow R$$

where R is an arbitrary regular expression over $\acute{a}Y\grave{a}$. Also there is an alternative formulation of regular hedge grammars. We obtain grammars of the same expressiveness by restricting each production to one of the following forms:

$$X \rightarrow \acute{a}Y\grave{a}Z \quad \text{or} \quad X \rightarrow \epsilon.$$

Example 2. The following is a regular hedge grammar where I is the start symbol.

$$I \to X \quad X \to (\acute{a}Y\grave{a})^*(\acute{a}X\grave{a})(\acute{a}Y\grave{a})^* \quad X \to (\acute{a}Y\grave{a})^*(\acute{b}Y\grave{b})(\acute{a}Y\grave{a})^* \quad Y \to (\acute{a}Y\grave{a})^*$$

The same language is obtained by the following productions.

$$I \to X \qquad X \to \acute{a}X\grave{a}Y \qquad X \to \acute{a}Y\grave{a}X \qquad X \to \acute{b}Y\grave{b}Y$$
$$Y \to \acute{a}Y\grave{a}Y \qquad Y \to \epsilon$$

The grammar generates the set of balanced strings over $\{\,\acute{a}, \grave{a}, \acute{b}, \grave{b}\,\}$ containing one pair of $\acute{b}$ and $\grave{b}$.

There is a regular hedge grammar that cannot be represented as an XML-grammar. The example above is indeed such a regular hedge grammar. Inversely, an XML-grammar can always be considered as a regular hedge grammar. We describe an XML validation algorithm of a context-free grammar against a regular hedge grammar in Section 3. This makes it possible to validate a context-free grammar against XML schemas such as RELAX NG which is more expressive than DTD. This validation algorithm has doubly exponential time complexity.

We introduce two new algorithms for deciding inclusion $L(G_1) \subseteq L(G_2)$ for G_1 a context-free grammar and G_2 either an XML-grammar or a regular hedge grammar. However, they do not extend known results on subclasses of context-free grammars for G_2, for which the above inclusion problem is decidable. Greibach and Friedman considered the inclusion problem for a subclass of deterministic pushdown automata called superdeterministic PDA [GF80]. They showed that it is decidable whether $L(M_1) \subseteq L(M_2)$ for M_1 an arbitrary nondeterministic PDA and M_2 a superdeterministic PDA. The complexity of their algorithm is doubly exponential in the size of the machines. It was also shown that generalized parenthesis languages studied by Takahashi [Tak75] are superdeterministic: a generalized parenthesis grammar is translated into a superdeterministic PDA, which is exponential in its size. Since regular hedge grammars are a subclass of generalized parenthesis grammars, their result is more general than ours and we can apply their algorithm to validation of a context-free grammar against a regular hedge grammar. However, if we naively estimate the complexity of the validation through a superdeterministic PDA, the complexity is triply exponential. This is one order of exponential worse than our validation algorithm.

Hereafter in this paper, we assume that a context-free grammar (CFG) is reduced. This means that every nonterminal is accessible from the start symbol and every nonterminal produces at least one terminal string.

This paper is organized as follows. In Section 2, we describe the algorithm of Berstel and Boasson, which decides whether or not every word of a context-free grammar is balanced. This is the basis of both of our algorithms. In Sections 3 and 4, we introduce our validation algorithms for regular hedge grammars and XML-grammars, respectively. In Section 5, we describe the implementation of the algorithms as backend validators of the PHP string analyzer and show our experimental results. Finally, we review related work and present some conclusions.

2   Checking Balancedness

One of the most fundamental notions of strings over a paired-alphabet is their balancedness. Knuth [Knu67] developed an algorithm to decide whether the language of a context-free grammar is balanced for a language with a single pair of parentheses. Berstel and Boasson [BB02] extended this for a language over a paired alphabet.

Proposition 1. *Given a context-free grammar G over a paired alphabet, it is decidable whether or not its language is balanced.*

This balancedness check is the basis of validation algorithms because a grammar G is valid against some XML or regular hedge grammar only if G is balanced. However, the original algorithm by Berstel and Boasson for this balancedness check was not efficient as it could be, so that we here give an improved version of their algorithm.

Berstel and Boasson started from the following observation. We say a string ϕ is *partially balanced* if it is a factor, i.e., substring, of some balanced string. If ϕ is partially balanced, we have $a = b$ whenever $\acute{a}\psi\grave{b}$ occurs in ϕ with ψ balanced. As a result, each such ϕ is always uniquely factorized into the following form with all ϕ_i balanced.

$$\phi = \phi_1\grave{a}_1\phi_2\grave{a}_2\phi_3 \cdots \grave{a}_n\phi_{n+1}\acute{a}_{n+1} \cdots \phi_m\acute{a}_m\phi_{m+1}$$

Let us define a partial function $\rho : \Sigma^* \rightharpoonup \grave{A}^*\acute{A}^*$ by

$$\rho(\phi) = \begin{cases} \grave{a}_1\grave{a}_2 \cdots \grave{a}_n\acute{a}_{n+1} \cdots \acute{a}_m & \phi \text{ is partially balanced} \\ \text{undefined} & \text{otherwise} \end{cases}$$

Observe that (1) ϕ is balanced iff $\rho(\phi) = \epsilon$, and (2) $\rho(\phi\psi) = \rho(\rho(\phi)\rho(\psi))$ if ϕ and ψ are partially balanced. This means that to determine whether all strings generated from a context-free grammar G are balanced, it is sufficient to check G under interpretation by ρ.

Example 3. Consider the following grammar.

$$I \to \acute{a}\acute{a}X\grave{a}\grave{a} \qquad X \to \grave{a}\grave{a}\acute{a}\acute{a} \qquad X \to \acute{a}X\grave{a}$$

The language of this grammar is balanced. A set of strings generated from X is $\{\acute{a}^k\grave{a}\grave{a}\acute{a}\acute{a}\grave{a}^k \mid k \geq 0\}$ whose interpretation by ρ is a finite set $\{\grave{a}\grave{a}\acute{a}\acute{a}, \grave{a}\acute{a}, \epsilon\}$. We can easily see that for each string ϕ in this set $\rho(\acute{a}\acute{a}\phi\grave{a}\grave{a}) = \epsilon$.

The idea of the balancedness check is to compute the finite set $\text{Irr}(X)(\subseteq \grave{A}^*\acute{A}^*) = \{\rho(\phi) \mid X \xrightarrow{*} \phi\}$ for each nonterminal X. As in the above example, given a balanced grammar this set is always finite. Furthermore, each length of

$\phi \in \mathrm{Irr}(X)$ is at most exponential to the size of the balanced grammar. These facts suggest that we can stop the computation of $\mathrm{Irr}(X)$ whenever some string $\phi \in \mathrm{Irr}(X)$ is found to be longer than a given fixed length. This is the idea of Berstel and Boasson.

Let us look at this idea more precisely. In general, for each nonterminal X, we have a derivation in the form $I \xrightarrow{*} \psi X \zeta$ such that both ψ and ζ are at most of exponential length to the size of grammar [1]. Now, the balancedness implies that $\rho(\psi\phi\zeta) = \epsilon$ for any ϕ such that $X \xrightarrow{*} \phi$. We can observe that this holds iff $\rho(\psi)$, $\rho(\zeta)$ and $\rho(\phi)$ are in the following forms, $\rho(\psi) = \grave{b}_k \cdots \grave{b}_1 \acute{a}_n \cdots \acute{a}_1$, $\rho(\zeta) = \grave{c}_1 \cdots \grave{c}_m \grave{b}_1 \cdots \grave{b}_k$ $(a_n \neq c_m)$, and $\rho(\phi) = \acute{a}_1 \cdots \acute{a}_n \grave{b}_1 \cdots \grave{b}_j \grave{b}_j \cdots \grave{b}_1 \grave{c}_m \cdots \grave{c}_1$ $(j \leq k)$. Hence we have $|\rho(\phi)| \leq |\rho(\psi)| + |\rho(\zeta)|$.

However, this bound is not always small, as shown in the following example.

$$I \to XY_n \qquad Y_0 \to \acute{a} \qquad Y_1 \to Y_0 Y_0 \qquad \cdots \qquad Y_n \to Y_{n-1}Y_{n-1}$$

We can see that $I \xrightarrow{*} X \overbrace{\acute{a} \cdots \acute{a}}^{2^n}$. Therefore, for this grammar to be balanced (e.g., define rules for $X(= X_n)$ by $X_0 \to \acute{a}, X_1 \to X_0 X_0, \ldots, X_n \to X_{n-1}X_{n-1}$), each ϕ such that $X \xrightarrow{*} \phi$ should be at most 2^n in length. On the other hand, the grammar is not balanced if we define the following rules:

$$X \to \epsilon \qquad X \to X\acute{a} \qquad X \to X\grave{b}$$

where $\mathrm{Irr}(X) = \{\acute{a}, \grave{b}\}^*$. Unfortunately in checking this unbalancedness, the algorithm by Berstel and Boasson tries to compute subsets of $\mathrm{Irr}(X)$ including words at most of length 2^n, i.e., $\bigcup_{k \leq 2^n} \{\acute{a}, \grave{b}\}^k$ whose size is *doubly* exponential to the size of the grammar.

We can relax this double-exponential behavior to exponential by a small modification to the algorithm. Let $\sqsubseteq$ be the minimal ordering over $\acute{A}^* \grave{A}^*$ satisfying

$$\phi\phi' \sqsubseteq \phi\grave{a}\acute{a}\phi'.$$

Our idea is simply to compute $\mathrm{Irr}(X)$ as far as every two elements are consistent wrt this ordering, i.e., if $\phi, \phi' \in \mathrm{Irr}(X)$ then either $\phi \sqsubseteq \phi'$ or $\phi' \sqsubseteq \phi$. Again assume $I \xrightarrow{*} \psi X \zeta$ and $X \xrightarrow{*} \phi, \phi'$. By the previous discussion, if $\rho(\psi\phi\zeta) = \rho(\psi\phi'\zeta) = \epsilon$, we have both $\rho(\phi)$ and $\rho(\phi')$ in the form

$$\acute{a}_1 \cdots \acute{a}_n \grave{b}_1 \cdots \grave{b}_j \grave{b}_j \cdots \grave{b}_1 \grave{c}_m \cdots \grave{c}_1$$

with only j differing. Hence $\rho(\phi)$ and $\rho(\phi')$ are always consistent wrt $\sqsubseteq$. In other words, we can stop the computation of $\mathrm{Irr}(X)$ whenever we found an inconsistent element. We obtain the algorithm in Figure 1 by extending Berstel and Boasson's algorithm with this additional consistency check.

---

[1] The depth of derivations to compute ψ and ζ is bounded by the number of nonterminals n of canonical two normal form [Har78] of G where only the productions of the following forms are allowed: $X \to YZ$, $X \to Y$, $X \to a$, and $X \to \epsilon$. Then, the sizes of ψ and ζ are at most 2^n.

Input CFG (V, Σ, P, I).

Output BALANCED or NOT_BALANCED.

1 For each $X \in V$, let $bound(X) = |\rho(\psi)| + |\rho(\zeta)|$ for some $I \xrightarrow{*} \psi X \zeta$.

2 Set $\mathrm{Irr}[X] = \{\}$ for each $X \in V$

3 For each $X \to \gamma[X_1, \ldots, X_n] \in P$ where $\gamma[]$ is a context made from terminal symbols, and $X_1, \ldots, X_n$ are nonterminals.

   – For each tuple $\phi_1, \ldots, \phi_n$ such that each $\phi_i \in \mathrm{Irr}[X_i]$,

     • Let $\phi = \rho(\gamma[\phi_1, \ldots, \phi_n])$. If this ϕ is undefined, return NOT_BALANCED.
     • If $|\phi| > bound(X)$, return NOT_BALANCED.
     • If $\phi \not\sqsubseteq \phi'$ nor $\phi' \not\sqsubseteq \phi$ for some $\phi' \in \mathrm{Irr}[X]$, return NOT_BALANCED.
     • Otherwise, update $\mathrm{Irr}[X] := \mathrm{Irr}[X] \cup \{\phi\}$.

4 If some $\mathrm{Irr}[X]$ has been updated, go to 3.

5 If $\mathrm{Irr}[I] = \{\epsilon\}$ then return BALANCED, else return NOT_BALANCED.

Fig. 1. The algorithm of balancedness check

To observe the complexity improvement, note that $\sqsubseteq$ is a linear ordering. So if $\mathrm{Irr}(X)$ only has consistent elements wrt $\sqsubseteq$, its size is bounded by the maximal length of strings in $\mathrm{Irr}(X)$.

The algorithm presented here still requires exponential time, i.e., $2^{O(n)}$-time where n is the size of the grammar. However, we conjecture that the balancedness check itself is even a PTIME problem. For this, the first step is to simplify the algorithm to check and remember only the maximal element of $\mathrm{Irr}(X)$ according to $\sqsubseteq$, rather than $\mathrm{Irr}(X)$ itself.[2] The remaining steps involve the use of a PTIME algorithm for the equivalence of straight line programs [Pla94]. We do not explain these details in this paper due to space limitation. Because the balancedness check is a subproblem of validation, and the complexity of our validation algorithms is exponential or doubly exponential, an improvement here will be canceled out in the analysis of total complexity.

3   Regular Hedge Grammar Validation

In this section, we give the first algorithm of XML validation for CFG. This algorithm determines

$$L(G) \subseteq L(G_{\mathrm{reg}})$$

where G_{reg} is specified as a regular hedge grammar. This algorithm runs in double exponential-time, i.e., time complexity bounded by $2^{2^{p(n)}}$ for some polynomial $p(n)$, to the size of inputs n.

3.1   Regular Hedge Grammar and Binoid

We first introduce a finite algebra called binoid. We believe that a binoid is a useful algorithmic tool to solve problems related to XML and DTDs. In theory,

---

[2] However, $\mathrm{Irr}(X)$ as we compute it here is still required in complete qualification of a grammar used in Section 4.

a binoid is similar to a deterministic tree automaton whose size can grow exponentially if we construct it from a nondeterministic tree automaton. However, as we will see in the experimentation section, binoids are fairly small for practical XML schemas. For example, we can construct a finite binoid for the XHTML strict DTD with only 58 elements.

Let $B(\Sigma)$ be a Dyck set, i.e., the set of balanced strings, over Σ. We have the following proposition.

Proposition 2. *(Existence of binoid) For any regular hedge grammar G_{reg} with alphabet Σ, we have a finite algebra $\mathcal{H}(G_{\text{reg}}) = (\mathcal{H}, \varepsilon, F, \hat{\ }(\_), (\_.\_))$ such that there is a (homomorphic) mapping $\_^\circ : B(\Sigma) \to \mathcal{H}$ such that*

(i) $\epsilon^\circ = \varepsilon$,
(ii) $(\acute{a}\phi\grave{a})^\circ = \hat{a}(\phi^\circ)$ for each $a \in A$,
(iii) $(\phi\psi)^\circ = \phi^\circ.\psi^\circ$, and
(iv) $\phi \in L(G_{\text{reg}})$ iff $\phi^\circ \in F$.

This algebra $\mathcal{H}(G_{\text{reg}})$ is called a binoid [PQ68]. Similarly to monoids, $(\_.\_)$ is associative and ε is its unit. A difference from monoids is that we now have a new operator $\hat{\ }(\_)$, corresponding to construction of tree node, or enclosure by parentheses. We can construct a binoid from a regular hedge grammar using a variation of the algorithm of tree automata determinization [Toz06].

Example 4. A grammar in Example 2 is captured by the following binoid with three elements.

$$\mathcal{H} = \{\eta_0, \eta_1, \eta_\top\}, \ \varepsilon = \eta_0, \ F = \{\eta_1\},$$
$$\hat{a}(\eta_k) = \eta_k$$
$$\hat{b}(\eta_k) = \begin{cases} \eta_1 & (k = 0) \\ \eta_\top & \text{(otherwise)} \end{cases} \quad (\eta_k.\eta_{k'}) = \begin{cases} \eta_{k+k'} & (k + k' \le 1) \\ \eta_\top & \text{(otherwise)} \end{cases}$$

We define the homomorphism $^\circ$ as $\phi^\circ = \eta_k$ if ϕ is a balanced string containing k occurrences, i.e., $0, 1$ or $\top$ meaning more than one, of pairs of letters $\acute{b}$ and $\grave{b}$. We can easily verify the requirements of binoid, e.g., $(\acute{b}\grave{b})^\circ.(\acute{a}\grave{a})^\circ = \eta_1.\eta_0 = \eta_1 = (\acute{b}\grave{b}\acute{a}\grave{a})^\circ$.

The homomorphism $(^\circ) \in B(\Sigma) \to \mathcal{H}$ can interpret an arabitrary balanced word as an element of $\mathcal{H}$ so that (1) constructors ϵ, vw, and $\acute{a}w\grave{a}$ for balanced words are preserved by corresponding operators ε, $(\_.\_)$ and $\hat{\ }(\_)$, and (2) the membership for $L(G_{\text{reg}})$ is preserved by the membership for F. We can judge whether a set of strings is contained in $L(G_{\text{reg}})$ without enumerating true strings in the set, but rather by enumerating elements of $\mathcal{H}$ computed by $\mathcal{H}$'s operators. This is the basic idea behind our algorithm.

3.2 Validation Algorithm

Assume that $G = (\Sigma, V, P, I)$ defines a balanced language. We also assume that we have a finite binoid $\mathcal{H}(G_{\text{reg}}) = (\mathcal{H}, \varepsilon, F, \hat{\ }(\_), (\_.\_))$ with a homomorphism $(^\circ) \in B(\Sigma) \to \mathcal{H}$.

As mentioned, the idea of the algorithm is to interpret a set of strings generated for each nonterminal of G using the algebra $\mathcal{H}(G_{\text{reg}})$. However, each string ϕ such that $X \xrightarrow{*} \phi$ is not necessarily balanced, but rather partially balanced. Therefore, we again use the factorization of ϕ. Assume that $\text{Irr}(X) = \grave{a}_1 \grave{a}_2 \cdots \grave{a}_n \acute{a}_{n+1} \cdots \acute{a}_m$. Each ϕ is factorized as follows:

$$\phi = \phi_1 \grave{a}_1 \phi_2 \grave{a}_2 \phi_3 \cdots \grave{a}_n \phi_{n+1} \acute{a}_{n+1} \cdots \phi_m \acute{a}_m \phi_{m+1}$$

where ϕ_i are balanced strings. Then, assume that a function ν maps a partially balanced string ϕ to $\nu(\phi) \in \mathcal{H}(\Sigma \mathcal{H})^*$ as follows.

$$\nu(\phi) = \phi_1^\circ \grave{a}_1 \phi_2^\circ \grave{a}_2 \phi_3^\circ \cdots \grave{a}_n \phi_{n+1}^\circ \acute{a}_{n+1} \cdots \phi_m^\circ \acute{a}_m \phi_{m+1}^\circ$$

Here $\grave{a}_1 \grave{a}_2 \cdots \grave{a}_n \acute{a}_{n+1} \cdots \acute{a}_m$ is a member of $\text{Irr}(X)$. Since G is balanced and $\mathcal{H}$ is finite, the set $\{\nu(\phi) \mid X \xrightarrow{*} \phi\}$ for each X is finite. Similar to the algorithm of the balancedness check, we wish to construct this set by induction.

Let us extend $\nu(\phi)$ to $\nu(\omega)$ for words $\omega \in (\Sigma \cup \mathcal{H})^*$. In the following rewrite rules, we assume $\sigma, \sigma' \in \Sigma$, $\upsilon, \omega \in (\mathcal{H} \cup \Sigma)^*$ and $\eta, \eta' \in \mathcal{H}$.

$$\upsilon \sigma \sigma' \omega \Rightarrow \upsilon \sigma \varepsilon \sigma' \omega$$
$$\upsilon \eta \eta \omega \Rightarrow \upsilon (\eta . \eta') \omega \qquad \sigma \omega \Rightarrow \varepsilon \sigma \omega$$
$$\upsilon \acute{a} \eta \grave{a} \omega \Rightarrow \upsilon \hat{a}(\eta) \omega \qquad \omega \sigma \Rightarrow \omega \sigma \varepsilon$$
$$\epsilon \Rightarrow \varepsilon$$

Now $\nu(\omega)$ is defined as a normal form such that $\omega \Rightarrow^* \nu(\omega)$ and $\nu(\omega)$ can no longer be rewritten by $\Rightarrow$. Here, the two rules on the left interpret a given word using $\mathcal{H}$'s operators. The four rules on the right canonicalize the word by removing all leftmost, rightmost and two successive occurrences of $\sigma, \sigma' \in \Sigma$. Since the rules on the left never introduce such occurrences of σ and σ', and they decrease the length of the word, this rewrite terminates. Similar to the discussion on ρ, we can see that (1) $\phi^\circ = \nu(\phi)$ if ϕ is balanced, and hence $\nu(\phi) \in F$ iff $\phi \in L(G_{\text{reg}})$, and (2) $\nu(\nu(\phi)\nu(\psi)) = \nu(\phi\psi)$ for partially balanced ϕ and ψ.

Example 5. Some examples using the binoid given in Example 4.

$$\nu(\grave{a}\acute{a}\grave{a}\acute{b}) = \eta_0 \grave{a}(\acute{a}\grave{a})^\circ \acute{b} \eta_0 = \eta_0 \grave{a} \eta_0 \acute{b} \eta_0,$$
$$\nu(\grave{b}\acute{a}) = \eta_0 \grave{b} \eta_0 \acute{a} \eta_0,$$
$$\nu(\grave{a}\acute{a}\grave{a}\grave{b}\grave{b}\grave{a}) = \nu(\nu(\grave{a}\acute{a}\grave{a}\acute{b})\nu(\grave{b}\acute{a})) = \eta_0 \grave{a} \eta_0 . \hat{b}(\eta_0.\eta_0).\eta_0 \acute{a} \eta_0 = \eta_0 \grave{a} \eta_1 \acute{a} \eta_0.$$

The rest of the algorithm is very close to that of the balancedness check. This is given in Figure 2.

3.3 Complexity

The dominant factor of the complexity is the size of $\text{Abs}[X]$ for each X. The number of iterations for the outer loop of the algorithm in Fig. 2 is bounded by the number of all pairs (X, ω) such that $\omega \in \text{Abs}[X]$. The inner loop for $X \to \gamma[X_1, \ldots, X_n]$ is repeated $|P|$ times, and the innermost for-each is repeated

Input CFG $G = (V, \Sigma, P, I)$ defining a balanced language, and binoid $\mathcal{H}(G_{\text{reg}}) = (\mathcal{H}, \varepsilon,$
    $F, \hat{\,}(\_), (\_\_\_))$.
Output VALID or INVALID.
1 Set $\text{Abs}[X] = \{\}$ for each $X \in V$
2 For each $X \to \gamma[X_1, \ldots, X_n] \in P$ where $X_1, \ldots, X_n$ are nonterminals.
    − For each tuple $\omega_1, \ldots, \omega_n$ such that each $\omega_i \in \text{Abs}[X_i]$,
        • update $\text{Abs}[X] := \text{Abs}[X] \cup \{\nu(\gamma[\omega_1, \ldots, \omega_n])\}$.
3 If some $\text{Abs}[X]$ has been updated, go to 2.
4 If $\text{Abs}[I] \subseteq F$ then return VALID else return INVALID.

Fig. 2. The validation algorithm for regular hedge grammars

$|\text{Abs}[X_1]| \times \cdots \times |\text{Abs}[X_n]|$ times. Computing $\nu(\omega)$ at most requires time polynomial to $|\omega| \log |\mathcal{H}|$. The maximal length of strings in $\text{Irr}(X)$ is bounded by $2^{O(|G|)}$. It is known that the size of $\mathcal{H}$ obtained from G_{reg} is at most $2^{O(|G_{\text{reg}}|^2)}$. Now for each X, the size of $\text{Abs}[X]$ is at most $\Sigma_{\phi \in \text{Irr}(X)} |\mathcal{H}|^{|\phi|+1}$, hence $2^{2^{O(|G|+\log |G_{\text{reg}}|)}}$. The O-notation absorbs all the other factors, giving $2^{2^{O(|G|+\log |G_{\text{reg}}|)}}$-time total complexity of the algorithm, which is doubly-exponential to the size of G.

4 XML-Grammar Validation

We develop a validation algorithm of a context-free grammar against an XML-grammar (or DTD) by exploiting its locality. DTDs and XML-grammars have locality in the sense that they can only describe a relation between an element (tag) and its children, as we described in the introduction. This locality makes it possible to decide the inclusion problem $L(G) \subseteq L(G_{\text{xml}})$ for a CFG G and an XML-grammar G_{xml} by checking local properties. As a result, we can obtain an XML-grammar validation algorithm with time complexity $2^{O(|G|+|G_{\text{xml}}|)}$.

To formalize the idea, we introduce the notion of the trace and the surfaces of a balanced string by Berstel and Boasson [BB02]. Every balanced string ϕ is uniquely written into the following form:

$$\phi = \acute{a}_1 \phi_1 \grave{a}_1 \acute{a}_2 \phi_2 \grave{a}_2 \cdots \acute{a}_n \phi_n \grave{a}_n$$

where ϕ_i are balanced strings. The *trace* of a balanced string picks up only the base symbol of the toplevel tags. The trace of ϕ above is the following string.

$$\text{Trace}(\phi) = a_1 a_2 \cdots a_n$$

The *surface* of a in ϕ is defined as:

$$S_a(\phi) = \{ \text{Trace}(\psi) \mid \acute{a}\psi\grave{a} \text{ is a substring of } \phi \text{ and } \psi \text{ is balanced} \}$$

This formalizes the set of sequences of tags under the a-tag in ϕ. For example, the string $\acute{a}\acute{b}\grave{b}\acute{c}\grave{c}\grave{a}\acute{a}\acute{d}\grave{d}\grave{a}$ has the following surfaces for a and b.

$$S_a(\acute{a}\acute{b}\grave{b}\acute{c}\grave{c}\grave{a}\acute{a}\acute{d}\grave{d}\grave{a}) = \{ bc, d \} \qquad S_b(\acute{a}\acute{b}\grave{b}\acute{c}\grave{c}\grave{a}\acute{a}\acute{d}\grave{d}\grave{a}) = \{ \epsilon \}$$

By using the surfaces of a string, we can decompose the validation of a context-free grammar G against G_{xml}. Consider the following XML-grammar as an example.

$$X_a \rightarrow á(X_a|X_b)(X_a|X_b)à$$
$$X_b \rightarrow b́X_b^*b̀$$

For the validation, it is sufficient to check the following inclusion relations for the surfaces of a and b.

$$S_a(L(G)) \subseteq L((a|b)(a|b)) \qquad S_b(L(G)) \subseteq L(b^*)$$

If we can obtain $S_a(L(G))$ and $S_b(L(G))$ as context-free grammars, the inclusion relations above are decidable since they are inclusion relations between context-free and regular languages.

We say a context-free grammar is completely balanced if $L_G(X)$ is balanced for every nonterminal of G where $L_G(X)$ is the set of strings derivable from the nonterminal X. If a context-free grammar is completely balanced, then it is balanced. The other direction does not necessarily apply.

Example 6. The following grammar is balanced, but it is not completely balanced.

$$A \rightarrow áb́Bb̀à$$
$$B \rightarrow \epsilon \mid b́b̀B$$

where A is a start symbol. It is not completely balanced because $B \xrightarrow{*} b́b̀$, and $b̀$ and $b́$ are *end* and *start* tags, respectively.

In the remainder of this section, we first show that we can compute surfaces if the grammar is completely balanced and then show that any balanced CFG can be converted into a completely balanced CFG with the same surfaces. Since the surfaces are preserved by the conversion, it can be used for validation. However, the language of the obtained completely balanced grammar may not be same as that of the original grammar.

4.1 Surfaces of a Completely Balanced CFG

We present an algorithm to obtain the surfaces of a completely balanced context-free grammar. To simplify the presentation, we restrict the format of productions of a completely balanced CFG to the following forms:

$$X \rightarrow áX_1 \cdots X_nà$$
$$X \rightarrow X_1 \cdots X_n$$

It is easy to transform a completely balanced CFG into one with productions with these forms. From a grammar in this format, it is relatively easy to obtain the grammars representing its surfaces. The first step is to obtain the productions to produce $\text{Trace}(L_G(X))$ for each nonterminal X. Each production in G is transformed as follows:

$$
\begin{array}{ccc}
G & & G' \\
X \rightarrow áX_1 \cdots X_nà & \Rightarrow & X \rightarrow a \\
X \rightarrow X_1 \cdots X_n & \Rightarrow & X \rightarrow X_1 \cdots X_n
\end{array}
$$

The first rule just picks up a since the strings derived from $X_1 \cdots X_n$ are under the start and end a tags. For example, the productions of the grammar G below are transformed as follows:

$$
\begin{array}{rcl}
\qquad G & & \qquad G' \\
A \to \acute{a}\grave{a} & \Rightarrow & A \to a \\
B \to \acute{b}\grave{b} & \Rightarrow & B \to b \\
C \to \epsilon \mid ACB & \Rightarrow & C \to \epsilon \mid ACB \\
D \to \acute{c}C\grave{c} \mid \acute{c}D\grave{c} & \Rightarrow & D \to c \mid c
\end{array}
$$

Then, we can construct the context-free grammar representing the surface of a in G for each $a \in A$. Consider $S_c(L(G))$ for the grammar G above. For this grammar, we have $S_c(L(G)) = \text{Trace}(C) \cup \text{Trace}(D)$ because a pair of $\acute{c}$ and $\grave{c}$ occurs only in the following two productions.

$$ D \to \acute{c}C\grave{c} \qquad D \to \acute{c}D\grave{c} $$

Therefore, $S_c(L(G))$ can be represented with a grammar with the following productions:

$$
\begin{array}{ll}
A \to a & \qquad D \to c \\
B \to b & \qquad I \to C \mid D \\
C \to \epsilon \mid ACB &
\end{array}
$$

where I is the start symbol. This grammar generates the following language:

$$ S_c(L(G)) = \{\, a^n b^n \mid n \geq 0 \,\} \cup \{\, c \,\} $$

The context-free grammars for $S_a(L(G))$ and $S_b(L(G))$ are constructed in the same manner. Then, we can validate G against an XML-grammar using the surfaces.

4.2 Transformation into a Completely Balanced CFG

The rest of our validation algorithm is to transform a balanced CFG into a completely balanced CFG with the same surfaces. This is the most involved part of the XML-grammar validation algorithm. The following grammar shows that there is a balanced CFG that cannot be represented with a completely balanced CFG [Knu67].

$$ I \to A\grave{a} \qquad A \to \acute{a} \mid \acute{b}\grave{b}A\acute{c}\grave{c} $$

This grammar generates $\{\, (\acute{b}\grave{b})^n \acute{a}(\acute{c}\grave{c})^n \grave{a} \mid n \geq 0 \,\}$.

We say that a context-free grammar is completely qualified if $\text{Irr}(X)$ is a singleton for every nonterminal X. Given a balanced CFG G, we can construct a completely qualified CFG G' where $L(G') = L(G)$ [Knu67]. Therefore, in this section, we assume a balanced CFG is completely qualified and write $\text{Irr}(X) = \phi$ if $\text{Irr}(X) = \{\, \phi \,\}$.

The transformation we introduce is based on the factorization of partially balanced strings. Consider the following factorization of a partially balanced string ϕ:

$$\phi \equiv \phi_1 \grave{a}_1 \phi_2 \grave{a}_2 \phi_3 \cdots \phi_m \grave{a}_m \phi_{m+1} \acute{a}_{m+1} \phi_{m+2} \cdots \phi_n \acute{a}_n \phi_{n+1}$$

where ϕ_i are balanced. We define the i-th factor $F_i(\phi)$ of ϕ as $F_i(\phi) = \phi_i$.

Let $G = (V, \Sigma, P, I)$ be a balanced CFG. We construct a completely balanced CFG G' with the same surfaces as follows. For each nonterminal X, we introduce nonterminals X_i ($1 \leq i \leq |\mathrm{Irr}(X)| + 1$). Let V' be the set of nonterminals X_i introduced above. Then, we define a function F from V to $V'(\Sigma V')^*$ as follows:

$$F(X) = X_1 \grave{a}_1 X_2 \grave{a}_1 X_3 \cdots X_m \grave{a}_m X_{m+1} \acute{a}_{m+1} X_{m+2} \cdots X_n \acute{a}_n X_{n+1}$$

where $\mathrm{Irr}(X) = \grave{a}_1 \grave{a}_2 \cdots \grave{a}_m \acute{a}_{m+1} \cdots \acute{a}_n$. This function F on nonterminals is naturally extended to a function on $(\Sigma \cup V)^*$ by $F(\acute{a}) = \acute{a}$ and $F(\grave{a}) = \grave{a}$ for all base symbol a.

With this function we can expand production $X \to \gamma$ of G as follows.

$$F(X) \to F(\gamma)$$

By construction, $F(\gamma)$ must have the following form:

$$F(\gamma) = \gamma_1 \grave{a}_1 \gamma_2 \grave{a}_2 \gamma_3 \cdots \gamma_m \grave{a}_m \gamma_{m+1} \acute{a}_{m+1} \gamma_{m+2} \cdots \gamma_n \acute{a}_n \gamma_{n+1}$$

where γ_i are balanced by considering that nonterminals are balanced. This is because G is completely qualified and thus $\mathrm{Irr}(\gamma) = \mathrm{Irr}(X)$. Then, we construct $G' = (V', \Sigma, P', I_1)$ where P' contains the following productions for each production $X \to \gamma \in P$.

$$X_i \to F_i(F(\gamma)) \quad (1 \leq i \leq |\mathrm{Irr}(X)| + 1)$$

It is clear that only balanced strings can be derived from each nonterminal X_i in G' since the right-hand side of each production is a balanced factor. Therefore, G' is a completely balanced CFG and the following are satisfied:

$$L(G) \subseteq L(G')$$

$$S_a(G) = S_a(G') \quad \text{for each } a \in A$$

We proved these properties for a CFG G in Chomsky normal form. The first property is easily shown by construction and the second is obtained from the following property:

$$\mathrm{Trace}(L_{G'}(X_i)) = \mathrm{Trace}(F_i(L_G(X)))$$

An expanded production $F(X) \to F(\gamma)$ above can be considered as a context-sensitive production rule. To obtain a CFG, we split it into several productions for factors. This is the source of approximation in the transformation.

Example 7. Consider again the following grammar considered by Knuth:

$$I \to A\grave{a} \qquad A \to \acute{a} \mid \grave{b}\hat{b}A\acute{c}\grave{c}$$

where $\mathrm{Irr}(A) = \acute{a}$ and $\mathrm{Irr}(I) = \epsilon$. This grammar generates $\{(\grave{b}\hat{b})^n\acute{a}(\acute{c}\grave{c})^n\grave{a} \mid n \geq 0\}$. We have $F(A) = A_1\acute{a}A_2$ and $F(I) = I_1$. Therefore, the productions for A are expanded as follows:

$$A_1\acute{a}A_2 \to \acute{a} \mid \grave{b}\hat{b}A_1\acute{a}A_2\acute{c}\grave{c}$$

From $F_1(\grave{b}\hat{b}A_1\acute{a}A_2\acute{c}\grave{c}) = \grave{b}\hat{b}A_1$ and $F_2(\grave{b}\hat{b}A_1\acute{a}A_2\acute{c}\grave{c}) = A_2\acute{c}\grave{c}$, we obtain the following grammar:

$$I_1 \to A_1\acute{a}A_2\grave{a} \qquad A_1 \to \epsilon \mid \grave{b}\hat{b}A_1 \qquad A_2 \to \epsilon \mid A_2\acute{c}\grave{c}$$

This grammar generates $\{ (\grave{b}\hat{b})^n\acute{a}(\acute{c}\grave{c})^m\grave{a} \mid n, m \geq 0 \}$. The constraint between n and m is lost by the transformation and consequently they do not have the same language. However, it is clear that it has the same surfaces as those of the original grammar.

4.3 Complexity

Let n and m be the sizes of a balanced CFG G and an XML-grammar G_{xml}, respectively. We assume that the length of the right-hand side of a production of G is at most two. As described in Section 2, both the cardinality of $\mathrm{Irr}(X)$ and the maximal length of strings in $\mathrm{Irr}(X)$ are bounded by 2^n for every nonterminal X in G. We define $\iota(G)$ for a balanced CFG G as follows:

$$\iota(G) = max\{ |\gamma| \mid \gamma \in \mathrm{Irr}(X) \text{ for some nonterminal } X \text{ in } G \}$$

The first step of the validation algorithm is to obtain an equivalent completely qualified CFG G_1. We can obtain G_1 with at most 2^{2n} productions by the transformation of Knuth [Knu67] in time $2^{O(n)}$. The length of the right-hand side of a production in G_1 is again at most two and $\iota(G) = \iota(G_1)$.

The second step is to obtain a completely balanced CFG G_2 that has the same surfaces with G_1. Each nonterminal X with $\mathrm{Irr}(X) = \acute{a}_1\acute{a}_2 \cdots \acute{a}_m\acute{a}_{m+1} \cdots \acute{a}_n$ in G_1 is translated as follows.

$$F(X) = X_1\acute{a}_1X_2\acute{a}_1X_3 \cdots X_m\acute{a}_mX_{m+1}\acute{a}_{m+1}X_{m+2} \cdots X_n\acute{a}_nX_{n+1}$$

We have $|F(X)| = 2|\mathrm{Irr}(X)| + 1 \leq 2\iota(G_1) + 1$. A production $X \to \gamma$ in G_1 is translated into the following productions.

$$X_i \to F_i(F(\gamma)) \quad (1 \leq i \leq |\mathrm{Irr}(X)| + 1)$$

It is observed that each production rule is translated into at most $\iota(G_1) + 1$ production rules and $|F(\gamma)| \leq 2(2\iota(G_1) + 1)$ since $|\gamma| \leq 2$. Thus, the size of G_2 is bounded by $O(2^{2n} \cdot \iota(G_1)) = O(2^{3n})$ and it is obtained in time $2^{O(n)}$.

Table 1. XHTML validation

programs	size		the numbers of		time(sec)	
	depth	Irr(X)	nonterminals	productions	binoid	surface
WebCalendar	8	4	102	170	0.0121	0.0492
marktree	∞	4	32	54	0.0023	0.0127
phpScheduleIt	15	8	24	42	0.0062	0.0191
mrtask	11	6	50	70	0.0059	0.0281

To validate a context-free grammar G_2 against an XML-grammar G_{xml}, we need to check $S_a(G_2) \subseteq L(R_a)$ for each $X_a \rightarrow áR_aà$ in G_{xml}. The size of the deterministic automaton for R_a has at most 2^m states. Because intersection emptiness between a context-free grammar and an automaton can be checked in cubic time, the inclusion relation for each surface can be checked in time $2^{O(n+m)}$. Thus, the complexity of the algorithm in total is in $2^{O(n+m)}$.

5 Experimental Results

We have implemented our validation algorithms as backend validators of the PHP string analyzer developed by Minamide [Min05]. The analyzer generates a CFG that conservatively approximates the string output of a PHP program. It is available from http://www.score.cs.tsukuba.ac.jp/~minamide/phpsa/. In our experiments, we checked the validity of Web pages generated by a PHP program against the XHTML specification. However, we ignored attributes in our experiments and only checked the constraints on elements imposed by the specification. As a preliminary step of validation, the analyzer eliminates comments, attributes, and non-tag texts from a CFG and obtains the corresponding CFG over a paired alphabet. The transformations for this simplification are implemented as string transducers.

In our implementation of the validation algorithms, we first extract the set of element names appearing in a CFG obtained by the analyzer and delete the elements from the DTD that do not appear in the set. Without this optimization, it takes approximately 0.2 seconds to construct the binoid for the XHTML DTD and this dominates validation time in the binoid-based validation.

We applied our validation algorithms to several PHP programs available from SourceForge and validated the top Web pages generated by them. We repaired several validity bugs in these programs and had to modify the programs to improve the precision of the analysis. The experiments were performed on a Linux PC with two Opteron processors (2.8 GHz) and 8 GB memory. The CFGs were validated against XHTML version 1.0 Transitional DTD[3]. Table 1 summarizes our experiments. The first four columns show the various information concerning the grammars over a paired-alphabet obtained by the analyzer. We checked the grammars and found that all the grammars are completely qualified. The

---

[3] The content model $(r)+$ was interpreted as $(r)*$ in the experiments to circumvent imprecision due to analysis of loops in a program.

columns 'depth' and 'Irr(X)' show the maximum nesting depth of elements (tags) and the maximum size of Irr(X). In the last two columns, the table shows the validation time for the binoid-based and the surface-based validation algorithms[4]. These do not include the time spent in obtaining the CFGs. These results show that both algorithms are fast enough for common server-side programs even if they have theoretically exponential complexity. We think that it is because the size of Irr(X) is small in practice, as shown in the table, and a regular expression in a content model of DTD must be deterministic.

It is interesting that the binoid-based validation is faster in these experiments although it has higher complexity. This may be because the implementation of the binoid-based validation is simpler than that of the surface-based validation. However, it is also straightforward to write an artificial program where both of the algorithms show their exponential behavior. Consider the following program where $x = $x.$x; $y = $y.$y; is repeated n times.

```
$x = "<div>"; $y = "</div>";
if (rand()) $x = $x."<p></p>";
$x = $x.$x; $y = $y.$y;
...
$x = $x.$x; $y = $y.$y;
echo $x; echo $y;
```

The grammar obtained for this program is completely qualified and the size of Irr$(\cdot)$ for the variables $x and $y is in $O(2^n)$. The surface-based algorithm shows exponential behavior for this program and it takes 1.0, 6.5, and 34.5 seconds to validate it for $n = 10, 11, 12$, respectively. On the other hand, the binoid-based algorithm shows doubly exponential behavior for this program because of the if-statement in the program and can validate it only when $n \leq 5$.

6   Related Work

The PHP string analyzer originally supported only the inclusion checking between a CFG and a regular expression [Min05]. This checking can partially support validation of dynamically generated Web pages by restring their depth. It is because the set of valid Web pages can be described with a regular language if we restrict their depth. The algorithms in this paper give more direct and general solutions to the problem.

The XML validation algorithms presented in this paper depend on previous work on context-free grammars over languages with parentheses. A parenthesis grammar is a context-free grammar over a language with a single pair of parentheses where each production has the form of $A \rightarrow (\theta)$ where θ does not contain parentheses. McNaughtotn showed that equivalence of parenthesis grammars is decidable [McN67]. Knuth extended the result and showed that there exists an algorithm to determine whether a context-free grammar is a parenthesis language [Knu67].

---

[4] We measured the time spent to validate a CFG 100 times. The table shows an average time calculated from the total time.

Berstel and Boasson extended the theory of context-free grammars over languages with parentheses to study the language described by a DTD [BB02]. In this paper, we have developed a surface-based validation algorithm by exploiting their results that the language of an XML-grammar has locality and can be characterized by its surfaces, and the regular hedge grammar validation based on their algorithm for checking balancedness of a context-free language.

Extensive studies have been done in tree-based validation of dynamically generated HTML/XML documents [CMS03a, HP03, HVP05]. The motivation of the work is the same as ours, but the validation algorithms developed in these works cannot be directly applied to our setting of string-based validation. As shown in Section 4, we can retrieve a tree-based language for a balanced CFG with the approximation preserving surfaces of the language. Thus, after the transformation, the methods for tree-based validation can be applied in principle. Brabrand, Møller, and Schwartzbach proposed summary graphs to approximate the set of dynamically generated XHTML documents [BMS01]. Although summary graphs can express constraints on attributes, they basically correspond to *completely* balanced CFGs. The validation of a completely balanced CFG can be considered as a variant of their validation algorithm for summary graphs.

7   Conclusion

We have presented two new algorithms validating a context-free grammar against a regular hedge grammar and an XML-grammar. Although both have exponential complexity, it is shown that they are efficient in practice. Our validation algorithms for regular hedge grammars and XML-grammars have doubly exponential and exponential time complexity. We plan to establish the lower bounds for these validation problems. For simpler problems, it is known that the inclusion problems for regular expressions and regular hedge grammars are PSPACE-complete and EXPTIME-complete, respectively. However, gaps remain between the results and the complexity of our algorithms.

We have considered validation against a subclass of balanced context-free grammars, such as XML-grammars and regular hedge grammars, but legacy server-side programs generate HTML, which is not in XML format. In order to validate those Web pages, we need to consider validation against a grammar that has an unbalanced language. Although the inclusion problem between two context-free grammars is undecidable in general, we think that it is possible to validate a context-free grammar against the HTML specification because it is designed to be unambiguous and where end tags are omitted can be determined.

References

[BB02]   Jean Berstel and Luc Boasson. Formal properties of XML grammars and languages. *Acta Informatica*, 38(9):649–671, 2002.

[BMS01]   Claus Brabrand, Anders Møller, and Michael I. Schwartzbach. Static validation of dynamically generated HTML. In *Proceedings of the 2001 ACM SIGPLAN-SIGSOFT Workshop on Program Analysis For Software Tools and Engineering*, pages 38–45, 2001.

[CM01]   J. Clark and M. Murata. RELAX NG specification, 2001. http://www.
            oasis-open.org/committees/relax-ng/spec.
[CMS03a]   Aske Simon Christensen, Anders Møller, and Michael I. Schwartzbach. Ex-
            tending Java for high-level web service construction. *ACM Transactions
            on Programming Languages and Systems*, 25(6):814–875, 2003.
[CMS03b]   Aske Simon Christensen, Andres Møller, and Michael I. Schwartzbach. Pre-
            cise analysis of string expressions. In *Proceedings of the Static Analysis
            Symposium (SAS)*, volume 2694 of *LNCS*, pages 1–18, 2003.
[GF80]   Sheila A. Greibach and Emily P. Friedman. Superdeterministic PDAs: A
            subcase with a decidable inclusion problem. *Journal of the Association for
            Computing Machinery*, 27(4):675–700, 1980.
[Har78]   Michael A. Harrison. *Introduction to Formal Language Theory*, chapter 4.
            Addison-Wesley, 1978.
[HP03]   Haruo Hosoya and Benjamin Pierce. XDuce: A statically typed XML pro-
            cessing language. *ACM Transactions on Internet Technology*, 3(2):117–148,
            2003.
[HVP05]   Haruo Hosoya, Jérôme Vouillon, and Benjamin Pierce. Regular expres-
            sion types for XML. *ACM Transactions on Programming Languages and
            Systems*, 27(1):46–90, 2005.
[Knu67]   Donald E. Knuth. A characterization of parenthesis languages. *Information
            and Control*, 11(3):269–289, 1967.
[McN67]   Robert McNaughton. Parenthesis grammars. *Journal of the Association
            for Computing Machinery*, 14(3):490–500, 1967.
[Min05]   Yasuhiko Minamide. Static approximation of dynamically generated Web
            pages. In *Proceedings of the 14th International World Wide Web Confer-
            ence*, pages 432–441. ACM Press, 2005.
[Mur99]   Makoto Murata. Hedge automata: a formal model for XML schemata,
            1999. http://www.xml.gr.jp/relax/hedge_nice.html.
[Pla94]   Wojciech Plandowski. Testing equivalence of morphisms on context-free
            languages. In *Algorithms – ESA '94 (Utrecht)*, volume 855 of *LNCS*, pages
            460–470. Springer, 1994.
[PQ68]   C. Pair and A. Quere. Définition et étude des bilangages réguliers. *Infor-
            mation and Control*, 13(6):565–593, Dec 1968.
[Tak75]   Masako Takahashi. Generalizations of regular sets and their application
            to a study of context-free languages. *Information and Control*, 21(1):1–36,
            1975.
[Toz06]   Akihiko Tozawa. XML type checking using high-level tree transducer. In
            *Functional and Logic Programming, 8th International Symposium, FLOPS
            2006*, pages 81–96, 2006.

A Practical String Analyzer by the Widening Approach*

Tae-Hyoung Choi, Oukseh Lee, Hyunha Kim, and Kyung-Goo Doh**

Department of Computer Science and Engineering, Hanyang University, Ansan, Korea
{thchoi, oukseh, hhkim, doh}@pllab.hanyang.ac.kr

Abstract. The static determination of approximated values of string expressions has many potential applications. For instance, approximated string values may be used to check the validity and security of generated strings, as well as to collect the useful string properties. Previous string analysis efforts have been focused primarily on the maxmization of the precision of regular approximations of strings. These methods have not been completely satisfactory due to the difficulties in dealing with heap variables and context sensitivity. In this paper, we present an abstract-interpretation-based solution that employs a heuristic widening method. The presented solution is implemented and compared to JSA. In most cases, our solution gives results as precise as those produced by previous methods, and it makes the additional contribution of easily dealing with heap variables and context sensitivity in a very natural way. We anticipate the employment of our method in practical applications.

1 Introduction

Strings are used in many applications to build SQL queries, construct semi-structured Web documents, create XPath and JavaScript expressions, and so on. After being dynamically generated from user inputs, strings are sent to their respective processors. However, strings are not evaluated for their validity or security despite the potential usefulness of such metrics [5,7,6]. Hence, this paper aims to establish a method for statically determining the approximated values of string expressions in a string-generating program.

1.1 Related Works

Previous efforts to statically determine the approximated values of string expressions have attempted to maximize the precision of string approximations.

Christensen, Møller and Schwartzbach [2] developed a Java string analyzer (JSA) that approximates the values of string expressions using regular language. An interprocedural data-flow analysis is first used to extract context-free grammar from a Java program such that each string expression is represented as a

---

* This work was supported in part by grant No.R01-2006-000-10926-0 from the Basic Research Program of the Korea Science and Engineering Foundation, and in part by Brain Korea 21.
** Corresponding author.

N. Kobayashi (Ed.): APLAS 2006, LNCS 4279, pp. 374–388, 2006.

nonterminal symbol. Then, Mohri and Nederhof's algorithm [8] is applied to approximate the context-free grammar with regular grammar. Eventually, the string analysis produces a finite state automaton that conservatively approximates the set of possible strings for each specified string expression. JSA tends to be adequate when every string value is stored in a local variable, but it falters when dealing with strings stored in heap variables. Perhaps the method could be extended to deal with such variables, but not in a straightforward and immediate manner.

To conduct string analysis based on regular expressions, Tabuchi, Sumii, and Yonezawa [11] created a type system for a minimally functional language equipped with string concatenation and pattern matching over strings. However, they failed to provide a type inference algorithm due to a technical problem with recursive constraint solving. Our analysis can be thought of as a solution to their problem based on a carefully crafted widening.

Thiemann [12] presented a type system for string analysis based on context-free grammar and provided a type inference algorithm derived from Earley's parsing algorithm. His analysis is more precise than those based on regular expressions, and though sound, his inference algorithm is incomplete because its context-free language inclusion problem cannot be solved. The weak point is that the grammar must be written in terms of single characters rather than tokens.

Minamide [7] also developed a static program analyzer that approximates string output using context-free grammar. His analyzer, which uses a variant of the JSA approach to produce context-free grammar from a PHP program, validates HTML documents generated by a PHP program either by extracting and testing sample documents or by considering documents with a bounded depth only.

1.2   Our Approach

Our work is motivated by a desire to statically determine which database application program accesses and updates which database tables and fields. Such information is particularly useful in maintaining huge enterprise software systems. To obtain this information statically, all possible SQL queries must be extracted from database application programs as strings.

Strings may be stored as field variables in object-oriented applications, thus a string analysis must be able to determine their value. For example, the Java application in Fig. 1 uses a field variable to construct strings. The class SQLBuffer is defined as a gateway for connecting to a database server. In this example, two SQLBuffer objects are allocated and each object has a separate string field, buf. To prevent the clouding of analysis precision, independent string fields should be maintained as such. Thus, heap memory analysis is required. Furthermore, the methods add and set are called multiple times in different contexts. As such, precise string analysis must also be context-sensitive. For the example in Fig. 1, our analyzer is able to distinguish possible queries as SELECT .* FROM .* and UPDATE .* SET .* = .*, while JSA is unable to do so and only gives .* that means any string.

Our string analysis uses the standard monotone framework for abstract interpretation [3,4], which allows for context-sensitive handling of field variables. However, use of the abstract-interpretation framework for string analysis requires the invention of a reasonable widening operator. Thus, to keep its precision as high as possible, our widening operator is designed with heuristics.

1.3 Paper Contributions

Our paper makes the following contributions:

- We design a string analyzer based on standard abstract-interpretation techniques. Until now, ascertaining widening operators for regular expressions has been believed to be difficult [2]. However, by selecting a restricted subset of regular expressions as our abstract domain, which results in limited loss of expressibility, and by using heuristics, we can devise a precise widening operator. String operators, such as `concat`, `substring`, `trim`, and `replace`, are treated uniformly.
- The abstract-interpretation framework enables the integration of the following tasks into our analyzer:
  - handle memory objects and their field variables
  - recognize context sensitivity
  - integrate with constant propagation for integers
- Our string analyzer is implemented and tested. The results show the proposed analyzer to be as precise as JSAs in all cases, and even more precise for test programs dealing with memory objects and field variables.

1.4 Overview

The rest of this paper is organized as follows. Section 2 presents our key abstract domain, the set of regular strings. Section 3 explains the analysis for a simple imperative language and extends the analysis for integers, heap-manipulating statements, and procedures. Section 4 shows the experimental results, and the paper is concluded by Section 5.

2 Abstract Domain

An abstract string value is modeled as a *regular string* from within a restricted subset of regular expressions, and string operations are given abstract semantics. We first define a regular string and then explain the abstract semantics of concatenation and the widening operator. We subsequently give the abstract semantics of other string operators: `replace`, `trim`, and `substr`.

2.1 Regular String

A regular string is a sequence of atoms that comprise either an abstract character or the repetition of a regular string, as shown in Fig. 2. An abstract character is a set of characters that is, in most cases, a singleton set. For brevity, we omit the

```
class SQLBuffer {
  String buf;
  Connection con;
  void set(String s) {
    buf = s;
  }
  void append(String s) {
    buf = buf + " " + s;
  }
  ResultSet execute() throws SQLException {
    Statement stmt = con.createStatement();
    ResultSet rs = stmt.executeQuery(buf);
    buf = "";
    return rs;
  }
}
public class Example {
  public void some_fun(String[] args) throws SQLException {
    SQLBuffer sql1 = new SQLBuffer();
    SQLBuffer sql2 = new SQLBuffer();

    sql1.set("SELECT");
    sql1.add(args[2]);
    sql1.add("FROM");
    sql1.add(args[0]);

    ResultSet rs = sql1.execute();

    while (rs.next()) {
      sql2.set("UPDATE");
      sql2.add(args[1]);
      sql2.add("SET");
      sql2.add(args[2] + " = " + rs.getString(0));
      sql2.execute();
    }
  }
  // ...
}
```

Fig. 1. Example

set notation for a singleton set; for instance, instead of $\{a\} \{b, c\} \{d\}$, we write $a \{b, c\} d$, which is equivalent to $a(b + c)d$ in regular expression. The meaning of a repetition is as usual.

A regular string is derived from a restricted subset of regular expressions, which is expressible enough for our purposes. The alternative operator $+$ is omitted, and the set notation is used to represent the collection of alternatives. Consecutive repetitions, such as $a^\star b^\star$, are not allowed. To force the termination of the analysis, the regular expression $a^\star b^\star$ is approximated as $\{a, b\}^\star$.

In an abstract state, each variable maps to the set of regular strings.

Collecting domain:
      Var x
      Char c
      Str s $\in \{c_1 c_2 \cdots c_n \mid n \geq 0,\ c_i \in \mathsf{Char}\}$
      State^{col} S $\in \mathcal{P}(\mathsf{Var} \to \mathsf{Str})$

Abstract domain:
      Chars C $\in \mathcal{P}^{\mathrm{N}}(\mathsf{Char})$ where $\mathcal{P}^{\mathrm{N}}(A) = \mathcal{P}(A) \setminus \{\emptyset\}$
      Atom a $::= C \mid r^\star$
      Reg p, q, r $\in \{a_1 a_2 \cdots a_n \mid n \geq 0, a_i \in \mathsf{Atom},\ \neg\exists i.(a_i = p^\star \wedge a_{i+1} = q^\star)\}$
      State σ $\in (\mathsf{Var} \to \mathcal{P}^{\mathrm{N}}(\mathsf{Reg}))_\perp$

Meaning:
      Atom $\to \mathcal{P}(\mathsf{Str})$ $\gamma_a(C)$ $= C$
                                                   $\gamma_a(r^\star)$ $= \{s_1 s_2 \cdots s_n \mid 0 \leq n, s_i \in \gamma_r(r)\}$
      Reg $\to \mathcal{P}(\mathsf{Str})$ $\gamma_r(a_1 a_2 \cdots a_n)$ $= \{s_1 s_2 \cdots s_n \mid s_i \in \gamma_a(a_i)\}$
      $\mathcal{P}^{\mathrm{N}}(\mathsf{Reg}) \to \mathcal{P}(\mathsf{Str})$ $\gamma_R(R)$ $= \bigcup \{\gamma_r(r) \mid r \in R\}$
      State $\to$ State^{col} $\gamma_S(\perp)$ $= \emptyset$
                                                   $\gamma_S(\sigma)$ $= \{\lambda x.s_x \mid s_x \in \gamma_R(\sigma(x))\}$
Order:
      Reg $p \sqsubseteq q$ iff $\gamma_r(p) \subseteq \gamma_r(q)$
      $\mathcal{P}^{\mathrm{N}}(\mathsf{Reg})$ $P \sqsubseteq Q$ iff $\gamma_R(P) \subseteq \gamma_R(Q)$
      State $\sigma \sqsubseteq \sigma'$ iff $\gamma_S(\sigma) \subseteq \gamma_S(\sigma')$

Fig. 2. The Abstract Domain

2.2   Concatenation and Widening

The abstract semantics of string concatenation is defined as follows: two regular
strings are sequentially ordered, except for when initial and subsequent regular
strings end and begin, respectively, with a repetition, as defined in Fig. 3. If the
two repetitions are the same, one is thrown away; otherwise, the two are brutally
merged.

The widening operator of two regular strings is designed minimize precision
loss while allowing for analysis termination. Two sets of regular strings can be
widened simply by widening every pair of two input sets, but with the possible result of an unnecessarily large string. For instance, consider where after
one loop iteration of $\{a, b\}$ becomes $\{aa, ba\}$. The most reasonable analysis solution should be $\{aa^\star, ba^\star\}$, so we would want to choose $\{a\nabla aa, b\nabla bb\}$ instead of
$\{a\nabla aa, a\nabla ba, b\nabla aa, b\nabla ba\}$. Hence, we define $P\nabla Q = \{p\nabla q \mid p \in P, q \in Q, p\,\mathcal{R}\,q\}$
to give total relation $\mathcal{R} : P \times Q$. The method for finding such a relation is dis-
cussed after the explanation of the widening operator for regular strings.

To widen two regular strings, we identify their common and different components, pick and leave unchanged the common parts, and then merge the different
parts. For instance, suppose we compute $acd\nabla abc$, where the common components are the bold characters in **a**c**d** and **a**b**c**. We first pick a, then extract $b^\star$
from the merger of ϵ and b, then pick c, and then extract $d^\star$ from the merger of d
and ϵ. Therefore, by concatenating the components, the two original inputs are

$$P \cdot Q \quad = \{p \cdot q \mid p \in P, \; q \in Q\}$$

$$p \cdot q \quad = \begin{cases} p'r^*q' & \text{if } p = p'r^*, \; q = r^*q' \\ p'\{c \mid c \text{ appears in } r \text{ or } r'\}^* q' & \text{if } p = p'r^*, \; q = r'^*q', \text{ and } r \neq r' \\ pq & \text{otherwise} \end{cases}$$

$$\sigma \nabla^k \sigma' \quad = \begin{cases} \sigma & \text{if } \sigma' = \bot \\ \sigma' & \text{if } \sigma = \bot \\ \lambda x. \{.p\nabla^k.q \mid p \in \sigma(x), \; q \in \sigma'(x), \; p\,\mathcal{R}\,q\} & \text{otherwise} \\ \text{for a total relation } \mathcal{R} : \sigma(x) \times \sigma'(x) \end{cases}$$

$$p.q\nabla^k p'.q' \quad = \begin{cases} pq \odot^k p'q' & \text{if } q = \epsilon \text{ or } q' = \epsilon \\ (p \odot^k p') \cdot a \cdot (.r\nabla^k.r') & \text{if } q = ar, \; q' = ar', \text{ and } star\text{-}height(a) \leq k \\ pa.r\nabla^k p'a.r' & \text{if } q = ar, \; q' = ar', \text{ and } star\text{-}height(a) > k \\ pa.r\nabla^k p'.a'r' & \text{if } q = ar, \; q' = a'r', \; a \neq a', \text{ and } |q| > |q'| \\ p.ar\nabla^k p'a'.r' & \text{if } q = ar, \; q' = a'r', \; a \neq a', \text{ and } |q| \leq |q'| \end{cases}$$
$$\text{where } |q| = n \text{ for } q = a_1 a_2 \cdots a_n$$
$$\text{and } star\text{-}height(a) \text{ is the depth of repetitions of } q$$

$$p \odot^k q \quad = \begin{cases} \epsilon & \text{if } p, q \in \{\epsilon\} \\ p^* & \text{if } p \neq \epsilon, \; q = \epsilon, \text{ and } star\text{-}height(p^*) \leq k \\ q^* & \text{if } p = \epsilon, \; q \neq \epsilon, \text{ and } star\text{-}height(q^*) \leq k \\ (.p'\nabla^{k-1}.q')^* & \text{if } p = p'^*, \; q = q'^*, \text{ and } k \geq 2 \\ (.p'\nabla^{k-1}.q)^* & \text{if } p = p'^*, \; q \neq q'^*, \text{ and } k \geq 2 \\ (.p\nabla^{k-1}.q')^* & \text{if } p \neq p'^*, \; q = q'^*, \text{ and } k \geq 2 \\ \{c \mid c \text{ appears in } p \text{ or } q\}^* & \text{otherwise} \end{cases}$$

Fig. 3. Abstract Concatenation and Widening

widened to ab^*cd^*. This method is problematic, though, as the different components of multiple regular strings may be determined with different results. For
instance, for cd and cdd, we can say that cd is common and the last d of cdd is
different: **cd** and **cd**d, or the middle d of cdd is different: **cd** and **c**d**d**. We solve
this dilemma by traversing the string from left to right. The marker . is used to
indicate the position of string traversal. That is, $p.q$ indicates that p has been
traversed and identified as different, and that q has not been traversed. Thus the
current atom is always next to the dot(.) on the right. There exist three possible
cases of string traversal:

- After one regular string has been completely traversed, we conclude that
  the two regular strings are different. Thus, we merge them with the mash
  operator, $\odot$, which is discussed below.
- When we find a common atom, we merge the two different parts on the left,
  widen the rest of strings on the right, and then concatenate them in order.
- When two current atoms differ, we pick the longer string (the string with
  more atoms) and move the dot one atom to the right in the picked string.

For instance, consider the case of $.abc\nabla.ac$. First, we find that a is common and
move to the adjacent string to the right, $.bc\nabla.c$, where the current atoms b and

c are different. Since bc is longer than c, we conclude that b is different: $b.c\nabla.c$. We again meet the common character c, so we mash b and ϵ to obtain b^*. In conclusion, abc and ac are widened to ab^*c, where a and c are picked as common string components.

The mash operator $\odot$ yields precise results for the following cases.

- When one of its operands is empty, the other non-empty regular string is most likely to be repeated. Thus, the repetition of the non-empty regular string is returned. If both operands are empty, an empty regular string is returned.
- When both operands are repetitions, regular strings in the bodies of the repetitions are widened, and then the repetition of the widened result is returned.
- When only one of its operands is a repetition, a regular string in the body of the repetition and the other regular string are widened, and then the repetition of the widened result is returned.

For other cases, two regular strings are brutally mashed to conform to the form of C^*.

During widening or mashing regular strings, we control the star height. The superscript k of widening operator ∇^k and mash operator $\odot^k$ indicates that the star height of the result should be less than or equal to k. In mashing two regular strings, k is decreased when we go one level deeper inside a repetition. When $k < 2$, instead of going one level deeper inside, we brutally merge two regular strings so that the star height of the result is one. In theory, we cannot guarantee the termination of our analysis without some form of star-height control. As shown by our experiments, however, our analysis seems to terminate without star-height control (i.e., $k = \infty$).

We now discuss in detail the clever widening of two sets of regular strings. The procedure aims to find the total relation of two sets so that similar regular strings are related. One pair of regular strings is more *similar* than the other if it maintains more common components. When the number of common components is equal, the pair with fewer differing components is considered to be more similar. The algorithm to find the total relation of two sets is as follows: (1) For each regular string in the smaller set, find the most similar regular string in the larger set and pick related pairs until the smaller set is empty; (2) The leftover regular strings in the larger set find their similar counterparts from the original smaller set. For instance, consider $\{a, b\}$ and $\{ba, bb, bc\}$. For a in the smaller set, we pick the most similar one ba. For b, since the leftovers bb and bc tie, we arbitrarily choose one bb. Since all regular strings in the smaller set are picked, the leftover bc finds the most similar one b from $\{a, b\}$.

Theorem 1. $\nabla^k :$ State $\times$ State $\to$ State *is a widening operator which satisfies the followings:*

1. $\sigma \sqsubseteq \sigma \nabla^k \sigma'$ and $\sigma' \sqsubseteq \sigma \nabla^k \sigma'$; and
2. *the ascending chain by ∇^k is always finite when the cardinality of sets of regular strings is bounded.*

We only sketch the proof of the termination argument. The widening sequence of abstract states is finite if the sequence of regular strings is finite for each variable, which can be proved as follows. We can consider every regular string p as a form $r_1 C_1 r_2 C_2 r_3 \cdots C_n r_{n+1}$ where r_i is an empty string or a repetition because we do not allow adjacent repetitions. For instance, $abc^\star$ can be considered as $\epsilon a \epsilon b c^\star$. By using the canonical form, we define the *size tree* of regular strings:

- $|\epsilon|^T = \langle \omega \rangle$ where ω is an arbitrary big tree, and
- $|r_1 C_1 r_2 C_2 \cdots C_n r_{n+1}|^T = \langle |r_1|^I, |C_1|, |r_2|^I, |C_2|, \cdots, |C_n|, |r_{n+1}|^I \rangle$ where $|C| = \mathsf{Int}(i)$ when i is the size of character set C.

where $|\epsilon|^I = \omega$, $|C^\star|^I = |C|$, and $|r^\star|^I = |r|^T$ if $r \neq C$. The order among trees is defined as: $\mathsf{Int}(i) \leq t \leq \omega$ for all tree t which is not an integer, $\mathsf{Int}(i) \leq \mathsf{Int}(j)$ if $i \geq j$, and $\langle t_1, t_2, \cdots t_n \rangle \leq \langle t_1', t_2', \cdots, t_m' \rangle$ if $n < m$, or $n = m$ and $t_i \leq t_i'$ for all $0 \leq i \leq n$. We proved that $|.p\nabla^k.q|^T \leq |p|^T$, and that $|.p\nabla^k.q|^T = |p|^T$ implies that $.p\nabla^k.q = p$. We also showed that every sequence $t_0, t_1, \cdots, t_n$ is finite when $t_i > t_{i+1}$ for all $0 \leq i < n$ because we limit the depth of the trees. Therefore, every sequence widened by ∇^k is finite.

2.3   Other String Operators

The abstract versions of string operators `trim`, `replace`, and `substr` are defined in Fig. 4. `replace`(c,c') replaces all occurrences of character c with character c' in the given regular string. `trim` removes blanks at both ends of the given string. However, for presentation brevity, we assume that `trim` removes blanks only at the front end. The abstract `trim` operator traverses the given regular string from left to right.

- If we reach an abstract character $\{'\ '\}$, we continue trimming.
- If we reach an abstract character C which includes a blank, we have to consider two possibilities: when the concretized character is a blank and when it is a non-blank.
- If we reach a repetition $r^\star$, we consider two possibilities: (1) when $r^\star$ becomes empty after trimming it off, we continue trying for the rest; (2) when $r^\star$ becomes a non-empty string, we trim r off and put the result in front only when the result is not empty.
- If we reach an abstract character which does not include a blank, we stop.

`substr`(i,j) extracts a substring from the ith position to the $(j-1)$th position of the given string. When we reach a repetition $r^\star$ when finding a substring, we also consider two possibilities: (1) $r^\star$ is concretized to an empty string, and (2) $r^\star$ is concretized to a non-empty string. For possibility (2), $r^\star$ is unfolded once to yield $r \cdot r^\star$, from which substrings are extracted. Other cases are straightforward.

Previous string analyzers do not properly handle string operations. In JSA and Minamide's analyzer, string operations other than concatenation use rough approximations to break cycles of string productions [2,7]. In our analyzer,

Abstract operator $[\![op]\!] : \mathrm{Reg} \to \mathcal{P}(\mathrm{Reg})$ for $op ::= \mathtt{replace}(c, c') \mid \mathtt{trim} \mid \mathtt{substr}(i, j)$

$[\![\mathtt{replace}(c, c')]\!]p = \{p\{c'/c\}\}$

$$[\![\mathtt{trim}]\!]p = \begin{cases} [\![\mathtt{trim}]\!]q & \text{if } p = \{'\ '\}\, q \\ [\![\mathtt{trim}]\!]q \cup ((C \setminus \{'\ '\})q) & \text{if } p = Cq \text{ and } \{'\ '\} \subset C \\ [\![\mathtt{trim}]\!]q \cup (\{r' \cdot r^*q \mid r' \in [\![\mathtt{trim}]\!]r,\ r' \neq \epsilon\} & \text{if } p = r^*q \\ \{p\} & \text{otherwise} \end{cases}$$

$$[\![\mathtt{substr}(i, j)]\!]p = \begin{cases} \{\epsilon\} & \text{if } i = 0 \text{ and } j = 0 \\ \{C\} \cdot [\![\mathtt{substr}(0, j-1)]\!]q & \text{if } i = 0,\ j > 0, \text{ and } p = Cq \\ [\![\mathtt{substr}(i-1, j-1)]\!]q & \text{if } i > 0,\ j > 0, \text{ and } p = Cq \\ [\![\mathtt{substr}(i, j)]\!](r \cdot r^*q) \cup [\![\mathtt{substr}(i, j)]\!]q & \text{if } i \geq 0,\ j > 0, \text{ and } p = r^*q \\ \{\} & \text{otherwise} \end{cases}$$

Fig. 4. Abstract String Operators

abstract string operations are applied during analysis on demand. Hence, with our method, it is not at all an issue whether or not string operations are in cyclic productions. For example,

```
x = "a";
for(i=0; i<10; i++) {
    x = x + "b ";
    x.trim();
}
```

Our analyzer returns the exact answer: $\underline{ab^*}$, while JSA gives the most imprecise answer: $\underline{(\mathtt{a+b+'\ ')^*}}$

3 Analysis

In this section, we describe our string analysis. We first define the analysis for a core imperative string-processing language. We next extend it to cover constant propagation for integers. Then we show how to handle heap objects. Finally, we close this section by briefly explaining the interprocedural version.

3.1 Analysis for the Core Language

The analysis of the core imperative language is defined in Fig. 5 based on the standard abstract interpretation technique. An expression may be a string constant s, a variable x, a string concatenation $e+e$, or another string operator $x.op$. For a string concatenation, we use the abstract concatenation operator $\cdot$ defined in Fig. 3. For other string operators, we use their abstract version defined in Fig. 4. A statement is either a no-operation $\mathtt{skip}$, an assignment $x:=e$, a sequence $t;t$, a conditional statement $\mathtt{if}\ t\ t$, or a loop $\mathtt{while}\ t$. For the case of a loop, we use the widening operator defined in Fig. 3 to compute a widen sequence until it is stabilized. Note that the boolean expression in conditional statement and loop is not considered.

$$\mathcal{E}[\![e]\!] : \text{State} \to \mathcal{P}(\text{Reg}) \text{ for } e ::= s \mid x \mid e\text{+}e \mid e.\,op$$
$$\mathcal{E}[\![s]\!]\,\sigma \quad = \{C_1 \cdots C_n \mid s = c_1 c_2 \cdots c_n,\ C_i = \{c_i\}\}$$
$$\mathcal{E}[\![x]\!]\,\sigma \quad = \sigma(x)$$
$$\mathcal{E}[\![e_1\text{+}e_2]\!]\,\sigma \quad = \mathcal{E}[\![e_1]\!]\,\sigma \cdot \mathcal{E}[\![e_2]\!]\,\sigma$$
$$\mathcal{E}[\![e.\,op]\!]\,\sigma \quad = \bigcup \{[\![op]\!]p \mid p \in \mathcal{E}[\![e]\!]\,\sigma\}$$

$$\mathcal{T}[\![t]\!] : \text{State} \to \text{State} \text{ for } t ::= \texttt{skip} \mid x\,{:=}\,e \mid t;t \mid \texttt{if } t\ t \mid \texttt{while } t$$
$$\mathcal{T}[\![t]\!]\,\bot \quad = \bot$$
$$\mathcal{T}[\![\texttt{skip}]\!]\,\sigma \quad = \sigma$$
$$\mathcal{T}[\![x\,{:=}\,e]\!]\,\sigma \quad = \begin{cases} \sigma[\mathcal{E}[\![e]\!]\,\sigma/x] & \text{if } \mathcal{E}[\![e]\!]\,\sigma \neq \emptyset \\ \bot & \text{if } \mathcal{E}[\![e]\!]\,\sigma = \emptyset \end{cases}$$
$$\mathcal{T}[\![t_1\,;\,t_2]\!]\,\sigma \quad = \mathcal{T}[\![t_2]\!]\,(\mathcal{T}[\![t_1]\!]\,\sigma)$$
$$\mathcal{T}[\![\texttt{if } t_1\ t_2]\!]\,\sigma = \mathcal{T}[\![t_1]\!]\,\sigma \sqcup \mathcal{T}[\![t_2]\!]\,\sigma$$
$$\mathcal{T}[\![\texttt{while } t]\!]\,\sigma = \text{fix}^\nabla \lambda \sigma'.\sigma \sqcup \mathcal{T}[\![t]\!]\,\sigma'$$

Fig. 5. The Analysis for the Core Language

3.2   Integers

String-manipulating programs sometimes convert integer values to strings. To increase the precision of our analysis, a constant propagation for integers is added to our analysis, as defined in Fig. 6. We assume that programs are well-typed. That is, we assume that each variable only has values of its type, and thus a widening operator may be applied to string-typed variables.

3.3   Handling Heap Objects

Our method uses a well-known technique [1] to handle heap objects: (1) a heap object is abstracted by its allocation site; for instance, two heap objects allocated at the same program point are summarized as one abstract heap object; and (2) for each abstract heap object, we record the number of heap objects that are abstracted. This information is used to strongly update the content of a heap object. If an abstract heap object represents only one heap object, we can strongly update its content; otherwise, we cannot.

In the extended abstract domain for handling heap memory, shown in Fig 7, the location domain identifies allocation sites. The value domain is extended to include locations and a null-pointer value. The heap domain is a partial map from locations to their possible objects. An object consists of one value because we only consider objects with size equal to one. In addition, every object is tagged to indicate whether it is unique.

The analysis extended to deal with three heap-manipulating statements is defined in Fig 7. The additional statements are an allocation statement $x\,{:=}\,\texttt{new}^l$, a load statement $x\,{:=}\,\texttt{[}y\texttt{]}$, and a store statement $\texttt{[}x\texttt{]}\,{:=}\,y$. Note that every allocation statement is marked with a label, the size of every object is always one, and we assume that the initial value for a new heap object is $\texttt{nil}$.

Abstract domain: Value $V \in \mathcal{P}^N(\text{Reg}) + \mathbf{Z}^\top$
$\qquad\qquad\qquad$ State $\sigma \in (\text{Var} \to \text{Value})_\bot$

Order:
$\qquad\qquad\qquad$ Value $V \sqsubseteq V'$ iff $V, V' \subseteq \text{Reg}$ and $\gamma_R(V) \subseteq \gamma_R(V')$
$\qquad\qquad\qquad\qquad\qquad$ or $V, V' \in \mathbf{Z}^\top$ and $(V' = \top$ or $V = V')$
$\qquad\qquad\qquad$ State $\sigma \sqsubseteq \sigma'$ iff $\sigma(x) \sqsubseteq \sigma'(x)$ for all $x \in \text{Var}$

$\mathcal{I}[\![ie]\!] : \text{State} \to \mathbf{Z}^\top$ for $ie ::= \ i \in \mathbf{Z} \mid x \mid ie \ iop \ ie$ for $iop \in \{+, -, \times, \cdots\}$
$\mathcal{I}[\![i]\!]\sigma \qquad = \ i$
$\mathcal{I}[\![x]\!]\sigma \qquad = \ \sigma(x)$
$\mathcal{I}[\![ie_1 \ iop \ ie_2]\!]\sigma \ = \ \begin{cases} \mathcal{I}[\![ie_1]\!]\sigma \ iop \ \mathcal{I}[\![ie_2]\!]\sigma & \text{if } \mathcal{I}[\![ie_1]\!]\sigma \neq \top \text{ and } \mathcal{I}[\![ie_2]\!]\sigma \neq \top \\ \top & \text{if } \mathcal{I}[\![ie_1]\!]\sigma = \top \text{ or } \mathcal{I}[\![ie_2]\!]\sigma = \top \end{cases}$

$T[\![t]\!] \ : \text{State} \to \text{State}$ for $t ::= \ \cdots \ \mid x := ie$
$T[\![x := ie]\!]\sigma \quad = \ \sigma[\mathcal{I}[\![ie]\!]\sigma/x]$

Fig. 6. The Extension for Integers

- For the allocation statement $x := \text{new}^l$, if there is no heap object previously abstracted as l, that is, l is not in the domain of the abstract heap, we add a new object to the abstract heap, initialize its content as `nil`, and tag it with 1. Otherwise, that is, if there already exist some objects abstracted by l, we weakly update its content by the initial value `nil` and tag it with ω.
- For the load statement $x := [y]$, we get the content of y from the abstract heap and update x.
- For the store statement $[x] := y$, if x points to a single, unique object, we strongly update its content. Otherwise, we weakly update the content of objects that x may point to.

These statements may be straightforwardly extended to other cases. For the loop case, we apply widening to regular strings in both the abstract state and abstract heap.

3.4   Interprocedural Analysis

The interprocedural version of our analysis employs a standard technique named 1-CFA [10,9]. We collect the possible states of each procedure at all of its call sites, making it possible to output states by computing the procedure body. The analysis result is achieved by a fixed-point iteration. If the procedure is called more than twice at different call sites, we separately keep the abstract state for each call site, and separately compute the procedure body for each call site. This is made possible by annotating contexts to abstract states. Since we use the 1-CFA technique, in which the context keeps the last call site only, the analysis precision can be blurred for nested calls.

$\quad$Since recursive procedures may induce non-termination of our analysis, we also compute the widening sequence of inputs and outputs of the methods.

Abstract domain:

$$\begin{array}{lll}
\text{Loc} & l \\
\text{Value} & V \in \mathcal{P}^N(\text{Reg}) + \mathbf{Z}^\top + \mathcal{P}^N(\text{Loc} + \{\texttt{nil}\}) \\
\text{State} & \sigma \in \text{Var} \to \text{Value} \\
\text{Uniqueness} & u \in \{1, \omega\} \\
\text{Content} & V^u \in \text{Value} \times \text{Uniqueness} \\
\text{Heap} & h \in \text{Loc} \rightharpoonup \text{Content}
\end{array}$$

Order:

$$\begin{array}{lll}
\text{Value} & V \sqsubseteq V' & \text{iff } V, V' \subseteq \text{Reg and } \gamma_R(V) \subseteq \gamma_R(V') \\
& & \text{or } V, V' \in \mathbf{Z}^\top \text{ and } (V' = \top \text{ or } V = V') \\
& & \text{or } V, V' \subseteq \text{Loc} \cup \{\texttt{nil}\} \text{ and } V \subseteq V' \\
\text{State} & \sigma \sqsubseteq \sigma' & \text{iff } \sigma(x) \sqsubseteq \sigma'(x) \text{ for all } x \in \text{Var} \\
\text{Uniqueness} & 1 \sqsubseteq \omega \\
\text{Content} & V_1^{u_1} \sqsubseteq V_2^{u_2} & \text{iff } V_1 \sqsubseteq V_2 \text{ and } u_1 \sqsubseteq u_2 \\
\text{Heap} & h_1 \sqsubseteq h_2 & \text{iff } \text{dom}(h_1) \subseteq \text{dom}(h_2) \\
& & \text{and } h_1(l) \sqsubseteq h_2(l) \text{ for all } l \in \text{dom}(h_1)
\end{array}$$

$$(\text{State} \times \text{Heap})_\bot \quad \bot \sqsubseteq (\sigma, h)$$
$$(\sigma_1, h_1) \sqsubseteq (\sigma_2, h_2) \text{ iff } \sigma_1 \sqsubseteq \sigma_2 \text{ and } h_1 \sqsubseteq h_2$$

$$\mathcal{T}[\![t]\!] : (\text{State} \times \text{Heap})_\bot \to (\text{State} \times \text{Heap})_\bot \text{ for } t ::= \cdots \mid x\texttt{:=new}^l \mid x\texttt{:=[}x\texttt{]} \mid \texttt{[}x\texttt{]:=}y$$

$$\mathcal{T}[\![t]\!] \bot \quad = \bot$$

$$\mathcal{T}[\![x\texttt{:=new}^l]\!](\sigma, h) = \begin{cases} (\sigma[\{l\}/x], h[\{\texttt{nil}\}^1/l]) & \text{if } l \notin \text{dom}(h) \\ (\sigma[\{l\}/x], h[(V \cup \{\texttt{nil}\})^\omega/l]) & \text{if } l \in \text{dom}(h) \text{ and } h(l) = V^u \end{cases}$$

$$\mathcal{T}[\![x\texttt{:=[}y\texttt{]}]\!](\sigma, h) = \begin{cases} (\sigma[V'/x], h) & \text{if } V' \neq \emptyset \\ \bot & \text{if } V' = \emptyset \end{cases}$$
$$\text{where } V' = \bigcup \{V \mid l \in \sigma(y), \, h(l) = V^u\}$$

$$\mathcal{T}[\![\texttt{[}x\texttt{]:=}y]\!](\sigma, h) = \begin{cases} (\sigma, h[\sigma(y)^1/l]) & \text{if } \sigma(x) = \{l\} \text{ and } h(l) = V^1 \\ (\sigma, h') & \text{otherwise} \end{cases}$$

$$\text{where } h' = \lambda l. \begin{cases} h(l) & \text{if } l \in \text{dom}(h) \text{ and } l \notin \sigma(x) \\ (\sigma(y) \cup V)^u \text{ where } h(l) = V^u & \text{if } l \in \text{dom}(h) \text{ and } l \in \sigma(x) \\ \text{undefined} & \text{if } l \notin \text{dom}(h) \end{cases}$$

Fig. 7. The Extension for the Heap

4   Experiments

We built a string analyzer for Java applications that employs our approach, and we tested its performance and precision for comparison with JSA. For a Java application with hotspots[1], our string analyzer produces a set of regular strings for each hotspot. We used Objective Caml as the implementation language and a Linux PC with an Intel PentiumD 830 processor (3.0 GHz) and 2 GByte memory.

The table in Fig. 8 shows the experimental results of 19 programs. The first 14 programs were those tested by JSA, and the final 5 programs were selected from sample programs in the BEA Kodo[TM] Enterprise Data Access library. Both JSA

---

[1] A hotspot is the program point where an interesting string expression is located.

Example	Lines	Hotspots	Calls	Objects	Loops	JSA(s)	OSA(s)
Switch	21	1	1	0	0	1.33	0.42
ReflectTest	50	2	15	2	2	1.6	0.43
SortAlgorithms	54	1	3	0	0	1.35	0.4
CarShop	56	2	8	2	0	1.39	0.51
ProdConsApp	3,496	3	1,224	311	34	9.95	25.12
Decades	26	1	9	0	2	1.91	0.47
SelectFromPer	51	1	16	0	1	1.61	0.39
LoadDriver	78	1	20	0	1	1.84	0.4
DB2Appl	105	2	26	0	1	1.74	0.48
AxionExample	162	7	76	1	1	1.83	0.59
Sample	178	4	47	0	1	2.08	0.55
GuestBookServlet	344	4	131	6	3	4.18	0.71
DBTest	384	5	127	13	3	2.88	1.19
CoercionTest	591	4	378	18	11	18.38	1.58
CustomFieldsMain	1648	17	451	24	4	2.96	0.93
CustomProxiesMain	477	9	76	8	1	1.97	0.72
CustomSequenceMain	280	9	38	3	2	1.12	0.47
ExternalizationFieldsMain	666	2	164	21	0	2.09	1.52
TextIndexMain	396	8	71	11	6	1.51	0.46

Fig. 8. Experimental Results

Example	JSA	OSA
CustomFieldsMain	Inserted: CustomFields<.*>:.* name: .* male: .* point: .* xml: .*	{Inserted: CustomFields<.*>:.* name: name.* male: false.* point: .*[x=1,y=2].* xml: .*}
ProdConsApp	.*	{Adv_SyncGet, Adv_SyncPut, .*}
SortAlgorithms	DefaultSortAlgorithms$(Counting+Quick)Sort	{.*}

Fig. 9. Precision Comparison

and our string analyzer were tested for comparison. The number of lines ranged from 21 to 3,496. To show the characteristics of programs, we collected the number of hotspots, the number of method calls, the number of new statements, and the number of loops. Columns JSA and OSA indicate analysis run times, in seconds, of JSA and our string analyzer. Our string analyzer completed analysis more quickly than JSA of all programs except the ProdConsApp, for which our analyzer was about 2.6 times slower. The speed-up is probably due to the implementation language used (Java versus OCaml). For the slower case, we guess that the large number of calls increased the number of times that method bodies were analyzed.

The results produced by our analyzer have been as precise as those yielded by JSA in most of the cases we have tested. However, the precision of some results differed, as shown in Fig. 9. For `CustomFieldsMain`, our analyzer gives more precise results due to its ability to analyze heap variables. For `ProdConsApp`, our string analyzer gives extra information than does JSA[2], as the two sets of regular strings are unioned when they are combined. On the other hand, JSA gives better results for `SortAlgorithms` because our current implementation ignores arrays.

5   Conclusion and Future Works

A string analyzer based on the abstract-interpretation framework is designed and implemented. A carefully crafted widening operator is devised to maintain the highest possible precision. Our solution generally gives results comparable to those of previous methods, and it understands heap variables and context sensitivity unlike others. We expect the method to be more suitable to practical applications.

Our string analyzer uses regular expressions that lack the expressibility required for checking the syntax of generated strings and for handling strings with escaped characters. Future work could aim to produce abstract string representations with more expression power while still employing the widening operator of our method.

Acknowledgement

The authors would like to thank anonymous reviewers for thoughtful comments and corrections.

References

1. David R. Chase, Mark Wegman, and F. Kenneth Zadeck. Analysis of pointers and structures. In *Proceedings of the ACM SIGPLAN Conference on Programming Language Design and Implementation*, pages 296–310. ACM Press, 1990.
2. Aske Simon Christensen, Anders Møller, and Michael I. Schwartzbach. Precise analysis of string expressions. In *Proceedings of the International Static Analysis Symposium*, volume 2694 of *Lecture Notes in Computer Science*, pages 1–18. Springer-Verlag, June 2003.
3. Patrick Cousot and Radhia Cousot. Abstract interpretation: a unified lattice model for static analysis of programs by construction or approximation of fixpoints. In *Proceedings of the ACM Symposium on Principles of Programming Languages*, pages 238–252, January 1977.
4. Patrick Cousot and Radhia Cousot. Abstract interpretation frameworks. *Journal of Logic and Computation*, 2(4):511–547, 1992.

---

[2] In theory, two results have the same precision. However, the extra information we get can be useful in practice.

5. Carl Gould, Zhendong Su, and Premkumar Devanbu. Static checking of dynamically generated queries in database applications. In *Proceedings of the International Conference on Software Engineering*, pages 645–654, May 2004.
6. Christian Kirkegaard and Anders Møller. Static analysis for Java servlets and JSP. In *Proceedings of the International Static Analysis Symposium*, August 2006.
7. Yasuhiko Minamide. Static approximation of dynamically generated web pages. In *Proceedings of the International World Wide Web Conference Committee*, pages 432–441, 2005.
8. M. Mohri and M.-J. Nederhof. Regular approximation of context-free grammars through transformation. In J.-C. Junqua and G. van Noord, editors, *Robustness in Language and Speech Technology*, pages 153–163. Kluwer Academic Publisher, 2001.
9. Flemming Nielson and Hanne Riis Nielson. Infinitary control flow analysis: a collecting semantics for closure analysis. In *Proceedings of the ACM Symposium on Principles of Programming Languages*, pages 332–345. ACM Press, 1997.
10. Olin Shivers. Control flow analysis in scheme. In *Proceedings of the ACM SIGPLAN Conference on Programming Language Design and Implementation*, June 1988.
11. Naoshi Tabuchi, Eijiro Sumii, and Akinori Yonezawa. Regular expression types for strings in a text processing language. In *Proceedings of Workshop on Types in Programming*, pages 1–18, July 2002.
12. Peter Thiemann. Grammar-based analysis string expressions. In *Proceedings of the ACM Workshop on Types in Language Design and Implementation*, pages 59–70, 2004.

A Bytecode Logic for JML and Types

Lennart Beringer and Martin Hofmann

Institut für Informatik, Universität München
Oettingenstrasse 67, 80538 München, Germany
{beringer, mhofmann}@tcs.ifi.lmu.de

Abstract. We present a program logic for virtual machine code that may serve as a suitable target for different proof-transforming compilers. Compilation from JML-specified source code is supported by the inclusion of annotations whose interpretation extends to non-terminating computations. Compilation from functional languages, and the communication of results from intermediate level program analysis phases are facilitated by a new judgement format that admits the compositionality of type systems to be reflected in derivations. This makes the logic well suited to serve as a language in which proofs of a PCC architecture are expressed. We substantiate this claim by presenting the compositional encoding of a type system for bounded heap consumption. Both the soundness proof of the logic and the derivation of the type system have been formally verified by an implementation in Isabelle/HOL.

1   Introduction

Modeling languages such as JML [25] allow the software architect to specify functional and non-functional behaviour of code modules. Typically, these languages comprise a variety of specification idioms such as partial-correctness specifications using pre- and post-conditions, termination measures, specification of exceptional behaviour, model fields, ghost variables and fields, invariants at object or class level, lightweight specifications, or the inclusion of pure (i.e. non-side-effecting) code in specification clauses. Although the precise interpretation of some of these features is still a matter of ongoing debate, a number of verification tools have been presented that validate code w.r.t. JML specifications [14]. Although the proposed formalisms mainly target Java source code, they can relatively easily be adapted to bytecode.

The adaptation of specification constructs to low-level code admits a smooth translation of high-level specifications into specifications of mobile code units. However, we do not expect that a similarly direct transfer of validation strategies such as verification condition generators would suffice for their verification, for two reasons. Firstly, bytecode that was obtained by compilation from languages other than Java may not be amenable to the same proof strategies, or may lead to different verification conditions if it has undergone an obfuscation routine. Secondly, a recipient may require transmitted code to be complemented by a proof certifying that the code is safe to execute [28]. Typically, the production of certificates exploits results of program analyses such as type systems. In this case, the validation of certificates by the code consumer is supported if the type system's structuring principles (invariants) are communicated as part

N. Kobayashi (Ed.): APLAS 2006, LNCS 4279, pp. 389–405, 2006.
© Springer-Verlag Berlin Heidelberg 2006

of the certificate [4,13]. Again, it is not guaranteed that these abstraction barriers are respected by a verification strategy for source code verification.

In this paper, we therefore propose a program logic for a bytecode language that satisfies requirements motivated by JML specifications and admits different verification strategies to be implemented, including strategies that are suitable for validating high-level type systems. More specifically, we present a formalism where partial-correctness method specifications can be complemented by method invariants and local annotations at intermediate program points whose interpretation applies to terminating *as well as non-terminating* program executions. Non-terminating executions are not covered by traditional (partial or total) Hoare logics, but are required for a faithful interpretation of JML code annotations. They are also desirable for proof-carrying code (PCC) frameworks: the significance of a certificate regarding the safety or the consumption of resources is increased if its validity does not derive from a partial-correctness interpretation - for example, consider a certificate purporting to guarantee an upper bound on the runtime. On the other hand, non-terminating program executions are often implicitly covered by program analysis formalisms such as type systems, but this fact is often not stated (or proven) explicitly, for example if the soundness proof is formulated as a syntactic subject-reduction proof w.r.t. a big-step operational semantics. In order to demonstrate the suitability of our logic for the interpretation of such type systems, we present the syntax-directed encoding of a type system for bounded heap consumption which covers terminating and non-terminating executions.

For presentational reasons, the program logic described in the present paper covers only a small fragment of the JVML. However, in collaboration with partners from the Mobius project [8], a variation of the logic has been produced that covers a more substantial subset of JVML, including virtual method invocations, static fields, arrays, exceptions, and various datatypes. At the same time, work is under way to translate JML specification constructs that are not considered in the present paper into the extended logic, in particular the constructs of JML specification level 0 [25].

Motivation and overview of assertion format. The format of judgements in a program logic is strongly influenced by semantic considerations, i.e. by the conclusions one may draw from a derivable judgement regarding the operational behaviour. Our logic aims to fulfill two sets of requirements. The first requirement concerns JML annotations at intermediate program points. Their common understanding mandates that an assertion A associated to a program point ℓ should be satisfied whenever the control flow reaches ℓ. At first sight, this interpretation motivates a notion of validity like

$$\forall s.\ \ell_0, s_0 \to^* \ell, s \Rightarrow A(s) \tag{1}$$

where s_0 denotes the entry state of the program fragment (e.g. method) and ℓ_0 the label of the first instruction. Indeed, this interpretation extends partial-correctness program logics by also applying to non-terminating program executions. Furthermore, the generalisation to binary predicates A, with validity defined by

$$\forall s.\ \ell_0, s_0 \to^* \ell, s \Rightarrow A(s_0, s), \tag{2}$$

admits assertions to refer to the initial state, as is required for the translation of idioms such as JML's old keyword [22].

Although program logics motivated by such an interpretation have been proposed [32,7,1], the resulting proof systems appear unsatisfactory, since they mandate the concurrent satisfaction of local conditions at all program labels, for a fully annotated program. For example, the proof rule for program points in Rinard's logic [32] involves a universal quantification over all predecessor labels. This, in our opinion, precludes local reasoning, by which we mean that the validity of an assertion at a program point ℓ should refer to the phrase represented by ℓ. Local behaviour is the source from which type systems for high-level languages draw their compositionality. In order to achieve our second goal, the interpretation of type systems, it appears necessary that this behaviour be reflected in the logic. Thus, an assertion at ℓ should constrain executions *from ℓ onwards*, irrespective of the path used to *reach ℓ*. While this demand contradicts a formulation following (1), it would enable us to exploit the syntax-directedness of typing rules in the proofs of derived proof rules, i.e. of lemmas for a syntactically determined subclass of assertions.

In Bannwart and Müller's logic [7], program points are decorated with (unary) assertions E that are interpreted w.r.t. a partial-correctness specification of the surrounding method. Assuming a fully specified program, each local judgement $\vdash \{E_\ell\}\ \ell$ is valid if the satisfaction of E_ℓ in the state prior to executing the instruction at ℓ guarantees the satisfaction of the assertions of all successor labels of ℓ:

$$\forall s.\ \ell_0, s_0 \to^* \ell, s \Rightarrow E_\ell(s) \Rightarrow \forall \ell'\ s'.\ \ell, s \to \ell', s' \Rightarrow E_{\ell'}(s'). \tag{3}$$

Thus, E_ℓ denotes a *pre-condition* for $E_{\ell'}$ and consequently (by transitivity) for the method specification (which is identical to the specification of the return instruction). However, this format does not admit a rule of consequence, as E_ℓ in (3) suggests that assertions could be strengthened, while $E_{\ell'}$ suggests that they can be weakened, which is also what one would expect from JML annotations. Furthermore, the fact that the final state is only mentioned indirectly, via the implicit reference to the method specification, is an obstacle to local reasoning: the method specification relates a final state of a (terminating) execution only to the *initial* state, but not the state at label ℓ.

Our proposed solution consists of introducing several assertion forms, with specific roles. Judgements explicitly relate a program point ℓ to a (binary) *pre-condition* A, a (ternary) *post-condition* B, and a (ternary) *invariant* I, and implicitly refer to a global table Q that assigns (binary) *annotations* Q to some program points (not all program points are required to be annotated). Informally, the interpretation of such a judgement asserts that whenever ℓ is reached from s_0 with current state s, and $A(s_0, s)$ holds, then

- $B(s_0, s, t)$ holds, provided that the method terminates with final state t
- $I(s_0, s, H)$ holds, provided that H is the heap component of any state arising during the continuation of the method invocation surrounding s, *including invocations of further methods*, i.e. subframes
- $Q(s_0, s')$ holds, provided that s' is reached at some label ℓ' during the continuation of the method invocation surrounding s, *but not including subframes*, where $Q(\ell') = Q$

In order to support the descent into subframes in the interpretation of invariants, partial-correctness method specifications are complemented by *method invariants* which relate the frame-initial state to the heap component of any state arising during the execution of the method (*including subframes*), irrespective of its termination behaviour. Both kinds of invariants are thus *strong invariants* in the sense of Hähnle and Mostowski [19]: they mandate that the property holds *throughout* the execution of a program fragment, instead of merely stipulating that the property holds upon termination whenever it was satisfied in the initial state. The decision to consider only a state's heap component in invariants is motivated by the fact that the operand stack and the (naming of) local variables should be considered implementation details of a method. For example, the substitution of a method by an improved implementation that uses different local variables should not affect invariants of surrounding methods.

The proposed format admits the expected rule of consequence where pre-conditions can be strengthened, while post-conditions and invariants may be weakened. Furthermore, JML annotations are directly supported as these may be collected in Q and will be satisfied whenever the annotated label is visited, irrespective of the termination behaviour. References to the frame-initial state are also supported, thus enabling the direct translation of specification idiom old. Finally, the format enables syntax-directed interpretations of type systems as all items involved in the execution of the code fragment *starting* at ℓ are available in the judgement for ℓ. Conceptually, the emphasis on syntactic structure that distinguishes our logic from the above-mentioned work appears similar to the difference between Hoare logic and Floyd's reasoning techniques for flowcharts.

Synopsis. The remainder of this paper is structured as follows: in Section 2, we present syntax and operational semantics of a small bytecode language which serves as our vehicle for presenting the logic. This allows us (Section 3) to formally define our notion of validity. We then present the proof system and outline its soundness proof. We demonstrate the suitability of the logic for giving interpretations of type systems that affect terminating and non-terminating program executions by outlining the encoding of a type system for bounded heap consumption in Section 4. Finally, we conclude and discuss related work. The material presented in Sections 2 to 4 is based on a development of the logic in the theorem prover Isabelle/HOL, including a formalised soundness proof and a formal derivation of the encoded typing rules. Following the approach advocated by Kleymann [24], the formalisation uses a deep embedding of the programming language syntax, while assertions are embedded shallowly in the meta-logic of the theorem prover. The corresponding Isabelle sources are available from [12].

2   Syntax and Dynamic Semantics

For the purpose of this paper, we consider instructions

$$ins ::= \text{Load } x \mid \text{Store } x \mid \text{Const } z \mid \text{Unop } u \mid \text{Binop } o \mid \text{New } c \mid \text{Getfield } c\, f \mid$$
$$\text{Putfield } c\, f \mid \text{Goto } l \mid \text{If0 } l \mid \text{Invokestatic } M \mid \text{Return}$$

where x ranges over a set $\mathcal{X}$ of (local) variables (also called registers), z over integer constants and Null, u and o over unary and binary operations (like isNull, add, mul,...), respectively, c over a set $\mathcal{C}$ of class names, f over a set $\mathcal{F}$ of field names, l over a set $\mathcal{L}$ of program labels, and m over a set $\mathcal{M}$ of method names. All these sets are assumed to be mutually distinct. Method identifiers $M = (c, m)$ combine class and method names, and program points ℓ are of the form $\ell = M, l$.

A method definition $(par, l, body, suc)$ consists of a list $par = [x_1, \ldots, x_n]$ of (distinct) formal parameters, the label l of the first instruction, a method body $body$, represented as a finite map from program labels l to instructions, and a partial function $suc : \mathcal{L} \rightharpoonup_{fin} \mathcal{L}$ that maps labels to their control flow successors.

A program consists of a finite map from method identifiers to method definitions. All notions in the remainder of this paper are formulated with respect to an arbitrary but fixed program, which we denote by P. For $P(M) = (par, l, body, suc)$ we also write $init_M$ for l, $M(l)$ for $body(l)$, and suc_M for suc.

The dynamic semantics is defined over a set $\mathcal{V}$ of values that is ranged over by v and comprises constants z and addresses $a \in \mathcal{A}$. JVM states $s \in \Sigma$ are built from operand stacks, stores, and heaps

$$
\begin{aligned}
O \in \mathcal{O} &= \mathcal{V}\ list & s &\in \Sigma = \mathcal{O} \times \mathcal{S} \times \mathcal{H} \\
S \in \mathcal{S} &= \mathcal{X} \rightharpoonup_{fin} \mathcal{V} & s_0 &\in \Sigma_0 = \mathcal{S} \times \mathcal{H} \\
H \in \mathcal{H} &= \mathcal{A} \rightharpoonup_{fin} \mathcal{C} \times (\mathcal{F} \rightharpoonup_{fin} \mathcal{V}) & t &\in \mathcal{T} = \mathcal{H} \times \mathcal{V}.
\end{aligned}
$$

The categories Σ_0 and $\mathcal{T}$ represent initial and terminal states which occur at the beginning (end) of a frame's execution. For $s_0 = (S, H)$ we write $state(s_0) = ([\,], S, H)$ for the local state that extends s_0 with an empty operand stack. For $par = [x_1, \ldots, x_n]$ and $O = [v_1, \ldots, v_n]$ we write $par \mapsto O$ for $[x_i \mapsto v_i]_{i=1,\ldots,n}$. Finally, we write $heap(s)$ to access the heap component of a state s, and similarly for initial and terminal states.

As in [7], the operational semantics is given by two judgements, a small-step relation $\Rightarrow \subseteq (\mathcal{L} \times \Sigma) \times (\mathcal{L} \times \Sigma)$, and its closure up to the end of the current frame, $\Downarrow \subseteq (\mathcal{L} \times \Sigma) \times \mathcal{T}$. Both relations are indexed by the current method. The (mutually recursive) relationship between these relations, and the rules for New, Goto, and Invokestatic are shown in Figure 1. The rules for the other instruction forms are similar.

$$
\text{NEW}\ \frac{M(l) = \mathsf{New}\ c \qquad a \notin dom\ H}{\vdash_M l, (O, S, H) \Rightarrow suc_M(l), (a :: O, S, H[a \mapsto (c, [\,])])} \qquad \text{GOTO}\ \frac{M(l) = \mathsf{Goto}\ l'}{\vdash_M l, s \Rightarrow l', s}
$$

$$
\text{INVS}\ \frac{\begin{array}{c} M(l) = \mathsf{Invokestatic}\ M' \qquad M' \in dom\ P \\ \vdash_{M'} init_{M'}, state(par_{M'} \mapsto O', H) \Downarrow H', v \end{array}}{\vdash_M l, (O'@O, S, H) \Rightarrow suc_M(l), (v :: O, S, H')}
$$

$$
\text{COMP}\ \frac{\vdash_M l, s \Rightarrow l', s' \qquad \vdash_M l', s' \Downarrow t}{\vdash_M l, s \Downarrow t} \qquad \text{RETURN}\ \frac{M(l) = \mathsf{Return}}{\vdash_M l, (v :: O, S, H) \Downarrow H, v}
$$

Fig. 1. Operational semantics: relations $\Rightarrow$ and $\Downarrow$ (excerpt)

3   Program Logic

3.1   Format of Assertions and Judgements

Judgements associated with program points involve formulae of the following three forms, where $\mathcal{B}$ denotes the set of booleans.

Assertions. $A \in Assn = (\Sigma_0 \times \Sigma) \to \mathcal{B}$ occur as preconditions A and annotations Q, and relate the current state to the initial state of the current frame.

Postconditions. $B \in Post = (\Sigma_0 \times \Sigma \times T) \to \mathcal{B}$ relate the current state to the initial and final state of a (terminating) execution of the current frame.

Invariants. $I \in Inv = (\Sigma_0 \times \Sigma \times \mathcal{H}) \to \mathcal{B}$ relate the initial state of the current method, the current state, and the heap component of a state of the current frame or a subframe of the current frame.

The behaviour of methods is described using two assertion forms.

Method specifications. $\Phi \in MethSpec = (\Sigma_0 \times T) \to \mathcal{B}$ constrain the behaviour of terminating method executions and thus relate only their initial and final states.

Method invariants. $\varphi \in MethInv = (\Sigma_0 \times \mathcal{H}) \to \mathcal{B}$ constrain the behaviour of terminating and non-terminating method executions by relating the initial state of a method frame to all heaps that occur during the execution of the method.

A program specification consists of two parts. The method specification table M : $(\mathcal{C} \times \mathcal{M}) \to (MethSpec \times MethInv)$ defines the externally visible behaviour. In addition, local annotations Q which constrain the behaviour at intermediate program points are collected in a partial map Q : $((\mathcal{C} \times \mathcal{M}) \times \mathcal{L}) \to_{fin} Assn$. For the remainder of this section, let M and Q denote some arbitrary but fixed specification and annotation tables.

3.2 Interpretation of Assertions and Judgements

In addition to the operational judgements defined in Figure 1, the interpretation of the program logic refers to two auxiliary relations. The first one, denoted by $\vdash_M l, s \Rightarrow^* l', s'$, is the reflexive and transitive closure of $\Rightarrow$ and is defined in the standard way. The second relation, denoted by $\vdash_M l, s \Uparrow s'$ and defined in Figure 2, extends $\Rightarrow^*$ by also relating l, s to s' if s' is a state that occurs later than s either in the same frame as s or in a subframe of that frame. This is achieved by the rule R-INVS that relates the call-state of a method invocation to the initial state of the subframe.

$$\text{R-Refl} \frac{}{\vdash_M l, s \Uparrow s} \qquad \text{R-Trans} \frac{\vdash_M l, s \Rightarrow l', s' \quad \vdash_M l', s' \Uparrow s''}{\vdash_M l, s \Uparrow s''}$$

$$\text{R-Invs} \frac{M(l) = \mathsf{Invokestatic}\ M' \quad M' \in dom\ P \quad \vdash_{M'} init_{M'}, state(par_{M'} \mapsto O', H) \Uparrow s}{\vdash_M l, (O'@O, S, H) \Uparrow s}$$

Fig. 2. Auxiliary operational relation $\Uparrow$

Definition 1. *A triple* (A, B, I) *is valid at* $\ell = M, l$, *notation* $\models \{A\}\ \ell\ \{B\}\ (I)$, *if for all* s_0 *and* s *with* $\vdash_M init_M, s_0 \Rightarrow^* l, s$ *and* $A(s_0, s)$,

- *if* $\vdash_M l, s \Downarrow t$ *then* $B(s_0, s, t)$,
- *if* $\vdash_M l, s \Uparrow s'$ *then* $I(s_0, s, heap(s'))$, *and*
- *if* $\vdash_M l, s \Rightarrow^* l', s'$ *and* $Q(M, l') = Q$ *then* $Q(s_0, s')$.

Note that the third clause applies to annotations Q associated with *future* labels l' in the same method M, and that these are interpreted without direct recourse to the current state s, although the proof of $Q(s_0, s')$ may exploit the precondition $A(s_0, s)$.

In order to store recursive proof assumptions during the verification of loops, proof contexts G may be used. These are finite maps which associate triples (A, B, I) to program points ℓ.

Definition 2. *Context G is called* valid*, notation* $\models G$*, if* $\models \{A\} \, \ell \, \{B\} \, (I)$ *holds for all $G(\ell) = (A, B, I)$. Similarly, specification table M is valid, notation* $\models M$*, if all M, Φ and φ with $M(M) = (\Phi, \varphi)$ satisfy* $\models \{A\} \, M, \text{init}_M \, \{B_\Phi\} \, (I_\varphi)$*, where*

$$A = \lambda \, (s_0, s). \; s = state(s_0)$$
$$B_\Phi = \lambda \, (s_0, s, t). \; s = state(s_0) \rightarrow \Phi(s_0, t), \text{ and}$$
$$I_\varphi = \lambda \, (s_0, s, H). \; s = state(s_0) \rightarrow \varphi(s_0, H).$$

Finally, program P is valid, notation $\models P$*, if there is a G such that* $\models G$ *and* $\models M$.

3.3 Assertion Transformers

In order to notationally simplify the presentation of the proof rules, we define operators that relate assertions occurring in judgements of adjacent instructions. The operators for simple instructions,

$$PRE(M, l, A)(s_0, r) = \exists s \, l'. \; \vdash_M l, s \Rightarrow l', r \wedge A(s_0, s)$$
$$POST(M, l, B)(s_0, r, t) = \forall s \, l'. \; \vdash_M l, s \Rightarrow l', r \rightarrow B(s_0, s, t)$$
$$INV(M, l, I)(s_0, r, H) = \forall s \, l'. \; \vdash_M l, s \Rightarrow l', r \rightarrow I(s_0, s, H)$$

resemble WP-operators, but are separately defined for pre-conditions, post-conditions, and invariants. In the case of method invocations, we replace the reference to the operational judgement by a reference to the method specification, and include the construction and destruction of a frame

$$PRE_{sinv}(\Phi, A, par) = \lambda \, (s_0, s). \; \exists O \, S \, H' \, H \, O' \, v. \; s = (v :: O, S, H') \, \wedge$$
$$\Phi((par \mapsto O', H), (H', v)) \wedge A(s_0, (O'@O, S, H))$$
$$POST_{sinv}(\Phi, B, par) = \lambda \, (s_0, s, t). \; \forall O \, S \, H' \, H \, O' \, v. \; s = (v :: O, S, H') \rightarrow$$
$$\Phi((par \mapsto O', H), (H', v)) \rightarrow B(s_0, (O'@O, S, H), t)$$
$$INV_{sinv}(\Phi, I, par) = \lambda \, (s_0, s, H). \; \forall O \, S \, H' \, H'' \, O' \, v. \; s = (v :: O, S, H') \rightarrow$$
$$\Phi((par \mapsto O', H''), (H', v)) \rightarrow I(s_0, (O'@O, S, H''), H)$$

Finally, the rule for the conditional jump instruction involves operators that take the dependence on the outcome of the branch condition into account:

$$A^+ = \lambda \, (s_0, s). \; \forall O \, S \, H. \; s = (0 :: O, S, H) \rightarrow A \, s_0 \, s$$
$$A^- = \lambda \, (s_0, s). \; \forall O \, S \, H \, z. \; s = (z :: O, S, H) \rightarrow z \neq 0 \rightarrow A \, s_0 \, s$$
$$B^+ = \lambda \, (s_0, s, t). \; \forall O \, S \, H. \; s = (0 :: O, S, H) \rightarrow B(s_0, s, t)$$

$$B^- = \lambda\,(s_0, s, t).\,\forall\,O\,S\,H\,z.\,s = (z :: O, S, H) \rightarrow z \neq 0 \rightarrow B(s_0, s, t)$$
$$I^+ = \lambda\,(s_0, s, H).\,\forall\,O\,S\,H'.\,s = (0 :: O, S, H') \rightarrow I(s_0, s, H)$$
$$I^- = \lambda\,(s_0, s, H).\,\forall\,O\,S\,H'\,z.\,s = (z :: O, S, H') \rightarrow z \neq 0 \rightarrow I(s_0, s, H),$$

3.4 Proof Rules

The proof system is presented in Figures 3 and 4, and has two judgement forms, $G \vdash \{A\}\,\ell\,\{B\}\,(I)$ and $G \vdash \langle A\rangle\,\ell\,\langle B\rangle\,(I)$. Both forms associate a program point to a precondition, a postcondition, and an invariant, relative to a proof context G. The motivation for using two judgement forms stems from the interaction between the rules that alter the flow of control inside a method frame (for the language considered in this paper only conditional and unconditional jumps, but in general also instructions that may throw an exception) and the rule AX that extracts such assumptions from G. Our approach separates the *usage* of an assumption from its *justification*. The axiom rule can only be used to derive judgements of the form that is required in the hypothesis of the syntax-directed rules, $G \vdash \langle A\rangle\,\ell\,\langle B\rangle\,(I)$. In contrast, the definition of verified programs requires us to discharge an assumption $G(\ell) = (A, B, I)$ by exhibiting a proof of $G \vdash \{A\}\,\ell\,\{B\}\,(I)$. Such a proof *cannot* simply consist of an application of the rule AX, but will necessarily end (modulo applications of the rule CONSEQ-F) in a syntax-directed rule. Consequently, the justification of an assumption is forced to inspect the corresponding code block, eliminating the possibility to insert arbitrary (incorrect) assumptions. In order to chain together a sequence of syntax-directed rules, we introduce a further rule, INJ, that turns a derivation of $G \vdash \{A\}\,\ell\,\{B\}\,(I)$ into one of $G \vdash \langle A\rangle\,\ell\,\langle B\rangle\,(I)$ – but no rule is given for converting in the opposite direction. The separation into two judgement forms thus represents an alternative to global well-definedness conditions on derivation trees, as it enforces that assumptions in G can not be justified vacuously by reference to G but only by inspecting the corresponding code block. Semantically, the judgement forms differ in bounds the number of operational steps for which a judgement is required to be valid.

The proof rules are oriented such that the conclusion is an unconstrained judgement and proof hypotheses refer to successor instructions. Hence, a verification condition generator may be defined as a proof strategy that traverses the program in the direction of the flow of control.

Syntax-directed rules. The syntax-directed rules are shown in Figure 3, and are motivated as follows.

Rule INSTR describes the behaviour of *basic* instructions.

$$basic(M, l) \equiv M(l) \in \left\{ \begin{array}{l} \text{Load } x, \text{Store } x, \text{Const } z, \text{Unop } u, \text{Binop } o, \\ \text{New } c, \text{Getfield } c\,f, \text{Putfield } c\,f \end{array} \right\}$$

The hypothetical judgement for the successor instruction involves assertions that are related to the assertions in the conclusion by the basic transformers presented in the previous section. In addition, the side conditions SC_1 and SC_2 ensure that the invariant I and the local annotation Q (if existing) are satisfied in any state reaching label l.

$$SC_1 = \forall\,s_0\,s.\,A(s_0, s) \rightarrow I(s_0, s, heap(s))$$
$$SC_2 = \forall Q.\,Q(M, l) = Q \rightarrow (\forall\,s_0\,s.\,A(s_0, s) \rightarrow Q(s_0, s))$$

$$\text{INSTR}\ \frac{basic(M,l)\quad SC_1\quad SC_2 \quad G \vdash \langle PRE(M,l,A)\rangle\, M, suc_M(l)\, \langle POST(M,l,B)\rangle\, (INV(M,l,I))}{G \vdash \{A\}\, M, l\, \{B\}\, (I)}$$

$$\text{GOTO}\ \frac{M(l) = \mathsf{Goto}\ l'\quad SC_1\quad SC_2 \quad G \vdash \langle PRE(M,l,A)\rangle\, M, l'\, \langle POST(M,l,B)\rangle\, (INV(M,l,I))}{G \vdash \{A\}\, M, l\, \{B\}\, (I)}$$

$$\text{IF0}\ \frac{\begin{array}{c} M(l) = \mathsf{If0}\ l'\quad SC_1\quad SC_2 \\ G \vdash \langle PRE(M,l,A^+)\rangle\, M, l'\, \langle POST(M,l,B^+)\rangle\, (INV(M,l,I^+)) \\ G \vdash \langle PRE(M,l,A^-)\rangle\, M, suc_M(l)\, \langle POST(M,l,B^-)\rangle\, (INV(M,l,I^-)) \end{array}}{G \vdash \{A\}\, M, l\, \{B\}\, (I)}$$

$$\text{INVS}\ \frac{\begin{array}{c} M(l) = \mathsf{Invokestatic}\ M'\quad M' \in dom\, P\quad M(M') = (\Phi, \varphi)\quad SC_1\quad SC_2 \\ \forall s_0\, O\, S\, H\, O'\, H'.\, A(s_0, (O'@O, S, H')) \to \varphi\, (par_{M'} \mapsto O', H')\, H \\ \to I(s_0, (O'@O, S, H'), H) \\ G \vdash \langle PRE_{sinv}(\Phi, A, par_{M'})\rangle\, M, suc_M(l)\, \langle POST_{sinv}(\Phi, B, par_{M'})\rangle \\ (INV_{sinv}(\Phi, I, par_{M'})) \end{array}}{G \vdash \{A\}\, M, l\, \{B\}\, (I)}$$

$$\text{RET}\ \frac{M(l) = \mathsf{Return}\quad SC_1\quad SC_2 \quad \forall s_0\, v\, O\, S\, H.\, A(s_0, (v :: O, S, H)) \to B(s_0, (v :: O, S, H), (H, v))}{G \vdash \{A\}\, M, l\, \{B\}\, (I)}$$

Fig. 3. Program logic: syntax-directed rules

In particular, SC_2 requires us to prove any annotation that is associated with the *current* label l, in contrast to the clause in the interpretation of judgements in Definition 1. Satisfaction of I in later states, and satisfaction of local annotations Q' of later program points are guaranteed by the judgement for $suc_M(l)$. Similarly, the rules for conditional and unconditional jumps include a hypothesis on the jump target, and side conditions for annotations and invariants. In the rule for conditional jumps, a further hypothesis models the fall-though case, and the dependency on the outcome of the branch condition is taken into account by the operators A^+ etc..

In rule INVS, the method invariant φ and the precondition A may be exploited to establish the invariant I. This ensures that I will be satisfied by all heaps that arise during the execution of M', as these heaps will always conform to φ. In contrast, the specification Φ is used to construct the assertions that occur in the judgement for the successor instruction. Both conditions reflect the transfer of the method arguments to the formal parameters of the invoked method corresponding to the constructions of a new frame in the operational semantics. Similarly, the return value and the final heap are (in a terminating execution) handed back to the invoking method, where they are used to construct the assertions for the successor instruction.

Finally, rule RET ties the precondition A to the post-condition B w.r.t. the terminal state that is constructed using the topmost value of the operand stack.

Logical rules. The logical rules are shown in Figure 4. We have rules of consequence

$$\text{CONSEQ-T} \frac{\begin{array}{cc} G \vdash \langle A' \rangle \, \ell \, \langle B' \rangle \, (I') & \forall s_0 \, s. \, A(s_0, s) \to A'(s_0, s) \\ \forall s_0 \, s \, t. \, B'(s_0, s, t) \to B(s_0, s, t) & \forall s \, H. \, I'(s_0, s, H) \to I(s_0, s, H) \end{array}}{G \vdash \langle A \rangle \, \ell \, \langle B \rangle \, (I)}$$

$$\text{CONSEQ-F} \frac{\begin{array}{cc} G \vdash \{A'\} \, \ell \, \{B'\} \, (I') & \forall s_0 \, s. \, A(s_0, s) \to A'(s_0, s) \\ \forall s_0 \, s \, t. \, B'(s_0, s, t) \to B(s_0, s, t) & \forall s \, H. \, I'(s_0, s, H) \to I(s_0, s, H) \end{array}}{G \vdash \{A\} \, \ell \, \{B\} \, (I)}$$

$$\text{INJ} \frac{G \vdash \{A\} \, \ell \, \{B\} \, (I)}{G \vdash \langle A \rangle \, \ell \, \langle B \rangle \, (I)} \qquad \text{AX} \frac{\begin{array}{c} G(\ell) = (A, B, I) \quad \forall s_0 \, s. \, A(s_0, s) \to I(s_0, s, heap(s)) \\ \forall Q. \, Q(\ell) = Q \to (\forall s_0 \, s. \, A(s_0, s) \to Q(s_0, s)) \end{array}}{G \vdash \langle A \rangle \, \ell \, \langle B \rangle \, (I)}$$

Fig. 4. Program logic: logical rules

for both judgement forms, the above-mentioned rule for mediating between the two judgement forms, and the axiom rule. As is the case in traditional program logics, the rules of consequence allow pre-conditions to be strengthened, while post-conditions and invariants may be weakened.

Definition 3. *P is* verified, *notation $\vdash P$, if there is a G such that $G \vdash \{A\} \, \ell \, \{B\} \, (I)$ holds whenever $G(\ell) = (A, B, I)$, and for all M, Φ, and φ, $\mathsf{M}(M) = (\Phi, \varphi)$ implies*

$$G \vdash \{\lambda \, (s_0, s). \, s = state(s_0)\} \, M, init_M \, \{\lambda \, (s_0, s, t). \, s = state(s_0) \to \Phi(s_0, t)\}$$
$$(\lambda \, (s_0, s, H). \, s = state(s_0) \to \varphi(s_0, H))$$

Note the correspondence of the latter condition with Definition 2.

3.5 Soundness

The proof of soundness establishes that verified programs are valid, and consists of two steps. We first prove that $G \vdash \{A\} \, \ell \, \{B\} \, (I)$ implies $\models \{A\} \, \ell \, \{B\} \, (I)$ under the hypothesis that all assumptions in G are valid, and likewise all method specifications in M. Following [29,5], this proof proceeds by introducing relativised notions of validity that restrict the interpretation of judgements to operational judgements of bounded height. The second step discharges the validity assumptions on G and M by proving that verified programs guarantee the validity of G and M for arbitrary bounds.

Theorem 1. *If $\vdash P$ then $\models P$.*

In particular, this theorem implies that for $\vdash P$ all method specifications in M are honoured by their respective method implementations. As the proof has been formalised in Isabelle/HOL [12] we omit the details.

4 Interpretation of Type Systems

In addition to supporting the verification of programs w.r.t. JML specifications, a program logic for bytecode should also support the compositional formulation of program
analysis results. In this section, we demonstrate how this can be achieved for analyses
phrased as type systems. As property of interest we consider static *constant* bounds on
heap consumption, with allocation-free loops. For this task, Cachera et al. presented an
abstract-interpretation-based analysis at the bytecode level which involves the formalisation of various program analysis tasks (identification of mutually recursive program
structures, identification of method calls in loops,...) in the theorem prover [15]. The
correctness proof of their analysis thus includes a verification of the inference mechanism. During the verification of concrete programs, the fixed-point iteration and the
calculation of solutions to the resulting constraints are carried out in the theorem prover.

In contrast, our type-based approach proceeds as follows. We first define an assertion
format that expresses when a code block whose initial instruction is located at ℓ is guaranteed not to allocate more than n memory cells. This results in a derived proof system
for bytecode in which all judgements are of the restricted form. Then, we consider a
simple (first-order) functional language and prove that code resulting from compiling
this language into bytecode satisfies the boundary asserted by a high-level type system:
derivability in the type system guarantees derivability in the specialised program logic
for the assertion interpreting the type. Thus, we avoid the formalisation of any inference
mechanism (type inference). Only the outcome of the inference, a digest of the typing
derivation, needs to be communicated from proof producer to proof consumer.

As a further difference to Cachera et al., our analysis is phrased at an intermediate language level. This is motivated by the fact that modern compilers perform many
analysis and optimisation tasks using intermediate code representations where additional program structure can be exploited. Given that our analysis as phrased as a type
system, we chose to employ a low-level functional language similar to A-normal form
[18]. The similarity between such languages and the imperative program representation
Static Single Assignment (SSA, [16]) has been observed by Appel and Kelsey [3,23].

Specialised program logic for bytecode. For each number n, we define a triple $[\![n]\!] = (A, B, I)$ consisting of a precondition, a post-condition, and an invariant.

$$[\![n]\!] \equiv \begin{pmatrix} \lambda\,(s_0, s).\ \textit{True}, \\ \lambda\,(s_0, s, t).\ |heap(t)| \le |heap(s)| + n, \\ \lambda\,(s_0, s, H).\ |H| \le |heap(s)| + n \end{pmatrix}$$

Here, $|H|$ denotes the size of heap H. We specialise the two judgement forms to

$$G \vdash \ell\ \{n\} \equiv let\ (A, B, I) = [\![n]\!]\ in\ G \vdash \{A\}\,\ell\,\{B\}\,(I)$$
$$G \vdash \ell\ \langle n \rangle \equiv let\ (A, B, I) = [\![n]\!]\ in\ G \vdash \langle A \rangle\,\ell\,\langle B \rangle\,(I).$$

Thus, the derivability of a judgement $G \vdash \ell\ \{n\}$ guarantees that the code located
at ℓ allocates at most n items, in terminating (postcondition B) and non-terminating
(invariant I) executions. For $(A, B, I) = [\![n]\!]$ we also define the method specification

$$Spec\ n \equiv (\lambda\,(s_0, t).\ B(s_0, state(s_0), t), \lambda\,(s_0, H).\ I(s_0, state(s_0), H)).$$

Specialising the logic to these judgement forms yields the following rules, with empty Q.

$$\text{C-NEW}\ \frac{M(l) = \mathsf{New}\ c \qquad G \vdash M, suc_M(l)\ \langle n \rangle}{G \vdash M, l\ \{n + 1\}} \qquad \text{C-INSTR}\ \frac{basic(M, l) \quad \neg M(l) = \mathsf{New}\ c \qquad G \vdash M, suc_M(l)\ \langle n \rangle}{G \vdash M, l\ \{n\}}$$

$$\text{C-RET}\ \frac{M(l) = \mathsf{Return}}{G \vdash M, l\ \{0\}} \qquad \text{C-GOTO}\ \frac{M(l) = \mathsf{Goto}\ l' \quad G \vdash M, l'\ \langle n \rangle}{G \vdash M, l\ \{n\}}$$

$$\text{C-IF}\ \frac{M(l) = \mathsf{If0}\ l' \quad G \vdash M, l'\ \langle n \rangle \quad G \vdash M, suc_M(l)\ \langle n \rangle}{G \vdash M, l\ \{n\}}$$

$$\text{C-INVS}\ \frac{\begin{array}{c} M(l) = \mathsf{Invokestatic}\ M' \quad M' \in dom\ P \\ G \vdash M, suc_M(l)\ \langle n \rangle \qquad M(M') = Spec\ k \end{array}}{G \vdash M, l\ \{n + k\}} \qquad \text{C-INJ}\ \frac{G \vdash \ell\ \{n\}}{G \vdash \ell\ \langle n \rangle}$$

$$\text{C-SUBF}\ \frac{G \vdash \ell\ \{n\} \quad n \leq m}{G \vdash \ell\ \{m\}} \qquad \text{C-SUBT}\ \frac{G \vdash \ell\ \langle n \rangle \quad n \leq m}{G \vdash \ell\ \langle m \rangle} \qquad \text{C-AX}\ \frac{G(\ell) = n}{G \vdash \ell\ \langle n \rangle}$$

$$\text{C-VP}\ \frac{\begin{array}{c} \forall\ M.\ M \in dom\ P \to (\exists\ n.\ M(M) = Spec\ n \wedge G \vdash M, init_M\ \{n\}) \\ \forall\ \ell\ A\ B\ I.\ G(\ell) = (A, B, I) \to (\exists\ n.\ (A, B, I) = [\![n]\!] \wedge G \vdash \ell\ \{n\}) \end{array}}{\vdash P}$$

Intermediate-level type system. The syntax of the intermediate language is stratified into primitive expressions and general expressions [18]. We include primitives for constructing empty and non-empty lists, and a corresponding pattern match expression. In order to simplify the translation into bytecode, we use method identifiers M as function names.

$$\mathcal{P} \ni p ::= i \mid \mathsf{uop}\ u\ x \mid \mathsf{bop}\ o\ x\ y \mid \mathsf{Nil} \mid \mathsf{Cons}(x, y) \mid M(x_1, \ldots, x_n)$$
$$\mathcal{E} \ni e ::= \mathsf{prim}\ p \mid \mathsf{let}\ x = p\ \mathsf{in}\ e \mid \mathsf{if}\ x\ \mathsf{then}\ e\ \mathsf{else}\ e \mid$$
$$(\mathsf{case}\ x\ \mathsf{of}\ \mathsf{Nil} \Rightarrow e \mid \mathsf{Cons}(x, y) \Rightarrow e)$$

A program $F : (\mathcal{C} \times \mathcal{M}) \to_{fin} (\mathcal{X}\ list \times \mathcal{E})$ consists of a collection of function declarations in the standard way. Figure 5 presents the rules for a type system with judgements of the form $\Sigma \triangleright p : n$ and $\Sigma \triangleright e : n$. Signatures Σ map function identifiers to types n. Apart from the construction of a non-empty list and function calls, all primitive expressions have the trivial type 0. This includes Nil which is compiled to a null reference. Program F is well-typed w.r.t. signature Σ, notation $\Sigma \triangleright F$, if $dom\ \Sigma = dom\ F$ and for all M, $F(M) = (par, e)$ implies $\Sigma \triangleright e : \Sigma(M)$.

Figure 6 defines a compilation $[\![e]\!]_l^C$ into the bytecode language. The result (C', l') extends the code fragment C by a code block starting at l such that l' is the next free label. Primitive expressions leave an item on the operand stack while proper expressions translate into method suffixes.

Semantic type soundness for primitive expressions now shows that an execution commencing at l satisfies the bound that is obtained by adding the costs for the subject expression to the costs for the program continuation.

$$\text{T-NIL } \frac{p \notin \{\mathsf{Cons}(x,y), M(x_1, \ldots, x_n)\}}{\Sigma \rhd p : 0} \qquad\qquad \text{T-CONS } \frac{}{\Sigma \rhd \mathsf{Cons}(x,y) : 1}$$

$$\text{T-CALL } \frac{\Sigma(M) = n}{\Sigma \rhd M(x_1, \ldots, x_n) : n} \qquad \text{T-LET } \frac{\Sigma \rhd p : n \quad \Sigma \rhd e : m}{\Sigma \rhd \mathsf{let}\ x = p\ \mathsf{in}\ e : n+m}$$

$$\text{T-COND } \frac{\Sigma \rhd e_1 : n \quad \Sigma \rhd e_2 : n}{\Sigma \rhd \mathsf{if}\ x\ \mathsf{then}\ e_1\ \mathsf{else}\ e_2 : n} \qquad \text{T-SUB } \frac{\Sigma \rhd e : m \quad m \leq n}{\Sigma \rhd e : n}$$

$$\text{T-PRIM } \frac{\Sigma \rhd p : n}{\Sigma \rhd \mathsf{prim}\ p : n} \qquad \text{T-CASE } \frac{\Sigma \rhd e_1 : n \quad \Sigma \rhd e_2 : n}{\Sigma \rhd \mathsf{case}\ x\ \mathsf{of}\ \mathsf{Nil} \Rightarrow e_1 \mid \mathsf{Cons}(x,y) \Rightarrow e_2 : n}$$

Fig. 5. Typing rules

$$[\![i]\!]_l^C = (C[l \mapsto \mathsf{const}\ i], l+1)$$

$$[\![\mathsf{uop}\ u\ x]\!]_l^C = (C[l \mapsto \mathsf{load}\ x, l+1 \mapsto \mathsf{unop}\ u], l+2)$$

$$[\![\mathsf{bop}\ o\ x\ y]\!]_l^C = (C[l \mapsto \mathsf{load}\ x, l+1 \mapsto \mathsf{load}\ y, l+2 \mapsto \mathsf{binop}\ o], l+3)$$

$$[\![\mathsf{Nil}]\!]_l^C = (C[l \mapsto \mathsf{const}\ \mathsf{Null}], l+1)$$

$$[\![\mathsf{Cons}(x,y)]\!]_l^C = (C\begin{bmatrix} l \mapsto \mathsf{load}\ y, l+1 \mapsto \mathsf{load}\ x, l+2 \mapsto \mathsf{new}\ \mathsf{LIST}, \\ l+3 \mapsto \mathsf{store}\ \mathsf{t}, l+4 \mapsto \mathsf{load}\ \mathsf{t}, \\ l+5 \mapsto \mathsf{putfield}\ \mathsf{LIST}\ \mathsf{HD}, l+6 \mapsto \mathsf{load}\ \mathsf{t}, \\ l+7 \mapsto \mathsf{putfield}\ \mathsf{LIST}\ \mathsf{TL}, l+8 \mapsto \mathsf{load}\ \mathsf{t} \end{bmatrix}, l+9)$$

$$[\![M()]\!]_l^C = (C[l \mapsto \mathsf{Invokestatic}\ M], l+1)$$

$$[\![M(x_1, \ldots, x_n)]\!]_l^C = [\![M(x_1, \ldots, x_{n-1})]\!]_{l+1}^{C[l \mapsto \mathsf{load}\ x_n]}$$

$$[\![\mathsf{prim}\ p]\!]_l^C = \mathsf{let}\ (C_1, l_1) = [\![p]\!]_l^C\ \mathsf{in}\ (C_1[l_1 \mapsto \mathsf{Return}], l_1 + 1)$$

$$[\![\mathsf{let}\ x = p\ \mathsf{in}\ e]\!]_l^C = \mathsf{let}\ (C_1, l_1) = [\![p]\!]_l^C, (C_2, l_2) = (C_1[l_1 \mapsto \mathsf{store}\ x], l_1 + 1) \\ \mathsf{in}\ [\![e]\!]_{l_2}^{C_2}$$

$$[\![\mathsf{if}\ x\ \mathsf{then}\ e_1\ \mathsf{else}\ e_2]\!]_l^C = \mathsf{let}\ (C_E, l_2) = [\![e_2]\!]_{l+2}^{C}, (C_T, l_1) = [\![e_1]\!]_{l_2}^{C_E} \\ \mathsf{in}\ (C_T[l \mapsto \mathsf{load}\ x, l+1 \mapsto \mathsf{If0}\ l_2], l_1)$$

$$\begin{bmatrix} \mathsf{case}\ x\ \mathsf{of} \\ \mathsf{Nil} \Rightarrow e_1 \\ \mid \mathsf{Cons}(x,y) \Rightarrow e_2 \end{bmatrix}_l^C = \mathsf{let}\ (C_C, l_N) = [\![e_2]\!]_{l+9}^{C}, (C_N, l_1) = [\![e_1]\!]_{l_N}^{C_C}\ \mathsf{in}$$
$$(C_N\begin{bmatrix} l \mapsto \mathsf{load}\ x, l+1 \mapsto \mathsf{unop}\ (\lambda\ v.\ v = Nullref), \\ l+2 \mapsto \mathsf{If0}\ l_N, l+3 \mapsto \mathsf{Load}\ x, \\ l+4 \mapsto \mathsf{Getfield}\ \mathsf{LIST}\ \mathsf{HD}, l+5 \mapsto \mathsf{Store}\ h, \\ l+6 \mapsto \mathsf{Load}\ x, l+7 \mapsto \mathsf{Getfield}\ \mathsf{LIST}\ \mathsf{TL}, \\ l+8 \mapsto \mathsf{Store}\ t \end{bmatrix}, l_1)$$

Fig. 6. Translation into bytecode

Proposition 1. *If $\Sigma \rhd p : n$, $[\![p]\!]_l^C = (C_1, l_1)$, and $G \vdash M, l_1\ \langle m \rangle$, then $G \vdash M, l\ \{n+m\}$.*

For proper expressions, the soundness result does not mention program continuations, since expressions compile to code blocks that terminate with a method return.

Proposition 2. *If* $\Sigma \rhd e : n$ *and* $[\![e]\!]_l^C = (C_1, l_1)$ *then* $G \vdash M, l \; \{n\}$.

Both results are easily proven by induction on the typing judgement. For presentational reasons we have omitted technical side conditions that ensure that the table M contains precisely the interpretations of Σ, and that the global program P contains precisely the translations of F, where for each entry, we reverse the list of formal parameters due to the order in which the translation pushes arguments onto the operand stack. Denoting these conditions by $[\![\Sigma]\!]$ and $[\![F]\!]$, respectively, we obtain overall type soundness, i.e. the verifiability of well-typed programs:

Theorem 2. *If* $\Sigma \rhd F$ *then* $\vdash [\![F]\!]$.

Again, the proof has been formalised in Isabelle/HOL [12].

5   Discussion

We presented a program logic for bytecode suitable for translating features found in modern specification formalisms and for interpreting type systems in a compositional way. Using a judgement format which separates postconditions, invariants, and annotations, the logic supports reasoning about terminating and non-terminating executions.

The necessity of complementing partial-correctness assertions by guarantees that apply to intermediate states and non-terminating computations has also been observed by Hähnle and Mostowski [19]. Based on an extension of first-order dynamic logic with trace modalities [9], they discuss the verification of transaction properties in the context of JavaCard. Similar requirements arise from object invariants [26] and idioms like ESC-Java's *validity* of objects [17]. The logics developed in connection with the LOOP tool (e.g. [21]) apply at the source code level, or a representation of source code and (JML) specifications in a theorem prover. Various termination modes are considered in [21], but some rules, such as the rule for while, can only be applied in special circumstances. The logic is formulated as a set of derived proof rules, so proof search may always fall back on the underlying operational semantics. In contrast, our formulation as a syntactic proof system admits a study of (relative) completeness, following the approach of Kleymann, Nipkow, and ourselves [24,29,5].

The usage of expressive program logics as a mediating formalism between the operational semantics of a low-level language and type systems was already explored in our previous work [13]. Here, we presented an interpretation in a partial-correctness program logic of a type system for bounded heap consumption where the amount of memory used may depend on the structural size of input data [20]. The encoding involved formulae that express the structured use of a freelist and enforce various disjointness conditions. Heap-represented data structures are required to obey a linear typing regime. The interpretations of the typing rules are formally derived in the theorem prover in such a way that the partitioning of the heap into regions holding particular data structures is performed once, during the derivation of the proof rules. Compared to the verification of application programs using separation logic [31], the verification using the derived proof rules proceeds at a higher-level, for the price of being limited to programs originating from high-level code that obeys a particular typing discipline. Compared to the FPCC approach of formalising type systems [4], the explicit use of a program logic introduces a useful abstraction barrier. Proof patterns arising repeatedly in the verification of program analyses (e.g. the verification of recursive program structures) can be dealt with once-and-for-all. Thus, the program logic may serve as a formalism in which different program analyses may be compared and integrated.

In contrast to our approach of interpreting typing calculi, Benton's logic [11] includes (basic) type information in judgements, extending bytecode verification conditions. Consequently, methods can be given more modular specifications that, for example, constrain the heap to the segment relevant for the verification of the method body, similar to separation logic [31]. In our approach, such local-reasoning principles would be formulated in the interpretation of type judgements, i.e. in derived proof rules [13]. As a further difference, Benton's logic is interpreted extensionally, by reference to program contexts. This enables Benton to prove that certain program transformations are semantics-preserving (see also [10]), while we primarily aim to certify intensional properties such as the consumption of resources [6].

A further approach to integrating types and program logics is proposed by Nanevski and Morrisett [27]. Following a two-level approach that separates effectful from pure computations, Hoare-triples describing side-effecting computations are injected into the type system using a monadic type constructor. The result is a rich, dependently typed reasoning framework whose operational soundness has been established using progress- and preservations lemmas. An extension that treats polymorphism and supports local reasoning using constructs from separation logic appears in [2].

As was mentioned in the introduction, our logic has already been extended to a substantial fragment of the JVML. The basis of this extension is the Bicolano formalisation of the JVML [30]. In connection with this effort, Benjamin Gregoire recently proposed a variation of our soundness proof that eliminates the auxiliary notion of step-indexed validity. Based on his observation, a new formalisation has been produced using the Coq theorem prover. In addition, work is currently under way to include further specification idioms, in particular ghost items and modifies-clauses, by translating them into the format proposed in this paper. It is planned to extend the logic towards multi-threaded programs. For this, we expect the form of invariants presented in the present paper to be particularly useful. Over time, we thus expect that the presented formalism will yield a solid foundation for the certification of functional and non-functional code properties.

Acknowledgements. This work was funded in part by the Information Society Technologies programme of the European Commission, Future and Emerging Technologies under the IST-2005-015905 MOBIUS project. This paper reflects only the author's views and the Community is not liable for any use that may be made of the information contained therein. We are grateful to all members of the MOBIUS Working Group 3.1 for the numerous discussions on JML and program logics, and on formalising these in theorem provers, and to the referees for the valuable feedback they provided.

References

1. E. Ábrahám, F. S. de Boer, W. P. de Roever, and M. Steffen. An assertion-based proof system for multithreaded Java. *Theoretical Computer Science*, 331(2-3):251–290, 2005.
2. L. B. Aleksandar Nanevski, Greg Morrisett. Polymorphism and Separation in Hoare Type Theory. In *Proceedings of the 11th ACM International Conference on Functional Programming (ICFP 2006)*. ACM Press, Sept. 2006. To appear.

3. A. W. Appel. SSA is functional programming. *ACM SIGPLAN Notices*, 33(4):17–20, 1998.
4. A. W. Appel. Foundational proof-carrying code. In *16th Annual IEEE Symposium on Logic in Computer Science (LICS), Proceedings*. IEEE Computer Society, 2001.
5. D. Aspinall, L. Beringer, M. Hofmann, H.-W. Loidl, and A. Momigliano. A program logic for resource verification. In K. Slind, A. Bunker, and G. Gopalakrishnan, editors, *Theorem Proving in Higher Order Logics, 17th International Conference, TPHOLs'04. Proceedings*, volume 3223 of *LNCS*, pages 34–49. Springer, 2004.
6. D. Aspinall, L. Beringer, and A. Momigliano. Optimisation validation. In J. Knoop, G. C. Necula, and W. Zimmermann, editors, *Proceedings of the 5th International Workshop on Compiler Optimization Meets Compiler Verification (COCV'06)*, ENTCS. Elsevier, 2006. To appear.
7. F. Y. Bannwart and P. Müller. A logic for bytecode. In F. Spoto, editor, *Bytecode Semantics, Verification, Analysis and Transformation (BYTECODE)*, volume 141(1) of *ENTCS*, pages 255–273. Elsevier, 2005.
8. G. Barthe. Mobius – Mobility, Ubiquity and Security. http://mobius.inria.fr.
9. B. Beckert and S. Schlager. A sequent calculus for first-order dynamic logic with trace modalities. In R. Goré, A. Leitsch, and T. Nipkow, editors, *Proceedings, International Joint Conference on Automated Reasoning (IJCAR'01)*, volume 2083 of *LNCS*, pages 626–641. Springer, 2001.
10. N. Benton. Simple relational correctness proofs for static analyses and program transformations. In N. D. Jones and X. Leroy, editors, *Proceedings of the 31st ACM Symposium on Principles of Programming Languages, POPL'04, Venice, Italy*, pages 14–25. ACM, 2004.
11. N. Benton. A typed, compositional logic for a stack-based abstract machine. In K. Yi, editor, *Programming Languages and Systems, Third Asian Symposium, APLAS'05. Proceedings*, volume 3780 of *LNCS*, pages 364–380. Springer, 2005.
12. L. Beringer and M. Hofmann. A bytecode logic for JML and types – Isabelle/HOL sources. http://www.tcs.ifi.lmu.de/~beringer/BytecodeLogic.tar.gz, 2006.
13. L. Beringer, M. Hofmann, A. Momigliano, and O. Shkaravska. Automatic certification of heap consumption. In F. Baader and A. Voronkov, editors, *Logic for Programming, Artificial Intelligence, and Reasoning, 11th International Conference, LPAR'04, Montevideo, Uruguay. Proceedings*, volume 3452 of *LNCS*, pages 347–362. Springer, 2004.
14. L. Burdy, Y. Cheon, D. Cok, M. Ernst, J. Kiniry, G. T. Leavens, K. R. M. Leino, and E. Poll. An overview of JML tools and applications. *International Journal on Software Tools for Technology Transfer*, 7(3):212–232, June 2005.
15. D. Cachera, T. P. Jensen, D. Pichardie, and G. Schneider. Certified memory usage analysis. In J. Fitzgerald, I. J. Hayes, and A. Tarlecki, editors, *FM 2005: Formal Methods, International Symposium of Formal Methods Europe. Proceedings*, volume 3582 of *LNCS*, pages 91–106. Springer, 2005.
16. R. Cytron, J. Ferrante, B. K. Rosen, M. N. Wegman, and F. K. Zadeck. Efficiently computing static single assignment form and the control dependence graph. *ACM Transactions on Programming Languages and Systems (TOPLAS)*, 13(4), Oct. 1991.
17. C. Flanagan, K. R. M. Leino, M. Lillibridge, G. Nelson, J. B. Saxe, and R. Stata. Extended static checking for java. In *PLDI '02: Proceedings of the ACM Conference on Programming language design and implementation*, pages 234–245. ACM Press, 2002.
18. C. Flanagan, A. Sabry, B. F. Duba, and M. Felleisen. The essence of compiling with continuations. In *PLDI '93: Proceedings of the ACM Conference on Programming language design and implementation*, pages 237–247. ACM Press, 1993.
19. R. Hähnle and W. Mostowski. Verification of safety properties in the presence of transactions. In G. Barthe, L. Burdy, M. Huisman, J.-L. Lanet, and T. Muntean, editors, *Proceedings, Construction and Analysis of Safe, Secure and Interoperable Smart devices (CASSIS'04) Workshop*, volume 3362 of *LNCS*, pages 151–171. Springer, 2005.

20. M. Hofmann and S. Jost. Static prediction of heap space usage for first-order functional programs. In *POPL '03: Proceedings of the 30th ACM Symposium on Principles of programming languages*, pages 185–197. ACM Press, 2003.
21. B. Jacobs and E. Poll. A logic for the Java Modeling Language JML. In H. Hußmann, editor, *Fundamental Approaches to Software Engineering, 4th International Conference, FASE'01. Proceedings*, volume 2029 of *LNCS*, pages 284–299. Springer, 2001.
22. C. B. Jones. *Systematic Software Development Using VDM*. Prentice-Hall International, Englewood Cliffs, New Jersey, second edition, 1990.
23. R. A. Kelsey. A correspondence between continuation passing style and static single assignment form. *ACM SIGPLAN Notices*, 30(3):13–22, 1995.
24. T. Kleymann. *Hoare Logic and VDM: Machine-Checked Soundness and Completeness Proofs*. PhD thesis, LFCS, University of Edinburgh, 1998.
25. G. T. Leavens, E. Poll, C. Clifton, Y. Cheon, C. Ruby, D. Cok, P. Müller, and J. Kiniry. JML Reference Manual (draft). http://www.cs.iastate.edu/ leavens/JML, May 2006.
26. K. R. M. Leino and R. Stata. Checking object invariants. Technical Report #1997-007, Digital Equipment Corporation Systems Research Center, Palo Alto, USA, 1997.
27. A. Nanevski and G. Morrisett. Dependent type theory of stateful higher-order functions. Technical Report TR-24-05, Harvard University, 2005.
28. G. C. Necula. Proof-carrying code. In *POPL '97: Proceedings of the 24th ACM Symposium on Principles of programming languages*, pages 106–119. ACM Press, 1997.
29. T. Nipkow. Hoare logics for recursive procedures and unbounded nondeterminism. In J. C. Bradfield, editor, *Computer Science Logic, 16th International Workshop, CSL 2002, 11th Annual Conference of the EACSL. Proceedings*, volume 2471 of *LNCS*, pages 103–119. Springer, 2002.
30. D. Pichardie. Bicolano – Byte Code Language in Coq. http://www-sop.inria.fr/everest/personnel/David.Pichardie/bicolano/main.html, 2006.
31. J. C. Reynolds. Separation logic: A logic for shared mutable data structures. In *17th IEEE Symposium on Logic in Computer Science (LICS'02). Proceedings*, pages 55–74. IEEE Computer Society, 2002.
32. M. Rinard and D. Marinov. Credible compilation with pointers. In *Proceedings of the FLoC Workshop on Run-Time Result Verification*, July 1999.

On Jones-Optimal Specializers: A Case Study Using Unmix

Johan Gade[1,2] and Robert Glück[2]

[1] Dept. of Mathematical Informatics, University of Tokyo
Tokyo 113-8656, Japan
jgade@acm.org
[2] DIKU, Dept. of Computer Science, University of Copenhagen
DK-2100 Copenhagen, Denmark
glueck@acm.org

Abstract. Jones optimality is a criterion for assessing the strength of a program specializer. Here, the elements required in a proof of Jones optimality are investigated and the first formal proof for a non-trivial polyvariant specializer (Unmix) is presented. A simplifying element is the use of self-application. Variations of the original criterion are discussed.

1 Introduction

When using a specializer, it is desirable to know how "strong" it is. Likewise, when engineering a new specializer, it is desirable to know when the design is "good enough". Jones proposed a criterion [6], now known as *Jones optimality*, for judging the strength of a specializer. Originally, it was presented as an aid for engineering a self-applicable partial evaluator [7], which led to some thinking this is its only value. Over the last decade, however, the notion proved useful as a standard for assessing other aspects of a specializer's strength. For example, a Jones-optimal specializer can overcome *inherited limits* [10], and it is a necessary condition for a specializer to be *translation universal* (i.e., for any compiler an interpreter exists such that the target programs produced by specializing the interpreter are as efficient as those produced by the compiler) [3].

Although the practical and theoretical implications of the criterion have become clearer, many specializers are still only *believed* to be Jones-optimal and, to our knowledge, only lambda-mix (a small partial evaluator for the lambda-calculus that does not use the usual polyvariant program-point specialization) has *formally* been shown to satisfy the criterion [15]. On the other hand, for some specializers, such as FCL-mix, it has been argued that they are *not* Jones-optimal [4]. Thus, while Jones optimality may be *plausible* in some cases, the question is usually not settled conclusively for more realistic specializers.

In this paper, the elements required in a proof of Jones optimality for non-trivial systems are investigated and Unmix, a system based on the classical offline partial evaluator Mix [8], is shown to be Jones-optimal (in a refined sense wrt a set of optimized programs, which also under suitable conditions implies Jones optimality [7]). With use of a partial evaluator that exhibits the essential

N. Kobayashi (Ed.): APLAS 2006, LNCS 4279, pp. 406–422, 2006.

features of offline partial evaluators in general, it is hoped that this study may serve as a useful guideline for investigating more realistic partial evaluators. More specifically, the contributions of this paper are to:

1. Establish that the self-applicable partial evaluator Unmix is Jones-optimal.
2. Confirm the need for variable splitting to achieve Jones optimality of specializers in languages with multiple parameters.
3. Give a framework for proving Jones optimality of more realistic specializers.
4. Explore practical issues for proving Jones optimality (e.g., textual equality vs. timed semantics and modularization of proofs by self-applicability).

The paper is organized as follows. Section 2 reviews specialization with focus on the arity of programs. Section 3 introduces Jones optimality and Sect. 4 presents the Unmix case study. Sections 5 and 6 discuss related work and conclusions. Familiarity with the basics of partial evaluation is assumed [7, Part II].

2   Program Specialization and Multi-parameter Programs

This section introduces the notation and terminology used in the paper, which should be fairly standard for readers familiar with partial evaluation. Nevertheless, to sensitize the reader to the effects of an arbitrary number of parameters, they are treated in greater detail than is usual. Understanding the subtle implications of multi-parameter programs is essential for proving Jones optimality of specializers for many untyped languages, including Unmix. A connection to the tagging problem known from specializing self-interpreters for strongly typed languages [2,9,10,16] will be made. The notation is adapted from Jones et al. [7].[1]

All programming languages in the text are assumed to be Turing-complete and untyped. In addition, every program has a fixed, but arbitrary number of parameters. Unless stated otherwise, the same language is intended as the source, residual, and implementation language of self-interpreters and specializers. We assume that the set of input values, D, includes the set of all programs, P, and all lists $(i_1, \ldots, i_n)$ where $i_1, \ldots, i_n$ are input values. The notation $\doteq$ denotes equality of partial values: Either both sides are defined and equal or both are undefined.

Definition 1 (Program evaluation, running time). *The result (if any) of evaluating a program* $p \in P$ *with arity* $n \geq 0$ *and inputs* $i_1, \ldots, i_n \in D$ *is denoted by* $[\![p]\!] \, i_1 \cdots i_n$, *and the* running time *is denoted by* $Time(p, i_1, \ldots, i_n)$. *The partial order* $\leq_{Time}$ *for n-ary programs* p *and* q *is defined by:*

$$p \leq_{Time} q \iff \forall i_1, \ldots, i_n \,.\, Time(p, i_1, \ldots, i_n) \leq Time(q, i_1, \ldots, i_n) \quad (1)$$

A *program specializer* is a program that given another program (the *subject* program) and some of its inputs (the *static* data), produces a *residual program* that gives the same result when evaluated with the remaining inputs (the *dynamic* data) as the subject program does when evaluated with all of its input.

---

[1] To make a clear distinction between evaluating programs whose input is a tuple (or more generally a list) from evaluating those with multiple inputs, the arguments are not surrounded by braces, e.g., in $[\![p]\!]$ (a, b) there is only one input, a tuple.

Definition 2 (Program specializer). *A program* spec *is a specializer iff for all programs* $p \in P$ *with arity* $n \geq 0$ *and for all inputs* $i_1, \ldots, i_n \in D$:

$$[\![[\text{spec}]\!] \; p \; (i_1, \ldots, i_m)]\!] \; i_{m+1} \; \cdots \; i_n \doteq [\![p]\!] \; i_1 \; \cdots \; i_n, \quad 0 \leq m \leq n \quad (2)$$

The specializer can specialize subject programs with any arity $n \geq 0$ where the first m inputs of the program are static. The specializer has two arguments (a subject program and a *list* of static inputs). There is no general agreement whether a specializer should always terminate. The above definition allows non-terminating specializers (the left hand side of (2) can be undefined in two ways: The specializer or the residual program may fail to terminate). For non-trivial specializers, as discussed in [7], equality $\doteq$ in (2) is usually weakened to: If both sides are defined, they are equal. (This is also the case for Unmix).

Central to the definition of Jones optimality is the notion of a self-interpreter.

Definition 3 (Self-interpreter). *A program* sint *is a self-interpreter iff it is written in the language it interprets, and for all programs* $p \in P$ *with arity* $n \geq 0$ *and for all inputs* $i_1, \ldots, i_n \in D$:

$$[\![\text{sint}]\!] \; p \; (i_1, \ldots, i_n) \doteq [\![p]\!] \; i_1 \; \cdots \; i_n \quad (3)$$

2.1 Effects of Multi-parameter Programs

The well-known first Futamura projection states that one can translate a program p by specialization of an interpreter. In the special case of a *self-interpreter*, the residual program, p', is written in the same language: $p' = [\![\text{spec}]\!] \; \text{sint} \; (p)$. Combining equations (2) and (3) yields

$$[\![p']\!] \; (i_1, \ldots, i_n) \doteq [\![\text{sint}]\!] \; p \; (i_1, \ldots, i_n) \doteq [\![p]\!] \; i_1 \; \cdots \; i_n \quad (4)$$

From the equation, it is evident that p' has *one* input, a list of values, while p has n inputs. Consequently, programs p and p' can never be textually identical: p' requires (at least) an extra function to unpack the contents of the input list, or worse, if nothing is done in spec to prevent it, all parts of p' will operate on a list and hence be *less efficient* than p. This is a consequence of the source language: In any language where programs have an arbitrary, but fixed number of parameters, the self-interpreters written in the language require a data structure, such as a list, to hold an arbitrary number of input values. This is a problem because Jones optimality [7] relies on the property that p' is not slower than p.

The issue can be viewed as an instance of the problem encountered when specializing self-interpreters for strongly typed languages, where the interpreted program's inputs must be *encoded* in a universal type *Univ*. In this context, even though strongly typed languages are not considered, the fixed arity of programs requires the inputs to be encoded as a list. A solution for typed languages was found [9] by placing the self-interpreter between a pair of encoding and decoding programs, that map values of different types to and from the input type, *Univ*, of sint: $P \times \textit{Univ} \rightarrow \textit{Univ}$. If the type of a program is $p: \alpha \rightarrow \beta$, then a self-interpreter $\text{sint}^{\alpha \rightarrow \beta}: P \times \alpha \rightarrow \beta$ for all programs of that type is defined by

$\mathtt{sint}^{\alpha \to \beta} = \mathtt{decode}^{\beta} \circ \mathtt{sint} \circ (\mathtt{id} \times \mathtt{encode}^{\alpha})$, where $\circ$ denotes composition of programs, $\mathtt{encode}^{\alpha} \colon \alpha \to Univ$ maps values of type α into the representation used by $\mathtt{sint}$, and $\mathtt{decode}^{\beta} \colon Univ \to \alpha$ performs the inverse (the program $\mathtt{p}$ need not be encoded, thus the identity $\mathtt{id}$). Hence, $\mathtt{sint}^{\alpha \to \beta}$ maps $\mathtt{p}$'s input of type α to $\mathtt{sint}$'s input type, and maps $\mathtt{sint}$'s output back into a value of type β. Nothing is changed in $\mathtt{sint}$; it is only placed between an encoder and a decoder.

Similarly, define a self-interpreter $\mathtt{sint}^{n} \colon P \times D^{n} \to D$ for n-ary programs by

$$\mathtt{sint}^{n} = \mathtt{id} \circ \mathtt{sint} \circ (\mathtt{id} \times \mathtt{encode}^{n}) \tag{5}$$

where $\mathtt{encode}^{n} \colon D^{n} \to D$ is given by $[\![\mathtt{encode}^{n}]\!] \; i_1 \cdots i_n = (i_1, \ldots, i_n)$. As all programs have the same output type, the decoder $\mathtt{id}$ can be omitted. Thus,

$$[\![\mathtt{sint}^{n}]\!] \; \mathtt{p} \; i_1 \cdots i_n \doteq [\![\mathtt{sint}]\!] \; \mathtt{p} \; (i_1, \ldots, i_n) \tag{6}$$

Translating program $\mathtt{p}$ using $\mathtt{sint}^{n}$ results in

$$\mathtt{p}'' = [\![\mathtt{spec}]\!] \; \mathtt{sint}^{n} \; (\mathtt{p}) \tag{7}$$

Combining equations (2), (3) and (6) gives

$$[\![\mathtt{p}'']\!] \; i_1 \cdots i_n \doteq [\![\mathtt{sint}^{n}]\!] \; \mathtt{p} \; i_1 \cdots i_n \doteq [\![\mathtt{p}]\!] \; i_1 \cdots i_n \tag{8}$$

Now, it is possible for $\mathtt{p}$ and $\mathtt{p}''$ to be textually identical. Therefore, $\mathtt{sint}^{n}$ is used to define a *multi-parameter* version of Jones optimality [7].

Definition 4 (Jopt-$\leq_{Time}$). *A specializer* $\mathtt{spec}$ *is Jones-optimal iff a self-interpreter* $\mathtt{sint}$ *exists such that for all programs* $\mathtt{p} \in P$ *with arity* $n \geq 0$, *and* $\mathtt{sint}^{n}$ *as defined in (5):*

$$[\![\mathtt{spec}]\!] \; \mathtt{sint}^{n} \; (\mathtt{p}) \leq_{Time} \mathtt{p} \tag{9}$$

3   A Framework for Proving Jones Optimality

This section discusses a variation of Jones optimality and proof structures.

3.1   Timed Semantics

Agreeing on a timing function may be difficult. However, any reasonable timing function should time textually identical programs identically. So, if one can prove textual identity modulo insignificant details, such as variable names, it is possible to conclude, irrespectively of any concrete timing function, that $\mathtt{spec}$ is indeed Jones-optimal. This was done for lambda-mix. In a more realistic context, even if insignificant details are ignored by a suitable *textual equivalence* $\cong$ on programs, it may not be possible to prove $\cong$-equivalence as realistic specializers typically perform further optimizations of the residual programs. The residual program may therefore be textually quite different from the source program.

A way to isolate the problem of the specializer being too powerful for textual equality to hold is to restrict the domain of programs for which a specializer is said to be Jones-optimal to an "optimized" Turing-complete subset P_{opt} of P.

Definition 5 (Optimized programs). *Let* opt *be a total translator such that* $\forall p \in P \,.\, \llbracket \text{opt} \rrbracket \, p \leq_{Time} p$, *then the set* $P_{\text{opt}} \subseteq P$ *is* $P_{\text{opt}} = \{ \, \llbracket \text{opt} \rrbracket \, p \mid p \in P \, \}$.

Definition 6 (Jopt-P_{opt}). *A specializer* spec *is Jones-optimal wrt* P_{opt} *iff a self-interpreter* sint *exists such that for all programs* $q \in P_{\text{opt}}$ *with arity* $n \geq 0$, *and* sint^n *as defined in (5):*

$$\llbracket \text{spec} \rrbracket \, \text{sint}^n \, (q) \approx q \tag{10}$$

The intention is that spec will not "over optimize" programs in P_{opt}, so establishing textual equivalence is isolated from how to define opt.

Once spec is found to be Jones-optimal on some P_{opt}, it follows that

$$\forall q \in P_{\text{opt}} \text{ with arity } n \,.\, \llbracket \text{spec} \rrbracket \, \text{sint}^n \, (q) \approx q$$
$$\Longleftrightarrow \quad \forall p \in P \text{ with arity } n \,.\, \llbracket \text{spec} \rrbracket \, \text{sint}^n \, (\llbracket \text{opt} \rrbracket \, p) \leq_{Time} p \tag{11}$$

If for any arity $n \geq 0$, spec can reduce away the static expressions in $\text{sint}^n_{\text{opt}} = \text{id} \circ \text{sint} \circ (\text{opt} \times \text{encode}^n)$, i.e., if $\llbracket \text{spec} \rrbracket \, \text{sint}^n_{\text{opt}} \, (p) \doteq \llbracket \text{spec} \rrbracket \, \text{sint}^n \, (\llbracket \text{opt} \rrbracket \, p)$, then spec is Jones-optimal in the sense of Def. 4 with $\text{sint}^n_{\text{opt}}$.

3.2 Self-applicable Specializers

To prove Jones optimality, it is necessary to analyze both the specializer and the self-interpreter to determine how the self-interpreter is specialized wrt source programs. This two-level problem can be simplified considerably when the specializer is *self-applicable*: Using the second Futamura projection to turn sint^n into a compiler comp^n reduces the problem to examining the compiler. Given $\text{comp}^n = \llbracket \text{spec} \rrbracket \, \text{spec} \, (\text{sint}^n)$ the program $p''' = \llbracket \text{comp}^n \rrbracket \, (p)$ is textually identical to p'' in (7). So, it remains to show that comp^n is an identity:

$$\forall q \in P_{\text{opt}} \text{ with arity } n \,.\, \llbracket \text{comp}^n \rrbracket \, (q) \approx q \tag{12}$$

In the best case, comp^n will be a straightforward implementation of an identity on programs making the proof simple. That is, to prove Jones optimality of spec wrt P_{opt} it is sufficient to show that a self-interpreter sint exists such that for all $q \in P_{\text{opt}}$ with arity $n \geq 0$: $\llbracket \llbracket \text{spec} \rrbracket \, \text{spec} \, (\text{sint}^n) \rrbracket \, (q) \approx q$.

For the equation to hold, both the generation of the compiler and the generated compiler must always terminate (although termination of the generation process is verified by the existence of the produced compiler, an argument is required to show that the compiler always terminates).

3.3 Structure of Jones Optimality Proofs

To prove Jopt-P_{opt} of spec one needs to: (1) give a definition of opt, (2) give a definition of textual equivalence $\approx$, (3) write a self-interpreter sint, and (4) argue that for any $n \geq 0$ the compiler, comp^n, generated using spec and sint^n, produces target programs that are $\approx$-equivalent to the source programs.

4 Case Study: Jones Optimality of Unmix

The Unmix system [12] is presented with a focus on the details necessary for proving Jones optimality. Unmix is a self-applicable offline partial evaluator for a first-order, purely functional subset of Scheme.[2] It was developed by Romanenko, and is a further development of the well-known partial evaluator Mix [8].

4.1 Structure and Properties of Unmix

The following diagram illustrates the structure of the Unmix system.

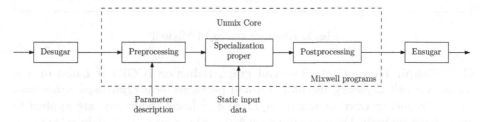

The core of the specializer works with the internal language *Mixwell* [8], so as first and last steps, programs are translated from Scheme to Mixwell and back (desugar and ensugar in the diagram). As the two steps are exterior to the partial evaluation itself, they will not be considered further. The proof of Jones optimality will be for the Unmix core, which consists of three main phases:

Preprocessing. The subject program is annotated according to the results of a monovariant binding-time analysis.

Specialization. The annotated program is specialized wrt the static input data.

Postprocessing. Three transformations are done on the residual program: (1) first call graph reduction, (2) arity raising, (3) last call graph reduction.

The Mixwell Language. Mixwell is a first-order, purely functional language. It has call-by-value semantics and is statically scoped. The abstract syntax is given in Fig. 1. A program consists of a series of *function definitions*, the first of which is called the *goal function* and defines the meaning of the program. The input to a program is given through the formal parameters of the goal function. The usual *static requirements* apply: (1) all function definitions have unique names, (2) all parameters in a function definition have unique names, (3) all variables occurring in the body of a function are defined in the parameter list, (4) the arity of function calls and function definitions must match, and (5) all functions that are called are defined.

The semantics of the constructs are like those in Scheme. The annotation construct `rcall` is functionally equivalent to `call`, which is a call to a function.

---

[2] Strictly speaking, a variant of Scheme because the language contains some macro facilities as well as certain annotation constructs not present in Scheme.

$\langle Program \rangle$	::=	$\langle FunDef \rangle^+$
$\langle FunDef \rangle$	::=	$(\langle Fname \rangle \; (\langle Vname \rangle^*) = \langle Exp \rangle)$
$\langle Exp \rangle$	::=	$\langle Constant \rangle \mid \langle Vname \rangle$
	|	$(\langle UnOp \rangle \; \langle Exp \rangle) \mid (\langle BinOp \rangle \; \langle Exp \rangle \; \langle Exp \rangle)$
	|	$(\texttt{call } \langle Fname \rangle \; \langle Exp \rangle^*) \mid (\texttt{rcall } \langle Fname \rangle \; \langle Exp \rangle^*)$
	|	$(\texttt{if } \langle Exp \rangle \; \langle Exp \rangle \; \langle Exp \rangle)$
$\langle UnOp \rangle$	::=	`car` | `cdr` | `null?` | `pair?` | `symbol?` | `not`
$\langle BinOp \rangle$	::=	`cons` | `equal?` | `eq?` | `eqv?` | `+` | `-` | `*` | `/`
$\langle Constant \rangle$	::=	$\langle Atom \rangle \mid (\texttt{quote } \langle \textit{S-expression} \rangle)$

Fig. 1. Abstract syntax of Mixwell

Call Graph Reduction. The call graph reduction (CGR) is based on the *automatic call unfolding* method [14] and performs *local expression reductions*, such as reducing (`car` (`cons` e_1 e_2)) to e_1.[3] Local reductions are applied to every function body. For every function call (`call` g $e_1 \ldots e_n$), reduced versions e_i^* of the argument expressions e_i are computed (this may involve further call reductions); then, the call is either unfolded or left in its reduced form. The unfolding strategy prevents infinite unfolding as well as call and code duplication. All calls *not* marked as cutpoints and *not* satisfying the check below are unfolded:

1. To *prevent infinite unfolding*, all calls to at least one function in each *recursive call chain* are suspended. Such *cutpoints* are determined by a call graph analysis. The *call graph* of a program is a directed multigraph, the vertices of which consist of the program's functions, and with an edge from f to g for each call to g in the body of f. A recursive call chain is a cycle in the call graph.
2. To *prevent call and code duplication*, the following check is performed for a call to a function g. If there exists a reduced argument expression e_i^* that is not an atom (or a quoted atom), and the corresponding formal parameter x_i occurs more than once in a branch of the body of g, then the call is *not* unfolded. This conservative strategy prevents call and code duplication.

The CGR is not idempotent: Applying it several times to a program can lead to further reductions. We will later use the following *always-true* function that is only unfolded by a second CGR after the reductions by a first CGR removed a code duplication risk.

Example. Consider the small program:

```
(f (x) = (if (call true-const (cons x x)) 'A 'B))   ; call as predicate
(true-const (y) = (if '#t '#t (cons y y)))          ; always true
```

---

[3] In general, the reductions do not preserve the termination properties of the program.

The local reduction of the first CGR attempts to unfold the call to `true-const` in `f`, but as `(cons x x)` in the call is not an atom and the corresponding parameter `y` occurs twice in the false-branch, the call is *not* unfolded. However, local reduction simplifies `true-const` to `(true-const' (y) = '#t)`.

The second CGR applied to the resulting program can now unfold the call to `true-const'` and perform a local reduction in `f`, producing `(f' (x) = 'A)`. Clearly, a third CGR does no more simplifications. It is easy to see that the example can be generalized to require any other fixed number of CGRs.

Arity Raiser. Arity raising is a method for *variable splitting*, which potentially *raises the arity of functions*. The arity raiser in Unmix [11] performs monovariant arity raising in the sense that it does not produce different variants of a function according to different usage patterns, but only one version that accommodates all usage patterns. The arity raiser will never discard unused parameters. A parameter is discarded iff, in all calls to a function, the corresponding argument has the same atomic value and the type of the parameter is not generalized; see usefulness below. First, the idea of arity raising is illustrated with some examples, and then a more formal discussion follows.

Example. Consider a program where an argument to `g` is constructed just to be deconstructed in `g`. This implies that the parameter `y` in `g` can be split.

```
(f (x) = (call g (cons x x)))          ; construct value
(g (y) = (cdr y))                      ; deconstruct value
```

Split parameter `y` and change all calls to `g` into calls to the new `g'`:

```
(f' (x) = (call g' (car (cons x x)) (cdr (cons x x))))  ; add selectors
(g' (y₁ y₂) = (cdr (cons y₁ y₂)))      ; split parameter
```

Finally, perform local expression reduction:

```
(f' (x) = (call g' x x))               ; simplify body
(g' (y₁ y₂) = y₂)                      ; simplify body
```

When to split. The example illustrates *how* splitting is done, but does not explain *when* a split should be made. To split a variable, two criteria must be satisfied:

1. *Feasibility.* It must be feasible to split, meaning that neither semantic errors nor code/computation duplication will be introduced. To ensure that a split is semantically valid, it must be impossible to split a variable whose value may be an atom during a program evaluation. For example, it is *incorrect* to split parameter `y` in `g`:

   ```
   (f () = (call g 1))     (g (y) = y)
   ```

   To avoid code/computation duplication, a split must *not* increase the number of *selectors* (`car`, `cdr`) in a program: All selectors introduced by a split must be eliminable by local expression reduction.
2. *Usefulness.* A split is deemed *useful* if the number of selectors in a program *decreases*. For example, it is *not useful* to split parameter `y` in `g`:

   ```
   (f (x) = (call g (cons x x)))     (g (y) = y)
   ```

Feasibility and usefulness. To establish feasibility and usefulness, two global analyses are performed. First, a forward analysis determines feasibility by analyzing the *structure* of the variables (*argument type analysis*); second, a backward analysis determines usefulness by analyzing the *use* of the variables (*parameter access analysis*). Both analyses use the following set of types to describe the structure of the variables (where $\mathcal{A} \in \langle Atom \rangle$):

$$Type \ni \tau ::= any \mid atom\langle\mathcal{A}\rangle \mid cons(\tau, \tau) \mid \bot$$

The set *Type* is equipped with a reflexive partial ordering $\leq$ (illustrated by the diagram) defined by $\bot \leq \tau \leq any$ for all $\tau \in Type$, and $cons(\tau_1', \tau_2') \leq cons(\tau_1'', \tau_2'')$ if $\tau_1' \leq \tau_1''$ and $\tau_2' \leq \tau_2''$. If $\tau' \leq \tau''$ and $\tau' \neq \tau''$, then the latter, τ'', is referred to as *more general*. It is easy to see that the set *Type* with $\leq$ is a complete partial ordering with no ascending chains of infinite height.

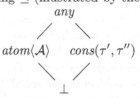

With the above types, the feasibility and usefulness criteria can be formalized:

Feasibility. A function parameter is deemed feasible to split if its associated type is of the form $cons(\tau', \tau'')$ for some $\tau', \tau'' \in Type$. The type is established by computing the least upper bound of the corresponding argument type in all calls to the function. The analysis is similar to a binding-time analysis [7]. For details, please see the original paper [11].

Usefulness. A parameter will be split if its associated type is of the form $cons(\tau', \tau'')$ for some $\tau', \tau'' \in Type$. A way to avoid the splitting will be to *generalize* the type to *any*. With this observation, the *usefulness* requirement is formalized as: A type should only be retained (not generalized) if it causes at least one selector (`car`, `cdr`) in the program to disappear.

The criterion is implemented as follows. If a variable has a preliminary type (as established by the feasibility analysis) other than $cons(\tau', \tau'')$, for some $\tau', \tau'' \in Type$, it is left unchanged, otherwise it is generalized to *any* exactly when all *access paths* in the *total context* for the variable are empty. The definitions of access path and total context are given below. For parameters of type $cons(\tau', \tau'')$, this implies that, if the parameter does not occur in the function body, the type will be generalized to *any*.

Definition 7 (Access path, total context). *An* access path *is a list (possibly empty) of selector names (i.e., a list where every entry is either* `car` *or* `cdr`*). The* total context *of a variable* x *in a function* f *is the set of all valid access paths. More specifically, for each subexpression* $(sel_1(sel_2(\cdots(sel_n \ x)\cdots)))$ *in the body of* f*, where* sel_i *is either* `car` *or* `cdr`*, the set of valid access paths is* $\{[], [sel_n], [sel_n, sel_{n-1}], \ldots, [sel_n, sel_{n-1}, \ldots, sel_1]\}$*. The total context is then given by the union of the sets of valid access paths for each subexpression.*

The *final type* of a variable indicates how many times a split will occur. A variable with a type containing n occurrences of *cons* will be split into n variables. For example, a variable with type $cons(\tau_1, cons(\tau_2, cons(\cdots, cons(\tau_n, \tau_n')\cdots)))$, where $\tau_1, \ldots, \tau_n$ and τ_n' contain no *cons*, is split into n variables.

4.2   Jones Optimality of Unmix

Following the approach in Sect. 3, Jones optimality of Unmix will now be shown. First, two basic notions are defined: The set of source programs and the textual equivalence. Next, the self-interpreter is introduced and the following characteristics are established:

1. The specific structure of the residual programs after specialization proper.
2. The first CGR does not unfold any calls in the residual programs.
3. Near textual equivalence of source and residual programs after arity raising.
4. Textual equivalence of source and residual programs after the last call CGR.

Set of Source Programs. As the goal is to show textual equivalence of source and residual programs, a set of source programs that cannot be "more optimized" by the specializer is sought. The program mwopt used in the definition of P_{mwopt} is defined by the following actions on Mixwell source programs:

1. CGR and arity raising are performed until no further changes occur in the source program. (This terminates as the arity of each function can only be raised a finite number of times and the CGR prevents infinite unfolding.)
2. Function definitions with textually identical parameters and body are replaced by a single definition and all function calls are updated accordingly. Function definitions not reachable from the goal function are removed, and every rcall is replaced by call.

Textual Equivalence. Two n-ary Mixwell programs p and q are *textually equivalent*, p $\approx_{\text{mw}}$ q, if their list representation is identical disregarding (a) the order of function definitions, (b) renaming of functions and parameters, and (c) an initial *forward function* of the form $(fwd\ (x_1 \ldots x_n) = (\text{call}\ goal\ x_1 \ldots x_n))$.

Self-interpreter. The self-interpreter mwsint is fairly standard except that the following issues must be addressed:[4]

1. Avoid unfolding of the goal function into the initial forwarding function.
2. For the arity raiser to raise the arity of a residual function to the level of the source function, the last parameter must occur in the body of the function.

The first issue is addressed by annotating the call to the primary function in the interpreter, exec, as residual with rcall. To address the last issue, the self-interpreter changes all functions $(f\ (x_1 \ldots x_n) = e)$ to $(f'\ (x_1 \ldots x_n) = (\text{if}\ (\text{call true-const}\ (\text{cons}\ x_n\ x_n))\ e\ x_n))$, where true-const is the *always-true* function from Sect. 4.1. This ensures that the first CGR does not unfold calls in the residual program, but it will reduce the body of true-const to '#t. The last CGR removes the dummy conditional in f', as discussed in Sect. 4.1.

---

[4] The self-interpreter source is included in App. A.

```
(define ($pe-exp-$2 svv-$1 svv-$2 svv-$3)   ; expression translation
  (cond ((symbol? svv-$2) ($pe-exp-$3 svv-$2 svv-$3 '| vs |))
        ((not (pair? svv-$2)) `| ' |,svv-$2)
        ((equal? (car svv-$2) 'quote) `| ' |,(cadr svv-$2))
        ((equal? (car svv-$2) 'car)
         `| (car | ,($pe-exp-$2 svv-$1 (cadr svv-$2) svv-$3)| ) |)
        ((equal? (car svv-$2) 'cdr)
         `| (cdr | ,($pe-exp-$2 svv-$1 (cadr svv-$2) svv-$3)| ) |)
        ...))
(define ($pe-exp-$3 svv-$1 svv-$2 dvv-$1)   ; variable translation:
  (if (equal? svv-$1 (car svv-$2))          ; generate variable access
      `| (car | ,dvv-$1| ) |
      ($pe-exp-$3 svv-$1 (cdr svv-$2) `| (cdr | ,dvv-$1| ) |)))
```

Fig. 2. Fragment of the translating part generated from the self-interpreter. The boxes mark the code being generated for the different constructs; also comments were added.

Generated Compiler. The self-interpreter is converted into a compiler by self-application of Unmix. The compiler consists of two parts: One part translating function definitions, and another part inherited from Unmix controlling the loop over the source program and ensuring that the compiler always terminates. A fragment of the translating part is shown in Fig. 2. As hoped for in Sect. 3.2, the translation of source programs is essentially an identity function (like the operator translation by $pe-exp-$2), except for details such as code generation for variables ($pe-exp-$3 generates a variable access). Not clearly visible from the fragment is the fact that all functions (except the goal function) in the residual program have only a single parameter (vs). Thus, in all residual calls, the arguments are packed into a list of values with (cons $rarg_1$ (cons $\cdots$ (cons $rarg_n$ '()) $\cdots$)), and instead of a variable in the source program, there is an expression (car (cdr $\cdots$ (cdr vs) $\cdots$)) that accesses the value in the value list. This representation is inherited from the self-interpreter, and specialization proper does not remove the overhead. This is a limitation of many offline partial evaluators and a reason why they may not be Jones-optimal.

Inspecting the compiler generated from the self-interpreter leads to the following theorem about the structure of residual programs before postprocessing.

Theorem 1 (Structure of residual programs). *Given* $p \in P_{mwopt}$ *with arity* j, *the residual program* $\tilde{p}$ *produced by specializing program* mwsint^j *with respect to the source program* p *has the form:*

1. ***Residual functions.*** *There is a one-to-one correspondence between the functions in* p *and in* $\tilde{p}$, *except for two additional functions. Let* $\tilde{f}$ *denote the residual function in* $\tilde{p}$ *that corresponds to the source function* f *in* p. *If* f *has arity* n *then* $\tilde{f}$ *has the form:*

   (exec-k (vs) = (if (call exec-$2 (cons (cons lv lv) '())) $rbody$ lv)

where k is a unique integer, lv is a variable access of the form given in 2a) below with m = n (or lv ='() if n = 0), and rbody corresponds to the body of f. *The two additional functions are a new goal function and an always-true function,* exec-$2. *Assuming that the goal function in* mwsint^j *is named* sintj *with variables* x1,...,xj, *they have the form:*

```
(sintj-$1 (x1...xj) = (call exec-$1 (cons x1 (cons···(cons xj '())···))))
    (exec-$2 (vs) = (if '#t '#t (cons (car vs) (car vs))))
```

2. *Residual expressions.*
   a) *For every variable occurring in the body of a source function* f, *assuming the variable is the m'th parameter of* f, *there is a variable access expression in the rbody of* f̃:

$$\text{(car }\underbrace{\text{(cdr (cdr }\cdots\text{ (cdr }}_{m-1}\text{ vs)}\cdots\text{)))}$$

   b) *For every call to a source function* f *with arity n, there is a corresponding call in the residual program, where* exec-$k *is the name of* f̃ *and* $rarg_i$ *is the residual code generated from the arguments in the original call:*

$$\text{(call exec-$k (cons }rarg_1\text{ (cons }\cdots\text{ (cons }rarg_n\text{ '())}\cdots\text{)))}$$

Proof. The proof is organized into one part dealing with residual functions and another dealing with residual expressions:

1. The correspondence between f and f̃ follows by inspection of the compiler (the compiler discards any unreachable functions and merges functions with identical body and parameter list, but $p \in P_{\text{mwopt}}$ ensures no such functions are present). The two extra functions are fixed pieces of the translating part (omitted from Fig. 2 due to space constraints).
   The form of residual functions is immediate from the main compiler loop and the function $check-function-$1 in the translating part (omitted).
2. That all constructs other than variables and calls are translated literally follows directly by inspection of the $pe-exp-$2 function.
   To prove property 2a), observe that for a variable access the recursive function $pe-exp-$3 in the translating part is called. In this function initially svv-$1 is bound to the variable that is accessed, svv-$2 is bound to the list of parameter names of the function f, and dvv-$1 is bound to the symbol vs. As the accessed variable is guaranteed to be in the list of parameter names due to the static correctness of p, a simple induction proves the property.
   The proof of property 2b) is obtained in two stages. Assuming f has the form (f (*vars*) = *body*), then the translating part will generate *intermediate code* of the form

```
(call (exec pgm body vars) (cons rarg1 (cons ··· (cons rargn '())···)) )
```

where $n = \text{arity}(f)$, *pgm* denotes the program text of the source program, and $rarg_i$ denotes the residual code generated for the arguments. The intermediate form follows from similar considerations as the variable access proof (from pieces of the translating part not shown). Finally, the main compiler loop replaces (exec *pgm body vars*) in the intermediate form by exec-$k where k is the integer corresponding to the residual function f̃.   □

First CGR. The first CGR does not change the structure of a program $\tilde{p}$. This follows immediately as the structure of the calls and functions in the residual program ensures that the duplication check is always satisfied (except for functions with arity 0; however they must be cutpoints as $p \in P_{\text{mwopt}}$).

Lemma 1 (First CGR does not unfold calls). *Given* $p \in P_{\text{mwopt}}$, *the first CGR does not unfold any calls in* p*'s residual program* $\tilde{p}$.

The CGR can perform immaterial (preserving the types in the arity raiser) reductions of the argument expression in a function call. Consider a call as shown in the structure theorem. If the arguments $rarg_n$ down to $rarg_i$ for $i \geq 1$ are static, then the innermost $n - i + 1$ cons'es will be replaced by a list of the static elements. The CGR will also, by design, simplify function exec-\$2 to (exec-\$2 (vs) = '#t) as discussed in the example in Sect. 4.1.

Arity Raiser. From the structure theorem, it follows that the only overhead not deliberately introduced in the intermediate residual programs is related to accessing variables and performing function calls. The following lemmas serve to prove that the variable access overhead and function call overhead is removed by the arity raiser. More specifically, it will be shown that raising the arity of any residual function $\tilde{f}$ to the arity of the corresponding source function f is feasible and useful (and that raising it higher is not).

Lemma 2 (Feasibility of arity raising). *Given* $p \in P_{\text{mwopt}}$, *the type assigned by the feasibility analysis to parameter* vs *of a residual function* $\tilde{f}$ *corresponding to a source function* f *with arity n has the form*

$$cons(\tau_1, cons(\tau_2, cons(\cdots, cons(\tau_n, atom\langle()\rangle)\cdots))), \quad \tau_1, \ldots, \tau_n \in \textit{Type}$$

Proof. According to the structure theorem, each occurrence of a call to the residual function $\tilde{f}$ will have a type

$$cons(\tau'_1, cons(\tau'_2, cons(\cdots, cons(\tau'_n, atom\langle()\rangle)\cdots))), \quad \tau'_1, \ldots, \tau'_n \in \textit{Type}$$

The type of the parameter vs is then given by the least upper bound of the corresponding argument types in all calls to $\tilde{f}$. This establishes the *feasibility* of raising the arity of $\tilde{f}$ to the arity of f or higher, depending upon the unspecified types $\tau_1, \ldots, \tau_n$. Note, if $n = 0$ the type is trivially $atom\langle()\rangle$. □

Lemma 3 (Usefulness of arity raising). *Given* $p \in P_{\text{mwopt}}$, *it is useful to raise the arity of a residual function* $\tilde{f}$ *to the arity n of the corresponding source function* f.

Proof. The feasibility lemma states that the parameter vs has the type

$$cons(\tau_1, cons(\tau_2, cons(\cdots, cons(\tau_n, atom\langle()\rangle)\cdots))), \quad \tau_1, \ldots, \tau_n \in \textit{Type}$$

Observe that the types τ_i for $i = 1, \ldots, n$ correspond to the types that would be assigned to the parameters of the source function by the feasibility analysis (of p). As $p \in P_{\mathbf{opt}}$, the arity raiser cannot affect the source program, and therefore any occurrences of *cons* in the types τ_i would be generalized by the usefulness analysis (of p). Hence, the usefulness analysis of the residual program will generalize the types. Therefore, without loss of generality, assume that none of the τ_i for $i = 1, \ldots, n$ contains any occurrences of *cons*.

To establish the usefulness, it is necessary to show that the type of vs is *not generalized* any further, i.e., that none of the n remaining *cons* are generalized. That is, it suffices to show that there is an *access path* $[\mathtt{cdr}, \mathtt{cdr}, \ldots, \mathtt{cdr}, \mathtt{car}]$ with $n - 1$ cdr's. As lv in the structure theorem part 1 is a variable access of the form (car $\underbrace{(\mathtt{cdr}\ (\mathtt{cdr}\ \cdots\ (\mathtt{cdr}}_{n-1}\ \mathtt{vs})\cdots)))$, the required access path exists and it is useful to split vs into n parameters. Note, if $n = 0$ the type is trivially $atom\langle()\rangle$ (in this special case, the arity will therefore be *reduced* to 0).   □

Last CGR. The following lemma ensures textual equivalence wrt $\approx_{\mathbf{mw}}$ since after unfolding all calls to `exec-$2` the conditional in the body of the functions becomes static, so the expression reduction of the CGR will reduce the bodies to code $\approx_{\mathbf{mw}}$-equivalent to the bodies of the source program.

Lemma 4 (Unfolding by the last CGR). *Given* $p \in P_{\mathbf{mwopt}}$, *the last CGR unfolds only the calls to* `exec-$2` *in* $\tilde{p}$ *and possibly the call from the new goal function to the original goal function.*

Proof. The only new edges in the call graph for $\tilde{p}$ as compared to p (where no unfolding can take place) are those to `exec-$2` and that from the new goal function to the original goal function. As `exec-$2` cannot be a cutpoint and none of the calls to it can satisfy the call and code duplication check it is always unfolded.   □

Theorem 2 (Unmix is Jones-optimal wrt $P_{\mathbf{mwopt}}$). *For all* $p \in P_{\mathbf{mwopt}}$ *of any arity, the partial evaluator Unmix is Jones-optimal according to Def. 6 with the self-interpreter* `mwsint` *in App. A, and the textual equivalence relation* $\approx_{\mathbf{mw}}$.

Unmix and Jones Optimality wrt *Time.* The theorem established that Unmix is Jones-optimal wrt $P_{\mathbf{mwopt}}$. Note how the question of a suitably timed semantics has been separated from the main task of proving Jones optimality, and now hinges on the definition of `mwopt`. In a suitably timed semantics, where program size does not affect the running time and each primitive operation takes a fixed number of time units, none of the actions performed by `mwopt` will worsen the running time of a program. In addition, as the binding-time analysis of Unmix annotates fully static functions as computable, `mwopt` will be computed at specialization time if made part of the self-interpreter. Thus, with these assumptions, Unmix is also Jones-optimal in the sense of Def. 4.

5   Related Work

Recent work on Jones optimality has focused on developing methods for tag-elimination when specializing self-interpreters for strongly typed languages

[2,5,9,16]. Type specialization [5] performs retyping as part of the specialization process, while other work [2,9,16] added an extra phase and sometimes relied on manual annotation. Often, the authors conjecture Jones optimality after a few experiments. To our knowledge, the only proof was given for lambda-mix, but it only allows programs with single-variable abstractions and no user-defined functions (a program is one lambda-expression) [15]. It was given by examining an annotated self-interpreter and arguing with respect to the semantics of the specializer.

These and related work indicate that Jones optimality is easier to state than to achieve in practice. The first implementation of a specializer that could remove the interpretive overhead was the offline partial evaluator Mix [13], but this required manual annotation for variable splitting.

Jones optimality provides a good property in general to identify inherited limits of a specialization method [10]. A formal status to the term "optimal" in the name of the criterion was given by showing that Jones optimality is a necessary condition for any specializer to be translation universal [3].

6   Conclusion

Despite the importance of Jones optimality for program specialization, few specializers have been shown to satisfy the criterion. In this paper, we addressed this unsatisfactory situation by investigating Jones optimality of more realistic partial evaluators.

Our aim was to identify and exemplify the main principles and issues involved in such an investigation. This was done by studying the partial evaluator Unmix. The system is non-trivial in that it consists of several transformation phases, includes polyvariant program-point specialization, an arity raiser and two call graph reductions, and allows for self-application and compiler generation; not all of these features are present in some of the smaller partial evaluators (e.g., lambda-mix, FCL-mix). As Unmix was not engineered with Jones optimality in mind, but merely to be "good enough" for compiler generation, various properties of the specializer had to be treated specially, such as ensuring that the arity of residual functions is raised to the arity in the source program. Unmix is a direct descendant of the classical partial evaluator Mix, which provided the basic techniques used in all offline partial evaluators. For these reasons, the issues addressed here are very likely to occur in larger systems (but with additional complexities), so further studies should be able to benefit from the steps described here.

The proof of Jones optimality for Unmix contains several important elements, such as the conversion of the self-interpreter into a compiler using the self-applicable specializer itself as a tool, which considerably reduces the amount of code that needs to be reasoned about, and the isolation of the timing semantics from the main proof to separate the concerns.

Acknowledgments. We thank the anonymous reviewers and Mikhail A. Bulyonkov, Andrei V. Klimov, and Sergei A. Romanenko for their useful comments.

References

1. D. Bjørner, A. P. Ershov, N. D. Jones (eds.). *Partial Evaluation and Mixed Computation*. North-Holland, 1988.
2. O. Danvy, P. E. M. López. Tagging, encoding, and Jones optimality. In P. Degano (ed.), *Programming Languages and Systems, LNCS*, Vol. 2618, 335–347. Springer-Verlag, 2003.
3. R. Glück. The translation power of the Futamura projections. In M. Broy, A. V. Zamulin (eds.), *Perspectives of System Informatics, LNCS*, Vol. 2890, 133–147. Springer-Verlag, 2003.
4. C. K. Gomard, N. D. Jones. Compiler generation by partial evaluation: a case study. *Structured Programming*, 12(3):123–144, 1991.
5. J. Hughes. Type specialisation for the lambda-calculus; or, a new paradigm for partial evaluation based on type inference. In O. Danvy, R. Glück, P. Thiemann (eds.), *Partial Evaluation, LNCS*, Vol. 1110, 183–215. Springer-Verlag, 1996.
6. N. D. Jones. Challenging problems in partial evaluation and mixed computation. In Bjørner et al. [1], 1–14.
7. N. D. Jones, C. K. Gomard, P. Sestoft. *Partial Evaluation and Automatic Program Generation*. Prentice Hall, 1993.
8. N. D. Jones, P. Sestoft, H. Søndergaard. Mix: A self-applicable partial evaluator for experiments in compiler generation. *Lisp and Symbolic Computation*, 2(1):9–50, 1989.
9. H. Makholm. On Jones-optimal specialization for strongly typed languages. In *SAIG '00: Semantics, Applications, and Implementation of Program Generation, LNCS*, Vol. 1924, 129–148. Springer-Verlag, 2000.
10. T. Æ. Mogensen. Inherited limits. In J. Hatcliff, T. Æ. Mogensen, P. Thiemann (eds.), *Partial Evaluation — Practice and Theory, LNCS*, Vol. 1706, 189–202. Springer-Verlag, 1999.
11. S. A. Romanenko. Arity raiser and its use in program specialization. In N. D. Jones (ed.), *ESOP '90: 3rd European Symposium on Programming, LNCS*, Vol. 432, 341–360. Springer-Verlag, 1990.
12. S. A. Romanenko. The specializer Unmix, 1990. Program and documentation available from `ftp://ftp.diku.dk/pub/diku/dists/jones-book/Romanenko/`.
13. P. Sestoft. The structure of a self-applicable partial evaluator. In H. Ganzinger, N. D. Jones (eds.), *Programs as Data Objects, LNCS*, Vol. 217, 236–256. Springer-Verlag, 1986.
14. P. Sestoft. Automatic call unfolding in a partial evaluator. In Bjørner et al. [1], 485–506.
15. S. C. Skalberg. Mechanical proof of the optimality of a partial evaluator. Master's thesis, Department of Computer Science, University of Copenhagen, 1999.
16. W. Taha, H. Makholm, J. Hughes. Tag elimination and Jones-optimality. In O. Danvy, A. Filinsky (eds.), *Programs as Data Objects, LNCS*, Vol. 2053, 257–275. Springer-Verlag, 2001.

A   The Self-interpreter

The Mixwell-interpreter `mwsint`[3] with goal function `sint3` written in Scheme (before translation into Mixwell). The goal function expects Mixwell-programs with three inputs. The omitted operations are similar to the cases shown.

```
; Interpret a program with three inputs.
(define (sint3 prg x1 x2 x3)
  (sint prg (list x1 x2 x3))) ; encode the inputs as a list

; Interpret a program with a list of inputs.
(define (sint prg vs)
  (let ((newprg (rewrite-prg prg)))
    (rcall (exec newprg (car (cdr (cdr (cdr (car newprg))))) (car (cdr (car newprg))) vs))))

; Interpret an expression.
(define (exec prg e ns vs)
  (if (symbol? e)              (lookup-val e ns vs)
  (if (not (pair? e))          e
  (if (equal? (car e) 'quote)  (car (cdr e))
  (if (equal? (car e) 'car)    (car    (exec prg (car (cdr e)) ns vs))
  (if (equal? (car e) 'cdr)    (cdr    (exec prg (car (cdr e)) ns vs))
  (if (equal? (car e) 'cons)   (cons   (exec prg (car (cdr e)) ns vs)
                                       (exec prg (car (cdr (cdr e))) ns vs))
  (if (equal? (car e) 'null?)  (null?  (exec prg (car (cdr e)) ns vs))
  (if (equal? (car e) 'pair?)  (pair?  (exec prg (car (cdr e)) ns vs))
  (if (equal? (car e) 'equal?) (equal? (exec prg (car (cdr e)) ns vs)
                                       (exec prg (car (cdr (cdr e))) ns vs))
  ...
  (if (equal? (car e) 'if)     (if     (exec prg (car (cdr e)) ns vs)
                                       (exec prg (car (cdr (cdr e))) ns vs)
                                       (exec prg (car (cdr (cdr (cdr e)))) ns vs))
  (if (equal? (car e) 'call)   (eval-call (lookup-fn (car (cdr e)) prg) prg e ns vs)
  ... '#f)))))))))))))))))))))))

; Evaluate a function call (call-by-value).
(define (eval-call fn prg e ns vs)
  (exec prg (car (cdr (cdr (cdr fn)))) (car (cdr fn)) (eval-args prg (cdr (cdr e)) ns vs)))

; Evaluate the list of function arguments and return a list of values.
(define (eval-args prg e ns vs)
  (if (null? e) '() (cons (exec prg (car e) ns vs) (eval-args prg (cdr e) ns vs))))

; Lookup the definition of a function in prg.
(define (lookup-fn fname prg)
  (if (equal? fname (car (car prg))) (car prg) (lookup-fn fname (cdr prg))))

; Lookup the value of a variable in (ns, vs)-environment.
(define (lookup-val vname ns vs)
  (if (equal? vname (car ns)) (car vs) (lookup-val vname (cdr ns) (cdr vs))))

; Rewrite the program so that the last parameter of every function occurs in its body.
(define (rewrite-prg prg)
  (if (null? prg) '((true-const (x) = (if '#t '#t (cons x x)))) ; add true-const to prg
      (let ((fn (car prg)))
        (cons (rewrite-fn (car fn) (car (cdr fn)) (car (cdr (cdr (cdr fn)))))
              (rewrite-prg (cdr prg))))))

; Rewrite function definition by adding occurrences of the last parameter.
(define (rewrite-fn fname fparams fbody)
  (let ((lv (last fparams)))
    `(,fname ,fparams = (if (call true-const (cons ,lv ,lv)) ,fbody ,lv))))

; Return the last element of lst.
(define (last lst)
  (if (pair? lst) (if (null? (cdr lst)) (car lst) (last (cdr lst))) lst))
```

Author Index

Abadi, Martín 253

Benton, Nick 114
Beringer, Lennart 114, 389
Birkedal, Lars 79
Bohr, Nina 79

Chicha, Yannis 323
Choi, Tae-Hyoung 374
Corin, Ricardo 253

Doh, Kyung-Goo 374

Endoh, Yusuke 131
Eo, Hyunjun 61

Felleisen, Matthias 270
Findler, Robert Bruce 270
Flatt, Matthew 270
Fournet, Cédric 253

Gade, Johan 406
Garrigue, Jacques 44
Gedell, Tobias 200
Glück, Robert 406
Gori, Roberta 234
Gustavsson, Jörgen 200

Harrison, William L. 97
Hofmann, Martin 114, 389

Kennedy, Andrew 114
Kim, Hyunha 374
Kim, Ik-Soon 61

King, Andy 166
Koopman, Pieter 148

Lee, Oukseh 374
Levi, Francesca 234
Lumpe, Markus 290

Masuhara, Hidehiko 131
Minamide, Yasuhiko 357
Mu, Shin-Cheng 340

Nakano, Keisuke 340

Palsberg, Jens 165
Park, Sungwoo 217
Plasmeijer, Rinus 148

Schmidt, David A. 183
Schrijvers, Tom 26
Simon, Axel 166
Stuckey, Peter J. 1, 26
Sulzmann, Martin 1, 26
Svenningsson, Josef 200

Tozawa, Akihiko 357

Vitek, Jan 307

Watt, Stephen M. 323
Wazny, Jeremy 1

Yamauchi, Hiroshi 307
Yi, Kwangkeun 61
Yonezawa, Akinori 131

Lecture Notes in Computer Science

For information about Vols. 1–4200

please contact your bookseller or Springer

Vol. 4292: G. Bebis, R. Boyle, B. Parvin, D. Koracin, P. Remagnino, A. Nefian, G. Meenakshisundaram, V. Pascucci, J. Zara, J. Molineros, H. Theisel, T. Malzbender (Eds.), Advances in Visual Computing, Part II. XXXII, 906 pages. 2006.

Vol. 4291: G. Bebis, R. Boyle, B. Parvin, D. Koracin, P. Remagnino, A. Nefian, G. Meenakshisundaram, V. Pascucci, J. Zara, J. Molineros, H. Theisel, T. Malzbender (Eds.), Advances in Visual Computing, Part I. XXXI, 916 pages. 2006.

Vol. 4283: Y.Q. Shi, B. Jeon (Eds.), Digital Watermarking. XII, 474 pages. 2006.

Vol. 4281: K. Barkaoui, A. Cavalcanti, A. Cerone (Eds.), Theoretical Aspects of Computing - ICTAC. XV, 371 pages. 2006.

Vol. 4279: N. Kobayashi (Ed.), Programming Languages and Systems. XI, 423 pages. 2006.

Vol. 4278: R. Meersman, Z. Tari, P. Herrero (Eds.), On the Move to Meaningful Internet Systems 2006: OTM 2006 Workshops, Part II. XLV, 1004 pages. 2006.

Vol. 4277: R. Meersman, Z. Tari, P. Herrero (Eds.), On the Move to Meaningful Internet Systems: OTM 2006 Workshops, Part I. XLV, 1009 pages. 2006.

Vol. 4276: R. Meersman, Z. Tari (Eds.), On the Move to Meaningful Internet Systems 2006: CoopIS, DOA, GADA, and ODBASE, Part II. XXXII, 752 pages. 2006.

Vol. 4275: R. Meersman, Z. Tari (Eds.), On the Move to Meaningful Internet Systems 2006: CoopIS, DOA, GADA, and ODBASE, Part I. XXXI, 1115 pages. 2006.

Vol. 4272: P. Havinga, M. Lijding, N. Meratnia, M. Wegdam (Eds.), Smart Sensing and Context. XI, 267 pages. 2006.

Vol. 4271: F.V. Fomin (Ed.), Graph-Theoretic Concepts in Computer Science. XIII, 358 pages. 2006.

Vol. 4270: H. Zha, Z. Pan, H. Thwaites, A.C. Addison, M. Forte (Eds.), Interactive Technologies and Sociotechnical Systems. XVI, 547 pages. 2006.

Vol. 4269: R. State, S. van der Meer, D. O'Sullivan, T. Pfeifer (Eds.), Large Scale Management of Distributed Systems. XIII, 282 pages. 2006.

Vol. 4268: G. Parr, D. Malone, M. Ó Foghlú (Eds.), Autonomic Principles of IP Operations and Management. XIII, 237 pages. 2006.

Vol. 4267: A. Helmy, B. Jennings, L. Murphy, T. Pfeifer (Eds.), Autonomic Management of Mobile Multimedia Services. XIII, 257 pages. 2006.

Vol. 4266: H. Yoshiura, K. Sakurai, K. Rannenberg, Y. Murayama, S. Kawamura (Eds.), Advances in Information and Computer Security. XIII, 438 pages. 2006.

Vol. 4265: N. Lavrač, L. Todorovski, K.P. Jantke (Eds.), Discovery Science. XIV, 384 pages. 2006. (Sublibrary LNAI).

Vol. 4264: J.L. Balcázar, P.M. Long, F. Stephan (Eds.), Algorithmic Learning Theory. XIII, 393 pages. 2006. (Sublibrary LNAI).

Vol. 4263: A. Levi, E. Savas, H. Yenigün, S. Balcisoy, Y. Saygin (Eds.), Computer and Information Sciences – ISCIS 2006. XXIII, 1084 pages. 2006.

Vol. 4261: Y. Zhuang, S.-Q. Yang, Y. Rui, Q. He (Eds.), Advance in Multimedia Information Processing - PCM 2006. XXII, 1040 pages. 2006.

Vol. 4260: Z. Liu, J. He (Eds.), Formal Methods and Software Engineering. XII, 778 pages. 2006.

Vol. 4259: S. Greco, Y. Hata, S. Hirano, M. Inuiguchi, S. Miyamoto, H.S. Nguyen, R. Słowiński (Eds.), Rough Sets and Current Trends in Computing. XXII, 951 pages. 2006. (Sublibrary LNAI).

Vol. 4257: I. Richardson, P. Runeson, R. Messnarz (Eds.), Software Process Improvement. XI, 219 pages. 2006.

Vol. 4256: L. Feng, G. Wang, C. Zeng, R. Huang (Eds.), Web Information Systems – WISE 2006 Workshops. XIV, 320 pages. 2006.

Vol. 4255: K. Aberer, Z. Peng, E.A. Rundensteiner, Y. Zhang, X. Li (Eds.), Web Information Systems – WISE 2006. XIV, 563 pages. 2006.

Vol. 4254: T. Grust, H. Höpfner, A. Illarramendi, S. Jablonski, M. Mesiti, S. Müller, P.-L. Patranjan, K.-U. Sattler, M. Spiliopoulou (Eds.), Current Trends in Database Technology – EDBT 2006. XXXI, 932 pages. 2006.

Vol. 4253: B. Gabrys, R.J. Howlett, L.C. Jain (Eds.), Knowledge-Based Intelligent Information and Engineering Systems, Part III. XXXII, 1301 pages. 2006. (Sublibrary LNAI).

Vol. 4252: B. Gabrys, R.J. Howlett, L.C. Jain (Eds.), Knowledge-Based Intelligent Information and Engineering Systems, Part II. XXXIII, 1335 pages. 2006. (Sublibrary LNAI).

Vol. 4251: B. Gabrys, R.J. Howlett, L.C. Jain (Eds.), Knowledge-Based Intelligent Information and Engineering Systems, Part I. LXVI, 1297 pages. 2006. (Sublibrary LNAI).

Vol. 4249: L. Goubin, M. Matsui (Eds.), Cryptographic Hardware and Embedded Systems - CHES 2006. XII, 462 pages. 2006.

Vol. 4248: S. Staab, V. Svátek (Eds.), Engineering Knowledge in the Age of the Semantic Web. XIV, 400 pages. 2006. (Sublibrary LNAI).

Vol. 4247: T.-D. Wang, X. Li, S.-H. Chen, X. Wang, H. Abbass, H. Iba, G. Chen, X. Yao (Eds.), Simulated Evolution and Learning. XXI, 940 pages. 2006.

Vol. 4246: M. Hermann, A. Voronkov (Eds.), Logic for Programming, Artificial Intelligence, and Reasoning. XIII, 588 pages. 2006. (Sublibrary LNAI).

Vol. 4245: A. Kuba, L.G. Nyúl, K. Palágyi (Eds.), Discrete Geometry for Computer Imagery. XIII, 688 pages. 2006.

Vol. 4244: S. Spaccapietra (Ed.), Journal on Data Semantics VII. XI, 267 pages. 2006.

Vol. 4243: T. Yakhno, E.J. Neuhold (Eds.), Advances in Information Systems. XIII, 420 pages. 2006.

Vol. 4241: R.R. Beichel, M. Sonka (Eds.), Computer Vision Approaches to Medical Image Analysis. XI, 262 pages. 2006.

Vol. 4239: H.Y. Youn, M. Kim, H. Morikawa (Eds.), Ubiquitous Computing Systems. XVI, 548 pages. 2006.

Vol. 4238: Y.-T. Kim, M. Takano (Eds.), Management of Convergence Networks and Services. XVIII, 605 pages. 2006.

Vol. 4237: H. Leitold, E. Markatos (Eds.), Communications and Multimedia Security. XII, 253 pages. 2006.

Vol. 4236: L. Breveglieri, I. Koren, D. Naccache, J.-P. Seifert (Eds.), Fault Diagnosis and Tolerance in Cryptography. XIII, 253 pages. 2006.

Vol. 4234: I. King, J. Wang, L. Chan, D. Wang (Eds.), Neural Information Processing, Part III. XXII, 1227 pages. 2006.

Vol. 4233: I. King, J. Wang, L. Chan, D. Wang (Eds.), Neural Information Processing, Part II. XXII, 1203 pages. 2006.

Vol. 4232: I. King, J. Wang, L. Chan, D. Wang (Eds.), Neural Information Processing, Part I. XLVI, 1153 pages. 2006.

Vol. 4231: J. F. Roddick, R. Benjamins, S. Si-Saïd Cherfi, R. Chiang, C. Claramunt, R. Elmasri, F. Grandi, H. Han, M. Hepp, M. Hepp, M. Lytras, V.B. Mišić, G. Poels, I.-Y. Song, J. Trujillo, C. Vangenot (Eds.), Advances in Conceptual Modeling - Theory and Practice. XXII, 456 pages. 2006.

Vol. 4229: E. Najm, J.F. Pradat-Peyre, V.V. Donzeau-Gouge (Eds.), Formal Techniques for Networked and Distributed Systems - FORTE 2006. X, 486 pages. 2006.

Vol. 4228: D.E. Lightfoot, C.A. Szyperski (Eds.), Modular Programming Languages. X, 415 pages. 2006.

Vol. 4227: W. Nejdl, K. Tochtermann (Eds.), Innovative Approaches for Learning and Knowledge Sharing. XVII, 721 pages. 2006.

Vol. 4226: R.T. Mittermeir (Ed.), Informatics Education – The Bridge between Using and Understanding Computers. XVII, 319 pages. 2006.

Vol. 4225: J.F. Martínez-Trinidad, J.A. Carrasco Ochoa, J. Kittler (Eds.), Progress in Pattern Recognition, Image Analysis and Applications. XIX, 995 pages. 2006.

Vol. 4224: E. Corchado, H. Yin, V. Botti, C. Fyfe (Eds.), Intelligent Data Engineering and Automated Learning – IDEAL 2006. XXVII, 1447 pages. 2006.

Vol. 4223: L. Wang, L. Jiao, G. Shi, X. Li, J. Liu (Eds.), Fuzzy Systems and Knowledge Discovery. XXVIII, 1335 pages. 2006. (Sublibrary LNAI).

Vol. 4222: L. Jiao, L. Wang, X. Gao, J. Liu, F. Wu (Eds.), Advances in Natural Computation, Part II. XLII, 998 pages. 2006.

Vol. 4221: L. Jiao, L. Wang, X. Gao, J. Liu, F. Wu (Eds.), Advances in Natural Computation, Part I. XLI, 992 pages. 2006.

Vol. 4219: D. Zamboni, C. Kruegel (Eds.), Recent Advances in Intrusion Detection. XII, 331 pages. 2006.

Vol. 4218: S. Graf, W. Zhang (Eds.), Automated Technology for Verification and Analysis. XIV, 540 pages. 2006.

Vol. 4217: P. Cuenca, L. Orozco-Barbosa (Eds.), Personal Wireless Communications. XV, 532 pages. 2006.

Vol. 4216: M.R. Berthold, R. Glen, I. Fischer (Eds.), Computational Life Sciences II. XIII, 269 pages. 2006. (Sublibrary LNBI).

Vol. 4215: D.W. Embley, A. Olivé, S. Ram (Eds.), Conceptual Modeling - ER 2006. XVI, 590 pages. 2006.

Vol. 4213: J. Fürnkranz, T. Scheffer, M. Spiliopoulou (Eds.), Knowledge Discovery in Databases: PKDD 2006. XXII, 660 pages. 2006. (Sublibrary LNAI).

Vol. 4212: J. Fürnkranz, T. Scheffer, M. Spiliopoulou (Eds.), Machine Learning: ECML 2006. XXIII, 851 pages. 2006. (Sublibrary LNAI).

Vol. 4211: P. Vogt, Y. Sugita, E. Tuci, C. Nehaniv (Eds.), Symbol Grounding and Beyond. VIII, 237 pages. 2006. (Sublibrary LNAI).

Vol. 4210: C. Priami (Ed.), Computational Methods in Systems Biology. X, 323 pages. 2006. (Sublibrary LNBI).

Vol. 4209: F. Crestani, P. Ferragina, M. Sanderson (Eds.), String Processing and Information Retrieval. XIV, 367 pages. 2006.

Vol. 4208: M. Gerndt, D. Kranzlmüller (Eds.), High Performance Computing and Communications. XXII, 938 pages. 2006.

Vol. 4207: Z. Ésik (Ed.), Computer Science Logic. XII, 627 pages. 2006.

Vol. 4206: P. Dourish, A. Friday (Eds.), UbiComp 2006: Ubiquitous Computing. XIX, 526 pages. 2006.

Vol. 4205: G. Bourque, N. El-Mabrouk (Eds.), Comparative Genomics. X, 231 pages. 2006. (Sublibrary LNBI).

Vol. 4204: F. Benhamou (Ed.), Principles and Practice of Constraint Programming - CP 2006. XVIII, 774 pages. 2006.

Vol. 4203: F. Esposito, Z.W. Raś, D. Malerba, G. Semeraro (Eds.), Foundations of Intelligent Systems. XVIII, 767 pages. 2006. (Sublibrary LNAI).

Vol. 4202: E. Asarin, P. Bouyer (Eds.), Formal Modeling and Analysis of Timed Systems. XI, 369 pages. 2006.

Vol. 4201: Y. Sakakibara, S. Kobayashi, K. Sato, T. Nishino, E. Tomita (Eds.), Grammatical Inference: Algorithms and Applications. XII, 359 pages. 2006. (Sublibrary LNAI).